The Journals of David E. Lilienthal

VOLUME V

THE HARVEST YEARS

A  BOOK

Books by David E. Lilienthal

THE JOURNALS OF DAVID E. LILIENTHAL
VOLUME I THE TVA YEARS 1939-1945
VOLUME II THE ATOMIC ENERGY YEARS 1945-1950
VOLUME III THE VENTURESOME YEARS 1950-1955
VOLUME IV THE ROAD TO CHANGE 1955-1959
VOLUME V THE HARVEST YEARS 1959-1963

MANAGEMENT: A HUMANIST ART

CHANGE, HOPE, AND THE BOMB

BIG BUSINESS: A NEW ERA

THIS I DO BELIEVE

TVA: DEMOCRACY ON THE MARCH

The Journals of David E. Lilienthal

VOLUME V

THE HARVEST YEARS 1959-1963

HARPER & ROW, PUBLISHERS

NEW YORK, EVANSTON, SAN FRANCISCO, LONDON

FIRST EDITION

STANDARD BOOK NUMBER: 06-012614-0

LIBRARY OF CONGRESS CATALOG CARD NUMBER: 64-18056

With abiding gratitude
and affection
this volume is
dedicated
to the memory of
Gordon R. Clapp
and
Nathan Greene

CONTENTS

—Trip to Argentina: cancellation of Argentine contracts—
Campaigning for Kennedy in the Tennessee Valley—Ideas on
foreign aid—Trip to Iran: landlords and land reform—Republic of the Ivory Coast

A section of illustrations follows page 206.

PUBLISHER'S NOTE

It is now obvious that man's two greatest tasks in the years ahead are the proper management of his environment and the control of his powers of self-destruction. For both of these crucial enterprises the earliest large-scale working projects were organized and directed by David E. Lilienthal—the Tennessee Valley Authority in the 1930's and 1940's, and in the postwar 1940's the Atomic Energy Commission and the Acheson-Lilienthal proposal for the international control of atomic energy.

Expanding logically from these pioneering achievements, Mr. Lilienthal in 1955 invented a new kind of corporate enterprise—a private profit-making business but with public service objectives—Development and Resources Corporation (D&R). Based in Manhattan, but with staff members functioning in four continents, D&R has assisted a dozen emerging nations in their efforts to improve the quality of life of their people during the past fifteen years.

Through all of his remarkably constructive career as an activist, Mr. Lilienthal has been also the tireless keeper of one of the great personal diaries of modern times. Its publication, begun in 1964 with the appearance of Volumes I and II of *The Journals of David E. Lilienthal* (covering the TVA and Atomic Energy Years), has been widely recognized as a major publishing event. Each succeeding volume, *Venturesome Years*, published in 1966, and *The Road to Change*, in 1969, has been a distinguished addition to what Allan Nevins has described as this "unmatched and probably unmatchable record."

The Harvest Years, in many ways the most intimate and revealing volume so far, is filled with impressions of wide-ranging events and candid conversations with illustrious personalities. The author, who had just turned 60 when these journal entries were originally written, resumed his active interest in public affairs while carrying on worldwide business commitments. Speaking out critically on such issues as the U.S. foreign aid program, the fallacies of disarmament, and the environmental hazards of atomic energy plants, he points the way to controversies still raging in the 1970's.

A practical visionary, a humanist, a man of extraordinary talent and energy, Mr. Lilienthal's contributions to our time are enormous, and in some ways unique. His Journals, forming a day-by-day personal account of history in the making, rank among his most significant accomplishments.

DIARIST'S NOTE

A man's focus, his interests, his mood and outlook on life, change over the years. He is not one person but many. These changes in his life are telling clues to the kind of man he is, to the vitality of his work, to the mark he leaves on others.

A journal such as this may be the best way to capture this series of changes, this moving picture aspect of a man's life. A retrospective autobiography or memoir can rarely do this since it is written at one age and one particular time.

Certainly the man whose work and personal life are recorded in this volume is a different individual than he showed himself to be in the four previously published volumes, which cover a period from his college days to his sixtieth birthday.

The entries in this volume, written between 1959 and the end of 1963, I read for the first time as a unit during the summer and fall of 1970. I had certainly changed since those earlier journals. I had become more exuberant, more confident, enjoyed life more keenly—even including the not infrequent crises and setbacks—in short, was a happier and more fully functioning individual.

But my method of recording events and reflections, from day to day, did not change. As in earlier volumes the jottings are published substantially as written; they continue to be highly informal, even casual, in style. They still were written in my Gregg shorthand, and at odd times, and in even more odd places, during a period of almost continuous worldwide travel. Many were written in airplanes or while waiting in airports, on commuter trains, in hotel rooms very late at night after long working days, or very early in the morning. One was written while in a private helicopter flying perilously in a deep moun- tain gorge.

Such casual conditions of writing do not produce polished or literary prose, but do make for a certain immediacy and validity. Because they are contemporaneous and impromptu, it is my hope they have the ring of truth.

Some of the unusually large output of journal entries during this period deal with the nuts and bolts of my work in the development of natural and human resources around the world. Not all of these entries have been included in this volume as being primarily of interest to professional men rather than to the general reader. (All these entries, however, have been filed with my collected papers in the Firestone Library of Princeton University.)

Some of the entries record moods of irritation or vanity or effusive- ness, or make uncharitable, even harsh, judgments. Of some of these I am now far from proud. Some predictions or judgments of people or events have turned out, in the succeeding years, to be wrong; a few express views I no longer hold.

I have, however, as in earlier volumes, left the entries stand sub- stantially as written for I want those who may read them—and *young people* particularly—to know that the willingness to risk making mis- takes is often the price one pays for making up one's mind, of not being wishy-washy, of being positive and affirmative.

Many entries in this volume deal with the workings of the enter- prise I head, Development and Resources Corporation, the creation and the early days of which are set out in Volume IV, *The Road to Change.* In this volume the D&R story is carried forward: the redevelopment of the vast and ancient Khuzistan region of southwestern Iran is well on its way; the Cauca Valley development in Colombia, having survived a trial by fire at the hands of a military dictator, is flourishing; in West Africa the Ivory Coast development has made a sturdy beginning.

In short, this volume tells a story of the first token harvest of the seeds of those unique concepts and methods of unified development whose origins were recorded in Volumes III and IV. The subsequent and increasingly heartening harvest yields I have recorded in journals I have continued to write. These are to be published in due course. These more recent journals will also tell of D&R's nearly four-year on- the-ground effort to further the nonmilitary economic development of South Vietnam and the Mekong River basin.

The period covered in the present volume was also marked by set- backs, by harrowing bouts of friendly brinksmanship with Iranian of- ficials and the World Bank, by political attacks abroad and financial troubles at home, and by the sudden death of my long-time partner and friend Gordon R. Clapp. It also records a number of exploratory trips to foreign countries where, as it turned out, D&R's services were not engaged, sometimes because of tragic and troubled conditions in those countries, or were withdrawn because of irreconcilable differences on business policies. The entries describing these seemingly nonproductive and frustrating efforts are retained, since such failures—and even professional pratfalls—were as significant and certainly as interesting, in a human sense, as the record of successes.

These journals, however, are basically a personal story. It is therefore appropriate that I conclude this foreword on a personal note.

This period—1959–1963—was one of the happiest and, by my lights, most productive of my life. This is reflected in many ways: how, after a quiescent epilogue to my AEC service and to my involvement in private business, I began once again to speak out on such controversial issues as the fallacy of preoccupation with disarmament, the euphoria over the "peaceful atom" and the neglect of its environmental consequences, the infirmity of a policy of foreign aid as a weapon against Communism. My exuberant mood in this period is also evidenced by an obsessive need for strenuous physical activity, and in an almost sensual satisfaction in the observation of natural beauty and the diversity and stimulus of life in New York City.

I wish once more to acknowledge, with gratitude and affection, the help I have received, in readying this journal for the printer, from my wife and lifelong partner, Helen Lamb Lilienthal. She has accompanied me on many of the trips here recorded, and contributed substantive ideas and criticism; she has carried the burden of checking and cross-checking a huge manuscript for factual accuracy and clarity. The index, so essential a tool in a book of this kind, is her work.

Once again, I am indebted to my secretary, Miss Mildred Baron, for her exceptional professional talents and unfailing good nature. She shared the exacting task of research on names and places, and performed a superlative job in the typing of a manuscript of nearly 1,100 pages.

The sympathetic understanding and assistance of Harper & Row, who have been my publishers for over thirty-five years, are gratefully acknowledged. In particular, my thanks go to that remarkable figure in the life story of publishing, Harper's Senior Editor, Cass Canfield, Sr., and to the patient editorial helpfulness of Mrs. Margaret Butterfield and Mrs. Beulah Hagen.

D.E.L.

One Whitehall Street
New York City
December, 1970

The Journals of David E. Lilienthal

VOLUME V

THE HARVEST YEARS

I

1959

World Bank agrees on loan for Dez Dam in Iran—
Khrushchev in New York—Agencies in underdeveloped
countries—Ideas for new style of TVA financing—D&R
reorganization—Trip to Iran: work in Khuzistan—Trip
to Israel—Conversations with: John Gunther; Ed Murrow; James Reston—Interest of Ivory Coast in D&R—
Democratic Party dinner: possible Presidential candidates—Eleanor Roosevelt—Trip to Colombia: achievements of CVC; situation in Colombia—Curaçao—World
Bank methods

JULY 22, 1959
PRINCETON, NEW JERSEY

Sixty may be even less a "dangerous" age for a man than some
other of a number of ages. But for me it is far from a period of emotional tranquillity. Certainly I'm not "through," or if I am I don't behave
that way, judged by my activities and plans for the future. Yet I am no
longer quite on the way *toward* something, not as I was, in my thirties
or forties. The achievement of *some* goals, within the limits of normal
ambition, has a strange and disturbing effect on me, quite contrary to
what I had expected; yes, 180 degrees from what I had expected.

Restlessness, the strong itch to be *do*ing something (sometimes,
doing almost *any*thing, just so I am *doing*) I thought surely would have
subsided by this time, by this age of sixty.

I remember my mother. I have in my system some of the physical
and emotional restlessness that marked her. So I realize that years are
not likely to quench this activism that keeps me moving about instead
of quietly absorbing life by making life come to me, not me to it

[1]

I am blessed with a wife with the gift of wit. Wit is not just the ability to tell an anecdote or repeat a joke well. Wit is—well, wit.

As we were driving home from the station, in the Nigeria-like humid heat, I thought I would trot out cheerful things that had happened since I went to New York yesterday, and mentioned the fine bill of health Dr. Dana Atchley had given me this morning, after studying all the tests. No cancer, blood fine, blood pressure "perfect," heart in fine condition. Of course, I added, out of superstition, I suppose, "that doesn't mean there is any guarantee I won't kick off tonight, but it is a mighty good report just the same."

Sez she, smiling gently, "In other words, if you do die, I'll have the consolation that you died a healthy man."

Last evening, after a long, hard but productive day of work in town, I went to the Century for dinner. Sat between Paul Herzog and Lewis Galantiere. Lewis is a man of fabulous range of knowledge and interests—a really civilized man. He asked about our work in Persia —how he had heard about it I don't know—and when we began to talk about the history of that country his knowledge was a delight to hear; he mentioned at least a half dozen books about Persia I had never even heard of, though we have been doing quite a lot of reading and book collecting. He knew that Persian, though written in Arabic script, isn't Arabic, which many people don't know. It was good to hear him talk with such ease about a subject far removed from his ordinary life and special interests.

Then I asked Dr. Shirley Fisk, Helen's physician, if he wouldn't like to join me in going to visit the Soviet Exhibition of Technology, Science, and Culture now on at the Coliseum. Which we did.

Much of the exhibit is given over to nuclear energy, hydro power, and big machinery. The emphasis on the atom, and on the sputniks (replicas of which greet one as one enters the great hall) is readily understood; but why they decided to make such a point of exhibiting cameras or combines or drag-lines (all big, and probably efficient) I don't understand, considering that these are things the U.S. has—only bigger, I suppose. And mink coats! And surgical scalpels, though Shirley said quietly: "Very nice; those were the kind my *father* used; today we use things like razor blades that can be thrown away after each operation."

AUGUST 10, 1959
MARTHA'S VINEYARD, MASSACHUSETTS

We got here Thursday night, after a long day of driving in a downpour. So this is really only my fourth day.

And you can have it, and the Vineyard too, and all periods of unraveling after a long, hard, but exciting period of productive work.

For the dark blues always descend, while I am getting my batteries recharged, or at least the first part of that nasty but necessary period. Add a lot of rainy overcast weather, and there it is.

But the sun will shine again, as it did most handsomely on Saturday; and the dumps will give way to renewal.

Actually the past several months have been a period of unusual concern and strain, particularly the past few weeks. The fate of the World Bank loan for the Dez Dam was the cause of the worry and exasperation.

This is a lot of grief, but it is rather satisfying to be in the middle of something so vital and *real*. I don't suppose the millions of people in Persia who will eat not much more than pebble bread tonight have ever heard of our worries and fighting; or ever will; but it is the thought of *them*, and the food in plenty their country *could* produce, that makes our work really worth the considerable effort.

Lilienthal's "concern and strain" about "the fate" of a World Bank loan for the Khuzistan development he described in a number of journal entries during April and May of 1959 in Volume IV. A major impasse had developed between Iran and the Bank, with Lilienthal and Development and Resources Corporation seeking to resolve the head-on conflict: on the one hand, the Bank's refusal to grant a loan for the Dez Dam (on which substantial construction work had already been begun) and the insistence of the Shah and his government that the Dam (key to the Khuzistan program) would be built, loan or no loan.

By late September, 1959, the World Bank and D&R had worked out the basis for an agreement for the loan, acceptable to Iran.

The details of this spirited negotiation were recorded by Lilienthal in a number of long, detailed journal entries during July and early August. These entries, expressed with considerable feeling, are not published here in extenso as they are too detailed for general readers, though of interest to practitioners of economic development and scholars; they are, however, retained as written in the Lilienthal Papers in Princeton University Library.

Some few excerpts, however, are set out below:

July 13, 1959: We go to Washington this week for another session with the World Bank. Their report, which lies before me, continues to take a dim view of the loan for the Dez, saying that there is an "alternative" that is more economical. Our figures will show that this isn't true, but, in any case, their report dismisses the fundamental factor: the rearrangement of the water regime of the region, which their "alternative" of a steam plant and some casual irrigation by pumping does not.

July 16, 1959: The all-day session with the World Bank was fun, in a way. It was also very disturbing.

Fun because we put a hole through the World Bank's cocky report big enough to drive a team of World Bank "experts" through. That is a story worth retelling in detail.

Disturbing, however, because of the feeling I had confirmed that this technical report was being used as a blind for a policy of giving Iran the brush-off on something that means so much to them, and therefore to the world.

August 1, 1959: The meeting with the World Bank technical group yesterday in Washington marked a real turning point for the Dez, and a favorable one.

The Bank staff told us they are now prepared to discuss the Dez Dam; their "alternative" they have dropped. They modified our proposal on irrigation and had another idea for an irrigation "pilot project" utilizing water stored by the Dez Dam. Gordon* and I said we would be glad to explore this with them to see if it was possible to find a 25,000-hectare section in the Dez irrigation area where this could be done.

The great achievement of yesterday is that it confirmed the wisdom of taking risks of "displeasure" in dealing with people who have such almost absolute power—the power of money to lend—by standing up to them and on what we believe. We did this in the TVA for years and it worked, and it is too late in life to change myself in this respect.

Now the Bank's hypothetical (and fanciful) steam plant "alternative"—actually a substitute—is no longer what we are all talking about. We are now talking about the Dez Dam. And that is infinite progress.

On September 1, 1959, the Journal records an "agreement in principle" with the Bank on a loan for the huge Dez Dam, with a pilot project scale irrigation development. The journal entry continues that "the important thing is that this would assure financing and successful completing of the Dez Dam." But Lilienthal adds a word of concern: "But Iran should not be forced to pay too high a price, as a condition of the loan, in the way of commitments demanded by the Bank that Iran change the whole legal and farming custom of that region, with only a little pilot project to provide the incentive and reason for such widespread changes."

AUGUST 27, 1959
MARTHA'S VINEYARD

I drink in the wonders of the natural world these days, like an alcoholic who feels he must get as much booze inside him as possible while

---

* Gordon R. Clapp joined Development & Resources in June, 1955, and served as president and chief operating officer. He had previously been Chairman of TVA, succeeding Lilienthal when the latter was appointed Chairman of the Atomic Energy Commission. See Volume IV of the *Journals*, pp. 4 *et seq.*—Ed.

it is there; it won't last long, so take it in fast and expansively. So I begin my day early, walking (bird glasses in hand), or swimming, or climbing to the top of Indian Hill, or cutting down trees back of the house (I charge this to prudence: "We will need the firewood next year," but actually because I love the feeling of the saw, the slow topple of the tree when it can no longer resist gravity as my cut goes through its body, the sight and touch of the tree rings on the stump, the little curious warbler who supervises what I am doing so early in the day with so much racket).

Then there is sailing. My proficiency has taken a big "step forward" this summer, so I no longer feel bewildered by the sometimes sudden "problems" of getting out of the harbor crowded with boats, or back to the mooring, or finding the place where the wind is most likely to be when it is light, or making the most exciting use of it when (as is often true this summer) it is strong and gusty. Watching the wind's reflection —or presence—on the water a half mile away, watching it come, observing the surface evidence of a running tide or two currents mixing and producing that special quality of turbulent water called so well a "rip"; or looking up at the proud sail high above me, or the pull, pull, pull, of a jib that is properly filled; or the dark-green shoreline (like the coast of England).

SEPTEMBER 4, 1959
MARTHA'S VINEYARD

Our wedding anniversary: thirty-six years. I had no other idea, that brilliant September morning in Crawfordsville [Indiana], than that this marriage would have no ending. But, at the age of just twenty-four I suppose thirty-six years would have been a period I couldn't have begun to comprehend.

This is a "happy" anniversary because, for one reason, this has been a wonderfully happy holiday. Not a long one—it will be about a month—and certainly not one marked by good weather, though we have had a few brilliant "Vineyard days," and plenty of good sailing breezes.

But the combination of keeping in touch with my reason for being, viz. my work and thinking, and of playing, has been, I think, about right.

I have really done a lot of "work," something almost essential every day, and sometimes spent at least half a day at it. But there has been no feeling of harassment.

The important thing is that I no longer look on a "vacation" as a time when I must completely cut myself off from everything that is part of my daily chores in business. I don't make a to-do about business telephone calls, of which I have had a great many throughout the month, or writing long letters.

Yesterday the early morning radio news featured the fact that Khrushchev had an article in *Foreign Affairs,* just published, in which he set out his views, apparently a substantive piece.

Quite enterprising of Armstrong;† and I wired him so. A good break for my own article too,‡ to be in the same issue, a "book" that will be in such demand among reporters, editorial writers, and the State Department.

SEPTEMBER 18, 1959
PRINCETON

This afternoon I watched one of the greatest practitioners of the most important of the "performing arts," the art of political acting before an unfriendly or, in any case, a wholly unsympathetic and fearful audience. In short, I was one of the guests who "watched" Khrushchev speak to some of the "leading" figures of New York City, at a luncheon in his honor at the Commodore.

What are the elements of greatness in the kind of test to which his TV appearance put him, before one of the largest audiences which ever watched one man? An audience as large as for the World Series, but with overtones somewhat more serious even than that great event to the American public!

First I would put his ability to kid himself, to use irony, directness, wit, to make contact with this audience before him, and the twenty-five million people who saw or will see him on television. This is one of the highest of skills. F.D.R. had it, in his way, and on occasion. But he never had to face such a buildup of enmity as this character did today.

Khrushchev said things that showed how sensitive he is to what *goes* in America. Nothing in his career as a revolutionary or a commissar I would have supposed would prepare him for this. For example, his praise of Eisenhower, delivered without script, showed a confidence and warmth, and a piece of shrewd salesmanship in contrast to the picture of the Russians as cautious, cold, logical, prudent. He gave praise to everyone, in the very manner of a politician making a whistle-stop speech, all the local references. He disclaimed being a diplomat, implied that the diplomats, his particularly, would be distressed by the way he talked, without regard to protocol.

These and many other "tricks" are not unfamiliar ones, but they

† Hamilton Fish Armstrong, editor of *Foreign Affairs.*
‡ "Enterprise in Iran," *Foreign Affairs,* October, 1959.

are certainly amazing in a man who is so strange to American customs as we thought he was, so out of tune with our way of "making friends."

If he were a handsome, striking man, this would be one thing. But he is one of the least imposing of men, when you think of great power, enormous power. Short, plump, really fat, a funny shaped head without a neck, the color and general appearance of a scrubbed pig. And despite these physical defects (in a dictator and a salesman) and the obvious disadvantage of having to have his words interrupted frequently for translation, he "got over," I thought, to a difficult audience, an audience that came out of curiosity and for the prestige of being selected out of all New York for attendance, and left, I think, shaking their heads as I did, about the kind of adversary we have in this man. He will no longer be as dark a mystery to the American people as before, and this is a great stroke for him.

God help us, I hope it will be a good thing for us, but I certainly have grave doubts about it.

Before I heard him I was much disturbed about having him visit America and getting all the breaks of propaganda and prestige this carries with it. Now, after hearing him, I wonder if there was any other way to begin to introduce new ideas into a hopelessly stalemated situation. I may end by acclaiming Ike's wisdom and courage in inviting him, instead of feeling that this was a risk without any compensating advantage.

The test will come, so far as his public impression is concerned here, when he has had another ten days of this. If he keeps his present line, doesn't rattle sabers too much, doesn't show the resentment that, of course, he feels about the U.S. (and which he showed once pretty plainly during his extemporaneous talk), he will have done a great job of obfuscation and perhaps even further the cause of peace. But he may crack under the strain of being genial, and make a big goof. After hearing him, I hope he doesn't; I can't see how a restoration of the flames of hatred and distrust can do anything more for the world than they have already done—which has been precious little.

But Ike has taken a long, long gamble, and the world along with him.

Lodge made a superb talk. Thanked Khrushchev for making us think afresh of the great heritage which is ours, renew our faith in what we have. An interesting evidence of this occurred during the playing of the national anthems, first of the U.S.S.R., then "The Star-Spangled Banner." Sentimental though it may be, I was struck that *this* time this sophisticated audience didn't fidget; as the music went on, a few began singing the words, then the whole audience. Somehow this seemed like the old and the good days of America even in that blasé audience. So perhaps Lodge is right; we may have Khrushchev's visit to thank for reminding us of how we do love our country, and perhaps beyond that, of causing us to give ourselves to our country and what it has stood for.

SEPTEMBER 23, 1959
NEW YORK

Last night Helen and I dined with John Laylin, Washington counsel for Pakistan, and his wife, at his invitation. Afterward we called on H. E. Manzoor Qadir, Foreign Minister under the present military government of Pakistan. A good many complimentary references to my having started an idea§ which the Minister indicated quite plainly was soon to become a reality—at least on paper in the form of a treaty, which to lawyers like Qadir and Laylin is often mistaken for reality; if an agreement is made, that is the end, rather than, as I realize, just the beginning.

We talked about the Indus; it was clear that Qadir's instructions, and perhaps his own convictions as well, were: it is my job to improve the relations with India rather than to fish up the old antagonisms and suspicions. This was quite in contrast to Laylin's aggressiveness about the way in which the Indians were trying to take advantage. A treaty is being drawn, and Laylin implies that he is in on the drawing, but I suppose there will be many drafts. This appears to be the home stretch of the first heat, to use the language of the harness race.

But Qadir's principal interest was in Persia, where he spent four days on his way to the U.S. He said he saw the Shah, and the Ministers, but out of this got no idea of how the people generally feel about that regime. He was a bit taken aback by the "palaces" he saw being built in Tehran and said—in a way I thought shockingly touched with propaganda and carelessness—that these palatial residences were built with oil revenues, but where do the people come in? There wasn't anything being done for them. I did what I could to indicate how this is hardly the case and that what he sees in Tehran is private real estate speculation such as we had in Florida in the twenties.

An interesting little man; harried; not accustomed to political affairs; much happier in a law court, but a stable, humble person, I would say. Since he will probably steer the Indus River treaty through, he becomes an important member of the cast.

§ In an article in *Collier's* in July, 1953, L. proposed a program that India and Pakistan jointly develop and operate the Indus Basin river system. This became the basis for a settlement of a grave water dispute between the two nations. See the *Lilienthal Journals,* Volumes III and IV.—Ed.

SEPTEMBER 25, 1959
PRINCETON

Lunch with John Gunther. A brave fellow, the way he has stood up to the impairment of eyesight resulting from his cataract operation. Had a pleasant visit. One of the foremost journalists of the time.

Told me a lot about Albert Lasker; Gunther is doing a book about him. In the course of this he became acquainted with André Meyer.

But John and André and a lot of other people have the notion, as sometimes I do, that we are immortal, that we will never grow old and die. I'm trying to get through my head that the time left us is our most important possession. But the habit of being active, busy, is a hard one to get over in favor of a more discriminating use of one's time and energy.

SEPTEMBER 28, 1959
WASHINGTON, D.C.

Here for the World Bank meetings, and to see people, from all over the world, who come to these gatherings.

As I passed Gene Black in the receiving line, he grinned hard and said: "Are you happy now, Dave?" I was taken off base at first; then picked it up and said, "Yes, I am happy, now." Aldewereld [head of the Bank's project division], with whom I had some rather strenuous disagreements earlier in the summer, was most affable, and said: "We are all set now." Hedayat⁜ saw Black and others this afternoon, just before seeing Gordon and myself, and reported that the whole discussion was about dates, schedules. It is expected that the actual negotiation will begin in early November.

That was a tough one, that struggle, and I hope it turns out to be worth it.

Hedayat was explicit in telling us how determined the Shah is about the Dez, how strongly His Majesty put it to Folk, of the Bank, just before Hedayat left.

SEPTEMBER 30, 1959
WASHINGTON

I have certainly been "doing" the convention chore at this Bank meeting and finding much of it fun. Seeing a great many people, which is the principal purpose these vast gatherings serve. I am trying to put

⁜ Khosrow Hedayat was Minister in charge of Iran's Plan Organization.

out of my mind—or the center of my mind—whether my being here and seeing all these people will produce anything in the way of new work for the company—which I hope it might—and concentrate on watching the spectacle and enjoying the meeting of old friends or associates, and new people.

At the Iranian dinner last night I had a couple of pleasant talks with Loy Henderson, who was ambassador to Iran and to India at trying times in each case. He recalled our trip to India when I spawned the idea of the settlement of the Indus Waters dispute; in fact, there has been a good deal of friendly and admiring comment about my part in what most people now rather *assume* is a settled issue. And it well may be.

Went to a luncheon this noon given by Paul Hoffman, now Managing Director of the UN Special Fund. Met Sir Roger Makins, who heads the British delegation here as Permanent Secretary to the British Treasury, a post he soon gives up to become head of the British Atomic Energy establishment. He seems to share my view that, as I put it, "the bloom is off the peach" of the atom; I added that I thought it was a good thing; the possibilities had been overstated.

The Minister of Finance of Ghana asked me when I was going to pay them another visit, and was very friendly. But when I mentioned the processing of chocolate, one of the projects Louis Reynolds was interested in starting in Ghana for his Eskimo Pie business, he was as cool to the idea as an Eskimo Pie. The employment of a few people, that was all Ghana would get out of it, as the consumption of chocolate there would be very small. Much better to export the cocoa and use the proceeds. I didn't argue about it, thinking to myself that he probably fears that the big cocoa buyers, the British, would raise ned about a competition from Americans. Komla A. Gbedemah was full of talk about Ghana, asked me to sit with him at table during lunch, said some interesting things, including a statement that they feel now that the Volta River scheme at last is on its way, "through a consortium" which, I gather, Kaiser is arranging.

Paul Hoffman made an impassioned talk to induce (or shame) the big countries to contribute what they had promised to put into the Special Fund, which is essentially a survey fund, utilizing the specialized agencies of the UN. What he said (and has been writing recently) was heavy on good will and much of it good sense, in a long-range point of view. But when he represents these surveys as ways of uncovering private investment opportunities as a "preinvestment" function, I think he overstates. He used as an example their first survey: a survey of electric power needs in Argentina. This one-fourth million dollar job, to be done by people drawn from the World Bank, he said might lead to hundreds of millions of investment in power in Argentina. But really it isn't the lack of survey that discourages investment in power (or other things) in the Argentine. The Argentines are convalescing (one hopes) from a sickness. Of course it is good to know how much power they need, when, where. But to think that to know the answer to such questions will result in "hundreds of millions of investment" is oversimplifying badly, I think.

Spent a half hour with Minister Bouabid of Morocco, in his suite, doing so at the suggestion of Jean Guyot [partner of Lazard, Paris], who reported that he was fearful that Bouabid "is drifting toward the East."

I never saw a man so changed. When I saw him, twice, in Rabat last July, he looked young, dynamic, hopeful, and cheerful. Whether it is because he is terribly tired or what, I don't know; but something is troubling him deeply. He looked worn out, twenty years older, dispirited. And certainly he was noncommittal about what I said about the content of our communication re Sous.†

OCTOBER I, 1959
WASHINGTON

A dinner companion last night was Alice Mary Maffry, wife of August Maffry, a vice-president of the Irving Bank, and a former government servant in the New Deal days.

Told me about her twenty-year-old daughter, who has been going to Radcliffe, then spent a year in Athens at a School of Classical Studies.

A classic story, this young woman, and I don't mean Greek and Latin.

"We never thought of letting her even go to Bloomingdale's alone; whenever she crossed the street [they live in New York] we held her hand. Then suddenly she is in Athens, on her own, and going to archaeological digs. Went third class, sleeping under a donkey blanket she bought, on the deck of a boat from Piraeus to Brindisi." Her mother, a pert little woman and most likable, shuddered and covered her face with her hands at this thought; yet it was evident how proud she was.

Marquis Childs phoned me yesterday. He was writing a piece, for his column about CENTO; called me for my impressions of the stability of Iran.

He asked about our son, David; I told him he had decided to leave D&R, to try his hand for a year at least at writing, combined with a

† On the invitation of the Sultan of Morocco, in July, 1959, I made a trip to Morocco to explore the possibilities of the development of a region in southern Morocco, the Sous. An account of that trip, and our recommendations are set out in Volume IV of the Journals.

couple of days a week on the *Vineyard Gazette;* that he had been invited to return to the St. Louis *Post-Dispatch;* that, though I think the invitation helped his morale, I doubted if he would do it.

Then Mark said: "Well, he's right. The big city newspaper is a dying business, like the railroads. The cost of production, and particularly the difficulties of distribution, compared to the competing medium of radio-TV, are going to be just too much for most papers. They won't die out completely, but the life is going out of them."

I remarked that apparently the local and regional papers were staging a comeback. He agreed; they didn't have quite the problem of the bigger papers.

Mark is given to gloom, verbally at least, but he knows a very great deal.

The first day we came, last Monday, we lunched with Marguerite Owen.‡ She was in top form, looked fine, and was exuberant as I haven't seen her in years. These past five years, with a new TVA Board committed to killing the TVA, have been a kind of nightmare, but the kind that brings out all of Marguerite's great sense of tactics, her inflexibility about principle, her great flexibility about methods, her capacity for reaching a goal by persistence.

She reported that the bill that finally became law dealing with TVA financing was a good law. Told me to my infinite satisfaction that it also included a little-noted provision by which the big municipalities of the region could build power plants with TVA engineering, and sell their output to TVA, issuing their own municipal and federally tax exempt bonds. This was the central idea she and I had discussed years ago, and upon which I think had I still been on the TVA Board we could have erected a decentralized ownership of the TVA system. But the present law carries TVA over a crisis, and that is very important. But the cost of money today and in the future will be very high compared with municipal bond financing. No point in regretting that lost opportunity now.

She said both Vogel, the Chairman, and Jones had become belligerent, even bellicose, on behalf of TVA; this is delightful, since Vogel was obviously sent down to break it up, and "get rid of those Communists," meaning most of the staff; and Jones was a less than ordinary little man from the Bureau of the Budget who didn't seem to have any fight in him about anything, much less this big and controversial TVA.

The basic idea of TVA was a good one, and it had a good start, otherwise it couldn't have stood up under the hammerings of a Republican Administration and its hatchet men.

‡ Miss Owen was TVA representative in Washington, D.C.

OCTOBER 10, 1959
PRINCETON

Visited by Dr. A. Peccei, of Italconsult, with two Fiat men from Argentina, one of whom, Ayerza, had accompanied the new Minister of Economic Affairs, Alvaro Alsogaray, to the States on a mission to find money, the old story, of course.

Peccei was apologetic for the delay in our getting an answer from Argentina about developments in Patagonia and elsewhere. Alsogaray wanted to see us Thursday; we said ok, but had no notion this meant a decision, favorable or otherwise. But Argentina does seem to be making headway against the fiscal and political sickness from which it suffers; I fear the convalescence will be a long one.

In any case, on Thursday afternoon Gordon and I, and Bill Voorduin and Walt Seymour of D&R's top staff—who had made the trip to the Argentine—called on the Minister in a suite at the Waldorf.

While we were waiting in the hall, an excited group of young Mexican military aides (the gold braid over the shoulder I assumed meant an aide) plus even more exciting young women, their wives probably, were being inducted into rooms down the hallway. The President of Mexico arrived in Washington today, and there is to be a big to-do for him in New York later in the week. All the turbulence that goes on around these junkets—what a story the Waldorf could tell, for they almost always make a beeline for the Waldorf, bag, baggage, aides, press agents, the works.

Alsogaray said he had been in office only briefly; that his first efforts were to try to stem inflation. Now the time is "ready" to assume some of the projects that are proposed for developing the country. One of these is that for North Patagonia. He is familiar with our proposal: he will study it soon, and let us know "yes or no" promptly.

A call from Adriano Olivetti, with his handsome, strapping big son Roberto, and another young fellow of the company. Olivetti has recently purchased one-third of the old standby, Underwood Typewriter Co., which has been losing ground—and money—for some years now. The only man at Lazard [Frères] he knew was Hettinger, who was away, so he called me. He talked by phone to Hettinger in Salt Lake, who told him he would remain on the Underwood Board. I said he ought to become acquainted with André Meyer and gave him some good and true reasons why: his broad background of American and European finance and industry, his creative, inventive mind.

I sensed that Olivetti had pretty ambitious plans about the American market for office machines, into which it has already made a pretty good dent with its Italian-made products, that perhaps some merger might be the answer for Underwood, or some other arrangements that would expand Olivetti activities in the U.S.

I find it interesting that an Italian firm should take over a debilitated (though famous) American outfit, and proceed, I have no doubt, to make something of it. This is the reverse of the gospel of American know-how being *exported*.

Another visitor: Abol Hassan Ebtehaj, full of bounce. How we miss him in our work!

He is busy finishing the organization of a bank in Tehran which he calls Iranians' Bank. He had lunch with André and tried to interest him in a warehouse business in Tehran. Those two are quite a team, and I like to think of them as characters in an international drama.

I told him I was rather discouraged about the way our affairs were going in Iran; not any particular thing, but the deterioration of the kind of drive from the Iranian side that we experienced under him. I didn't tell him how harassed we had been about the advance payments, the delays and uncertainties, and the mounting gossip that our accounts were not acceptable. Actually, we got $2 million during the week and are promised another seven by October 20; the full amounts were due September 20. Hedayat says this will improve when we change the due dates, which are unfortunate in relation to the time when Plan Organization receives its funds. But it is more than that, and it will be like pulling teeth to keep the payments on time from here on, I fear.

Went to dinner with the Australian Ambassador, Howard Beale, a bubbly, jolly politician-type fellow, a dinner in honor of the Minister of State for External Affairs, Lord Casey. This latter is *quite* a man. He was a distinguished Australian soldier in the First World War; then in the British Finance Ministry, where he met Ebtehaj in Persia, and admires him greatly. "So *un*Persian he is" is the way he sums up his admiration. He was Governor of Bengal (65 million people) for two years. What he hasn't done!

The party, at River Club, was for about sixteen people. It was the evening when the results of the British elections were coming in; there were two small radios at the table, people listening eagerly, and soon with great joy: "the Tories are in" (they used the term "Tory," which I thought had completely gone out of use).

OCTOBER 12, 1959
PRINCETON

Not too happy about the stage we are in with the company. Gordon is tired and tense—and no wonder. He has had hardly any time off, has had a tiring trip to Persia; we have been on the griddle about funds, and will be, I expect, from now on. Our diversification efforts have thus far produced no results. I wrote a long memo on this subject last week, to try to put on paper the rather bleak outlook, so far as we can now *see*, for a broader foundation for the work. Something will probably turn up, but just how or where it will come from is something I can't see. I just want to try as hard as I can to bring this about, so if it doesn't I won't feel I haven't done whatever I knew how to do.

I should not fret because I am not in the midst of operating discussions and decisions, in the company. That isn't my chief role, whether in this job or any other. I have been best as one who sees ahead, who sees the whole, who conveys an emotional excitement about goals. That's enough of a job to satisfy anyone, or should be. It is, that is, if it is done well, and it can't be done well, that kind of half-poetic, half-evangelic job, if one tries to be too active in straight management chores, important and interesting as they are.

When you start looking up the ages of other men in *Who's Who*, this must be a sign that you are feeling your years—or something. I did this just a bit ago, finding to my surprise that Marriner Eccles (with whom we spent an evening last week) is sixty-nine, and so is Ferd Eberstadt. They are both going along as active as can be, so I guess I will too. But every once in a while I mistake ordinary fatigue, after a rough week at the office, or three days of transplanting and digging in the garden, for antiquity. I forget that fatigue, at any age, is normal, and that the kind of heavy spading I do—or beating the squash ball around hard as I also do—is tiring, albeit fun.

OCTOBER 14, 1959
PRINCETON

Yesterday Helen and I spent a concentrated period of talking about the prodigious records and files I have here, and how she can continue the job of organizing them to be most useful. I have been rummaging through the files themselves, just hit and miss, from Fred Arvin's earliest letters to me in 1913, some of my letters to Helen before we were married, on to editorial comment on my AEC confirmation ordeal.

But what will I do with what this material represents by way of *experience* rather than records? This is still not certain in my mind; in a way it is a good thing to take my time deciding on a course of this kind.

OCTOBER 19, 1959
NEW YORK

Called on today by Salvador Araneta, of Manila, a member of a wealthy family, with whom I've had correspondence lately about consulting work in that country. Araneta turned out to be a very personable, to-the-point man, of obvious great ability, enormous admiration for F.D.R., for TVA ("Roosevelt's greatest monument"), and yet he has a strong businessman's approach. He says he will arrange an invitation to me to visit the Philippines, sponsored by a number of organizations in Manila, and cover the cost.

OCTOBER 23, 1959
WASHINGTON

Saw Gene Black for a half hour this morning. Said I wanted to give him some background about the Cauca Valley, and of the opportunity the CVC§ might offer as a demonstration of some important principles; that I knew he believed that the World Bank could at times, by its lending policies and technical guidance, go way beyond what unimaginative straight "lending" could do. He had little specific knowledge about CVC, asked me to send him the report I made proposing El Plan, names of people etc.

He asked how things were going in Iran. I said all right, I thought; that the Bank's ideas about a pilot irrigation scheme as a beginner, we thought a constructive and sound idea and were recommending that Iran adopt it.

Lunch with Scotty Reston. Such a wise and happy man, so happy in his family, his work. Not often does one find anyone these days who gets such satisfaction out of life. We talked a good deal about Oppenheimer; I introduced the subject, but he was glad to talk about it. Scotty's breaking of the story of the AEC suspending Oppie's clearance was one of the important newspaper events of the past ten years.

He asked me about how things were going in Persia. I tried to give him a general idea of progress, but without too much sales talk, as I don't want to seem to take advantage of his friendliness toward me and what I am trying to do.

He feels very low indeed about Eisenhower. Such a fine man, so "good," but he just isn't sufficiently interested in doing any more than living out his term, while the country suffers. We talked a good deal about how limited a virtue good intentions are, where there is no policy and no follow-through. This stimulated me to talk about the importance of *method*, of *how*, in these international development activities. He remarked that the International Cooperation Agency (Point IV) is a good illustration of Ike's lack of interest in anything that goes beyond words.

§ The Cauca Valley Corporation (CVC) was a regional development authority with headquarters in Cali, Colombia. I was advisor to the CVC from its initial phases; later D&R was engaged by CVC as technical and managerial consultant. It was known in the region as "El Plan Lilienthal." See *Journals*, Volumes III and IV.

Ike really *believes* deeply in foreign aid, but when the new head of ICA has his head cut off because he isn't a Republican it never seems to occur to the President that this is an issue to be fought out, or all the good sentiment about foreign aid is of no avail.

Short visit with William Iliff, who is handling the Indus Waters business in the World Bank. Most cordial, and an impressive fellow. He showed me part of the draft of treaty between Pakistan and India now being worked on here in Washington, pointing especially to a provision about "common purpose" and how they expect to raise the billion dollars it will take. Interesting to see how large the contribution is from the British Commonwealth countries, even New Zealand pledging $2.6 million. He commented that as the pressure grows on India to get this waters issue settled, due to the troubles with the Chinese, the Pakistanis push harder for more and more. Which was what I feared, and I wonder if John Laylin's influence in this is too good; he is a strong and able advocate, by nature, and at this point he can get the Paks so steamed up about the past "crimes" of India that they will win the argument but may lose the goal itself.

I am still troubled in my mind about D&R being the contracting party on this big Dez Dam. I want to change our relationship to that of supervising the main construction contractor, but having the construction contract itself between Plan Organization and the successful bidder. I feel unhappy about our getting farther and farther away from the original unique D&R concept of integrated development and closer and closer to doing the kind of direct engineering work that others do, and do at least as well.

My thought now is that we begin the process of transition from managerial ultimate responsibility toward something less than that, and if we could do it beginning with the main construction contract for Dez, I would like that very much. I don't want to break with Clapp and Voorduin on this issue, if I can possibly persuade them, so it would be their preferred course too. But so far little headway; perhaps circumstances will solve the impasse.

OCTOBER 31, 1959
PRINCETON

The Power of the Word.

In wondering about giving more time to actual writing and less to the exciting business of doing, I come on more than one instance of what may be the truth: that writing may also be "doing." Writing need not be *withdrawal* from the purpose of my life: to effect changes, get things done that need to be done.

Some examples:

1. The Prime Minister, Moulay Abdallah Ibrahim, of Morocco is now in this country; made a quick trip to TVA—at *his* insistence, not the State Department's. He said that fifteen years ago he had read my TVA book, published in 1944. At that time he was just another Moroccan "intellectual"; today he is a leader in a new country. And he remembers this book and it becomes a part of his thinking. The *words* of that book have certainly had an effect, in this particular country.

2. I wrote an article in *Collier's* about the Indus Valley's waters, and the effect of a continued dispute over them upon the life and peace of that part of Asia. Eleven years later a treaty is being drafted between those two countries, that was initiated by the words I put on paper so long ago. That is hardly the case of "mere" writing as a "withdrawal" from life.

But my writing should be *personal*. I am not a historian nor a social philosopher nor a journalist. I want this to be *me*, looking out on the world and saying things that may be useful. (Useful perhaps because some of the ideas will seem so clearly wrong, but provocative in their wrongness so that people quarrel about the ideas and/or think about them in the process of consigning them to the junkpile of errors.)

So we start with a *personal* record. But this can be a very sound idea. For each man is at the center of the world. Not only at the center, each man *is* the center. From that center he has experiences, disappointments, achievements, pain, frustration. But the emotions are his, they happen to him, to him the *center*, though the events themselves may be, usually are, things in which he himself doesn't actively join.

This is the view of the world of all but a rare species of men who have an objectivity that makes them either saints or eunuchs, spiritually speaking.

So the world is something I see from my center, from me outward. In this sense every piece of writing can be said to be personal.

What I write should be an attempt to distill out of my experience in active affairs, out of the life that I have lived as well as intimately observed, what it means *to me*, what principles or themes of life it makes me feel are valid; and particularly, what it might mean to those young people ignited or encouraged or weakened by what I say.

Why do I think young people might find what I have to say stimulating and clarifying or provocative? Because so often they have.

Beatrice Tobey and I had an evening together this week, seeing the Bayanihan Dancers from the Philippines (exquisite!) and dinner and much talk. After years of struggling to paint, and working hard at it, while carrying her duties as a mother and homekeeper, she has had professional recognition. One cover for *The New Yorker* last summer, two more accepted. She is so excited and happy it is wonderful to be with her. A kind of rebirth of her youth, as I remember her so well when I was a law school student and she was just a kid.

Bede is essentially a person of impulse, of feeling. And as an artist this is as it should be. But her eagerness about life—and, God knows, she has had her share of the rough things life has held for almost all of us—is a great help to so basically cautious a fellow as I am, with all my taking long shots.

"As a young fellow, you were helped on your course," she reminded me, "by older people, by something they said to you at a certain moment, by encouragement, by their taking you seriously, by their listening to you and your hopes. Now it is up to you to pay that back, not to them, of course, but to other young people who need your time and interest just as you did those of, say, Frank Walsh, or some of your beloved teachers."

And paying this debt she applied to the importance of my doing more writing; that my fear of its being mere reminiscence, hollow, self-prideful, need not happen.

As I got out of the elevator yesterday noon, after lunching with Gordon, I saw right ahead, on the little settee opposite the elevator door, one of the most luminous faces I have ever seen. It was the face of Dr. A. Wiener, who heads Israel's water planning. Our talk with him about our forthcoming trip to Israel showed that the face was a true reflection of the *spirit* within the man, of his extraordinarily sensitive and understanding grasp of what his role as an engineer should be in that "poor country."

We had said that we did not want to spend time on strictly engineering things. This led to a brief but satisfying discussion of the technical man's inadequacies, when technical things were the be-all and end-all of his life and work. I suggested that some technical men seemed to want to have some technical problem to get at, build something perhaps, because that was something they could grasp and could do. But to come to grips with the whole meaning of things was so difficult, and they felt so inadequate for it that they turned from it or downgraded its importance.

"What a good many technical people need," I said, "is more Shakespeare, whereas we are told on all sides what we need are *more* scientists, more engineers. What we need are more *men,* more men (engineers or technical men, among other disciplines) who are capable of understanding things that go beyond that limited area." I went on to say that the educators, responding to this lack in technical people, were beginning to include and indeed emphasize "Shakespeare," poetry, history, etc. But not as integral to the making of a good engineer; it was like having a cake baked and ready, and then putting some fancy and nonfunctional frosting on the top.

Have been going crazy about our garden, putting in new roses and planning and plotting the future of our herbaceous borders. Planting, for me, means mostly getting the soil ready, putting in this and that, mixing and stirring, trying to make things just right for that particular plant. What a joy it is.

Back of this joy of preparation is the dazzling feeling of wonder of the miracle I shall see, come spring: out of an almost dead stick or root, now dormant, and these lovely ingredients of soil and humus and bone meal (I'm a great believer in bone meal) will come the glories of a deep-dark rose, fragrant, delicate in contour; or the gaiety of a cluster of campanula bells tinkling along the stalk, giving off their sound to the eye rather than the ear.

Last week I memorized a little poem of Thomas Brown's:
"A garden is a lovesome thing, God wot" . . . It is, indeed.

NOVEMBER 2, 1959
FLYING THE ATLANTIC
FIVE HOURS OUT OF NEW YORK

The pains of *thinking* have not been adequately described. It is a bitter-sweet pain. In the midst of the uncomfortable striving to get things straight in one's mind, to clear up conflicting and often contradictory ideas, there is the warm, exciting satisfaction of using one's mind and imagination, the fatalistic instinct that, in the end, clarity and satisfaction will come out of the Sturm und Drang.

All of which is prompted by my efforts, rather intensive these past few days, to find out what I think about the prospects for "world development," for the improvement of the condition of the two thirds of the peoples of the world who are hungry and just hanging on—while I and my fellow passengers in this palatial ship of the skies dined this noon, 37,000 feet above the sea, on caviar, rock Cornish hen and Port Salut.

The particular concern for the grinding of the gears in my mental crankcase is a speech I am to make in Cleveland on January 14, before the Council on World Affairs, the Newton D. Baker Lecture.

A history of the development of the *expression* of a particular idea, expressed in words, of course, rather than in paint or sculpture, would be an interesting thing to try to do. There is a *process* to this kind of creation, and it is the process that I have never heard or read described.

In any case, I am going through it now—over the Atlantic; at the break-fast table talking back and forth with Helen this morning early (I left the house at 7 A.M. for Idlewild) and many other times in the past few days, wandering into her room, or talking it out with her while she was cooking our food; or sweating it out alone in the "salt mine" in the basement office.

I have never been able to regularize these struggles for clarity, to develop a *system* for eliminating or testing ideas. It all seems hit or miss, at this stage at least; one idea or theme canceling out or seeming to be at odds with an idea or theme held, with equal fervor, just the day or hour before. But out of it all come some of the most satisfying experi-ences of life, for me: finding expression, somehow, for the things that are inside me that I believe and want others to believe.

NOVEMBER 3, 1959
LONDON

Gordon and I lunched with Ed Murrow.

We talked about the function he thinks we can supply to his *See It Now* film on Iran, now completed except for the interview with me. "Want you to supply the vision that could make this a rather extraordi-nary thing. It may be the last one I will make," he added, and went on to describe how brittle are his relations with CBS. He thinks they would like it if *he* resigned, but he says, No, that would confuse the issue. The "issue" is something he has been debating with what he calls his "su-periors" for a long time: the responsibility which the *network* must take for the content of what TV shows, rather than pass that on to ad-vertisers ("sponsors").

About the Shah, with whom he spent five hours of filming (!). He thought the whole place, i.e., the people surrounding him, were in-effective in the handling of things; this may be simply any reporter's reaction when everybody doesn't immediately drop whatever he is doing to attend to a reporter's needs. He looked at me, raising his eyebrows (in a way now familiar to millions of people) and said, "I would say it is a rather brittle regime."

I told him I didn't want to confine what I had to say before his camera to Iran and the Khuzistan; that I had been thinking as hard as I knew about the whole position in which we in the U.S. find ourselves in respect to helping the hungry of the world and would like to include that in what I say because Iran is only one segment of a great worldwide panorama. And most of what I had to say concerned the moral back-set the U.S. is suffering by reason of the fact that helping others is a policy today without a rudder, losing its way all the time, and without any clear motivation, the kind of clear motivation that once drove the American people to take world leadership in helping others.

He was all for broadening it as much as I liked.

Then he said something that warmed my heart: "There have been other dams than the one you are building on the Dez. This is just another dam, however dramatic the setting, in the great gorge. The important thing to you goes beyond that—what a dam or any other physical change can do, or be used to perform for people, as in TVA, the dam a symbol of ideas and ideals."

NOVEMBER 8, 1959
PARK HOTEL
TEHRAN, IRAN

By the time we had reached Beirut, at sundown, on our daylong flight from London, I knew it was not something I was imagining: I definitely had a fever. The next morning (that would be Friday the 6th) I ached all over. But I *had* to go through with the CBS filming that day, that's all there was to it.

Our big office had been turned absolutely inside out. Cables coiled ominously all over the place, like huge, black headless snakes; this illusion was made the more effective by the fact that they disappeared out the windows.

Without any rehearsals and not a piece of script or cue card in the place, we set off, Winston Burdette of CBS, and I, on a close-up sequence of me. Reel after reel of questions, and my answers, or comments, some of them quite long. By 6:30 I was burning up, and was sent home, where at last I took my temperature, and saw that I had done it again—dammit. It was definitely flu; two and a half degrees of fever. Remembering my long period of getting over the flu two years ago, I hope I'll manage to recuperate faster, and avoid relapses.

What I tried most to say on the interview was the American motivation for aiding the needy.

I have never made any impression on the public mind with ideas where I have been too cautious, made too many qualifications as if I were writing a contract rather than expressing my feeling about things. And it was in this mood that I talked into the camera Friday.

NOVEMBER 10, 1959
TEHRAN

I am essentially a promoter and evangelist of ideas; my interest in administration and management is secondary; my capacity for administration is greatest when it is the promotion of *ideas*, of *how* to get things done, rather than the satisfaction of the task of actually managing things.

If this analysis is, roughly, a correct one, then it explains my diminishing enthusiasm and absorption in this Persian enterprise, as we have moved steadily toward more and more straight administrative tasks.

When the pilot project idea for the Gebli irrigation area came along, this perked up my interest again. The area was far smaller than the whole Dez scheme. But the chance to work out ideas—about tenancy, production methods, education, health, and administrative devices— appealed to me far more than the prospect of spending years simply building canals to get water to land in a more or less conventional irrigation scheme. And as for the actual construction of the Dez Dam, which so excites Bill Voorduin and Gordon, this leaves me not cold, but cool. Not that it won't be one of the world's greatest. But what most interests me is the opportunity it gives to develop ideas about the *meaning* of the dam, the effect it can have upon things far more important than putting one yard of concrete on top of another.

NOVEMBER 11, 1959
TEHRAN

Had our first conversation with Hedayat this afternoon—and my first excursion out of this room in about five days. The cursed flu.

For some months my chief misgiving about our role in this Khuzistan program has been growing. It is that we are the party directly contracting on a sugar mill, construction of the dam, etc. While Ebtehaj was managing director, this could be made to work; with him gone, my concern mounted.

This seemed to me a mistake in *function*, for most of our energies would be expended in the details of management of far from unique enterprises (e.g., a big dam, a sugar refinery, etc.) and less and less on those aspects of policy and of ideas and inspiration for which our background gives us, I think, a rather unique position.

From today's session with Hedayat it appears that by reason of Plan Organization's initiative (though they probably don't recognize the full implications yet) we may be in a position where we shall not be the prime contracting party on the dam.

The *result* would be something I think is right, namely, that we get out from under these direct contracting and *disbursing* functions and back to our real job: of igniting people with ideas and ideals and ways of getting important things done.

NOVEMBER 14, 1959
TEHRAN

We met with Hedayat and his staff this noon.

I don't think Hedayat had any idea that we would practically announce a clear about face on carrying the full executive and fund disbursing function as we have to date.

I feared that we might be seriously divided among ourselves about how drastic and blunt we should be. But yesterday and the day before, in our visits among ourselves, and particularly between Gordon and myself, there was complete meeting of minds on this. The readiness Gordon showed to accept, and espouse, these basic changes amazed me, considering that for so long he has made it almost a moral issue that we must be the contracting party, that we *must* disburse the funds to the contractor; otherwise we cannot discharge our responsibilities, to "discipline" our subcontractors to keep to our schedules.

Hedayat wouldn't accept the changes, wanting time to think about it.

I'm not happy, God knows, that this new posture threatens the liquidation of our Persian excursion, for it looks more and more like a first stage of liquidation.

But, whatever the consequences, we have already injected some ideas into the Persian scene that are of great importance. As I said to Gordon, it is nothing less than false pride to feel that if we don't *finish* in every detail the execution of ideas we have failed. He said, rather significantly, and almost under his breath, "Sinful pride."

As I see the workmen shuffling by, in their ragged, utterly ragged clothes, little round hats, and then think of millions of hungry, kicked-around people throughout this country, my perspective returns. There is so much to do to help these people, and so many obstacles. Most of them somehow they will have to remove *through their own efforts*.

NOVEMBER 16, 1959
TEHRAN

There is something quite funny, not to say ridiculous, in the kind of session we had yesterday afternoon with Prime Minister Egbal.

As the old-fashioned lecturer says: "Imagine, if you will . . ." a group of earnest people sitting in a half circle while important questions affecting them all were being discussed with many words. But while there were many words, and emphasis, and gestures, and this goes on for an hour, for most of the time I didn't understand a word; and only a very little of this spate of discussion—of *us*—was translated, just a bare summary, if that.

I sat there, next to the Prime Minister, and admired his most hand-some huge head, his theatrical eyebrows and crinkled gray hair, aris-tocratic mien, and didn't know what in the hell he was saying—since he spoke in Farsi (though his English is quite good). Then Hedayat, looking uneasy and on the edge of his chair, talking at length, but what about I knew not.

A relatively small room, in a blond kind of wood, with the easy chairs covered in a hideous skin of plastic. A picture of the Shah, not in his gold-encrusted uniform but looking like a young college boy.

Finally Mostafa Mozayeny, of the Plan Organization technical staff, was bidden to translate—this was after at least a straight half hour of Farsi.

"His Excellency believes that the Dez Complex is a good project. It must go ahead. But because of our financial difficulties, the cane sugar project must somehow be managed so private money can finance it. But it must not stop, it must go right ahead. We want and need your help in this."

I made some inane diplomatic remarks, vague and purposely general as if I were at a cocktail party or ceremonial, that of course we wanted to be helpful; that the cane sugar project, as to the mill and refinery undoubtedly, could be turned into a private and money-making venture.

But as Gordon pointed out when we got back, he was concerned that these general expressions of good will were construed to mean that we would stay by the sugar cane project. So I didn't help much.

But without the funds there is only one thing we can do and that is cancel the refinery and turn the whole thing back to them. Judging from the conciliatory and outwardly friendly attitude yesterday (in contrast to the Prime Minister's chilly little lecture the last time we had a session) it may take a good deal of firmness to get out.

NOVEMBER 17, 1959
TEHRAN

Still another meeting with Hedayat and his staff yesterday after-noon.

He has not agreed yet to our proposition that the administration of the Dez contract should be *their* responsibility, not ours, which is a consequence of our position that we will not sign the contract with Impresit, the Italian low bidder.

If we come out of this difficult situation with any good will toward us left, it will be a miracle. But this is the course we simply must follow. This has happened so swiftly, though it has been coming, in my mind, and I think in Gordon's too, for a considerable period (since

Ebtehaj's removal, I suppose), that Gordon says Bill Voorduin still doesn't understand what's going on and will press us to get the contractors into the canyon and piece along somehow. Bill's passion to build that dam— a commendable one for him—has had a lot to do with the unwillingness to face up to the implications of our being the direct contracting party, even if it became pretty clear that funds to meet the obligations were going to be increasingly difficult to come by.

It would be rather easy to become cynical and pessimistic about what lies ahead for such countries as Persia in their development efforts. But I reject this position, both with my heart (which should come first) and with my mind. For these are episodes, natural ones, along the always rocky road toward fulfilling deferred needs and hopes.

We met with Ambassador Wailes this morning, early. It seemed important to let him know, directly from us, what he would hear, probably in garbled fashion, from others, including the Persians, to the effect that we were "letting them down." I described the situation very briefly and with some vigor.

I got some insight into the life a diplomat leads. After being at night parties all week, given for the visiting President of Pakistan, Ayub ("that man is a work horse; a party every night and it doesn't phase him!"), they were on their way to the airport to see someone off, or on. "That's what we are doing all the time," he said, with signs of fatigue on his usually cheerful and bouncy face. Then there are forty-seven people from Washington due today to lay plans for our President's arrival here on December 14—security officers, pilots to try the airfields, etc. And CENTO is meeting here today, with the Presidents of Turkey and Pakistan, and the Shah holding forth. The American Ambassador will have to do something about that too, mostly attend more parties! The diplomatic life needs a recorder who will tell just what an ambassador's life is like. Of course some people like that part of it, and hate the rest, the study of documents, the negotiations.

Wailes made a good point, in our little talk, apropos our saying that certainly the Italian low bidder would make terms of credit in order to get the Dez contract. Wailes said: "We want the other countries to bear some of the burden of aid we have carried almost alone for so long. But there is another side to it. If the Western European countries do take a more active part in aid programs, this will also step up the activities of their commercial interests in offering all kinds of credit, bidding against each other with such countries as Persia delighted at the prospect of having competition for their business. And whatever discipline in fiscal matters we now have, or the World Bank tries to maintain, will be greatly weakened."

NOVEMBER 19, 1959
FLYING TO TEL AVIV

A remarkable visit late yesterday with a remarkable man: Ebtehaj. This was at the home of Mozayeny. We told him that the basic arrangement we had worked out together was being fundamentally changed, on our intiative, but forced by the fact that Plan Organization and the Government did not have the funds, or was unwilling to allocate funds, to ensure carrying the work forward.

After an hour of being restrained and cautious, we finally talked about the crux of the matter: that the Government of Persia was moving away from the idea of devoting most of its oil revenues to development, in the direction of other uses for those funds, including expansion of the military services—but also including such things as a very expensive new Senate Building, a radio and TV station.

When the Government (i.e., the Prime Minister) tells us that the Khuzistan program must be cut back—or, rather, that they want it to go ahead, but fail to provide funds for it, a neat trick if you can do it— it is always on the thesis that Ebtehaj overcommitted the amount of money available or did not know what money there was. In point of fact, when they decided to cut back Plan's (i.e., development's) share of oil revenues to a maximum of $131 million for the balance of the second seven-year plan (less than 50 percent of oil revenues), it was inevitable that Ebtehaj's plans, based on 60 to 80 percent of those revenues as provided by law, could not be fulfilled.

Ebtehaj was fearful of policies about expanding the military services, with the disrupting effect this has on the whole of Iran's economy and at the expense of development. But he blamed, equally, U.S. policy in encouraging or going along with such ideas. Almost $200 million of U.S. funds is to be spent on an Iranian airfield and barracks now well along near Andimeshk.

The basic truth is *not* that there is a "financial stringency" of a temporary character but that the present Government does not believe sufficiently in putting development *first* to see to it that such funds as they have are put in for that purpose over every other.

NOVEMBER 21, 1959
HAIFA, ISRAEL

An extraordinary day yesterday.

We began the day very early, flying north to Mahanaim, and then drove to Kibbutz Ayeleth Hashahar (Morning Star). After seeing how people work and live in this remarkable settlement, we walked down a road to a slit trench on the brow of a hill, looking out over the Jordan Valley and the hills of Syria. A young man sat in a "hole," over him a corrugated iron roof, beside him a submachine gun and binoculars. I stepped into the observation post, looked through a telescope. Across the Valley I could see activity: a group of brown-clad soldiers, Syrians, stirring out of *their* observation post to see what was going on across the way. This is a farming operation; children playing all around. Yet all under the range of gunfire; here many men have lost their lives on both sides. The tragedy of it all was overwhelming. Tragedy for everybody.

This is Shabbat. The observance of the Sabbath is extreme for some things—no smoking in this modern hotel; you serve yourself breakfast, and none of it cooked. How strange it all is to me, how alien I feel, *except* when the Israeli engineers talk about how they are managing the limited water of this arid land.

NOVEMBER 23, 1959
FLYING VIA EL AL
TEL AVIV TO PARIS

This trip of less than five days has been so crowded, with travel, new impressions, new personalities and ideas that I haven't been able to keep a day-by-day record. But here are some notes, fragmented impressions, set down at the time.

Ezra Dannin, an expert on fish ponds. His eyes hooded like a hawk's; slow way of speaking, hardly moving his lips, never gesturing or emphasizing by tone of voice. My surprise that he is "Adviser to the Foreign Minister, on Arab Affairs." My question: "What do fish ponds of carp have to do with Arab affairs?" His philosophy about the Arabs, and what he does about it. His 125-year family background in Palestine. The all-carp meal served us, dessert included. The closeness between this huge mountain of a man and his bright-eyed Russian-born wife. His wealth and the modernity of his house, and his farmer traits; his respect for a "good farmer." His talent for experiment—the South American poplars, which he feeds with precious water and sheep manure.

Levi Eshkol, Minister of Finance—square-built Russian, bouncy, full of drive; the pioneer who began, not so long ago, as a day laborer, now a Minister of Finance. The Jewish joke: "We lost the holy Wailing Wall—now in Jordan's part of Jerusalem—but *there* is our wailing wall" (pointing to the Minister of Finance), where so many people go asking for funds for this and that. Eshkol says: Everything about Israel has a "but" about it, always something wrong, some limitation.

Prime Minister Ben-Gurion—looking like my Uncle Szold of Chicago, but without his Hungarian fire. A relaxed musing man, *very* short, full of doubts.

Horowitz of the Central Bank, bright snappy blue eyes, wise-looking, great pride in having made his start in Israel standing in a swamp to his armpits, a day laborer helping drain a swamp—and look at this—where we were dining in the fanciness of a leading Tel Aviv hotel. The "ambivalence"—too high a standard of living, he says. "We Israelis have a progressive income tax, but it doesn't help cut down consumption and thus protect against inflation—we need a "less equitable tax." Pride that he has been able "by hook or crook" always to meet every obligation of borrowing to the day; warmth about the Bank of America lending them $12 million when the outlook was not bright.

Doron: Deputy head of Tahal, the water agency. Small, intense, quiet-spoken, complete master of his job, wonderful sense of encouraging his subordinates—like the young fellow who had worked out the idea about pumping near the sea in a way that did not bring in sea water but used the interface between salt and sweet water.

The Lachish settlement near ancient biblical Ashkelon. The vehemence of Raanan Weitz, director of settlements. His theories that you must not "pulverize" the patriarchal social pattern the Oriental Jews at Lachish brought with them from Persia, Iraq, Morocco, Yemen. Separate them into communities—but use the school and center *to unite.* My comment that though from many separate countries and cultures they had a uniting force in a common religion. His response: they fight most *among themselves* about their religious differences *within Judaism!*

The children in the schoolyard and in class—some as dark as Moors (which they probably were). The final destruction of any idea that there is such a thing as a Jew, as a racial type: Saguy, the German with an Oxford background; Doron, a Romanian with an English accent; the many blond people among the Jews at Lachish and everywhere.

The house of the head of the Persian clan, a tailor from Tabriz, greeting us with the Persian bow, the hand over the heart, the double hand clasp—strictly Persian even after six or seven years in a country dominated, as Eisenstadt put it, by "East Europeans by way of Russia."

Young men in uniform, on the roads, and very smart-looking women, carrying weapons, as part of their conscript military training.

The problem of the Arabs surrounding Israel, the millions who had lived there, had orange groves, etc., who fled—or were driven out. The proud references, like old soldiers, of young men, to the "war of the Liberation." The road to Jerusalem from Tel Aviv lined with the wrecks of armored cars, ambushed in the effort to "relieve" Jerusalem.

The fad, or rage, for archaeology among laymen—a way of satisfying the question "Why am I here"—effort to establish a link with the past to make the present seem more understandable.

The night club in Tel Aviv—nice-looking and well-behaving young people dancing in a crowded space to Dixieland jazz. Saguy's remark: "When I was in the Youth Movement we wouldn't have been found dead in a place like this."
The palatial movie palace ("15 meters high") being built out on the plain in the midst of people of the most primitive background, and how this happened—the International Ladies' Garment Workers' plaque on the front—the proud little principal, who had plans to provide both culture and tea to those who came to see the movies.

My most intense personal impression: the contrast between my unlimited admiration for the great job these folks have done with their resources and the basic idea of a Jewish state, a political entity in which religion and the state are not distinctly separate.
Even with large outside help, mostly from the U.S., of course, it is still a kind of miracle: the tiny strip of land, much of it just rocks or desert, has been made to yield a living, to give birth to sophisticated cities and universities, to culture, in so few years.
But I left Israel with the same feeling I have had for many years, that the idea of a state, a political unit, that centers around a racial or religious theme is retrogression, more than justified in an emergency but not sound in principle.
It is required as a means of ameliorating the suffering of Jews in many lands, suffering inflicted upon them because of their racial or religious heritage. As a rescue operation it is admirable, extraordinarily well done. But the direction is destructive: a withdrawal from a world seeking unity; an acceptance of the outdated idea of a *political* unit based upon non-political factors. It is a retreat from something I hold very dear, the idea of *diversity*.
But as time goes on diversity will surely reassert itself in Israel and in the rest of the world. I can't face the prospect of a world in which all the people *in each country* are all the same—whether that "sameness" is religious, racial, cultural, or ideological.

NOVEMBER 28, 1959
PRINCETON

Although still rather tired from the "long journey home," went into the office yesterday to see a man from the Ivory Coast; André had phoned about him on Thursday. Name of Diffre, Executive Secretary of the Cabinet. A French civil servant who has been in the Ivory Coast some years. His purpose: to sound us out on undertaking a search for minerals in the small country, part of the "French Community" of West Africa.

I found what he said very interesting because he demonstrated how bitterly the Ivory Coast Frenchman, at least, and probably the Africans "in charge" of the Government under France feel about the rising tide all around them: French Guinea, their neighbor on the west, no longer a colony, and her President Touré getting big kudos in the U.S. (he spent a good deal of time with Eisenhower, offers of help, private bank loans, etc.) as well as in Moscow, where he is now visiting. Then on the east Ghana, independent, headed by an aggressive politician, Nkrumah, who is trying to give a picture of West African "unity"— which Diffre pooh-poohed.

Much of this French civil servant's talk was political, and politics produces no minerals if Nature hasn't. The Ivory Coast is openly and wholeheartedly "on the side of the West," whereas, said Diffre, Ghana and Guinea are taking money and support from both sides. And so on.

My enthusiasm for undertaking this is something less than 100 percent. Part of the reason, I suppose, is that a country in West Africa that is wedded to the French colonial system still—and, despite all the talk about the "French Community," that is what it is—is highly vulnerable; it is fighting the tide of independence.

But we will make a preliminary look-see.

DECEMBER 5, 1959
PRINCETON

A long visit with Baron Coppée, of a distinguished industrial and financial family of Belgium. He had talked to André about American participation in a European Community study (survey) in of all places the *Belgian* Congo. Coppée is a young man—perhaps thirty-two to thirty-five, plump, a shrewd eye, smooth manner of the Continental.

His idea: a group of Italian, French, and Belgians, chiefly the "consulting engineer or economist" type, to be joined by D&R, we to have a one-third interest, to make a study of the future development of the Belgian Congo. This is an outgrowth of a study his engineering firm has made for the Belgian-mandated territory in the heart of equatorial Africa known (unbelievably) as Ruanda-Urundi. Now, says he, the Minister for the Belgian Congo, Auguste de Schryver, a young man, wants to and is willing to extend this to the Belgian Congo; Coppée and his people want an outstanding American participation, and are persuaded we would be the best available. Peccei of Italconsult and SOGEP group of France and Kochs of Germany would be the lot.

I was very tough and almost unmannerly with him, in an effort to find out, quickly, what goes on. I dealt with the Belgian Government for the Congo, and the business interests who are synonymous with that great region (Union Minière, etc.) during my duties as AEC Chairman; I know they are hard-boiled, and want no one else than Belgium in the Congo. Why now do you think we should believe that they would welcome, and pay for a survey by a group, including Italian, German, French, and American interests? That doesn't ring true, I said.

He took this like a man, his very blue and shrewd eyes sizing me up, knowing too I was trying to squeeze the realities out of him. "A year ago," he said, "that would have seemed as unlikely as anything could be. But since then the Congo has been a ferment. Today a younger group of men are in charge, in the Belgian Government, chief among them being the new Minister for the Congo, De Schryver, a close associate of mine."

"But why do you want an American firm?" I asked. "We don't have anything of a technical character that you can't get in Belgium. The Belgians *know* natural resources in the Congo and how, technically, to develop them, every bit as well as Americans and better than the French or Italians."

"There are two reasons," he said; "we think that your assistance would improve the chances of major American investment; second, are political reasons. It is important to overcome the colonialism tag (those were not his words, but that was the point) and the inclusion of a group that represents the European Community *plus* a famous American such as yourself would have an important political effect."

Well, that was the kind of candid talk one doesn't often get from Europeans.

If in fact the Belgian Government is prepared to spend money and give standing to a multinational group of Europeans and Americans to stick their nose into the Congo, this is important indeed. It is important because it might be one of the very first evidences of Western European *Community* efforts in multinational aid to underdeveloped countries, and second, it might be the beginning of a New Deal in the richest European "colony" in Africa.

DECEMBER 8, 1959
5:45 P.M.
LEAVING IDLEWILD FOR CALI

Helen and I to the dinner of the Democratic Advisory Council "honoring Eleanor Roosevelt" last night. In the main ballroom of the Waldorf, scene of so many such meetings. But it was gay—all lighted up in Christmas tree style. And the meeting was happy, even light-hearted. First time I have been at a Democratic gathering for a long, long time when happy would be a word you would use to describe its spirit.

We sat in the first row of tables; at our table, one seat from me Governor "Pat" Brown of California; one of the "hopefuls" for the Democratic presidential nomination. When I was introduced to him he said: "I have heard so much about you and your work. Read your book." I didn't say a word; stupid. Helen remarked on my silence. But later we talked about the great north-south water project he has finally put through the legislature.

A $2 billion undertaking. Very proud of what he has accomplished; but is worrying about getting it under way. Two big worries, troubles: first, the limitation by law of not more than 160 acres to one settler. On this he says, very sensibly, I think, let's not let that divide us; the thing to do is get ahead with the project. The second is the continuing dispute between the north, where the water of California comes from, and the south, which benefits directly from it. This is a real problem, of course, in almost all cases where the water regime of Nature is changed. Didn't think much of his little five-minute speech, but he was a pleasant and rather substantial man to talk with.

Also visited with Stuart Symington, who was exceedingly cordial and is certainly handsome. His speech was excellent, though his voice has a lightness and nasal quality that doesn't convey the force he has, as I know; nor does his appearance disclose that, in fact, he has handled two tough executive assignments with far-above-average administrative ability.

Senator Jack Kennedy's wife, Jacqueline, sat at our table; a quite lovely and very young-appearing, slender, dark-eyed woman. She was tense and anxious. Kennedy's talk was poetic and moving, but there was no electrifying quality. I talked to him in an intermission; taller man than I thought, and not so young looking "close up" as the impression created by his pictures and TV appearances. His hopes have had a very tough blow, administered the other day by the statement of the Roman Catholic Bishops against providing birth-control information to foreign countries as part of aid programs; entirely gratuitous on their part, as nothing of the kind is going on, I understand. But it certainly put the Catholic religion into the campaign with a bang. Kennedy made a very good comment to me about Senator Norris: that the great thing about him had been that he fought for TVA although he was not from the South, nor from the Northwest, where there is waterpower, but from Nebraska. I liked him.

Humphrey spoke briefly—which was deliberate because of his well-deserved reputation for being a terrific talker. He showed dignity, fire—the best performance I have ever seen him give.

The star of the evening was clearly Adlai Stevenson. Of course, this was *his* audience, because of his great popularity in New York City among those who put up much of the money for campaigns, and who worship him. But, quite aside from that, he showed much of the eloquence, humor, and understanding of the nuances of public affairs, plus conviction, that made him such a figure during his first campaign, and which I thought was lacking in the second. Unless some figure emerges soon, it is far from nonsense that the Convention may, in the end, pick him again. He said some very witty things, and he looks much better than when he was heavier.

Mrs. Roosevelt is a great figure, for what she has done, for her symbolic importance, which is worldwide and deserved. But what she *says*—as last night—is so often the vaguest bunch of clichés ever assembled; in this like Ike, in his extemporaneous style, except that she *does* finish sentences.

I haven't laughed as riotously since my last W. C. Fields movie, when I nearly was thrown out of the theatre as a one-man riot. The occasion: a remarkable night club monologist, Mort Sahl: a very slender, intense, pert young fellow. A Will Rogers Broadway 1960 style. His rippling on about Ike, Nixon, *everything*, had everyone in stitches, even Mrs. Agnes Meyer, who also sat at our table.

With the coming of a definite invitation from Araneta yesterday, our trip to the Philippines is about set. Gordon is going to see if he can determine how Ambassador Romulo feels about it. Romulo is an explosive and expansive little man, and if he thinks Araneta is "bad auspices" he will tell us so. But whatever he thinks, I am quite confident the trip is on.

Tomorrow morning sometime I will be back in the Cauca Valley.

DECEMBER 9, 1959
9:15 A.M.
PANAMA CANAL ZONE

The humid, oppressive heat of the tropics bears down on you, even in an airport stop of an hour.

But within the airport a phonograph keeps playing: "Jingle Bells, Jingle Bells, ta, ta, ta, ta, taaa - . . . through the snow," and, inevitably, "Iyam dreeeming uva wite grismas,' etc.

DECEMBER 12, 1959
CALI, COLOMBIA

This has been a real "homecoming," these days in Cali and Valle del Cauca.

Yesterday late afternoon I talked to a public meeting, mostly students and faculty of the young Universidad del Valle del Cauca.

What is really remarkable is that CVC has survived, has so much accomplishment to its credit, despite the fact that the Calima Dam Project wasn't begun, that national government financing has been mighty little, and that the powerful landowners of the Valle have been opposed, and at times bitterly opposed. Their reason chiefly a puny little land tax put on them for two purposes: to support the CVC's reclamation activities and, second, to begin the process of forcing them to use their land more intensively, rather than hold it for the great rises in land value that go on in this amazingly rapid rise of population, industry, etc.

There is no question about *how* I get some of the keenest and deepest satisfactions of life. To see a people struggling with the problems of how to live more decently, to get an education for their children, to overcome the human failings of greed, madness for power, sloppiness and inefficiency, inability to get things done, above all, to *prove to themselves* that they can achieve things: to see such things, and then come up with an idea which *they* embrace, and do something about, and particularly to see the beginning of results—how could there possibly be, for me, a source of greater satisfaction and fulfillment? How lucky I am that in my lifetime this sequence of events has actually happened to me—not just a fantasy, but actually happened!

This is just what has happened in the five years since Helen and I first entered Colombia at that squalid tropical Conradian port of Buenaventura, and before our visit was over launched the idea of a regional development for the Valle del Cauca. I thought it would surely die when the dictator, Rojas Pinilla, ran amuck, we pulled out, the CVC was double-crossed by the General, and I thought General Manager Bernardo Garces would give it up.

CVC has become a going concern, thanks partly to their continuing with limited but useful reclamation work and a rather ambitious rural extension program. CVC is an idea in action, ready to do a bigger job should Calima Dam be authorized and financed. I am coming up daily with ideas on how to persuade the World Bank to do that financing, rather than piddling along with one little steam plant after another, which is their preference, for banking reasons perhaps but for no reasons that are good for Colombia.

DECEMBER 13, 1959
CALI

Yesterday visited an orphanage, Instituto de San José para la Protección de Niños Desamparados (abandoned children), twenty-two small boys, with Mrs. Alejandro Garces, one of the founders. Had a happy time with these wonderful shining faces, of all colors and sizes. One, quite small, with his hands thrust deep into his first pockets (I guessed) reminded me so much of our grandson Daniel.

I didn't just go through; we stayed, talked to them for a long time, had them play with my Minox (which is an unfailing conversation piece), listened to music (guitar and a toneless—to me—kind of singing). They followed me out in a body to the car as we hurled Adióses, and Felices Navidades at each other. Though it had been a hard day before this—6 P.M.—I never felt fresher.

A similar experience this morning. After meeting Señor Presidente Lleras at the Air Base, he went off to see some extensive housing undertakings; I was in the cavalcade.

Mired in deep mud are these streets full of people we would call squatters. Huts—and people and people. This is a problem of justice and of *doing something* that really gets you. But, whereas in India (Benares or Calcutta) it may seem almost hopeless (though it would be a crime to admit that defeat is possible) here the young men around Lleras have been doing something remarkably good.

Particularly, the building of low-cost housing. We saw a cooperative housing development that is like nothing I have ever seen. The Government (the Rehabilitation Institute, under a quite young man, Llama Picón) provides a small piece of land for a house, and requires ten pesos as a down payment (that is less than U.S. two cents). The Government lays a block of concrete the size of the house, provides sewage, CVC undertakes the drainage problem, leading the storm sewers into a canal. In some cases the Institute builds four brick walls and a roof, and the owner completes the house—"do it yourself."

But along a good many "streets" a third method was being used. Only the block of concrete, the foundation. Then neighbors buy brick together, and work on each other's houses, or trade skills: one fellow knows how to lay bricks, another to make cement, etc.

We watched a number of groups busy working together, with enthusiasm and persistence, the houses going up. And while *their* house is being built (with work at night, on Sundays and holidays) the families were living in a poor little hut on a piece of the little plot of land that now is *theirs*. But how slicked up and decent most of them are, and how many women who can only be described as ladylike: in their Sunday best, washing the children—and they are beautiful children.

So many pictures I wish I could record. One that almost made me weep. A hut; the new mansion not yet started. The lady of the house on the concrete foundation slab carefully *sweeping* the empty foundation slab. Theirs.

Or, two men working side by side on adjoining lots. To hold the line to keep his bricklaying straight, one put a brick on the end of the line. The man next to him on the adjoining lot said: "That's all right, putting that brick there, but just remember it is on *my* property."

Running into U.S. Senators on these trips is getting to be the thing. This time Senator Wayne Morse of Oregon, a long-time fighter for TVA.

President Lleras today looked older by far than when we had him for dinner at our apartment in New York three years or so ago. When I chatted with him at the Air Base, as he was taking a helicopter to see CVC works, I said: "A good deal has happened, since we talked together in New York." He grinned and said: "Was I right?" He had remembered the predictions he had made—the fulfillment of which certainly seemed unlikely at the time—that the dictator would be overthrown. He certainly was right, and he had most to do with making that prediction come true.

I brought up the question of more intensive use of the land of this valley, against the opposition or lethargy of the owners, and cited my experience at Fruco. This is a 200-acre tract between here and Palmira. When I saw it three years ago it employed one man and there were a half dozen scrub cattle on it. The owner was holding it for a rise in value.

CVC got through a land tax, and has been pressing the idea of more intensive use of land. The owner has now leased this land to a corporation farming group to produce for a cannery here. I saw the payroll station; there are now 145 men employed on that 200 acres. They are raising tomatoes, peas, onions, prodigious yields and bearing right through the year. That produce helps keep other people employed at the cannery, which sends its products all through Colombia, and provides a market for a can-producing plant.

The President asked me how CVC is coming along, saying he was lunching with me in Bogotá Tuesday when we could talk about it further. I started off with a general approval—and the need for financing of Calima Dam. I must use whatever prestige I have to keep the World Bank from financing a *third* small uneconomic steam electric plant (Yumbo III) and go right at Calima. But it will be uphill business, for the same reasons as in Khuzistan. The Bank's staff apparently have general orders to expand electric expenditures as slowly as possible, because it is a capital-eating animal. But it is the most productive kind of capital investment there is.

CVC is in wonderful hands. Bernardo Garces is one of the best minds and spirits I have ever known, earnest, wise, thoughtful, and yet not a "lecturer."

Went to a huge reception for the President tonight, and met scores of people, including the Beauty Queen of the Valle—and *what* a beauty she is. The "friends" of Plan Lilienthal try to outdo each other in saying poetic and dramatic things to me, about how appreciative they are. One little man, said to be "the richest man in the Valle" (I have heard that term applied to at least four other people), Llamese Caicedo, a sugar king, said among other things (this in Spanish): "You are our second Discoverer."

The stark contrast between the well-to-do and the very poor was dramatically demonstrated tonight, after the sights I saw this morning. A new country club, looking, as Alejandro Garces said, like a modern airport building rather than a "country" club. Vast; a huge racing pool, luxury rampant. And on those hillsides against the shadow cast by the moon people in hovels; and they keep pouring in—8 percent increase a year—from all the miserable villages and hillsides of the whole of western Colombia.

Explosive difficulties. Many of these immigrants are part of the wreckage of bandit "warfare," which is probably just brigandage pure and simple with no particular political aspect.

DECEMBER 14, 1959
CALI

One thing that seems to have happened to the Plan Lilienthal is this: Only the Departamento del Valle del Cauca is really actively interested any more. Caldas sees no benefit, or has been shown none. Departamento del Cauca to the south, very poor, contributes nothing in the way of funds, and I gather is hardly part of the story any longer —that is, at this stage.

The way American official visitors, Senator Morse, for example, are herded closely by our Embassy people so they hardly see anyone but Colombian officials is a sad but common story. Too bad Morse couldn't have walked about in the mud in that home-building spree we saw yesterday, or through the slums and side streets, as I did. But officialese practice usually makes this something that rarely happens. Here is something someone should have a "project" about: how can *serious* visitors really see what goes on in a country?

And yet Morse will go back, I'm sure, convinced that he has "seen" Colombia, and can look down his nose at his Senate colleagues who talk about Latin America without his "firsthand knowledge."

DECEMBER 15, 1959
BOGOTÁ

Just back from the Palace, and the small luncheon Lleras gave in my honor. One of the pleasantest and most stimulating and heartening experiences—to see the kind of mind and heart that man has, at close range.

When we arrived he took me off in a corner of the room adjoining the dining room. When I was last in this room, I was sitting next to General Rojas Pinilla—and could there possibly be a greater difference between two men, in every way, than between these two Colombians!

Lleras looks you right in the eye, intently, with no wavering of attention, both when he listens (and unlike most Presidents, he is a good listener, invites comments), and when he talks, which he does with such simplicity and yet depth of feeling.

The President has taken particular pains with the military. When he was in Cali, he stayed at the Air School. He had the Commander in Chief of the Air Force at the small luncheon he gave for Senator Wayne Morse, Ambassador Dempster McIntosh, and me. He had his military aide with him; I was amused, however, to note that after he arrived the aide changed to civilian dress, and so did the General in charge of the Air Force. One of the stories most often told about Lleras, in the stirring days of his take-over, was to declaim to the military men: "Here, I hand you back the democratic Army of Colombia, taken from you by a dictator."

When I saw him first at Cali, about to take to a helicopter, he looked quite worn and much older. But after a long, long day in Cali, being greeted with warmth and love by the poorest people, and feted in a grand party at the Country Club by the rich, respected on all sides, he looked like a man of forty (actually he is only fifty-two). All signs of fatigue gone. Except for a stoop, and a rather frail-looking slight body, he looked as vigorous at the end of the day (10 P.M.) as he had looked worn at the beginning. Such are the mysteries of nervous energy, and the refreshment that springs from man's emotions. And at the Palace he was gay, no sign of strain in his manner, and so friendly and informal and considerate.

He is certainly not at all what one thinks of as a Latin, a South American. His eyes are a soft shade, hazel or brown; there is nothing Spanish I could detect in his appearance or manner, or way of thinking. But he can be eloquent as his speeches attest (a collection of which I have in my bag for reading) and his *physical* courage during the overthrow of Rojas is the kind one might call Latin, if it were not also the kind of complete disregard of personal consequences that also characterizes all brave men, dedicated men, of all races.

He has a lively, almost mischievous, childlike grin, which shows him at his best; a simple man, without flamboyance or "side."

His *understanding* of CVC surprised me. He sees CVC as a case of decentralization, one to be supported for that reason. He said to me, quite spontaneously: "We in the National Government have never interfered with CVC; that is the way it should be. We should help, but CVC should run its affairs. Decentralization in a Latin-American country is more important even than in other places, because of the history of military dictatorships. If we can demonstrate it in the Valle . . . well," and again that grin.

In connection with his forthcoming visit to the U.S., his first as President, of course, he told me he said this to Gene Black: "I don't want to come to the U.S. to ask for something. I want the question of a loan to Calima to be out of the way before I get there, or after I leave. I don't like the idea of heads of countries coming to the U.S. and always asking for something, as if that were their only reason for coming. There are some fundamental issues to discuss, in conference and in public statements: these I want to concentrate upon, not loans and aid."

The reason Lleras has made such a great impact on me, I suppose, is that his ideas, better expressed, are so close to my own observations on life, and his bravery is what I would hope I could emulate if the occasion arose, as I guess in frankness one should say, it did, in a less physical way, when I have been called upon for the one great indispensable of courage: willingness, without hesitation or calculation, to *risk everything* on being yourself.

In Lleras' case, risking everything included his life; but also it is worth remembering that he was a man with a good income (as head of the Pan American Union), when he gave it up to come back to fight it out for the democratic future of Colombia, taking the post of Rector of the Universidad de los Andes, at practically nothing per year.

His simplicity is genuine and affecting. I referred to a discussion with the Minister of Obras Publicas, and not being sure of his name (Virgilio Barco, actually) I said. "His Excellency." With that delightful little grin, he said: "There are no Excellencies around here."

At lunch he sat at the head of the table. Looking down the line of perhaps ten people, he called out to me, "And what do you think of the age of my Ministers?"

I said they looked decrepit to me, and of course we all laughed, for one is in his late twenties; the other two in their middle or early thirties.

He made many trenchant comments. "I don't try," he said, "to see all the problems there are. Only those we can do something about. I don't think of us as appointed 'guardians of the human species.' "

As we left the Palace in a big car, two cows were grazing along one street, a man in a ruana splashing water on his face on the edge of the street; an Indian woman barefooted—in the midst of modernity.

DECEMBER 19, 1959
CURAÇAO, NETHERLANDS ANTILLES

Must be getting rested; happy and interested in every little thing; a newly arrived German family, for instance. The grandfather, looking like a Himmler on a holiday without the uniform and the stern visage. Three little blond kids. How can it be that such human beings as these —affectionate, home-loving people, became such beasts?

Curaçao is different from any place I have ever seen. At this time of year at least, the visitors to this hotel are very cosmopolitan: a good many Dutch, some French, German, and of course American. The hotel itself is built within the great stone walls of a Dutch fort. To complete the picture, they have reinstalled old cannon of the eighteenth century in the wall openings.

The town is divided by a very deep but narrow channel, the harbor lying rather deep within the island. Through this channel come and go the oil tankers from the Venezuelan fields of the Royal Dutch Company, and carry away the products of the refinery here.

The people, very black and very intelligent looking, seem to live well. The market is partly waterborne.

The sailing vessels are moored to the channel as a dock, at a 45° angle, their bowsprits pushing over the walk. The wares of fruit and fish are then sold, under awnings spread from the ships themselves. The schooners are rather a larger kind of long-boom schooner than those in and about St. Croix.

DECEMBER 21, 1959
EN ROUTE TO NEW YORK FROM
WILLEMSTAD, CURAÇAO

I have had a feeling, a perverse desire to differ perhaps, that all the hoorah to the effect that foreign aid to underdeveloped countries should be through international agencies only, has some buncombe in it, some exaggeration or oversimplification.

But it was Bernardo Garces, in his careful, understated, non-Latin, and highly specific attack on problems that brought this hunch into the realm of conviction.

So I got Bernardo to talk about the UN agencies as the antidote for U.S. (or U.K., for that matter) technical assistance.

He told stories of actual episodes in his experience in CVC that illustrated the realities about UN as the cure-all.

He underlined what I have known, vaguely, about the World Bank staff—the elite of international agencies. The European staff are jealous of the U.S. position in that organization.

To preserve their international character, the international agencies must allocate a *quota* of non-Americans to the staff of the Bank, whether they are as good as U.S. or U.K. or not. This is a variation of the patronage system; necessary perhaps but certainly not a demonstration of the completely cure-all, pure, *nonnational* character of the UN.

This produces strange results, Bernardo says. For example, application was made by Colombia to the UN (WHO perhaps) for public health help. Result: two Ecuadorian public health "experts" were assigned to help its neighbor Colombia with Valle del Cauca public health problems. Said Lleras: "Do the Ecuadorians know any more about public health than our own people? Considering how severe are the public health problems of our neighbor Ecuador, if they have people to spare, wouldn't they be better employed to stay in Ecuador, which they know and where they are needed, than come to Colombia where they have much to learn?"

Another illustration of the limitations of exclusively United Nations technical assistance: Would a newly independent, anticolonial country (Ghana or Morocco or India, for that matter) want to have the UN assign an "expert" from Holland or France, say, whose whole basis of expertise had been in the atmosphere and philosophy of colonialism?

The UN mantle isn't as holy as the international phobiacs would make it appear.

In Bogotá I had about a two-hour visit with Lauchlin Currie. The meeting was initiated by the Minister of Public Works, when he saw me at Cali. Wanted advice about the Magdalena Valley. Currie, who headed the World Bank major mission to Colombia years ago, had been asked to "coordinate" the studies of the Magdalena Valley.

Currie was Marriner Eccles' chief assistant at the Federal Reserve, and generally regarded as as able an economist as there was in the Government. Then he became one of the six administrative assistants to F.D.R.—the anonymous six. Bob Garner picked him to head a general mission to Colombia, about the first of the nationwide planning missions of the Bank under the Black-Garner regime.

After completing, for the World Bank, the "Currie Report on Colombia," Currie stayed on in Colombia, bought a finca on the savanna of Bogotá, married a Colombian wife, became a Colombian citzen.

Lleras brought him back into "planning," Currie told me. He was pretty disconsolate about making any sense of the Magdalena Valley.

But what he talked about most of all (in addition to the impossibility of this task) was a curious commentary on man's foresight. As a result of his recommendations in the Currie Report, transportation, financed by World Bank loans, is being put through the heart of the Magdalena River Valley. The completion of the railroad and a highway are scheduled for the immediate future. (I got the impression that if he had it to do over again, with greater knowledge of realities, he would have omitted the railroad in place of more highways—and I think I would too.) With improved access, squatters are pouring into that Valley by the thousands, burning the hillsides to make little farms, dynamiting the fish in the streams, cutting down trees, etc. Nothing being done about it. Nothing in the Currie Plan specifically foreshadowed this consequence, or proposing affirmative alternatives to this destruction.

So his preoccupation is some way to *prevent* people from doing things—cutting trees, killing fish, destroying natural resources. The TVA way would be to get busy providing affirmative ways for people to live in that new-found region so they would be less likely to destroy. To police the kind of Verboten he is thinking about would take the whole Colombian army.

Every new human being one gets to know, even if casually and in a transitory way, opens another door, a door through which one sees just a bit more about the world than he knew before that person crossed his path.

In some cases the door that is opened is one that leads into almost another world; a better, more whole comprehension of *this* world is perhaps the way to put it. A world that otherwise would have always been unknown, even unimagined. I can think of a good many people, friends, teachers, intimates of one sort or another, who did this very opening-up for me.

And then, if one is truly alive every moment (as I am certainly not), even a few hours opens a new avenue; even though one never sees that individual again, the door, the window perhaps, is opened, and actually life is never completely the same.

The two young Dutchmen I met and visited with at Willemstad, as casual examples. Because of these apparently aimless poolside talks here at Curaçao I better understand the young man who is sent out from a small country, representative in an important way of both his company and his country.

The deep and direction-turning people—Helen as a single but pervasive example: the profound mind-opening, heart-developing effect of such people—this is fairly well known. What is new to me is how much one can get by casual, limited touches with people along the way.

The moral of this is that avoiding people because they may be bores shows a lack of imagination, an unwillingness to take risks—the risk of boredom by people who simply don't have *any*thing. And that is the way I regret to say I lived a good part of my life.

Less and less I write of really *personal* things in this journal; more and more it becomes a history of ideas, or record of things seen, "important" people talked to.

Perhaps that is just as well. But it makes it quite incomplete, and less the kind of release or form of expression with which this started when I was a boy in my teens, when the first "diaries" and later the journals began.

To be fully satisfying, however, this should be a place where one says something, within the limits of good taste and one's own inhibitions (not a bad thing, inhibitions!) about how the inner man feels, thinks, dreams, believes, at the time, without worrying one bit whether that will sound silly *to me* if read a year or ten or twenty years later.

Thus: for a couple years now, from time to time, I have found myself filled with the urge to pray to the Lord. Now, the sense of God is nothing new or strange or recent to me; I can't remember the time when this wasn't part of me. But praying, that is, talking with the Lord as best I know how, has grown on me. And then, more recently, I have found this more satisfying, more real, if I kneel by the side of my bed as I prepare for sleep. This is old-fashioned, and I could make a good deal of fun of the childishness, or childlike quality of kneeling, alone, in my bedroom. But it helps in the outpouring of my heart; this is partly tradition, a picture of what praying should be. But perhaps it is deeper than that. In any case, even on this holiday I found myself in that posture.

And what do I pray about? Almost always on one theme. No matter where my thoughts and feelings began: thankfulness, an overpowering sense of gratitude for the wonders of the world, its beauty, its mystery, its infinite and magnificent variety, a thankfulness that I have lived this day, this year, this decade, this lifetime in a world so wondrous that only a divine hand could have shaped it, a divine will have created it, a divine imagination made it so unpredictable, so changing, so worthy of one's best efforts, one's love.

DECEMBER 29, 1959
NEW YORK

When I come to town I stay late at the office; rather pleasant here, when the city outside has quieted down, and the streams of people have started on their way to Long Island, etc.

Part of the ritual is asking Nate Greene in for a drink and talk.

This evening this wise and delightful man made a point I need to ponder.

We were talking about the difficulty some men have in "disengaging themselves from life," after a life of action, while others seem to look forward to such inactivity. But what *is* disengagement? Writing about the life that goes on in this explosive period can be functioning, actively, almost as much, or in the same sense, as participation in events. I mentioned George Kennan's life of contemplation and writing as a kind of withdrawal. Nate disagreed; he *is* functioning, actively, in what he writes, and thinks, about problems to which he can contribute more than almost anyone else.

I agree: it is possible that contemplation, reflection, and writing *can* be a form of active functioning almost as much as the kind of decision making and responsibility carrying that I have ordinarily considered the only way in which an active life can be lived.

DECEMBER 31, 1959
11:15 P.M.
PRINCETON

Went to bed quite early, to try to get caught up on the intense and highly stimulating three days and two nights in New York, but sleep hasn't come. Perhaps what is barring sleep is a sense of unfinished business; for so many years I tried to sum up the year, at its end.

Is such a verbal summing up ever even an approximation of the truth? At the end of 1940, for example, did I know enough to evaluate, to measure in words or thought, the things that had happened to me, as an individual, during that year? Certainly not. The same thing is probably true this year.

But what stands out in my mind that is possible to bring close enough to the surface for words, these things I could enumerate:

First, I suppose, is that this was a year full of life, just as the year before was almost drained of any of those robust, vigorous, straining, and salty exuberances that go with really being alive. The year before I was holding back, and learning somehow to bear that half-life.

Not so 1959—from beginning to the very end.

I traveled into parts of the world new to me: with Helen to Morocco, Ghana, Nigeria. To Persia and Israel and the Cauca Valley. Great rich additions to the sum total of experience, perspective. The experience of finding—perhaps creating—energy sufficient to go to these places, do strenuous things, meet many, many new people, affect them, their thinking, and outlook, with the flaring off of enthusiasm for ideas and people that I like to think is the thing I do best and get most satisfaction from, the thing that justifies my existence.

The year had strains and worries, too; the long battle with the World Bank to get them into a position such as now exists, when Persia's Khuzistan is finally described by Knapp—as it was a few days ago in a phone call to me here—as having the "top priority in the Bank" —that too was a thing to remember 1959 for.

I have tried throughout the years of these journals to write them for myself, to help clarify my own thinking about events and my relation to them, in my life. The most important things of all though, even in a personal journal, are difficult to put down; it is only rarely, as I look back, that the most significant emotional and intimately personal events, or even "facts," find their way into this half-therapeutic personal record.

Life is repetitious. I find that at sixty I have many of the marks of immaturity, of less-than-adulthood that I had as a college student or at thirty. And without characterizing it as immaturity or any other noun, the way I react inside to the ups and downs, the comings and goings of fortune from day to day, the highs and the blues because of this or that moving of the dial of one's daily life—these seem to be not much different today than thirty or twenty years ago.

The way a year looks at its close is very much affected by the plans that agitate one about the year that will begin in ten minutes. Here things look exciting. Today Helen and I worked out further plans about another trip around the world. Helen has for years been fascinated by the ruins in Cambodia known as Angkor Wat, and Nehru made a great point that we should try to see the cave paintings in the Ajanta caves. This trip will try to include both, and the prospect that I can repay Helen for her enormous help and her companionship and affection, by these trips, buoys me up considerably. And in the end I will find that I enjoyed this "sight seeing" too, greatly, as I did the great sights at Tarquinia of the Etruscan burial vaults, and many other places I went to please Helen, and found that I had added a great deal to my own satisfaction quite independently of the pleasure of seeing her enjoy these ancient things that mean so much to her, emotionally and intellectually.

II

1960

California Water Plan—Around-the-world trip—Colonial-
ism in the Philippines—Rural Cambodia; Angkor Wat—
Iran: U.S. military aid; the Shah and Lilienthal discuss
Dez Dam and large-scale agriculture—Brussels: young
Belgians' ideas for a new Congo—Madrid—Lilienthal's
idea of a multinational corporation—The Soviets and the
Summit Conference—Lilienthal on Board of FIDIA—
Democratic Convention—Murrow on Israel—Indus River
treaty signed—D&R and the World Bank—Trip to
Argentina: cancellation of Argentine contracts—Cam-
paigning for Kennedy in the Tennessee Valley—Ideas on
foreign aid—Trip to Iran: landlords and land reform—
Republic of the Ivory Coast

JANUARY 9, 1960
PRINCETON

This morning wakened with a beaut of a bronchitis. But happy.
Why do I feel so much alive? Why have I, for almost two weeks, been
in a state of—vibrancy? What a good feeling, this sense of being fully
alive.

Certainly the excitement of working out the Newton D. Baker
Memorial Lecture (what a solemn way to describe a speech) has had
something to do with it. For that job of finding out what I *think* about the
underdeveloped countries has been one that has stirred and challenged
me, because it deals with certainly the most important issue of this
time—economic and social improvement for the coming-up nations. And
the excitement of launching an idea—for there is an idea in this speech
—works on my insides, as it always has since I was in my teens.

JANUARY 16, 1960
PRINCETON

The "underdeveloped countries" speech◖ in Cleveland has come
and gone. It was a hard one to work out, and perhaps I put too much
effort into it. But I got a great satisfaction out of shaping it, and the
reception my words received by the audience in Cleveland was as close
and intent and (I thought) in agreement as anything I can remember for
a long time.

Have just come from visiting a few minutes with Bob Goheen, the
new President of Princeton. He has just been through a Board of Trustees
session, which I am told he handled masterfully, but he looked far less
like a young handball player than when I had seen him before. It was
fun for me to see this young fellow, and get better acquainted with him,
for if we continue to live in Princeton I want to have more to do with
Princeton people, both town and University.

JANUARY 23, 1960
NEW YORK

In theory at least, in five minutes Helen and I should be starting our
second trip from "New York to New York," this time going westward.
We're both pretty excited, each in our own way. This trip comes
at a crucial time for me, personally, emotionally, and for my "decade of
decision," the sixties—the century's and mine.

Important step along the way in the idea evolution of Development
and Resources was confirmed in the past two weeks.
The move away from becoming just another conventional engineer-
ing and management company is well along to a complete program.
What began as an effort on my part to persuade myself, first, and then
Gordon that we were getting too deeply into direct, *detailed* management
has now pretty well gone full circle.
We are returning more nearly to the original concept of D&R—a

◖ In this speech Lilienthal questioned the basic rationale for American "aid"
to the underdeveloped countries, namely, ". . . if we do not provide the poor and
needy countries with economic help they will probably go Communist." He asserted
this policy "is not practical. It has not worked, and I believe it cannot be made to
work." He proposed a re-examination of our aid program to take account of the
"wondrous spirit of independence and pride [that] has gripped" the underdeveloped
countries.

An adaptation of this speech before the Cleveland Council on World Affairs
was published as an article in the *New York Times Magazine* for June 26, 1960,
under the title "Needed: A New Credo for Foreign Aid."

small, compact enterprise. We had to depart from that concept, pressed by Ebtehaj—almost four years ago now—when he insisted—wisely under the circumstances—that we accept responsibility not only for developing a program but *executing* it. Helen listened to Gordon's and my solemn discussion of the Ebtehaj proposal, then smiled in a pleasant but slightly mocking way: "I recall hearing you two, in Paris (it was at the Meurice Hotel, on a snowy day in February, as I recall it) talking about the concept of D&R. Well, it seems now you are going to have to *revise your concept*." So "revise your concept" is a phrase Gordon and I have adopted as a kind of partnership joke.

So long as we work for Iran we will have considerable direct management responsibility; this will be particularly true of the Gebli irrigation area (the pilot project effort) and the fertilizer program. But we are, happily, doing less and less of direct management, once we have moved our ideas (which is our forte) into action and projects. Examples are the PVC (plastic) project; complete responsibility for the Dez, as distinguished from the more limited role of supervision of engineering and construction which we anticipate will continue as our role; our successful sugar cane program—all are gradually dropping away, in an overall management sense. How relieved I am that we are beginning to get back on the track, and that this was accepted without any differences developing that were not adjusted by talking things over quietly and persistently.

Last Monday Gordon and I had a delightful and memorable luncheon meeting with André. For the first time in a couple of years, I thought, he showed a keen interest and responsibility for seeing that D&R got ahead, rather than listening to us in a friendly but mildly dubious and rather negative way. He took the ball, as we neared the end of our lunch, and carried it for a straight half hour, pouring out ideas, possibilities, and all of this with an eagerness and charm that made me think of the André I knew five years ago.

One set of his ideas concerned Italy. Enrico Cuccia, of Mediobanca, thinks a lot of us, he said. Cuccia has managed to get Pirelli, Fiat, Snia (the synthetic textile outfit) and other private companies of that character to form an organization "for the development of Italy." The initials of the group are FIDIA. This was something I had urged on Cuccia and Carlo Weiss on our first trip to Italy five years ago, feeling that the government agency, Cassa per il Mezzogiorno, could do little for the South except agriculturally perhaps, because (1) Italy's government is so heavily bureaucratic, and (2) because only the industrial North could develop the South industrially, and (3) in agriculture larger units, combining farming with processing, were essential in a country where land was scarce and was already held in too small parcels to be truly productive.

Well, at that time Cuccia had said to me, in that skeptical Sicilian way of his: "Getting Italian industrialists to work together is impossible; they don't trust each other." But, characteristically, apparently he hasn't given up trying.

André continued: "They want two 'foreigners' on the Board. One is Jean Monnet, the other [turning to me] is you. Are you interested?" Of course I would be glad to go on the Board, even without knowing anything more than what he had said.

André continued: he had word from the Prime Minister (I think he said "President") of the Ivory Coast, saying he would like to see him, i.e., André, in Paris about D&R getting involved in the Ivory Coast. When I got back to my office there was a letter from the Directeur du Cabinet de Ministre Diffre, who had called on me here, saying that our proposal was in the hands of the Prime Minister; he had directed the Minister of Finance and Economy to discuss it further with us.

JANUARY 27, 1960
FLYING THE PACIFIC FROM
SAN FRANCISCO TO HONOLULU

A family visit in Beverly Hills Saturday and Sunday.

My beloved Aunt Hermine Szold, soon to be ninety-two, was a pathetic figure. Not because she is in pain or ill, or even feeble. But this once proud, benevolent tyrant is now only fleetingly in the here and now, her memory like a wisp of cloud that drifts across the light, her former fire and determination only showing now and then.

This morning a highway patrol officer of California drove me over to Sacramento to see Governor Pat Brown.

Brown is a hearty man, quite young looking, and showing confidence and self-assurance.

At luncheon the Governor talked about the sources of opposition to his water plan, which must be approved by a referendum in November, at the time of the general election. He seemed to be low in his mind about the prospect of getting the $1,750,000,000 issue approved. "Any organized minority can kill a bond issue in this state, and it doesn't have to be a very large group either."

The group that he seemed most worried about was labor; and the strange part is that the issue the labor leaders chose was a farmer's issue, a small farmer's issue; the limit of 160 acres as the largest amount of land which, under Federal law, any user of water can own to entitle him to water from a Federal irrigation district. This limitation would make the water plan unworkable in this state, since so many of the water users are large corporate farmers. The public power issue seemed to loom less important, and it is evident that Brown has made his peace with the two big utilities in the state on this issue.

I got a strong impression that he seemed quite scattered rather than orderly and organized, intellectually; his imagination and capacity to create images or emotions in others seemed less than one would wish for in an important leader. But on the water plan he did show great resources of practical political wisdom; he was able to get it through the legislature, a real achievement of human understanding, or understanding of legislators would be a more accurate way of describing it.

Governor Brown wanted to talk national politics, and did. He had seen most of the "candidates," i.e., Democratic, while on his Washington trip. He is lukewarm about Stevenson: "Doesn't talk in the way that gets to the ordinary guy; good for intellectuals." He thinks Kennedy will "clobber" Humphrey in Wisconsin, and has by far the best organization for the political situation. He asked me about my preference. I said I thought "present company" should be taken seriously. No, he says: "I'm a favorite son, not a candidate; when you run a horse for big stakes, first he'd better get some trials in the county fair circuits."

About Nixon (this was walking across the park to where we had our lunch), he said: "He is not a sincere man, and he is lined up, and always has been, with the most reactionary interests in this state."

FEBRUARY 2, 1960
WAKE ISLAND

Honolulu was dominated by the erupting volcano—Kilauea on Hawaii—miles away: the air has smoke haze, it is the number one topic of conversation.

The "new state" of Hawaii seemed in some ways like the "old state" of Florida, in mind and in the appearance of the tourists. Waikiki, as I remember it nine years ago, was a rather quiet, almost tranquil piece of shore and park; now as crowded as Coney Island, almost, and hotels and apartment houses going forward in all directions, mostly up. The boom spirit is all over the place.

The staid long-established first families still own things; but they are being elbowed by professional managers they have hired, like Boyd MacNaughton of Portland, now head of C. Brewer & Co., Ltd., and his brother Malcolm, who has just been made head of Castle & Cooke, Inc. The Scots shall inherit the earth.

The exception is Walter Dillingham and his brother (or is it son?) Harold. Walter D. sat next to me at the luncheon Brewer gave for me to meet Honolulu businessmen, and a finer figure of a man I have never seen at any age; yet he is eighty-seven, straight as an arrow, huge in build but certainly not fat, eyes as sharp and dancing as a youth's. It *can* be done, extending "middle age" into the period of great years.

(Wake Island, this little hunk of land in the middle of the Pacific, is very quiet tonight; nothing but machines rolling up to our plane, like little pigs moving in on mamma sow at feeding time, giving us our fuel and water and food, each at a different aperture.)

Talked at considerable length with Boyd MacNaughton—very much a modern management star—about the study they have made of vegetable raising in Puerto Rico, something we suggested to them. By a lot of questioning I finally found out why they seemed so serious about a field that is foreign to them (they being sugar cane people first and foremost). MacNaughton said they would only consider the vegetable project because it would give them a foothold in the Puerto Rican sugar picture, which has some advantages of location, quota, transportation charges, etc., in the U.S. market.

FEBRUARY 5, 1960
HOTEL MANILA
MANILA, PHILIPPINE ISLANDS

I am now in the state that occurs on every one of these closely scheduled trips, where so much is expected of me (by my hosts—and by me) that it all seems pretty confusing. I have ideas, but they form no pattern, being pulled and hauled by the pros and cons, by the evidence of things seen and only partly understood.

I have often been exposed to the pageant of a country struggling to find itself, having attained its independence. But here there is a new factor, new to me. That is the American business community. This is one place where the ex-colonialists are American. And they are really a good, decent lot, but their viewpoint doesn't vary too much from that of any people who are making money in someone else's country and think there is some law of nature that makes this the right and proper thing to do.

There is great dissatisfaction even in this country where American influence is on the whole far better than in some colonial areas. The Filipino First movement here is one manifestation of what is going on more violently all over the world.

The high point so far was a visit yesterday to Feati Industries. Young Filipinos in a makeshift setting manufacturing a great variety of finished articles—electric fans, vacuum sweepers, transformers, castings.

What was encouraging was to find that these men, winding armatures for motors or working in foundry sands casting bronze or iron fittings, were vocational school and technical graduates who had no reluctance to get down and get their hands dirty—contrasted with the way we have seen Chinese and Indian engineers perform. This is an American talent, this getting into dirty clothes and learning by doing, rather than finding it beneath the "dignity" of a technically trained man.

FEBRUARY 6, 1960
FLYING TO MINDANAO, PHILIPPINE ISLANDS

Yesterday was a heavily tiring day, and by dinnertime I was pretty well exhausted from a series of more or less courtesy calls: the Speaker of the House, the presiding officer of the Senate, the Vice-President, a luncheon conference and meeting with the management and board of the National Power Corporation, the Acting Secretary of Agriculture and his staff, then the Director of the Bureau of Mines. They were indeed a varied lot.

The Vice-President, Diosdado Macapagal, who heads the Liberal Party, the party opposite to the prevailing one, the Nacionalista, turned out to be an extraordinarily alive and handsome young man, to whom I responded with warmth and the enthusiasm I enjoy. He is immobilized as Vice-President, but I daresay will be heard of for many years in this country.

The presiding officer of the Senate is the "grand old man" type; slits of eyes, the slick amused chronic smile of the pro among politicos, short, squat, very Malayan in appearance in contrast to the Vice-President.

The National Power Corporation is headed by a Cabinet officer, but is run by the man who is seated at my left here in the plane, Filemon Zablan, a quiet-spoken, earnest, long-suffering type, a good engineer but with a kind of resignation to the troubles that beset a man trying to do a technical job in the midst of a Government filled with small-bore General Accounting Office types, with their preoccupation with detailed criticism and audit, with how much you pay your secretary (he says this issue about his own private secretary has been pending for months *before the Cabinet*).

We are headed for the southernmost island of the archipelago, Mindanao, where there is a great deal of unused land, and hydro capacity.

I spend a good deal of time thinking about what I can say in a speech to the Rotary Club here next week, a speech in which it is expected that I will actually *say* something. It is a difficult spot. I am not in my own country; I must not appear to be too critical of the U.S. and the American businessmen here; and yet my sympathies are so strongly in favor of the efforts the enterprising people of the Philippines are making to set up their own industry.

FEBRUARY 7, 1960
SUNDAY
MINDANAO

We've just returned from the land of the Moros, a beautiful and fascinating experience.

The trip was by jeep wagon on the roughest road imaginable, through rough terrain, climbing from sea level to 2,100 feet. At one point we ran into a mud bog, where road machines had left a mess, and the hard, hard rain had turned it into something literally impassable. So we waited until the Acting Governor arrived, with a huge tractor and we were yanked and hauled through hub-deep mud for an hour. All the while it was pouring. Past us, as we crawled and lurched along, were carabaos pulling sleds of copra, boys with banana leaves over their heads, women and men in the sarongs the Moros wear, some young men carrying their shoes; a wonderful parade it was.

We were joined by two handsome young Moros, complete in Western dress, except for their cocky dark purple velvet caps, resembling the Pakistan cap, except it was velour rather than black lamb.

One of these is the Acting Governor of the province, now called Lanao del Sur, of which the capital city is Marawi City. He had studied for a law degree at Cornell; his companion on the "reception committee" had studied sociology at the University of Kansas.

The sociologist is preoccupied with the traditional way of life of the Moros, his people, the way in which their traditional organization, which is tribal, i.e., based upon family kinship, conflicts with or can be harmonized with "constitutional structures of government." He wants to preserve that tribal tradition and form of organization.

But the Filipino slogan (and the "image" in America throughout my boyhood and youth) is summarized in the Filipino soldier's phrase: "A good Moro is a dead Moro."

When we entered Marawi City we were joined by two jeeploads of soldiers, in full battle dress, including Thompson submachine guns. When I commented about how well protected we were, even when we walked through the partly built City Hall, the Acting Governor said, diplomatically, that this was intended as a mark of courtesy "to a great visitor"; but Colonel Gavino, our escort, told us later troops were sent, with these high-powered arms (not just side arms) because "the Area

Commander doesn't trust the Moros and didn't want any trouble to happen to us."

Two things stand out: one was the extraordinary beauty of the area, the clarity and freshness of the air, the green, green, green of the hills, the white water in the Agus River rushing through the rapids on its way to the majestic Maria Cristina Falls, the purplish blue of the sky, the delicacy of the great banks of cloud or fog lying between the ridges, and below one of the most magnificent lakes I have ever seen. Incomparable.

The other was the picture of the people, the Moros, gathered on the muddy streets as we walked around in Marawi City. The men and women each wearing a wrap-around sarong, though that is not the Moro term. Turbans, caps, one red fez, white burnous-like headdress.

That the Moros are a Moslem minority in a predominantly Catholic country may explain much of what we saw of arrested economic development in the Moro region.

(While I am writing this, in the big living room of the resthouse, Filipino technical men are gathering for a meeting on high technical matters concerned with the steel plant, the chemical plant, and the hydro system. Their leader and boss, Filemon Zablan, is a most intelligent man, full of his job, has none of the flamboyance or emotional tension we often attribute to the Filipino. The dark and earnest young faces—there are now about fifteen men in the other part of the room— are as intent and serious as any gathering you ever saw.)

This morning we saw the tumultuous beauty and power of the Maria Cristina Falls, about a hundred meters high, the water falling in an unbroken deluge, to break and leap high on the rocks below. Penstocks are almost all that are required, leading the water down from the river above. The whole river could be made to yield about what the Dez at full capacity will, i.e., about 500,000 kw.

I got the feeling that Mindanao presented a great opportunity for a regional integrated development.

I was overwhelmed with the unrestrained fertility of the red soil, as we bumped and ground our way through the back country headed for Moroland. We saw corn just coming out of the ground, and right next to it, on the same tract, corn in tassel, and next to it, corn being harvested. Corn grows the year around. Bananas and cassava grow virtually wild, breadfruit, grasses—what a wild burst of natural vitality, topped off with orchids and bougainvillea growing rank.

Are the "human resources" up to this scale of technical development? I am sure there are skeptics but I would guess the answer is yes.

Our two Moro friends said: "Why can't we have some of this power for our city, and for use by farmers along the road?" They have a local power plant, but it operates only part of the day, and not enough for even any small industrial use. I encouraged this idea, of course, to the embarrassment somewhat of Zablan, who finds the Moros pressing enough without encouragement. But it is the rain from *their* hillsides that makes the river so full of energy. And what electricity could do, particularly for refrigeration and small industry, is just as attractive in Moroland as in TVA land.

There is hardly a ten-minute period in our constant discussions (for I am excited by things I have seen the past couple of days and am full of questions) in which this typical sentence doesn't occur:

"Yes, we export lumber (or iron ore, or copper, etc., etc.) to Japan (or perhaps the U.S.) and then buy it back after it has been processed in Japan (or the U.S.) and at many times what we sold it for, and for much more than we could produce it for right here."

This happens again and again. Plywood—which the P.I. already make—being imported, made in Japan out of P.I. logs; sheet steel from P.I. iron ore, copper cable from P.I. copper, etc.

This is the old, old story of colonialism the world over; the story of our own South, for that matter, for a long, long time.

The trip today and yesterday's long rough drive from Cagayan de Oro City to Iligan are the highlights of the whole trip thus far. The use of planed lumber in a most attractive and tasteful way in the houses along the road impressed us greatly. It was only today that we saw primitive conditions (some of them very much so indeed). The fishing villages along the sea yesterday were particularly attractive, though simple, with their long narrow boats, with outriggers, drawn up on the shore; the high stilted houses gave the impression of a rather well-developed life. We passed two fiestas. In one there was dancing that reminded me of the dances in the Bayanihan troupe I saw in New York in late December. In another village there was a funeral procession, resting on the main street, "waiting for the priest," as Zablan said.

FEBRUARY 8, 1960
FLYING BACK TO MANILA FROM MINDANAO

Such an expedition as this (particularly the past two days on Mindanao) is *really* strenuous. There is the constant excitement and strain of new sights, new people you meet or see, new and strange customs, and above all the effort to understand and learn enough to put the pieces together and get some over-all idea of the meaning of what one sees.

FEBRUARY 9, 1960
MANILA

I have just had a most sobering and disturbing experience. It was one I went out of my way to have, by *insisting* that I wanted to see something of the slums of Manila. Well, I've seen them—or some of them—and I am still shaking.

With our Filipino driver and friend, Ben, I drove out to an area near the harbor front, and then we parked the car and walked down narrow, ugly little bystreets as they branched off; just wandering.

God have mercy, the conditions under which human beings live, right next door to wealth, for there is great and ostentatious wealth in this city.

I won't try to describe the hovels, just wood and thatch and old galvanized sheet iron thrown together. Like the refugee camps of Karachi. But what got me more than anything else were the ditches of filth, half-filled with standing water, water with a scum over the top, stagnant, with the bubbles of decomposition coming up from the bottom. Into these ditches or pools alongside the houses everything had been dumped—scraps of vegetables, broken bottles and cans, every kind of refuse including that of human defecation.

After all, the jube in Persia is *running* water.

But it is the first impact that rocks me to my heels. My impulse, even when hit hard by an ugly fact, is to look for some saving grace, some light that means hope or improvement; such is my faith in men that even in this horrible mess (made more horrible because much of this the City of Manila could correct) I saw things that brightened the picture.

For example, the clothes of the people, children, women, men, were clean, remarkably clean. Washings hang out everywhere. And the children were so bright and happy looking, playing in these messy streets. As we passed one of the worst of the streets, a young fellow came running out carrying a couple of books, and through one of them a long try square; he was on his way to night school.

I just can't get it through my noggin that these people live this way day after day, night after night, that there are millions upon millions of human beings whose lot is no better, some worse. After what I have seen in Calcutta and Old Delhi and Benares, or the squatter areas of Cali only last December, it is surprising that I can be shocked by *anything* any more. And I hope I shall never get to the place where such sights don't shock and disturb me.

FEBRUARY 10, 1960
MANILA

We have just come from dinner at the home of Salvador Araneta. Not just a beautiful and luxurious house; it is a house in the style of a Spanish grandee or an Italian prince in the old days. Filled with religious statues—antiques, most of them—and rooms the size of a golf course. A greater contrast with the slums of yesterday would be hard to imagine.

Today was a potpourri of everything. Visited an elementary school in the barrio of Lagona near the municipality of Calamba, on the way to the School of Agriculture and Rockefeller Foundation supported research center known the world over as Los Baños. The village children were a delight, and everyone so friendly and excited. Colonel Gavino said that Americans rarely visit these places, and this was pretty evident; he went on to say that our visit would be talked about for six months as a big event.

We certainly enjoyed it, the people especially, their desire to be hospitable (something to eat at each stop). We stopped at a place where duck eggs were being prepared for the delicacy known as balut, an old Chinese custom. Fertile duck's eggs are incubated until the embryo is good size, then boiled. I cracked the egg, drank the fluid and then chawed into the embryo and egg. I must confess I felt a little uneasy for an hour afterward, but my sampling the product was the thing to do, the lady of the house being very pleased with the whole affair.

By 9:30 A.M. we had arrived at the college, Los Baños, and at ten I spoke entirely off the cuff to a really inspiring audience: eager, intent dark young faces (men and women, for the schools are co-ed) who are studying to become farmers, or at any event to be the agricultural leaders of the country. They filled the hall, and the overflow stood at the windows and looked in, hundreds of them.

Then we raced on to a feudal but very modern estate of thousands of acres, owned and dominated by a little, soft-spoken benevolent tyrant by the name of José Yulo, formerly Speaker of the legislature, a distinguished corporation lawyer, and a man of enormous wealth apparently. He took us, after lunch at his home (it is a kind of tropical poem), through his empire: a Santa Gertrudis herd of chestnut aristocrats; grassland; alfalfa; huge coconut plantations; and oceans of sugar cane, being processed in the Central.

The man himself was the most interesting part. A man of the world, familiar with every capital, the friend of many important figures, regarded this whole complex operation as his personal toy. "It keeps me from thinking about things," he said. He ran for President at the last election, at sixty-seven, but lost. He has built a shrine for his late wife that made me think of a Philippine Taj Mahal.

FEBRUARY 19, 1960
MANILA

This fortnight in the Philippines clarified my views about "economic nationalism," precipitated by what I have seen here; and written, in hot haste but not badly, in a single day, last Wednesday, in a speech delivered before a SRO Rotary Club meeting yesterday. The theme was simply a restatement, in current terms, of Governor William Howard Taft's phrase of years ago—"the Philippines for the Filipinos."

This was a success; it made me say what I have been thinking for a good many months now but never had the direct occasion to ignite those ideas; it gave the Filipinos a lift, and among some Americans you could see that I had hit the bull's-eye of truth, however little they liked the idea of my doing so.

A two-hour visit, before and during breakfast, with President Garcia, this morning. This was in our honor at the Presidential Palace, a grandiose place indeed, set in an elaborate park, the former official residence of a series of American Governors General.

Breakfast was set for a couple dozen, in a vast room. The "conversation," if it could be called that, was the kind of polite nothingness that marks the most formal affairs anywhere, with the honored guest travelworn and the President's mind full, no doubt, of the coming election. Helen talked to her table partner about our visit to Mindanao, and how it would lend itself to a TVA kind of development. This stirred her partner, who called across to the President: "You must hear this." But we found that the President, overweight, fatigued, a solemn chunk of a man, was silent on all subjects.

FEBRUARY 20, 1960
FLYING OVER THE MEKONG RIVER, INDOCHINA

I never see another great river (even though it be at 6,000 feet) but that an excitement, almost a trembling, takes hold of my whole being.

My confidence that something concrete and useful, perhaps profitable, for D&R will come out of my hectic straining of the past two and a half weeks is somewhat diminished. For toward the very end of the trip I became aware that Araneta, keen, and full of ideas as he is, is essentially a promoter (as, I suppose, essentially I am) but unless he is willing to accept critical analysis and careful managerial restraints and tests of his ideas, and to accept the idea of priorities, he may not be too good a business partner. He is one of the most imaginative and enthusiastic men I know; but I must be careful not to assume that he knows the pitfalls which only careful second thought and managerial disciplines provide.

FEBRUARY 23, 1960
SIEM REAP, CAMBODIA

Across the field outside our balcony the saffron-robed figures of Buddhist priests walking in the cool of the morning, their begging bowls ready to pick up the day's food. Yesterday afternoon, under our window, two elephants, one of them bossed by an aggressive eight-year-old, helped in building an addition to this old-fashioned colonial French-type hotel. From below I can hear the women, in ragged dirty sarong and head covering, begin to mix concrete and carry it, in the Chinese-type shoulder carrier, to the masons. Over the tops of the trees of the jungle, on the horizon but very plain and clear, the towers of Angkor Wat. One of the most remarkable feats of art and mathematics and design and construction, built by the Khmers, remote ancestors of these diminutive people, about the time of Chartres, then lost in the jungle and not uncovered until the nineteenth century.

The kind of poverty one sees in Southeast Asia has been going on a long, long time. And yet there did exist the ability of administration, art, and living that produced such great works as Angkor Wat and such a palace of sensual living for the rich as we saw yesterday, Angkor Thom. A huge pool, still beautiful although covered by the jungle for centuries until it was unearthed, in which the King and the princes had "fun and games" with their concubines—and all the rest of the evidences of rich and easy and brutal life. All this was carried on the backs of the people who still carry burdens as they did then.

But today there is a difference, thanks to the West. These people now sense, many of them, that there *is* another way; the turbulent "politics" of this part of the world grows out of this largely unintended "contribution" of the West that burdens can be lightened, that others than the kings and princes can have some of the product of work.

FEBRUARY 24, 1960
SIEM REAP

This morning we drove in a jeep through the sand "roads" into the jungle to see Banteai Srei, a particularly beautiful and old Brahman temple. For the first time I came to visualize what the towers of Angkor

Wat and Angkor Thom, which look so much like slag heaps except on close scrutiny, must have looked like in the days when the artists and craftsmen had just finished their work, eight centuries or so ago, and before the banyan tree, with its gray serpentine roots, had rent them stone from stone.

For this little temple, far back in the jungle, is still adorned with Indian-type sculpture clear to the tops of the towers; the bas-relief so deep and fresh, almost like three-dimensional carving; the piling up of little temple upon temple as decoration for the main temple towers, black with age or green and gold with moss. But there they stand, in a circle of the quietest most remote forest, almost as if their priests and devotees had just left.

Perhaps as interesting as anything—I guess most worthwhile— was the picture of rural and village life during the dry season in the real back country of Cambodia, and probably characteristic of much of Southeast Asia. This was genuinely *primitive*. The children ran like wild animals to the shelter of the thatch houses on stilts, for quite evidently not many people in cars get into this back country. Their parents peered out from the darkness of the "second story," or the open area beneath the houses which serves as the place of work, of storage, of congregation. There were clan gatherings at noontime, under a thatch covering in a yard. Life is simple and unaffected by modern living as anything I have seen.

As we approached a village we saw an occasional bicycle or a little "store" in the dark shadows under a thatch. Here and there a brave little patch of green garden, surrounded by spiked sticks, about half the size of our living room, with lettuce or mainly tobacco.

Woodsmen came down the roads with strange-looking axes and an occasional curious kind of saw. The only mechanical devices were these strange saws and axes, and varieties of devices to pound rice, all driven by human energy: a boy bouncing up on a log that, when it fell, pounded the rice or a woman pushing a handle that in turn turned some kind of rice-grinding machine.

FEBRUARY 25, 1960
BANGKOK, THAILAND

Writing these notes while seated on the lawn before the Victorian portal of the Oriental Hotel. Directly across the river is a good-sized sailing vessel, very old and weathered and Chinese-y, with a sharp upturned bow and a high, high poop deck aft, but low amidships. Something of the feeling, in the poop, of the galleon of Columbus' time. Her forward mast rakes to the bow, and in rough unseamanlike folds, a dirty sail.

The women do the hard work around here and do it well. The women who push the frail little sampan "taxis" across the current of the wide river are just plain strong.

But one change I see is that even these girls evidently put up their hair in curlers before making their appearance as water spirits. In fact, it is noticeable even in the back country how much more attention to their coal-black, heavy hair the gals are taking.

About sundown, while Helen and I were sitting on the river-front lawn, I decided *this* was my chance to ride one of these sampans, propelled by these remarkable women whom I have watched with fascination so many times. A sturdy-looking woman in a red sarong invited me into her sampan, although I was obviously a "tourist." To her surprise and that of everyone else on the landing, I got aboard, motioned to the opposite shore and away we went, just the two of us.

On the way over, the female Charon hardly stroked her long oar at all. We went a long way up the river, and then half drifted across; when we got almost to a landing on the other bank, I motioned to her that I was ready to go back.

Coming back she kept close to the yon bank, where the current was weak; this added to the fun for me, for we went right alongside boats in which families were getting ready for the evening meal; young bucks and kids were swimming in the water around these boats. Some people were on the edge of the water having a bath with soap (these are the bathingest people).

A launch, a working boat or two went by, kicking up quite a wake and the men in them, obviously amused by the outlander riding in this beat-up little boat yelled pleasantries at my boatwoman, which must have been somewhat on the ribald side, for she answered with a good deal of spirit as if to say she could give back cracks as well as they could make them. But it was all as friendly as could be; I grinned and they grinned (or laughed).

When we had gone as far along the quiet shoreline as possible, Miss Charon struck out into the current, which was strong, and with a stiff breeze too, the water rather rough. She grunted and pushed and feathered, and did her dance of three steps forward, leaning hard on the long oar. I watched her with the greatest interest, for here was real skill. Then suddenly she stopped, picked up a crude paddle and tossed it toward me; I grabbed it, turned to face forward, i.e., toward the bow, and started to paddle on the side opposite her long oar. She uttered some cries that were plainly meant to say: No, not that way, dope. I thought this way I could help keep the bow headed across the current while she provided the motive power in the stern. So I changed to paddling off the same side, starboard actually, and she grinned hard and said the universal Esperanto "OK." And this is the way we came back, me digging into the water and feathering bow canoe fashion, and she bearing down with her long oar. I got a kick out of it, and the landing was full of Thais having a big time seeing the strange tourist, and giving my propelling companion quite a reception. I stepped ashore, paid her well, she took a little naked youngster aboard, her child probably, and started off across to supper.

My hair not having been cut for five weeks, I finally thought I had better do something about it, since it was curled about my head like Foxy Grandpa. The barber here was wearing a face mask. A fine-looking young man, tall for a Thai, and with long, slender, delicate fingers, fingers that in another time, long ago, designed and placed the beautiful porcelain of the temples that we see towering against the horizon.

He did a careful job, trying to follow my instructions not to cut it too short. My eye wandered to the list of prices for various things to be done—shampoo, etc. In English. At the bottom this: "Ear cleaning 10 baht." My curiosity and sense of humor were both aroused, so when he lisped a question about "year thleaning" I said yes. It was quite an experience. He dug and probed in the most delicate way, and when he came up with a find of a hunk of wax, he couldn't have been more proud if it had been an emerald I had mislaid somewhere. Then something that seemed like an electric vibrator, that kind of feeling and noise, went buzzing in my ear. I rared back; he giggled and finally showed me what was going on. He had put a tiny cotton stick into my ear, and was vibrating it by a tuning fork that he had set strumming. When he was all through, he gave me what I thought was going to be a sitting judo exercise, flexing my arms, gouging my shoulders. And to finish things off, hitting the back of my neck with the side of his hands in a way that made a terrific hollow sound like castanets. As I paid him, he gave me a bow with the hands peaked together, Chinese style. Quite a haircut.

FEBRUARY 26, 1960
BANGKOK

This letdown period has set me to reliving, in vivid memory, the early days of our courtship, and marriage. It has been a pleasant exercise, for the DePauw days come back so clearly.

My first "date" with Helen. The days when she would go with me to Meharry Hall, in the evening, while Professor Gough made me go over and over the gestures or intonations for my "State Oratorical Contest" oration. The hectic days of the student election campaign, in which I organized a party and was elected president of the student body. The hard work over Galsworthy's *The Mob,* in which I played the intransigent dissenter against the Boer War, a role and a play that either helped shape my subsequent career or was a brilliant piece of casting by our coach, I'll never be sure which. How Helen nursed me through the rigors of that experience, and a dozen others.

Well, so the recollections pile up: the early days of our marriage, when we had no money whatever, but were happy and busy, I writing articles on the table in the "kitchenette" on East 67th Street, in Chicago, and Helen editing and suggesting. The sudden calamity of her typhoid fever just before Thanksgiving Day only a few weeks after we had been married; the anxieties of the first financial adversities that began with the depression, when I had already established a considerable income, at age twenty-nine; the call from Governor Phil LaFollette and his asking me to leave Chicago to go on the Wisconsin Utility Commission; the night in Madison I spent walking around and around the capital square until the 4 A.M. train left for Chicago debating a change in our life that proved decisive; Helen's calm and strong and instant conclusion that she could manage the change very well if that was what I wanted to do. Well, so it goes on and on.

FEBRUARY 27, 1960
BANGKOK

This morning's Bangkok *Post* carries a column of Walter Lippmann's that makes me feel good. It follows the theme, and even the sequence of ideas, in the Cleveland Council Speech and ends with the conclusion I wrote into that statement. But whereas I made only passing reference to the point that our aid, when given to combat Communism, often simply lined us up with regimes that were on their way out, he tackles the "military assistance" fraud and hypocrisy openly.

He pussyfoots a bit about the military aid business, by saying we must continue it for a while. What I wish he had said is that to provide military aid to support a regime is something that will bring on civil strife *within* such countries, where the military are a privileged class and hated by many, and therefore we are forced to continue to give such aid and increase it, provide U.S. military "advisors," etc.; otherwise we threaten the stability of the regime into whose future we have poured so much money.

MARCH 1, 1960
TEHRAN, IRAN

Tiny fresh green leaves on a little tree before our D&R office on Pasteur Avenue; the weeping willows a mist of falling green; even some cherry blossoms. Spring, somewhat early. (But not too early; spring can never be too early.) The rosebushes putting out their deep red earliest leaves. In the Khuzistan, I am told, it is early summer, the desert abloom its one time of the year.

Tehran seems changed even since November when I was here last, more new skyscrapers and hotels and office buildings on their way up, more cars on the streets. And yet plenty of evidence that this is definitely not Milwaukee or Des Moines. Three huge chesty Kurds, their turbans and dark graceful coats making the Western-dressed Persians seem like foreigners; a herd of sheep, their backs marked with henna for identification, right in the midst of the rush of auto traffic on the main thoroughfare.

The course of true love may not be smooth, as they say, but certainly neither is the World Bank loan. This morning we talked to Khodadad Farmanfarmaian, who headed the Iran negotiating delegation in Washington. He is trying to get the Loan Agreement and the Side Agreements through the Council of Ministers. The Finance Minister protested strongly over a provision in which Iran agreed, in effect, to behave itself, fiscally; this set off a storm in the Council, as one could have anticipated, about invasion of Iran's sovereignty. So they amended the language; this may cause things to be sticky when word of this gets back to the Bank in Washington.

Safi Asfia, whom we saw Monday morning, was as usual sparing in words, most cordial and appreciative ("It is because of you that we got the Dez loan," he said, which is quite a long sentence for him) and said there was no question whatever that the Majlis would ratify and also pass the legislation about the pilot irrigation project. Farmanfarmaian now has become converted, could hardly believe his eyes, he says, when he visited the work recently. He has become a strong supporter of the project, and of the way it is being done.

MARCH 5, 1960
AHWAZ, IRAN

The gathering at the Ahwaz airport waiting for the Shah's plane to arrive was an astounding one, from my point of view. The dignitaries were mostly sheiks of considerable power, heads of clans, owners of many villages; some from near the Iraqi border probably have slaves. Yet with one solitary exception there they were in long-tailed coats (heavy broadcloth) and striped pants, some with high, shiny top hats. The English being aped in a land where they never had much of a following, and when the clothes many of these men wear at home are so picturesque. The holdout was one handsome old sheik in his tribal garb. One huge expanded man, the chief of the Ahwaz clans, was the biggest thing in a morning suit I have ever seen, and next to him a little wizened character, ditto tailcoat, from whom we bought the land for the sugar project. He has twenty-one wives, all probably at home doing the work.

The "Imperial Plane," in light blue, appeared in the skies after all of us had been standing in the hot sun for an hour or more. Then the usual review of the honor guard, and the Shah and the Queen came down the line of carpets, stopping now and then to hear some *read* speech from a mayor or clan leader.

The Queen was, of course, the center of much attention, including mine certainly. She wore a notable costume, the very latest thing from Dior no doubt. Light blue. A very high domelike hat. An impassive sweet face, very young. A tall slender woman. She who now wears an imperial crown, her picture on the walls all over the country, was only a few months ago just a young architecture student. Not much preparation for listening to interminable speeches, cutting endless ribbons, dedicating silos (such as the one here). When Hedayat, perspiring freely, read his speech about the power substation, to be dedicated, the King looked resigned, but the Queen kept her eye on the script Hedayat had in his hand to see how many pages more there would be. What a life a sovereign leads, I thought.

I stayed back although some of my Iranian friends kept prodding me forward. Finally, they escorted me to the end of the line at the substation; when the Shah saw me, he gave me a warm smile as to an old friend, shook hands, and in a soft and rather tired voice asked me how long I had been in the country. I said what a privilege it was to try to serve him and his country. He said: "The cooperation has been most helpful and most courteous." Then looking at the switchyard and gear, he said: "This is the first fruit, but there will be much more to come."

The cry of the Arab women as the Shah's big black Chrysler passed them, a solid row along the road from the airport, made me think of the rebel yell; then I recognized it: it was the Indian yelp, the kind we used to make as kids, moving our hand over our mouths to give that undulating wail.

Then there was the young man racing along the roadway trying to catch the Shah's car, just ahead, being pushed away by a soldier in the car immediately alongside; then someone reached out and took a small piece of paper from the fellow, who then subsided. Such a scene occurred several times; then I was told "a petition to the King" is apparently a common practice, except that with automobiles you have to run somewhat faster than you used to when the King rode a horse.

MARCH 6, 1960
AHWAZ

At the outdoor party at the Railway Club, though there were chairs for them, the Shah and his young Queen stood by a table set with candelabra, eating and chatting. Helen and I stood, with all the other people, at a little distance.

While we were eating the Court Chamberlain came across the strip of lawn separating all of us from Their Majesties, to say to Helen and me, "His Majesty would like you to come to talk with him." We made a further dab at our plates, put them down and walked across the brilliantly lighted lawn. The greeting we had was very cordial; the Shah's ease and charm were at their best, and he talked to Helen as pleasantly as if we were new neighbors on the block. The Queen shook hands and smiled, a quite lovely but rather shy smile, but said nothing; I think she only speaks Persian and French.

"No," Helen said, "this isn't my first trip to Iran! I have been here four or five times." I said she had been with us on our very first trip exactly four years ago.

The Shah asked some questions about the sugar operation, and I enthused about alfalfa. He turned on Hedayat: "Does the Ministry of Agriculture know of this?" Then he asked: "Does your organization have an animal husbandry department; could they help us to improve the breed of water buffalo, animals such as they have in India and Pakistan?" I shied away from this; the story back of it, Anderson told me, is that some ICA enthusiast did provide money for a herd of fine buffalo, but since there was no one in the Department of Agriculture here who knew how they should be cared for, or would care for them, they were about to pass out.

After more talk, partly personal, partly about alfalfa, and the trip coming up today, we excused ourselves and went back across the lawn, skyrockets banging overhead.

I realized that being picked out for this "honor" was intended to be just that. I didn't realize till the next day what an impression it made on our Ahwaz "constituency" who saw this.

MARCH 7, 1960
FLYING FROM AHWAZ TO DEZ CANYON

I am writing this in a fairly large helicopter, seating six. Facing me are three Iranians: Minister Hedayat, Dr. A. Kazemi, and a man from the Pan American Oil Co., which supplied this craft. Wearing big muff-like ear devices (to cut the rather considerable noise) and dark glasses, we looked like the Hear No Evil, See No Evil, etc., trio.

Below us, at not a great distance, are the broad unbroken plains, very dry and brown for this time of year: there has been a severe rain shortage this winter, and the herds of sheep are already looking very puny, as we saw the other day, on the ground, on our trip across the plains.

Now it is very white below, the nasty saline lands, the birds everywhere, in great flocks, doves, storks, etc. Soon we will be beginning the climb to the uplands that rise so rapidly from the upper Khuzistan plains.

We have just hovered inside the narrow canyon itself, flying so deep into the awesome canyon that the walls of the canyon are *above* us; *what* an experience!

This is our big day; as it will be the first time the Shah has seen the Dez canyon. I have no doubt he will be much impressed.

After seeing the canyon and, I hope, driving down through the miles of tunnels to the point where the dam's top will be, there is lunch at the camp, then we fly to Haft Tapeh—our sugar cane operation (so the plan goes)—to await his arrival by plane.

Our helicopter put us down at the village on the plateau's top, where we waited a long time for the arrival of Their Majesties, by car from the new airfield near Andimeshk.

I was much entertained by a long line of Lurs, in their tribal dress, who have been workers on the dam from the very beginning. These are among the most ancient pure Persians in the country, their famous Luristan bronzes go back three and four thousand years. Their dress is a knee-length coarsely hand-woven coat, gray with dark striping, with a wide white ceremonial sash around the middle, and topped with a little brown felt skullcap; their shoes are the pointed white cloth shoes so common throughout Persia.

They had big banners, and the flag of the Lurs flying, standing there waiting for hours for the arrival of their King. Their clan leader, a big, distinguished-looking man with a week's beard, wore a heavy dark woolen Western-type suit, and a dozen or so of the men in the line also wore ordinary clothes—quite a contrast. No Lur women about.

Across the road were three musicians. The busiest was blowing, heartily, till his cheeks puffed like a frog who would a-wooing go, on something like a clarinet, a wooden pipe, uttering the shrill and, to my ears, somewhat sad wail of Oriental primitive music. He was accompanied by a man with a crude drum; his drumstick had a curl instead of a knot at the end. The third had a kind of violin; three steel strings, but the body was simply a small, boxlike affair, circular, the whole thing mounted on a metal rod, carefully carved. During the dancing that followed, however, the "violinist" didn't play, but egged the dancers on by displaying paper Iranian money that people watching—mostly other Lurs, though Dr. Kazemi contributed too—would hand him to encourage the dancers.

The dancing began almost as if they were getting tired just standing in line; four men formed a line, a straight line, joined hands (not arms linked, but hands clasped) and began a kind of heel-and-toe step, quiet and rather slow, the music the same. Then others from the long line would join, until after a while there were perhaps a dozen dancers, the tempo increasing somewhat, but the movement was not changed from the heel-and-toe back-and-forth step; the vigor and beat came from thrusting their arms out, up, then back, hands still firmly grasped together. It was as if the Radio City Rockettes did their rhythmic, synchronized kicking with joined arms instead of the famous long line of legs kicked in unison.

Then a man came from the nondancing line, faced the dancers, and began a very graceful dance which seemed to set the pace and pattern for the "line," but his steps and particularly his body and head movements were quite different. Whereas their movement was rather restrained and repetitive, he flung himself, head, torso, arms, in what, after the tempo increased, was a dance of strong feeling, a kind of passion, his face not impassive, as were those of the "line," but like that of an actor telling a story in pantomime. In one hand he carried a colored cloth which he waved as his body twisted from side to side; his other hand was held by the man at the end of what by now was a straight line of perhaps more than a dozen men. I asked: "Is he perhaps dancing the part that would ordinarily be that of a woman?" No, I was told, there are no women in this dance; this is the way it has been danced without change that anyone knows about for centuries and centuries back in these mountain areas of the Lur tribe.

Not long after ten o'clock there were flumes of dust across the hills, where the access road winds its way; an electric thrill went through the little group: the Shah and the Queen were approaching, there were only three cars, no outriders. The Shah's car stopped where the Lurs were lined up, the Shah got out, no longer resplendent in gold braid: just a slight, well-built fellow in a gray suit, without a hat. The leaders of the tribe kissed his hand, read from their scroll the little speech of loyalty, the Lurs clapped and clapped and yelled.

Hedayat and I scampered into our car, pulled into the line and we were off, literally in a cloud of dust (it was *very* dusty on that plateau) and rolled down the road to Lookout #1, where Bill Voorduin and a couple of the engineers were waiting. Again the King, and this time the Queen, got out of their car, and we walked together to the iron rail to look out at the wonder of this gray vastness, down, down, down to the trickle of the river we are damming. Bill explained the layout of the tunnels by which one reaches the canyon floor. "All tunnels," the King said in an aside to the Queen, the first English I have heard him use in speaking with her. Then, after much picture taking, back into the cars for the journey halfway down the canyon, to Lookout #2, which will be the place where the dam tops out, when the concrete is placed, about November, 1962.

This is the first time I had seen this lower view, and it is truly fantastic; not quite so dreamlike as flying about in this narrow chasm, as we had just done, but certainly strange and awesome. Bill asked Their Majesties to put on white hard hats, which pleased the photographers. Two of them scrambled back of the protective railing, out on the canyon's edge; out of the corner of his eye the Shah saw this, a look of alarm and concern spread over his face and those expressive eyes, and he spoke to them in Persian to get back. This wasn't the only time he was the one most active in watching out lest someone get hurt in the jam of people and the excitement of having the King and his young Queen visiting the Khuzistan.

We were leaning on the rail together, looking out over this site when he turned to me, his eyes and features almost thunderstruck; then he grinned and said in an undertone almost, "Have you ever seen *anything* like this?" I said no, and no one else ever had, that this was a unique site. Then he spoke again of the long tunnels we had just traveled to get to this place, halfway down, as if he now knew where all that money and effort had been spent before a dam was even "begun," for to the layman the building of a dam is the pouring of the concrete, whereas actually most of the work is done, ordinarily, before that, and when you start placing concrete the worst and most difficult part is over.

Bill's explanation of things was restrained; he looked the part of a distinguished engineer—which he is. The Shah, turning to me, said: "And this is only one of many, not even the biggest?" "Yes," I agreed; "we hope that this one will help to season Iranian engineers so that as the series are built over perhaps a generation, they will design and build them." "That's too long a period though," he said, looking out over the canyon.

Across the canyon I saw a fly speck which I knew must be a man working with a drill on the face of the perpendicular wall; above him was a line which was probably around his waist. "To give you a sense of scale," I said, "you can see that man across there." He didn't believe it; someone handed him a pair of field glasses; he was all agog, handed the glasses to the Queen, and for some time they watched this and other men working where a false move would be their finish. This gave some sense of reality to the job, for by order of the Crown security forces all the machinery had been parked in the tunnels, so nothing would be going while the King was present.

The Shah asked Bill how hot it gets; when he heard that people worked here at temperatures of 130° at times, he shook his head; how do they stand it? Bill confessed he didn't know, but they did. His Majesty asked questions about summer temperatures several other times during the trip, particularly at the sugar plantation, and the workers' houses there.

MARCH 8, 1960
AHWAZ

I am determined to write in some detail about one of the most re- markable days of my life, the trip with the Shah yesterday, not only because of the unusual opportunity it gave to watch this remarkable man, but because of the crowds, the wild, hand-clapping, exuberant—and at one time violently exuberant—crowds, colorful; the Oriental potentate in Western dress and casual manner—the obvious awe at what we had been able to do, the feeling of having accomplished something.

March 7 was a history-making day, I really think, in the story of our Persian venture.

We returned, through the tunnels, with their occasional spectacular "windows" looking out on the gray grandeur of the canyon, to the prin- cipal house on the plateau, the house where Helen and I stayed when we were last here, when it was barely finished; I remember that the draperies were being hung the night we opened our suitcase. The King and Queen went to a bedroom, where they had their meal together.

Six of us sat down to lunch—and what a lunch! Black partridge; the choicest sirloin of beef, cooked to a Queen's taste I suppose I should say, and the yellow rice—chelow—beautiful, delicate, with aromatic herbs. Our voices were hushed, for we assumed the royal personages were trying to get some rest.

But promptly at the time our schedule called for us to leave, we were summoned on the porch of the little house, the soldiers came to attention, and the slightly gray-haired handsome man and the tall, rangy dark-eyed girl came back into the world of state. At the door were the Martin children, the only two children who had lived on the plateau from the beginning, with the perennial bouquet. The Queen smiled in a brilliant way, the Shah acted as if this was the first time they had been greeted by little girls with little bouquets, shook hands with the children, and the mother, and they were back in the world of Raritania.

We drove to Andimeshk, there to get aboard the royal train for the trip of perhaps an hour to Hosseinabad, thence to the sugar plantation.

The Shah's car was not preceded by a security car, but led the procession of only four cars, Hedayat and I being in the third. As we entered the town, the place was jumping. It was a real mob scene except for this important difference: these people jamming the streets were friendly. Yelling, wild faces, bizarre dress, women, men, all jumbled together in my eye, as we crept along. Then the crowd, already filling the street right to the fenders of the cars suddenly broke and followed the Shah's car, so his car, and ours, of course, had to stop, and they simply crawled all over us! Literally. And howling, chanting, running, pushing each other. The police were a mess; they pushed each other, shrieking, but had no effect on the crowd. Finally, after starting and stopping, starting and stopping, the Shah's car reached the turnabout of the railroad station. Officers of the military got frantic, one colonel fainted, the whole business was out of control. We jumped out of our car and, following Hedayat as interference, as a halfback might a fast guard or fullback, I found myself pushing and shoving and elbowing so we wouldn't get left off the train.

All went well enough, jumping over iron chains and other obstructions, until we got to the door of the station. Then a real moment of truth. One enthusiastic excited young man had just about got through the door, right ahead of us, when a soldier, a country boy with a rifle, with ugly bayonet bared, not only tussled with him; the soldier got wild and brought his gun down to stick the young fellow with his bayonet; the intruder (or "individualist") responded by trying to tear the gun out of the soldier's hands, and we were in the middle of a bayonet fight. The soldier was so wild that he would have split the fellow in two if he could, and then things would have been lively. But Hedayat, with me pushing him, got between the antagonists, and we sailed through the half-open door into the comparative quiet of the station. We clambered aboard the train.

When we reached Hosseinabad, a little mud village, there was another spectacle. Lined up two deep were tribesmen in their turbans and robes, all on horses, at least two hundred of them. As a lover of horses, this really set me off. And on the roofs of the mud houses little huddles of women, in brightly colored clothes, transfixed by the biggest thing that had ever happened in that village of perhaps 300 people.

In addition to the horses there were two pale "beige"-colored camels; the tribesmen brought them there to cut their throats as a "sacrifice" to honor the King; but when he heard about it he forbade it. In the line of clan leaders one man fell to the ground and tried to kiss his feet; the

Shah pulled him up as fast as he could, but not before the fellow had accomplished his ancient rite. And even so sophisticated a man as Yamin Afshar, the electrical engineer, told us with glistening eyes that he had had an opportunity to kiss the King's hand *twice*, once at the substation ceremony, again somewhere else.

Then the Shah (the Queen stayed aboard the train), Leo Anderson, Dr. Kazemi, and I got into the helicopter waiting at the trainside, and off we went, to circle the sugar plantation and irrigation works, and then set down on the road near a stand of sugar cane, and an exhibit of various varieties we have found best. The Shah pulled a big stalk of cane down and tried to break it with his hands; someone produced a knife, and cut it for him: he asked if it tasted sweet. So a slice was cut off ("Be careful not to cut yourself," he said to one of our young technicians). He chewed it meditatively, as I have seen little Colombian kids do as they amble down the road. He turned to me: "Have you ever tasted it?" I was so nonplused by this casual manner that I mumbled something. "Better try it," he said. So they cut a piece for me. I chewed, a "royal command performance." He grinned in this most un-Darius way: "Sweet, isn't it?" I don't know what he expected of sugar cane, but I had to admit it was sweet.

I asked the Shah to cross from the sugar cane to the plots of alfalfa. Digging my arm deep into this wonderful stuff, with its blue blossoms and succulent stalks, Anderson told the facts about number of cuttings a year (ten) and yield in tons. Leo said: "You could tie a water buffalo in the middle of this little plot [about 12 feet, by 12] and he could live a whole year." And I emphasized that this was without fertilizer, just water and the proper handling of water.

We went on to the big pumping station we had designed and supervised, where the water of the Dez is brought in, lifted perhaps 20 feet by a huge battery of diesel pumps, put into a great canal that circles the entire plantation. "And a year ago there was nothing here," the Shah said, which is literally true.

Then we flew by helicopter to where the Italian contractors have their work camp for road construction, more maps and talks, and then back by air to the trainside. The Shah sat opposite me, looking very thoughtful and intent. I said to him: "These are just some of the evidences that Iran is moving ahead, rapidly, very rapidly." "Yes," he said, with the only note of bitterness of the last two days. "Yes, but your American newspapers don't know it." I wisecracked: "They will be the last to know." But this does rankle with him, as earlier audiences with him in the Palace have made so clear.

Before we went into his train, he took me aside and said some very good things to hear. In a very quiet voice—he never raises his voice— he looked at me intently and said: "This has been confirmation of what we set out to do. And the cooperation must continue. We must not slacken the pace. The sugar program must go head; to do otherwise is something we won't consider. And the other dams." Then he said some words of appreciation for what I had done to instill confidence in Iranians in what they can do and what the country can do, not just talk about; these words were compensation for many of the headaches. He takes his job very, very seriously, that is certain. And I take him very seriously too.

I went out for a walk, and ran into a wonderful East Tennessee woman, Mrs. Eulis Pearson, tall, rangy, full of that naturalness and disdain for "putting on airs" or pretending to be something she isn't that so endeared the Tennesseeans to me, and made a bond with them that has lasted ever since.

She and a friend, Mrs. Betty Nydell, our doctor's wife, have been working in an orphanage for girls here. Her stories about how they have enjoyed cleaning these little waifs, giving them better food, and toys ("beat-up ones, but it was the first toys anyone had ever given them") was really the theme of my pompous Cleveland speech, but *lived* out. She remarked about how some few of the Americans here treat their servants ("I never had servants in Chattanooga, and I do my own work here") and by contrast the way others are showing what Americans at their best can be.

MARCH 9, 1960
ANDIMESHK

The day began at six this morning, and Helen and I have traveled many miles, through dust, mudholes where we got stuck fast, and some of the roughest "roads" I have ever known—and we also traveled back to the ninth century, and earlier, visiting villages and going into mud "homes" quite unbelievable—and unforgettable forever and ever.

As the biblical oath has it, "Let my right hand wither" if I ever forget how some of the most attractive of my fellow human beings live —are living tonight, only a few kilometers from here, where we visited them this afternoon.

We drove the full length, south to north, of the Gebli "irrigation pilot project" to which I am committed, through D&R and Khuzistan Development Service. It took a long time, for the ruts called "roads" right across the plains would often end in a deep mudhole where the irrigators irrigated the *road* as well as the fields—something that the pilot project, designed properly and operated as a unit, will prevent. Our Chevy fell into deep holes or scraped its bottom on a ridge, where it hung suspended, until our drivers got out a jack and eased it off, or the jeep that escorted us pushed or somehow hauled us out. All this in the middle of absolute nowhere.

And yet I am as sure as I am writing these notes that this pioneer area, this beginning of only 45,000 acres, swallowed in the vastness of the Khuzistan, will become as well known as, say, Salt Lake City, founded by a handful of dedicated men in a pass of the great Rockies.

This is the happy and sustaining part of such an experience as we had today: that through a strange turn of the wheel of fortune I have the opportunity to do something useful, perhaps decisive, in giving these wonderful but terribly poor men, women, and beautiful children a chance to put their latent powers to work for their own betterment. This is not one of those oversimplified stories of a Robin Hood: attacking the rich and thereby making the poor better off; it is a rational reasoned *program* that will enable these people to raise more food, bring medical care to them and their babies with the eye sores and fly-*covered* faces (faces that I will never, never forget)—and a series of things which have been set down by us in the cold unemotional type of "reports." These sights today spur me into a fire of determination; I have seen the reality of what needs to be done, and have more than ever a conviction that "it *can* be done."

We concluded our long day by a visit to the ancient bazaar of the ancient city of Dizful, near here. Cobbled streets so narrow that two people can hardly pass at places, little shops, men making wooden combs with implements they hold with their toes, a great imposing man with a majestic hennaed beard and a green turban passing the time of day with some of his cronies. And children—many with evidences of trachoma—everywhere. Dizful is known as the city of the blind. It was certainly out of another world.

MARCH 10, 1960
5:45 A.M.
ANDIMESHK "REST HOUSE"

All through the night the picture of what people who are poor, terribly poor must endure, caught in the web of circumstances not, God knows, of their own making, has haunted my sleep, or lack of it. The poverty and wretchedness I have seen in India, in Sicily, and in Colombia, didn't affect me so much. Perhaps the reason is that here I feel directly responsible for doing something to change all this. All thought of *not* pressing ahead—despite all difficulties—to bring water and light and something like health to these people has disappeared.

I am in this for the duration of my powers.

I jumped primitive irrigation ditches yesterday, the edges slick, the sides rather high. But by this jumping and prowling and climbing up mounds I went over, carefully, the existing seven or more parallel main canals from the existing brush dam take-off just below the bridge at Dizful, that ancient town that looks as old as old—and is. And I saw where our irrigation engineers have decided to provide the new take-off, which under our scheme will substitute for these multiple small canals or ditches a *single* main canal, to carry the then controlled Dez Dam water.

There is a symbolic importance as well as engineering economy in this. Now, each year, it takes as many as eleven men to throw back *one* shovel of silt, cleaning and keeping *each* of these separately owned canals open and operating. The man in the ditch would dig one shovel, throw it up on the steep bank; there another man would pick it up and throw it farther up the bank, to still another man, and so on till the eleventh man had put it on the top of the mound. It is this that accounts for the high, wandering, more or less parallel hills that line the sides of the separate canals.

Under our program there will be one canal, properly engineered, and from this one, built with machines, an irrigation district will administer the water, letting it in on those lands that need it, shutting it off, and the district charging for it—i.e., a cooperative endeavor. Such cooperatives as have existed before, so Morteza Vakilzadeh, our Iranian mentor on this trip, told us, have failed because the "good" landlords found that the not so good ones just didn't pay their share, or do their share, so separate canals were resorted to when actually everyone knew that a single one would have been better and cheaper.

MARCH II, 1960
AHWAZ

Last night it rained some, and right now, accompanied by a strong wind, it is raining again, this time quite steadily. This is cause for hosannas, or the Persian equivalent. For it has been a terribly dry winter, and our last two days of driving, which included dry farming areas, was quite sad: the grass about gone, the herds looking very peaked, with prospects for the summer for most of its animals, and therefore the people, pretty grim. As Leo Anderson, D&R's mainstay out here—he a North Dakota dry-land farmer—said this morning, "You worry and worry about no rain, and say, 'Well, it is too late to do any good even if it comes now,' and then it comes and it isn't too late." Certainly pray this is true; otherwise there will be real suffering, hunger, and loss of herds by June.

Our experience in the villagers' huts on Wednesday threw me into a deep pit. I hovered between despair, which is an emotion I consider a sin, and anger, which doesn't do too much good.

But almost as if it were the script of a drama, Thursday (yesterday) began on a note of hope; more than hope, a conviction that all of this activity of the past four years can reach its goal, which is *not* building a big dam or improving the strains of sugar cane, or methods of irrigation, but somehow doing these, and many other things, *in such a way* that the people who live in these clusters of mud huts called "villages" will have an increasing benefit from all this activity.

As is so often the case, there was a man, one man, who walked onto the stage—or, rather, we walked onto *his* stage—yesterday morning early, who represented this hope.

We drove to a village known as Ghaleh Ghazi. Vakilzadeh had told us candidly this was the best of the villages, and the owner (i.e., the representative of the family) the best of the landlords. But still I wasn't prepared for Ali Kamali.

A very broad-shouldered man, an air of command, not the overseer or military air, but rather the wide-eyed, alert, proud and responsible aura of command some men have. He had a grizzled beard, with his great head on these massive shoulders; you felt you were looking at the kind of man whose Persian forebears once ruled the world.

When we came on him Kamali, bareheaded, in rubber boots, in the midst of his villagers, was preparing a good-sized plot for a planting of "wood garden," i.e., trees to be grown for wood rather than citrus or nuts. A pair of young heifers was pulling a plow, the plowman bent over the short handles, so as to push the point into the soil; making the deep furrows two men working together, one pushing in the wooden hoe, the other pulling it back with a rope attached to the hoe. Vakilzadeh, whom Kamali knows well, introduced us. Kamali bowed in that indescribably proud and yet respectful way that is special to the Persian.

Later, when he was showing the new bathhouse for the village, Kamali said: "Of course, this isn't the way you did things in the Tennessee Valley, but we are trying, we are beginning." I asked: "Do you know about the TVA?" "What a question," he said, "everyone [again "everyone"] knows about the TVA." I would be a damned liar if I said that this kind of comment, way off in the middle of the Khuzistan plain, meant nothing to me!

Kamali took us through his citrus "garden," his nursery of citrus and other stock, showed us the villagers' own gardens. This is something that the system of khish, the practice of moving the tenant each year, from one plot to another, ordinarily prevents. But in this village each tenant family had part of a hectare for the family to use and to sell part of its produce. One of the basic propositions in the new Gebli project is, by law and agreement with landowners, to change this practice of complete lack of tenant tenure.

Kamali had recently installed a rice mill, powered by a diesel, and from the little power plant he was running crude wires that provided electric light for the village; also there were water pipes, though mostly the villagers seemed to prefer the ancient way: to get their water in jugs from the canal rather than the "faucet."

We left Kamali and drove on, along a "proper" road that bisects the 20,000-hectare Dez pilot area, the only road actually, and on to the tiny town of Andimeshk.

MARCH 14, 1960
TEHRAN

The story of ideas in the unfolding of our Persian program is filled with encounters with the perennial and never-ending problem of finding and holding people not only capable but put by us into the right place for their particular talents, and under a scheme of organization that brings out the best they have.

There has been a good deal of this "trying and fitting" during the past four years out here; what John Oliver calls the slaphappy period of new organization.

We have just been through the latest episode, with the requests for resignation of several top staff.

But amputation, important as it is in building an organization and shaping it, is not the answer to making an organization function; it is often just the beginning, however necessary. A new and affirmative answer has to be provided. This we are on the way to providing, I think.

This is really the first time in D&R that I have been in the middle of an important organization and personnel selection process. This I have usually left to Gordon and Oliver. Out of this current shaking-up, and his handling of the budget approval and financing problems we have been going through these past two weeks, I have developed an increasing respect for John Oliver's talents. A real talent for dealing with program through the *figures* that represent or state the program. Not imaginative nor articulate in the field of general ideas, but receptive to them. A good temperament, a fellow who enjoys what he is doing even when things aren't going entirely as he wants them to.

MARCH 15, 1960
FLYING TO GENEVA

Last evening in Tehran a cocktail party for us by the sweet Mozayenys, father and son, and their families. A long talk with Engineer Asfia, perhaps the most candid, and on his part the most enthusiastic I can remember, for he is a very reserved man.

I reminded Asfia of our joke on Voorduin about Asfia's enthusiastic statement about the sugar project, which he visited for the first time only a month or so ago. Asfia had said, with a great grin, "I thought what I saw at Haft Tapeh even more impressive than Dez Dam," and we joshed Bill Voorduin about this, I said. Asfia picked this up: "As I saw what had been done out in the middle of the desert, where only a year ago there had been nothing, nothing but space, I said to myself: 'But this cannot be Iran.' " That comment I find touching and full of meaning, from so reserved and cautious a man as this, the ablest of the Iranian technical and administrative men in the Plan Organization.

I said that when I returned all our friends, and particularly the women, would ask me questions about the new young Queen. Asfia said, "I know the Queen; she was in school with my daughter; I know her since she was [then he gestured] a little girl that high. A charming, fine girl, a good mind, intelligent and capable." I was glad to have the reserved Asfia's comment, since the only times we saw the Queen she was either so fagged or preoccupied, in public ceremonials, carefully remembering her instructions about how in her new role a Queen should behave on these interminable and surely boring trips of "inspection." But we have had one glimpse of her as a natural and "human" young woman. That was when Helen and I were "invited" to go to their table at the dinner in the garden in Ahwaz. Then she flashed a smile on us that was enchanting. And after we returned to our places, she and the King had an animated conversation, as if they were not being watched— every moment—by the big circle (at a distance on the edge of the garden beside the lavishly laid tables of food), by a host of people. They looked like two people enjoying each other's company, completely absorbed in each other, laughing at the give-and-take of their exchanges.

MARCH 16, 1960
BRUSSELS

How much truth is there in the following thesis about the art of negotiation?

A negotiator, a very good practitioner of the art of negotiation, must be objective, must be able to see the strong and weak points of both sides. But his purpose, *unlike* that of the advocate, is not to see both sides in order that he may destroy the opposite side but so that he can weigh and analyze the strong and weak points, not secretly in his mind (as the advocate is likely to do) but in the presence of all. Out of such objective dealing with the strengths and weaknesses, the pro and con implications of varying points of view, he can bring together into agreement the previously disagreeing and dissonant positions of the parties.

This is not *mediation*. The negotiator enters into discussions committed to producing an accommodation, not by being neutral as is a mediator, who urges the two opposing parties to give here and there.

The negotiator is trying to find the materials from which he can *create* a solution, an accommodation between the views held when the discussion began, and views that will resolve conflict in a way that will further the basic objectives of *both* sides, or all sides.

Nate Greene said his once great chief, the corporation lawyer Alfred Cook, when asked by someone puzzled that he did not seem to be acting as an advocate for the people employing him, whom he represented, replied: "I represent *the situation.*"

MARCH 17, 1960
BRUSSELS

Spent most of the morning on the proposed European-American group, of which D&R has been invited as the Americans to try to affect the future economic course of the Belgian Congo.

The meeting was in the office of the young Baron Coppée. An apple-cheeked, rather heavy-set young man, but with a real light in his eyes. His office is in one of those extremely formal European financial institution offices: at 8:30 A.M. there were men in long *tailcoats* scurrying about with mail. His office is huge, and from the walls the full-length paintings of his forebears look down on a picture they probably wouldn't stand for: the idea of *dealing* with the Congolese ("the blacks" is the term they would have used, and one that Coppée still uses, now and then). The whole notion of letting anyone else into the Congo, that private preserve of the Belgians, is so revolutionary that I'm afraid I don't fully appreciate what a shock and a blow it is to the Belgians.

What the Belgians (i.e., those in Coppée's group only) would like to do is to call in a group such as we have formed, that would indicate that the future development of the Congo, for the benefit of the native Congolese, is not just a disguised form of colonialism but something quite new. The risk Gordon and I take in having a hand in this is that while Coppée and Cracco and some of the younger men in the Government may have this idea, what will emerge will be the use of this device to aid the determined intention of the Belgian Establishment not to give up one single thing. I said frankly that I was sure that they would expect to continue to dominate the industrial and commercial picture; to take any different position would be unrealistic. But this is a long way from the old story, when no one could set foot in that colony except Société Générale, or some lackey of theirs in the so-called colonial administration.

MARCH 19, 1960
BRUSSELS

Last evening's soirée at Baron Coppée's removed whatever lingering doubts I may have had that the dramatic offer—even insistence— of the Belgian Government on political independence of the Congo ("Congo for the Congolese") was seriously meant.

Coppée had brought together some of the leaders of the "permanent staff" of the Government concerned with the Congo or men who though now in private life came from that setting and still are very active in the development of policy.

The most voluble man was Baron Albert Kervyn de Lettenhoven. About thirty-five, perhaps even younger. Wavy hair, very intense, not the Belgian "type." Now Chief of the Department of Economic and Social Planning of the Belgian Government—a recent innovation, I gather. He is now deep in Congo economic problems, sitting each day with the young and educated Congolese here in Brussels, preparing the way for the second Round Table Conference (as they call it, in English) between Belgians and Congolese, this time on economic matters. The first such Round Table was on political problems (they separate these two quite inseparable items with a French exactitude).

Out of the first Round Table came the offer by Minister de Schryver, the political Minister for the Congo, of independence now.

I said that I simply couldn't understand this apparently complete turnabout in Belgian Government policy toward the Congo. When we were guests at a dinner tendered by the Minister of the Congo (on the initiative of old Sengier, uranium king), Société Générale and Union Minière du Haut Katanga were the real rulers of the Congo; the several Ministers and other public officials who were in attendance were considered as superfluous front for the Union Minière and the other big companies.

Now the Belgian Government has insisted on giving the Congolese political independence right away; the elections are supposed to be concluded and the new Government take over June 30. I asked if this was considered by the man in the street and in the counting house as a maneuver, a gambit, since the Congolese have no experience whatever in government (thanks to past Belgian policy, which everyone at the soirée freely admitted as "our mistake") and only a handful of Congolese who know "which way is up" (as one fellow put it last night).

No. The new policy represents the will of most of the people of the country, I was told, with complete agreement all around. More than that, when it is proposed that the Belgian people give technical and other help (which costs money) to a new Congolese Government, there is no dissent; on the contrary, it is considered the "thing to do."

An affecting litttle episode. One of the men who came in "for a drink" was Louis F. J. Camu, now chairman of the Banque de Bruxelles, about fifty-five, formerly "Chief of Cabinet," i.e., Permanent Under Secretary of various ministries, head of the Belgian "Hoover Commission," etc. Said he felt he owed me a special debt; he then recited this story:

"During the occupation of Belgium in the last war, I spent two years in a German concentration camp. As a result I lost the use of my eyes, and was unable to read for a long time after I was released. Good medical treatment brought back my vision. The first book that I read after I could manage once more to read was a very remarkable book you wrote about the Tennessee Valley. This was such a hopeful book, yet so graphic and practical, so full of ideas of great importance for the whole world, that it restored my spirits. I have ever since wanted to thank you for what this did for me."

Baron Snoy (Jean Charles Snoy et d'Oppuers), a leader in the Common Market and Benelux movements, made a comment that gave an interesting interpretation of current developments in Belgium. When I expressed my amazement that the Belgian people should be apparently so willing to give up their political control of the Congo, he said: "The idea of owning a part of Africa was entirely old Leopold's, fifty years ago or so. Neither the people nor the Parliament took to the idea, and when on his death he willed it to Belgium—the Congo was the King's personal property—the country was far from enthusiastic. So in a sense the present position is a return to an earlier, historical one."

Kervyn said he didn't agree. This is not a return to an older position; it is a new position based on new factors. Snoy was inclined to agree that his historical interpretation didn't fit what was happening; that it isn't that the Belgians don't want the Congo, but that they see that the Congolese must run their own country, politically.

There was a good deal of discussion about "the mistake we Belgians made." The crux was that they had not trained a civil service capable of running a government, as the British did in the India Civil Service, considered one of the best functioning bureaucracies in the Empire or Commonwealth. As a consequence no one can foretell how the emerging Congo political parties, once the election has been had, will manage the complexities of government. For example, independence will increase the importance of the balance of payments problem, yet in talking to the educated Congolese in these Round Tables, Kervyn said that the whole concept of balance of payments was one wholly new to them. But he was full of praise for their natural talents, even used the term "brilliant." They lack the experience that produces judgment, but ability they have, and "they will learn how to run things, and learn it fast" was his opinion.

As the discussion proceeded, I could see that joining in this technical group, as proposed, was not for D&R or for Gordon and me, certainly not at this stage. But it came over me strongly, nevertheless, that one day we would see we had probably missed an opportunity to *try* to be helpful to that minority among the Belgians who saw the handwriting on the wall. So I suggested we separate the survey into a reconnaissance first and then, after that look had been taken, we would be in a better position to discuss next steps.

FLYING OVER THE PYRENEES MOUNTAINS

We are in Spain, over the lovely Pyrenees, on a clear, crisp day.

As a "collector" of the world's great rivers, I was much taken with our magnificent view of the Gironde, as its broad expanse, even at 15,000 feet, wove its way across the alluvial plains of France, to the Atlantic, past Bordeaux. Then the snow-covered mountains, looking more like a cloud bank. We have passed the pleasure domes of Biarritz, and are at last at San Sebastián, and Spain!

MARCH 20, 1960
HOTEL PALACE
MADRID, SPAIN

For quite a long time I have considered myself an aficionado of the bullfight. But I got over this today, a brilliant Sunday afternoon in the greatest bull ring in the world, that of Madrid.

The pageantry, the great excitement as the black bull comes charging into the ring, 28,000 people yelling and storming, the beautiful movements of bull and man in the cape work, the sense of reality—for this is no "fixed" entertainment, like wrestling. The matador was badly gored and trampled in the first fifteen minutes of the first bull.

But these unique attractions of this primitive sport were eclipsed by the dreary butchery that occurred at the end of three successive bulls, until I had my fill. The matadors had tough and doughty bulls, but the trouble—from the viewpoint of the artistic, pictorial magnificence of the struggle of man and beast—was that the young matadors simply could not put the sword into that vital spot between the shoulders; as a consequence all three bulls kept fighting their tormentors —for that is all they seemed to be—long after they should have been dead, quickly, by a single courageous thrust of the sword. They tottered about the ring, the matador having the sword pulled out dripping red, and trying again and again, then the dagger dug into the poor beast, who still kept rising to his feet and defying them all. There was no doubt that the crowd was for the bulls, who got the greatest applause as, finally, the three mules dragged them across the ring and out. It was at the end an abattoir.

So that's the end of my bullfighting enthusiasm. *Unless,* of course, some great matador comes along and I have a chance to see him fight the bull, and kill him decently.

MARCH 25, 1960
MADRID

During the past week I have tried to forget the excitement of the weeks in the Philippines and Persia, and be a 100 percent "tourist." We hired a car and driver, and put in hours seeing Ávila, Segovia, and part of the stupendous pile of El Escorial. The countryside, even in the cold of early spring, was delightful, in some places very rocky and grim, in others rolling, green, and sweet to the eye. The villages we went through, especially on the way to Ávila, were windblown—a strong wind always blows in the mountains—but charming, with flat angle tile roofs, remarkably clean and tidy. In Segovia we arrived on a market day. At the corners dark clusters of most serious-looking men, caped often and always with black berets, talking business, the business of trading cattle, feed, land, etc.

APRIL 3, 1960
SUNDAY
PRINCETON

Tuesday about 5 P.M. Beatrice "escorted" me through a remarkable exhibition of the paintings of Claude Monet at the Museum of Modern Art, and beautifully laid out. For example, four paintings of Rouen Cathedral, in four different kinds of light—morning, noon, etc. Beatrice's enthusiasm and feeling, deep feeling, about what goes on *within* such an artist as Monet, and which he portrays by his brush, is a contagious thing. So what might have been just looking at famous paintings became, through her comments and presence and understanding teaching, an experience, an opening of the eyes of the spirit.

APRIL 9, 1960
PRINCETON

A very full and exciting week this has been.

Monday memorable for the swift flow of emotional energy, and new confidence I felt, and demonstrated, rather dumbfounded me when I recall how, only two years ago, things seemed about up with me in all departments.

I am overjoyed that I seem to have tapped energies and drive and zest I haven't felt, in the same measure, for a long time. A subtle thing, and yet probably very, very simple: a return to a more "natural" outlook on life, a rejection of the doctrine so long held by me that one must ration and withhold and "conserve," and in the process probably drain more energy and electricity of the soul than I saved.

Much to go over with Gordon, who has pretty well shot his bolt after that terrible negotiating spell with the World Bank, and must get away and rest and renew himself. But on all the things we discussed: Iran, Congo, Ghana, the same comfortable feeling of being with a man with whom many things are shared.

Tuesday, Jean Kennedy, the producer of the David Susskind Sunday night discussion show, *Open End* called me. Would I go on their program this coming Sunday (tomorrow night) as one of a group intended to provide a "rebuttal" to the extraordinary performance of five Soviet members of the U.S.S.R. delegation to the UN who were the guests on the 27th of March? I asked for the transcript and concluded I'd better not stay so completely out or back away from this. My first reading of the transcript made me spluttering mad: the gall of these Russians in blandly asserting things that are so contrary to what everyone surely must know about their performance in world affairs since the end of the war.

A telephone call from Baron Coppée from Brussels. The Société Générale people have brought great pressure, he said, on the Minister for the Congo to put them on the Belgian team that is intended to be one of the members of the multinational "survey" group. Coppée said if this happened he would withdraw himself.

I took no time to let the Minister know, through Coppée, that these maneuvers confirmed my concern that the purpose of this survey was not primarily the Congolese but to protect Société's interest in the wealth of the Congo; that if the project were not carried out strictly in accordance with the new deal in Congolese affairs, as represented by Coppée and his friends—and I thought the proposals and pressures of Société made clear that this was *not* the present intention—then the Minister should know that we were out.

The crux of the whole matter was the purpose, the motivation, of this so-called survey. If it was to help the Congolese through the transition period until they can assume control of their economic life, that is something I would be willing to take considerable chances of failure or frustration on; if we were simply made part of a false front to protect Belgian commercial interests and nothing more, the whole thing is doomed to failure in the end, and, in any case, it is not for us.

APRIL 12, 1960
TUESDAY, 4:30 A.M.
NEW YORK

The impromptu dive last Sunday into the cold water of a Susskind TV program on a most touchy subject was a good experience for me, whatever it may have been for the people who watched the program.

Susskind tossed the discussion to me to start off. That what I said was causing Susskind pain and surprise was apparent almost from the first. He *wants to believe* that disarmament, complete—much in the air these days—is on its way; he wants to believe that the Russians have changed so much that we can begin to trust them in vital matters, as we already are beginning to in minor though not inconsequential ones. And when I didn't go along with this at all, he felt let down by one he says (and I believe him) he admires for what he *thinks* is my record. Ah, well.

APRIL 20, 1960
11 P.M.
PITTSBURGH

The paper I have called "The Multinational Corporation" I have been working on for months, with David Schwartz doing a good deal of the actual drafting, is about a reality. I saw it in final form this afternoon and thought: Now, that was worth doing. Whether I will think so when we get through the Carnegie Tech Symposium here I don't know. But it is a pretty solid piece of work and contributes some ideas on a surprisingly wide range of subjects, showing that "management" can be the focus or nucleus for *general* thinking, as well as mere craftsmanship. And the other participants include some interesting and stimulating people.

Pittsburgh is greatly changed and for the better; it is not the city it was as I first remember it twenty years ago, or even ten years ago. What a sense of civic responsibility can do!

APRIL 21, 1960
10:30 P.M.
PITTSBURGH

I don't know quite what has come over me, but whatever it is, it is certainly a new me: more sure of myself, less apologetic and falsely modest, an extraordinary lack of cautiousness so characteristic of the me of yesteryear, and a kind of spur-of-the-moment vitality.

This self-praise, for that it is, of course—obnoxious even in a private journal—is occasioned by my performance today in an all-day session of the Symposium of "big brains" at Carnegie Tech. Only the record of the colloquy, which was taken by tape, will establish whether this is imaginary or whether the plaudits of my colleagues and the audience were just politeness. But I think I am the one who would know first, and I feel released somehow, less timid to express myself, to take on people (I was the only one today who gave Friedrich von Hayek, the *Road to Serfdom* gloomy gus, a scornful kidding about how he has mellowed since the predicted serfdom failed to show up).

APRIL 30, 1960
SATURDAY, 7 A.M.
PRINCETON

An exciting week—superexciting.

The "range" of excitement was a wide and rich one, and my joy of living, usually high in the miracle of spring, was at about its highest.

In business: André managed to work out the merger with Philipp Bros., the ore and metal people, which will add $6.5 million pro forma, to the earnings of Minerals & Chemicals, making it now a rather sizable company.

Instead of merely writing about the Multinational Corporation (as I did in a Carnegie Tech lecture) this merger brings into my personal orbit just such a corporation dealing with raw materials all over the world.

The Finance Minister of the Ivory Coast finally accepted our proposal, made at their request, that we survey their minerals, and added something I liked: that we take a look at certain "problems of planification" in the resource-rich but wholly undeveloped southwest region of their country.

At the same time a letter from Baron Coppée accepting with reluctance (and a good deal of argument) my refusal to stay in their group for a survey of the Congo. There is clear evidence that the "established interests," i.e., the Union Minière, etc., were getting their stooges into the act, and certain knowledge that sooner or later the Congolese would repudiate the whole business as just a maneuver to keep the Belgians in a little longer.

Monday we had dinner, Helen and I, at the Nat Eliases in Washington Mews, the other guests being Commissioner Bob Moses and his wife, and General Edward Greenbaum and his distinguished sculptor wife, Dorothea.

Bob was in good form, cussing out his enemies with his old verve. He is somewhat defensive these days, for him, because a scandal of sorts in the private insured housing field was turned against some of his close coworkers and even against him. Apparently he "told off" the *New York Times* editorial lunch about it, and made a roaring Mosaic speech about attacks on public officials at the newspaper editors' meeting in Washington last week.

He talked at length about the Long Island Railroad. His disdain for the intelligence or integrity of the characters who built railroads on Long Island was Gargantuan.

MAY 17, 1960
PRINCETON

A week ago or so I wrote a piece for the North American Newspaper Alliance predicting the "impending debacle" of the Summit Conference, and the fallacy of such a dream-world way of going at the promotion of peace. At that time that statement seemed like sticking out one's neck on a prophecy that might have proved wrong, or ambiguous. So when yesterday morning, the 16th, the opening of the Conference in Paris produced a blowup, the full hurtful implications of which it may take years to assess, my judgment about major strategy was confirmed. Why the blowup was inevitable, why it actually was a saving of the peace it will take some time for the world to appreciate. Naturally, I feel reassured.

Last Sunday's *New York Times*, to my half surprise and entire delight, had my NANA piece, a column and a half, prominently displayed in the first section, along with lively news about the Summit Conference. My timing couldn't have been better, and as I reread the piece I thought it made sense. It will make me unpopular and a renegade with those who like to classify people as liberal and therefore trusting of the Soviets—which classification is nonsense. But this is what I think, and that is what is important. And it has got me out of the position of supercaution and immobility about important public questions concerned with security and war.

MAY 21, 1960
PRINCETON

This week—with some prompting from Sylvain Bromberger, our son-in-law—I thought hard about what to do with my papers, not the least of which are the Journals, now almost thirty looseleaf notebooks—and reached a decision after talking things over with Helen. The decision was to write articles but not to attempt to write a book or books in the next few years, drawing upon the Journals, and in any case not do any writing on a continuous all-out basis.

This has been—still is—a most beautiful spring season. Our herbaceous border, for the first time, gives us great delight as gardeners; it is assuming a form, a design too, and the hard work of improving the soil—basic to a good garden—is beginning to show definite results. The mixing of all the ingredients: peat moss, bone meal, liquid fertilizer. Breaking open what was once the stubborn Jersey clay and seeing the pieces part and crumble. The whole process of getting my hands into the soil, which I have loved for so many years, never seemed more delightful or full of meaning.

Is there really any steady pleasure, day in and day out pleasure, greater than a flower garden? It is particularly delightful for us because it is actually the only outdoor interest Helen and I have together. She has become an avid lover of the garden, works diligently at it, down on her knees—the posture of all true gardeners—and seems to get great satisfaction from it.

Last Sunday a cocktail party for about twenty-five people. Among the guests: Joe Johnson, President of the Carnegie Foundation for International Peace. He said: "I'm leaving for Paris tomorrow to be on the edge of the Summit." I said, quite seriously: "You'd better hurry if you expect to get there before it is over." He thought this was intended as a joke; it turned out to be far from a joke.

The story of the blowup of the Four-Power Summit Conference, and the humiliation of finding our country in so defensive a position that people were "sorry" for us, was a painful thing, and the pain has not left yet, of course. The important thing now is to learn something basic from this past two years of hoopla and complacency. Will we? Or will we concentrate on such intrinsically irrelevant things as the U-2 "spy" plane incident and neglect the fundamentals?

We should not look for easy deliverance by Summit or any other kind of one-shot expectations. This is a long and grueling road.

And yet, right after the blowup, Madison Square Garden was filled with people cheering for an end to aboveground atomic weapons testing as The Solution; among the speakers were people who should know better.

Because we want something badly doesn't mean that it is to be had for the wanting. How long will it take people to understand that?

MAY 22, 1960
PRINCETON

Years ago—it must have been as long ago as 1936 or so—a man representing the Delaware River Study Commission—something of the sort—came to see us at TVA. He told me with the utmost seriousness that the TVA method of developing a river for all its possibilities simply would not do; that it deprived the states of their authority, etc.

Now after twenty-five years the Delaware is still in increasing trouble with pollution, flooding, the works; the states, bless them, have still their "rights"—but the plan to do something of a coordinated sort with this river is about where it was. But the Tennessee River, thanks to TVA, is under control, and the seven states of the Valley not only still have their "rights," but have a better river and valley than before 1933.

JUNE 6, 1960
PRINCETON

Last weekend my beloved cousin Bernardine Szold Fritz with us. Had such a hearty and happy visit with her.

In the course of this vivid talk we recalled so many things of our past, when we were both very young and very idealistic and rebellious—she the rebel more than I for she had much sterner parents, and being a girl her more flamboyant "conduct" was more subject to censure by her elders.

JUNE 14, 1960
CAMBRIDGE, MASSACHUSETTS

Yesterday morning Helen and I took a long walk through old familiar places. That is, places in Cambridge where we walked, and shared the dreams we had for the years ahead, way back in 1922-23, when we were students and before we were married, in September, 1923. Yes, that would be thirty-eight years ago!

The Quadrangle of Radcliffe was quite lovely, and so also the Harvard Yard, for it was an unusually fine late spring day with a fresh easterly breeze. But what just about "broke me up"—indeed brought

me to the verge of tears really—was going into now empty Langdell
Hall at the Law School and walking into the large lecture hall. I went,
almost automatically, to the very chair in the very row of this amphitheatre where I attended my first law school class; Professor Williston
was just as plainly sitting behind the desk in the back of the half circle
as the day I first saw his twinkling grin and heard his clipped voice. This
too was the great room where I heard Joey Beale cut off people's heads
with relish and without batting his eyes, eyes like a fish, but the face of
a cherub. And I could see Bull Warren, red-faced and portly, bellowing
and storming.

It was at the Law School that I woke up, intellectually. It was here
that for the first time I sensed that there was a long history of ideas
and of a great company of men with ideas—part of my inheritance.

JUNE 15, 1960
HOTEL COMMANDER, 9:30 P.M.
CAMBRIDGE

Too tired tonight to write a real description of today's events at the
Radcliffe Board of Trustees' meeting. Enough to say, at this point, that
my "new personality" came to the fore again, and as a result I ignited
a Trustees' meeting in staid Radcliffe. In a brief but quite emotional
talk I pictured President Polly Bunting's proposal for an Institute of
Advanced Study—for truly creative *women*—in a perspective of the
greatness of the idea's potentials; as a result the nit-picking that was
going on about details was silenced, and the proposal got an enthusiastic
endorsement. A motion was immediately put and carried.

I am inserting at this point an excerpt from the Clerk's minutes
about my remarks at the meeting:

> Mr. Lilienthal spoke most warmly in support of the plan, calling
> it a "history-making proposal." Many persons are, he said, aware
> of the waste of talent of women, and this [proposal] is in his
> opinion a means of interpreting public thinking about women. It
> is as important, in its way, as the very establishment of this college
> itself. What we are talking about in terms of democracy is putting
> this talent to the use of the full potential of human beings. That
> such a proposal should emanate from Radcliffe, makes him proud.
> We will not raise the money necessary, however, in the way in
> which we should if we start worrying at this stage about details of
> the proposal. Its fundamental importance should be recognized.
>
> It was recommended that the Institute be enthusiastically
> endorsed by the Trustees.

JUNE 17, 1960
NEW YORK

The morning paper tells the details of the latest debacle of visits of "heads of state," i.e., so-called personal (to wit, grinning) diplomacy. The cancellation of the President's visit to Japan tells more about how asleep and dopey we have been to what is going on in the world than about conditions in Japan and the Far East.

Well, "fame" is both ephemeral and geographically "confined." But this morning I picked up a cab at the Plaza, and in talking to the obviously Spanish driver about the weather (which is hot and humid today) he said: "Where I come from it is *dry* and never like this." So I asked where is this. "Colombia," he said, "Cali." I told him I have often been to Cali, have many friends there. "What is your business?" he asked. "Developing valleys, such as the Cauca." Then he eyed me: "What is your name, please?" When I told him, he nearly fell out of the cab. "Ah, yes, I know the Lilienthal Plan; Bernardo Garces Cordoba is my cousin." His name was Herman Cordoba Marino.

JUNE 18, 1960
SATURDAY, 6 A.M.
PRINCETON

A visit yesterday afternoon with Enrico Cuccia about FIDIA, the new Italian consortium he has formed, and of which it is expected that I will be elected a director.

The areas he is studying actively for a beginning of ventures that will make money but in a way that will move Italy along—and particularly the South—cover quite a range. The growing and canning of vegetables and fruits is one. Italy uses very little beer, compared with almost any other European country, to say nothing of America, so this is another. Department stores are another. And so on.

On my trip to Italy about six or seven years ago, I developed a thesis to him and Carlo Weiss. It was that the only hope for the South was through the existing well-developed industrial organization of the North of Italy. Yes, Cuccia said, we agree. But we can't get the big industries together and make them work together. But we'll try. This FIDIA is now intended to be that try.

One problem he mentioned, in that characteristically spicy way he uses to make a point: before a canning plant can begin operations in an Italian community it must have a license. Who decides whether such a license shall be issued? The local Chamber of Commerce. And if any member feels that another plant, for any reason, is against his own business interest or might render obsolescent plants or products of their members, the political people who actually issue or deny the license just don't do it. This is a form of cartelization—or stagnation—that shocks one, though in Europe the cartel (or "rational production" phony that is used to justify the practice) is common enough, of course. But to apply this not to heavy capital industries but to consumer goods or a department store is intolerable, if they are to get ahead.

I told Cuccia that I was only interested in becoming a director of FIDIA if there was a function for a foreign, American director to perform. He expects American participation in these new enterprises. Not as to capital; he placed his hand on his heart to swear that the financial risks the Italian members would take. But the *how*—that was to be the contribution. For example, he had spent a good deal of time with Fred Lazarus of Federated Department Stores on how to get that kind of merchandising going. Incidentally, he said that the IBEC, the International Basic Economy Corporation sponsored by Nelson Rockefeller, had considerable difficulty getting a supermarket established in Rome because of this licensing gimmick, that it is opposed by existing stores, asserted through political channels.

JUNE 22, 1960
5:10 A.M.
NEW YORK

Sunrise over the heart of Manhatttan has a strange, impersonal grandeur. A great band of very pale-blue sky to the east, with darker blue above. The reflected light of these early dawns on the silent towers, the city's mountain peaks, all about me here in the middle of this great city. Like sunrise on Indian Hill on the Vineyard, this, too, is evidence of the breathless beauty of living one more morning, one more day.

Helen's and my trip to Niagara Falls and the New York Power Authority's power project as Bob Moses's guest was well worth the day and a half it took. Moses was most genial and friendly. His speech at the noon meeting of the New York State Newspaper Editors' convention was partly a recitation of the origins of the project, the long, long delays while the power companies fought the horrid idea of "public power."

The part of what he said that moved me most was pure Moses, heaping hot coals of contempt upon those who had held things up, and a preliminary dose of same for the Chicago Drainage District and its diversion of Lake Michigan water into the Des Plaines and Mississippi Rivers.

Helen said afterward that she couldn't see why it was so heinous for Chicago to use the water of Lake Michigan for important public purposes, or any other city along the Great Lakes, if the only ill effect was that it might increase somewhat the cost or diminish the amount of power available from the installations at the Falls. Well, considering that most of the power goes to a few private industries on the Niagara Frontier and that slightly higher costs for them and somewhat less coverage for bondholders wouldn't ruin either, I must say I thought she had a point.

We saw the building operations at Niagara at their best time, while things were really stirring, huge trucks, rock crushers, and concrete placement all over the place. The long conduit to bring the water of the river *around* the great falls and rapids is of a magnitude I have never seen before.

At the Century ran into Ed Murrow, looking extraordinarily fit, very brown and lean, but otherwise himself, to wit, predicting doom for America in well-rounded phrases. He spoke of himself with Murrowian self-deprecation but when I asked about that handsome red-headed son Casey (Charles) he was all glowing again, and full of stories of Casey's repartee, in the best tradition of the proud father that he is.

JUNE 23, 1960
EN ROUTE TO NEW YORK FROM PRINCETON

My departure for the Democratic Convention is only two weeks off. The edge that Kennedy appears clearly to have at this point could be dissipated when the rival candidates get together to pool their resources, if they do. But they will have to act pretty promptly in deciding who they will go for as a "fusion" nominee, or this incredibly active and able young man will be in. Johnson wants the nomination badly, he feels he is entitled to it but he will have to show great strength fast or throw his support to Stevenson or Symington fast. Otherwise it will be a short convention.

JUNE 30, 1960
NEW YORK

Tuesday night Helen and I saw *The Best Man*, starring Mel Douglas. Afterward we went backstage to see Melvyn. He was in a horrid, ugly little dressing room (most of these look like a cubby hole that the sheriff had just cleaned out of all furniture because it wasn't paid for). He said he had watched the Susskind program. "I never saw a man who seemed more tormented than you were." I assumed that meant he didn't approve of my dismal view about the prospects for accommodation with the Soviet based on those Summit talks, exchange of visits, etc. Unfortunately, my hunches so vigorously expressed as convictions were all confirmed and all too soon. But why "tormented"?

Gradually, piece by piece, the last remaining difficulties between ourselves and the World Bank staff are being worn down and got out of the way. Agreement on the disputed design features of the dam, as between their consulting board and our engineers, is about worked out, through John Oliver and Gene O'Brien's patience and skill largely. Now there is a row about some provisions of the "rules and regulations" of the to-be-created Khuzistan Water and Power Authority, as it relates to water use and charges. *Then*, Inshallah, the first disbursements from the loan should begin. It has been a long road, and as full of trouble as the life of man, but it has been worth it.

JULY 4, 1960
PRINCETON

Rising at 5 A.M. to a day of brilliance of sunrise and warmth of shadow, I took a walk and then returned to the labor that has consumed me for the past several days, that is, finishing the article the North American Newspaper Alliance wants from me.

When I get steamed up by the necessity of saying something that means a good deal to me I find I invariably do my best in the "early, early" morning. In hotel rooms in New York last week, at dawn and usually without my coffee, this to and fro went on.

This very early morning concentration on ideas reminds me that I wrote the first chapter of my TVA book in one sitting in a room in the Hay–Adams in Washington. More than a chapter, it was the theme of the book complete.

When one is formulating ideas or words, there are times when the frustration, and even agony, is so great you wish to hell you had spent your time doing something less wearing and exacting. Then an idea begins to develop, seems almost what you have been seeking; the joy, almost the sensual joy, of this process.

The article is rather strong medicine; whether Catledge will print it in the *New York Times* I can't be sure.* But of this I can be sure, and it pays for all the sweating and wrestling: it does represent what I think. More than that, it represents a side of me that for ten years or more has been congealed or in suspended animation. I mean a willingness, even an eagerness, to speak my mind on controversial subjects, even ones where I know I am vulnerable to the snide kind of innuendo

* The article appeared in the *Times* on July 8, 1960, under the headline: "Lilienthal Says U.S. Faces Peril of Gradual Enforced Isolation."

attack that I had to put up with so long in TVA and AEC. I developed a kind of caution and a withdrawal from controversy that I rather assumed would be with me the rest of my life. But recently I have become less fearful, even inviting risks.

Last Friday Dr. Robert Lively and I had a definitive talk about my papers and journal manuscript. He said he wanted to use the materials, including the row on row of files of letters, speeches, memos, etc., as the basis for a study of the dynamics of recent history in which I took a part.

I agreed that he could have access to the whole file. I would not now even consider transfer of the title of the files to Princeton.

He made some comments of an enthusiastic and almost awed nature about the scope and depth of this material. In this he included, with a high rating, my letters to Helen during the first two years I was at the Harvard Law School (where so many later New Deal figures were —without their then knowing it, of course—being "trained" for public affairs). He was even fascinated, as a historian, by the nickel-by-nickel expense accounts I kept in our early and impecunious days.

But the tone, ideas, and the reflectiveness of the journals seemed to impress him the most. "I am familiar with most of the collected papers of public figures, but except for two of the Presidents, I don't know of anything like the material you have in this house."

JULY 5, 1960
PRINCETON

On the dot of 10:30 this morning, a big Princeton University truck pulled up, accompanied by the University librarian, William Dix, and Professor Lively. Thirty-six file drawers, constituting much of my life on paper, went into the truck, the Librarian signed a receipt, and so began the first serious work on these "papers." This afternoon I saw them in their new home, a big seminar room in the beautiful Firestone Library. There "I" shall rest, until the archivist, graduate student, and Lively go through them and begin to reorganize and classify.

JULY 8, 1960
FLYING WEST, TO LOS ANGELES

Spanning this vast continent in five hours is an exciting thing just to think about. There she lies: America, far below us, 30,000 feet below us. But I have never felt closer to my country than this morning.

Met Quincy Howe, on the plane; he is now (and for many years) a radio broadcaster as well as writer. I don't think I have actually seen him since I was a student in the Law School and he was a student in Harvard College. We met at the home of Isabelle and Bert Wilde. Which brings back memories, too, of the happy times Helen and I had at the Wildes' little house, appropriately on Joy Street, at the back-of-Beacon Hill. I remember a rather confused but important Sunday afternoon there, and it makes my heart melt for all today's groping young people, learning what life is about.

Yesterday Gordon, John, and I had most of an hour with André.

André asked: "Who is your candidate?" I said I thought very well of Kennedy, particularly his performance in the past few weeks. André was shocked, particularly when, to my surprise, Gordon joined in, and quite strongly. To elect Kennedy, André said, would be nothing less than a disaster for the country. He has no "authority" not only in this country but particularly in England and France. We left the subject and went on to our business; but as we left André, who is always so friendly and considerate toward me, said, "I hope you don't mind what I said about Kennedy but I couldn't help being shocked that a man of your standing and authority . . ." Of course I didn't mind.†

We told André of the good reception that Professor Ralph Grim, our geologist, and Tom Mead had had in their visit to the Ivory Coast, a visit André made possible. Gordon told him what our proposal, the one requested by Minister of Finance and Development Saller, would include. It also gave me a chance to describe the difference between the way we go at one of these surveys (whether minerals or what) and the usual specialist way. We would not, as French geologists tend to do, look under every pebble and for every mineral. Instead of spending great amounts of money on an exploration of all the resources, our survey would be far less extensive and expensive, because it would be *selective*. And the selectivity would be on the present economic or *market* importance of *particular* minerals. Copper is running out of the world's ears right now, as is iron ore, but chrome and manganese are in short supply. So our efforts would be to get the facts about such minerals, including bauxite, the cost of access, etc.

Wednesday, late afternoon, went to a "reception" given by Averell Harriman at his Manhattan home on 81st St. Bill Fulbright answered questions from the living room full of serious thinkers, mostly Stevenson-

† Mr. Meyer later became a great admirer and supporter of Kennedy. See entry in this volume for December 19, 1963.

type supporters. The purpose of the meeting was to raise funds for Syd McMath's campaign for Governor (of Arkansas) against Faubus. If Faubus wins, then two years later he may oppose Fulbright for the Senate. If Faubus beats Fulbright on the segregation issue, this would be a national disaster in both foreign relations and our racial progress in this country.

I visited with McMath, a handsome, vigorous, straightforward young man whom I haven't seen since I left the Tennesse Valley.

Averell and I had a good talk; he walked me to the corner of Madison and got me into a cab. He looks so well and vigorous and self-assured. I remember so well how tense and apprehensive and self-conscious he seemed when I saw him in Paris in 1950, at his apartment, with Jean Monnet, when Averell headed the Marshall Plan program.

If Averell had somehow had the sense of assurance to repudiate DeSapio and take over leadership of the Democratic Party, I think, with Finletter as senatorial candidate he might have beat Rockefeller. But caving in as he did with the thought that this was the "practical politics" of it, not only didn't win the election but tied him to the kite of an "organization" that was even then on the decline; today everyone can see that DeSapio's days are numbered. Averell was never *himself*, win, lose or draw, in that campaign four years ago, and this is always self-defeating and unhappy.

JULY 9, 1960
HOTEL AMBASSADOR
LOS ANGELES

Last Thursday at lunch Gordon added something to my information about Dr. A. E. Morgan.

In the very earliest days A.E. called in Floyd Reeves, A.E.'s selection as "Director of Social and Economic Planning" as well as Personnel Director and ordered him to hire X; Reeves asked how did Morgan know that X was who was needed or had the proper qualifications? "I have studied his *picture* and I know," said A.E., impatiently. "Picture!" said Reeves. Then it turned out, as A.E. explained at some length, that A.E. was firmly convinced he could pick the best people just by looking at their pictures.

Reeves was nonplused, talked to Gordon, then his assistant. They put together a number of pictures of people, all of whom had been interviewed, most of whom were in the TVA, and laid them before A.E. to pick out the ones we ought to employ, those we shouldn't, to test the "system."

"Don't pick that one, no good," said A.E. without a bit of hesitation (he never doubted his own powers, that is sure). This turned out to be

Roland Wank, TVA's great architect whose work was later acclaimed as setting a new mark in designing beauty into functional structures, such as dams, bridges.

"There's a man you ought to get," A.E. said, pointing to another picture. This man had been employed, and fired for, as Gordon said, "making love to the wrong wife in a public way." And so on. I expressed astonishment but Gordon went on: "Oh, that's just one of A.E.'s instinctive methods of always being able, himself, to pick 'the best people in the country,' to use a phrase he used until I got fed up with it.

"Actually, he wanted us to hire a phrenologist, a guy who determined character by reading the bumps on your head." Gordon went on.

The preconvention business is in a just-before-the-battle period of expectancy. Some important caucuses tomorrow, at which Kennedy may make some headway, perhaps enough to ensure his nomination. The resentment of the Johnson people is obvious; they feel that Johnson deserves the post whereas this young man Kennedy has muscled his way in; this feeling will preclude a coalition to agree on someone that might beat Kennedy and probably the agreement will come too late; otherwise it is Kennedy. If Johnson would make up his mind that Stevenson is better *for the party* than Kennedy (and this could be true) Adlai could be nominated. But Johnson looked awfully grim and angry tonight and so did Sam Rayburn.

From all sides here I hear the earnest approval of my NANA piece, about wishful thinking in dealing with the Soviets, the strength of the way it was put and the content and timeliness. Most of this came from newspaper people who are notoriously niggardly in approving anyone else's writing, particularly about public events. I feel it was well timed, in relation to the convention, and the content just specific and just critical enough to make an impression.

This evening Bernardine [Szold Fritz] and I drove up the hills to a huge party given by Jules Stein, the head of Music Corporation of America, a little, sharp-looking man. It was an extaordinary mixture of people. Bernardine and I were lucky to have gone together for she knew most of the movie contingent, and I the political. For three hours I talked to politicians like Sam Rayburn and movie celebrities like Gary Cooper. The latter a very self-conscious fellow, considerate and modest, much shorter than I had thought—shorter than I am. I told him I had benefited by his knowledge of his craft for a long time and wanted to thank him. He was obviously thinking that my own work was more important, and said: "Well, it's been a good kind of life, I guess, but without any responsibility."

Perle Mesta asked me to sit down with her on a circular bench effect, so she could take a load off obviously uncomfortable feet. She turned on me and said: "Are you a Republican?" I said no, that I had served through the Administrations of F.D.R. and Truman. "Well, somehow," she said, "you *look* like a Republican."

Sam Rayburn was heartiness itself in greeting me, recalling our visit at his home in a little cotton town in Texas, pointed to Lyndon Johnson, who had accompanied him to this gathering, but saying nothing about his candidacy; then Mr. Sam retreated to a corner of the terrace and stayed there until he and Johnson left.

Governor Meyner was a bit heavier than 1953 when I last saw him (and it was he who remembered when and where this was—these politicos and their memories). His wife, extremely handsome, with an extraordinary voice and presence. The Governor introduced me to her as "our neighbor" in Princeton.

The star performer was Eddie Albert, a great friend of Bernardine's, who told us about a project he is in the midst of in Honolulu; to change the curriculum of teaching out there through the use of closed-circuit television. He throws himself into everything he does, and with such eloquence, his enthusiasm is hard to resist, and I didn't, particularly when he spoke about the sixty racial strains being brought together in this new state.

Danny Kaye, hugging people all over the place, usually women, bright as a dollar and bouncy as a rubber ball, a most attractive person, I thought; Leonard Lyons prowling for bits for his column, as he might on 45th Street; Hedda Hopper with that waxlike face of hers; and so on and on, even Edgar Bergen and Gosden (Amos of *Amos n' Andy*) which is where our radio life—everyone else's, I guess—began back in our little apartment on 67th Street in Chicago in the mid-twenties.

JULY 10, 1960
LOS ANGELES

Yesterday morning began by my going to the Headquarters at the Biltmore. Big signs: Unite with Symington, A Leader to Lead the Nation (Johnson), Win with Kennedy, etc. People milling about, most of them the old-timers who saturate this strange piece of Americana, Los Angeles.

Ken Galbraith, stooped and picking his way through the corridor like a crane with sore feet, stopped to speak many kind words about what I had to say in the *Times* piece of last Friday.

So many newspaper and radio-TV people around, and handsome bronzed California-type gals with startled looks and Kennedy hats; seeing all this hub-bub, it is hard to believe that this is a decision-making event of the gravest importance to the whole world.

As I wandered into the big hall, the Johnson people were all over the place. I was a bit startled to have a good-looking Johnson gal grin and say, "Have a kiss?" Well, of course, she was carrying a basket of wrapped candy kisses but by the time I realized what the gag was I was on my way, again puzzling about the circus atmosphere.

Then I went to Prospect Park across from the Biltmore, ostensibly to watch Symington arrive, wave his hat, look handsome (as he is) — and somehow irrelevant at this point, which I rather think he is too.

But the real purpose was to be with the unique kind of Southern California crowd that practically lives in that Park. Not a city park crowd, such as used to gather in Hyde Park in Chicago years ago, or in Hyde Park, London, now. These are county seat, courthouse square loafers or resters, people waiting it out after a life of hard work somewhere else, Iowa, Indiana, etc. Some playing chess, more often checkers, enjoying the deep circle of "audience" packed in around them, showing off by expansive gestures as a decisive move in checkers would be made. Only one knot of "debaters," and they weren't talking politics, but some curious amalgam of religion and lay philosophy, I suppose it might be called, charitably, also heavily marked with the strong attention-getting traits of children rather than people who had grown wise as they grew older.

JULY 11, 1960
10 A.M.
LOS ANGELES

Yesterday was full of meeting people, and the growing reports of a Kennedy early nomination. Bernardine and I went to Mr. and Mrs. Sidney Brody's home, on invitation of Mary Lasker, Mrs. Brody's stepmother. Standing about the sunny, grassy edge of a pool, I had visits with so many people I rarely see, and whom I enjoy talking with: Bob Wagner, unharassed; Hubert Humphrey; the controversial Paul Ziffren, just fresh from a stormy caucus of the California delegation.

Bernardine and I went to the huge dinner (in two ballrooms). It was not too well managed, with painfully overlong introductions (Dore Schary was the worst offender). Finally brief speeches. Kennedy, spirited and magnetic, but his voice somehow didn't have the ring one would wish for (neither did Lincoln's!). Symington, who made the best speech and gave an impression of strength. Adlai Stevenson, witty as always, and impressive with his eloquence and essential dignity and awareness. But I wondered: is he tough enough, decisive enough? Can he appeal to the American general public enough to lead them? The answer is probably yes, but again I had doubts. Lyndon Johnson was a great disappointment, as to appearance, what he said, his way of saying it, his manner. A legislative master of the first water, but his appeal as a teacher and therefore a leader—well, I don't rightly know.

JULY 12, 1960
LOS ANGELES

Yesterday, beginning at 5:30 P.M., I saw my first national convention. The Sports Arena here is an immense oval. The equipment of "communication" dominates the place: great long-barreled telephoto lenses, cameras, TV cameras, microphones, a screen high above the speaker's head flashes his face 100 times life size, while way down there he waves his arms like a tiny toy, or someone seen through the wrong end of a telescope.

I wandered around a lot, as did everyone else. For this is a kind of electronic county fair, and people just naturally crave a look at real people, after all the marvels of electronics that flash only synthetic images and voices harsh with the distortion of a public address system. Could W. J. Bryan possibly have swept a convention with microphones and TV?

Kennedy seems quite clearly the candidate, probably on the first ballot tomorrow night. Part of this reason is strength as a vote getter and organizer of a preconvention campaign. Part is that the other candidates don't have the same quality.

Johnson is a disappointment. He seems to be spoiled by his period of unquestioned "leadership" in the Senate, so he seems to resent critical questions rather than take them as part, a serious part, of the job as Kennedy does. You can't be a great teacher and be impatient of your pupils' questions, can you? And a great teacher is what we need. Kennedy isn't one now, but I think he has a better chance of becoming one than anyone else here.

JULY 14, 1960
I A.M.
LOS ANGELES

Just back from the Sports Arena, the Democratic Convention hall, and one of the most vivid experiences of my life. A convention that was pretty dead and rather boring to attend came to life with a shriek and howl. The galleries, clear to the roof, were filled with Adlai acolytes, devoted, inspired, and "dedicated" young people, screaming and chanting at the delegates, quite sure they were going to change the course of political history and put Adlai over as the candidate by the force of the noise alone. This was triggered off by an extraordinary speech by Senator Eugene McCarthy of Minnesota, one of the best forensic efforts I have ever heard, far, far better than the keynote speech. But as I well knew, in spite of the excitement in the air, the chants, the banners, the wild hysterical goings-on all around us in the gallery, few votes would be affected—not more than a dozen, I'd guess.

Some of the old warriors of the Party are sitting in wobbly saddles at this moment, and about time, I say. Sam Rayburn is a wonderful man and has served his country well, but what does it mean to us today to hear him say that he had been in Congress longer than any other man ever had, and what kind of introduction to Lyndon Johnson's campaign was that? The boys of the *old* New Deal who advised Rayburn to use that piece of *East Lynne* just don't understand what has happened in the world. Nobody cares (I hope) how long you have been this or that in the past. What you are going to do about today and tomorrow, that's what should count. And the *average* age of the party workers in the Democratic Party will go way down (I saw some of these new Kennedy staff boys in the lobby—wow!), since this terrific Jack Kennedy was so overwhelmingly nominated.

I was sorry to see Mary Ellen Monroney and Eleanor Roosevelt— both devoted to Stevenson—leave the hall almost in tears. But hanging on has nothing to do with the law of life, which is change.

Four years ago—it is in my *Journals* somewhere‡—I pleaded with Stevenson to tell the old heroes to go fishing; that he was running the Party and running it for the future, not to glorify the past. I don't think he believed that course a practical one. Perhaps he does now, after Kennedy has "taken" the lot of them, Truman, Roosevelt, Lehman, and a lot of the others.

Whether Kennedy can win is another question. But he is a remarkable man, no doubt about it, and if the war crisis doesn't upset the country in Nixon's favor (it shouldn't logically, *but* . . .) he should win handily.

The impression I formed of Kennedy over the last few months has been more than confirmed by the way he has handled himself out here. My affection for Stevenson and his eloquence and wide-ranging spirit hasn't diminished; but this is a time for decisiveness, for knowing where you stand without too much "on the one hand and on the other," for a capacity to organize, and to pick people who know how to organize and get things done.

So the result makes me happy. It is time we got this Catholicism issue out of our system; it is time we decided that the South will not

‡ This is recorded in Volume IV of the *Lilienthal Journals*.

hold a veto over the Democratic Party and therefore over the nation's slow motion toward decency about the Negro and his rights. The Southerners did their best to lick Kennedy and he took it in stride, winning the nomination on a really good platform without any concessions. I am sure time will prove this right.

JULY 16, 1960
LOS ANGELES

Look Homeward: this seems to me a good theme these days. To understand and appreciate anew the miracle of this our own country is as important as to understand the rest of the world, perhaps more so because of our preoccupation with "foreign affairs" at a time when the future of the world depends upon greater guts and realism and moral strength right here at home.

This was brought home to me in a rather dramatic or overdrawn way when, at Bernardine's insistence, I was taken to the International Communications Foundation office. This is the establishment that Larry Van Mourick has set up with the financial help of the Babcock and Reynolds fortunes. Then that evening I sat at dinner at Bernardine's with Larry and his beautiful young wife Terry. The questions they poured at me were about the Convention, a session of which Larry attended as my guest.

Larry hadn't the faintest notion of how the delegates had been chosen, why their home folks had selected them or how, what a precinct was, or a precinct worker. They were to him, as he put it, just a "bunch of politicians." When I protested that politics is the art of government, and that government and democracy are part of the same concept—participation in the decisions that affect people's lives—he was as confused as if I had suddenly started talking Nepalese. Then it came over me that this handsome young man—graduate of UCLA, and who as an infantry platoon leader had been instructing prisoners of war in Korea in the rudiments of democracy—simply didn't understand democratic institutions or history or philosophy. As the questions kept coming in more and more, proving that this hunch was right, I became dismayed.

I wondered if this lack of interest or knowledge of the way representative democracy really works—works well or works badly—is typical of their generation. If this is true of this wonderful couple, *what goes on* at UCLA or Berkeley or wherever their generation gets "educated"? For Larry and Terry—idealistic and highly motivated—are going around to the far places of the world and through the splendid foundation supported by Reynolds money are preaching international communication; but what do they really have to communicate about the source of the strength or the weaknesses of American political institutions, in the local communities, where our representatives and ultimately (as at this convention) our President is chosen?

JULY 18, 1960
SAN FRANCISCO

One of the high points of this trip was a visit to see Bernard ("Bud") Szold, the athletic hero of my youth. An internationally known athlete— football and track—and an artist and theater director. He seemed to be well over the worst of the attack of angina he had some months ago. Handsome as ever, more so in fact, with his mane of iron-gray hair. It was a great comfort to see him, even though I was distressed to see how tense and worried Betty, his wife, is.

Beatrice Tobey was in San Francisco and I asked her if she would drive down to Carmel with me, for Bud and she were great friends. So I rented an open car; we had an interesting drive along the sea, and I think she enjoyed seeing Bud as much almost as I did.

An intense and serious young girl, Beatrice is still that as a mature woman. Her appealing eagerness to learn and to live fully has been sustained against obstacles that would have floored a lesser person. She has gone to the New School to take courses where she will be exposed to and stimulated by ideas. "I didn't want to become a vegetable sitting around with other women talking about nothing but our children."

As I talked about some of the things I have been doing over the years, she followed this with a hunger for new things to understand and absorb, in areas far, far away from the life that has been hers. A complex woman, of grit, not knowing how to whine, alive with the ideals of learning and living fully that marked her as a very exceptional person even forty years ago when I talked to her (I was then a law school student) about my ambition to get to know Frank Walsh and become a "labor lawyer."

JULY 28, 1960
DENVER AIRPORT

This morning I called Palmer Hoyt, publisher and editor of the Denver *Post*; he asked me to come over right away. He spent yesterday with Lyndon Johnson, he said, going up to the Cheyenne Frontier Days celebration which the *Post* sponsors. Full of feeling about politics. "Ike —I was close to him at first, thought he was a great man; forgot that he was a general; thought he was not like other generals. Will have nothing to do with him now.

"Nixon can't win. When I tell my right-wing Republican friends that, at first they have a fit, then when I tell them that *no one* connected with Eisenhower's Administration can win they soften up. Do you know that right here in this little city a petition for Rockefeller was signed by 10,000 people?

"The reason I am so off Nixon is a simple one: the man has no deep convictions about anything; he is eaten up by his personal ambition for power. The other day he accepted everything Rockefeller had insisted on, for the Republican platform (their convention is now in session) after having made speech after speech recently condemning all Rockefeller's ideas.

"I'm about to come out for Kennedy and Johnson, not because I think Kennedy is any great shakes, but because this country can't afford Nixon and survive."

The sky, as we fly across the country through thunderclouds, is of that soft, soft warm blue that so moved me as my train from San Francisco to Denver wound through the Glendale gorge heading for the Continental Divide. What a wondrous trip that was in *every* way. First through the Feather River gorge, from Oroville (where as part of Pat Brown's State Water Plan a big dam is planned to handle the floods into the Sacramento River), and then the brilliant gorges of the upper Colorado and the Rio Grande, across the Divide at 9,000 feet plus, through the Moffat Tunnel, and then the miracle of seeing the stream along the train's track rushing to the Gulf of Mexico many, many miles away, instead of the Pacific as it was on the yon or west side of the Divide.

It is good to see one's own country, and particularly the great expanses and majesty of the West. It is particularly healthy to do so when one spends as much time as I now do seeing countries other than my own.

NEW YORK

A talk with Arthur Dean, head of Sullivan and Cromwell. Arthur is one of the very few men who have ever negotiated with the Chinese Communists. He expressed a startlingly optimistic picture of what they have already accomplished and are capable of accomplishing in their country, given their disregard of human life, forcing people to work for sixteen hours a day. I made a point of the essential importance of having our own observers, *non-State Department* (people, as Dean put it, "like you and me") to see at first hand what the Chinese are doing, for our own information. Dean agrees heartily with the point.

AUGUST 2, 1960
1 A.M.
NEW YORK

Just back from my first night-club hop with a columnist.

I was taking a short walk before turning in when Leonard Lyons stopped me on Park Avenue. Why not come with him and see the Four Seasons, a supergrand restaurant across from the Gladstone? So I did. I was told, by this city slicker, how—think of it—they changed all the flowers every season; phlox and spirea were displayed as if they were something exotic. And this to me, a gardener. And all about the bronze hangings. Really very handsome it is too. I asked, "Do you serve *food* here—haven't heard anything about food yet?" Which almost broke up a beautiful friendship with the proud headwaiter.

Then on to Sardi's, where I met a flock of theatre and TV people— Sam Levenson, John Osborne, etc. Then to a modest joint on Eighth Avenue "because Shelley Winters usually stops there." She certainly did, and quite a gal, handsome as all get-out, and with a brain and convictions about politics to say nothing of a figure worth observing. With her was Norman Mailer, the novelist, who told a story well, very well, about how he coached Shelley for her first TV job—a nice piece of kidding himself.

Then to the Stork Club, which I resisted. Miss Winters had said to Leonard: "You're not going to take that nice guy through a picket line, you're not." Well, there was no picket line, but so far as I am concerned the Stork Club you can have; except for Leonard's amusing anecdotes.

AUGUST 4, 1960
MARTHA'S VINEYARD

How many, many times I have looked out from this hilltop, to the Sound and islands to the west and the blue wall that rises against the south horizon—the sea, and next stop Portugal.

Each year it is a different *person* who sees this great panorama of green, and blue; the view remains much the same, the viewer does not.

I was "born" on July 8, 1899, in the little town of Morton, in Illinois. But one is not born but once; not me at least. One is reborn again and again.

Certainly I feel quite reborn; I am simply not the person I was three months ago; or even one month ago. It has been a period of revision, basic revision, and it is not romantic or sentimental to call this a rebirth.

I arrived late on the evening of the 2nd, in a deep (and quite beautiful) fog, having landed in a 400-foot ceiling at Hyannis, then a taxi ride to Woods Hole, then standing for hours waiting until the ferry came through the "soup," looking like a big fat frog, and sounding like it.

The following morning I took my ceremonial walk, to the young beech grove (now looking like an adolescent boy, vigorous and pushing its neighbor trees about) then through the meadow, newly mowed, the gleaming mailbox on its new locust post, the repaired road up our hill.

AUGUST 6, 1960
MARTHA'S VINEYARD

Ludwig Jesselson, president and sparkplug of Philipp Brothers (and now head of the Philipp Division of M&C) had been trying to reach me some couple of weeks ago. Our meeting on August 1, first with him and later with half a dozen of his associates (now *my* associates) was the outgrowth of his request to talk to me about Iran.

The specific subject Jesselson wanted to discuss was a chrome mine in southeastern Iran, in the Province of Kerman, near the port of Bandar Abbas, a desolate hole on the Persian Gulf. Jesselson thinks the deposits there, based on their own geological reports, are perhaps the largest and purest available to the free world, probably better even than those in Turkey. Chrome at the moment is a drug on the market; but like a good businessman, it is when things are in excess supply and therefore can be had at a good price that he gets interested in acquiring properties and preparing to expand operations, knowing or being convinced that the dip is a temporary one, a matter of a few years at most.

What Jesselson wants to do is to expand the present mining operations. An Iranian owns 51 percent of the stock of this now relatively small mine, Philipp the balance. "We never go into a country except with a local partner who owns the majority; we wouldn't think of controlling a company dealing in natural resources in a foreign country."

I told them I didn't see that they had any problem, given those facts. Iran, I should think, would be pleased to see an expansion of industrial activity in Kerman, one of the very poorest and most bereft provinces.

Jesselson, like the other older men of that group, was born in South Germany. He is bald, small boned, and under average height, with extraordinarily bright eyes, and an intense, enthusiastic driving temperament. He says he speaks his own mind, whether he is right or wrong, and expects others to do the same. I had ample evidence in the two and a half hours we had together that this is just what he does. For twice his juniors came to him, in my presence, and told him he should not take a course he had rather impulsively and enthusiastically decided upon; in both cases he listened carefully and agreed with them.

He is a sophisticated man, as one might expect for one who deals with situations all over the world. His strong preference and confidence in *private,* i.e., nongovernmental, ways of getting things done is not a pious ideology, as is true of so many businessmen I know, who talk private enterprise and then move in on any governmental support or risk bearing they can find or create.

I find Philipp Brothers' worldwide operations in ores fascinating because they deal with the *functional realities* of the modern international world of business.

AUGUST 10, 1960
MARTHA'S VINEYARD

I have been here just a week. A couple of days of overcast weather, during which I very sensibly slept much of the time. And then sailing, on four consecutive days, a record.

What a delight it is to sail that little boat. We had a good breeze each time, and on one day a stiff 20-knot puffy gusty wind. I made most of the mistakes which, so Callahan (my text-book mentor) says, are part of the fun of being a sailor. But the delicious, almost sensuous pleasure of casting off the mooring with the little dinghy dropping away behind me, and slicing through the water, weaving through the boats that fill the harbor—these are pure joy, these sensations.

AUGUST 20, 1960
MARTHA'S VINEYARD

Yesterday I had lunch with Ed Murrow. As to his sabbatical year, so widely publicized at the time it was announced, he said it was like the girl whom you fell for so hard when you were in high school: better in anticipation than in realization. But it did break the routine. He is going to do only a half hour a week on radio instead of his daily "stint," which would be a great relief. "Now I can see the first act of plays for the first time in many years." But he and Fred Friendly are putting on twenty-six CBS Reports, hourlong shows about public questions— that is, one every two weeks; quite a "stint."

I pressed him for an account of his trips, and he was full of stories, mostly about Israel.

He and Janet spent a day in Cambodia. He told with relish about an American tourist, his chest festooned with four cameras, looking at the erotic and quite beautiful carved figures of dancing girls that are one of the chief features of the great temples. The tourist selected one camera, took a sight through the finder, then turned soberly to his guide and said: "Say, haven't you got this in bright sunlight?" On the other hand, he spoke feelingly about other Americans of whom anyone could be proud.

Another picture that impressed him was a gathering of Ben-Gurion's Cabinet, plus some scholars, that sat around a table, with a huge map of Israel before them, engaged for hours in debate, at times rather heated. About what? About the probable itinerary of Samson at some juncture in his life. But the thing that interested Ed was: can you imagine Eisenhower's Cabinet sitting down with scholars discussing a point of history?

Israel made the biggest imprint on Ed of any of the countries they visited. There everyone "puts up an argument about everything" from ages eight to eighty. He attributed this to the fact that in the countries from which many of them came you couldn't argue about the Government or with your neighbors. I am not so sure that this love of argument isn't a kind of Talmudic heritage, having nothing to do with the new-found freedom of being in a country they feel is "theirs."

Of the ten days they spent at St. Moritz, he spoke with some contempt. "The high altitude parasites," he called the denizens.

Ed told one anecdote that appealed to me. He was being given a big send-off in some private group; Ed interposed with the usual disclaimer: "all those fine things really aren't true, after all I'm just a reporter," etc., in short, the kind of head-ducking and shoe-top looking that one goes in for when subjected to this sort of formal praise. Ed says he was interrupted by the following: "Don't be so damned modest; you're not *that* good."

AUGUST 21, 1960
MARTHA'S VINEYARD

Spirited dinner party here at Topside last night, with Walter J. Levy, perhaps the world's greatest authority on the practical economics and politics of international oil (and his wife), Roger Baldwin and Evey, Nat Elias and Leona Baumgartner, New York City Health Commissioner, David and Peggy, and Tom and Rita Benton. Tom is finishing his murals for the Truman Library, and the designs for the Niagara Power station. A good lively group, with good talk, much raising of voices, much plying with questions.

I was put in the witness chair, as an advocate of Kennedy; not that any of these people will vote for Nixon, but they would like, as Leona put it, to have some reason *for* Kennedy other than that he isn't Nixon.

I made the point that Kennedy was a man who espoused the politically unprofitable cause of India long ago (as these things go); who was for organized labor strongly, and yet had earned the enmity of the racketeering kind of labor leader, e.g., Hoffa; was for the use of government power and revenue for social purposes; had been able to attract intellectuals (Leona discounted this by saying that some of these were the kind who would hop any promising bandwagon as quickly as any low-grade local politico). One of my principal points was, and is, that Kennedy is the candidate of the Party which will be predominant in the Congress; that we cannot become an affirmative, positive, decisive force in the world if the Executive and the Legislative are not of the same Party.

Roger Baldwin, strangely enough, was deeply concerned about the religious issue against Kennedy. Since Roger has no use for any religion, starting with the Protestant, this isn't because he is prejudiced against the Catholic religion. But he says people are bothered; and that there should be a declaration that Kennedy will not have a personal representative at the Vatican, that there will be no Papal Nuncio in Washington, etc. But such a declaration is defensive. For Kennedy to define his stand more explicitly is fine; I have a letter from the young Congressman from South Bend, John Brademas, indicating that efforts to get Protestant leaders, like the greatest of them all, Bishop Bromley Oxnam, to accept Kennedy's position are in the works.

But the big to-do was an argument between Roger and me, with Leona and Nat throwing fast ones right along, on the broad and, I thought, dogmatic assertion of Roger's that it was the *white* people who were responsible for the terrible state of affairs in the world today. The white skins had conquered the dark skins, had exploited them, enslaved them, and (with their "civilization," said he scornfully) had invented the means of destroying the world.

Well, this was too much for me. My voice quieted down, for I recognized here a great liberal but one who I thought was fighting yesterday's battle (never wholly won, of course) when there was a new phase of freedom that was *today's* issue and tomorrow's.

To understand the world, I said, we must remember that all people, white and dark, are human beings of the same kind. It is not the whites who have a monopoly on exploiting other people or a record of oppression. This is part of the *human* problem. I tried to remind Roger that it was dark-skinned people who sold blacks to the slave traders, that it was brown people (say, Genghis Khan or Tamerlane) who swept down on Asia and destroyed and butchered and obliterated the civilization of, say, the Aryan Persians. But Roger would have none of that—"I'm talking about *now*, not some other period."

So I took another tack. The problem these newly independent nations now face is no longer, acutely, the domination of the British or the French, but the domination of one group or class of dark skins over *other* dark skins. Color of skin is not the measure of oppression or being oppressed.

If the new nations, mostly dark skinned, wish to escape the problems of living together among themselves, eliminating exploitation of one newly independent man by his brother Moroccan or Ghanaian or Congolese, by acting as if the issue is still getting rid of the British or French or Belgians, then it is the duty of real neighbors like ourselves to challenge this evasion of reality.

If we liberals go along with these newly independent people who try to solve their problems of today's exploitation—and tomorrow's (and tomorrow treads more closely on the heels of today than ever before in history, I believe)—by concentrating on their justified hatred or distrust of their *once* masters, the whites, we do them a disservice. We thereby characterize liberalism as a lazy form of prejudice and ignorance.

I didn't persuade Roger, I fear.

AUGUST 30, 1960
MARTHA'S VINEYARD

The world is greatly astir these days, almost everywhere. The most spectacular and perhaps the most meaningful goes on in Africa, and particularly in the Congo.

To think that such a change could occur in the period of a few months since we were in Brussels talking about a technical mission to the Congo.

No point in trying to keep up with the day-to-day events, in this journal; enough to say that it illustrates two points, chiefly, to me:

1. The rapidity of change. Cuba is an instance. My point about Cuba, in the July 8 article for NANA, does not seem "wild" now. At the time I'm sure many people must have thought I was irresponsible in suggesting that Cuba might well become, and we should be prepared for its becoming, a Soviet base of operations in this New World.

2. The notion that a "world government of law" embodied in the UN would, by a "surrender of national sovereignty" to a world government, solve the problems of the peace has in my view been exposed for its shallowness by the Congo eruption.

It just isn't that simple: a world government—and presto the evils of political strife are over. A strong UN is the best way to demonstrate that a world government, even if a limited one, is not the end but rather the beginning of a long process of education and of conflict, even of war, the very thing that the zealots about World Government insist will be prevented by their formula.

SEPTEMBER 5, 1960
(LABOR DAY)
MARTHA'S VINEYARD

Late yesterday afternoon the Lilienthal junior family came out to help us celebrate our wedding anniversary. David was in fine fettle, relaxed, very handsome, and with a greater show of confidence than I have seen in him for a long time. Their anniversary gift touched me so deeply: copies of two of his short stories, and to them attached a cluster of toy balloons, symbol that the children were part of the giving. He has never before shown us any of his writing, since he came up here more than a year ago to try the most chancy kind of career, that of a free-lance fiction writer.

SEPTEMBER 7, 1960
NEW YORK

Events have been moving along in the D&R story.

The World Bank has finally released the first payment on the Dez loan, after many ups and downs, some of them almost opéra bouffe—the nit-picking performance of the international consulting engineering board, the insistence that the Prime Minister himself sign a letter on a detailed engineering question about design of the spillway tunnel, and other rather fantastic tales. And worries, of course, continue.

The Ivory Coast has accepted our proposal—even enlarged on it—so that seems pretty well settled and we will have a crow's nest seat, or lookout tower, in West Africa.

Argentina: a signed contract for a survey on the Rio Colorado; our proposals for the Salto Grande, a joint enterprise with Uruguay and through a joint commission, are still being debated by them against the bids of others; the Patagonia business, now confined to the Valley of the Rio Negro, has been revived; a new proposal is being made (jointly with Italconsult, as was the Salto Grande) and has a chance of acceptance. If two of these three should come through, we would certainly be active in Argentina.

Most important in the D&R story is the primacy the foreign economic development issue has assumed in recent weeks; everyone is trying to be more sweeping than the next guy in asserting that *this* is the great issue of our time. Which makes me feel rather good about the foresight of the opening chapter of that book I wrote back in 1943—a long time ago— stating categorically that *this* was the issue which the politicians and statesmen must treat as the central one of our century.

It is, however, one thing to be right *before* your time; it is another to be *effective in your time*. This is the question about D&R that is both difficult and challenging.

I think that five years ago, in creating D&R, we set up the framework of an *institution* well designed to *function* in a strong and principled way, chipping away at the issue now described by all as the primary one of the time: the improvement of economic and social conditions in more than half the world. But can we make it work, will we manage to get the opportunity to do so, without sacrificing what we regard as our own principles of fitness and integrity? This we don't yet know for sure.

A long talk with Beatrice, an effort on my part to catch something of the understanding of the meaning and implications of art. Art isn't a series of canvases, sculptures, etc., she tried to tell me. It isn't just museums. It will take me a long time perhaps to understand how broad and all-embracing a concept it is, but that it is involved, as a kind of unifying theme, even in those things that I do that are creative, she was firm about.

This gave me for the first time a clue—but just a clue—of the set of limitations that makes the engineer, and scientist, typically, unfitted for a major role in a time of vast change.

The engineer and the scientist believe that there *is only one way*—the way of "knowledge," they call it. *But* there is not just one way—that's the point.

The engineer is trained, one might almost say *conditioned,* to believe that things are fixed and certain, as indeed the *materials* with which he works are; that the engineer's job is putting those fixed things together in a predetermined manner and sequence. Anything else gives him a sense of frustration and confusion.

But that isn't the way of art; art believes that there are *many* ways, *different* ways. Nor is that the way of life itself, nor of those who understand people; nor is it the way of a lively functioning human institution.

SEPTEMBER 12, 1960
PRINCETON

A gale blowing outside, our part of hurricane Donna sweeping up the coast, after having hit Florida a terrific wallop. The very tall, very slender locust trees to the east of our garden whip and pirouette; the smaller trees—the Franklin magnolia, the dogwood—swirl and cringe, as the full 60-mile gust hits them, twisting and covering their faces like tormented souls.

Which reminds me of the cypress paintings of Van Gogh, with the swirls in the background: these could be "abstractions," as under-

standable as if there were nothing identifiable as trees; the abstract idea
of tumult of mind and spirit, put down in oil on canvas.

The roar of this gale is like the wildness of the sea in a great storm.
Have decided I'm going out in it with my foul weather gear; too good
to miss.

Later: it was an exhilarating experience, with the bursts of nature
full in my face, wind and driven rain. Trees breaking off, some of them
slowly settling on their sides before my eyes. Came back full of respect
for the power of unleashed nature. I'm rather a fool, I guess, to want
to go out in this kind of turmoil, with a certain dash of danger—such
as falling trees.

Helen said to me: "I think you like danger and risk; and you tend
to make it *seem* to exist, because you prefer it that way, whereas I tend
to minimize it and try to dismiss it, or not dwell on it."

SEPTEMBER 13, 1960
NEW YORK

There is a great opportunity for a revival of Persian art in a modern
setting in the walls of the great control room of the underground powerhouse at Dez Dam. Gordon found that a conventional mural had been
designed, on the commission of Voorduin *et al.*, by some Philadelphia
designer. I was horrified. What a denial of everything we are trying to
say about this dam being "for the people of Persia" to have some meaningless (in Persian eyes) American mural on those walls. I discussed
with the attractive young new Ambassador to the United States the idea
of a mural chosen after a national competition among Persian artists.
He, I'm sure, will pass this idea along to the Shah.

SEPTEMBER 15, 1960
WASHINGTON

Luncheon with John Laylin of Covington and Burling, and counsel
for Pakistan through the long, long contest about the Indus waters.
Showed me a copy of the treaty which is to be signed on the 19th.

He said something that fits so well into my idea of what I ought
to be saying again and again to young people. This is the story:

When he was at the Harvard Law School, all of his close friends
were aiming toward going into New York law firms, in what was then
known as "issue" work, that is, providing legal opinions, etc., on bond
issues. The same thing was pretty well true of the leading members of
my own class, somewhat earlier.

Laylin, however, decided that what he wanted was international legal work. His contemporaries thought this was strange. But now the "issue" side of corporate practice has dwindled to little importance, relatively, whereas international legal business is an important one indeed.

Laylin's law school contemporaries went for "issue" work because in the minds of their *fathers*, many of whom were distinguished lawyers, *that* was the great thing in *their* day and time, and therefore would be for the time of their own sons' careers.

I chimed in to say that we have got to learn that most of the things that are gospel in our youth, now in our maturity, are no longer true or valid or workable. The *proof* of their invalidity or their workability may not be forthcoming for a little while; but when we are thinking about our young people we must not let them assume that the verities of today, or our day, are any longer verities.

At the Iranian Embassy talked to young Tehrani, who was for a while our lawyer in Tehran. A handsome, delicately featured, alert face. He said a characteristic Persian thing: I asked him how he liked Washington; he did very much; not a big city like Tehran[!]. Then he said, quite softly: "In Persia we have gardens in our cities, but each family's garden is enclosed behind a wall, a compound, so the city is made up of many such enclosing walls and their gardens. But Washington itself is a garden [and he looked out at Rock Creek Park and Massachusetts Avenue]. The city is the garden, and the buildings of the city are set in the garden which is the city."

No wonder I warm so to these poetic people.

SEPTEMBER 19, 1960
PRINCETON

A cable from the President of Pakistan, Ayub, of appreciation for having started the breaking of the deadlock about the Indus:

David E. Lilienthal, Development & Resources Corp.
50 Broadway, NYK:

It must indeed be a matter of profound satisfaction to you that your idea of a cooperative approach to, and an engineering solution of Indus Water dispute has today fructified into a elaborate treaty between Pakistan and India. We in Pakistan deeply appreciate your great contribution to the cause of peace and amity between nations which this settlement between our two countries represents. You have cause for legitimate pride in fulfillment of your cherished desire for harmony and understanding between the two neighbors.

The Ambassador of Pakistan, Aziz Ahmed, phoned. "This is not India's victory nor Pakistan's victory, but *yours"; he said this in several different ways. "You should rejoice that you have done something so directly related to the peace of the world, and of the people of the sub-continent of India. I tell you most seriously," he went on, "that if you had not made your most fortunate trip to our countries, and made your grand and imaginative proposal, this dispute would never have been resolved and war would have ensued."

Well, anyway, it was "good listening."

I'm getting a deep commitment to this idea: that it is the responsibility of those of us who should be leaders of thought and direction (I said "should") particularly for the young people, to be presenting ideas and interpretations that deal with *what things will be like* five or ten years hence. To look ahead—that is the key to thought and idea and concept leadership, not to interpreting today but tomorrow. Those who can't see ahead are good only as historians.

The normal objective of diplomacy and the efforts to "substitute law for force" as between nations was essentially a negative one: to keep things from getting worse is one way to put it. To hold the line. To prevent the outbreak of violence, etc. An adjudication or negotiation limited to preventing something bad from happening, i.e., the use of force between nations, is certainly a worthy and noble goal.

BUT, aren't we ready, more than ready, to look ahead to an affirmative, positive objective, adding to the strength of peoples, increasing the sense of unity by affirmative and probably technically based methods now available to us? I think so.

The strengthening of the Indian subcontinent, through better use of the waters of the Indus, so largely going to waste still, is a more modern object for negotiations between countries than the more negative one of preventing the outbreak of violence, i.e., holding the line.

SEPTEMBER 20, 1960
MIDNIGHT
NEW YORK

The air of the East Side has been filled with the screaming of sirens as the "men who rule the world" go tearing by, to and from the great meeting at the UN. This is probably the *least* diplomatic diplomatic gathering in history. How Metternich and Clemenceau would have bugged their eyes out at the picture of Khrushchev hugging the bearded Castro, twice his size from the ground anyway, and all the other shenanigans. Not the least impressive are the gangs of picketers with their signs MURDERER addressed to Mr. Khrushchev.

SEPTEMBER 24, 1960
WASHINGTON

"The misery of a cold": I am a living (partly living) example of same at the moment. Rotten feeling, and with it my voice has about given out, due to overstraining it last evening at a huge (1,500 people) "reception" given by the World Bank. The Bank staff, after being half angry with me for having got them into the seemingly endless Indus Waters dispute, now all smiles; and people from many countries, as well as the Bank staff, crowd in to congratulate me on my "victory"— which is the word mostly used. Well, all pleasant enough.

The cheers about the Cauca Valley Corporation's great success, which even the Bank technicians are now showering on CVC and on me, I receive with a good deal more satisfaction. For that is indeed a living and a growing thing, and its timing today is as pat as anything could be, when the very issues of CVC, of organization, local control, local taxation, agricultural education, etc., are uppermost, now that the U.S. seems (I say "seems") about to recognize that Latin America can't be fobbed off any more by visits of the President's brother and other public relations type superficiality.

For this complete change of heart I suppose we have Castro to thank. Castro, of all people, an antibody to a certain worldwide sickness. History has a strange way of making use of whatever is at hand. Castro is the subject of more talk hereabout in this World Bank meeting than even "Mr. Khrushchev," at the center of the stage.

In his "great debate" with Nixon last night—the first of the series —Kennedy pointed to TVA *three times* in the course of his part of the hour, to make certain points about his own philosophy and program. Gordon and I heard the program together, so it was a memorable occasion for us.

SEPTEMBER 28, 1960
WASHINGTON AIRPORT

A stimulating three-hour visit with Chester Bowles. Bowles was relaxed, his voice low, his manner as easy as, at times, I have remembered it as tense. They have rented a pleasant house in Georgetown on Q Street at the corner of 26th.

He said Nehru was most somber and pessimistic about Mao Tsetung, the Chinese leader. Most. Could see nothing but disaster ahead if the Chinese continue their present course, which he thinks they will.

Chester discards the idea that we should try in some way (as some in the State Department seem to think) to drive a wedge between the Chinese and the U.S.S.R. "The only way I can see that we can make any headway with the Chinese is by working through the Soviet." This statement takes a lot of thinking about, I must say.

Should we "recognize" Red China? That, I said, would have been the first question in the nineteenth century or even the forepart of this one. I thought this far too legalistic for the conditions we face. Sooner or later they will be "recognized" (formally or, as the phrase has it, *de facto*). But I wonder why not consider *that* at a much later stage, not as an opening premise or question. They have great needs; their resources are inadequate for their 600 million people. Ours, in food, are an embarrassment of riches. Why not make a massive offer of food, forgetting about "recognition" for the time being? This would arouse a terrific storm from Taiwan, but we must face that.

SEPTEMBER 30, 1960
ON THE PENNSY, ABOUT TO LEAVE FOR PRINCETON

Met late afternoon yesterday with Jonathan Bingham, Walt Rostow of MIT, et al., who had an assignment to work out a "serious" statement for candidate Kennedy "on foreign aid."

My chief contribution to the discussion—I left after the first hour —was this: That the statement and any assistance which, as "experts," we might provide would have to be made to fit the fact that Kennedy was in the midst of a campaign, that what he said about foreign aid would have to be of a piece with the theme of his whole campaign; that it would therefore have to *attack*, to take an initiative and make Nixon be apologetic or yes-but-ish about the losses the U.S. had sustained in the Eisenhower years in our total position abroad.

If the price for intensity and depth of feeling is pain from time to time (along with the equivalent of intense joy and fulfillment), then if there were a choice I would gladly take the pain. But for some of us there isn't a choice. We go the road our natures take us.

And that nature changes so little. This evening I read some of the long letters I wrote to Helen from the Harvard Law School back in the winter of 1922, when I was twenty-two years old, almost forty years ago! Such intensity. So little acceptance of the second best. So little use for serenity and peace and making terms with life. Phrase after phrase, I found as I read on, I could have written today, in essence. There is today as little cynicism and surrender in me, basically, as there was forty years ago.

Some of the letters are love letters, letters of longing and loneliness for the girl I wanted to share my life—and who has. But many of them are the opening of a heart that is so set upon experiencing life, at its tumultuous height, that it is hard to believe that they were written by an inexperienced youth. What is even more difficult to believe is how little, in these respects, I have changed during the intervening hard years, years that even then I actually predicted would be filled with enemies and battles and sacrifice. It is almost as if I was *looking* for those bumps, as indeed I suppose I was, seeking them.

OCTOBER II, 1960
OVER THE SEA, 10 MINUTES OUT OF IDLEWILD,
HEADING FOR BUENOS AIRES, ARGENTINA

D&R will not make any real money out of this proposed work for Argentina. But the timing is extraordinarily favorable. Latin America is now, at long last, receiving the attention it deserves from the American Government. Castro's foray, by no means over nor even at its peak, will keep that attention and concern. This is a bad basis for a policy on our part, but perhaps that is the way of history.

The tools in the hands of the Latinos for development and self-improvement in Latin America have been improved very recently, e.g., the Inter-American Development Bank just established. Too bad our Government opposed it so long, but in any event it underlines the importance of the timing of D&R's entry into far South America, the first since CVC, in Colombia.

4:30 P.M.

The illimitable vast sweep of green that is the jungle of Brazil. Boundless as the sea, yet unlike the sea, not empty, not overwhelming.

The captain tells us that that great majestic river, way below, is the Amazon! Another river to my collection—and *what* a river!

OCTOBER 12, 1960
HOTEL PLAZA
BUENOS AIRES

Met at the plane last night by the blinding lights, TV cameras, flash-lights, and sundry dignitaries, with recorded TV and radio interviews to follow. It was 2 A.M. before I got to this room and to bed. Up early this morning for conferences with our Italian partners in the three regional undertakings we expect to have signed up before I leave in a couple of days.

After seeing the schedule they had worked up, my hosts gave me time for a siesta this afteroon, and this I have just wakened from, wakened by the sound of a service, the music of boys' voices and organ, in the big church that is just outside the window of my living room.

The prestige that TVA, and my part in it, commands throughout the world has never been more remarkably exhibited, for me at least, than in the past few hours in Argentina.

In accordance with my custom I arrive in a country at the same time as a crisis. I can't flatter myself that I create them, but the coincidences are piling up!

The military (or part of them) are holding a gun to President Frondizi's head these past two days, demanding God knows what—a new Cabinet, named by them, etc. And threatening to take over by arms if he doesn't agree. The "guard" in the government buildings has been trebled today, and there is the feeling of trouble in the air.

But what a beautiful city—a touch of Paris in South America. And though October, here, far south of the equator, it is early spring. The enchanting green of the earliest leaves.

OCTOBER 14, 1960
11 P.M.
BUENOS AIRES

I have been living in the atmosphere of a threatened military coup d'état in this lovely and incredible South American city. The rumors, at fifteen-minute intervals, of how the President is standing up to the demands of the Generals fill the air; I have seen the crowds stand around the bulletin boards before the newspaper offices. And yet there is a holiday or devil-may-care atmosphere. As one man said to me tonight at the big "reception" for me, "We get so used to these crises we take them for granted."

My extemporaneous speech to what I was told was a distinguished audience was not a technical one—as was expected. It was an expression of philosophy and feeling. As I warmed to the task, it came out as the expression of faith that is the basic tenet of my personal and official life. Toward the close the audience of perhaps 300 people "froze"—not a movement, a cough, as if they were painted on a screen —and I knew that my impromptu words were making an impression, even though fully half of the audience did not understand English and had to depend on awkward simultaneous translation through earphones, or the emotional atmosphere I was creating—and feeling. Under the circumstances of a crisis of major proportions, a drama going on between a former professor and the outmoded but powerful generals, this speech in the rotunda of the Capitol was an experience of high drama.

A very youthful journalist came up to me at the "reception" (600 people from the whole gamut of Buenos Aires life came out to look at this strange North American creature) and said one of the most touching and helpful things that has ever been said to me: "You were speaking *to* my generation, and *for* my generation." I almost wept, because that is exactly what I want to do, to keep the viewpoint of the younger generation and to be able to communicate with them.

Well after an hour's speech, and four hours of standing up shaking hands with 600 people *twice* I'm pretty tuckered—so to bed.

Thursday at about 6:30 P.M. I had a brief "audience" with President Frondizi.

Frondizi has a professor's look, and indeed he does have an academic background. As he sat at the long heavy table in a gigantic room, he looked quite small; somehow the picture of a Venetian statesman who *wiggles* through things—and preferred to; in fact, rather enjoying the flavor of danger and of outwitting his opposition. About his eyes were dark circles, but he looked quite able and very much composed, not knowing at that moment whether the big garrisons had taken over the essential services that would bring the country into the Army's hands or whether fighting might not begin at any moment between the Army and the Air Force, which latter apparently has been siding with the President.

He said some complimentary things, chiefly about "the miracle in Tennessee." I responded with a comment about what a remarkably good impression his personality and views had made in the United States at the time of his visit—what is it, perhaps a year ago? I said something about the importance of resource development, referred to the three regions considering our services: the Colorado, Negro Valley, and Salto Grande, and our partnership with Italconsult.

The President's enormous and high-ceilinged office is dominated by a huge fireplace. Great decorations in brass wind their way over it and to the ceiling. Everything is dark—except the brass—and very heavy. What a contrast to the office of the President in the White House. That office is open to the green and the sky, with the President's desk small and simple, the room itself graceful and unpretentious. This office—which Perón occupied—is intended to impress both the occupant and those who call on him.

OCTOBER 15, 1960
BUENOS AIRES

A remarkable part of my trip was an hour's talk this morning with General Pedro Arámburu, at his apartment.§

He is a short and slender little man, a natty dresser in a blue shirt and impeccable suit. He looks quite young on first sight, with his hair slicked back and his quick, brusque movements. Some time ago he became a private citizen, so though he is addressed as El Presidente or General, he is technically a private individual.

Arámburu was leader of the revolution that unseated Perón. He became the first President after the overthrow of Perón, and, I was told by Peccei, yielded his power as head of the Army so that an elected President could take over and resume "constitutional" methods in Argentina after twelve years of Juan and Saint Eva Perón.

During the crisis of the past few days he was offered the post of War Minister, which he declined; is thought to become the Provisional President should Frondizi resign, as the Generals insist. So he is a central figure in an eruption which is bound to cause some misgivings in the U.S. about the vaunted new stability of this recently dictator-ridden country.

The General considers himself quite frankly as the mediator between the Army and the President. He gave the clearest and most disingenuous exposition of the viewpoint of the military in this (and similar Latin countries). It was a classic of rationalization of desire for power, and of naïveté about the world as it is today that deserves to be preserved word for word, point for point. A medieval outlook under the conditions of today, and yet all over the world this still goes on. Professional soldiers, the only fully organized center of power in civil matters trying to justify their invasion of political processes by assumptions of their superior wisdom and judgment. Completely totalitarian. The irony is that the Army (taking Arámburu as interpreter and defender) actually presents itself as the foe of totalitarianism, against the duly elected officials of a Government.

Peccei was with me, and introduced the subject on which I wanted to be informed, i.e., the General's summary of the crisis which was so alarming and confused.

General Arámburu referred to his statement to the press about the relations between the Army and the President; then said he would go into that "more deeply."

§ On May 30, 1970, the press reported that General Arámburu had been abducted from his apartment; on July 18 his body was discovered in a farmhouse many miles from Buenos Aires, and on July 19 he was buried with full military and civil honors.

He spoke in Spanish, and Peccei translated.

"You should have in mind that the Army is the oldest institution in this country, and that it has the longest traditions of continuity; that it represents the views and position of Argentina's middle class, of which it is constituted. It is an institution that is not only military, but is the one stable and continuous expression of the middle class in *every* field. [I recalled then that the Army is deep in such things as manufacture, minerals, etc.]

"After twelve years of the chaos of Perón and the two years of provisional government before the election of Frondizi, the people needed clear leadership; they needed a leader as President who would have a definite and fixed policy and program, and one that the people understood would not be deviated from.

"But Frondizi has not provided this. Instead he has departed from time to time from the platform on which he was elected, to propitiate this and that element in the country. This has been bad for the morality of the people, and for peace of mind. They began to feel that the President, when he took a position or followed a policy, meant something else. He is too much like the Borgias."

These things were delivered with great emphasis, his two hands gesturing as if he were measuring something before him.

"As a consequence the people have lost confidence in the Government. The only institution they believed in was the Army.

"The Army felt that it was its traditional duty to represent the interests of the country, and that when the President departed from the interests of the country, the Army should exert pressure on the President to force him to do what he should do in the interests of the country.

"The Army knows, through its civilian agents, that the Government has in it many Peronists and many Communists. This fact was forcefully brought to the attention of the President; he did nothing about it.

"Thus a *cleavage* [great emphasis and gestures] arose between the people and the Government, which it was the duty of the Army to try to bridge by its pressure upon the President. The Army insisted upon the dismissal of these subversive people.

"Then the President made a provocative radio address to the nation. [This was made the morning of my arrival here, the 12th.]

"This broadcast turned loose all the forces of propaganda of the press against the Army and confused the people even more.

"The people were not told that the Army was trying to protect the people from the evasive and dual deception of the President, but it was claimed that a coup d'état to take over the Government was the Army's purpose. This was not true. All the Army tried to do was to bring pressure on the President to see that he followed the right course. That course should make absolutely plain that Argentina is with the West, without any doubt of any kind. And yet because of the existence of Communists in the Government, where Argentina stood wasn't made clear to the world. So the Army insisted that these Communists should be dismissed at once, both from within the Cabinet and in other positions."

I said: "You have explained why the Army seeks to put pressure on the President, and that part of the necessity for this pressure is explained by the fourteen years of absence of constitutional government. But during that same fourteen years, particularly the twelve under Perón, labor unions were greatly strengthened, so they, I get the impression, also became what you call 'a force' [this was the expression he used about the Army, a "national force"]."

I asked: "Will not the exercise of pressure by the Army in a certain direction stimulate the use of pressure by the unions in another direction?"

"The answer is No." This was barked out. "If the unions tried to exert pressure, the Army will grind them out."

This was Peccei's translation, but it didn't take any translation to see the glint almost of anticipation with which the General said this.

I said: "I understand what you have said about the Army's motive in exerting pressure. But Argentina now has a Congress, a Senate and House of Representatives. Is it not their function to keep an eye on matters in the Executive branch with which they did not agree, rather than the Army's?"

"No," the General said, with increased emphasis. "Most of the members of the Congress are no better than the Executive; they are filled with people who are pro Perón and pro Communist, so we can expect no help from them. Besides, we have not had parliamentary government for a long time. Later, after another election perhaps."

After this we discussed "development." Here the General was in complete agreement with my own statement about its importance; that if the country was fully occupied with developing its natural wealth there would be less frustration and more concentration on nonpolitical things, such as the three valley developments we were agreeing to participate in.

OCTOBER 17, 1960
12:30 P.M.
MONDAY

An hour ago we left Asunción, in Paraguay. A beautiful plain, with a great river, and warm sunshine during our hour in the airport.

I spent most of the day yesterday, in the countryside. It was good in October to see the spring *again*, to see flowering quince in full luscious roseate bloom, while *our* quince is without leaves and preparing for winter, to see delphinium and roses (including a Peace) in their first bloom. There is a kind of symbolism in these *two* springs. For I too am having a second spring—and how lucky I am, how blessed and fortunate I am that this is so.

Late yesterday afternoon, after returning from the campo, I spent an hour and a half with the President's nephew, a young and serious and intense and intelligent young man.

The President, Frondizi Jr. said, thought it necessary for me, "as an outsider," to have some background about Argentina, before trying to state, in summary fashion, the consequences of the crisis to date.

His principal emphasis was on three points:

First, that Argentina was in a transition period between an agricultural raw material exporting economy, and the political and economic institutions this promoted, and a modern state, in which industry played a principal role. This transition affected everything that was taking place, for in the President's view, until Argentina had achieved a place as a modern industrial country, the outlook of its people, including the Army, would be tied to an outmoded and passing way of life.

Second, there are no political parties in the Argentine, in the sense that there are in the U.S.; this is partly due to the Perón period, partly to the strong influence—nefarious and selfish, he said—of the British.

Third, in the absence of mature and clearly defined political parties and procedures, and a transition in economic conditions to a modern state, the Army as an institution did "reflect" the views of a good many of the people of Argentina, on nonmilitary matters, and therefore must be dealt with as a kind of mirror of upper- and middle-class opinion. When political parties were better established and their principles more clearly defined, the necessity for listening to the views of the Army on civil matters would decline.

The President, his nephew said, was compelled under the circumstances, to pursue a "zigzag" course (this phrase was illustrated with gestures resembling a snake's movements) in order to preserve the fundamentals. He had to contend with many forces, among them the rearguard fight of the British business interests to maintain their hold on the Argentine economy and political life, as they had done so skillfully for many years.

I asked whether American business interests had engaged in activity that was, in this sense, objectionable, by way of interference in political affairs and preventing normal growth of Argentina's economy along lines dictated by their own rather than Argentine interests.

I prefaced this by saying that I felt that Castro, objectionable as he was for the future of the Cuban people as well as of Latin-American unity and decency, was a product that some critics might label "made in the U.S.A." Why? Because some American business firms had earned unconscionable profits and interfered in the internal affairs of Cuba, such as in supporting Batista.

No, said young Frondizi, American firms on the whole had not followed the English practice. It is true that until quite recently there were no important American business interests in Argentina, but thus far there is no sign that they are acting otherwise than in a way that is in the interests of Argentina as well as their own interests.

We have now signed two contracts, jointly with Italconsult. First is a small preliminary study on the Rio Colorado. The second is a substantial task of reviewing what has been done in North Patagonia, and what could be done in developing the region—the "zone of influence"— roughly being the drainage basins of the Limay and Neuquén Rivers, and the river into which they flow, the Negro. We are well along the road to a formal contract with the Comisión Tecnica Mixta, made up of members representing Argentina and Uruguay for a project report and for detailed design of a huge dam on the Uruguay River. I met with the members of the Joint Commission, gave them a pep talk about the importance of what they have been working on now for fifteen years, the impact of the construction and the dam itself on the economies and the opportunities of both countries.

During the first days of November Lilienthal and Clapp took the initiative to cancel the contracts with Argentina for valley development in valleys of North Patagonia (the basins of Rio Colorado and of Rio Negro). These contracts had been signed by Lilienthal for D&R on his trip to Argentina in mid-October, 1960, described in journal entries beginning October 11, 1960.

It was also decided that D&R should not accept an award of contract with the Joint International Commission (Argentina and Uruguay) for the great Salto Grande project.

These agreements had been entered into in a partnership venture between D&R and an Italian consulting firm (Italconsult) headed by a distinguished and highly respected industrialist, A. Peccei, later Managing Director of Olivetti.

The decision to cancel and withdraw, following discussions with Peccei, also included termination of all joint venture understandings with Italconsult.

The reasons for these actions by D&R were basic differences on business practices between D&R and its Italian partners which proved to be irreconcilable.

While sensitive ethical issues concerning conduct of development in foreign countries were at stake in this episode, Lilienthal has concluded that to publish the full record at this time would not be in the best interests of American-Italian relations.

OCTOBER 23, 1960
LEAVING NEWARK AIRPORT FOR CHATTANOOGA

And so begins a return to the Tennessee Valley quite different in every way from any other I have made over these years.

This is my first adventure in "taking the stump." A whole series of speeches, receptions, handshakings, TV appearances, newspaper interviews to promote the election (I hope) of the Democratic nominee for the Presidency. I, who so completely eschewed anything resembling political activity while I was head of TVA, and of AEC, now am straining at the leash to persuade as many people as I can to vote Democratic. But now I am a completely private citizen whereas before I was a public servant.

OCTOBER 28, 1960
JOHNSON CITY, TENNESSEE

I am fast getting to be a barnstorming political speaker. Just completed a speech to a "wildly cheering" dinner meeting of 300 in this center of Republicanism, following close on a TV appearance and a nonpolitical political tour of points of pride here; and day after day for five days through Tennessee this has been going on, sometimes three or four speeches a day.

I have enjoyed this thoroughly, with one exception and that was Oak Ridge. But when I was out among the real Tennesseans (as at Fayetteville in the old-fashioned courthouse, or a rural electric cooperative meeting—of 1,200 people—or in Tullahoma) I enjoyed myself very much, and find my free-wheeling style more natural, more fiery, and more fun.

When I have had hours and hours of the kind of excitement and tension and emotional "output" that I enjoy, when I am on a trip of this kind, I do put out a lot, and of course there is fatigue. Yet the excitement of seeing people who quite obviously like me, and with whom I feel at home, plus eating some sugar (there was no liquor to be had; this is "dry" territory) revived me completely, so that I put on some of the most spirited and fiery speeches of the whole "campaign."

Fear of fatigue is, I conclude, a *cause* of fatigue.

How much I felt at home in a community life that is nonintellectual; how well I was able to express even abstract ideas and philosophy so that people were interested, as I could tell by the almost eerie closeness of their attention.

In Chattanooga and Nashville the press coverage has been excellent, so that on the whole I think I probably have done some good. The Democratic organization people, many of whom are young people who formed the spearhead of the Kefauver primary campaign this summer, seem to think that I have helped a lot.

But the impact of the issue of religion continues to remain the big question mark in my mind. For, as they say, this is the Bible Belt. The lay preachers and the Baptist and Church of Christ ministers are really bearing down, with tons of stuff that is just plain bigotry and hatred against Catholics. Rather frightening, really.

OCTOBER 30, 1960
FLYING TO NEWARK FROM KNOXVILLE

The dinner "rally" in Rockwood was an overflow business. I shook hands with almost everyone. This is really fun, for in the feel of the rough hands of the women—who are workers in their homes—and the weather-beaten and rather shy faces of the men you get back to the essence of small-town life—for this was distinctly a small-town group, towns I used to visit time and time again, as a part of what I was trying to do in this region years ago.

As people went by, in the little routine of greeting after the talk, they said some amusing or heartening things. The heartening things—as has been true all through this strenuous week—have been what the other speakers and "introducers" have been saying: all indicating that these rather reserved people want to express their confidence that it was *they* I had in mind and heart in my TVA work, and that they just plain like me. But occasionally there would be a gem. A schoolteacher, saying she had never before seen me in the flesh, said she taught her children about me, had my picture on the wall of the schoolroom, and then: "And I have even taught them how to spell your name correctly!" No mean achievement, this last.

But the expression I like the most came from a farmer in Tullahoma. I had been talking over there chiefly about foreign policy—or the defects of such, in the present administration—which is not too simple a proposition to talk about to that kind of non-egghead audience.

He said: "You sure can put the hay down where we can eat it."

This morning early, at the Knoxville airport restaurant, I was greeted like an old friend (as he is) by a porter who has been my friend and confidant for a good many years. Name, LeRoy Porter. We had an enthusiastic reunion, and later I went outside to meet some of his other colored friends, and to talk about Negro politics. He said that the Negro Masons were working hard for Kennedy, as they had for Kefauver; that 67,000 Negroes had been registered to vote in Shelby County, that they would vote, and vote Democratic.

What was most interesting was what he said about the "progress of our people." I had expressed disappointment that the changes toward equality of opportunity had been so slow. Yes, he agreed, they are slow. "But I keep preaching: *prepare* yourself." By that he meant, do everything to get an education, to go on through high school, to go to college. Of his five children, two daughters are now in college.

NOVEMBER 1, 1960
PRINCETON

The election now only a week away. The excitement is mounting—certainly mine is. On the positive side, i.e., positive *for* Kennedy, is the feeling I have that when a people are as uneasy about so many things as I believe the American people are, the *ins* have a hard row when opposed by as fighting a heart as Kennedy's.

The big question mark continues to be the same: will enough people be opposed—or uncertain—about him because he is a Roman Catholic to offset his other advantages? Will the anti-Catholic vote be canceled out, partly or wholly, by the number of people who will vote for him because he is a Catholic?

The first thing I heard on my radio this morning was that Queen Farah had a son! This will strengthen Iran more than ten divisions and improve the Shah's position no end with his own people. It has nothing to do with logic, economics, and all the involved reasoning of complex people, but the impact of it I am sure will be great.

NOVEMBER 3, 1960
1 A.M.
NEW YORK

Ike and Dick Nixon ("my boy") rode into New York today on a billion bales of confetti dumped out of the windows and parapets across the street from our office, and a hundred others. And the President misused his great office to "warn" the country that a vote for Kennedy was a vote for war, about as desperate a piece of panic sowing as we've seen since his speech the other day saying that Kennedy would devalue the dollar, cause our gold reserves to disappear, etc. Fortunately (I think) the American people are immunized pretty well to such extreme talk, even from the esteemed war hero.

To the Horse Show tonight. I always enjoy the international jumping contests, and tonight they were quite exciting. From my experience as a Congressional witness, I think I know how a horse feels when he faces impossible barriers, with everyone watching to see if he stumbles and faults.

NOVEMBER 8, 1960
ELECTION NIGHT, 11:30
PRINCETON

What an enormous relief! Ever since Connecticut reported (at about eight) a big margin for Kennedy, and then Philadelphia with 260,000, it was clear that we had seen the last of Nixon and Ike.

Ohio is still uncertain. Tennessee (and this is a bitter pill) has apparently again gone for the Republicans as has Indiana; this is certainly where the anti-Catholic sentiment did its work.

NOVEMBER 12, 1960
PRINCETON

Our grandson Daniel has had dinner with Helen and me tonight, while his parents are out at some party, and his brother Allen is in New York. He is the most enchanting child I have ever seen. He has a smile that comes on suddenly and, like the sun, lights everything and everyone; his dark eyes are so warm, and his single dimple and sidelong look simply bowl me over.

Heavy gardening today, the second day in a row; transplanting, improving the soil with compost, planting bulbs, widening borders, moving shrubs, and generally having a wonderful time. I smell of cow manure, deliciously, despite a hot bath, for the fragrance lingers. What a joy gardening can be. The buds of the lilac and bush azalea are swollen, with the leaves gone with the frost; I run my fingers over these proofs, this promise, that life goes on even when the world seems to be going into a sleep.

Have been taking a before-breakfast walk on these frosty mornings. The fields nearby are covered with a hoarfrost; in the light of the early-morning sun, this is pure magic, and I revel in it. The air is crisp in the early morning, and these walks are something to relish and long to remember. Reminds me of the days when Mac◖ and I used to set out on a morning ride, *both* of us feeling that we could lick the whole world.

NOVEMBER 15, 1960

7 A.M.

NEW YORK

Yesterday afternoon spent two hours with John Brooks, who is doing a "profile" of me, for *The New Yorker* Magazine.

Brooks's thesis is apparently: "What happens to a guy after he leaves a life of public service?" And since, as a writer, business interests him inordinately, this may have been what induced him to invest a large amount of his time (and mine!) in this writing.

I said to Brooks that business, and the making of a substantial amount of money, hasn't changed my basic outlook, nor has it cost me my freedom to be the kind of person that I was when I was building TVA.

The reason I felt confident in setting that thesis (with which he may in the end not agree, may even make fun of it) is that my critical and freedom-loving friend Nate Greene has said just that. "How fortunate you are," Nate said, in an unprecedented burst of approbation and personal candor, "that you have spent ten years down here in Wall Street, have made a very considerable amount of money, and yet have not yielded your principles, or anything of the things you stood for while you were in government. You should know that it rarely happens. Mostly fellows leave the government and say to themselves: 'Well, I'll put those things I believe in aside for the time being, conform and make myself part of this money-making community, and *then* I will be able to afford to return to the principles I believe in.'

"But that almost never happens. Freedom," Nate said, "has to be earned each day."

His approbation meant more to me than I can say, for he himself has maintained his independence, despite being personal counsel to André Meyer. And André is a forceful man who usually gets the people who work with him to do things his way. If a man can work closely with André, as Nate has, in a relation of great confidence and trust for twenty years and still be independent in a spiritual sense, he is quite a man. And Nate Greene is just that.

◖ Mac was the horse I owned while living in Norris, Tenn.

Beatrice Tobey gave me the rough sketches indicating what could be done with the powerhouse at Dez, in the way of murals or mosaics. This was accompanied by a list of conditions about the physical media. Altogether a good job. The purpose of the sketches is to be able to suggest to Iran what *their own artists* might be able to do. To this was added a rough sketch from Barney* of his idea of a sculptured frieze high on the walls of the Dez canyon.

NOVEMBER 16, 1960
BOSTON

What a horrible thing to change the name of the *Copley* Plaza to Sheraton Plaza. Makes me furious.

Drink and dinner with Walt Rostow, apropos my foreign aid letter to Senator Kennedy, which Rostow says Kennedy asked him to talk about with me.

Quite a satisfactory talk, about two hours. His ideas make much sense. He gave me a memorandum Max Millikan prepared for Kennedy on the subject, which I have just read. As a statement of principles it is quite right; but it is filled with the academic way of solving problems— by phrases. The *how* of getting there is mercifully not gone into.

NOVEMBER 17, 1960
EN ROUTE BY TRAIN TO NEW YORK
FROM CAMBRIDGE AND BOSTON

I make my share of bum guesses and hunches but my warmly enthusiastic, even ecstatic speech to the Radcliffe Trustees about the Institute at the last meeting before today's was not one of those lapses.

I feel, if not a pioneer, at least like one of those who backed a pioneer before anyone else did. For the Institute (despite the "doubters") is now definitely a fact.

This is the big news about today's Board of Trustees' meeting. It was an hour of triumph for an idea, an idea that was not mine but President Bunting's, but that perhaps needed my intense emotional support to get through the Trustees. Today President Bunting announced that the Carnegie Corporation had made a grant of $150,000 over a five-year period; together with Agnes Meyer's gift of $50,000. The plan is well along and will be announced next Sunday.

An interesting-looking and obviously talented gal of about thirty-

* Barney Tobey, husband of Beatrice, is the well-known *New Yorker* magazine cartoonist.

five, a professional writer, Mrs. Bryant, had prepared a competent statement of what the program was about. On this I offered some comments and criticisms. For example, something was said about the need for married women of a high degree of training, interrupted by marriage and children, "to return to a productive career." I asked that this be changed; there is no more productive function than heading a household and bearing and rearing children. The place almost broke into cheers, in Radcliffe's staid Longfellow Hall, at this from a mere man.

Early this morning I phoned Walt Rostow my reactions to the M.I.T. Center for International Studies memo to Kennedy on foreign aid prepared by Max Millikan.

I told Rostow that I was very happy about some of the recommendations, e.g., that putting everything into the UN was an error. The UN was already overloaded; its fate might be decided by the Congo, where it has bittten off a big bite; to add most of the "foreign aid" program to the UN load might hasten the collapse of the UN—a sad event that would be too.

But what Millikan's paper did recommend was far from that "bold new approach" that we had been hearing about and that was promised.

I told Rostow that the report, from the viewpoint of an executory or operational man like myself, was more an essay in development economics than a call to action or a framework for getting something done.

He responded—on this one—that necessarily it was that kind of paper because they didn't *know* about execution and I did. He said he hoped I would put my ideas about execution "on paper." But I don't want to be one of those many academics who have been asked to write memos about which nothing whatever is done, not even a reading of them.

I said I had two ideas just offhand that might be worth including in the paper.

One idea is the establishment of a bilateral, i.e., U.S., or multilateral "lenders' club" agency devoted to development only, but in which the *interest rate* was 1½ or 2 percent, rather than the 6 or 6¼ percent of the World Bank, Development Loan Fund, etc. The difference between the 6 percent and the 2 percent could be made up by subsidy, but could make considerable difference in tax receipts and improvement of international balance of payments that would be more than worth the "subsidy."

The other idea was *selectivity*—pick an area or region *within* a country, do an intense *demonstration* there that would provide a pragmatic case in administration and development such as could not be provided by diluting the effort to cover a whole country—but only "once over lightly."

NOVEMBER 18, 1960
9:40 A.M.
IDLEWILD ABOUT TO TAKE OFF FOR LONDON

Life seems pretty wonderful at this point; the sky, the people, the sense of *continuity*—Helen, the children and grandchildren: that comes as near to immortality as anything, I suppose; the flush of continuity in seeing my work in TVA go on and on into a new period, something built, as are the dams, not only into the shoulders of the hills but into the lives of five or six million people and the consciousness of many people. To be respected in one's lifetime.

NOVEMBER 21, 1960
TEHRAN, IRAN

A happy man. The desert sky is so blue, the air so *breathable*. A feeling of rightness within me and about me.

We saw Ebtehaj yesterday morning in his new offices as head of Iranians' Bank. Still full of bounce and drive. But economically the country is in a bad way, so he says. (This is *not*, however, the version given me by William Taylor, the American Embassy economist, ordinarily so lugubrious.)

Ebtehaj's views are full of wisdom, but are they now largely those of a banker? Bankers usually take too seriously the temporary or transient or current state of *fiscal* affairs, not giving enough weight to the real things happening in the mind and innards of a country. Certainly as Managing Director of Plan Organization Ebtehaj was anything but a conventional banker.

NOVEMBER 23, 1960
TEHRAN

Some reflections on a new foreign economic development program.

Don't give too much attention to reorganization in Washington, i.e., top management. A really good man can make almost any top arrangement work, a poor one won't make much good come out of the most beautiful "reorganization."

The place we must concentrate our thought on is what happens *within* the countries and regions, rather than the top offices in Washington.

As to this, we need *not* go back nostalgically to the Marshall Plan and Point IV, but forward to a concept and program that will result in things happening in the highly diverse conditions which each country or even regions within countries present.

I think to lay the foundation for a new program *out where things happen* we must demonstrate the fallacies and myths of our present policies before we can develop an alternative that will be appealing and persuasive.

Fallacy one is that the reason for the relative ineffectiveness of our foreign aid program is that our people "don't know the language" or they don't crawl into the mud huts and make themselves loved. This is part of *The Ugly American* theme, which has done a lot to contribute to confusion.

The main reason Leo Anderson is effective is that he knows what he is doing, that he goes out and works at his job rather than hanging around making himself friendly with Persians or talking Farsi.

Another fallacy is also dramatized in *The Ugly American* and to some extent in much of what is said about programs in India, etc., namely, that what people need are primitive improvements, such as that bamboo water wheel in *The Ugly American,* or other simple ways to *keep people primitive,* when what they *want* is to become modern.

Another fallacy, related to this, is providing "aid" that does not deal sufficiently with *fundamentals.*

Some years ago, for example, Anderson said, the Point IV Mission here was overly concerned about how small were the eggs and scrawny the chickens. So they had a planeload of Rhode Island Red chicks and roosters sent over, trading them for the scrubs, till they had pretty well covered the country with the new poultry. Anderson thought this was fine—but ephemeral.

The roosters, according to Anderson, were chiefly killed off to eat, since people in the villages rarely get food of that quality. Most of the chickens that were raised or bred died because there was no feed for them. Instead of starting with increasing the source of feed, the Point IV people started with chickens, so he said.

So with "improving the breed" of livestock. Like the scrawny chickens, the scrawny scrub cattle could survive on almost nothing, whereas the handsome highly bred "improved" cattle died. Cattle improvement, etc., before *feed* is an illustration of not making basic changes, of trying to do something spectacular and quick.

A friend of Anderson's, a famous grass man, was sent to Turkey by ICA (i.e., Point IV) just a few weeks ago to work with the Turks on cattle. His entire Turkish audience was made up of forty veterinarians; not one man who was working at providing food so the improved breeds would have a chance.

Wayne Morse in Cali, talking to President Lleras in my presence last December, illustrates another fallacy. Morse was ecstatic about the electric sheep shearing he saw Point IV demonstrating to the Bolivian hill people: "a revolution before your very eyes," he said.

But an electric sheep shearer without electricity to operate it, or a broader base than the technique of sheep shearing, will be mighty short-lived.

So much for fallacies. But what is a better way? There are certain essentials, I think.

One is selective and concentrated areas, where people will learn by doing, in the context of all the *interrelated* factors that affect development rather than only one or two, whether it is poultry or fertilizer or highbred cattle. The fancy Dan intellectual calls this a "systems approach"; but a good farmer understands it through experience.

Another alternative way: the countries which receive help must develop their own program for these areas; they, not Americans, must select the area they think will be best, what the resources are that are most important, what the goals should be. They should have technical help in developing that program but it should be *their* judgment, their choice.

The area of activity and of geography must be *large* enough to include enough of the interrelated factors to make the case a valid and pervasive one.

Is a village such a unit? I doubt it; unless the purpose is simply to make primitive village life more bearable, more tolerable. And if this is the purpose, this runs into the fallacy earlier described, i.e., that the object of a development program is to make people satisfied with being primitive, whereas most of them have had their fill of being primitive.

NOVEMBER 25, 1960
TEHRAN

Yesterday morning, from ten until about twelve, we met with Abdol Reza Ansari. He is the newly named Managing Director of a child conceived by us and born of the Majlis this last summer. The offspring is called Khuzistan Water and Power Authority (KWPA). We proposed it as the Iranian regional agency that would, as promptly as they thought they were ready, take over the functions and responsibilities D&R has been carrying and still carries: operating the "tools" we are building—the dam on the Dez, the sugar plantation and refinery, irrigation facilities, the obligation to collect water charges, the power system, and so on.

The personality and talents, therefore, of this youngish man, Ansari, could be crucial in determining the course of this big undertaking into which both Iran and D&R have poured so much energy, and for which such great hopes are entertained.

Ansari is extraordinarily handsome, and a "collected" man, to use the word we apply to a well-trained and tense horse. About forty, I would say, a clean profile, exceptionally well dressed, large dark brown Persian expressive eyes set off by fair skin. He speaks colloquial American and employs the shades of meaning of American words beyond the capacities of most native Americans.

What I hoped would come out of this meeting was some concrete expression of what the Prime Minister, as well as Hedayat and the Plan Organization, is thinking about the extension of our contract. This expires next March 29.

The basic issue is not whether the contract is to be extended, but whether the fundamental principles of our original arrangement of five years ago (come March 29) will be modified. Will we be asked to agree that the discretion and flexibility to get the job done in the way we find best will be curtailed? I was determined that this meeting with the new rising star, Ansari, would not close without our getting some light on this proposition.

Ansari began in the most pleasant and friendly manner. He must have sensed my impressions and disquiet over the delay in getting down to exchange of views in the two weeks since Gordon has been here, the five days since I have been in Tehran. He made no direct reference to this, but said something along this line:

"There are some people, of course, particularly among the newspapermen but others as well, who will criticize you for trivial things, spending too much money for this and that, and the like.

"But this is not really important, such criticisms about small economies. The important thing is that the great work is actually being done, and done well and rapidly. Whatever the little newspaper critics may say, this country has great confidence in you, Mr. Lilienthal, and in your organization. We know that they have worked hard and effectively, and we hope it will continue to work for Iran for many years to come."

The theme of criticism about cost was embellished by his pointing out that the value of saving time was far more important than minor economies. Presumably the Board of Control and its financial representative have been calling attention to this and that item which might have been smaller, or done in another way. I'm sure an operation of this size couldn't be carried on, particularly so far from home, without being subject to valid criticism of this kind.

I recalled our early meetings with the Shah; his emphasis on speed; his remark to the Economic Council "that for the first time I found Americans who worked as hard in Iran as they do in their own country."

Anderson and Clapp added comments about what kind of work, and under what conditions (heat of 130°, dust, poor housing and food, absence from home, etc.) had to be overcome to produce, for example, a large irrigation system and the beginnings of a sugar complex *in a year*, etc.

As to whether Iran wanted D&R to continue, Ansari met the issue explicitly:

"First, you surely must know, Mr. Lilienthal, that there isn't one chance in 10,000 that Iran does not want you to continue. As a matter of fact, we want you to help Iran for many years to come, because there are many other dams in the Khuzistan to build; also I hope that the same methods and the same organization you head will work in other regions of the country."

I said his statement disposed entirely of that question. We could treat that as settled.

As to the question of method, Ansari said, "it is difficult to find just the right formula that will permit you to continue those methods that have proved so successful; but we are trying to find a way of stating it that will make these unusual conditions of flexibility which you need less open to attack and criticism."

"Make them less vulnerable," I put in.

"Make them more palatable to critics," he amended, smiling that handsome half-smile, half-grin.

So then we knew what was going on behind the scenes within the Plan Organization. There is probably one group, including members of the Board of Control, who would like to wipe out the discretion we have.

There are others who, quite sincerely, are questioning, as Mozayeny put it, "whether D&R methods under which we had been operating under the present contract should be modified to take into account the fact that the Majlis had just enacted a charter for a new Iranian organization, the KWPA."

We are in a stronger position than we have been in earlier periods on this issue of method. For now there are *results* to see: before there were only projections. And in recent years Iran has been disappointed so often by promises for the future, unfulfilled.

There are people within the government who wanted an explicit contract provision that D&R could not *start* projects on our own. This was proposed, one Iranian said, "for bureaucratic reasons" since we can't do this under our existing contracts, and no one takes this possibility seriously.

So I said I could think of language that might serve that "internal" purpose without raising substantive questions; asked for a piece of paper, and wrote something in my Gregg shorthand. Eyebrows went up across the table, which was filled with Farsi-covered pages. I tossed the shorthand sheet across the table and said: "Here is my suggestion as to language, if any of you can read Farsi." It was good for a laugh, and at such a time, when the tension was off, a laugh seemed good. Then I showed them how my name looked in shorthand: David Lilienthal.

Said I: "Looks like a Pepsi Cola sign in Persian script."

The whole subject of contract terms to prevent our starting projects on our own was dropped, never revived.

NOVEMBER 26, 1960
TEHRAN

Ansari phoned this noon that tomorrow at 1 P.M. they would be prepared with a revised draft of contract for discussion; that on Monday Hedayat and Asfia would see us.

Leo Anderson, now our Chief Representative in Iran, is a very exceptional personality, deserving of extended description. He is what one would call a "natural," a person who defies any category. His chief experience has been in the civil agricultural service of the U.S. Government: Soil Conservation Service regional director in eastern Oregon or Washington; a farmer in North Dakota, where he also has a very successful seed business and still has farms.

He is one of those men who always think in concrete terms, cases, instances, illustrations. Broad general statements he shies away from. He does not live in a world of words, and finds great difficulty in expressing himself except through a torrent of words and considerable repetition too; but if you listen patiently to this overwordy and apparently disorganized way of stating his views you see a pattern of conviction emerging.

I asked to see him this morning, to talk about the discussions that have recently been had with ten "representative" landlords of the Gebli area. What about improvement of tenure (khish) for the farmers, those who out here are called peasants, the landless ones who live in the landlords' villages and by long custom receive one-fifth of the crop for their labor—the other four-fifths going for water, seed, draft animals, and the landlord's share as owner?

Anderson's entire preoccupation in a land reform program is the very same one that impels me. Increased productivity, not dividing up of the land. "We could have started by proposing a subdividing of the land owned by the landlords of each village or group of villages. But this would have stranded the farmer-peasants, as they have been stranded in the Shah's program for Crown lands. There the peasant, with considerable fanfare, gets handed a deed. Big deal! He flexes his muscles. 'I am a free man, I am no longer a slave.' He feels wonderful.

"Then the poor fellow finds that the interest and pay-back for the land he has been 'given' leave him with *less* than he had when he didn't own land, when he was a villager working some landlord's land. This makes him mad as hell.

"And he no longer has the landlord's khadokah—the manager for the landlord—to help him with problems. He isn't used to being on his own. He is worse off than he was before. This causes bitterness all through Iran.

"No, we didn't want that. So in the law and the Charter of KWPA, we established that the landlord had a *responsibility*. [While he was saying this, Anderson was drawing furiously on the back of a big envelope, making a village area, and punching his pen at it to make his points.]

"That responsibility was that the landlords should see that their manager and their tenants produced more. Four times as much was the target. That meant that the tenants had to be better farmers, had a lot to learn. We didn't want our on-site assistance, through KWPA, or D&R, to take on the job of teaching the farmers; if we did that, the landlords would be happy, go off to Tehran, and let us hold the baby. But we couldn't just work entirely through the landlords' people either; we had to get their on-site assistance (that's what we call it, instead of extension service, the term we use in the States) right onto the land."

As he spoke, the picture of these villages Helen and I had visited last March came back to me so clearly, and I was thankful I'm also the kind of guy who likes to think things through in specific, concrete cases.

As an administrator or manager, Anderson has some great traits: he "cares" greatly about everything that goes on. He is a bearcat for following through details, instead of tossing them off as not important. His shortcoming as a manager is that he loves the details so much that he has difficulty in not boring into every one of them, and of course, the defect of finding it difficult really to delegate. By "really" I mean that when you delegate a duty you can't be poking at it yourself all the time, or the boys down the line with whom you have dealt directly will be arguing endlessly among themselves as to just what it was the boss said, what it is he wants, and the whole idea of delegation and responsibility is shaken.

NOVEMBER 28, 1960
TEHRAN

The strain is over. After fifteen minutes with Asfia and Ansari, we adjourned, all the points raised and disposed of yesterday with Ansari were confirmed; even on the fee. Ansari simply said, "This is agreeable to us." No haggling, no lectures about "economy."

This contract now must receive the approval of the High Council and probably of the Board of Control. Both Ansari and Asfia said it would be forthcoming, they thought, but that it would take a week. There is sure to be a row, and a lot of Farsi will bubble over the dam before the approval is given. But I have no doubt of the ultimate outcome.

Now our immediate task is to keep our people here in a frame of mind and attitude to help Iranians in every way toward our goal of *Iranians taking over*, through KWPA, and keeping Ansari fully occupied with important things until that time. There are many such important things, including perhaps a trip to the U.S. to induce Iranians over there to come home and go to work for Khuzistan. We want Ansari to take an active part, with us, in recruiting Persians here, in setting up standards by which to judge their merit and advancement, and to see that their *jobs* are ones in which their supervisors and associates are "training" them; this to be distinguished from formal classroom type of "training" which is of limited value but which is so often taken to be synonymous with, or the exclusive meaning of, the term "training."

Just before lunch I had a talk with General Daimeri on his meeting with the landlords in the Gebli area.

He has a most affecting face. The other day one of his brothers died suddenly, and the days and days of funeral and memorial services had him in an upset state of emotions. "But," he said, straightening his big shoulders in his uniform tunic, "I am a soldier, and if you wish me to resume my work with the landlords at once I will do so. I am a soldier."

He has the dark and most expressive eyes of the true Persian, something quite special and different from the eyes of a Latin American or Spaniard. He has acquired a great respect for Leo Anderson, and two different-appearing men with more widely differing backgrounds it really would be difficult to imagine. But they have a common link, as I said to them: their concern for the land and for people, whether they are living in the poverty and squalor of some of the Gebli villages or in North Dakota.

We should not by any means discount patriotism, love of country, in trying to find ways to make effective this pilot project area. It will take a lot of technical knowledge, of course, but when the key is inducing people, whether landlords or farm tenants, to join in an enterprise involving the land and water it takes more than technical knowledge. People's emotions must be moved, and love of country is one of those springs of emotion. There are others, but it shouldn't be assumed that there is not a great deal of latent patriotism among these people, cynical or disappointed as so many of them have become with the corruption and sloth and greed of which they have seen so much, particularly among the well-to-do and among parts of the official class.

It is these new young men, the men like Ansaris, the Samiis, the Farmanfarmaians, in whom the hope lies. How it will come out no one can be sure. But there is a real, a solid hope.

NOVEMBER 29, 1960
6:15 A.M.
FLYING OUT OF TEHRAN

The most spectacular dawn I believe I have ever seen: our DC-8 jet, springing from the earth, like a bird released to freedom from its cage, and then there was the magic white cone of Mount Demavand against the glow of the predawn. God, how beautiful is this world you have made.

Now, on to the west, and to the joys that await me back home.

What should be the role of America and Americans overseas? This has been much on my mind. It is part of my job, my function, this question. It is not a purely academic or "writing" question. It sharpens the cutting edge of one's mind as almost nothing else does—to have a function, a responsibility from day to day about a question which might otherwise be simply "something to write about."

(Now we are over Turkey, the brown old, old creased mountaintops.)

There are some things about Americans overseas my experience seems to confirm. One is that Americans, whether they are businessmen or foreign service officers, should be *themselves*. If they are from Dubuque, say, then they should act the way that a good, well-liked and relaxed Dubuquean acts at home.

The prevailing "intellectual's" view about this is that Americans whose work life is abroad should strive to "adjust," that the measure of their acceptance and effectiveness is the degree to which they are more like Finns or Persians or Indians than themselves. (I overstate—but not much.)

I disagree and with conviction. The *purpose* of being abroad is more than a personal question pertaining only to the individual; it is part of carrying America to the world, which surely is part of an American's role in life.

One can't disagree that being multilingual, genuinely able to speak in several tongues, is a good thing in every way. But to give ability to speak the language of a country such a high priority is to confuse linguistics with communication.

Moreover, many adults, faced with a "must" about learning a new language, will find that this pre-empts time and energy that would otherwise go into learning more about their job, the country, the way the world wags, their home country. If there must be this choice, and there usually must be, learning more than the rudiments of a new language is all that should be attempted.

Talking through an interpreter is a good way to cut down prolixity, enforce precision, give breathing space between paragraphs.

I had a good illustration of this yesterday. Anderson, not a man gifted with language, was saying some things to General Daimeri, our intermediary with the Gebli landlords. Anderson spoke in measured and elegant sentences. Both Gordon and I attributed this complete change from the torrent of words, almost to the point of being inarticulate, with which Anderson frequently "thinks aloud," to the fact that he was speaking a few sentences at a time through Vakilzadeh as his interpreter.

Besides, in many countries one must know not one language but several dialects. In Italy an interpreter is needed to interpret one kind of Italian to other Italians. We saw this happen in our trip in the South of Italy with Carlo Weiss and his Milanese driver, some years back. When we got to Sicily, neither Weiss nor his driver knew what the dickens the Italians of those parts were saying in response to their simple questions put in North Italian, asking "Where is so-and-so?"

NOVEMBER 30, 1960
4 P.M.
AT CIAMPINO AEROPORTO, ROME

I am waiting to take off for Milano, after thirty hours or so in Rome. And what a golden, colorfully warm city it can be.

I was met at the airport yesterday morning, arriving from Tehran, by Dr. Stringher plus driver, from Mediobanca, and an abrupt little man, named Raup from the U.N. Food and Agriculture Organization. Then followed a daylong session at Food and Agriculture Organization (FAO) devoted to Egypt and D&R's possible involvement in the development of its desert oases.

The cast of characters of these sessions was fabulous. A tall White Russian, with a fringe of gray hair sticking up over his head, a gangling, wordy, ineffectual, but terribly interesting man. Two Egyptians, one fresh in from the FAO Regional Office in Cairo, Mr. Farouki (with whom I got along famously; he appreciated my rather coarse sense of humor); and a curly-headed man, Ghonemy by name. And an assortment of Americans—a bit tired and cynical except for cocky Raup. A couple of Chinese (what in hell *they* were doing there I never did know) and some who were there just so they could say they "had sat in a conference with Dr. Lilienthal." Among the lot were that strange pair who accompanied us on our very first Khuzistan trip, little swart beaming Dewan, an Indian soils expert, and a Dutchman, J. A. Bakker.

The upshot of this meeting (that is, where it came out), I stated after fifteen minutes of discussion.

It was (a) that what the United Arab Republic Desert Development Authority was commissioned to do was a mattter of great importance to Egypt, during the strained period while the Aswan Dam is being built; (b) that developing certain great oases in the western desert as a pilot project in resettlement of farmers from the densely populated delta area, and thereby reducing the pressure in that region, was important in itself, and feasible, despite the present isolation of the oasis areas and (c) that before I committed myself to an advisory role for D&R, I should test how seriously the U.A.R. people themselves took this (or was it a political gesture?) and how feasible it seemed. So: I said I would be willing to do a two weeks' reconnaissance to find out if there was anything to "advise" about.

Farouki will take this message to Cairo.†

This is an overwhelmingly beautiful flight. The glow of the sunset with this remarkably clear sky. The Italian peninsula dark and brooding, jutting out into the sea like crouching animals of the forest's darkness.

DECEMBER 1, 1960
MILAN

In Milan to attend the special Directors' meeting of FIDIA. Last night I had dinner at Savinni's in the great galleria beside the brooding Duomo. With us was Count Faina, head of Montecatini; Leopoldo Pirelli, head of the worldwide rubber company of that name, and son of one of Italy's important figures; Franco Marinotti, a tough extraverted Italian peasant (as I always think of him), head of the Snia Viscosa, biggest of the synthetic fiber people of Italy. And of course, the wise and lively Enrico Cuccia of Mediobanca.

---

† No invitation to do such a reconnaissance was extended from Cairo.

9:50 P.M.
ON THE LOMBARDY TRAIN TO PARIS, IN MILAN STATION

A fog so thick in Milan that the planes didn't take off. But the delay made it possible to visit Carlo Weiss' home, see his delightful very American wife (Chicago; Smith College) and his bilingual children. Also a cousin of hers, whose young husband is about to take her on a trip via Volkswagen to Iraq and Iran and Turkey. Their purpose is to find materials for a Ph.D. thesis on a thirteenth-century dynasty, an offshoot of the Mogul domination of that part of the world. Such handsome young people.

The Board meeting of FIDIA today was a strain, as my Italian is not adequate to really follow the discussion, which was spirited, mostly about supermercatos. Spent most of the morning with Cuccia discussing just how I could "cooperate."

DECEMBER 4, 1960
PARIS

A rainy, rainy Sunday in Paris. And a long, long day.

What a two weeks it has been, since I took off on a Friday morning from Idlewild. I have traveled more than 15,000 miles. More than that, though, has been the variety, the utter diversity of ideas and places in that short period. The give-and-take, the parry-and-thrust of the week in Tehran; the long talk with Gordon, perhaps the closest and most congenial we have ever been, as friends. The return to Italy, that strange and wondrous and often exasperating country. The discussions about the desert oases of Egypt with that group of FAO men, who seem so removed, somehow, from the stream of life, despite the fact that they deal with land and water. Actually, it is because they deal with *reports* more than with food production and people that I get this sense of unreality when I am with them. There is a built-in factor of frustration in their purely *advisor* role.

Because I didn't want to spend another evening reading I decided to see the Folies-Bergère, night before last. This used to be the thing no American male visiting Paris was supposed to miss or there was something wrong with his virility or such.

The hall made me think of my boyhood, of the "Opera House" in Valparaiso, Indiana, the first theatre I ever saw in my life. The same ugly iron pillars supporting the gallery; the same worn-out creaky red-plush seats that threatened collapse.

But there the similarities with Valparaiso and my boyhood stopped.

It was a revue, of course, so there was a rapid succession of very different kinds of "spectacles" or acts. In some the costuming was very beautiful and sumptuous—Empress Josephine period, some medieval, etc. And in some there wasn't any costume at all. But the sexy part, that is the nudity which was supposed to start one's eyes popping, was not funny nor light, which is what I thought the French idea of sex was. It was just gals without clothes; and they could get out of a dress and suddenly be naked so fast it was like Houdini.

Well, not exactly a great art production, but at least I can check *that* off.

Spent a good deal of time yesterday in the small galleries in the Latin Quarter not far from this hotel, looking at pictures, some abstract, some not. And this morning I spent a delightful hour or so at the permanent exhibition of French Impressionist paintings at the Louvre, Cézanne, Van Gogh, Manet, and some wonderful Claude Monet. Felt rather frustrated seeing this alone, there was such a richness about it and so many questions I wanted to ask.

Then I found my way down to the lower depths, to the "Iran" exhibition. (Why "Iran," why not Persia?)

How this excited me. A great column, topped with the double bull, from Persepolis; gold work; votive figures; almost all (except the bulls) from Susa, in the heart of Khuzistan.

But what stirred me the most were the painted terra-cotta figures of fierce lions, from the palace at Susa, which now seems in my "neighborhood." The most beautiful and living things in inanimate form I have ever seen. I could hardly keep from shouting. I was all alone, for it was Monday morning, and besides I don't think too many people get way down there, though the pieces are among the finest things that French archaeologists have ever excavated.

DECEMBER 11, 1960
SUNDAY AFTERNOON
PRINCETON

The first snow. Sudden: this is a word I had not before thought of about a first snow. The earth covered with the benison of snow. How utterly beautiful it is: the off-white blanket over everything; my garden lying contentedly beneath the protecting cover of winter. The stirring of spring will bring back to life and green those roots now resting so serenely beneath the gray-brown of the frozen soil.

How damned good to be alive, awake and awakened. As if there were only a few hours, weeks, days, before the end. But like the glory of a late sunset, the more refulgent for being something that one realized will have only a brief time to glow—but the more glorious because of that realization. This is something that in the timeless or non-time world of youth one doesn't savor, for in the time of youth there is always "forever" ahead, so one's perceptions are not as vivid nor precious nor desperately exciting as in middle life. Or is what I now have "middle life," my sixties? Is it more nearly spring in autumn?

DECEMBER 16, 1960
NEW YORK

At dinner at the Century by chance Judge Charles Wyzanski sat next to me. I could hear some lawyers across the way predicting the end of the Republic because Kennedy today had appointed his kid brother as Attorney General; "that smart Irish kid, with no experience as a lawyer, the head of the judicial system, appointing Federal judges," etc., etc. Well, I didn't think it was a good idea, but I remarked that somehow the judicial system had survived Daugherty and a lot of other mediocrities and worse; I was impatient with the way lawyers assume that a Cabinet post is not part of the political and administrative system, that the law is created for lawyers.

I introduced myself (rather meekly, for Wyzanski is a great judge, I think). "Oh, yes, I know all about you; I quote your book on *Big Business* in my antitrust opinions. But there is something about you I know that even you may not know: I was President of the Harvard Board of Overseers at a time when you were named a professor at Harvard—but you didn't take the job. I was sorry you didn't take it, but I think you were right, considering what you have done since." So the rumored offer of a Harvard professorship was more than an offer; it had actually been taken for a vote to the Overseers and the Corporation.

After a long talk, the Judge and I went over to an adjoining table to greet Professor Austin Scott. Wyzanski said: "Here, Scotty, is a further proof against your contention that no man who doesn't get an A, who isn't on the Law Review, will ever amount to much. One of the most distinguished graduates the Law School ever produced, and he only got a B; true, a high B."

DECEMBER 22, 1960
NEW YORK

To the Biltmore Hotel for a session lasting from three until six with John Brooks of *The New Yorker*, who is working on a "profile" of me. He referred to my suggestion that he might wish to talk to Dr. Dana Atchley about me. I said something to the effect that Atchley had helped me to understand my emotional nature. Brooks sat up and looked sharply at me in that sidelong way of his: "Do you mean that you ever have an emotional crisis? I got the strong impression that you don't have emotional ups and downs, particularly downs. Do you mean that there were times during the postpublic service period [this is the one he is concentrating on] when you had self-doubts about what you were doing, and so on?"

"God, yes," I said.

"But you give the impression—and that is what people who have written about you always say—that you are self-confident, sure of yourself in every way, never get flustered or in doubt, and that this is part of the secret of your ability to do so many things"—words to this effect.

Well, I know that is my reputation. The fact is, of course, that I do stew and fret, and emote.

To this should be added, however, that when there is a decision to make I rarely am in any kind of quiver about it, or full of doubts at all—on the contrary.

But apparently had I not said this, even after the hours Brooks and I have been talking together, he would have put me down as a fellow whose emotional "curve" is a straight line.

CHRISTMAS EVE, 1960
DANIEL'S 4TH BIRTHDAY
PRINCETON

Nancy's boys here all day. They got their first full-scale lesson in boxing from their grandfather, complete with new boxing gloves. They are learning, too, and beginning to learn the most important thing that boxing can teach anyone: you have got to expect to be hurt by the other fellow now and then, and be prepared against and for it, or you had better not go in for anything competitive, which almost means staying outside life itself.

Have been reading a collection of the Essays of Robert Louis Stevenson. One on John Knox, the great Reformer and churchman, is an extraordinary and revealing work, dealing with Knox's relations with women, which were various, intense, and hardly consistent with the picture of a reformer of religion, unless you know that what makes a great preacher also makes a passionate and emotionally charged man. Stevenson's concluding sentences:

"The attraction of a man's character is apt to be outlived, like the attraction of his body, and the power to love grows feeble in its turn, as well as the power to inspire love in others. It is only with a few rare natures that friendship is added to friendship, love to love, and the man keeps growing richer in affection—both giving and receiving more—after his head is white and his back weary; and he prepares to go down into the dust of death."

DECEMBER 28, 1960
NEW YORK

Yesterday morning a stimulating and heartening report on the beginnings of D&R's work on minerals in the Ivory Coast.

Present, Dr. Ralph Grim, so wise and experienced and sensible, and his two associates, also consultants of D&R's: Carozzi, an intense young Italian, a member of the University of Illinois faculty in geology, a likable youngish man with heavy glasses and a quizzical look; Agocs, a hefty square-built man of about forty, a geophysicist, the modern man with the magic wand.

One of the chief hazards of geophysical methods of locating probable mineral reserves is that it seems like some kind of necromancy to most people. They rather expect that with these mysterious instruments and esoteric methods of discovering what is in the earth by avoiding it, i.e., flying over it, the magic devices can actually somehow *produce* minerals that are not there.

Grim outlined what the report they had drafted would include.

My one concern was: in what way could we make this geologic report to be quite different from the conventional geologic "survey"?

I expressed the conviction that geology can be made to serve ends—and at least equally important ones—that go beyond finding, or looking for, minerals. It can be one of the means of helping the people of the Ivory Coast make their political independence a solid thing. Geology can be made one part of the very foundation of political independence, an affirmative building of the strength of their country, building the skills and the confidence of their own people, building new or strengthening old institutions acquired from the French colonial period.

For example, part of the proposed D&R-Grim program calls for about a dozen field survey crews, exploring for minerals. The heads of each of these groups must necessarily be trained geologists. There are very few among the Ivory Coast Africans. But we should see that training and seasoning for the top posts in these parties should not be deferred but begun at once, *an integral part of the job of geology.* Even in a geological investigation there can be a human and political philosophy and conviction.

The same proposition I stressed when we were told of the proposed report's program for a minerals laboratory in which geochemists would assess the content (for beryllium, manganese, etc.) of the samples these field forces would be sending in.

At present, under the French system, such samples must be sent to Dakar or some such place, and it may be two months or more before the results are known by the field investigators. In the meantime they really must sit on their hands. Grim *et al.* have in the program a lab for this purpose right in Abidjan, or nearby.

I poked into the question of how long it would take to provide Ivory Coast Africans to man all but perhaps the top two or three posts, since much of the work is only partly technical. I urged that we recommend a definite *program* to bring this about, in the initial report.

For D&R's basic task, we must understand and our "clients" must see, is not just finding minerals (if they exist) but finding and equipping the talents of these people launched on their new adventure, an adventure that has swept almost the entire continent of Africa.

Searching, by modern techniques, for ground water was also on the agenda of the program. This can be just a matter of pumping, to provide potable water for the field parties or for later industrial utilization of the mineral perhaps. But, as Grim was quick to point out, this can also provide remote villages with water and open up a new way by which geology can serve and "aid" the people these things are intended to strengthen.

We do *seem* to be on our way to another significant and concrete demonstration of what the principles of "how to do it" can be made to effect.

DECEMBER 31, 1960
PRINCETON

For many, many years I have been writing a year-end summation. (Actually this began in December, 1918, forty-two years ago, predating the beginnings of what has since become an extensive library of journal notes, almost filling two file drawers.)

But this hour isn't a good time to give a view of the year, for this hour is too close and therefore too dominated by a seemingly (though only seemingly) sudden change in my life.

There were unhappy episodes during the year, certainly. Rejection or dilemma or frustration (whatever the term) causes acute suffering.

On the other side, however: this year has contained some of the most intense and overwhelming periods of happiness and freshness I can remember. To know that I am still *capable* of intense experience, even if for a month, much less a year, has been a fact of the year that almost dominates the twelve months.

Someone told me recently that I have a trait of substituting what I *want* to be true (about people or events) for what is real. Still, when I am forced to stand up to reality—through the route of an enforced choice—I can become hard enough, however painful. Kenneth Mc-Kellar, Wendell Willkie, and A. E. Morgan, among others in my past, learned this.

Some people never have this problem. They see things just as they are. By this they gain a good deal, I suppose; I can also testify that they lose a lot, both of vision and joy, and of despair and pain.

III

1961

Reflections on the young generation—Robert Oppenheimer—Inauguration of Kennedy—Chester Bowles on
Southeast Asia—London—Spain—Iran: D&R contract
negotiations; Iranian student demonstrations—Republic
of the Ivory Coast: French domination—Nigeria: Easter
in Lagos—U.S. foreign policy—Ghana—Bay of Pigs—
Tragedy and overextension in Laos—Ideas on "multinational barter"—Corning Conference—Beginning of Peace
Corps—Visit with Dean Acheson—National Conference
on International and Social Development—Nigeria's
Prime Minister in Washington—A-bomb tests—Russia:
war scare—Paris: Jean Monnet's views on unification of
Germany and the European Community—Iran: peasant
village health program; audience with Shah—Rome—
Harrison Salisbury on Russia—Milan: Cuccia on Russia,
on China—A surprising Princeton student seminar—
Trip to Colombia: President Lleras on Organization of
American States, Castro, and Latin America—Critique
of World Bank

JANUARY 4, 1961
NEW YORK

At dinner tonight, Scotty Reston, looking more and more like
W. C. Fields would if he were a temperance man: the bright eyes and
mischief in his smile. Also Tom Hamilton, who covers UN for the
New York Times. Cuba was much in the discussion, with Ike's termination of diplomatic relations being the "news" of the day.

Would it have been better never to have spent the years in business out of which financial independence has come? I have no doubt this was an important part of my "education" quite aside from the financial results; and, further, that the financial independence *is* in itself a good thing.

But other men, with a background of public service and strong intellectual and creative interests, have gone another direction. Reading Dean Rusk's quietly sensible testimony before the Senate Foreign Relations Committee yesterday gives one stellar example. A solid and splendid man, whose integrity is "built in" whether he has financial independence or not, he can "do as he believes," for that comes naturally to him, and always shall.

JANUARY 13, 1961
PRINCETON

In his "Introduction" to *The Education of Henry Adams* (a book that occurs and recurs in my thinking), James Truslow Adams says: "*. . . books last longer than statesmen.*"

A phrase that sticks in my craw: it is only out of *conflict* that we know what "values" we believe in. We ourselves don't know about "values" except as we are forced to make *choices of values* and that comes, usually, through a *conflict between values*, forcing such a choice. A tough doctrine, perhaps, but right; the fact that it is tough means that it is right *for the young*.

JANUARY 15, 1961
PRINCETON

"Maturity": what a lot of fraud is committed in the name of this so popular word these days.

What most people really mean by "being mature," when lecturing young people who "haven't yet grown up," as they say, haven't yet become mature, is simple: by maturity they mean *resignation*.

God help me—and even if He doesn't—I don't intend ever to become resigned, and if that means I will never be "mature," well, make the most of it.

I said to Helen a few moments ago, half joking, "Do I seem like Dave Lilienthal to you?" meaning like the fellow with the hair low on his forehead she knew as "Dave" so many, many years ago. Without losing a moment or even looking up in surprise from her washing of the breakfast dishes, she said, "Yes, in all of his various personalities."

There certainly isn't just one Dave Lilienthal, whether one thinks of *time* (the Dave of 1917 and 1937 and 1961) or *within* a particular segment of time, even within a single day.

And I suppose almost everyone is like that; this is the interesting point to me. I may be more chameleon-like than most, but it is just a matter of degree.

In the serenity and grace of this house and home, I think of an experience I had on the subway recently.

I started for the office on the Lexington Avenue subway at a bad morning rush hour. The *crush* of human beings was not only stifling, there was a kind of degradation about it. It was an experience a modern man should not miss. The struggle to live, the capacity, the infinite capacity of ordinary people to endure perhaps two or even three hours on these jam-packed trains each day is a curse, but a tribute to their durability too.

Human beings are really wonderful; there is nothing else in Nature—not the arching sky nor the vast and awesome sea, nor the leafing of early spring, nothing in Nature—quite so wonderful as the ever-changing wonder of mankind living together.

Two hours ago Robert Oppenheimer came in, out of the sleet and rawness of the night, the first real visit we have had alone for a long time.

Since our first meeting, years ago, was about disarmament, which is now again so much in the center of things, we naturally talked about this.

He said he was relieved to notice in this morning's paper the recommendation of a Kennedy "task force" that nothing be done about disarmament discussions for six months, until a coherent policy had been developed.

I agreed, but went on to say that disarmament is not only a problem of infinite difficulty, but we must recognize that at particular times some problems are simply not solvable, however urgent; that it is the part of wisdom not to try to devise "solutions" at a time when there is nothing that could be called a solution. It was this that had troubled me about the nuclear *test ban* discussions; that since they didn't go to the heart of things at all, and the main problem of war and peace wasn't presently solvable, nor could it even be ameliorated, as things now stand, then just doing *something* however superficial wasn't very sensible and might prejudice later efforts that would go to the core of things.

There are some terrible issues that must be lived with, perhaps for a long time; to ignore this possibility on the ground that the mental tension is too great to permit living with it, or that if we can't find an answer we should at least busy ourselves with peripheral issues that show our desire to make things better—this didn't seem a wise course to me. Did Oppie disagree? I don't know.

JANUARY 16, 1961
ON THE PENNSYLVANIA TO NEW YORK

Robert's visit last night still sticks in my mind. How utterly sad, tragic, his face is at times. The burden of having been the first man to look into that burning pit that is the release of the energy of the atom is marked on his face and manner as much today, I think, as it was years ago—when that event was so close.

I said to him that I had little confidence in much of the "expert" work going on in so many universities: the international centers all over the place, where men with little sense of the world but with great knowledge of a special kind of technical tricks were assaulting a deep problem as if it could be "solved," as an engineering or scientific problem could. Particularly I mentioned Henry Kissinger and his recent book. I expected Robert to "rar" back and look at me sadly for my ignorance. He has done this more than once. The most recent time was just after my NANA article about our self-delusion about the Russians. He had said, "So you have become a pundit." This he said bitterly though I know he is as fond of me as one who is as far ahead of me, mentally, as he is, could be.

But last evening when I mentioned Kissinger on nuclear strategy he began pacing about our living room: "A lot of nonsense; such nonsense that almost before the book was out he had written *another* book taking it all back. As for the other experts," he said, looking down on me, unlit pipe in hand, "to think that these are troubles that can be solved by the theory of games or behavioral research!"

NEW YORK

Lunch with Jim Conant. "You may remember," he said, "that I was one member of your Advisory Committee of the AEC, perhaps the most emphatic one, who was pessimistic from the beginning about the prospects for genuinely economic atomic energy. Well, I hate to be one of these 'I told you so' fellows, but it certainly has worked out that way."

Which reminded me of my long-delayed article about the fiasco of the euphoria about atomic energy for peaceful purposes. "I have often thought I would like to do a muckraking job on this. The trouble is that for that kind of thing to have any effect you have to put the blame on some one person; I don't like that sort of thing, and I don't know that the blame goes to anyone, unless it is to those few scientists who became so overenthusiastic."

He talked quite a bit about the H-bomb discussions of eleven years ago. "Bob Wilson [formerly of Standard of Indiana] who is now a member of the AEC Board came up to me and said, 'I can't understand how you fellows on the Advisory Committe made such a foolish report.' "

Jim went on: "I said it wasn't a foolish report. At that time the method proposed for making that kind of bomb seemed slim. Fermi thought so emphatically, and he was right; it wasn't made that way at all, which proved to be impossible, but in quite another way, as you must know."

JANUARY 19, 1961
WASHINGTON

Another inauguration—and *snowing* like mad!

And a strike in the harbor of New York spreading to the railroads, so we may, and then again we may not, be able to get back home Saturday.

In the meantime, I hope we will enjoy the massing of people from all over the country that is one of the happiest parts of this kind of pageantry. How the parade tomorrow will fare with this snow—well, I guess the nation will survive, even if the spectators don't.

JANUARY 20, 1961
INAUGURATION DAY, 7 P.M.
WASHINGTON

Now it is *President* Kennedy. To think that it was just twelve months ago that we sat at table with Jacqueline Kennedy, beautiful but tense and ill at ease, a year since I talked to the serious, almost solemn young Senator at the Waldorf dinner for Mrs. Roosevelt. And after a whirlwind year I saw him, via television, take the oath as President, make an effective address about "cooperation" with the East in the war against poverty, etc.

Went out to the parade. It was bitter cold, the wind cutting. But it was *fun*, great fun that made me feel quite gay: to see these fellow Americans from all over, and the pageantry (though at times repetitious) of bands, marching outfits, etc., from all the states.

A year ago, in a speech in Cleveland, I said we must change our policy of using foreign aid to buy friends or "stop Communism." We must give aid, I said, because "we must, because we are that kind of people." To find this adopted so wholeheartedly in the President's inaugural, almost the key of it, gave me considerable satisfaction. This is a great change, 180°, of course, from the policy of self-interest and "stopping Communism" to an affirmative moral tone. I won't be ashamed of the time and effort I put into that Cleveland speech. It is a matter of satisfaction, too, that he wrote me, back in January, such a strong affirmation of the thesis of that speech.

JANUARY 22, 1961
NEW YORK

In the parlor car seat next to me yesterday, returning from Washington, was the sad, worn, weary-looking man who for a couple of years was known as the husband of Marilyn Monroe, or sometimes as "Mr. Monroe." The great American playwright Arthur Miller. The mystery of his courtship and marriage to the American synonym for Love (sex division) is even greater after one sees him at close range.

Have just noted in today's Sunday *New York Times* that while we were noting Mr. Miller's saturnine look his wife had appeared in a Mexican court to obtain a divorce on grounds of "incompatibility of temperament." So no wonder he looked rather worn and inward-seeming —whether from relief, or regret, or some other emotion, or several emotions.

JANUARY 23, 1961
NEW YORK

Yesterday (Sunday) Helen and I went to the Metropolitan Museum chiefly to see the wonderful special exhibit of Thai works of art. It added to the joy to learn that Indiana University had organized and manages this exhibit as it goes about the country. Thanks largely to Chancellor Herman Wells, the old picture of Hoosierdom as provincial, suspicious of "art and artists," must yield, too, along with a lot of other stereotypes.

Then we had a wonderful hour doing what I most enjoy, I think, in an art museum wherever it is: looking once more upon the great paintings of the late nineteenth and early twentieth centuries—Picasso, Matisse, Seurat, Claude Monet, Van Gogh. Each time I see some of these paintings I get a bit more satisfaction and understanding of what they have put on canvas. And I try to remember that most of these painters, now so "conventional," in their lifetime were regarded as experimenters, or even as no-counts trying to palm off something way-out as art. This makes me more sensitive and more humble about the puzzling abstract paintings I am trying to learn about, feebly and inadequately, but trying.

Kennedy's beginnings couldn't be better. An inaugural address that was certainly *not* written by Clark Clifford, say, excellent pedestrian draftsman as he is, but of a high order of eloquence and feeling. His salutes to poets and to intellectuals, the general atmosphere of respect for all achievement, not alone, as with Ike, the achievement of men of business—these are heartening and clearly genuine.

Whether these intellectuals around Kennedy are also men who will learn to be actionists is another matter. Happily Kennedy has also a great respect for politics as an art, and politicians are closer to the realm of action than intellectuals.

Remember this about continuity: the unbroken strand, the lane that stretches back to beginnings, through darkness and light, stretching back and well remembered—this quality of an individual's life may at times seem dull because well worn and predictable. But continuity is precious; a unique gift of the gods.

JANUARY 26, 1961
NEW YORK

Had a lengthy talk with André Meyer about how to make more effective the original concept of how D&R and Lazard could work together.

André repeated what he had often said, that D&R's consulting and management services, standing alone, could hardly be described as "a business." It meant very hard work, required a large, permanent organization, and produced relatively little money, after taxes.

"You have an exceptional imagination about natural resources; no one in the world has a better, nor a more impressive record in TVA and in other things since. Now if you will put that imagination to work on business situations you will find me more than willing to consider them and find the money to invest in them."

I said I had thought a good deal about this for five years, since D&R was founded. "As is so often true between men with strong views which appear to be divergent, I think we were *both* right, each from our own viewpoint. To you, who know how to make money, by big deals, that yield capital gains, D&R's business of collecting fees doesn't seem to be business." And the salaries we receive must seem very small indeed, not worth the strenuous effort and worry through which we must go to earn them.

"So from your viewpoint you are right.

"But my primary interest in D&R is the *satisfaction* it gives me, responding to an urge inside me. You approve the goals of our work, but to you that is not, as with us, primary. And the salaries we receive, while small by any standard except perhaps that of public service, are adequate compensation. So we are both right as to whether D&R is a 'business.'

"This doesn't mean that we don't want to uphold our end of the partnership by trying to find collateral activities that will yield a capital profit for Lazard and for us. We believe in that, but it is not our primary interest."

I tried to make him see that, unless D&R is exposed to business opportunities and put in the middle of them through the route of our consulting services, the chance of turning up collateral business opportunities was almost nil; one couldn't just sit in a room and use one's "imagination," a word he so frequently uses to describe what it is that will make money.

President Kennedy (how good it is to be able to write it that way) continues to make sterling appointments. Henry Labouisse as head of ICA is terrific; Harlan Cleveland, George McGhee, Paul Nitze—these are men with a record of good performance, who are proud to serve their country, and have the brains and dedication for the most important of all tasks, public service. They are the kind of men who reflect great credit on the public service and on Kennedy's concept of his task.

JANUARY 29, 1961
PRINCETON

Spent an hour yesterday with Gardner Patterson, head of the Woodrow Wilson School, and Professors Ward and Lively, at their request, to discuss selection of men from abroad who might become Fellows at Princeton, under a new foundation set up by a businessman, Albert Parvin, a friend of Justice Bill Douglas' from the West Coast.

No one has a clear enough picture why such a "Fellow" should be interested in spending a year at Princeton, more than the vague rhetoric of the donor and of Justice Douglas. Parvin and Douglas say that the purpose is "to promote better international relations." Well, certainly. But just how ten men spending a year at Princeton will do this, men from Nigeria, Iran, etc., needs a good deal more *concrete* thinking than has been given to it, or I fear, is likely to.

I said I would be on the lookout for likely people on our forthcoming trip, which is about what they wanted from me. But I threw in this idea: that they consider artists, creative writers, sculptors, etc., as well as "public affairs" people.

Ed Murrow has just been designated as head of our overseas information (USIA) and thereby influential on foreign policy (considering the strength of this man, and his enormous prestige). Reminded me of his talking about Red China with me and Alexander Kendrick at lunch. Ed said: "If we in the U.S. decided to recognize Red China, it wouldn't cause any particular surprise nor any great furor at home."

What is it you want, want most? This is the question I've put up to myself with special sharpness, a question I've tried to answer with the greatest honesty I can summon. Being completely honest, intellectually, with others is difficult enough; with oneself the contravailing impulse toward self-deception is trebly difficult to withstand.

It is apparent—I was fully aware of it—that beginning a year ago at least the idea that I might want to re-enter public service came drifting into my mind and emotions. A new Administration seemed likely, one that would have my sympathy and confidence. I had achieved the goal of financial independence; I had a respite of ten years from the rigors and the power intoxication of high public office.

So there has been this divided mind and emotions: to be asked to return to public service by a fine Administration, and the contrary pull—keep your freedom of action; don't "repeat yourself"; you can eat your cake of influencing the course of events, through writing, being consulted, the not-so-elder statesman role, and *have* your cake of freedom of action, time to reflect and write without having to "clear" everything. This kind of pulling and hauling between these two desires was compounded by the desolation I felt if I had to live in parochial Washington.

But a man simply MUST NOT at his peril be of two minds for long, and even more hazardous is to be pulled and hauled between two emotional states.

It is becoming more and more clear that while I want both of these two worlds—as I always have, I guess—since there *must* be a choice, the choice is clearly on the side of continuing in private life; or more explicitly, of not re-entering public service, on any long-term basis.

So let's consider this as settled, and as the English say, "carry on."

JANUARY 30, 1961
PRINCETON

Have just heard (and seen) President Kennedy's State of the Union message. I don't know when, if ever, I had such a sense of witnessing a country turning itself around—I don't know any other way to express it. In every way this was a break with the sluggish, complacent past of the Eisenhower period, plus a cultivation and sense of intellect that Truman, for all his strong qualities, never had.

FEBRUARY 4, 1961
NEW YORK

Snowed in—this time in New York City. And what a wild and beautiful "blizzard" it has been. Struggling to get to Princeton and then struggling to get back makes no sense. Cut off this way, I don't feel frustrated, and certainly am physically comfortable. The two skinny chambermaids on this floor, who had to *walk* down the middle of the streets to take care of us slugs, or the waitresses whose patience is so admirable, these *are* the people; I was quite proud to see them on the job after a terrific night of snow, impassable streets, delayed trains. People are really good, most of them, and no gloomy Gus can tell me otherwise.

FEBRUARY 6, 1961
NEW YORK

A call this afternoon from Chester Bowles, the Under Secretary of State, from Washington.

He said: "David, I have an idea that I want you to think over carefully. We want an Assistant Secretary to run the Latin-American program, so it won't end up in a lot of memoranda pushing around Washington. I mentioned your name to the President, who received it warmly.

"Things are beginning to move down here, and I want you to be in the middle of it, and make it amount to something."

The idea is far from unpleasant to have a chance to provide leadership for that part of the world I consider closest to us, as to our needs and resources and the great need of their people. But as I said to Chester, what I am now doing (i.e., D&R) seems to me clearly public service, in very concrete ways. The allure of having "22 Ambassadors and Missions for which you would be responsible," to use his words, doesn't appeal to me as it might once have done; the kudos and "power" stage of my life is something I have had.

FEBRUARY 8, 1961
PRINCETON

This noon another phone call from Chester Bowles.

He said he had the word I gave his secretary this morning that on full consideration I should *not* be considered as available for the Assistant Secretaryship for Latin America.

"I must respect your conclusion. But I have another idea.

"Our most troubled spot in the world is Southeast Asia. The President would like to name you Ambassador to Thailand, so you could create the atmosphere and steam behind the development of the Mekong River, a big Southeast Asian TVA."

I didn't want to be Ambassador, I said, offhand and without hesitation "but," I went on in the same sentence, "but I like the idea of producing stable conditions through economic development and particularly of a great river. I would be glad to go out there to develop that river as a TVA, to help in the troubles of Southeast Asia, using my company as the means, but with me giving it personal attention."

"Let's take it up from there," he said. "You would be a consultant either to the U.S. Government or perhaps the World Bank." I put in another reference to having this done through the medium of D&R; that I was off on a two-month trip but could be reached; and if he wanted me to, we could go to Southeast Asia during the trip.

FEBRUARY 12, 1961
HEADING FOR LONDON BY PAN AM

Ideas and an emotional commitment to them should be the theme of this latest voyage on which Helen and I have set out, one that will take us to England, Spain, Lebanon, Iran, West Africa, France, and Italy —a roving kind of existence that should create ideas.

Gordon, my closest professional associate, quite different in temperament, is concerned and preoccupied with *knowing* all the "facts"—or most of them. He has a genius for absorbing and remembering facts, most of them of the kind that I would call "details" and he would probably call "knowledge in depth." It makes him uneasy about me when I start off on an enthusiasm or drive before I know "all the facts."

But knowing all the facts is one of the best ways to suffocate in me that almost spontaneous insight which I here call "an idea," or at other more formal times "a concept."

The illustrations are not difficult to find.

The idea of an Indus River development between Pakistan and India. All the "facts" I had were obtained in a few days of observation and perhaps a day or so of reading.

The idea of the Cauca Valley regional corporation resulted from a week's visiting the area and talking to the people; at a moment of despair a hint, a "lead" from Helen reassured and guided me; and from this came the CVC. Facts on facts were added *later* to the few I had available. If I had *started there,* steeping myself in facts, wanting to be sure that other facts were being gathered, the insight would have been blanked out.

The basic idea for the Khuzistan regional development came after a week or less of seeing the country and a few people, brooding a bit about the ancient life of the region, and seeing some of the remnants of that glory. The "facts" we had at that time were most meager, and as it turned out mostly *wrong*, e.g., the FAO experts' "facts" that this desert region's soil was too saline for a flourishing agriculture.

Another example: the concept behind my decision about TVA electric rates, an innovation that upset the electrical industry, I announced in early September, 1933, only a couple of months after TVA was created. This was based on some kind of insight ("an idea") rather than an exhaustive rate analysis. That idea was ridiculed at the time; but it has held up. We *created* the supporting facts after the idea had been born and expressed. The concept changed the facts is one way of putting it.

Now comes the possibility that we may be called into the Mekong River development in Southeast Asia. This may not come to fruition.‡ But my letter to Bowles of the 9th, confirming what I said on the phone, is again based on a sense of what *can be* made of the Mekong Valley rather than a knowledge of what is.

Gordon was disturbed when he saw the draft of my letter (and wrote me his comments to that effect) because I might be "stimulating" something that might not, on further investigation, prove to be possible. But that isn't my way of working. Of course, I make mistakes this way.

But mistakes, occasionally, for this reason are, I think, better than the usual fate of the overcautious, i.e., inaction, good reports and no-good inaction. It may be unfair to say so, but I can't help recalling that Gordon, a great master of fact-finding, interpretation, and exposition, wrote an extraordinarily good report on the Arab refugee problem, but nothing happened.§ Perhaps—it is indeed likely—the political conditions between Arabs and Israeli made this literally impossible. But whether it could have been *made* to happen had there been more drive and less caution, more flair and enthusiasm and emotion, about getting something done, no one can prove or disprove.

FEBRUARY 14, 1961
HOTEL CONNAUGHT
LONDON

Luncheon at Lazard Bros. in the City. Preceded by a talk with Tommy Brand, now Viscount Hampden. But despite his accession to

‡ It did but not until 1966, by which time the United States had become heavily involved in South Vietnam; this is recorded in the *Journals* for 1966-1970.

§ A UN Commission (for the Economic Survey of the Middle East), headed by Gordon R. Clapp, in late 1949, subsequent to the establishment of the State of Israel, recommended four projects for the development of streams, chiefly for irrigation. These included one project on the Litani, a major river in Lebanon, and one on Wadi Zerqa, an eastern tributary of the Jordan River between Lake Tiberias and the Dead Sea, lying in Jordan.

so august a title he still looks more like "Tommy." His eyes are blue and knowing and twinkling, his soft collar, as always, slightly out of center, his necktie not quite pulled up, his hair, now white, bushed out around a quite nobly shaped head. In short, Viscount Hampden is still Tommy Brand, with the simplicity and cordiality and straightforwardness of manner which have always appealed so much to me, and to many others.

And businesslike. Immediately we sat down in his tiny office, he started on Nigeria: whom would I like to see when I'm there that they would know? "We've just had a man back from Nigeria and we'll talk to him before you go." He didn't mention that "the man" was Lord Kindersley's son, now a partner, a tall spare hatchet-jawed young man, the Hon. R. H. M. Kindersley who will inherit his father's title, I *assume,* since I am less sure when I visit England these latter days that there will indeed "always be an England."

Lunch with the partners. A hearty lunch, too, none of this eat-in-an-uproar sort of thing to which I am accustomed when in New York for lunch. A delicious smoked fish, entire, and then roast beef, which everyone ate in large amounts.

Tommy spoke of our work in Iran, how it was getting on, something about his most recent visit as a director of the new Iranian Industrial and Mining Development Bank. "I'm afraid your work out there is making inflation even worse, bad as it is." I turned this aside by saying I am at the moment more troubled by another "underdeveloped country," my own, "than about Persia."

Tommy, who spent much of World War II in Washington, on behalf of his Government, knows the American scene better than any other Englishman I know. Will the present Administration insist on backing your notes (meaning our currency, I supposed) with gold; only country in the world—perhaps Holland is an exception—that does it any more. I opined that if unemployment doesn't decline, indeed increases, the Administration will do whatever it thinks is needed, but I hoped tinkering with the currency wouldn't be among the first, at least.

Then he said the sort of candid thing I have grown to expect of Tommy Brand: "Of course, everything you Americans do to strengthen the dollar weakens sterling."

About Nigeria, Lazard have decided against opening an "acceptance" business out there. On the whole they took a dim view of the investment climate now, in Nigeria and other parts of Africa. "Either you have the whites supreme and running things, or the blacks supreme and running things." He referred to Kenya. "The blacks don't know how yet, and the whites are on their way out. It doesn't look like an appetizing place to invest money or energies."

I find London quite exciting. To see One Threadneedle Street, or Ye Old Cheshire Cheese, or Fleet Street, or the St. James's area, even in the middle of winter (though the weather here is mild) is still a thrilling experience.

A prayer: Dear God, keep me always a "country boy" who never loses the sense of excitement when I see new things, and sees again old things that once excited me. Protect me from becoming blasé. Amen.

FEBRUARY 17, 1961
GRANADA, SPAIN

Alhambra!

What corny images that word invokes—thanks to Washington Irving. And today Helen and I have seen that wonder. Unlike most overtouted "wonders," this one lived up to our expectations.

This trip to the south of Spain is a kind of birthday present from me to Helen; believe it or not, on April 3 she will have her sixty-fifth birthday. How unreal that sentence seems, particularly when I see both of us clambering up the many steps and roadways, walking for hours through the voluptuous beauties of this jewel of the Sultans.

FEBRUARY 18, 1961
GRANADA

A delightful morning in the city. Going through a market, in the early morning when the housewives are picking and choosing, is one of the best ways of learning about a country and people, the sellers, the buyers, and the produce of the sea or land.

This trip to southern Spain has stirred anew a favorite private puzzle. Why is it that in a certain country and at a certain time human energy, creativeness, and restlessness explode and flourish and then subside and almost vanish. Spain is a chief example.

There was a time when Spain was full of inventiveness, drive, creativeness of a political and military kind. The world—or most of it—was hers and her people's. South America, Philippines, much of North America, etc. Then a long eclipse, a long one: that drive has never returned.

It is important to us, a young country, to know that such things happen and to be guided by a sense of the evanescence of the things we think are forever ours because we are *we*. The Spaniards were explorers, they absorbed other peoples and cultures, they produced great artists. But look at them now! I think our young people could learn a good deal if they would know and ponder on the reasons for the decline of Spain.

FEBRUARY 21, 1961
HOTEL MADRID
SEVILLE

Seville was once one of the centers of the world. Up this dingy riverfront came the wealth of the Indies. From this city adventuresome, greedy, restless men went forth to perform feats that even the highly touted astronauts will have difficulty duplicating.

Why *then*? And why has this never reappeared?

This mystery of why greatness and high skills appear in a people, then disappear, was borne in on me again in a visit I paid the Archivo de Indies.

Housed in a large building of its own, here are thousands of packets, millions of words, reporting in longhand the exploits and discoveries of the whole line of conquerors of the days of Spain's greatness: Magellan, Amerigo Vespucci, Cortez, to say nothing, of course, of Christopher Columbus. Maps and charts for the steerer to use at the mouth of the Rio de la Plata (which I saw so recently), i.e., Montevideo, and nearby Buenos Aires. Sophisticated engineering plans for water aqueducts, the fortifications for Cartagena. There are hundreds of such volumes dealing with "Santa Fe" (which must mean what we now call Colombia).

Seeing these remarkable documents prepared centuries ago has fed the flame of my intense curiosity and interest in this strange and exciting phenomenon: the explosion of restless energy at a particular time and place.

FEBRUARY 22, 1961
SEVILLE

I spent one and a half hours walking through a "working class" area across the river, known as Triana. On some of the little streets I peeked into the darkness of a charcoal shop, the proprietor's face smudged, his customers carefully picking over the pieces of charcoal as if they were vegetables. A stalwart spit-in-their-eye countryman came along the narrow street, a very long pole in his hand carried upright, behind him two magnificent, black Andalusian steers, dignified and contemptuous, pulling a two-wheeled cart loaded to the sky with green branches of pine. The drover started to turn into a very narrow street, to deliver the branches. A minuscule motor truck was standing in the way. He stalked over, the lord of creation, to tell this creature to make way for a real form of transportation. Seeing the oxen (I would judge no longer a familiar sight in the streets of Seville), a little boy pulled his hand away from his grandmother and clapped and danced. I heard a flute, or pipe, high and clear, repeating the same series of notes: the call of the knife and scissors grinder. I felt that he was prouder of his ability on the flute than in sharpening knives.

Wandered through an open food market, halfway under the bridge known as Puente de Isabel II, over the Guadalquivir River. This was bedlam. Young boys were carrying part of some merchant's produce in their hands, the better to accost the housewives, and yelling at the top of very healthy lungs; in the background the clerks who were there to cut up an octopus or ladle out some lard, also yelling happily. People were jammed in so closely I felt like part of a mob scene. Songbirds, some little ones, all neatly plucked except for their sad and drooping heads. Strange strips of stuff I rather assumed were fish eggs. There was a big bulletin listing all the vegetables—perhaps thirty—for sale in this public market, on a blackboard. In the column of maximum legal prices there was a complete blank all down the line. I'm sure "there is a law," but I doubt if anyone pays attention to it, and especially the merchants and customers.

FEBRUARY 24, 1961
FLYING FROM ROME TO TEHRAN, IRAN

There have been journals other than mine written with far greater literary quality and greater intrinsic interest. But I wonder: has there to this date ever been a series of journals written at greater altitude, greater *distance from the earth* (we are now at 40,000 feet, a paltry distance for a sputnik, but quite high for a passenger vehicle), *or* from as many different places?

FEBRUARY 26, 1961
TEHRAN

Yesterday I learned that only a few days before we arrived a new Managing Director of the Plan Organization had been named, Mr. Ahmad Aramesh, a well-known and active politician and "public figure." But the important thing is that he had been one of Ebtehaj's most violent enemies, both official and personal—and vice versa. He had frequently bitterly criticized the D&R contract and the entire Khuzistan program, in public and in private, through the press.

The talented young men in the Economic Bureau headed by Khodadad Farmanfarmaian were aghast; said they would resign.

Said Farmanfarmaian, with an utter sadness and despair which only the Persian eye and demeanor can convey, "You are meeting me in my last time in this building; I am leaving the Plan Organization." So filled with pent-up emotion, frustration, the very things that in much younger men—and with less cause—led to the protest "disturbances" that have been going on at the University here, with hundreds, sometimes two thousand students, marching six abreast, condemning the present Administration.

When I learned that the D&R contract extension, upon which agreement had been reached when Gordon and I were here in the fall, had not been signed by Plan Organization, I got the wind up. It was important to take the initiative at once. I told John Oliver that we must take this position: that the question was not whether they would sign the contract, and when, but whether *we* would sign it and agree to continue; that they must persuade us to stay rather than we persuade them to sign the agreement. He was in a mood to accept this position, even though it might mean—as I well knew, and he too—that if the position failed not only would we begin to pull out of Persia right away, but D&R might, at this juncture, not be able to survive.

The risks and stakes of taking this initiative were high, but it was clear to me that we must not let *them* decide about the contract: this must be our decision.

John suggested that I go with him to his Ansari appointment. After some preliminary chitchat I laid it on the line with Ansari. If Aramesh felt that he did not now want to sign the previously agreed-upon contract, but wanted "time to think about it" or "time to study it," Ansari, whom I believe in, should understand this: that under those circumstances we would not sign the contract, and it would not be necessary for Aramesh to "think it over" at all.

Ansari's face went gray, the lines between his brows deepened, but he held his temper. He then explained how violently Aramesh had opposed Plan, and us in particular. But he gave the background as explanation: that Aramesh believed Ebtehaj had secured a decree from the Shah forbidding Aramesh from attending meetings of the Board of Control to which he had been named by the Majlis. That naturally this humiliation produced a reaction by Aramesh against everything Ebtehaj did. But he, Ansari, had been discussing the whole Khuzistan program with Aramesh since his appointment; that he believed Aramesh, now that he had responsibility, would support it. Ansari said so wisely, "Ministers come and go, but the program is the thing."

I said that before I would agree to sign any contract to stay on in Iran I would have to hear these things directly from Aramesh. Thirty minutes later we were in a session with the new Managing Director.

A tall, lean-faced, shrewd, quite un-Persian-looking man of about forty-five. Yes, he had been a severe critic of the Plan Organization and of the Khuzistan program. He felt differently now. He did feel that the people of the country didn't understand what the Khuzistan program meant to them; "they know more about TVA in Iran than they do the Khuzistan program."

He gave quite a lecture (speaking from notes) to the effect that public understanding was essential for public activities; that it was a lack of public understanding of Khuzistan rather than the way we were doing the job that was its most serious defect. He proposed to correct that. And, having been a severe critic, his views might be taken more seriously than if he had always favored the undertaking. I responded with a vague diplomatic speech that this faith in an informed public was at the very heart of a real democracy, so that what he said was reassuring. It was our duty to provide the information to the Plan Organization and to Ansari, and this we must do. But it was not proper for guests and foreigners to carry this information to the people of Persia; *that* was for Persians.

I said that we should come down to specifics: there still was no signed contract; if we did not have definite word soon, we would have to start liquidating.

Then he said, "We will sign the contract tomorrow at five o'clock."

I said we would be there, ready to sign. I again made the point that progress in turning the actual management of the undertaking over to Persians had been our original objective; that the creation by the Majlis of the Khuzistan Water and Power Authority had been a landmark in that direction. Most important was the appointment of so able a young man as Ansari, who in turn would be able to attract other qualified Persians into the work. This was the real measure of whether our work was successful—not the building of dams or sugar production, but how quickly the undertaking could be successfully managed by the people of Persia.

This would serve to assure young Persians that there were opportunities in their own country.

He picked this up, speaking of the importance of the "rising generation." Rising is right. Last night the students at Tehran University burned the big car of the former Prime Minister, Manoucher Egbal, as it stood in a parking place on the campus. The amount of disaffection among young people is certainly rising; the incipient revolt among the staff of the Plan Organization at the appointment of Aramesh is another straw in the wind.

At 5:15 this afternoon Aramesh and John Oliver signed the contract extending D&R services for eighteen months, so that is that. Apparently the funds will be in our New York bank in a day or so.

Nothing should be allowed to drag on as long as this has after essential agreement had been reached. Bad handling and a bad sign.

At the meeting after the signing today Aramesh discussed with more guile than candor the future relations of the U.S. and Iran, stating quite explicitly what the Soviet is offering Iran by way of economic aid "seeking nothing in return." For example, a 500,000 ton-year steel plant, to be repaid in steel. He recognizes that this would involve danger of Soviet infiltration, but if the "West is unwilling to do anything for us and the World Bank keeps saying it is 'uneconomic,' what can we do but accept the Russian offer?"

On the question of accepting Russian aid I was on a spot. But I not only reminded them of what they already knew, that is, the danger of having the Russians use this to support and fan Communist sentiment in Iran but, on the other hand, that India had accepted aid from the Soviet without endangering their internal situation. They were faced with risks, the risk of Russian domination in this way against the risk of too slow economic development resulting in destruction of an Iran as they knew it by the dissatisfaction of their own people. Which was the greater risk is what they had to decide.

FEBRUARY 27, 1961
12 NOON
TEHRAN

I have just come from an hour's audience with the Shah, in his office in the Residence.

His personal warmth toward me, and what we have been trying to do for Iran was never more marked. I was glad Ansari (complete with cutaway coat, high hat, and court manner) was there to see it, for it made a great impression on him.

The Shah looked trimmer, somewhat thinner, moved about more quickly than I can remember. As the discussion got into the realm of the future of American policy toward Iran, he displayed tenseness. As he recognized candidly the possibility of "subversion" by Communists, or more likely pseudo Communists within his own country, the clouds hung over his face.

I sat at his elbow, at his invitation, and he began by asking me what was my impression and feeling about the Khuzistan program to date. I made the biggest point of the results of the yields of the big sugar cane operation for which D&R had been responsible, which look like an average of not less than 100, perhaps 118, tons per hectare, against earlier forecasts of 50 to 75. "This soil is remarkably productive, as these actual results show. It is described by sugar cane experts such as the Brewers of Hawaii, as the best in the world."

I said this meant not only that there was a great opportunity for cane sugar, as in the olden days, but that this soil was like a gold mine that had been lying neglected and unappreciated for many years. And it must be remarkable soil. I gave him some of the salient facts: that from 2,200 hectares (about half of what we had planned, i.e., 4,000 hectares, to plant but couldn't because of money shortage) there will be produced substantially as much actual sugar cane and sugar as we had estimated for the full 4,000 hectares; and instead of requiring one and a half years for maturity, this cane could be harvested in twelve months.

I said the program had been beset by difficulties about money and other competing interests and demands; no developing nation had enough money to provide for all the expanding needs of its people. He interjected that it wasn't a matter of other demands, because Khuzistan had the top priority.

I spoke of the Dez Dam schedule, which is only one month behind, despite floods and fund shortages. But that we were not complaining about the difficulties and extra costs that fund stringencies had produced; these were part of the inherent difficulties of the task.

When I said that I wanted to talk about my strong impression of American lack of understanding of what he and his country are trying to do, his face darkened, his eyes lighted up, and from then through the rest of the hour he sat forward on the edge of his chair, at times with his elbows on his knees. His voice was full of overtones of an almost fierce frustration and anxiety.

I said that I thought that among American "opinion formers" in the papers, magazines, TV, etc., and the "experts" (of whom we have so many) there was less confidence expressed about the future of Iran, more critical, even cynical, comment about his regime, than at any time since I first came to Persia almost exactly five years ago. And the occasion for this, I said, surprised and made me somewhat indignant, but there it was, and I thought he should know it. Because it will be in that atmosphere that the new Kennedy Administration must function.

For example, I thought the setting aside of the elections by order of His Majesty was an act of courage attended by real risks, which would only be done by a sovereign who wanted to improve the system of free elections and do something to instill confidence and respect. But in the American press the critical comment and cynicism mounted, rather than abated, and in a self-righteous tone. It was as if rigged elections (the charge against both the earlier and the most recent one in Iran) was something quite unheard of in American political affairs, whereas we know, e.g., Boss Crump in Memphis, that keeping elections pure is a constant struggle with us, not always successful by any means. As for corruption, also widely assigned by our news media as a reason for lack of faith in his regime, I said I was sure that there was some corruption in Iran (I should have added, for it is true, that D&R has never once had any intimation or hint or solicitation of a bribe from us in all the five years we have been working in Persia). But there is some corruption in the government of New York City, for example, but no one for that reason believes that the Administration of Mayor Wagner is about to fall.

In dealing with the new Kennedy Administration there will be many new faces. Quite a few will be men from academic life, a rather sheltered existence, who will be brilliant but not always practical nor wise. Many of them have yet to learn how tough the world is by going through rugged experiences, as I have, and as he has. (At this he gave a knowing, quiet half-smile.)

But I was confident that there would be a thoroughgoing re-evaluation of American foreign policy, including that vis-à-vis Iran. In the course of that re-examination, our people will see how hard Iran is struggling to achieve an improvement in the state of the country, something that should have the moral support and sympathetic understanding of Americans, particularly as we reflect on the many debts we of the West owe to Persian culture and way of life, all the way from art and architecture to—well, to the rose.

Then he opened up—as I hoped he might. He was extraordinarily fluent and with an excitement in his voice that was positive, rather than complaining.

"America should certainly see what a potential asset to the world of free men Iran presents. America should look at Iran as it *can be* twenty years hence."

He dwelt at length, and quite movingly, on that theme of the future. (There flashed through my mind, as he took this stance, that in our very first presentation of our conclusions about the potentials of development of the Khuzistan, five years ago, I built it all, as Helen had suggested, on a picture of what *could be* in ten years. Much of that prediction is proving to be the reality.)

"This is a country in which twenty years from now forty million people, not twenty as now, could live happily on living standards comparable to that of industrialized European countries. We have the land, we have the water, we have minerals, most especially we have a talented people capable of anything. This nation once ruled India, large parts of the world. That took real ability, real men. The present-day Iranians are of the very same stock. This time they do not want to rule other countries; they want to develop their own."

I broke in to tell him of the Iranian "hot line" crews repairing high-voltage lines while they are "hot" and deadly. These maintenance crews of Iranians D&R had trained in a very brief time to do some of the most exacting and dangerous of all industrial occupations, requiring cooperation within a group, courage, and carefulness. As I told this story, he leaned far forward, smiling in a happy way. To make such an obviously troubled King happy even for a few moments was worth a good deal to me.

I really believe in this man. Whether he can manage the difficult chore that is his destiny, whether he can attract and pick able people is a question for the future. But of this I am sure: he means business.

And he had better mean business if his regime and his country are to get through the hazards of these times, living in the very midst of such birds of prey as the Russians and Nasser.

He continued: "The prospects that Iran will be leader for the free and prosperous races in Asia are greater than in any other country. India will do well if it can keep its additional population from starvation. We have no problem of overpopulation; we are underpopulated instead.

"And look at the strategic importance of Iran in relation to *Africa*. Look how far the Russians have had to extend themselves in going to Egypt and Morocco but Iran is the gateway to Africa, by sea and air."

I suggested that perhaps there were some international regional approaches to economic aid that might be both economically and politically attractive to the countries directly concerned, and would make economic aid from the U.S. and the West take on a new face—meaning that it might have a better chance of achieving support. As an example I cited the development of the port of Bandar Abbas and rail and road connections that would enable products not only of Iran but also of southern Afghanistan and western West Pakistan to reach the sea and the avenues of ocean commerce.

He looked at the floor, seemed to be controlling himself, then said in that clipped way of speaking he has at times: "Yes, we have thought of that, but the World Bank says that Bandar Abbas isn't needed, isn't economical." Obviously he disagreed.

I responded that what the World Bank said initially, before a full presentation and some persistence, wasn't necessarily the final answer, reminding him that they once turned down the Dez Dam loan.

By this time we had been together an hour; twice the great doors of his library had opened to admit a low-bowing secretary with some message about his time, I would guess, and twice he sent him on his way. So I thought we had better be going, though ordinarily it is for him to indicate that the audience is at an end.

Before we left, said I, I wanted to say a word about art, because that might bring some relief from the constant serious burdens a King must bear. He smiled that rueful little smile of his, whereupon I opened the large envelope I had brought with me containing Beatrice's sketch suggestions about murals in the Dez visitors' room and Barney's sketch suggestion for a bas-relief of the Shah, on the canyon walls at the damsite.

We pored over these for a time; he obviously was quite pleased. I reminded him that the creative art of Persia was one of the great debts the West, indeed the East, too, owed to ancient Persia; these quick sketches were intended only as suggestive, so that Persian artists of *today* might, through a competition of some kind, actually provide an artist's bridge between ancient and present-day Persia. He turned to Ansari, who sat silent and resplendent in his striped pants throughout the hour, and said, in English: "I want you to follow this up. The sculpture would be a very big undertaking, but perhaps it can be done."*

He took me to the door, commenting that "I appreciate all that you have done for my country, and I hope the cooperation will continue for many years to come." And with a broad grin he saw me through the door and out into the opulence of the Palace stairway.

MARCH 2, 1961
6:30 P.M.
AHWAZ

Today, a journey to the "reed villages" in the Euphrates marshes due west of here, and my first (and so far as I am concerned, my last) wild boar hunt and my first (and it could be last) dunking in the waters of the Euphrates.

It was a vast, utterly flat expanse of desert through which we first drove, with only here and there a small herd of camels; not even any goats. Yet at one time, so an archaeologist who is here says, there was once a large city here; and we passed over depressions where there had once been canals bringing water from the Karkheh into this area. The canals were only partly silted up. How easy it must have been for invaders or bandits or enemies or even competitors to cut off the supply of water in such canals and leave the people utterly stranded.

Then we came to the river. The houses of the village strung along both banks of the river are made of the tall, sturdy reeds that grow so profusely in these marshes. Later in the year the houses will be moved bodily to islands in these marshlands.

In a cavalcade of four boats we glided through the marshes. The boats, graceful, very narrow, and as skittish as a canoe, had only about an inch of freeboard, so that now and then we would ship water.

Leo Anderson, who loves to hunt, brought his gun, and he had

---

* A competition for Iranian artists was held; the winning designs in colored tile are in place in the public room overlooking the control center of the power-house.

several shots at wild pigs. As we were on our way back, skimming through the narrow channels between the reeds, our bow poler, all excited, pointed to one huge boar. Leo insisted on my taking a shot. I stood up in the frail, strange, two-ended primitive craft and banged away. Leo insisted that I had hit the boar; I doubted it.

I was way up in the bow as I fired. The recoil of the shotgun or my awkward stance rocked the little boat; it began to take in water like mad. Before we quite knew what was happening, the boat filled with water and slowly sank beneath our feet. All I could think of was keeping the gun high over my head out of the water, as I went in up to my armpits, the boat settling beneath our feet in the mud of the marsh. The boatmen began emptying the boat by splashing it out with their garments. I transferred to another boat. As I poured water out of my shoes it suddenly occurred to me how funny this was, and I started to roar and whoop with laughter. This set up laughter, first by our Arab "crew," then the laughter spread to the three other boats' crews, and we had a merry time. When we got back to the village from which we had set out our boatmen shouted the news of the inundation to the villagers who lined the bank. Again we all had a laugh. As I got out of my dripping shirt into a dry one (I had to wear the sopping pants, etc., as we had nothing for me to get into) I was surrounded by an entire village of grinning, laughing people, men, women, and kids.

We had seven and a half hours of very rough jeeping, two and a half hours in the sun (I am very red), and no lunch. Yet I feel refreshed, for every other thought was set aside during this fascinating trip into the world of people who live almost exactly as people lived in those marshes a thousand years or more ago.

MARCH 4, 1961
7:30 A.M.
ANDIMESHK, IRAN

The "accommodations" of this D&R resthouse are hardly those of the Plaza. There is a bathroom, since I am the "boss-man," but the water for my toothbrush I must pour out of a green metal teapot, since the tap water isn't "safe." But this little D&R resthouse (made out of an old Persian house) is a center of luxury and comfort compared to the way it was three years ago when we first came. A look out the back window makes one realize how well off one is: people here still live in the midst of squalor and sadness and mighty little in the way of food or clothing. Last night taking a walk down the "main street" I saw a row of dark bundles on a terrace before a building: men wrapped up to sleep for the night. And it was cold.

AHWAZ (GHOLESTAN)

As I swung over the canyon of the Dez on a rickety platform suspended from the overhead cable, the Dez canyon took on a new splendor, a sense of the everlasting, and of the majesty of man who undertakes to master this behemoth beside which he seems like an ant.

Whether this voyage in mid-air, almost on a broomstick (and not a very stable one) should be classified as "foolhardy" or a part of my job I should not miss, it is too late now to say, except that I felt this was something I *had* to do. The trip was accomplished with only slight concern: when the damn platform first tipped at a crazy angle in mid-air, 600 feet above the canyon bed.

Half of one of the planks of the platform had broken, leaving a hole too big for comfort. We seemed to be up there by levitation and faith.

When Chief Engineer Williams told me that Voorduin and Clapp had refused to cross on the cable, I knew that even though there were considerable objections raised (it was getting late, it wasn't safe, the operator was off duty, etc.) I *was* going to make that trip.

The sight of the canyon from the little rickety platform hung way up by a cable was an unbelievable one, beautiful and moving beyond expression. The pitting of the walls of the canyon looked like cuneiform writing. The men hundreds of feet below, too small to make one believe that anything so diminutive would drive scores of kilometers of tunnels through those walls to bring in great machines that could handle that swift-rushing ribbon of water and foam below.

From the cableway I could see snow on the tips of the mountains to the south; the slopes were greener than I have ever seen them, because of the unusual rains. On the southern slopes the yellow and lavender flowers were breaking out of what seemed solid rock; tiny delicate little ferns were making their way to the sun, for their short period of growth before the blistering summer sun hits them.

Yesterday we saw our handiwork: what was so recently a bleak desert now green and waving with sugar cane (eight square miles of it, flourishing, the *first time for many centuries*) and such cane: twelve feet and more high, some of the best in the world.

And today the Dez Dam, steadily rising.

The reflection from these two happy days was much the same: how wonderful it is to be able to see one's ideas and words take root and become real things, things as real as miles of sugar cane, a great factory shiny and eager to go, a great dam rising where before was emptiness like a crater of the moon.

This is the deep satisfaction I crave: not reports and books and writing and rhetoric (important as they are, and much as I like to create them) but to see things actually happen as a result of one's ideas. That is a flowering from one's own, one's very own inmost seed.

MARCH 6, 1961
TEHRAN

Back to Tehran after midnight last night, after a fourteen-hour day of intense activity, with not one moment to draw my breath—nor any inclination to do so!

A highlight, related to the meaning of my "function": a talk to our D&R senior staff directed to perhaps twenty to twenty-five "overseas" men, about five British or Dutch, the balance Americans. Of these about a quarter were new since last year.

The people of our D&R organization in Ahwaz are worried and upset. These men are worried sick about things *at a distance,* in accordance with a formula I have seen enacted over the years, i.e., they are worried about the Persian regime, about D&R relations with Plan Organization in Tehran, about D&R financial problems. Yet the problems that to us in Tehran and New York seem almost insurmountable they here tackle and lick: how to grow terrific sugar cane despite frost; how to build a dam in a tricky and nightmarish canyon; how to get people to use and pay for electricity who have never even had kerosene lamps—these problems these men here take in their stride.

The farther you get from the center of troubles the worse they seem.

It is a curious commentary on human nature.

The causes of this state of affairs are various. Some are inherent in overseas life for people without experience in being completely out of their home environment; most, apparently, was due to brooding over "uncertainty" about the continuity of the work because the contract with Plan Organization had not been signed, the payments to D&R were behind by about thirty days, the World Bank loan payments had been held up pending approval of conditions that they had fixed; the student "demonstrations" in Tehran—the whole complex of fact, gossip, rumor and worry about someone else's responsibilities that prevent people from concentrating on their own part of the job.

So I began my talk with some of the facts about our own work, facts that are reassuring unless one is simply determined to worry no matter what the facts are.

I reminded them that the crisis through which D&R had just gone was not nearly as severe as earlier ones: the World Bank had for months turned down the Dez loan, yet it came through after long and persistent effort; that the sugar program was in such bad shape for funds that we had made plans for liquidating it entirely and yet there were now eight square miles of 12-foot cane ready for this fall's harvest; that the World Bank experts' predictions were that our electricity use program was bound to fail because people in Iran were not in the habit of paying their bills; the gloomy view that favoritism and corruption were a "necessary" part of doing things in Iran; that in Iran "nothing can get done and no one expects that it will." But the fact is that *none* of these things were true or had happened.

But the heaviest shafts I threw dealt more with an outlook on life in these days than with the specifics of our "program."

My object was to provide that old cliché known as "perspective." I thought the best way to do this was to take them away from Khuzistan or even Iran, to describe the state of the world today, a world in sudden and violent change, with unrest or restlessness everywhere, turbulent, filled with tensions and anxieties. "If anyone thinks," I said, "there is someplace in the world, including the U.S., where he can crawl into a cave and escape the uncertainties of life in these days, let him forget it; there is no place to hide. If any one of you here wants a stable, sure, secure life, in which you can predict just what will happen to you, all I can say is that you were born at the wrong time; there will be no such world of serenity and certainty and predictability within your lifetime or mine; and with great weapons being forged almost beyond imagining in their destructiveness, it may be one hundred years before the human race can live without the risk of sudden catastrophe hanging over our collective human heads.

"As for student unrest and protest and demonstrations, and questions about the viability of this regime or that outside the U.S. and Britain, this very thing is true in most places in the world. Africa, where I am soon to go, is an obvious illustration; South America is another, and of course, all of Asia is another.

"This is the way it is. Don't fool yourselves. If you can't live with this reality, whether in Iran or anywhere else, you will have a difficult time wherever you are.

"But I happen to believe in the creativeness of conflict; that it is out of periods such as this, full of tension and change and the clash of widely differing philosophies and ideas, that great things happen. I am grateful that I have the chance to live in such a period. I believe this is a lot more fun, that one can be much more *alive* in every sense at such a time than in a more serene and sure and therefore uneventful time.

Each man for himself about this, whether to love to be alive in such a time or hate it; but this is the way it is and those of us who enjoy it are the fortunate ones; we are the realists."

About this time the faces of some of my shocked technical men in this group began to lose that glazed look and several began to light up and to nod their heads in agreement.

MARCH 10, 1961
FRIDAY, 10 P.M.
BEIRUT

The Mediterranean is roaring and pounding just beyond our window; a sudden blow that came up within an hour.

What is it I am searching for? The moment I'm not active, physically, the sense of looking for something I don't have comes over me; not a pleasant or happy sensation; a feeling of being lost emotionally. Will I ever be able to *do* something about it? Is this just one of the inevitable consequences of being a questing sort of person?

MARCH 11, 1961
SATURDAY, 5:30 A.M.
BEIRUT

Off for Paris at 7:45 this morning, first leg on the trip to West Africa. I'm more than ready to start for home instead.

A man's education begins at his birth and continues throughout his life. But what is it he is educated *about*?

The whole unrolling tape on which are recorded what he sees and feels and understands and finds perplexing—these things are part of his education: how people behave, and why; about the beauty of the night and the inner warmth that spreads through him when he sees, say, the first dogwood of spring; about impulses within him and in others, good ones, kind and considerate, evil ones, suspicious and mean.

MARCH 12, 1961
PARIS

"Springtime in Paris": what a hackneyed piece of sentimentality this phrase has become. But today the expression became reality for me. The sun came warm, the haze lifted. Along the Seine the chestnut trees passed a miracle, for you could almost see the opening of the upside-down bunches of tiny green grapes—for this is what the chestnut bud appeared to be today. The chestnut leaves began to unfold their lupine-like, carefully folded packages of pale green. Forsythia was so far along that the leaves began to compete with the gold of the blossoms, almost past their prime.

But mostly it was springtime inside of me. And where else except within a human being's heart and spirit is there spring, a sense of renewal, of new beginning?

Tonight at about midnight we start on the long air trek to West Africa, almost twelve hours of flying across France, and then the Sahara, the rain forest, and the jungle, to Abidjan where the next phase of the working side of this thus far successful trip begins.

Helen became exhausted yesterday—my fault, for I was so eager to have her see the little galleries of modern painting, the Sorbonne students, the whole colorful life of this spirited, lively part of Paris that I didn't notice how tired she was. And then laryngitis grasped her by the throat. But by staying quiet today (except for an hour at the Louvre, where we saw the Susa exhibits) she seems much better and we're going ahead with the plan for the night flight.

How does one take care of one's health on such expeditions as this one, where each night we move from one bed to yet a different one, flying at all hours, work seven-day weeks, eat sometimes strange food, breathe strange dust, live outside the comfortable and familiar surroundings of home and office?

"Well" (as President Kennedy would say at a press conference), it takes some doing. I keep up my calisthenics, morning and night, and this seems to improve my well-being and certainly my morale. The big change in technique has been the result of Dr. Atchley's "instructions": to *schedule* breaks along the way, schedule them just as one would put a flight or a conference on a schedule. This doesn't mean that I become inert and "rest" during these breaks; actually, in Spain and then again in Lebanon, we scurried about a lot: two whole days of sightseeing in Lebanon, for example. But it breaks up one reason for tension and fatigue. And fatigue, with me, seems to be mostly a matter of emotional and not physical expenditure.

MARCH 13, 1961
PARIS, ORLY AIRPORT

I have never, I think, been a member of so cosmopolitan and variegated a planeload as is assembling aboard this Boeing, headed for Dakar, Abidjan, and connecting thence to Brazzaville in the French Congo.

Two young women with tiny new babies, and all the paraphernalia of baby travel: cribs, bottles, blankets. One of these was having such a time that Helen and I carried the crib for her. Where are they going, these white women and children, into an Africa that is no longer theirs? And a considerable number, in first class, of men of dark skin, some of them definitely not "Africans," i.e., having the voice and laugh of Americans. A big delegation came to see some dignitaries off; my guess is that two of them, looking like Malayans, complete with the telltale black Homburg required by "diplomacy" (what rot!) are UN people, headed for the troubled Congo, as are several others on the flight.

The flight has been altered for a stop at Roberts Field, near Monrovia, Liberia. There is an "Excellency" aboard; I would guess he is President Tubman, of Liberia, the U.S.'s only remaining colony; rather a colony of American rubber companies.

At Dakar, where we were for an hour, there was an array of a Senegalese guard of honor; even in the dark these crimson uniforms and high caps, the men with long drawn sabers, were impressive, until you looked at some of the boys more closely; the "guards" looked mighty sleepy.

MARCH 14, 1961
D&R OFFICES, ABIDJAN
REPUBLIC OF THE IVORY COAST

My good luck in "collecting" experience has held on this part of our trip. The plane on which we arrived from Paris brought the President of this country, Dr. Felix Houphouet-Boigny and his party from the meetings that have been going on in Paris about French economic aid to the former French West African "colonies," now independent states. This meant that there was a vivid turnout at the airport. A cermonial band, dressed in a combination of gay Shriner costumes, French Empire-style cockades, and a Saturday night meeting of the Sons-and-Daughters-of-I-Will-Arise in Harlem. Plus a band of drummers in yellow robes, beating frantically, and a large mass of women in gay draperies dancing a restrained kind of shuffle.

The American Ambassador suggested I call at 11:30; I thought of it as a "courtesy call." When he brought us into his little office (the Embassy has only recently been established, of course), sitting with his chair tilted back against the wall was a very tired-looking "Soapy" Mennen Williams, now Assistant Secretary for African Affairs. He has been going through Africa now for a month, and this is about the end of his "tour." He asked about our company and then volunteered an opinion about the need for the kind of service we try to supply.

"Back home I'm not exactly considered a pal toward private business, but what these countries need most are managerial skills, and someone to help them to select and put together *private* activities; well, that isn't what ICA—the once Point IV—is qualified to do. What these countries really need is someone to advise them who can stand between ICA—which has to represent the interests of the U.S.—and their own country."

I didn't get what he was driving at at first. So when he asked me what other countries we operated in, I told him, but went on to add that we had never done any work for the U.S. Government foreign aid agencies such as ICA, but might consider it now that the American point of view appeared to be changing to one that identified itself more fully with the recipient countries.

When I described the sort of thing we were doing in Iran, such as the use of modern irrigation systems to change landlord-tenant relations, he brightened up, the haggard, almost exhausted, look left his face, his tired voice lifted. Said that it was knowing how to combine government with private effort that was most needed.

When I told him I was going on to Nigeria next week, he said, "Nigeria is a place the U.S. ought to pour a lot into. They *think* development."

People in the U.S. could see, in a general way, why Latin America was important to them, being in the same New World. But I wondered if the same sense of its being important to them would apply to Africa, where it was the French and British who had been most active and the U.S. rather remote.

He agreed it wouldn't be easy, but "I think Chester Bowles is right, that here again the people are ahead of their leaders. After all, 10 percent of Americans are descendants of Africans, and that 10 percent is increasingly interested in Africa. African development and history, too, give these black Americans a new sense of prestige and of belonging."

I got a good impression of Williams; he will work hard, will welcome fresh views and ideas, though how well he will understand the "operational mind" I don't know.

On the not-so-good side—there *always* is one—is the absence of Minister Saller. Saller, a French civil servant though a native of Martinique and not really an Ivorian, apparently runs the economic show here; but he is almost always away somewhere (usually Paris, I gather). He has not returned from the important negotiations between France and the Entente of West Africa. This is a major trouble, for he will decide about the program we have outlined for mineral investigation.

I visited today with two African officials, in this still French-run capital. One was the Minister of State. Heavy gold-rimmed glasses against a burnished black skin, an earnest and pleasant man (I always find it strange to see French gesticulations as these Africans talk). He took my visit more seriously than I had intended, spoke of the problems the African states have in keeping a "barrage" against Communism, not because Africa is fertile soil for Communism but because of their great need. America should help, and there is little time, etc.

As we left, we asked him to see if we could see another African, Delforsee, Chairman of the Social and Economic Council, a strictly paper organization at this stage. No, he is busy with a delegation from the Government of Poland. Later we saw four "burly" (I'm reading too many spy thrillers) guys leaving that office, the Communist Poles. Tom Mead remarked with a grin: "We hear all about the horrors of Communism and how the Ivorians are fighting against them, and then run into a delegation from Poland."

The Minister made the first reference to Chinese Communists I have heard out here. He said: "If the Chinese continue their move into Africa, where there is plenty of land and other things the Chinese covet, in ten years there won't be any Africans left in Africa."

I don't set this down as representing wisdom; it just struck me because the idea of a serious threat to Africa by the Chinese seems so outlandish; and yet they are very active in neighboring Mali (formerly the French Sudan) which has great resources, e.g., of manganese.

MARCH 18, 1961
ABIDJAN

I have been going through a spasm of "righteous indignation."

The French middle class sit on top of all the comfortable things around this capital city. The beautiful food in the wonderful restaurants: sea urchins and oysters and baba au rhum flown daily from Paris. The big apartments. The banks, the high government posts, the cars, the art books in the beautiful bookstores—you name it, the French have it here.

And the Ivorians have what? A good many of them, as outside our door here, sleep all night stretched out on a piece of paper on the pavement; they sit in the "native" market haggling over a piece of smelly fish. They are the dark and beautiful creatures who serve the food in the fancy restaurants, under the irritable eyes and voices of the French proprietors; they haul the loads and supply the towels at the beach club where we were this afternoon.

Racial segregation? Not a bit. At the Park Hotel where we had our dinner last evening there was a beautiful young Ivorian girl, a receptionist at the American Embassy with a middle-aged Frenchman as her escort. No, it is not exclusion. It is just that all—or most—of the benefits are in the hands of the French, who built this city with their money and their brains and enterprise until it is quite a fine city indeed. But it does give me an acute case of indignation. There is "another side." But at the moment I'm not in a mood to give it much weight.

This is France, middle-class France. The handsome black figures are on the outside looking in. Except in the villages and on the tawny beach by the pounding surf. There *they* are the people. I watched fourteen dark figures launch a long, ceremonial canoe into this towering, hungry surf this afternoon, and plunge the narrow dugout into the Gulf of Guinea. Fourteen shoulders, fourteen arms dug into the sea as one man, as they bore that little sliver of craft into the clefts between the huge waves. And in the villages we visited yesterday—a great day it was for me too—they have learned to live with their environment, and live well; and that might be called a great educational achievement, just that.

For a day, yesterday, I was out of the stuffiness of Abidjan, this artificial French island, disguised so it is sometimes difficult to realize that it is a part of Africa.

Tom Mead, happy and excited to be back among Africans again, was like a schoolboy the first day of vacation. We drove a couple of hundred miles. on wonderful, wide, and well-built roads (thanks to the French!) winding through the grandeur of the forest. At Aboisso we stopped to "pay our respects" to the Commandant, that is, the Governor of the province. A very black, keen, young-looking man, Ivorian of course, very bright and friendly eyes. We told him we were on our way to see the newish hydro dam at Ayame, way back in the forest. His comment was: "Don't fail to see the new village we built for the people who were forced to leave their land because of the backwater of the dam."

So I commented: "People are more important than dams"—a TVA dictum, and one he and his dark associate seemed to savor.

Visited the dam about noon—a medium-sized concrete gravity and earth fill, total capacity about 30,000 kw; only one of the two generators now being required. When we arrived the only person on duty was an intelligent young African, at the power-control board. The French technicians, quite a group, some of them students, were at the canteen having an apéritif. After lunch, with the engineer in charge, a Frenchman, we returned to the power station; again the only man around the place was a tall, friendly, handsome Ivorian.

Said the homesick French engineer: "We can't trust the Africans with so complicated a thing as a dam and powerhouse; they must always have someone watching over them."

Nuts.

While he was saying this he and his quite beautiful bride of three months (from Nancy in Lorraine) were giving us an elaborate and delicious luncheon, served with elegance in the heart of the forest. Down in the powerhouse the men "who couldn't be trusted" and had to be "watched every minute" were tending to the production of electricity. A sense of indispensability and superiority is an essential of being a good colonialist.

But how lonely this French couple seemed, the girl especially. While we were lunching there came on a furious deluge; he said sadly, "In a week the rains begin, and then it will be raining like this almost all the time for weeks." She looked as if she might cry. "And no one to talk to," she said. Three months married, I would have supposed there wouldn't be a problem of anyone to talk to, but I suppose that is a romantic notion.

On the way back we drove through miles and miles of sand roads. These are a glowing reddish ribbon, made more red by the surrounding towering green. A lovely sight.

We went through a few settlements; finally stopped for a visit at a little village. Tom knows this sort of thing perfectly, from his great success as a district commissioner in Ghana. Tom is so naturally friendly, and the people were utterly warm and cordial and full of laughter and curiosity. It was *we*, white visitors, of course, who were the strange objects, not they.

The Chief sent word through one of his Elders that he would be pleased to have us stop and drink a potion and visit awhile. So we gathered under a reed awning for this little ceremony.

The Chief turned out to be a very cross-eyed, very old man; his sign of office wasn't a fancy headdress but a battered old cloth *cap*. But we drank beer together; Tom passed around cigarettes; we laughed and visited. I made noises for the amusement of the little naked kids who popped out from around their parents in the circle of dark bodies that surrounded us. It was very pleasant and relaxed, and we got a send-off that was warming. I'm sure that at first they thought we must be tax collectors or some kind of officials and were cagey; when it was clear we just wanted to visit, things warmed up and everyone had a good time. I invited them to a return visit in "my village," and since this presents some difficulties, Tom countered by giving them his address for a visit in Abidjan.

A letter of great interest from Beatrice, telling of her initial reactions to a reading of some of the journals. It has meant a great deal to me, on this long safari, to have letters from her: a lively, spirited, original personality; I'm very proud of her.

MARCH 20, 1961
ABIDJAN

Last evening about 8:30 Helen became acutely nauseated. I had no thermometer, but feeling her pulse it was evident she had a fever.

I was frantic. Tom Mead has no phone, I couldn't speak French, so I couldn't call a doctor. I went out into the dark streets about midnight, located a "medical clinic" building, and began ringing doorbells. This brought a sleepy-looking fellow on to a balcony, but he had no English. I persisted trying to make him understand; soon a man in night clothes showed up on an adjoining balcony and English never sounded better. He was a doctor, and came right over in his pajamas. Found no evidence of pneumonia, but he said, "You are not fit to travel; you cannot go to Lagos tomorrow morning."

I haven't been out of my clothes all night, reading much of the time, resting on a couch alongside Helen, where I could keep an eye on her. At 3 A.M. I found her sitting bolt upright, against the wall, saying, "I feel fine; I can go tomorrow, otherwise all the plans will be unsettled."

Of course I told her, "Plans be damned; there is only one question and that is how to get you well, and then to get on home."

For a couple of anxious hours I realized as acutely as I'm capable of realizing anything how closely our lives are entwined, how much it means to me that she should not be unhappy, much less in some danger. It was a feeling that ran all through my limbs, a combination of tenderness, pity, and just plain fright.

ACCRA, GHANA, AIRPORT
ABOUT TO TAKE OFF FOR LAGOS
4 P.M.

Quite a bad night for Helen, poor darling. And for me. This morning the doctor came in, found her nausea over, blood pressure O.K. etc., and said she could go. But it has been an ordeal, she as weak as a kitten, with no food and those hours of spasms of vomiting, and unbelievable heat, the long wait at the airport in Abidjan; again, a long wait here in Accra. But let's hope that we shall be in Lagos, in a hotel, in another three hours, say, and that much farther on the way.

Helen has been plucky and uncomplaining, but of course she looks bad, must feel terrible. I'm worried about her, but there is nothing to be done but see this through.

MARCH 22, 1961
FEDERAL PALACE HOTEL
LAGOS, NIGERIA

Just talked to Washington by phone; a call from Sargent Shriver, the President's brother-in-law, who is organizing the Peace Corps. A carefully formulated statement: the President, in view of my extensive experience in such matters, etc., etc., wishes me to serve as one of three vice-chairmen of the National Advisory Council of the Peace Corps. Bill Douglas is to be Honorary Chairman, Ellsworth Bunker, Chairman, the other "vice" are Mrs. Mary Bunting and Thomas Watson of IBM. Since it is not full time and yet is intended to help shape the program (a great idea, but it could run an awful cropper) I said I would be glad to serve.

An extremely interesting time last night; our host Joel Bernstein, head of the ICA Mission here, a levelheaded and sensible man. The guests mostly Americans, economists and planners attached to the Ministries.

Only two Nigerians, and I must say they were about the ablest men there; they had to listen while they were told how Nigerians think, what they should eat, etc., by an Indian, Dr. P. S. Narayan Prasad (economic development advisor to the Prime Minister, loaned to Nigeria by the World Bank), and three theoreticians from the University of Michigan and the Ford Foundation.

They are men of great good will and purity of motive. But is there any unconscious arrogance as great as that of an "educated" man who doesn't understand anything but the neat logic and symbols of his trade? And of all such, economists can be the worst, the kind who have had no experience with reality, whose knowledge is all in their tabulations. When they go "into the field" they only see what they want to see that will support conclusions they had reached before they saw a Nigerian village or villager.

Three economists the Ford Foundation is paying for are preparing a detailed five-year development plan for Nigeria, this bouncy land of forty million people, almost every villager having had more experience in *living with his environment* than the three of them put together.

Nigerians, like most Americans, are pragmatists, guided by experience, inclined to be "untidy" (in a special sense in which I like to use that term, i.e., taking things as they come, having one thing lead to another, etc.).

After this dose of theoreticians it was refreshing to call on two

remarkable and contrasting figures. Nigerian businessmen: Chief Ade-
bayo Doherty, a lively extravert, a black lion cub at sixty, full of laughter,
confidence, forthrightness—a real "character" who seemed American
to me. He is a "wheeler-dealer," an entrepreneur organizing small groups
and taking on all kinds of business: cement, "cinema," department
store, you name it, he's in it.

The other, by contrast, was a reserved, distinguished-looking, highly
intelligent and responsible man, Sir Odumegwu Ojukwu, O.B.E., described by Lazard of London as probably the most powerful businessman
in Nigeria, Chairman of the Nigerian Produce Marketing Co., of several
banks, etc.

We called on Chief Doherty at his home, which is also probably
his place of business. The parlor was ornate, with very pink antimacas-
sars on the overstuffed chairs, a fancy sideboard (as we would call
it in Indiana) with gold-leafed legs and a gold-leafed mirror over it.
A television set, artificial roses, and snapshots stuck everywhere on
everything; a copy of his daughter's diploma from the Pitman Business
College in London. The room was not African; more what I would suppose a prosperous Harlem insurance man might have had twenty years
ago.

Before we saw him he was with a group of Nigerians in an adjoining room. Everyone talking *at once* in loud but laughing, friendly,
argumentative voices. His house is at a busy intersection of a commercial
area of African houses—not the new snazzy ones now being built. The
"background noise" in the street was terrific, with that vitality and
hubbub that is characteristic of this vital, noisy city.

We had a good time with him. Americans? Well, Nigerians preferred to do business with the English: "We know their tricks and they
know ours; when they say something, we know exactly what they mean
and they know what *we* mean. But Americans; well, we think they are
here to exploit things and get out. But I think that's changing somewhat,
changing a bit. No, I have never been to America; maybe I'll go someday."

When Mead reached for his cigarettes, the Chief rared up—"Oh,
no, smoke my cigarettes, wait a minute." He left the room at a half
run (I saw later that he never moved except at this half trot) and
came back with some fine English cigarettes for Tom; the Chief himself
doesn't smoke any more. "This lung cancer thing," he said.

He didn't think that our business friends would have much to
interest them here because Nigerians don't invest large sums, just
interested in small business, and don't invest ordinarily through corporations, but through groups of friends who get together. "Big investments: that is through the Government, and D&R might be able to be

very helpful in some of those things. But all that big stuff is so technical; I can't understand it, it makes my head tired. I am more interested in business I can understand."

The contrast with Ojukwu could hardly have been greater if he had been a professor of philosophy and the other guy a denizen of the forest. Received us like an English banker (though he is very black) in the half dark of a most discreet office. But so cordial, handsome in his over six feet of height and beautifully tailored clothes, sitting behind the inevitable desk with buttons to call his minions quietly (Chief Doherty would do as Franklin Roosevelt used to: throw back his head and yell for whomever he wanted). He was very explicit: just what did we do and how did we go about it? We met a very talented man.

MARCH 24, 1961
AT A RESTHOUSE JUST OUTSIDE IBADAN
NIGERIA

A long rough and *very* hot dry day, driving most of the time. First to the largest Negro city in the world (500,000), Ibadan, in the Western Region. Then after meetings and lunch with the Chief Secretary, head of the region's Civil Service, Chief Adebo, to the town of Ife, through many interesting but (to my eyes) chaotic villages.

In Ife are the famous Benin bronze heads, origin not certainly known but extraordinarily beautiful. But what I found more interesting was to *walk*—*not* ride—through the streets, greeting people with our one Yoruba word. Almost everyone is selling someone something, whole families under the reed shades of the street with something to sell. I suspect this is partly economic, but mostly a social activity. When I first appeared, strolling along the street, one of the million little naked boys pointed at me, his eyes popping out, and said a word. The young man from the Ministry, a very refeened civil servant, laughed; I had to insist hard before he told me what the boy said, "Oh, look, a *white* man!"

MARCH 25, 1961
LAGOS

Drove back from Ibadan late last night, getting here at 1:30 A.M. Didn't look in on Helen lest I disturb her. But this morning I found she had been very sick beginning at four yesterday afternoon, with chills and fever. Got hold of Dr. Davenport, a young, inexperienced woman doctor; she said congestion in the lower lungs, pushing up her heart rate. God knows what this means: a form of pneumonia, I fear.

I am sick with anxiety for her. Of course we can't take the plane this afternoon, nor probably the one Sunday. So we are here for a while; the important thing, the desperately important thing, is that she takes the right turn in this illness.

Helen is utterly miserable; for the *only* time I can now remember, she's depressed. When I tried to divert her by telling about the "brain trust" TV program I heard in Ibadan last night, she finally made it clear she couldn't manage being cheerful. "It is just too much trouble," she said, turning her back on me and inviting me to leave—which I can well understand.

MARCH 27, 1961
LAGOS

The acute stage of Helen's illness seems abated; but she's almost completely prostrated, the curse of post-flu, as I myself know so well. When she will be physically able to undertake the long journey home is very much in doubt. I am not a good "waiter" in any case, and this would hardly be the place to wait if I were.

This is accounted "the worst time of year in West Africa" because it is so very humid. But the rains are due, and *that* is said to be even worse, steady rain hour after hour. The first rain has just begun.

MARCH 28, 1961
LAGOS

This morning I had our driver take me into the open market. Food being cooked in kettles, for sale, along the edge of the main open sewer. I nudged my way through the narrowest aisles of these tiny stalls. Women with these cute bumps of babies looped to their backs, so I passed along between babies, looking up at you with their big eyes, or dead asleep, their heads fallen back like wilted flowers. A great chaotic hubbub. The heads of bullocks, brains cut out, horns still "in place," all over the stalls in the meat section. And a gamey stench over all, a mixture of rotted food, "fecal material," and all the rest.

APRIL 1, 1961
LAGOS

From my window I can see the never-ceasing flow of Nigerian women, papooses snuggled against their backs, walking under head loads, occasionally with a walking stick. The lagoon is very quiet, the sky overcast. The rainy season is about upon us.

Pleasant visits with Ham Fish Armstrong of *Foreign Affairs* magazine and his sprightly slender, young wife. It has been a godsend to have them to talk to, now and then, and once we went to the beach for an afternoon of sun bathing and talk. The prodigious surf is too dangerous for swimming.

A visit with the Minister of Mines and Power, Maitama Sule, an intense, alert, diminutive man of about forty. Dressed in a white robe, a nightgown kind of garment; his features were rather delicate. And of course speaking in as Oxford a brogue as any don.

I told him something about myself, and about D&R. He was very clear and precise: The future of the country is very closely tied to the proposed Kainji Dam on the Niger. An abundance of cheap electricity was essential if Nigeria (which now has high power costs) was to make her place as an industrialized nation competing with other nations. A study of the Niger has been made, and will be submitted soon.

I was amused when he said he was probably going to New York. He was for a time on the UN Nigerian delegation. Like most of the Ministers throughout West Africa, so far as I can see, they prefer to be somewhere else than West Africa.

And now I'm back at the hotel, waiting for the "specialist" I insisted on having, a Dr. Skinner. The question we want enlightenment on is *when* and by what *means* Helen can *safely* travel. She seems to have gone through the acute stages of this miserable thing. Poor girl, she is very low in her mind, bored beyond words and worried that she's upsetting my plans. "The way I feel now," she said this morning, "I'm perfectly content to settle down and stay at home." But *of course* this is a temporary feeling.

APRIL 2, 1961
EASTER
LAGOS

The second visit of Dr. Skinner brought encouraging news. The relief of not having a definitely *negative* prognosis was such that I felt all caved in and a thousand years old. Helen sat up in a chair fifteen minutes at a time, for the first time in ten days.

Dr. Skinner is something new to me. He is one of the few "European" specialists left here; the others were worked to death and so is he. He is perhaps forty-two or so, stocky, has a toothy grin and long, horse-shaped face. He came yesterday in a sticky costume of short sleeves and pants that I thought were going to fall down. This morning our cardiologist was in brown khaki shorts. His bedside manner isn't exactly Harkness Pavilion. "Now let me see your belly, mother," was one of his choicest. I was glad to see that all his hup-hup amused Helen; she gave me a big wink as he hauled the sheet off her to poke, etc.

APRIL 3, 1961
LAGOS

I have been churning and boiling over emotionally, about my country and the posture we present to the newer countries. That "posture" is one of bending over, with a sign on our bottoms which reads, "Please do me the honor of kicking me—here." Then, in the fine print, we Americans say: "Be assured I will not kick back, nor resent being kicked, nor will I say anything that indicates why *you* need to be kicked now and then. My purpose is to prove that I am your friend."

Our stale, outdated type of idealism cherishes this "kick-me" viewpoint. Why the hell should we Americans feel it is up to us to lean over frontwards and be kicked, verbally, for being *what they want to be*? We are far from poor (which is what these countries don't want to be either); we are militarily strong (which is just what these countries want for themselves). We are well organized for production and education (which is what they also want). We can produce more food than the world has ever seen before, in a world that is half hungry, but why should we be defensive about that? We do not prey on our poor, as the *native* rich do on theirs in these countries. And, most important of all, we in America have a social objective never before attempted on such a scale: providing the opportunity for the exceptional person to move to that level of economic or educational advancement for which he is qualified.

Well, enough of this spluttering.

I think the time is more than ripe for Americans to get up from that bottoms-up posture, where we can talk back firmly, even belligerently if need be, certainly in a forthright way. We will lose our own self-respect if we continue this brand of apologetic pseudo idealism. It is just as much an obligation of friendship that the peoples of the underdeveloped countries—India, for example—show some understanding and admiration for American achievements of a social and cultural kind as it is for us to try to *understand them.*

As things now stand, the nations who have contributed the most toward a humane and decently organized society, the U.S., Britain, and France, are the objects of derision and apology by some of our own liberals and intellectuals because we have succeeded so well!

If this is the net result of liberalism, then it is a phony.

NOON

This is a holiday—the day following Easter. Since early morning I have seen going by my window an unbroken stream of people in gaily colored robes, mostly walking alone, a few on bicycles, in family groups or alone, heading for the nearby Bight of Benin, which this particular part of the coast of the Gulf of Guinea is called.

7:30 P.M.

That river of people kept right on flowing, swelling in size as the afternoon went on. Out of this extraordinary happy hegira of tens of thousands of very black heads came one of the most heart-warming, friendly experiences of my life.

At about 2:30 I decided I would join this colorful procession.

Within an hour I had seen what must have been 50,000 people thoroughly enjoying themselves in the most charming and childlike way. People entertaining themselves just by being together.

As I stood in the midst of this molten lava of ebbing and flowing people I was literally overwhelmed. Such gaiety, good humor, utter lack of sophistication—or maturity either, for that matter.

A sober-looking man of about my age spoke to me. He wore a yellow cap and a plain toga. Rather searching eyes. We got to talking: about how it came that there were so many people (a four-day holiday period); where they came from (from Lagos, on foot, but also from as far as Ibadan, his home town); his business—a carpenter, working for himself.

As we were talking, standing in this swarming, rolling tide of people, the crowd in front of us suddenly began to run, scatter, from a center. I wondered what I might be in for. My new friend took my hand in his as you would a child's, and said, "There's no harm," and led me to a nearby sand eminence. The scattering had been caused by a group called "The Cowboys," young men, a few women, dressed in a Nigerian cum American movie version of cowboys. When they had made a space on the sand, they began tromping in a circle, a monotonous kind of trudge, rather than the rhythmic body-swinging dances that were going on, impromptu, at other places. But all this Western cowboy stuff was accompanied by the singing of a native song, led by the "captain," a big fellow in a black sombrero, pulling a toy six-shooter out of a holster such as kids get at Christmas. This performance fascinated the circle of black heads; then they broke into a routine of yelling and hitting each other with whips, painlessly, but it was evident that this, too, was considered part of the American cowboy way.

My friend and I exchanged names, his being W. A. Osihilalu, which he wrote out for me on a scrap of paper we found in the litter on the beach. He insisted on taking me around to see all the sights, and stopping or being stopped by his friends and introducing his friend "from America."

When I thought it was time to come back he said he would accompany me, he wanted to greet my wife. He collected his bicycle, and we walked the quarter mile back to the hotel. The river of people coming to the "picnic" had increased, if anything.

His forthrightness was like a child's, with no sophistication. "I could see you were a good man. I could see we were going to be natural friends. All of us are children of God, isn't that right? Your wife will be well; you must have faith. I want to come back to see you again. You will promise to write to me when you get back to America?" Which I shall.

Now night has fallen. The stream has become a rivulet; they are trudging homeward.

"Everyone is here having a good time because it's Easter," my friend Osihilalu said.

One of the enchanting and also at times highly entertaining sights about this marble palace of a modern hotel is the Nigerian families who foregathered here during the Easter holiday season. Almost all in their native dress. For men this is a voluminous toga, sometimes in bright browns or gray blues, topped often with a beautifully embroidered caplike head covering. Some of the men tilted these caps far over to one side, to give an individual slant to them, the way a salty sailor will make something distinctive of his little round white hat. The women, also in gay swathings like a floppy sari, others as if they were trying to carry everything in the way of textiles they own, a huge wad around already ample hips. The West African taste runs to amplitude, both above and below the waist. The headdress is usually the exotic floating Yoruba turban.

As a concession to the modern setting of the hotel, sometimes the baby is carried in arms; I even saw a *father* carrying a sleeping infant. But if they come as a family the baby—there always is one—is in the back, held against mother by a wrap around her middle. Last night one very fashionable younger woman had a baby in the pouch this way, but the baby had a little pink bonnet on, so all you could see for sure was this wide-brimmed little bonnet sticking out behind. When the women sit in a chair, toting babies, they just rar forward a bit, and all's well.

APRIL 4, 1961
LAGOS

A clean bill of health for Helen! She made the trip to the hospital (a raggedy place), the X ray was made, and the result: chest clear, heart perfectly O.K.

Dr. Skinner said he had just seen a "fellow countryman of yours" and had to order him home. "Browned off." Someone from the University of Michigan, I suppose part of the ICA setup. Said he: "Between the slowness of the Nigerians in catching on, and the hard job of keeping up the spirits and efficiency of his American administrative staff in this terrible climate—it is a terrible climate to try to work in—he just fell apart, in five months." This is what the "glamour" of working overseas sometimes means.

APRIL 5, 1961
LAGOS

What excitement I have generated within myself (and in Tom Mead) by the prospect of a crack at the development of the Niger River system!

Last night I read my first summaries of the facts as presented in pedestrian NEDECO (Dutch) technical reports.

The "Feasibility Report" on the Niger River development is technically mediocre and uninspired; the language the usual dull stuff in such reports. But the vision I have that here could be—is—a great international river, affecting the lives and future of a half dozen new African states—this *is* inspiring; here again a river can bind up the wounds; not only help ameliorate latent tribal hatreds within Nigeria; it can help prevent some of the wounds that threaten so hideously, between tribes in the Congo; it could help prevent strife between Guinea, Mali of the old French Sudan (these are nations now strongly influenced by the Soviet), as well as Dahomey, Niger Republic, and Nigeria. The river could bring together the former British and French possessions and backgrounds; a grand multinational enterprise from which only good could come for each and for all of them.

APRIL 6, 1961
ACCRA, GHANA

We were met at the airport by Francis Russell and his wife; since January he has been the U.S. Ambassador to Ghana.

For a man who has spent the past three years in the serenity of our foreign service in New Zealand, he showed great composure about the turbulence and mercurial quality of Ghana—or, more accurately, of Kwame Nkrumah.

Nkrumah tried to seize on to the Congo revolution as a way to consolidate his position as the leader of the Soviet-aided African states. He had—or thought he had—an alliance with Guinea and Mali; to add the Congo, via Lumumba, would have put him a long way toward his goal. But the Congo failed him, the UN went in, Lumumba was humiliated and ultimately killed. Russell said that for a time Nkrumah was sour and in a foul mood on every subject. Then apparently he made up his mind to "cut his losses," made his trip to the U.S., was given a big hello by President Kennedy, and finally winds up (but *not* finally, for he isn't that kind) supporting the UN, and contributing Ghanaian troops.

Russell was full of delight at the way President Kennedy "took Nkrumah into camp." He not only met him at the airport; he bounded up the steps and met Nkrumah almost before he could get out of the plane. Then a big to-do at the White House, meeting the family, his "help" (as Nkrumah later described McGeorge Bundy and Walt Rostow to Russell!).

Just coming from Nigeria, a big bouncy country, with real parliamentary government (however opéra bouffe at times), it is hard to believe that the leader of so small a country as Ghana can become the leader of black Africa without an out-and-out alliance with the Soviet of a kind that would not appeal to most of the other countries.

But apparently the Kennedy Administration, and Kennedy's White House constellation of brains, is plunking for Nkrumah or doesn't want to antagonize him. On the Volta scheme, Russell said that George Ball, the new Under Secretary for Economic Affairs, was insistent on the World Bank granting a loan, though Eugene Black, who is a realist, was "most reluctant because of the way the country as a whole is handling its affairs—prestige expenditures like airlines and so on." But Ball is persuaded, so said Russell, that the thing to do is to build up Nkrumah.

I have plenty of reservations about this gambit. One can (and should) have "reservations" about anything so unconventional and new a condition as that of these new states of Africa. On balance perhaps it is necessary to take the risk and do something, rather than wait until events force an action that may be even more costly in money and freedom. But this is a long-shot risk.

APRIL 14, 1961
PRINCETON

Oppenheimer said he had a call from Bernard Baruch the other evening, who said: "I hear that disarmament has now become a fashionable subject. I'd like to get your views about it."

"Fashionable" is the word; but at this stage becoming a game, an intellectual game, an effort to erect what is essentially an ethical and moral issue into some kind of exact "*science* of armament control." This, I think, if continued, will discredit the whole effort, in time.

APRIL 21, 1961
PRINCETON

The first *real* gardening is beginning, and how luscious it is to get my fingers into God's soil, improved by Dave Lilienthal's efforts, if I may say so without blasphemy.

Beautiful as is the golden sunshine on the gay daffodils, it is a sad and somber and humiliating day. The repercussions of the Bay of Pigs, that dismal Boy-Scoutish hypertension "invasion" of Cuba, are coming in. The President's pathetic speech of yesterday was clearly something out of the wreckage of a major lapse of American judgment.

Some of the President's advice comes from men whose record shows they become too readily excited. They behave like children playing a game of good guys and bad guys in a world in which the U.S. is no longer unquestioned top-dog. Put it all together and we have the makings of grave setbacks and more transparent lies of which this fiasco may be only the first.

But it does no good to lament. We seem now committed to turning the Cuban civil war into another Spain. The effect of this brand of intervention on the whole of Latin America is something Ike didn't understand but I had hoped Kennedy would. He hasn't, through the worst possible advice. By God, Bowles and Rusk, so the *New York Times* stories indicate this morning, were dead set against the course our decisive President chose.

This is not an irretrievable blunder; nor is the mistake (as I see it) we are making in staking so much on Laos, where we *can't* win, but can so extend ourselves everywhere that we shall be strong nowhere.

Gordon talked to me about the next approaching crisis on our advance payments from Iran. Seven million due April 22, tomorrow. We can only continue, without taking the first steps of liquidation of the D&R Khuzistan operation, for another ten days or so.

I phoned Chet Bowles; Wednesday at six Gordon and I were ushered into the new offices of the Under Secretary. Cold offices they are, compared to the dignity of the old Army-Navy State offices next to the White House, where I first saw Byrnes and Acheson in 1947 about the atom.

Bowles looked pretty tattered. It had been a very rough day, between Laos, Cuba, and what not.

We told him that D&R would be forced to pull out of Iran by about May 10 unless the advance payments were received. We made it plain that we would not ask him to do *anything* about it, specifically, because we didn't know what could be done. I said: "We think you should know the situation directly, from us; we don't want you to say later: 'Why didn't you tell me what was in the offing, in time for us to do something about it?' " He said it was "unthinkable"; that, though we were a private company, and our costs were paid for entirely from Iran's own oil income, the U.S. was inevitably involved. (Just before we saw Bowles, a man on the Iran desk in the State Department, Bowling, had said: "No use being technical about it: the name Lilienthal is something to conjure with in Persia these days; if that project collapses because you withdraw, it will hurt American standing even more than the Helmand Dam fiasco did in Afghanistan." But that was a Morrison-Knudsen dam, paid for by U.S. Export-Import Bank funds, quite a different story from the Dez Dam, paid for by Iranians.)

"What troubles me is our whole way of making policy in these matters," Bowles said in a troubled and rather humbled way. He carries a huge responsibility, so much different from writing a book about what American policy *should* be, however good a book, and Chester Bowles *has* written some very sensible things indeed.

"We here say: We can't slacken military aid to Persia; the Iranians won't like *that*, even though we think it doesn't make too much sense.

"So we *drift* along. We have got to find a way to develop policies because *we* like them. But," he added dolefully, "there are so many things to do, so many emergencies, that the chance to think of something new and fresh isn't good.

"But there are two things I want to talk to you fellows about. First is the Mekong. I'll send you some material about that; I may go out there soon. That river may be a way of doing something that could arouse some feeling among the Laotians and Thais for their own country. Right now we can't get 3,000 Laotians willing to serve in the guerrillas; we may even have to use our Marines rather than just let the place fold. They just don't seem to care."

Hard lines, I thought. And some support for my concern that we may be spreading ourselves out so thin that we won't have the strength for the absolutely vital spots.

"The second thing is the Congo. I want one of you; I don't care which, you can flip a coin, to go out there as ambassador.

"Our relations with the UN aren't good, about the Congo, not good at all." Those cavernous eyes deepened; the sag in his mouth fell even more.

"I think if we send someone out there with stature, who knows how to get along with people, and who could begin to talk, too, about the great resources of the Congo River—why, I understand it probably has as much power as all the rest of the rivers of Africa combined—perhaps we could make headway. Right now the whole UN structure is threatened by the Congo.

"We need you fellows back in government; you've been out long enough."

Well, Gordon and I both thought this was a reaction rather than a thought. And of course neither of us would consider it. It isn't a good idea to begin with, that some "man of stature" can change the Congo picture. And even if he were successful, it would place the U.S. again, not the UN in the middle of that responsibility.

An exciting addition to my "business" experience. Actually, it turned out to be an opportunity to develop nascent ideas I have had of ways to overcome three economic problems in the context of a single pattern: modern multinational barter.

These three are:

1. Our great capacity to produce more food than we can possibly use, surpluses of food which should be used, not "burned" or plowed under or given away, making the recipient feel like a charity patient.

2. Our increasing weakness in minerals essential to our modern life, a weakness that has grown not only because we are chewing up our own minerals so rapidly but because more and more areas of such raw materials become increasingly politically shaky as sources for us (e.g. Chile, Peru, Bolivia for copper, tin, iron ore), and increasingly expensive, as labor costs in developing countries go up, as they should, and their own needs increase.

3. The need to find some way to meet the problem of shortage of hard currencies. This "foreign exchange" hurdle, dear to the "sound" banker's heart, is and always has been a means of controlling what people want and need, but are told they can't have because they are not "credit-worthy" by bankers' standards. (See the Populists in our own history, or the underdeveloped countries today.)

So, use our surplus food and their minerals in *barter* deals.

I spent two and a half hours discussing such ideas with Ludwig Jesselson and Ralph Meyer of M&C-Philipp. Both are past masters in the practical side of multinational trade through barter. They were full of everyday incidents that tend to confirm my hunches about how the elements of multilateral barter can be brought together into a working policy.

What I have in mind could make of "barter" something as important as it was in the simpler days when barter, not commercial paper and currency, moved goods across the trade routes of the world. But in a setting modern and exciting.

APRIL 23, 1961
PRINCETON

A further word about the session with Jesselson and Ralph Meyer:

I find myself fascinated by "personalities," whether in business or elsewhere. And Jesselson is certainly one of these special people.

He was talking about Geiger, who with "another Hungarian" (as he put it) built up a huge Chilean iron ore business, called Santa Fe, in a few years, from virtually nothing. "These Hungarians," he said, rather gently and quizzically, "you have to understand that they are different, that they are sensitive, even in business; but they are very able. A banker negotiating with Geiger walked out of a meeting with Geiger not long ago, quite angry, because he doesn't understand the European mind, and particularly the Hungarian mind. But I have learned that you must give Geiger plenty time to tell you what is bothering him, what his fears are, what goes on inside his mind. So I have spent lots of time with him. He doesn't like to be hurried, in an office conference."

In any case, some kind of "option" on Geiger's Chilean mine was worked out, and engineers (Bechtel) as well as accountants, etc., are examining the property and books.

"Mind you," said Jesselson, grinning at me behind his shiny glasses, his sharp alert face full of fire, "if I were buying the Chilean iron ore mine as a private business, without all this thing of being a public company, I wouldn't bother with an engineering report. These good engineers won't find out anything I can't see with my own eyes, not as much. I would make up my mind right away. As it is I'm afraid these engineers will have all kinds of questions that have very little to do with the real question: whether this is a good business. I *know* it is a good business and that this is a good deal. Of course it has risks. We're businessmen; we're supposed to take risks. Taking risks is how you make money."

APRIL 24, 1961
HOTEL GLADSTONE (6:45 A.M.)
NEW YORK

As if the Black Wednesday of Cuba last week were not enough of a setback, yesterday morning I picked the *Times* off the steps at home to read of civil war in France. Not civil war in its classic European or Western sense but an attempted coup by the very Army whose leadership made General de Gaulle dictator of France.

So I left the sun-blessed springtime of Princeton for the City with a heavy heart.

That I had come so close to identifying, characterizing, our present situation as long ago as last July was small comfort. In that North American Newspaper Alliance piece I had used the war term "clear and present danger" to describe where we were. At that time the country was filled with an Ike-induced complacency that it seemed unlikely would be jarred, though Kennedy came close to doing so in the campaign, or so I thought. But I was wrong: he won the election (though by a whisker) but he had not aroused the people. Did Cuba do that? Will the humiliating events in France do this? Will a stock market slide do it?

What will arouse us, prepare us to do what needs to be done?

Back in May I decided to speak out about how much we had been softened by Khrushchev's "peaceful coexistence" line. It wasn't the Russians that softened us; *we did it to ourselves.*

It is almost impossible for us to face the fact that *we have almost lost the capacity to risk our lives for what we believe.*

Our American Big Bomb Zealots, with their idea of a war of terror, have scared not the Russians; if they have scared anyone, they have scared *us* to the point where deterrence has lost any meaning except that we are deterring ourselves.

APRIL 28, 1961
(6 A.M.)
NEW YORK

This week's *New Yorker* contains John Brooks's Profile about me. I was expecting a basically friendly and sympathetic piece. But I was flabbergasted with the article itself. Not just that it made me out a far more impressive "personality" than I *know* I am. What impressed me most is that he was able to catch and record the *pattern* of life I deliberately chose to create for myself, one in contrast to public service yet not in contradiction to my years in public service.

MAY 6, 1961
PRINCETON

The clouds have been hanging desperately low over our "body and soul" efforts in Persia of these past five years. The clouds have grown more and more ominous as the recent days have drifted by. Aramesh, the new head of the Plan Organization, has made violent attacks on me in the Majlis, and on D&R and the Khuzistan program.

We stuck to our position: we should tell Iran in writing that on May 15 we would cease making disbursements—the first steps in the "liquidation" of a great enterprise.

Then this morning I read of the fall of the Sharif-Imami Cabinet, which presumably will carry Aramesh with it. The ostensible reason was a big antigovernment demonstration before the Houses of Parliament on an issue of teachers' salaries. Actually, I suppose, what was really involved was the mounting dissatisfaction with the government, this being the issue chosen for the demonstration.

So, with a former ambassador to the U.S., Ali Amini, as the new Prime Minister, we enter a new chapter in this modern tale of Persian Nights. It couldn't be worse; this may be much better.

Some satisfying letters and messages about the *New Yorker* Profile. And extraordinary activity in M&C-Philipp stock—on two successive days it was about the most heavily bought-and-sold issue on the Big Board. As usual on the Stock Exchange, no real economic reason for this, as witness a *Wall Street Journal* comment that the "only apparent reason . . . was publicity given the company in a *New Yorker* magazine Profile on David E. Lilienthal, a Minerals & Chemicals director."

It has been a week of furious and delicious gardening too. All day yesterday and today I have been going through the mystic ritual of mixing soil (rubbed between my hands as an ancient priest might have prepared the ingredients of some magic ceremonial) and then putting "into the hole" bone meal, peat moss, and cow manure; then the sweet moment when, having poured the hole full of water, in goes the plant— iberis, coral bell, phlox, or what. And overhead the flowering apple trees. This is the season of life renewed, of looking forward to the future symbolized by the plants and seeds one so lovingly entrusts to the earth.

MAY 8, 1961
PRINCETON

A cable from John Oliver from Tehran. Ansari "claims" that Asfia will become the new head of the Plan Organization. Asfia is a redoubtable little man, a flyweight with the punch of a heavy, like some of those lightweight "greats" I recall from my boyhood. What is equally to the point, John reports that the prospects for the April payment are now "reasonably good."

Short of a coup, I wonder what else could happen to us in this Persian task?

Last night I listened for a solid hour to a TV program, presided over (in a manner of speaking!) by Mrs. Roosevelt. Chet Bowles was one of the participants. A knowledgeable face, that man, and an incisive kind of eloquence. Then there was Barbara Ward (of *course;* how could there be a "conference" without Barbara Ward?). She is keen and forthright (but she starts from answers in the "back of the book": this I think is her sole limitation in this difficult area). And Max Millikan, who with Rostow undoubtedly authored the so-called new foreign aid policy and the President's message about it. Very academic type, pleasing in manner, sensible as a man can be. I was much taken by him, angry that people couldn't see that money spent for "preinvestment," his favorite phrase these days, was the only true light. *How* that "preinvestment" money is *spent,* that is, by people with what level of perception and experience, doesn't seem to trouble him, as it does me, I confess. He is as fine a soul as I know, and his insistence that the Marshall Plan was simply *restoring* what was there, whereas development is *creating* something that has never before existed, is a real contribution to the fuzziness of this analogy so loosely made between the Marshall Plan and economic development of less-developed countries.

MAY 11, 1961
NEW YORK

The Minerals & Chemicals-Philipp Board meeting was another interesting chapter in that "life of a business" story. We discussed at great length a proposal to put millions of new money into a plant that would crush, screen, etc., a stratum of limestone that lies under our Marblehead land on Lake Erie, a deposit we didn't know was there. I found it fascinating, especially the play of personalities, ranging from Ullmann, a puffy-eyed Jewish Buddha, with business wisdom going back, way back, to his ancestors of a thousand years ago; the quick darting mind of Jesselson; the soft-voiced but extraordinarily fluent and articulate doubts of Ralph Meyer; the very formal and conventional (but necessary) questions of Frank Howard, formerly head of Esso research; the big bluff handsome Fraser of Ventures, Ltd., with a sense of authority and experience in his every tone and phrase; the clear-headed and conservative views of Jim Deshler, who presided; this was a play well staged, with a diverse cast.

Carl Sandburg wrote: "The people—yes." The *people* are business, just as the people (yes) are any instiution.

MAY 13, 1961
NEW YORK

Helen and I to Cass Canfield's last night. Cass is head of Planned Parenthood and this small dinner party was for birth-control "experts": Sir Julian Huxley, now the troubadour of birth control; Dr. Harrison Brown, of Cal Tech and the lecture platform, and his tall, cool, youngish wife; a Chinese woman, also a birth-control crusader; a tall Englishman, Cadbury, of that wealthy family, and the Lilienthals.

Huxley is a prodigious man; his energy and exuberance, his great skill in telling a story, the actor in him which is so strong, and the professional "British lecturer"—these have all but blotted out the scientist, according to my observation.

Some reference having been made to India—(how could it be otherwise in a group of birth controllers)—I said that the Indians look down their noses at everyone, and get away with it, except for one person present in that room, who has finally decided she won't take it any longer: meaning Helen. I quoted her as saying the Indians are so sensitive to *any* criticism of them, yet so quick to be supercritical of us. Helen looked a bit flabbergasted, as well she might, at my throwing her into the middle of the arena. But she took it up. "I'm tired," she says, "of having the Indians or anyone else criticize Americans for the very things of which they themselves are guilty. So when they say accusingly to me that 'you Americans' have a race problem, I say 'Indeed we do, I am sure that you can understand how difficult it is to deal with such a long-standing problem, since you are still struggling with the caste system in India, now outlawed legally, but still very much influencing most Indians, I understand.' They don't like to be reminded of this."

Well, Helen's comment turned the tide of the usual intellectuals' adulation of everything Indian. Which led Mrs. Canfield to tell a story about the fabulous Krishna Menon, Nehru's right-hand man.

She thought it would be friendly to ask him to a small dinner at their house, set for eight o'clock. He accepted. Then the secretaries began calling: Mr. Menon does not eat this and that. Can Mr. Menon bring his physician with him? Later, can he bring his secretary? (She turned out to be a blonde Scotch young gal whom he stroked warmly during the evening.) At well after eight o'clock he and his entourage arrived, with sirens screaming, and then said all he wanted was a cup of tea.

MAY 18, 1961
EN ROUTE TO CORNING
IN THE CORNING GLASS WORKS PLANE

On our way to a conference on modern industry and the individual, sponsored by the Houghtons of the Corning Glass empire.

Have just been talking with a man on this Corning Company plane Dr. Cornelis W. de Kiewiet, who knows all about bees about which I know naught and didn't think I wanted to. But how fascinating *everything* about life, about the world, can be.

It turns out that the man who knows so much about bees, and raises them, is also an expert on Africa. How *good* it is to be interested in other people; how often it develops that if *you* are interested, you will find the other fellow interesting.

Another example: I had to wait quite a long time at the airport before this plane was ready to take off. It happens I was full of good will and even love for everything and everybody and as a reward, instead of being bored by the long delay, I "discovered" another world, through the means of a quite ordinary-looking man. I spoke of gliding, since I knew that Corning, where we're headed, is a center of this sport. The man turned out to be a tow pilot for gliders. He had some fascinating things to say about them, though I am sure *he* didn't think he was being fascinating; after all, to him gliding is just gliding.

On board, at my left is John Brooks, of *The New Yorker*, Amory Houghton, Jr., who was with David at Harvard, and Mr. and Mrs. Arthur Houghton, a great patron of the arts. Young Houghton brought along his three-year-old daughter Sarah. She asked whether there were lollipops on the plane; there were. I guess she knew it. Being well brought up, before she sucked hers, she came up to us to ask if *we* didn't want a lollipop. *That's* the right way to begin a conference of high-level thinking!

MAY 19, 1961
CORNING, NEW YORK

Professor Raymond Aron of the Sorbonne and I had breakfast together this morning. He said something rather startling: "You may not know it, but the reason you are so well known in Europe these days particularly is not just because of TVA—so much admired—but because of your views on big business. That an American liberal should have the perception to see that liberalism and small business are not synonymous, that bigness can be made responsible—by these ideas you have become identified as the leader of a more mature American

The completed Pahlavi Dam, 1963.

The Shah and Lilienthal with Voorduin and Ansari left, Greene in foreground, discussing progress of construction of Dez Dam, October, 1961. In 1963 Dez Dam was named Mohammad Reza Shah Pahlavi Dam.

The Shah of Iran orders the initial bucket of concrete poured at the damsite on October 30, 1961. In 13 months the Dez Dam reached its full height of 646 ft. above the canyon floor.

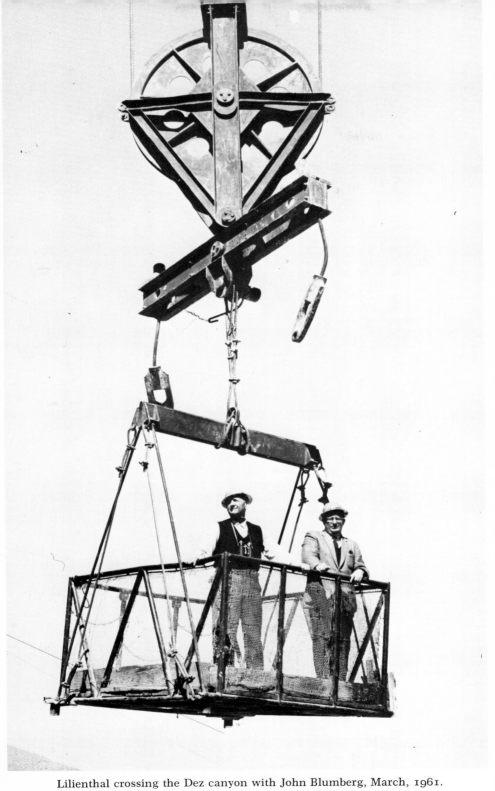

Lilienthal crossing the Dez canyon with John Blumberg, March, 1961.

David Jr. and David III, 1962.

Daniel Bromberger, grandson, 1959

Lilienthal in his Princeton garden.

Pamela Lilienthal, granddaughter, 19(

Mrs. Lilienthal on Martha's Vineyard.

On Martha's Vineyard, summer of 1960. (*Photo by Howell's Studio*)

President Kennedy at Muscle Shoals, May 18, 1963.

Nathan Greene.

André Meyer.

Governor Brown explains the State Water Plan, January, 1960.

Eleanor Roosevelt. (*Wide World Photos*)

Dr. Leona Baumgartner, Commissioner
of Health of New York City.

Dean Acheson, in 1961.
(*Wide World Photos*)

John Oliver (left) and John Burnett. (*Photo by Ron Appelbe for* Business Week)

Lilienthal and Clapp in Tehran.

The Shah and the Queen at Ahwaz, March, 1960, with Lilienthal and Iranian electrical staff.

Desk of His Imperial Majesty, the Shah of Iran; Volume IV of the Lilienthal Journals in top shelf of bookcase.

A reed village on the Euphrates.

Lilienthal is dunked in the Euphrates marshes. Described on page 176.

Vice President Lyndon Johnson in Tehran, August 1962. Prime Minister Alam at Johnson's right. (*Wide World Photos*)

Demonstrating machine sugar cane harvesting on the Haft Tapeh plantation.

Zurkhaneh (Athletic Club), Tehran.

President Lleras of Colombia visits the slums of Cali, December, 1959.

President Alberto Lleras of Colombia greets Lilienthal in Bogotá, December, 1959.

The President of the Philippines with Lilienthal, February, 1960.

Peccei of Italconsult, Lilienthal, and Voorduin of D&R in Buenos Aires, October, 1960.

His Excellency Felix Houphouet-Boigny, President of the Republic of the Ivory Coast, 1962.

Abidjan, capital of the Ivory Coast. (*Courtesy, Embassy of the Ivory Coast*)

liberalism." Europe is heading for the "economics of scale," i.e, bigness, if it is to survive.

Rather caught me off base, and I had nothing to say.

The Corning Conference has turned out, contrary to my expectations, to be a pleasurable and stimulating experience. There are ninety participants.

We adopted as a focus a subject offered by Huxley: In what ways in the modern world can the process of industrialization be so guided and encouraged as to favor the fullest development of individuals?

I understand that John Brooks has been comissioned to prepare a book putting into perspective the variegated views of the group‡

The people in our round table, one of three, included two extraordinarily articulate men, Julian Huxley and Judge Wyzanski. The latter's noble prose, spoken without notes, is a real tour de force, even majestic in the march of words and ideas. For example, he said: "The man with the sense of adventure is more to be relied upon than those who have a sense of repose." Wyzanski was magnificent and extraordinarily learned, in the classical style, and eloquent in an old-fashioned way (but most impressive way) in everything he said.

A bright and facile young psychiatrist, Dr. William Glasser of Los Angeles, and a brilliant, warm, outgoing writer, Alfred Kazin were among the most interesting.

One of the most articulate spokesmen for industry—in a dull, colorless voice—was Roger Blough, Chairman of U.S. Steel. A number of times he said that personally he likes the simple life; he and his wife, he explained, have bought an old house not far from Pittsburgh, in a town of 2,000; that is where he likes to be. He confessed a kind of "nostalgia" for those good old days of small towns and the preindustrial civilization. When the conference broke up, Bernie Kilgore said Blough was hurrying away in *his* (i.e., U.S. Steel's) plane; Kilgore was taking us to the airport to take *his* (i.e., the *Wall Street Journal's*) plane. Said Kilgore, "Roger is in a hurry because he is going to go fishing in a trout stream near that little town he keeps talking about. The plane will get him there in thirty minutes."

This is the same nostalgia most people feel, intellectuals included, who glorify the good old days, the simple life, before industry ruined everything. But they use planes (or their equivalent) as a matter of course so they can live the kind of life they really want, while enjoying the glowing feeling that they are at heart Thoreau-like people.

---

‡ The book was later published by Harper & Row (1962) under the title *The One and the Many—the Individual in the Modern World.*

MAY 22, 1961
WASHINGTON

Visit with a keen reporter from the *Courier-Journal*, Pearce. Question: Should he, and the *Courier-Journal* take out after TVA for its growing preoccupation with electric power? I told him I thought he should; that the TVA staff had developed hardening of the arteries and needed a swift dose of criticism *from friends*, and explained why. John Fischer of *Harper's* joined Pearce later; apparently Pearce is planning an article for *Harper's* on this theme and Fischer wanted to know if the factual and legal basis for the TVA justifications were true: I said that on the whole they were not.

Breakfast with Sargent Shriver, head of the Peace Corps. Full of fire and enthusiasm, a well-set-up and colloquial guy, the sort I like. I said I thought the Peace Corps might invigorate the foreign aid agency, ICA, which has grown cautious and dispirited, largely because they are now only advisors, not doers.

And something happens—not good—when the impulse to do is frustrated and denied. It happens to institutions—like the UN Food and Agriculture Organization. And to people. It could happen to me, and did for a time—in the early days of my "consulting" period.

Shriver is an operator. Considering that we were talking about a maximum of only 1,000 volunteers in the first year, he certainly used his "position" as the President's brother-in-law to the fullest. Actually, he is a fireball, with good administrative judgment and enthusiasm. But being the President's brother-in-law helps; rather. For who else could arrange a luncheon in the palatial new State Department dining room, with the Secretary of State, the Under Secretary, the head of ICA, etc., present; who else could use the Cabinet Room (to add glamour) and have the President of the United States walk into an Advisory Committee meeting?

The plain white door opened partway; and a tall guy with chestnut hair looked around the corner of the door rather tentatively. It was the President. I was seated not at the Cabinet table but in the back row, so I saw him first and started the movement to rise.

The President, looking somehow as if he were still looking for votes, rather than carrying the burdens of the White House, came in slowly —his movements are almost in slow motion. When he stopped to shake hands with me, and I spoke my name, he looked me over with that cool yet interested look he can give people, the vague suggestion of a smile, but none of this big grin stuff, said simply: "Glad to see you again," then went on to shake hands with the people on "his" side of the Cabinet table.

Being in the White House again, for the *first time* since I left the AEC, at least ten years ago, gave me no feeling at all—this is the fact. I thought it was because I was tired after yesterday's long session of the Peace Corps National Advisory Council.

But the fact is: the glamour of public office hath departed.

Even the Cabinet Room, where I hardly dared breathe so awe-stricken was I the first time I was there, back in 1934, F.D.R. presiding, seemed commonplace. Just another "board room." Perhaps this is good. But surely it doesn't mean that I have lost the wonder and the inner excitement about the works of government, and particularly of the launching of a new enterprise, so filled with gargantuan question marks and unsolved problems as this Peace Corps venture. But the allure of being where important things are done—by less than life-size people as a matter of fact—that kind of snobbery or little-boy dazzle is gone.

I know, for one thing, how little these able and brilliant people really know about how to face up to and organize their problems. This Advisory Board, supposedly made up of experienced men and women, or at least people who had arrived, showed at times a startling lack of perspective, fussing about what I confess I thought were picayune oddments. Some of these were very important to them, no doubt. For example, the chaplain of Yale, a breezy, talkative big fellow, Dr. William Sloane Coffin, worrying out loud about whether volunteers of the Peace Corps overseas had house servants. He cited the case of Chester's children, both volunteers, Sam and Sally Bowles; if they didn't have servants they would be the only secondary school teachers who didn't, and they would get robbed in the markets; if they *did*, what happened to the noble idea that the Volunteers should live a pioneer life of hardships? And so on and on.

This did it. I had heard enough of these detailed questions of worrying about things that have to be left to administration. So I got up in the Cabinet Room and in a voice that surprised me, I said: "Let's not spend our time and energy worrying about what is going to happen tomorrow or a week or a month hence; we are the trustees of a great and important idea that has yet to be set in motion, yet to be tried. Let's keep our minds on the big issue right now, and later meet the day-to-day problems as they arise." And then I added a word of highest praise for the quality of the staff Sargent Shriver had brought together from *other* existing government agencies, saying I had organized a number of staffs, of which I was proud, but this was as dedicated and capable as any I had ever seen; if the Peace Corps had done nothing else than show what talents and energy the Government is able to draw upon it has justified itself.

I was glad of a chance to see Dean Rusk, the first time since he has been made Secretary. His news pictures made him look very bad, as if he "had had it." Quite wrong, for he was certainly bouncy yesterday, greeted me with warmth, seemed quite well. He is not the conventional picture of "a forceful man," but he may well have the kind of stamina, the inner *strength*, that the task requires, and an ability to conserve himself, not to worry about the many advisors and ambassadors at large all over the place, the Harvard White House Palace Guard, once-greats of other Administrations. Washington is full of unofficial secretaries of state these days. Some men would erupt over this and thus make themselves less effective. (*I* would, God knows, and have.) Not Dean Rusk, I think. Which may at this point be an important attribute.

For example: Vice-President Lyndon Johnson is now going up and down Asia making informal commitments all over the place—which Dean will be held responsible for in the end. How we can run our foreign affairs this way, I don't know, though of course even Wilson did something of the kind, via Colonel Edward House. But then there was only *one* Colonel House, and he was professionally a kind of anonymous character; these people who go around "representing" the U.S. are far from quiet, far from selfless, far from anonymous.

Justice Bill Douglas sat on my right, at the Advisory Council luncheon; Mrs. Roosevelt on my left. Mrs. Roosevelt repeated to me the thesis that unless the wealthy top layer of Persia "accepted their responsibilities" no progress could be expected. I told her about peasant progress in the Gebli area; I don't think she caught quite what I had in mind. For I didn't use the language of *personal morality* to which she is accustomed ("responsibility"); I used instead the language of how you get results, through increased productivity that is equitably *shared*.

Mrs. Roosevelt is so full of energy and sweetness, and so willing to spend those energies on individuals whose troubles, or imagined troubles, she takes to her overflowing heart.

Bill Douglas has taken on a ruddy, too ruddy, color, big swollen nose. He talked to me about the great Chinese leader, Jimmy Yen, and his mass literacy movement. The fact that this great "movement" made not one whit of a dent on Communist China, from which Yen fled, never raised the question in his mind—as it does in mine—whether literacy or the lack of it is as important as all that, in the tense and rough world of the emerging countries.

One of my favorite people in the world, Leona Baumgartner, made the day, had there been nothing else. We rode together to the State Department, with Mrs. Roosevelt wedged with us in a tiny, smelly, yellow taxi; leading a cavalcade into the White House grounds, complete with police escort. The former Mistress of the White House. No one of us thought it incongruous. This is a touch of democracy a European or an Asian would have plenty of trouble understanding.

MAY 31, 1961
NEW YORK

I put a question, point-blank, to Paul Kieffer, president of the Century. "I would like to invite to lunch a distinguished Nigerian. Would it be against a house rule to have a Negro to lunch in the big dining room; and even if not against a rule, would it create an embarrassing situation?" He was explicit. *Of course* he would be received, without incident. "What we shall do about Negroes as members is something that lies ahead." Strangely, this very question of membership in the Cosmos Club, for example, is causing a deal of perturbation in Washington, considering how many black Africans from the new countries now hold the rank of ambassador. There is a good deal of irony in all this.

JUNE 2, 1961
NEW YORK

We have, i.e., D&R, just signed a contract with the Inter-American Development Bank for a study of how to get power supply in Haiti off dead center. And then comes the dramatic news that Trujillo, on the same island of Santo Domingo, has been assassinated. The Haiti business may be close to another storm center of the almost-forgotten Caribbean —almost forgotten until Castro came along.

The word from Persia continues to be good, in that the new broom of Prime Minister Amini seems for the present at least to have swept quite vigorously. As to our affairs, they have improved because (a) Aramesh, our "enemy," is out; (b) Asfia is in, with the redoubtable Farmanfarmaian, and (c) Iran is probably going to get an additional $50 million grant, from Uncle Sam. Whether the current wave of arrests of generals will begin a period of downgrading the status of the Iranian military, or whether the hostility of the generals will precipitate a coup —this is in the lap of the gods. I would guess Iran will pull through this one, too, one way or another. This morning's *Times* had a somber editorial, as have other papers; the net of this is: here is Persia's last chance. But this has been said before, again and again, over the centuries—but *Persia endures*.

JUNE 3, 1961
PRINCETON

A hectic and disturbed morning.
Up quite early again (4:30 yesterday, 5:30 today); at 7:30 a special delivery from the office; with it word from Oliver and Burnett in Persia.

Clapp and I had agreed, after the most explicit and at times rather strained discussion, that we should give notice to Plan Organization that D&R would no longer continue the responsibility of disbursements of funds to our subcontractors—that they should look to Plan Organization for payment, not to D&R. Burnett took along a proposed draft in which this was one of the principal points.

Now comes a letter dated May 30 by Oliver to Plan, omitting this basic point entirely, Burnett's covering letter saying that John had decided against it. There hasn't been any cable indicating that such a "shift of position" (actually an *abandonment* of position) was recommended. I was furious; tried unsuccessfully to reach Gordon in San Jose to get more facts.

A letter dated May 28 was described by Burnett as giving the "reasons" why the basic position we had taken had been "shifted"—a euphemism if ever I heard one.

So this is the way I steamed this morning. I told Helen that I would resign from D&R on the basis of this kind of disregard, without consultation, of our policy decisions. But having got that out of my system (although at the time I felt it genuinely) I now see that abandoning my own child isn't the answer; the answer is first to be sure I know *why* so responsible a man as Oliver felt he could disregard a basic policy decision without consultation and then, having determined that, to get a clearer understanding of the scope of discretion we vest in people about policy.

I believe so wholeheartedly in giving the "man on the ground" a wide range of discretionary authority and room for judgment that when I blow up, or boil up, about such an episode it is somewhat ironic. But this seems, on what I now know, to be a pretty bad case of poor communication or poor judgment or my poor management of this enterprise.

JUNE 9, 1961
PRINCETON

It seems like "old times" again; by which I mean the days of my public service, when someone (or more than one!) was always throwing barbs at me—and I was thinking about how to handle and, if possible, return the barb.

A couple of days ago Senator Andrew Schoeppel of Kansas arose on the floor of the Senate to take a crack at Development and Resources, with me as the target. This "lobbying" organization, said he, was making $78 million out of foreign aid in Iran: this was the burden of his attack. He based this on a report of the Attorney General administering the Foreign Agent Act, in which the *disbursements* we have made to others, as agent of Iran, were apparently listed as if they were fees to us.

Then he put into the *Congressional Record* a newsletter, "Human Events," I think is the name, in which by name I was attacked as using Iran as a "personal gold mine."

This is probably just the beginning, since my old adversaries in public life are the same people, more or less, who will be opposing the foreign aid bill. But I was more provoked by the most recent crack in this return of the "old times," a letter in the *Times* this morning.

The authority, a Mr. Harry Kern, is most sympathetic with Iran, and takes the *Times* to task for a recent critical editorial, saying that the *Times* should be encouraging the Shah and Amini rather than be supercritical. I agree with this. So I was particularly annoyed that he appears to blame Clapp and myself for squandering funds on "massive projects" rather than "local projects that would have brought some tangible benefits to the people." He goes on to say that the "U.S. cannot escape some responsibility here, particularly when the largest project in Iran is under the direct charge of David Lilienthal and Gordon R. Clapp. I was told in Tehran in April," he goes on, "that this organization has an arrangement by which it is not obliged even to show its books to the Iranian authorities." Which is untrue, of course. But this sort of thing, while inescapable, even though we *aren't* using any U.S. funds, renews a period of controversy and fighting, so in a way we might as well be in Government service again.

Which, I suppose, is only to say that no one, however "private," except perhaps the corner grocer, can escape from the necessity of standing up to public criticism, or being involved in the governmental process.

I don't welcome this prospect, as one might suppose I would, as most of my public controversies have brought me great satisfaction in return for great harassment, since I prevailed, or was vindicated, in all of them. But my first impulse is the usual one for me *before* I get into any fight, to say: oh, go away and leave me in peace.

When one can be greatly amused, be filled with robust, even noisy laughter, and a sense of fun, about things that are deep and important, then one is a well-developed and a full-blooded human being, then one is at one's best. To be filled with laughter at self, laughter because of the absurdity and ridiculousness of oneself—then adolescence and immaturity have been left behind.

JUNE 15, 1961
WASHINGTON

Dean Acheson is, to me, one of the most impressive of men. Perhaps it is because he has so many of the qualities I feel I *don't* have and, I suppose, covet unconsciously: a distinguished appearance, an air of ease and sophisticated gaiety, a self-assurance and fluency.

I have just come from an hour's talk with him at his law office, a meeting I asked for. I wanted his opinion about ways in which I might serve this Administration, where they thought I could help, *without* accepting an "appointment," a salary, an office, etc. He has been doing this for some months, sometimes spending most of his time on a "spot assignment," sometimes less formally.

The things he said—and even more, implied—are strong within me.

He sees Kennedy as a very attractive and likeable man, and one who has consulted him a good deal since he was nominated and since he was elected, so there is no question of sour grapes.

But the picture of Kennedy I get from Dean is that of a man who is bewildered, who has a long way to go before he has his job in the foreign field in hand. "I am scared to death" is the best summary of how Dean feels about the capacity Kennedy has to handle the task that has fallen to him, if "fallen to" is the way to describe the story of a young man who has pursued the Presidency as ferociously as Kennedy has.

Dean delivered this conclusion with the light and relaxed touch that is part of his sometimes sardonic and sophisticated outlook on human affairs. But it was based on two or three specific experiences. One should apply the salt of skepticism to some of his comments since of course on some important matters Kennedy has probably disregarded Dean's advice or asked for it and not really listened; under those circumstances even the most objective of men can see dark disaster.

His most specific cause of alarm was the planning about what we should do in the Berlin showdown. Dean was asked by the President to review these plans. "They were terrible, and I said so. Ever since then I have been scared to death." He said this with that composed, relaxed mask (or is it a mask?) he wears, but the *words* were not relaxed.

Rusk as Secretary hasn't yet had time to really run the Department of State, "which is still in a mess, a mess." And this comment despite the fact that " I am the one who is responsible for Dean's being made Secretary; Kennedy had never heard of him before I recommended him, and neither had Bob Lovett, for that matter." The relevance of this about Lovett is that Kennedy tried hard to get Lovett into his Cabinet, as Secretary of the Treasury.

I began by stating the problem I had: should I accept the overtures to go back into the Government, pressed on me by Bowles, supposedly speaking for the President and Rusk? I told Dean I had said no to the suggestion of Assistant Secretary of State for Latin America, some months ago. I gave my reasons. One was that this Administration should be manned by men of another generation than mine (and Dean's). I didn't think my reasons were purely protecting a rather satisfactory and productive way of life—my work continued to be of a public service nature though it was not within the Government.

Dean heard me out, and then, with that quizzical look of his said: "Mr. Justice Acheson concurs in that result, but for other reasons."

His chief reason for agreeing that I should stay out of this Administration, except on spot special jobs, was this: "You and I have worked under Presidents who knew what they were doing, and knew how to get it done. This one doesn't yet know what he wants to do, and doesn't know how to organize to do it. You and I would be no good in this kind of setting, just no good. Now, when I take a special assignment, and decide that I'm getting nowhere, I don't need to resign, and blow up a furor; I have nothing to resign, and just don't do any more work. You and I were used to something better than what is going on here now, and we can't adapt ourselves to this amateur touch.

"I talk to the President—until late January I called him Jack, for he is a neighbor and I like him a lot, but now I call him what he is supposed to be called, Mr. President—I talk to him and I have a feeling he isn't listening. Not a matter of agreeing or even understanding, but not listening. This is alarming, really. For instance, he signed a Security Council order the other day about the continuing need for American ground troops in Europe [an Acheson conviction]. I said: 'Mr. President, we worked for a month on this proposition about ground troops in Europe, and look at this paper; apparently our work was wasted.' 'Well,' the President said, 'I guess I missed that point in the paper!' "

Dean commented on the Cuba mishap, the Bay of Pigs debacle. He said the President can't yet understand what happened to him. "Like the fellow," he said, "who knew little about boomerangs; throwing one around, was knocked out cold by the one he himself had thrown. Kennedy can't yet believe that he had been hit in the head by his *own* boomerang."

Dean said Kennedy asked him about naming a Secretary of the Treasury: Kennedy was determined to get Bob Lovett. "I told him, Bob won't take that job. He hates banking and figures. [Lovett is and long has been a partner of the bankers, Brown Bros. Harriman!] What he *loves* is that railroad [meaning the Union Pacific, of which he is chairman—a family passion]. He loves to go out and buy locomotives and talk to conductors and such. *If* you asked him to take over the Defense Department and see to it that it is run by civilians, that might intrigue him and he might do it. ["Intrigue" is a word that sounded strange on Dean's patrician tongue.]

"But Kennedy said no; he wanted him as Secretary of the Treasury.

He sent Clark Clifford to New York to put it to Bob; Bob armed himself thereafter with all kinds of doctor's certificates that he was on his last legs; a wily fox."

I apply a certain discount to Dean's comments about the Kennedy Administration. In the first place, there is his love of irony and the pungent expression.

Then, having himself been Secretary of State, and having been hit fore and aft in the process, and considering himself as he says "an elder statesman" and Kennedy a youthful administrator just learning the facts of life, he takes the kind of cry-havoc view you'd expect of someone who knows his advice won't be taken, and who is sure he would do better, which of course he certainly would—and how. So I discount about 50 percent the distinctly dim view he takes.

After all, in the early days of F.D.R., as there are around the White House these days, a lot of people were wandering around with ill-defined authority and questionable sophistication; in the end it settled down pretty well, as this Administration will too. Truman "spoiled" Dean in that Truman understood the importance of trusting a strong man— and Dean was that—and standing by him come what may. So Dean Acheson *was* the Department of State. Whereas now Rusk is Secretary but the place is running over, as Dean puts it, "with Harriman off here on his own, and Adlai running a separate circus down there in New York and in South America, and even Lyndon making all sorts of commitments—as they must seem to the Asians."

But I don't forget that after making full discount to Dean's appraisal, here is America's most experienced foreign officer and one of the ablest minds of the country, who feels anything but happy about what he sees.

"I don't know," he said as I left, "whether it is better to be on the outside, worrying that what is going on may be terrible, or on the inside (as I have been on some recent issues), *knowing* that things are terrible."

Much of this discussion with Dean was precipitated by an episode this morning just before the opening plenary session of the conference on foreign aid.

Bowles, as the opening speaker, was standing against the wall, preparatory to the members of the panel going to the dais. He saw me, asked me to step out of the meeting room.

With a much interested 400 people gawking at this curbstone conference, we got off to one side. He looked quite distraught: "Spaeth has walked out on us on the Latin-American Secretaryship [he referred to the published reports that Carl Spaeth, Dean of the Stanford Law School, had been selected for the Assistant Secretaryship; then this morning a front-page story that he had found some "obstacle" that prevented his accepting].

"Will you take that post?"

I said that for me nothing in the meantime had changed; the answer was the same. A respectful no. Would I be willing to come in for three months to do a reorganization job? No, I said.

I don't feel any differently about joining this Administration than I did before, in any regular capacity. And getting into a reorganization job for a short period could mean that I would be on the sticky flypaper. If I thought that the Administration would be capable of defining responsibility and authority for this prodigious big task, and vesting it in one man, that would be one thing. But they won't; they aren't built that way; there are too many mothers' helpers to permit it. Only necessity will compel that kind of clarification. And that will come, but later.

As I went down to eat my dinner in the Hay-Adams forlorn dining room (elegant as it is) a great tall, Lincolnesque figure appeared in the elevator. I looked up the long reach of rumpled white jacket to find that this was Ken Galbraith, now transformed from a Harvard economics professor whom Clarence Randall and Sinclair Weeks were trying recently to throw out of Harvard, into the Ambassador of the U.S. to India.

"I came back from India to find out what all those cables from the department I've been getting mean." A pretty good summary, I thought, of the realities of ambassadorial life.

He grinned down at me (he must be 6-feet-6 at least) and said: "Kennedy talked to me about becoming Ambassador to India, and I hesitated quite a while; I had a new book half finished and so on. Then I began to hear with increasing frequency the name of Lilienthal and that helped me make up my mind, fast"—and laughed.

I told him he need have had no cause for concern. Actually no one had ever mentioned this possibility to me. My lukewarm enthusiasm for the life of an ambassador continues to be what it always was, only more so.

In fact, it seems to me I have about as good and useful a life as a man can have, right now.

JUNE 16, 1961
PENN STATION
WASHINGTON

It all seemed too painfully familiar: a President of the United States, surrounded by all the pageantry of his great office but unable to use his legs.

This time he is young (though not by any means as young looking as a year and a half ago, or even a few weeks ago, when I saw him at the Peace Corps meeting). But the shock of recollection of F.D.R. was a strange and unpleasant feeling. Not because Kennedy is ill or disabled as Roosevelt was; the shock is the realization that this symbol of power, the head of a nation in peril, should be just another human being, who like myself could develop a terribly painful back ligament, so painful that in the eyes of the whole world he must propel himself on crutches, dragging his left foot.

But when he was seated in the middle of the long "head table" at the Shoreham luncheon he was as handsome, vigorous, intensely sincere as ever. This meeting was part of the National Conference on International Economic and Social Development. I was at the head table, perhaps five or six places removed from the President, put there because I was one of the speakers.

Watching an audience that in turn is watching a President is an interesting experience, particularly, I think, for one who as a speaker has professionally watched so many audiences, over a long stretch of years. I remember watching the great pre-election audience at Madison Square Garden when I was sitting on the stage back of F.D.R. It was during his campaign against Willkie the night he "slayed them" with the phrase "Martin, Barton, and Fish." F.D.R. stood with a kind of awkwardness; one noticed this particularly from the rear, for his big fine handsome torso was propped up on nothing much more than steel braces.

But Kennedy sat for his speech, handing his crutches to one of the Secret Service men. Looking down the table I found his manner of handling his script interesting—again I suppose the "professional" preoccupation.

Typed in large type, four spaces between the lines, in a looseleaf binder. At times he did follow the text with a glance now and then, as one learns to do after long practice. At other times he would go off for twenty seconds at a time, or more, making a point with the greatest fluency, and then returning, after quite an excursion, to glance once more at his script.

More Americans have witnessed this President's speaking manner and mannerisms than they have those of any other President in history: the TV debate with Nixon, of course. But seen close up and at full profile, as today, I got the full effect of the intensity of the man while he speaks. Not a relaxed gesture, never a real break for humor or change of pace. He moved his fine, strong hands over the pages before him, almost as if the pages were wrinkled, and he was trying to smooth them, a way of letting off energy or nevousness perhaps. Then that single speaking gesture of moving one hand, the right, in a horizontal jerky way. At one time this hand struck a glass of iced water, spilling some, but not overturning the glass. He didn't glance at the glass, though it made quite a sound.

While we sat waiting for the President to arrive through a door just outside his place at the "head table" the scarlet-coated Military Band was all primed, at our left. As the time drew nearer the band leader complete in gold braid and white gloves, took up a position out among the diners (why don't we say lunchers?). His eye was kept sternly on the door, and the signal he was to get. Then for five minutes, I would guess, the baton was held high, at attention, until finally the air was split with the "Hail to the Chief." We don't have much pageantry in American life; except for football games these more recent years, this is about the total of what we do. And instead of a man in a field marshal's uniform, say, in comes a slender youngish man, with a drake's tail tuft of hair that never will lie down with the rest of his hair—and this is the Head of State.

What the President said I thought was excellent. Not a fighting speech, not a speech to arouse the country or even that audience—there was applause at only one point.

The country won't be lifted up by this kind of speech, nor by the President's speaking style. In fact, that is just it: it doesn't have a style, if that word means something distinctive and, in the case of a great leader, warmth, radiance.

Kennedy's speaking manner lacks warmth, and so does his manner before an audience. He more than makes up for this by the sheer intensity he pours into everything he says. In time this close, intense contact with an audience, which he has when he shows himself to crowds, will find itself in his speaking and "platform" manner.

Woodrow Wilson comes to mind. Wilson was an eloquent man; some of his speeches are among the great ones of political history. But apparently it was a long time until emotion showed through. This is what a friend, speaking of my effect on audiences, calls "the emotion of truth."

I pretty well threw away my MS this morning. But I would be a silly fool if I pretended that the audience that filled the terrace ballroom —at 9:30 A.M.—wasn't moved by what I said, and by the fact that it was I who said it, since they knew, as I do in my candid if immodest moments, that I probably know more about the *realities* of economic development than anyone in this government; perhaps than anyone, period.

JUNE 18, 1961
SUNDAY
PRINCETON

Washington is full of geniuses these days. In the word department. The other day I dreamed up a phrase I thought characterizes the period. We have become the Fluent Society; obviously a take-off on the phrase of Ken Galbraith's *The Affluent Society*. Webster says fluent comes from "to flow," akin to the Greek to boil over, or "readiness of utterance" or "ready in the use of words."

At the luncheon on the 15th at which the President spoke, I sat next to George Meany. I had a good time with Meany. He *looks* rather stuffy and solemn, but actually we had a jolly time. He probably had me down as "one of the serious ones"; so many people do. What a lot of fun I have missed by acquiring—and probably earning—that sobriquet.

Meany and I settled down to talk about what he called leaders of "the movement." I made the banal and obvious remark that *history is people* and that this applies particularly to the labor movement: the distinctive *personal* characteristics and temperaments of the men and women who constituted the labor leadership explain what happened, or didn't.

So recalling my Chicago background Meany asked: "Did you know John Fitzpatrick, who was head of the construction labor unions; Vic Olander, secretary of the Illinois Federation; and Andy Furnseth of the Seamens?" Of course I did, and then I responded with a few words about each, and asked him about this one and that whom I knew, of those days—Petrillo of the Musicians, Davy Robertson of the Firemen's Brotherhood, clients of mine as a cub lawyer in the twenties.

This talk about individuals he knew made Meany come entirely alive; we had a good time, and in the process exchanged ideas, through our comment about these distinctive men.

He made an interesting comment about Sam Gompers, whom neither of us ever knew. Gompers was the beginning of a real American labor movement. Up to that time the leaders were European immigrants who were just carrying forward their experience and philosophy from Europe. Gompers also was a European immigrant—a cigar maker by trade—but he insisted on a distinctive American kind of unionism, not one that was political, as in Europe, but *economic*.

The fact that it took guts and creativity for a cigar-maker immigrant to have such ideas, at that time, hadn't occurred to me before, I must admit.

JUNE 22, 1961
NEW YORK

Further chapters in the D&R Persian story, this week.

Word just received that $40 million was on its way to Persia from the U.S. Government. This will relieve Iran's hard-pressed financial picture. The grave troubles, even the threat of some kind of coup in Iran, have filled the air and the newspapers here for weeks. It appears that the Kennedy Administration has decided to put its reliance on the vitality of the Amini Cabinet, and on certain fiscal reforms which have the Shah's support.

Today we had a long session at the office—in which it was firmly (I hope!) agreed that Gordon and Oliver on their early trip to Iran will begin at once the process that I thought we had previously agreed to and understood, i.e., transfer on an orderly but rapid basis of many of *our* functions (such as disbursements) and personnel to the newly created Iranian agency, the Khuzistan Water and Power Authority.

Perhaps it is unnatural for an administrator to be so cheered as I am that my organization is beginning to liquidate some of its functions and forces or to cut them back severely at least. The "rule" is that a public administrator is prehensile; he follows the pack-rat impulse. Always increase your organization (is it Parkinson's Law?), try to add to functions, never to cut back until compelled to do so, thereby increasing your "status."

I *think* my record in TVA and AEC is in the contrary direction. In any case, I have been pressing all along on transferring our functions in Persia *to the Persians* as soon as possible. Now Gordon, who shares the views I have to the hilt, has really worked out an agreement, a timetable and a procedure for getting this done.

In a letter to Dr. Enrique Penalosa, the new head of a regional agency just created in Colombia (for the savanna of Bogotá) I made the same point in a different form: that the crucial contribution D&R can make is to begin at once assisting him in the building of a *Colombian* organization to which he can turn over responsibilities.

JUNE 24, 1961
PRINCETON

A message from John Blumberg of our staff in Ahwaz. An Iranian member of our staff reported that Radio Moscow in its broadcasts, in Farsi, beamed to Iran had been giving us hell. In part, as follows: "The Lilienthal and Clapp company is spending and wasting a lot of money, supposedly building Dez Dam. The construction of this dam has already taken a long time and is not likely to finish very soon. The Americans in Iran are attempting to stop every major project and are trying to run down the economy of the country." Blumberg, in a memo dated June 16, goes on to say: "It is always difficult because of the implications to find an Iranian staff member who will admit that he was listening to this particular station, Radio Moscow."

JUNE 25, 1961
PRINCETON

What I prize highly about our American way of living is its diversity —diversity of the *sources* of power, of culture, of decision.

Now, isn't this what is going to happen in the whole world? But hardly through further international centralized power in *public* agencies such as the UN. The preoccupation with the furthering of internationalism through international *governmental* agencies, treaties, etc., gives an inadequate and perhaps misleading picture of our progress. For there are a hundred, yes, or a thousand sources of power arising in the internationalization that is going on in the world. Many, probably most, of these are not governmental at all.

It is an error to think that the only way to serve the vital cause of a world that can "get along" is through the State Department of this or any other country, or the UN.

JUNE 30, 1961
6:30 A.M.
MARTHA'S VINEYARD

A short swim at noon at Miss Emma's; the water unbelievably frigid (the nights have been at 60° or less), so cold that I gasped for a full minute after I was in, and my legs and arms actually ached with the cold. But every "first plunge" is always like that, whenever one plunges into any kind of cold water!

Then in the afternoon we had Pamela and Davey, and they stayed for dinner. This was sheer joy, a fantasy of a sweetness and charm I could hardly believe.

I am so proud of my grandson David III. A foot taller than his contemporaries—he will be six in about ten days—a strong, straight body. Big capable hands. He loves to do things with hammers, saws, drills, etc. We got the "makings" together, in the so-called garage beneath this room (we never put a car in it). After carrying on serious conversation about his "work" with me, he started on a "project" and I returned to the living room. I could hear him below, singing softly to himself, as the whack of the hammer and rasp of the saw accompanied him. He came up soon with an "injured" finger, but a bit of attention and a band-aid and he returned, full of importance, to resume. Then he invited me to use some of "his" nails and a hammer, and build me something. What I did, under his now and then approving eye, was what I might sell to the Museum of Modern Art in New York as a piece of what-do-they-call-it? collage, an abstraction in old lumber.

Then Pam, a story-book picture she is with her golden hair and sweetness, invited me to go to her "childhood" favorite spot, Signal Rock, within sight of our house. Whereupon, with much figuring on hand-holds and toeholds, she began to climb up the steep face of the rock. She made me understand she wanted no help, nor did I volunteer any. The look on her face as she did what she had never before been able to do explained Hillary of Mount Everest and Amundsen and other explorers who will perform feats of daring and hardship just for the satisfaction of doing something difficult.

This is the way we grow and become worthy of this beautiful, difficult, frustrating, but utterly wonderful world.

JULY 3, 1961
(4:45 A.M.)
MARTHA'S VINEYARD

Since four have been reading Anatole France: *The Crime of Sylvestre Bonnard*. I reached for my notebook, as the birds began to tune up to greet the dawn, to record a sentence from Bonnard: ". . . for in spite of my tranquil mien, I have always preferred the folly of the passions to the wisdom of indifference. . . . Our passions are ourselves."

A few pages earlier, he speaks of Goethe. "The great Goethe, whose own vital force was something extraordinary, actually believed that one never dies until one really wants to die—that is to say, when all those energies which resist dissolution and the sum of which make up life itself, have been totally destroyed." In other words, Goethe believed that people only die when they no longer desire to live—but not before.

JULY 5, 1961
MARTHA'S VINEYARD

Yesterday was a day of glory. Clear, bright, gay sunshine. My first single-hand sail of the year. A sweet northwesterly breeze to set out in; as the morning wore on the breeze came up, became quite stiff and exciting. *Lili-put* performed beautifully, that is, the two of us did. Is there any sound quite so evocative of things deep inside a man as the sound of a small boat parting lively salt water as the wind bears the boat smartly along? To me an elemental kind of satisfaction.

JULY 6, 1961
MARTHA'S VINEYARD

A great envelope of fog over all when I went out my door at 6 A.M. I made some coffee, spiked it with Jack Daniels, got into my bathing trunks and heavy cherry-colored sweater and made for the shore. The walk across the moor in the sweet soft fog, the conversation of the gulls lost somewhere overhead in the mist, the sting of cold water as I plunge in, the unbelievable sensation of swimming distances underwater, seeing my arms come forward into what seems a plastic substance (for it is so magical out on that shore that it isn't just "water"), the wild feeling of ecstasy on coming back to the beach and rubbing down, feeling more like a tiger than a man. Then to a huge breakfast Helen made for me— swordfish *and* a *thick* slice of ham, with eggs, and very hot coffee.

JULY 7, 1961
MARTHA'S VINEYARD

Much excitement in me, yesterday; *inter alia,* because the announcement about the great Italian firm of Montecatini becoming associated with Minerals & Chemicals-Philipp Corporation was the top industrial news of the day. We are really on our way in that company.

Ferd Eberstadt phoned: "Dave, I'm sorry to say that our catalyst plant is not working, the pellets are only 76 hardness, and our company is in a hell of a shape." Then he laughed that short, half-chuckle of his. It was his way of reminding me, his former companion in trouble, of the days when as fellow directors we in M&C lived from day to day, never knowing whether the company would survive the series of blows, disappointments, etc. "Now," he said, becoming serious, "we have a solid company in every way, and it is good to be able to say this to you who went through the troubles, on this important day."

Each time something comes along that is as fascinating as getting a major Italian firm to join in an American enterprise I get a touch of a fever of excitement that has nothing to do with making more money. For now there really is no point in making more, really; we certainly will have more than enough for our needs. No, the fascination is related to the passion that I have observed in some men who have completely "arrived" in business: perhaps just plain competitiveness (or sinful pride?) that stirs a certain kind of man and keeps him going.

I find myself continually interested in diaries and journals, whether by men of affairs or artists (it is the latter who have far more time and interest in writing journals). The reason is obvious: I am still trying to think through the opus I would really like to write about my own life and times, and also find a way, prior to that book, to make use of some of these journals, pretty much as they stand.

The latest such journal to come to my eye is that written by Willard Straight, and made use of as part of a life of Straight by Herbert Croly, one of the founders of early American progressivism.

Croly says Straight was "primarily a man of action. He was dissatisfied unless he was being carried along on the tide of some spacious event. But neither was he satisfied with behaving merely as the creature of the event." Hence he recorded what he saw and much of this found its way, as a young man in the Orient, into this diary.

I have reached the place in this chronicle of a young American in the Orient when he has returned to New York with his wealthy wife (a Payne Whitney), his first project in China having failed. That project was to involve American banking interests in the economic development of China, through railroad building.

He went into Wall Street, with J. P. Morgan, became an officer of a "development and resources corporation" (not literally, of course, but the analogy isn't as farfetched as it sounds, considering the times, i.e., 1914 and 1915) designed to promote international trade through American private business interests.

But he couldn't get "steamed up" about private business, in New York, working in America.

". . . he needed to be traveling towards a goal which commanded his devotion and which was bathed in an atmosphere of public service. His work in Wall Street lacked such a goal. The transactions of private business could no longer keep him hitched. He had become more than ever a man who needed, in order to put forth his uttermost efforts, the stimulus of a disinterested and resplendent social objective. . . .

"For his temperament an experience or an action was left incomplete unless it was perpetuated in a record and communicated to its appropriate public. . . . He needed to communicate, *but he needed to communicate the fruits of action.*" (My italics.)

JULY 9, 1961
MARTHA'S VINEYARD

To dinner last night at Roger and Evie Baldwin's. Their house guest Dan Chapman, head of Achimota, a remarkable school in Accra, Ghana. A remarkable man, so composed, so handsome, so courteous, and we learned in Accra, so thoughtful.

The picture he gave of Ghana in these latter days of Nkrumah was anything but a pleasant one, though he spoke without any rancor or stridency whatever; sadness more than anything. Nkrumah has changed in the past couple of years since Helen and I were first guests there; this was evident, but Chapman, who was Nkrumah's classmate, was able to cite the change with greater precision. Part of this is his self-elevation to something like a god, with the title not of Prime Minister but the native equivalent of High Priest or, in political terms, à la Hitler, the Leader.

Chapman said: "I want to make them feel uncomfortable about all this new trend, all this putting of the opposition in jail that is going on. I say these things to Botsio of the Cabinet and he says: 'It is a political necessity.' No such thing; quite unnecessary. The fact is they believe, Nkrumah and those around him, that they must plan on staying in power forever; otherwise they will have to leave the country after their term has expired; it would not be safe for them in Ghana. So they take measures to see that they will always be in power."

There is a clue here to why dictatorships in so many countries seem always to move toward more and more arbitrary power and more and more stealing of public funds by the men in power; they feel that *someday they may no longer be in power* and must leave the country, but fast, and have a fortune waiting for them outside somewhere. General Rojas Pinilla, General Pérez in Venezuela, etc. The list could easily be extended.

Roger told us something about Thomas Hart Benton, the great painter, a Vineyard neighbor. He has finished the two great "commissions" on which he has been working: for the St. Lawrence Seaway and the Truman Library. "He knows there probably won't be any more large commissions to execute. He is restless and unhappy for not having some big work to do."

Then he added a poignant sentence: "Tom no longer paints to please himself."

Which brought me back sharply to a concrete illustration of the difference between serious painting and commercial painting. Beatrice has said how much she wanted a chance to paint what *she* wants to paint, to say through painting what will give her satisfaction, whether anyone else (such as *The New Yorker*) likes it or not, or whether art collectors or curators like it.

As a writer of fiction, David would have the same problem: writing something he believes is good, for the satisfaction it gives him to express himself that way, as against writing with an eye, yes, with both eyes, on what a magazine editor, etc., wants and what will please him.

Can an artist divide himself into two parts this way? Many have certainly done so; many great paintings were done as "commissions" of patrons. And yet there is a sad note and perhaps an important lesson in this: Tom Benton began as a very poor young artist, enduring privations so he could paint the way he felt. Then as the years went by he became preoccupied with getting these big commissions for murals, being half a businessman and half an artist. And in the end perhaps he is no longer *able* to paint to please Tom Benton.

JULY 17, 1961
MARTHA'S VINEYARD

Last night read Crompton's *The Life of the Spider*.

Well, the female spider needs the male for a certain function; otherwise there wouldn't be any more spiders, and she likes one thing (only) the male spider can do for her. But once he has done what he *has* to do, she eats him, like any other "prey," Crompton says. Even while he is providing her with his life substance she begins tying him up securely, trussing him up with her silken threads. He *knows* what the female will do to him, he is skeered to death, but he is on the prowl for a female anyway. "Till death do us part," says the female spider to the male, just before she kills him.

Nature, say the conservation zealots, is so wise a model for human conduct. We human beings must not disturb the holy "balance of Nature," they say.

Woke full of high spirits, almost a joking jag; the cute Bromberger grandchildren came up the hill, in striped shirts, each with a striped parka over his head, looking like two candy figures in a musical comedy. I invited them in (knowing they had been told they must *not* disturb the grandparents). And we had some great laughs, fights, games, etc., together, and breakfast supplied by the kindest of all grandmothers.

JULY 18, 1961
MARTHA'S VINEYARD

An hour and a half ago Peggy produced "a baby"; no longer just "a baby" but now Margaret Lamb Lilienthal.

A granddaughter, and a quite beautiful one, big, pretty and pink, not wizened and out of shape as new babies often are.

JULY 21, 1961
MARTHA'S VINEYARD

At dawn the fog enfolded everything, so warmly, gently, silently. I walked across the moors; out of the void gulls appeared, vague as in a dream, flying with slowly moving wings, yet seemingly motionless and unreal. The Sound was rolling, but so dense, so omnipresent was the fog that only the white line along the shore was visible. It was so moving, I could hardly bear it. And then, after a short swim, as I came back across the moor the sun broke through, lighting up the glistening leaves, stirring the birds into song.

In a "Speaking of Books" column J. Donald Adams in last Sunday's *New York Times* commented on Hemingway as a writer and an individual. He was a writer because of the kind of individual he was, was his general point; he compared Hemingway to Byron.

"Both," says Adams, "were fundamentally men of action who were at the same time endowed—or burdened, if you like, with a sensitivity which made them writers also." And "Like Byron, Hemingway craved sensation. He would have applauded Byron's remark in his *Journals*: 'The great object is sensation—to feel that we exist, even in pain. It is [this] which drives us to gaming—to battle—to travel—to intemperate, but keenly felt pursuits of any description, whose principal attraction is the agitation inseparable from their accompiishment.' "

This I understand.

JULY 24, 1961
(10 P.M.)
NEW YORK

The Prime Minister of Nigeria, Alhaji Sir Abubakar Tafawa Balewa, is an extraordinary man. His dress, his way of relaxing, his dignity, his British reserve which I managed to break through at the last. Here is a shrewd and cautious man, but one who can be aroused; the art is, in a brief encounter (I was with him about forty-five minutes) to probe for those things that would get him stirred, and to thinking, and this happened.

When I was admitted to the huge living room of the Waldorf Presidential Suite, he smiled most pleasantly, spread his long legs out beneath the sheet-like gown he wore and said something like this: "Well, heah we ah." (His English is very British, his voice extraordinarily low and vibrant.) I admitted we were. Then he said: "And have you ever been in Nigeriah?" Then I *knew* that this line, which is the opener in almost all such nondescript conversations, indicated he didn't know why the hell we were together. I said I had.

After a bit more vague chitchat I thought I'd better get down to cases. So I told him about my company's interest in the Niger, something of my background in TVA and navigation, our work in Persia and Colombia.

Then suddenly he remembered that *he* had asked for this talk, and that it was about the Niger. From there on it went well. He made it as clear in the way a shrewd man would (and these Northern Nigerians particularly are as shrewd as an animal stalker) that we were being considered.

A cable from Gordon in Iran that the transfer of our functions discussions had reached the point of agreement, at last. Transfer to the Iranian agency, that is. Praise Allah.

With John Burnett, chiefly about the present posture and future of D&R. A very sensible man, impatient and restless as I am, but also with a sense of perspective and timing. Net result: D&R is not doing too badly; we have a number of business flirtations going on, and some of them may "take"; we have added quite a bit to our workload, all interesting things. The lack of intensive and good management in the little New York group is the most troublesome to me.

JULY 25, 1961
HAY-ADAMS (10:32 P.M.)
WASHINGTON, D.C.

I have just watched, and heard, the President of the United States talk to the world about "The Berlin Crisis," and what steps he proposes to be ready for a Soviet crunch.

Then I turned off the TV and looked out from my window here to a scene so much like a stage set that I was a bit shocked, so solemn was the meaning of what he said, so theatrical the sight.

Yonder the White House across Lafayette Park; beyond, lighted and stark against the blue sky of a summer night, the Washington Monument. A full moon, looking painted on a set.

But there is no play-acting, nothing theatrical about the positive position the President has taken from which there is little room for retreat. There could be a war before the year is out, if Khrushchev feels it now incumbent on him to make a similar no-surrender speech. We may well be not too far from a *war of calculation*—not of miscalculation, as the phrase usually has it.

The deterrent power of bigger and bigger bombs about which I have been so skeptical for so long looks pretty thin tonight. We have said we are not ready for war but will get ready. The Soviet may feel that the time for a "preventive" war is now, the very horrible idea that our military people—and some "statesmen"—wanted to wage on the U.S.S.R. when, in the 1940's, we had a monopoly of atomic weapons.

These are the possibilities for 1961. But the risks of a world war in the next five years I believe probably less than if we rushed to the shelter of an unreal "spirit of Camp David," or any of the utterly rational but utterly woolly-headed proposals for negotiation, without first taking a very strong diplomatic position.

In the President's speech I detected the hand of those who still have great faith in the NATO alliance and the Atlantic Community. I wish I could dispel the uneasy feeling that once again we are prisoners of a set of ideas that have no present-day practical value; that we are not thinking along new lines but simply copying the bulldoggedness of Churchill and Truman, because in the past that was effective.

Aren't there any new, fresh ways of looking at these things? Everything in my experience tells me that some men, whatever their age, play out, their inventiveness isn't sustained, and they fall into the postures of a time that is past.

Before I turn in, and while it is fresh in mind, I want to write my impression of the President today at the White House, a day when in his TV address on Berlin he laid it on the line in as serious a committal as this country has made in a long time.

There were perhaps one hundred men, mostly from the Government and from the Nigerian party, at the White House luncheon, given in the huge East Room. An interesting mixture of Americans: "Ev and Charlie" (Senator Dirksen and Minority Leader Charley Halleck)— Ralph McGill, Sargent Shriver—and so on. The Marine Band played the usual music as the President, looking grim and rather puffy, I thought, escorted the heavily robed Sir Abubakar. We passed them in the reception line. The President presented me as "Mr. Lilienthal, who built the TVA." The Prime Minister's face lighted up: "Yes, we met together yesterday."

The President had a heavy double line between the eyes, and seemed heavier in the face than I can remember. He has a short torso, compared to his long legs, and a rather bunched-up way of carrying himself.

But what a proud figure, so young and confident, despite the great weight that rests on him. A man must really pursue the Presidency "implacably," as Ed Murrow described it, to have the confidence and decisiveness without which a man would go to pieces, as Hoover did when the Great Depression upset everything he thought he knew.

I was near enough to the center of the long table to see the President, across the board, during a very good luncheon. He listened attentively, indeed tensely, to the Prime Minister. The contrast with F.D.R. is marked. Roosevelt would have smiled, told stories, and monopolized the time as a good host should, perhaps. Kennedy's eyes, seen at the angle I had from where I sat, have an especially large amount of white, something approaching protuberance, for so handsome a man.

As I was leaving the White House the President moved over to me, on the North Portico, and asked me: "What about Iran? The Shah is putting the heat on us about his need for increased military aid. What do you think—does he really need that kind of help?" I was noncommittal, knowing nothing about military needs; and suggested to the President that I generally haven't much confidence in military assistance for a developing country. The President was obviously worried; his question to me, I sensed, was rhetorical and to show that he identified me with Iran.

JULY 26, 1961
WASHINGTON

Had a visit with Eugene Black in the late afternoon yesterday.

He is very much frustrated and puzzled about the way the foreign aid policies of the Administration are going. I agreed that, while a new policy had been announced, the *action* so far was still so largely the old song of making loans, etc., to keep a nation from going to Moscow; whereupon, as in the disgusting case of Ghana and the Volta, they no sooner get their money by pressure and threats than they go playing footsie with the Soviet. So the words and music have changed but the action remains the same, rooted in the belief that you can give aid to buy friends.

Black said he was against *all* bilateral aid. Its purposes were to make political hay, or to sell the goods of the "aiding" country. Neither of these worked out. To lend money to a customer because he can't otherwise afford to buy your goods doesn't make sense; lending money in return for political alliances hasn't worked. So he favors *only* multilateral aid.

But he is realist enough, I think, to see that bilateral aid will continue and probably expand. "I don't know what I can do beyond what I have done. Most of the fellows in the Administration I talk to will agree privately, but they can't agree publicly because now they are Democrats."

Generally, he agreed with my statement that I thought Nigeria was the most likely new nation in Africa; that the Prime Minister wasn't inclined to use Nkrumah tactics to get aid, but the pressure would be on to get loans, and whether he, the Prime Minister, liked to bear down on us or not, he would be compelled to; or the U.S. would urge aid on them. I said I detected in the Prime Minister's demeanor a sensitivity about Ghana's success in getting money for the Volta, by methods he well understood.

Black was prepared to defend the Volta as a good deal, because the power had a market, a huge aluminum complex. As a sole criterion I found this rather curious! "But when the State Department learned that Nkrumah was going to Moscow they said we had to get the World Bank Ghana loan all buttoned up before he went. So, though they had asked the World Bank to put the transaction together, they wouldn't wait on the Bank's finishing its study, and announced loans from the U.S. Development Loan Fund and the Export Bank, and in a hurry."

4:15 P.M.

The Vice-President's luncheon for the Nigerian Prime Minister was held in the old Supreme Court Room, in the Capitol. It was here in this beautiful chamber the Senate heard Daniel Webster argue the Dartmouth College case. Here Chief Justice Taney sat while the Dred Scott case was argued and the decision delivered. Few could have foreseen what bloodshed and heartbreak would follow upon that case. In that same room this noon I saw a black man sit on the Justices' rostrum; a tall young-looking Texan, the Vice-President of the United States, listened closely to his British accents of reason and wisdom; next to him the shining bald head of the Texan Speaker of the House, diligently spooning down his ice cream, having arrived late but not being one to neglect his victuals. Perhaps thirty-six men sat at tables in the room where I first saw Holmes and Brandeis sitting on a case, hearing Paul Miller in 1934 move my admission to the bar of the Supreme Court.

It all seemed unreal. The members of the Nigerian Cabinet and delegation in their colorful robes, some with the embroidered caps, the Prime Minister still tightly clutching his worry beads, folded into the fist of his left hand.

A great shock. At the TVA offices learned from Betty Godfrey that my dear brave loyal Martha Jane Brown§ had died last Friday. I knew when I didn't get a birthday card on the 8th that things weren't going well. Such a really great human being, so full of faith and good cheer and grit. If *she* doesn't get to heaven, wherever that is, God is going to be lonely up there, for there never was a better person.

11:45 P.M.

Farmanfarmaian called to say that the Iranian Prime Minister wanted me and Black to know that Aramesh has been put in jail—not for his attacks on us, but the turn of the wheel is interesting nonetheless.

§ Miss Martha Jane Brown was my principal secretary at AEC.

JULY 28, 1961
NEW YORK

Sat next to the smooth and handsome Albert Gore night before last, at Rusk's dinner for the Prime Minister of Nigeria. "That was a fine thing you did, Dave," he said, "coming down to campaign for us in Tennessee last fall." Actually, I had never had any previous knowledge that Gore or Kefauver had known I had been on the stump. I made some comment that it hadn't apparently done any good. Gore: "Well, we were in a very difficult situation down there, very difficult. And it will be every bit as bad in '64 if the Catholic organizations don't stop pushing for aid to parochial schools." He looked glum, his usual half-grin gone for the moment.

When the Navy orchestra members scattered along the tables playing tzigane violin music—a kind of informal touch that didn't (I thought) go too well in the opulence of the State Dining Room—Albert looked very very appreciative. I remembered that he would know whether this was good fiddling, being a fiddler himself. He grinned. "Have you ever been in the Monseigneur restaurant in Paris? They do this same thing there. After a couple of bottles of champagne about three o'clock in the morning I took one of the players' fiddles and joined in."

Gore is unhappy about the continuation of the atom test ban talks; thinks they should be called off. I remarked that they should not have been given such importance, since they didn't go to the main issue: a health measure but not disarmament.

JULY 29, 1961
MARTHA'S VINEYARD

It was curious to walk into a government building, stepping out of a government car, with Ed Murrow as a public servant rather than a "reporter"; go into *his* office rather than he into mine, as in the "old" days in Washington.

He is quite thin and worn looking, more and more mournful, with those knowing eyes and droopy jowls. But his one-sided grin comes easily, and I got the distinct feeling that he is enjoying his new role. But every once in a while I noticed that he hasn't yet made the transition completely, from being a reporter looking for cracks through which he can see what is going on to the guy who is *doing* what is going on.

He will do a first-rate job; his courage and independence as well as his great and earned prestige will ensure that.

When we settled down in his office he pulled his necktie down and opened his shirt at the collar. How familiar a gesture, when I used to watch him just before he went on the air in his nightly radio news show. After some personal exchange, I reminded Ed of how he had helped me get *out* of public service, out of the AEC, how we had met, by arrangement, in Philadelphia to work over a statement I was to release explaining the reasons for my resignation; that one of the chief reasons, and one that he, Ed, had suggested be included in the text itself, was that I wanted to be more free to express my views to the public than anyone could while in a public post. He chuckled—in a toothy way known to many millions now that he has become a TV familiar, his arms on his knees, looking up at me with a big grin through the furrows of a really noble brow.

"But," said I, "I haven't come through on that pledge to speak out. I got my freedom, but I haven't really *used* it."

"You said it, I didn't," he said. "But you're right. The reason is that you are a doer, not a sayer. But you haven't made the use of your 'freedom' that we thought about in that statement, that's true."

"So many of the men around the President in this early period," I said, "are wordmakers, extremely articulate men, and well motivated and with keen minds. But words and ideas were their field, not doing something about ideas. This lack of operational men will cause the Administration plenty trouble, already has."

Ed took it up from there, with *relish.* "I know just what you mean, and you are so right. A good many of the fellows around here, especially from the universities and colleges, have never had to *run* anything, don't know how, don't think running things amounts to much. They have never had that kind of responsibility."

Ed talked a bit about Iran. The United States Information Agency had made up a colored film about Persia; it had been shown at the Palace. The Shah liked it. Ordered a showing throughout Iran. "So I had it canceled. Anything that pleases them so much as *that* can't be completely accurate reporting. We'll try another one."

JULY 30, 1961
MARTHA'S VINEYARD

A good deal of TVA on my trip to Washington, centering on a long visit with Marguerite Owen.

She was greatly displeased and angry. "I am not amused with the attitude of John *Fitzpatrick* Kennedy and the rest at the White House," said the gal who has done as much to get TVA through the slough of Dwight Eisenhower as any other person—to say nothing of being largely responsible for my winning my fights during the TVA period.

She told of the meeting of the TVA Board and President Kennedy a couple of weeks ago, when the Norris Centennial "rate reduction" was made a big thing. At that time Kennedy lectured the Board, telling them that they must not rest on the laurels of past achievements but show that TVA still is bold and imaginative. Marguerite said the Board was on top of the world, to be received by the President and to make the front pages. But *she* felt they had been insulted. She said: "Dave, what have we done that is wrong?"

She attributes the critical attitude of the White House—and it's just that—to personal or partisan forces: as an example, Senator John Sherman Cooper, who wanted a steam plant located in his state (and got it, finally, I notice). She even took out against local leaders who want tributary streams and basins, e.g., the Upper Duck, the Elk, etc., developed, a subject on which the TVA management is dragging its feet.

She showed me the report the TVA Board made to the President in April. This was in response to a request from the President for a statement of what TVA is doing that shows that it is thinking *ahead*, not just warming itself before the achievements of the earlier days of the TVA. She seemed to think the report impressive; I told her, after reading it, that it was the story of carrying on activities that had been going a long time, doing them well; but that for a pioneering organization it showed a lack of imagination about new things, hardly what you would expect of an organization with the record of innovation that is TVA's.

I commented, for example, that the announcement that the resale rates of TVA's distributors could be 8 percent lower might have been big stuff and courageous in 1933, when rates that low were a big gamble; this was hardly world-shaking or adventuresome in 1961. As for TVA as an example for underdeveloped countries, the trips that foreign groups were taking to TVA had fallen into a repetitious regular routine. This was hardly living up to the great worldwide excitement about TVA.

I'm afraid I sense what was wrong with TVA. For ten years at least we have wrapped ourselves in the cotton wool of self-admiration and complacency over a good job well done. New ideas don't spring from such a soil.

JULY 31, 1961
MARTHA'S VINEYARD

Sunrise, throwing its glow into the puffs of clouds and the early blue of a new sky and a new day. Why, this day *could* be a new beginning: that is why I relish the dawn even more than the flamboyance of even the loveliest sunset.

Last week we had talks with John Burnett about D&R and its

future. Burnett has the enthusiasm and judgment, the imagination and toughness that we have had too little of during the past couple of years, so it seems to me. The drive and persistence to give to the building of this unique enterprise, the attention to *significant detail* that it takes to get others who are responsible to you to act; it is in this area I have been lacking.

Burnett is the best thing that has happened to D&R for a long time. If D&R becomes an "institution" rather than just a vehicle for Lilienthal and Clapp it will be, perhaps, because Burnett is determined that it should be so and is giving of himself so unstintingly to try to bring that about.

Institutions flourish or fade depending upon individuals. This is true of small ones, as this little company is, or big ones like AEC or General Electric. From such a man as Burnett energy is generated, new people as well as ideas emanate, the men who are tired or repetitious (and already we are in danger of just this) are either fortified or ultimately replaced.

Last evening, after dinner, went to the Eliases in Menemsha (Leona Baumgartner's idea) to visit with Jerome Wiesner of MIT, for the past six months Kennedy's chief advisor on science. His attractive wife, Laya, in her yellow frock, slender neck and fragile face, somehow like a wild canary.

Wiesner is anything but birdlike. A heavy, *solid*-looking youngish man, outwardly relaxed, sucking at a pipe, not garrulous, and yet very articulate, quite proud of his position, as he should be.

We discussed the current controversy: should the President order a resumption of the testing of A-bombs?

Wiesner said: "If left to himself, without the pressure of a dozen people, half of them on the Congressional Joint Atomic Energy Committee, the President would not order resumption of testing. I don't know whether he has any choice, though, with these pressures."

I said this is about the way the H-bomb crash program issue developed eleven years ago, when I was still Chairman of AEC. By the time the pressures had accumulated Truman felt he had no alternative but to order it to go forward.

Wiesner nodded, over his pipe, looking very thoughtful. He went on to say that there is hardly a member of the Joint Committee on Atomic Energy who doesn't have some local reason for his vote on anything to do with the atom: Gore with Oak Ridge, Anderson with Los Alamos, Jackson with Hanford, and so on.

I remarked that this atomic pork barrel was bad enough, and might be decisive about the test ban; but it was even more deadly about continuing to make weapons that were no longer the most useful kind, such as some kinds of manned bombers.

He picked this up: "This is terrifying. When we cut back on [naming some bombers] the phones rang all day from Senators in whose states these bombers are made that the military itself finds no use for. I don't see how we can expect much in the disarmament talks with this sort of thing."

I said I was nonplused to find so much good hard intellectual technical work on disarmament, by university people mostly, without mention of this political and industrial vested interest in making arms.

AUGUST 6, 1961
MARTHA'S VINEYARD

I make little reference, in these journals, to the prevailing ambiance of uneasiness about war (not to say pit-of-stomach fear). Whether this feeling is experienced by many others I don't know.

But all the reassuring communiqués and news magazine articles can't obscure the fact of Soviet advances, of our own inadequate initiatives, of troubles of our Allies. Tunisia and Algeria make our relations with the French increasingly difficult. This morning Khrushchev announced another successful space flight, and a conclusion by the Soviet bloc that a treaty will be signed with East Germany. These are all discounted as simply the "setting" for negotiations over Germany; but it would be absurd to ignore the fact that positions are becoming frozen long before the negotiations begin, that the push to some acts of force, some military action, is stronger now than any time I can remember since the end of the war.

That this exuberance and aggressiveness by the Soviet may be their undoing is a comforting thought: it has happened more than once before that success has ruined the plans of power in men and peoples: Napoleon, Hitler, *et al.* But look at the irreparable damage that resulted before that "ruin" came.

AUGUST 7, 1961
MARTHA'S VINEYARD

I have been trying to find some rationale that would make more acceptable my state of turbulence, inside, reaching out for something I do not have or something I greatly want, long for. Or the strain, far from comfortable, of trying to work out ideas.

The most comforting thing I can find to say is negative, oblique: that a *satisfied* person, or mind, or soul, is not as likely to produce something good, distinctive, perhaps original, as a *dissatisfied*, writhing person.

AUGUST 8, 1961
MARTHA'S VINEYARD

The reports of Khrushchev's speech about Berlin are pretty doleful. The arms race quickens. At last there is a specific issue drawn between the Soviet and the West, at a particular place and with a kind of time deadline. For a long time it has been difficult to point to any specific quarrel of the kind that in the past has precipitated war. Now we appear to have one. The longer Khrushchev can drag this one out— assuming it doesn't get away from him or his own team doesn't draw his claws—the better for his purposes, I suppose. Certainly a war scare, whether consciously intended that way or not, helps Kennedy in his basic effort, as I see it, to arouse the American people, inculcate a sense of sacrifice, and begin to call for definite sacrifices.

So on both sides a real war scare is to the advantage of the leaders, and a real war scare is what we shall have. Whether it will get so far along the road that the scare can't be called off is something I wouldn't bet too much on. But one must live on some kind of assumptions; mine is that some *modus vivendi* will be worked out as to Germany, one not yet proposed publicly certainly, but the tension will not let up, perhaps during my lifetime.

AUGUST 12, 1961
MARTHA'S VINEYARD

A great sail yesterday. To Edgartown (and return!) with Pete Mitchell. A brisk southwester about fifteen knots; then on the return ran into a squall; very turbulent water between Oak Bluff and East Chop. I held *Lili-put*'s nose right into it, and she would shake her head and come back for more; I sailed in a gusty blow without easing her off, either by sheet or tiller; for ten minutes at a time the gurgling, hissing water came over the lee rail (or what would be a rail if this weren't a tiny little boat). Such a wind and sea. The spice of danger was there, but for the first time I felt fully confident that I could sail in almost anything. Famous last words perhaps. But it was as close to sheer ecstasy at times as anything—of that kind at least—can be.

AUGUST 13, 1961
SUNDAY
ON BOARD NE AIRLINES AT MARTHA'S VINEYARD
READY TO TAKE OFF FOR NEW YORK

Sailed *alone—not* around the world, like Captain Joshua Slocum— but across the Sound to Falmouth. So yesterday was a new high in my sailing life. It wasn't exactly a reckless thing to do, for there was a stiff but steady northwest breeze, and I kept watch of the currents and drift. When I had reached the big bell buoy I saw the mainland over my bow, and thought to myself: Let's go across; you'll probably get back, if the wind holds out.

A bit pathetic and adolescent, for a gent late in life to get such satisfaction in becoming a small boat sailor, a single-hand sailor.

SEPTEMBER 1, 1961
MARTHA'S VINEYARD

Learning to negotiate with the Russians: this is a theme that most concerns everyone, with the end of the A-bomb test "ban" by the announcement of the Russians that *they* were resuming testing.

I have all along been dubious about the desperate emphasis some of our people have put on a moratorium on atomic weapons testing. For three years many people were agitated about the stopping of testing as if this was or could be the beginning of disarmament. It wasn't then and isn't now. And when testing begins again this makes it seem far more ominous than it would have been without all this long talk.

Don't get involved with the Russians unless you are sure it is important. What is happening in Berlin, etc., seems to me to underline the fatuity of Pugwash-type meetings. Americans come back from such meetings with an inner assurance that the Russians *really* are disposed to be free despite what their rulers do or say. But I can't help feeling that meetings of intellectuals, such as those at Pugwash, are parts of the *weakening* process. Weakening of *our* will, and sense of reality, I mean.

SEPTEMBER 4, 1961
LABOR DAY (OUR *38th* WEDDING ANNIVERSARY)
MARTHA'S VINEYARD

Saturday with Jack Daggett on a cruise to Tarpaulin Cove, an event looked forward to a long time. Left here at 8 A.M.; returned at 9 P.M.—thirteen hours: but this was *not* our intention. What we intended was a quick sail over, from Vineyard Haven; I was very proud to bring that 15-footer into the Cove. I have looked at Tarpaulin from our hill for so many years. Anchored, jumped overboard, and swam to the beach, walked about the wild moors, saw a picnic meeting of the most queer assortment of people, swam back, ate our lunch aboard *Liliput*.

By 2 P.M. we set off to go through Robinson's Hole, thence into Buzzards Bay in plenty of time to catch the easterly tide.

But the wind died. A flat calm. Then a deep, deep fog. Hours of creeping along steering by a compass we weren't too sure about. After hours of this Jack heard surf; decided it must be the Vineyard north shore. But by this time the tide was foul, and though a riffle of wind came up, it was hardly enough to move us against that increasing tidal current. It was going to be dark soon; we decided against going into Tashmoo, holding that out as an extremity we could repair to if all else failed. About 7:30 as night was falling a small outboard gave us a wild tow; a time or two I was sure we wouldn't make it, for by this time at West Chop the tide was running like mad, swirling and clawing at us and at our friend in his little outboard. To our mooring at 9. Greeted back home, six hours overdue, by anxious people.

SEPTEMBER 10, 1961
SUNDAY
PRINCETON

A shaking—and revealing—experience yesterday, from a source that was quite unexpected. And, too, it was the "surprise" element that makes the impression so deep.

Jim Szold, my distant cousin, a partner in Lehman Brothers, sent me a copy of a forthcoming biography of another quite-distant "cousin," the famous Henrietta Szold. I supposed that the book would be like the other biographical sketches of this "dedicated woman," dedicated, that is, to the cause of a national home for the Jews in Palestine, to the Jewish children escaping from Europe; the scholarly, erudite, and utterly self-controlled woman, her entire emotional life devoted to her work. This was the picture I had, and I daresay most people had.

This biographer, however, had been given full use of Miss Szold's journals, diaries. From these he found something quite remarkable. At the age of forty-four, when she was already a noted woman, editor, etc., she fell utterly and completely in love. A man thirteen years younger than she suddenly awakened the woman in her. This was platonic, in that it was without any "lovemaking." After four years in which she was utterly joyous when she was with him, or working on his literary needs like an abject slave, she discovered that he did not love her, as a woman, and never had given her any sign that he had. He announced his engagement to a twenty-two-year-old German girl—and Miss Szold was shattered.

It was the effort to write to herself, in her own journals, to analyze her predicament and "sublimate" her frenzy that interested me, of course. Here was a story of a woman who to the outside world seemed objective and utterly devoted to intellectual life who tried in her own journals to *erase or understand* a personal emotional experience, an experience that was both joy and devastation.

The creative power of pain, emotional pain, is something that I'm

sure varies from individual to individual. Was it this pain and frustration that made her so great a force for the good of others?

How little we know about what goes on behind the faces and
demeanor of those we assume are composed, fulfilled, "in control"!

The first A-bomb was exploded at Hiroshima in early August, 1945.
A month or so later I was invited to a conference at the University of
Chicago to discuss what could be done to prevent this new discovery
becoming the scourge of mankind. From that time on, until I left the
AEC in February, 1950, this was precisely my sole preoccupation. The
horrors that hung over the world that I pictured to others were pictured
to me, were part of my sleep and my unsuccessful efforts to sleep.

The Soviet has resumed testing of bombs, within the past week so
that, together with the acute tension about Berlin the anxiety I once had
to carry, because I was in a position of some responsibility, *everyone* now
shares.

This extreme uneasiness was manifested at a luncheon of the
M&C directors last week, dominating the conversation. Naturally they
wondered how I felt, asked me direct questions. One was: Is it "talk"
that these weapons are different in kind, not only in degree, from those
we have previously used? It is, I said.

But mostly I tried to steer the conversation toward the essentially
emotional inward questions: How do you live under this shadow? What
is your fundamental attitude? And then I expressed mine. It hasn't
changed much in the intervening years.

We must live a day at a time. We must do the best we can with the
jobs and commitments, spiritual and physical, that we have. We have to
make certain assumptions. One such assumption is that the world will
not be destroyed by the outbreak of a vast nuclear war; that this is not
in the stars. But that possibility must not be absent from our inner
conscience, any more than it is absent from our innards that someday—
perhaps tomorrow, perhaps thirty years from now—each of us will
surely cease to live, not because of bombs but because death is the part
of all who live, it is an antiphony of life itself.

So live today; expect to live tomorrow.

This is not a satisfactory response for the very young, of that I am
sure. And they are terribly important.

SEPTEMBER 13, 1961
AT LOGAN AIRPORT

The meeting with Max Millikan at the Center for International
Studies at the Massachusetts Institute of Technology was revealing,
reassuring, and more than worth the trip in this heat.

Millikan is square. A square head, a square cropped haircut, square shoulders; even his candid warm eyes seem not round but cubes, square on a side.

I started to tell him about D&R but he was way ahead of me. He knows it "well," with real understanding. But most pleasing and surprising: he isn't one who thinks that economists are all that are needed in a foreign aid program. I have never known an economist with a better sense of appreciation of the "nuts and bolts" of administration, of management, the things that are necessary to get something done.

Explained that we as a company had been doing development work as advisors or managers, for some six years now, but never as part of the foreign aid program of the United States. This, I said, was because of a conviction that we could be of the greatest help, if we are wholly independent, advising (or managing) on behalf of the undeveloped country that engaged us, with responsibility solely *to them*.

He was forthright. He said that those at MIT who were consulting and advising about foreign aid, in the top level, felt just as we did: that *lenders* to a developing country, as in the Development Loan Program, should not *also* be the development *advisors* of a country; that this was a mixing of functions. He was distressed that the World Bank is setting itself up, through an institute, to become development advisors. The country that received this advice would be certain that it was being proffered as a condition of a loan, no matter how much the Bank denied this.

I quoted Gordon's phrase about the limited "absorptive capacity" of an undeveloped country to utilize foreign "experts"; we embroidered this theme. He used the classic case of Ghana, overrun with experts supplied "for free" from other countries, with one hundred Indian engineers as railroad advisors when the total rail mileage in the country was less than 200 miles!

When I spoke of the importance of management, he said: developing theories and language and concepts was comparatively easy; following through on them was what was hard and the real test. I never expected to hear *this* kind of talk from an economist in this field!

A point I wanted to make strongly to Millikan carries the leaden-footed pretentious word "selectivity." Not trying to cover *everything* is a precept I've lived by in my work these many years.

An example: the sudden expansion of the Indian Village Community Program to cover *all* villages (or 5,000 at least) without waiting until things had been learned in a few. He told me that he had worked a long time in India, had found that the pilot selective approach had to be used, so that what Bowles was sure was right "because it concerned itself with people, in the villages" turned out to be unworkable when started on a wholesale basis.

SEPTEMBER 14, 1961
NEW YORK

Diplomacy is dead, I fear. Certainly as between the Russians and ourselves. Later it will also be true with the mainland Chinese. What we know historically as "the art of diplomacy" just doesn't have any place in these days except as a façade. The Soviet are warring on us; and after a war has begun traditional diplomacy is out, functionless.

Yesterday, in Cambridge, I attended an Executive Committee meeting of the Radcliffe Institute of Advanced Study, a meeting that continued until five and resumed with a dinner for the new scholars— the first batch—of the Institute.

Everyone calls President Mary Bunting "Polly." No one has less of the superficial, glad-hander surface so often seen in a college president. A twinkle in her eye; when she disagrees a cloud comes over her face, and you know exactly what her disagreement or qualification is. With a farm girl manner when she is in motion, not "feminine" in the conventional sense, she has, thanks to the Institute idea, become one of the foremost American women almost over night. I mean *not* just as an educator, but as a *woman*. This is one of those ironic twists that makes life so interesting.

The Institute idea is now on trial. For the idea has aroused interest throughout the whole country. It is important, for it is going to call attention to the special *modern* status of gifted women.

SEPTEMBER 15, 1961
NEW YORK

The last thing I thought I would be doing with this day was to think hard about TVA. But so it was.

A letter from Barry Bingham of the *Courier-Journal* enclosing five articles written by John Pearce of their staff. They recounted the rising criticism of TVA, chiefly because of the failure to begin dams and regional development on small tributaries, notably the Elk and Duck rivers.

Gordon was furious about the articles; thought they were hopelessly unfair. He was particularly upset by quotations from me saying that TVA could build these dams "if they really wanted to."

We had a rather spirited but in the end friendly disagreement about my basic uneasiness about TVA. But I wrote a long, long letter to Bingham making plain that, while I was indeed critical of TVA about being wedded too closely to doctrines that overstressed power economics that may now be no longer useful, I disavowed any attack on the motives of the TVA.

There is more than one way to get a complacent "successful" organization to move; my way may not be the best but it has its points.

My talking to the *Courier-Journal* man, Pearce, was taking a risk that some of my friends in TVA would be offended and alienated by. But I'm *not* one, any longer certainly, to believe that you should always play it safe and cautious.

SEPTEMBER 19, 1961
(11 P.M.)
WASHINGTON

Discussions today about Nigeria with the ICA heads for Africa, chiefly Marcus Gordon. Handsome, gray hair, a worn look, the harassed, almost hunted appearance of those men who have survived so much uncertainty trying to make "foreign aid" work and with so little appreciation and thanks. And later in the day with the Assistant Secretary for Africa, "Soapy" Williams, tall, football coach type, but with the shrewd disarming eye of an expert politician.

Governor Williams' secretary came out to explain that he would be a bit late. "There's a big flap on around here today." The "flap" was what may prove to be a disaster for the UN, the death of Hammarskjöld in a plane wreck in the Congo. The situation there was so desperate Hammarskjöld felt the head of the UN had to be there to try to work it out. Now there is no UN, temporarily, and before he is replaced it may be worth serious reassessing whether, as Gordon puts it, we shouldn't begin putting our support and faith in regional organizations (like OAS), rather than watch the UN gutted by a combination of the U.S.S.R. and some of the "neutrals."

SEPTEMBER 21, 1961
NEW YORK

Ed Murrow had that unmistakable fire in the eye that marks a full functioning human being. He came out into the reception room at his offices yesterday to greet us, his necktie pulled down, shirt collar unbuttoned, coatless, of course—the Ed Murrow who set a new standard (and one that hasn't been matched) in the electronic reporting business.

At my suggestion we went to the Cosmos Club. As Ed walked into the dining room, handsomer than ever with gray now in his bushy eyebrows, heads turned, people gently whispered to each other. He has the special quality of an actor, a good one; when he comes on stage, no matter where, he brings something electric with him, around him.

"We still don't know the power of terrorism," he said apropos the series of Soviet A-"tests." "It may be greater than we think."

Ed said that in the President's councils he had tried to delay the resumption of A-bomb tests, for a few weeks; otherwise we would get little "credit"—or the Soviet less censure—for *their* resumption of testing. But he didn't persuade those who had to decide.

History may record, he said ("if there is any history"), that "the retreat of the West began on August 13. That was when the East Berliners put up barbed wire at the border. They did it with factory militia. I was there and I saw them, fellows in half uniforms. If *right then* we had said—to these fellows—with a few men and a tank or two: 'Boys, poop off,' they would have pooped off, in spite of the several divisions the Russians had spread out, like a crescent, around the border. But we didn't do that, and that may have been the beginning of the end for us."

OCTOBER 1, 1961
PRINCETON

One constituted as I am must constantly recast his goals, every year or some other short period.

The flow of events, from the outside (e.g., the Berlin crisis, one's job with the atom or Persia or Wall Street) or his close personal relations, rain down impulses on one's emotional roof, impulses which ask: "What you wanted and were willing to strive for so hard yesterday, or last year, or ten years ago—do you really want that *now*?"

OCTOBER 2, 1961
PRINCETON

Tuesday, September 26, I went to the Waldorf Towers for a "social" gathering, on the invitation of Secretary of State Dean Rusk. I put "social" in quotes because at a time of great tension and public interest, a small gathering of serious men (and these were) with the Secretary of State (or any other equivalent man of "temporary power") turns out, of course, to be anything but "social." As Ernest Gross said, after interrogating Dean Rusk, in a circle of men each of whom was watching his every word like a cat stalking a wild bird: "A talk with the Secretary of State always ends up as an interview."

Rusk is in New York for a series of "exploratory" talks with Andrei Gromyko. The two men are oddly alike in this at least: they are both pros, with long training and experience in what is left of diplomacy.

As I listened to Rusk, and watched him for an hour and a half, I was greatly impressed. He is dealing with an impatient and untried Chief, on the one hand, and a chesty, cocky, saturnine Russian, on the other. What is now always referred to as the "crisis" in Berlin he said with firmness "is a *real* crisis."

I saw in Rusk not the slightest touch of flamboyance, of a temptation to make phrases or to impress the perhaps twenty men who were there, at his invitation. They were invited in order that they should be impressed—I am not so naïve about these things as not to know that. Yet he stood so quietly, his voice so steady (and tired), and mood so analytical that I got the feeling that he had command of all the elements of fact and of risk and of background. That something quite original and creative will come out of this husky, shaggy head on a husky frame I saw no evidence. He is not the inspired actor that Ed Murrow is, for example; but he doesn't have the strong touch of irony (so close to skepticism) of Acheson. He has a good mind, but not a clever, facile one. Isn't this to the good? I think so, definitely.

It was an interesting group. Young Orvil Dryfoos of the *New York Times*, still resentful that George Woods, a *Times* director and trustee, was scared off being foreign aid administrator. Henry Cabot Lodge, looking so young and buoyant he could be my son, whereas he is himself a grandfather. Paul Hoffman, his blue eyes and earnestness the same, but a little more aware of how complex things are. Ham Armstrong, avuncular and somewhat academic, but a seasoned expert in things that may no longer be quite so important at being expert about, in the foreign field. Max Ascoli, editor of *Reporter* magazine, peering smugly from behind his heavy glasses; but the appearance of being smug is an illusion; he really cares and can get angry.

OCTOBER 3, 1961
PRINCETON

My fifth consecutive day at home. The respite from the clang and crush of New York has been pleasant. But I shall be glad to get back to the delirium and humanness of New York.

I never thought I would think of New York as human. But it is so; one's sense of compassion for others, and the excitement of seeing so many people of so many different kinds, struggling just to live the day through is a kind of heady tonic. They are modern human beings, living life as it is today and, with urban congestion growing the world over, as it will be tomorrow for many, many other peoples around the world.

OCTOBER 5, 1961
NEW YORK

Luncheon this noon, at the Century, with Jim Geraghty, art director of *The New Yorker*. I have rather enthusiastically seconded his name as a member of the Century, and wanted to talk to him about that. But more than that, he is a man of the most wide-ranging interests. He said, in what seemed to me a quite penetrating comment, that in thinking of his successor as art director (someday) what it is the man should have. Curiosity, he said, and not knowing too much, i.e., have too many *facts*. Good qualifications for any kind of leadership, I'd say.

A good session with Dr. Atchley this morning. What a piece of good fortune that I should have a physician who understands my emotional nature as he does. One would never guess it to look at him. Son of a Baptist Minister; rather frail and bent looking, physically, though his face has the twinkle and bite and conviction we usually associate (sometimes quite wrongly) with youth. "Only one life," he said; that's the way he looks at things, and wants me to do the same, as my physician.

How fortunate, he said, to have things enter one's life that give it added meaning and depth, and just plain "fun"—I quote "fun" because it is not a word you often hear, certainly not from so distinguished a scientist and teacher and healer.

In talking to me about how I function in the work I now pursue, Dr. Atchley said: "Don't fuss that you aren't at your office a given number of hours or days. Do the things for which you are peculiarly equipped; leave it to others to do the other things. If I may use a military figure of speech: You are best at leading the charge, at taking the forward trench. Leave it to others to 'occupy.' There are few people—I don't know another one—whose experience and emotional temperament is so good at leading the charge. And that is quite enough of a function, more than enough."

OCTOBER 9, 1961
PRINCETON

In two short weeks I shall be on my way to Persia.

Last Thursday evening (the 5th) the Century Club was literally overflowing with that special kind of "successful" man that this club stands for. I enjoyed the cocktail hour; it was a subway rush in dinner jackets.

The high point for me was meeting Lewis Strauss. I walked over, put my hand on his shoulder, and greeted him. He grinned in his best manner. We were a picture of amiability. But it does no good whatever to carry grudges or grievances unless you are still in a fight over some issue worth fighting about and need fuel for the furnaces of your wrath. Which certainly I don't so far as Strauss is concerned.

Attended a dinner for Willy Brandt, the Mayor of West Berlin, Friday night. A young bull of a man, with the heavy shoulders and square head of a human battering ram. A big grin, dimples, a rumpled hairdo. Gunther compared him with Wendell Willkie, in manner. I would not agree with that; Willkie was full of zest and vitality, but impulsive. Brandt has a restrained, a grave and judicious quality. Perhaps it was because he knows that, at this very hour, the future of his city hangs in the balance. And the world?

Brandt was called to the telephone, while he was making his speech, called in peremptory tones. He colored, went hastily, returned not long after. In the Sunday *New York Times* I learned that the call was from President Kennedy, but, as Brandt explained to us, it was not completed "for technical reasons."

OCTOBER 10, 1961
NEW YORK

A call from one of my favorite of all people, Augie Heckscher: could I possibly have lunch with him and Gunnar Myrdal, the great Swedish economist? Myrdal is doing a big job for the Twentieth Century Fund about Asia.

So I trotted down to the Century. Myrdal is not at all what I expected. (*Where* did I get the idea that all Scandinavians are restrained, reserved, unenthusiastic, without passion?) Myrdal is full of the juice of life. He talks so rapidly, with such excitement.

One thing he said that pleased me coming from a "great economist." "The *facts* about much that is going on in the world, particularly in the less developed regions, just aren't important. In the first place, they change so rapidly. Also in the first place, there is no vocabulary to describe the facts, so they mean almost nothing. For example, the term 'unemployment' simply has no definable meaning in India."

I confess I have been prejudiced against the kind of economists who have their pat categories into which everything *must* fit or it is not worth considering. That has roused me to some pretty broad—*too* broad—expressions of ennui for economists. Well, here is one who is beginning to recognize that what is real and what is recorded and analyzed by economists have little similarity in most of the world.

To the Biltmore, and a visit from Salvador Araneta, our host in Manila eighteen months ago. I told him frankly that people were uneasy about the Philippines for two of several reasons: the feeling that corruption was widespread and therefore a handicap to private business and investment out there; and second, that the position of the Far East was in greater danger than ever before, the troubles in Laos, for example.

OCTOBER 14, 1961
PRINCETON

Last evening to the opening performance of *Saint Joan* (Shaw) at McCarter Theatre, here. We took Pamela, though we knew some of the long talk fests (which are such good reading) might be both tiresome and perhaps too subtle for so young a person. And it went on until 12:45 A.M.

But Pam is an enchanting twelve-year-old. "Everyone seems so tall," she said, shaking back the bright gold of her hair, which she wears à la Alice in Wonderland, down her back, her green eyes with a whimsical half-laughing light in them. Perhaps it is a long time since she has been with a crowd of people all of whom are adults.

Pamela has a mind, an interesting one. Yesterday afternoon, after bantering me about my ignorance about "seven based numbers," she got me quite interested in the way this Princeton school teaches mathematics. As I looked at the mimeographed book they use, it was evident that to these teachers math is *not* arithmetic (i.e., adding, subtracting) but an adventure in the reasoning process, a method of reasoning taught through a concept of numbers and how they can be analyzed; that actually this is a course for twelve-year-olds (junior high) in some of the basic tools of the world of science in which they must—and should be glad to—live.

What a world lies between this kind of instruction and the arithmetic of my childhood, and the repulsive and ill-understood algebra of "Professor" Jesse in my first high school days in Valparaiso. The changes in the world of thought and the processes of analysis and projection since 1912 could hardly be more startlingly demonstrated.

I have just come back from a ten-minute walk to the edge of the Institute grounds.

To be as full to bursting, with joy, even for a few moments is worth almost any amount of un-joy. And how lucky not to live always on the level of equanimity, where rarely does anything really distasteful or painful cross the threshold, but also never is there this explosion of joy within one's heart. And to be capable of this long after the days of my youth have come and gone. What a treasure this is indeed.

OCTOBER 21, 1961
PRINCETON

A good piece of advice, warm and knowing, as I prepared to set out for a strenuous trip to Iran:

"Don't set out grimly on this trip, rushing to get it over as soon as possible, dashing through it tensely. Absorb the joys of different sights and people. *Savor* this experience, bit by bit. See, look, observe—don't dash by the wonders you will see *if* you look, if you savor and relish.

"And don't be overly impressed with anyone. The Shah, you know, is lonely and troubled, sovereign that he is. Don't forget that behind the medals and the air marshal uniform and the bowing there is a man, a man who will respond to the warmth you have as part of your inheritance, who wants a friend as much as any powerful man does. The more impressive the façade and reality of power the more they will appreciate your *interest in them as people*.

"The physical demands of such a trip are great, true; but the nervous energy demands can be turned to the plus side if you set out to enjoy and relish and observe."

OCTOBER 24, 1961
EN ROUTE TO PARIS BY AIR FRANCE

We have been over the Atlantic four hours; the western sun is on "our tail"; the pink and white and rose on the high clouds below look celestial, as if some French or Italian baroque fat little naked angels will appear any time, floating about half perpendicular, with a wisp of cloud of chiffon draped decorously across their middle. Like a confectioner's version of a Paul Manship, or a Paul Manship sculpture in confectioner's sugar.

Here I am, a guy who feels deeply, and always has, for those who are short-changed in this world (remember my oration on "the Predatory Rich" way back in my high school days?). Yet I fly the Atlantic in the first-class cabin *and* gorged with paté, caviar, champagne, two kinds of French red wine, then fall back, after so heavy an absurdly luxurious luncheon, into a midday sleep. More attendants waiting on me (including two exceptionally fetching French gals) than on a minor seventeenth-century Duc of France.

Absurd, isn't it? The purpose of my trip is to try to further our six-year effort in Persia, to get more millet and rice and wheat and schools for people of such poverty as can hardly be imagined, or tolerated; and en route to my task I fall into this nonsense, this hand-and-foot attention and exotic food.

Something wrong somewhere.

This trip is different from any I have ever taken, in this: I feel more sure of myself, and complete within me. Less secure feelings will come but right now I feel that I shall let the world of the great and powerful and the people who are neither partake or not as they choose of the radiance of good feeling and love I feel for everything and everyone.

And now far below darkness over the vastness of the Atlantic Ocean.

OCTOBER 25, 1961
HOTEL PONT ROYAL
10 P.M.
PARIS

The joys of knowing only one language.

All the grim "improve-yourself" talk about the need to speak the other fellow's language in order to "communicate"—well, of course, there *is* something to it. But not all that much. There is another side. For example: how good it was tonight to sit in a tiny restaurant—just off Odéon circle—for a couple of hours and be able to observe and savor and sniff the way people look at each other, and their food, how they gesture madly, how they raise their eyebrows and shoulders—and not understand *one damn word*. Had I understood I would probably have heard much the same kind of banalities I would hear in Ye Olde Coffee Shoppe in Stamford. Here, not knowing French, I could let my imagination take over: it was drama and comedy undiluted. How nourishing to be with all these distinctive people, each one so sharply different, and keep the impression—or illusion—that what they were saying to each other was part of a play.

The gestures of the French are impossible to exaggerate, seen at close range, in a 14 x 14-foot bistro. A man of about fifty came in with a young man of perhaps thirty, tall and eager he was, with a heavy sweater, long legs, awkward. The older man, more sophisticated, ordered oysters from the bins outside, as I had. (They are very small, but sweet of the sea.) The younger man had never eaten oysters; went outside to look at them in the shell in their little bins. Was very skeptical. His gestures as he tried the first one offered him were something to behold. *Then* his face began to light up.

Spent more than two hours at the Petit Palais this afternoon, seeing "7000 Ans d'Art en Iran," the magnificent exhibition of Persian art opened by the Shah a couple of weeks ago. Many of the objects—of gold or ceramic or Luristan bronze—I had seen before, in Tehran or New York or the Louvre. But most were new to me; overwhelming in their variety and richness.

The City, though overcast—and tonight raining a light Paris-winter drizzle—was so beautiful. Everywhere, just across the Seine, i.e., on the Right Bank, floated the pale blue and white flag of the Republic of Gabon. When I asked the taxi driver—by pointing, for he spoke no English—why all the mass of police and flags, he said something about the President of Gabon, and gave a skeptical shrug, as if to say—along with the rest of us—here is De Gaulle taking the day off to honor a little make-believe "Republic." Starting at the bottom, as does Gabon, in the African world of newly independent politics, is like no other starting at the bottom the world has ever seen. Indeed, *they* start at the top, sharing the grandeur of De Gaulle.

One Sunday early last spring—in March—I walked along the Embankment of the Seine just below the Louvre, which is just across the river from this little hotel. It was a warming and happy kind of day. The chestnut candles were beginning to open. Men were sleeping in the bright sun, after an ugly winter of Paris' usual "overcast."

I felt the real impulse of spring, a sense of the magic of renewal, outside and in, that is, within me. I sat on a bench along the river's bank and wrote, in a lyrical note so deeply felt. Today I sought out the same place, the same bench. Now it is autumn; the buds of spring are now leaves; not the pale green of spring. But the impulse, the magic remains, sturdy, enduring.

OCTOBER 26, 1961
PARIS

It is only two or three years ago that we were in Ghana. Guests of Nkrumah. Sitting on his right, at his table. Sitting with him in the evening on the terrace of the old fort he occupied as the legatee of foreign rulers, he asked me questions about education, etc., intent with bright-eyed interest at my replies.

Then, so short a time ago, the chief brains in Ghana, and the most influential by far, were two men. One the tense and loquacious Sir Robert Jackson; the other K. A. Gbedemah, Minister of Finance, and therefore of planning, etc.

An obscure little story from UPI, from Lagos in this morning's international *Herald Tribune* says: The Action group denies knowing where Gbedemah is; he had to flee Ghana to Nigeria, after having been dismissed as a minister last month.

8 P.M.

Just back from an hour and a quarter with Jean Monnet, at his home office on Avenue Foch, 83.

I had forgotten how short a man Monnet is. Since I saw him last, only three years or so ago, he seems to have lost the air of delicacy and slenderness, diminutiveness, I should say. He has become much more stocky, almost square, in face and figure. My picture of the typical French peasant rather than the intellectual. But what a mind and political imagination!

What Monnet said to me about Germany was the most consequential topic of our talk together. He is perhaps the most mature and seasoned mind thinking about Germany today. Has anyone, certainly since Talleyrand, so profoundly induced *action* that is European (Pan-European?) rather than action geared to the separate nations of Europe?

When I first saw him in May, 1950, the European unity idea had made some headway as an idea; it was then called the Schuman Plan. We had just come from England, where we witnessed a debate in the House of Commons. A motion had been made to censure Atlee's Labour Government, as I recall it, because it would not bring the U.K. into the Schuman Plan. The motion to censure lost heavily. Churchill as well as the Labour people agreed that because of Britain's obligations (and advantages) as head of the British Commonwealth, Britain should not join anything that identified her as an integral part of Europe, rather than of the Commonwealth.

The assumption throughout the debate was that *without* Britain the Schuman Plan for Europe could result in nothing.

Due largely to Jean Monnet—and the course of events—action in several areas did move toward a common basis for Europe. The Coal and Steel Authority as a start; now the treaties for a so-called Common Market which has created a political as well as economic force of Europe so great that Britain realizes that, sooner or later, it must join, on the same basis as the other lesser countries within Europe.

Now, I asked Monnet, how does a divided Germany, divided between the West and the Soviet, fit into this picture of a steadily greater unity of Europe? How can Europe be said to be a new force, as a unit, when the most important single industrial, and one of the first political factors, in Europe is divided? Not only divided; divided in a way that any strong effort to bring Communist East Germany into the European Community would almost surely bring on war? Is this not a very serious counterforce to the one which has achieved such great success under his guidance these past ten years?

He settled his folded hands across what is now quite a pleasant little paunch, looked down, put his glasses on, then off (the only "nervous gesture" this outwardly composed little giant has).

"The question is for me?" I must have sounded as if I had asked a rhetorical question. I agreed; I was asking for his view. I liked this genuinely modest touch.

"In the first place, let me say that the division of Germany between East and West is the important question, and the critical one. Not Berlin but West Germany and East Germany. Most of the talk and heat is about Berlin, but that is not the central question.

"Then, I should say that I don't think the division of Germany works against the increasing strength of the European Community. *Provided* [and at this point he looked up and the low voice and restrained manner changed for a moment to a sharper pitch] provided West Germany continues to be treated in every essential respect as an equal, in every way, with the other countries—France, Belgium, the Netherlands, later on U.K. In every way, with the possible exception of atomic weapons, and even there I am sure some way can be found, will be found, to work that out.

"If West Germany—if Adenauer, say—should feel that West Germany is not to be part of the new Europe, then nationalistic forces *within Germany* [he repeated that phrase] within Germany will make it difficult to keep West Germany from moving away, moving toward the Soviet perhaps.

"So instead of this division of Germany being at odds with the European Community, the European Community can save the day for peace, be keeping West Germany *with the Western countries.* [He emphasized these last words strongly.] Of course that isn't the whole story. But the rest of the story depends on that proposition. That at least is my opinion."

Monnet so often uses this expression, "this is my opinion," or judgment, as if it were not the best informed and most solidly supported, by his record, of any in the Western world today.

"The rest of the story is that Germany will someday be united, West and East.

"But *not* today."

This was said with that look of *accepting* a fact, without resignation, indignation, perturbation, righteous wrath—just accept it as one accepts the fact that today it is raining, say.

I particularly noticed that each time he said it would not be united, he didn't say "now," but "today."

"But this does not mean that it won't be united. I am sure it will. The *hope* that it will must be kept alive, by the West. There shouldn't be too much talking about it, but the hope must be kept alive.

"Germany cannot be unified today without war. And West Germany must not, cannot, go into the Russian orbit without war. If West Germany leaves Europe, Europe itself is lost. The West has lost.

"On the other hand, if East Germany today should go to the West, through unification or because its people abandon it to go to West Germany, the Russians will use force; they must. If East Germany goes, the other non-Russian satellites will go. There must be time for the Russian people to become increasingly critical in their minds, turn gradually away not from Communism but from dictatorship.

"It is individualism, not dictatorship, that is natural for men. Communism can change the form of government and economy by dictatorship, but it cannot long change human nature, which always craves individualism.

"Look what the Soviet dictatorship is facing. First, there will be a Europe of 300 million people, one country in time, and not too long a time, politically. If you [meaning America] join us, this will create a political unit so great as to be the most powerful force in the world. And by 'force' I mean political force, not military.

"See what else the Russians are facing. They can impose Communism on Russians, almost indefinitely. But imposing it on another people—the Czechs or East Germans, say—this they can do only so long as they use force. Once that force is removed those countries will go back to their own kind of life, which is not dictatorship. It may be Communism as we see it, but it won't be totalitarianism. They will have trouble with every people except their own, given time, and this will be true of the East Germans.

"Now all of this assumes no accident. If there is an accident [he gave his shoulders the slightest shrug, for he is as un-Gallic in gestures as almost any man I know], well, that's another matter."

It is, indeed! But one must make certain basic assumptions; if we *assume* there will be a general war, whether by accident or otherwise, then why bother with any ideas or program?

But all this had been preceded by almost an hour of discussion of other things.

He asked me about our work in Persia. I said the need for change was very great; that there were some Persians who believed in that and were willing to work for it. "But only a few; more are needed, of course."

"No," he said. "At first it is better to have just a few, I think." His eyes lighting up as they do when he hits on a point that touches on his fundamental philosophy.

"If there are too many, at the outset, there is a lot of talk, but nothing gets done. If there are only a few, changes can be made. Then the *many* will carry out the changes just as conservatively as they carried out things before the change. All you need is the change; the administration of change can be left safely to men who were against the change, or indifferent to it.

"That is the way it is today in Brussels"—referring, of course, to the capital of the European Community.

More than once, talking about change—and who knows more about it?—Monnet said something to this effect: "Don't press too hard. Let things work themselves out. Don't be too grim about it. If what you are doing is right, and events are going to force it to happen, just relax a bit. But this is only if what you have is a good idea, a real idea."

In talking about Persia, I told him by way of illustration some point about an idea in which I believe. This concerns the development of a port at Bandar Abbas in Baluchistan, in eastern Iran, so it can be used *jointly* (i.e., on a regional *international* basis) by Iran, Pakistan, and particularly Afghanistan. The relations between Afghanistan and Pakistan have recently become so bad that the Afghans have no recourse, apparently, but to export through the U.S.S.R. Iran and Afghanistan are now not on good terms. The tension has become so great, so I read, that the President has sent one of the best of our diplomatic corps to try to work something out "along diplomatic lines"; whatever that means.

Monnet asked: "Can't you persuade Iran to make this port an international one?"

I said that the World Bank had sent some economists to look over the site; and they reported: it was "not economic."

How well I recall the bitterness in the Shah's voice and demeanor when I talked to him about that regional port idea last time I was in Persia (where, inshallah, I shall sleep tonight!). "Yes," the Shah said, "we have had that idea; but the World Bank says the port is not economic"—scorn and almost revulsion.

"Not economic," said Monnet, with that half-amused lilt in his voice I enjoy so much—great part of his charm, actually. "Of course it is not economic; none of these important thing are; they *become economic after they have been done.*"◖

That is the briefest way I have ever heard one of my favorite points made.

I said that the UN was in trouble. It was therefore important to develop regional international activities—real working things—as a hedge against UN failure, a point Gordon makes.

Monnet agreed with the object but not with the reasoning, quite. "The UN is a forum. But it is not a way to get things done. Too general. We must fix on specific things, courses of action. That talk about 'co-operation.' I don't know what that means. But *common action,* that I understand. That is what your international port could be, if it could be administered jointly.

"People have to be consulted. Because he didn't understand that, Nasser was thrown out by the Syrians. He tried to run Syria with Egyp-

◖ A modern port has since been built at Bandar Abbas though not an international one.

tians; that doesn't work, and in the end it won't work for the Russians. People have to be consulted, have to have their views considered."

I know he told his wife that I was there, because of the manner of my leaving. He had taken me to the outer door. There he shook hands two or three times, thereby establishing his French citizenship beyond any doubt. I had reached a landing far below when both he and his secretary hailed me. "Mrs. Monnet would like a copy of the book you wrote," he called down to me. "She read it and liked it so much and would like a copy." I was a bit puzzled. "What book?" (As if I had written as many as Horatio Alger.) "The one about the Tennessee Valley." So I said I would be delighted to send her a copy, and I shall.

OCTOBER 29, 1961
TEHRAN

Sitting in the desert sunlight that literally pours forth from a sky that is *solid* blue.

All seems set for the ceremony of pouring the first concrete into the foundations of the Dez Dam tomorrow morning.

I get on the special train at about 2:30 P.M. and then will begin a busy-ness, talking with all kinds of people on that train, mostly Iranians. Now that the Khuzistan program, despite all the earlier disbelief, is a reality, more and more Iranians want to "get into the act"; all to the good.

Yesterday morning I had a good visit with the new American Ambassador, Julius Holmes.

Holmes is quite a contrast to his two predecessors whom I have known since coming here: Selden Chapin and Edward Wailes. Brisk, almost birdlike in the quickness with which he moves his head, hands, with his ruddy cheeks and sharp gray mustache, he made me think of the picture of a British military man, in mufti. Sharp blue eyes, a candid manner.

I wanted to know, if it was permissible for him to tell me, a private citizen, whether the U.S. Government had a position about the Shah and his regime, and if it had, what it was. In explanation of this direct question I referred to my last meeting with the Shah in February. Then, for the first time the King had seemed definitely unsure about the attitude of the American Government. He complained about the critical American press and about something new. He said, with great fervor, that the U.S. Government was supporting "my enemies." I didn't understand clearly just whom he meant; I assumed His Majesty meant his Iranian enemies.

Holmes picked up the question without any hesitation. "Yes, your impression of last February was correct. He *was* unsure. Definitely.

"And he had reason. The student demonstrations, the reactions about the elections, the financial troubles, the pressure from Russia— these were part of it.

"But what really upset him was what Kennedy had said in his speeches during the campaign, and some of the same things said by Bowles and others. The U.S. was for 'revolution'—that was the word and the theme. The Shah interpreted these words to mean just one thing: we were going to support a revolution in Iran. Well, when I got out here, I explained that what President Kennedy meant, *of course*, was social revolution toward higher living standards. This put a new face on it. But that wouldn't have been enough if we hadn't confirmed it by our financial help."

I commented that our people in D&R did agonize a great deal about whether we should "pull out" because Iran had fallen so far behind on payments to us. "I didn't worry too much about it; I believe in delegating my agonies," I said, rather fatuously. "Like Dean Rusk," Holmes said, almost under his breath, but with a twinkle. This comment told me a good deal about the contrast between Dulles and Rusk. Dulles had his finger in everything. So much so that no one dared *do* anything about anything.

The answer, Holmes said, is that the U.S. Government stands behind the Shah and believes he is Iran's best, perhaps only, bet; and that the interests of the U.S. are interwoven with the independence of Iran from Russian domination.

This led me to raise the question of military aid to Iran, the "inadequacy" of which the Shah always speaks of to me.

"Yes," said the Ambassador, "it is a familiar argument the Shah has made. He says, 'The Afghans and the Iraqis both have jet fighters; we have none, etc. If there is a general war, the U.S. will be in it. But Iran may be attacked not by the Soviet but by our Soviet-supported neighbors; and now we don't have what it takes to resist.'"

Holmes added: "I have just come back from Washington. Washington knows full well what Russian ambitions and plans are about Iran. These have a long history. The Molotov-Ribbentrop Agreement of 1939."

"Even as far back as Peter the Great," I broke in to say.

"It is obvious that if they can take over the oil of Iran—and your beautiful new dam [at which he grinned] they can block us out of all Middle East oil. Perhaps more serious, and less understood, they will then outflank Turkey. Even worse, with Iran they have access to Africa, particularly all of East Africa. So the West *can't* lose Iran, simply can't.

"The Shah made a clear speech not long ago that puts him out of the 'neutral' fringe. There is no alternative to the Shah in this country. The National Front Party doesn't amount to anything. It is either the Shah or Iran goes under.

"You can be sure what the answer is about where the U.S. stands: we are with Iran."

Visited at length today, and yesterday, separately with two correspondents whom I had arranged to have here for the dedication at Dez Dam, and then stay on a while. One is Harrison Salisbury of the *New York Times*, the thoughtful scholarly man who has spent so much time in Russia and is full of ideas—almost dialectics—about Russia. (Dialectics are contagious, as a way of thinking.)

OCTOBER 30, 1961
6:15 A.M.
ON THE SPECIAL TRAIN ABOUT AN HOUR FROM ANDIMESHK

Dawn and the morning star over the desert of lower Khuzistan. The glow of dawn and with it the outline, against the dazzling east, of what could be ancient Saracen castles—in reality strange, uneven, gravelly hills rising abruptly in the plain. During the night the dying moon lighting up the great Bakhtiari mountains through which the sheer *will* of the Old Shah drove this remarkable railroad.

AHWAZ

Twelve hours ago I was having breakfast on the special train. Since then I have been awed, hushed, by the power of puny man who has used his knowledge and courage to change the face of the earth: the foundations of the arc that in a year will rise to a majestic 630 feet of concrete to control the waters of the Dez River.

Of all the rushing impressions of this vivid day, the one that somehow struck me most took place on the floor of the canyon, almost 1,200 feet below the edge of the plateau from which five years ago Bill Voorduin had first peered over into the chasm and said: "This is the place."

A tent had been set up, a tent not greatly different from what Darius might have used as a headquarters while on the move, or Alexander, or any of the long succession of potentates and chieftains. Before this tent, and under a great flag of Iran, were spread, on the bare rock, two huge flower gardens of carpets. These lovely carpets were themselves an incongruous note, in the midst of huge construction trucks.

The final contrast was a very large gold-upholstered chair for the Shah; more nearly a throne than a "chair." Beside the golden chair on a low table, a telephone, also of bright gold. After listening to speeches from Asfia and Ansari, the Shah in his blue and gold Air Force uniform picked up the phone and called to the bucket operator a mile away. Very slowly, across the chasm, we could see the great iron bucket begin to lower, slowly, down and down until it was out of our sight. The first concrete had been placed on the foundation of the Dez Dam, to be the highest in the Middle East.

What *good* will this dam do? Well, it has already done a great deal of good. The Persians have had a glimpse of what *can be done* in a country that has so often been shaken by its own disbelief in itself. But all around there will be other evidences of a stirring in this ancient region.

As I witnessed this ceremony my own reflections were rather banal, I fear. How much just plain worry and stubbornness, on our part, and patience and daring and some vision lay behind this actual placing of concrete; or in the broad fields of sugar cane we saw in the distance on the way to Ahwaz; or the electricity in the villages here.

It was only five years ago that Gordon, Helen, and I came down on that train for our first look at a part of the world I had never before heard of. To see the very earth move because of ideas that came out of our heads was something that still gives me a sense of incredulity.

When, that morning, the Shah's car stopped at the high overlook, some of us were lined up to be greeted. At the head of the line, I received one of those warm and informal smiles that would mark this man off as attractive even if he were not a world figure, the center of what could become a terrible struggle for the middle of Asia. He seemed more than usually thin, but less worn and troubled looking than the time I saw him in March. "Great day," he said.

The Shah and I stood together on the overlook, peering down into the canyon, while Bill Voorduin, looking every inch the engineer, explained the row of red silos on the edge of the slope, which is the cement storage, the aggregate bins, the complex mixing plant; then, at the lower levels, we saw the deep arch cut that is the foundation, with men like specks below preparing to receive the first ten tons of concrete (literally not quite the "first," for there had been some experimental placing a few days before, to test out the concrete).

As the Shah and I talked, I spoke of what one usually avoids in showing off a big construction undertaking, that is, the cost in lives, the amount of courage it takes to work on a job where there are bound to be a good many fatalities. Indeed there was a note of sadness, particularly among the Italians, for only yesterday a rockfall killed two Italian skilled men and badly injured four others. The rock came careening off the wall of the canyon and fell on the very place where Bill and his foundation consulting board had been standing just a few days before.

OCTOBER 31, 1961
AHWAZ

Dr. F. G. L. Gremliza, our boyish-looking German doctor, grows on you. He and his wife had spent seven years in the saddest spot I know, the Susangard area almost on the Iraq border. These abjectly poor Arabs had been given no attention for—well, never. He ministered to them, they adopted a little Arab girl, learned how confidence and respect and love are won, among the desperately poor—or anyone.

Then we brought him into the Khuzistan program. The American high-powered experts on public health didn't think much of him and his methods; too much emphasis on field work, not enough on research, I gather. But he turned out to be right. Bilharzia is *not* the major problem the experts asserted it might be. It is manageable and only one of the environmental difficulties of the people of the Gebli area.

He described his methods of work in the Gebli area. He has personally visited every one of the more than fifty villages. And been in every house, usually for an overnight stay. As a doctor, and one they trust, Dr. Gremliza can ask questions no census taker could ask and get a genuine answer: How many shoes do you have? How much sugar do you use in a day, a week? When you have a chicken or some eggs, do you eat them, and if not, where do you take them to sell?

He has become, as he puts it, "a doctor who is part of a team of nondoctors"; the way he functions is explained by his concept of the development of this pilot area: to understand in great detail the facts about how people live, and on what they live, so "impressions can give way to facts." This love of fact-gathering among Germans particularly can get to be an end in itself—economists too! But in his case he is protected from this by the fact that the other men in this "team" are practical D&R agricultural and irrigation people. With Leo Anderson to guide them in this search for what actually happens to water, and food, and health, these men are getting a knowledge of the people of that area in a depth greater than anything I know of. Our area demonstration projects in the Tennessee Valley are the only analogy I can think of, but that was on the surface compared with this digging.

And what is the good of all this highly detailed knowledge of the people and their ways of living Gremliza is diligently gathering? Well, on nutrition alone, it is an important addition to our development of methods and processes of transforming the economics of a people. Gremliza finds in detail, for example, how little of the things these people raise they eat themselves. Having no cash income they create it by taking to the bazaar at Dizful, say, the chickens and the milk, etc., which they badly need themselves for their diet, but not as much as they want a bit of cash. For example, he leaves a tube of "ointment" so those afflicted with the eye disease, trachoma, can treat themselves, after he has seen them. He finds that most of these tubes go straight to the bazaar for cash or in trade for something they want more.

I assume his report will make clear what they do with the cash. Does it go for a bicycle? For clothes? Does it go into the ground, hidden someplace as a reserve? I would like to know.

Add $100 a year in cash income for these families, by increasing production (as of course our activities will) and these patterns will change. Perhaps there will be some capital formation (i.e., savings), perhaps it will go back into the land, if they get tenure. Perhaps it will go into education. But $100 added cash a year can produce almost a revolution in this design of living.

I began this day—after a long one yesterday—talking with and listening to the men who make this program what I think it is: one of the greatest, most distinctive achievements I have ever had responsibility for.

I want to write in some detail about these men when I get a chance; but at the moment, as I prepare to take a car to Abadan and return to Tehran, I can't restrain the sense of joy and satisfaction and the deepest kind of stimulation (to my kind of person, at least) that I can not only be a witness to the blossoming and early fruit of my ideas but a participant in them, a responsible participant.

And how good it is that one is respected. I say respected when what I suppose I really mean is that people warm up to me and I to them.

A day with the agricultural staff at Ahwaz, together with some long and intense (intense on both sides!) talks with Leo Anderson, made a deep impression on me.

NOVEMBER 1, 1961
TEHRAN

Yesterday's *New York Times* here in Tehran the day after it appears in New York. Includes a story by Harrison Salisbury about the Dez ceremony—and a good one.

The same paper has a report of the Soviet's big superbomb "test," their "H"-bomb, and a statement from the White House that such a big bomb makes no military or other kind of sense—a terror weapon. But our own first H-bomb, of half that size, I thought, in 1950, would be nothing more nor less than a weapon of limited *military* value. This I tried, unsuccessfully, to persuade the advocates of a crash program for an H-bomb eleven years ago when the H-bomb controversy was raging—in secret, unfortunately.* Instead of stopping and insisting that the world take a look at where we were going in what some of us thought was sheer futility and madness, Strauss and Brien McMahon and "Scoop" Jackson—and the press—shoved all such ideas aside. And now, of course, the Russians also have an H-bomb. So where is that security that was promised?

I'm tempted to be a bit "I told you so" about this latest chapter. Not that discussions of the H-bomb *before* it was made would necessarily have changed the course of events. But January, 1950, might—just *might*—have proved a turning point in human history. But no; the issue was decided by this simple formula: If the Russians could possibly get such a weapon, i.e., the H-bomb (of 20 megatons), then we *must* have such for our security. Now must we, too, produce another series five times as big just to "keep up with the Russians" no matter how foolish they are?

Have just come from an Iranian gymnasium, called Zurkaneh, or House of Strength, a veritable Temple of Muscle. Extraordinary place. A mosque-like room, square, very elaborate and Oriental. In the center a pit; spectators sitting on shelves along the four sides. In the pit "strong men" doing Iranian dances—some of them whirling, some throwing huge dumbbells high into the air. In other rooms weight-lifting like mad.

Great shouts, in unison. The usual garb: red, plaid-like shawls and sarongs. One guy, though, thought a loose T shirt the right get-up.

Everyone very friendly and pleased to have us; the headman, a giant, made us a little speech, at the conclusion, with graceful Persian gestures.

NOVEMBER 3, 1961
TEHRAN

Yesterday was one of those sixteen-hour days again.

Up at six, then the following:

At 7:45 to the elaborate offices of the Prime Minister. Is this the place where the practice of "rolling out the red carpet" began? Or did they copy it, say, from the British? Anyway, with all the smooth marble staircases to climb, the carpet is a help, and rather impressive too.

At 9:45 going between the huge Palace guards, past the Shah's sports car that is always at the door of the Residence; passed on from one bowing attendant to another, finally at 10:05 through the copper bound doors to an "audience" that lasted until 11:35.

* See Volume II of *Lilienthal Journals* under index heading "H-bomb issue."

At 12, after driving through the fantastic Tehran noon traffic, stopping for a little chat with the British Ambassador. He gave me the impression that he was weightless, like the men in the rockets to outer space. He probably *was* weightless.

At 3 P.M. started for Ebtehaj's home on the side of the mountain, a palace, designed by his rich and talented wife, still being built, in the very best Persian taste, with glowing tile and a million mirrors. Such grandeur. Had a stimulating talk with him, sitting in the sun on his beautiful tennis court.

No one else present at the audience with the Shah—the first time this has happened to me. From the very first moment of my entering his huge study—he was standing opposite the door to greet me—I was struck by the contrast between this man and the worrying, troubled man—and sovereign—who had received me in February.

This *was* a bad time, February. But pessimism and foreboding are what one hears on every side still today. Indeed some of the younger men who were lifted up by the appointment of Amini as Prime Minister, at about that time, are now quite disenchanted and upset. Certainly the visual evidence that the economic condition of the country is worsened is more obvious today. Nevertheless, the Shah's demeanor and tone were utterly different than in February.

I don't refer only to the extraordinary warmth and "man-to-man" informality. He seems much more a man who has himself and his task in hand. He seemed thinner, but his voice not so thin. In a uniform, as I saw him at the Dez ceremony Monday, he has what we call a "military bearing."

He began the conversation, after the amenity of expressing pleasure at seeing me. "I was greatly impressed—as you must have noticed—and deeply pleased by the progress made on the dam since I saw it about a year ago."

I responded by saying: "We went out on a limb in the promises and assurances we gave Your Majesty now almost five years ago, with very little tangible evidence to support them at that time. Assurances about the potentialities for productivity of the soil of the Khuzistan; about the excellence of the damsite, a very difficult place to build a dam in the time we promised; assurances about the way the people would use electricity if it were provided and the service was reliable; and that we could somehow induce competent Americans to join our organization. Well, those promises and assurances have been kept. So this gives me enormous satisfaction."

"I now realize," he said, "the truth of what you said in the beginning: that the compensation for rebuilding the Khuzistan could not be money. You are not just 'contractors.' You really have the interests of my country at heart. I think most Iranians are beginning to sense this. The criticism is dying down, now that people can see what extraordinary things are being done and will be done.

"I have the greatest confidence that Khuzistan will be so productive, and the work so well done, that it will in only a short time change the whole face of Iran."

I said: "I want to call Your Majesty's special attention to the importance of the so-called Gebli pilot irrigation area just south of Dizful. After your forthcoming visit to inaugurate the sugar plantation and factory, next month, I hope you will keep in mind a day's visit to the Gebli undertaking. In my opinion it may be the beginning, the prototype, of the most significant agricultural and social progress in the entire Middle East.

"Irrigation has proved to be a curse as much or more than a blessing in parts of Pakistan, in India, in the Helmand Valley of Afghanistan, in many other dry areas. The reason is that the irrigation has not taken advantage of what is now known about land leveling, about drainage, about accurate measurement of water use and other things. So the tragic fact is that the net effect of vast irrigation projects—in the Indian subcontinent notably—has been that millions of acres of once productive land have become dead, destroyed by salt, through the rise of the water table. The net effect of irrigation has often been destruction of the land.

"Even when the agricultural experts *know*, technically, what should be done, they have not known how to teach that knowledge to the actual tillers of the land.

"What is going on in Gebli is to reverse all this. There is a preoccupation with teaching farmers about the day-to-day handling of water, or fertilizer.

"The net results are already beginning in better understanding by landlords that incentive must be provided the sharecropping tenants (and those who work for the tenants); that is not an easy lesson to learn; the Communists have had a hard time learning it, haven't fully learned it yet.

"Then there is the trial farm we have established, and other methods of demonstrating the benefits of a *different kind* of irrigated farming. Not only will yields be increased, I should say three or more fold, because there will be water and fertilizers, but a new generation of farmers will be developed. I prophesy and promise that the Dez area will be watched throughout the world."

The Shah looked hard at the floor, his face darkened, brows pulled together: "I don't want to interrogate you about American Government policy, but I hope your Government will make up its mind about Iran.

"Iran could be the showcase for the whole of Asia. America can't spread its assistance into every country and every place. Here is the place with the best prospects of a great transformation. India—do you know that by 1990 [I think this is the date he used] India's population will have almost doubled? Here Iran, with Khuzistan to feed and energize the country, could hold four times as many people today. There is no population problem in Iran."

This was not said in complaint. He must be quite reassured about present American intentions toward his country, for he said nothing by way of complaint about the extent of aid for the next Five-Year Plan, though I am sure he is far from satisfied. But his basic reservations are certainly not at the surface of his mind.

"As one human being to another," I said—and here I quote notes in my black book I made thirty minutes or so later—"and as one friend to another, I know you have great problems as the leader and sovereign; but there is one thing about Iran that must be a great solace and encouragement. This country does have a solid foundation in its rich natural resources as has been already demonstrated in the Khuzistan and elsewhere."

He gestured lightly. "Yes, I do have troubles, but I don't worry much about them. The future is secure."

He went on to say that early in the Kennedy Administration he was puzzled by some of the campaign speeches about "furthering revolution" and such things. "I was concerned that the President was surrounded by some men who were professors and might not be realistic about what revolution means out here, about how evil subversion by the Soviet can be."

I responded that these expressions about "revolution" did not mean in America what they might mean when used in Iran. But I went on to say that idealists—that is, those who seek to preserve idealism in the kind of world the Soviets have forced on us—"must be made aware of the malignancy of the heart of which some people are capable."

"What about the bomb; will the Americans yield in Berlin?"

I said we would not; that of course there was some anxiety as a result of the Soviet terror campaign, called bomb "testing"; I thought the test was not of weapons but of our nerve and that of Europe.

"Does this anxiety you speak of mean you will yield? If you give way on Berlin the Russians will nibble away, a piece at a time, and Europe will be next. I know them."

I said I didn't think it meant more than natural anxiety about the danger of war. "But in my opinion this does not mean we are going to yield because of that danger or these threats."

I went on to say: "We Americans must realize that we must take risks. If we do, the prospect is good that the Russians will back down, as they did when Iran stood up to them back in 1946 and got their army out of the country. But for my part, I wish we would accept and take on the smaller risks, risks that *could* grow into a major crisis, rather than wait until the risk is a horrendous one. Life is always a balancing of risks, of course, some great, some less great. For example, Your Majesty took risks in stepping out among crowds of your people, as you did on the ride back from Dez Dam, risks your security people must worry about. Yet you realize that the risk of *not* being seen close at hand by your people is an important one; besides I am sure you enjoy getting that close to the ordinary people of Iran."

I might have added what is probably true: that he is a fatalist because of his religion and upbringing; that he has survived five bullets fired at point-blank range, just as the country has survived all kinds of disasters.

I made some reference to the new American Ambassador, Julius Holmes, saying I thought he was a good man. At this he brightened, "Yes, he *is* a good one. His experience in military intelligence means he will know what we are up against in contending with intrigue and subversion. He is strong and energetic. Yes, he is a good man."

I said that unfortunately, in most cases, the role of ambassador has been reduced in importance because of the ease of communication. "The teletypewriter you might say has made the Ambassador less and less important. Many of the important decisions that an ambassador might have made a generation ago are now made by someone in a subordinate rear echelon at a desk in Washington, the young men who screen and prepare position papers, etc., for overworked superiors."

I thought it was long past time for me to go, but there was no sign from him, and I couldn't very well make the first move. So the talk went on.

I used the term "land reform," saying very frankly (too frankly?) that just driving out the landlord or dividing up land and giving title to small pieces to peasants was not the whole or even an important part of the first step. I thought I might get slapped down for this comment for His Imperial Majesty handing out deeds to small plots of his royal estates is a familiar story of the past few years. I said: "It takes a certain amount of land in a single operation to get high yields." The Shah broke in to agree: "Large size and competence in handling land and water and seed are needed to get production." I had long mistakenly assumed that he thought these deed-giving ceremonies were the sum total of his idea of land reform. "Land reform," he said, "must be more than a slogan."

The Prime Minister "received" me at eight on this same morning I visited with the Shah. An extraordinary-looking man of about fifty-five.

Rather wild eyes, a handsome swath of gray hair which lies back from his low brow as wheat does when the reaper cuts it in the field. His eyes bugged as he tried to explain his formidable task.

His family, Amini, as I understand, were related to or supporters of the dynasty that the "old Shah" upset. He came in at a difficult time. The "elections" had produced a very bad reaction, so bad that they had to be called off, canceled, and the Majlis dissolved. The Prime Minister began on a high note of reform: he said he was arresting a lot of corrupt generals and public officials. He clamped down on foreign luxury imports to save the dwindling foreign exchange. His ban on foreign female "entertainers" got great publicity in the U.S.

The younger intellectuals hailed the new Prime Minister. He got rid of the incredible Aramesh, before Aramesh could get rid of D&R.

But two things combined to make his present position far from a success. One is inherent in the task of slowing down on imports; this hit a lot of bazaar moguls, who are powerful and more influential even than landlords. These merchants and moneylenders have been making a killing for generations but never more, I would guess, than now. They are behind the Persian version of our own Zeckendorfs, the people who have been building hotels, skyscrapers, luxury apartments, etc., in the Houston-like boom of Tehran. A mere 10 percent equity has given them control of these vast investments in buildings. Cutting back on imports has reduced the rental value of the hotels, etc., preventing completion of many at halfway; and causing a good many businesses and stores to sweat blood. All these business speculators crowd in on the Prime Minister.

The second trouble for the Prime Minister is the rise in vocality of the intellectuals; many of these are students and teachers.

I had in the back of my mind an instance of his method which a Persian critic had referred to, with contempt and disdain, on the train trip to Andimeshk. "The Prime Minister doesn't know how to spend his time. Imagine! He has been mediating between the students and the faculty at a small teachers' college on what should constitute a passing grade, a D or a C." The Prime Minister said he must make people realize he is concerned with their problems and cited his intervention in this school "grade" dispute as an example, and one of which he seemed proud.

He said he is "besieged" (he speaks English very well) by people (the waiting room was full of them) who say they will go bankrupt if he does not make an exception of them; they will have to close their stores, their factories, etc. "I must try to make them understand—but it is quite impossible—that it is my job to think of the whole country, not just of their business."

I must say I understood and sympathized. But the real question is whether he has a line of *policy* he can try to explain, and stick to. If he decides each case on its own facts, or can't or won't explain the *why*, he is sunk. Perhaps he is anyway. The Shah will certainly respond to pressure against Amini by changing faces. Whether this will happen in the next couple of weeks or months I don't know, but certainly Amini or anyone else who tries to ride out this kind of storm can't last too long.

Have just taken a long walk through the "Sunday evening" (that is, Friday) streets of this always puzzling, fascinating city. Only two blocks from the hotel—away from the chief business district—and you are in a medley of village scenes, a raw frontier town, and only a few marks of a Western city.

NOVEMBER 4, 1961
6:30 A.M.
MEHRABAD AIRPORT, TEHRAN

This is about as much of an East-West mixture as I believe I have ever seen. Two benchfuls of sad, dragged-out-looking Pakistanis or Arabs, sitting impassively in the very same posture since I came in a half hour ago (the Americans can be distinguished at once; we are the ones who pace around while waiting). A Japanese mother with two of the cutest kids, not looking like babies, they are so much like what we are accustomed to as "Japanese dolls."

NOVEMBER 4, 1961
HOTEL EDEN
ROME

Have just returned from a long walk in the twilight of Rome. What a hopelessly romantic city it is to look upon, and yet actually as hard-boiled and cynical as any in the West. And, God, how handsome the Roman young woman is. Those bold dark eyes, the strong nose coming forthrightly from the brow, not a pinched aperture for breathing but a noble prominence. And the utter blackness of the hair, the confident aggressive set of the head on strong shoulders. But they have little appeal to me as a male, these strong, bold, untamed creatures. I think I can say the same for the typical Latin beauties of South America. Wonderful to see, but warmth and rapport I don't sense, nor sexual attraction. I can't make so negative a statement about Frenchwomen, except for that large dowdy class that abounds in Paris. But whether their features and figures are good—and it is rarely splendid as I have observed them —among Frenchwomen there is such animation and vitality, and I suppose a long experience in pleasing the male and amusing him—as well as running him. But the running is done by subtle means, I would guess, whereas the Roman woman is more dark and forthright; in other words, she is indeed the strong sex.

One of the delightful and stimulating parts of this trip in Iran was the chance to listen closely to Harrison Salisbury. I say "listen" because I avoided seeking to pour him full of my own enthusiasm about Khuzistan. He is too famous and established a correspondent to care for that kind of "influencing"; when he wanted my opinion, I knew he would ask for it, which occasionally he did.

But he was eager to talk about Russia. Salisbury at one time spent five and a half years in Russia, consecutively, longer, I suppose, than any other correspondent.

His chief point was this: what is going on in Russia today—and it is plenty—must be judged primarily on the basis of the internal politics of the Soviet, which means the politics within the upper reaches of the Party. Khrushchev is not particularly interested in the effect of his acts —such as success of the space program, or these huge bombs, or Berlin —upon the West or the neutrals. His every move is intended to buttress his position *within Russia* and in the bitter fighting within the top group.

The second point he made—that is, second in importance in my mind—bore on the continued failure of the Soviet to raise enough food. Our emphasis in the Khuzistan on *incentives* for the peasants hit him hard; this he said the Russians were being forced into, even though contrary to much of their dogma.

There was a third point that interested me very much, because of my experience with the problems of decentralization, or rather the difficulty of getting people to live and work in less developed parts of any country, whether Persia or the Tennessee Valley. This was a constant and stubborn problem in Russia. Men who were brought out to some factory or farming operation away from the big city areas would disappear—just "get lost" by the thousands. Able or ambitious administrators, or scientists, didn't want to live in those far parts and were afraid that if they did they would be forgotten for promotion, or knifed more readily if they weren't in Moscow or someplace closer to the center of power in this terribly centralized huge nation.

He made me feel that the Russians, as their society "loosened up," would be likely to be more like all the rest of us than we could now believe possible.

NOVEMBER 5, 1961
ON THE RAPIDO TO MILANO FROM FLORENCE

The youngish "balding" man in the seat opposite me spoke a very familiar British English. After a brief conversation he said he taught at New York University, that his field was archaeology. I spoke of a visit Helen and Carlo Weiss and I had paid to the beginnings of a dig in Sicily, Morgantina. I referred to one of the more brilliant of the men we met there as being a Turk.

"I was at that dig and I am that Turk," he said. His name is Erim: he has been in charge this past summer of an extensive dig in Turkey, not too far from Izmir, a beautiful Greek temple, stadium, and city known then as Aphrodisia, as the temple was in honor of that goddess. He says those who come to visit the operation and the finds are known as "The Clan of Aphrodisiacs." I told him that when I felt the need I would join the clan.

I have listened to archaeology talk since we left Rome at 10:45, and mighty interesting it was too.

NOVEMBER 6, 1961
HOTEL PRINCIPE E SAVOIA
MILANO

Was met at the Rapido by Dr. Cuccia, the beaming "slip of a man," his hat on the back of his head, almost his trademark with me; and by Carlo Weiss, looking older by far, far more sure of himself.

We sat in the bar and talked there until 8:30 or so, time for an "early" Italian dinner. Cuccia is a remarkable man, a truly remarkable and, I think, unique personality. He has become, according to André, whose standards are impossibly high and judgments stern, "the best banker in Europe." For an American banker to say that about an Italian is a great concession. But this Cuccia is a *modern* banker just as André is.

By this I mean what?—that he is a modern banker. I mean that he has a curiosity and appetite for ideas in a far broader spectrum than how much collateral is there back of this loan or what were the earnings last year or last quarter if he is considering a deal.

Cuccia is an easy man to underestimate, on casual acquaintance. He wears a big grin—the word "grin" isn't adequate, it is an entire facial contortion, his Sicilian eyes sparkling as they bore right through you as if the grin-smile-laugh is intended to evoke some response in you which he wants, in his shrewd way, to observe and note. Add to this a nervous laugh and a habit of saying something quite serious in a tone of wit or banter, usually at his own expense, not someone else's. But he is essentially a serious, terribly ambitious, and furiously curious man. He tries out ideas, and solicits them from me, avidly, his hand and gestures getting faster as he proceeds.

Last August, he told me, he visited Russia. Like a good many other Italian businessmen recently, he went there to look for business, in his case handling the financing services for the growing trade and business between Italian firms and the Soviet. He gave me an account of a visit with a Communist banker, head of the central bank for a large trading trust. This trust wants to export to Western countries. "But they don't know how to go about what has been heretofore only a capitalistic technique, such things as determining credit worthiness of the buyer, short- and medium-term loans and all the rest of the paraphernalia that bankers use to further the needs of those who buy and sell."

His Russian host said Cuccia did not understand his problem; the Russian described himself as an employee only of the state bank whereas Cuccia was "a capitalist making a profit out of the transaction."

Cuccia, his hands fluttering up against his chest—meaning he was referring to himself, in a way I have learned is characteristic—said: "No, we are both the same. I make nothing out of what Mediobanca does except my salary. You and I are just the same, we are both employees; we should be able to understand each other." While I found this a bit disingenuous, Cuccia thought the Russian warmed up considerably after this.

Cuccia talked a good deal about China, i.e., Communist China. Many Italians are going to China these days looking for business. I said that no American had been permitted in Communist China in any capacity, but that I clung to the bullheaded determination that someday I would go to China to see what is going on, particularly in the handling of rivers and the food program. I thought the capacity to increase food production in such a country as China was the basic issue there, as it was in India and Pakistan; that some of the techniques and concepts we had developed in Persia—as, for example, incentive for production versus emphasis on title in the tiller of the land—gave me a new look on the whole problem of the future of these huge countries.

ON THE NIGHT EXPRESS
MILAN TO PARIS

Standing out on the platform waiting to board this train with me, Jean Monnet (who grows on me, as he has on Europe!) put into simple words what is wrong about the conventional economists' concept of "planning," something I have been trying to say for more than twenty-five years—as in the TVA book.

"To plan you must, of course, have a goal. But the very first *step* you take toward that goal in itself brings about *change*. So any decision you take—call it 'planning'—about what you will do in the future changes things even before you have taken that first step."

He says these things in such a very quiet way and yet with such authority. He can convey conviction without raising his voice one decibel or looking strained or intense. Great difficulties that one sees ahead he dismisses by saying—"that can be worked out when the time comes."

His philosophy about major political issues I described in a journal entry written after my visit with him in Paris recently. Much the same is the frame of mind with which he confronts issues of private business. And it was the Jean Monnet of business that I sat with all day today, in the FIDIA Board meeting.

For example: there was rather chaotic discussion at the Board meeting over one item on the agenda with disorganized and repetitive gabbing going on by one or two directors particularly. Cuccia was quite upset by the waste of time, and I think a little humiliated with his two foreign public figures present at the meeting. Monnet said: "No, Cuccia, I thought it was a good meeting. Some things were decided. As for all the disorder—well, there is never anything done unless there is disorder."

NOVEMBER 7, 1961
ORLY AIRPORT

Yesterday's meeting of the Board of FIDIA, plus the prior discussions with Cuccia about the topics discussed and decided deserves a place in the "sorta second life" of D.E.L. in the business world. Missing, at last, was the familiar question: what in the hell am I, the boy orator of Hoosierdom, doing here, in this business discussion? This despite the fact that all my fellow directors were European, indeed all Italian except for the cosmopolitan and wise Jean Monnet. Here is a huge aggregation of Italian capital and industrial and financial experience with two "public directors," something of an innovation in any corporation, much less an Italian one.

The setting of the meeting was as nonbusiness by American (or British) standards as could be imagined. Mediobanca's offices are in an old palacio, the Managing Director's office and the Board room opening through French doors onto a lovely enclosed green garden of laurel and statuary, and utterly quiet. You enter the building itself not from the clamor of a busy street but through a court of perfect proportions.

At one end of the Board room is a huge marble carved fireplace. Massive and now rather yellow. Over the main door, which must be 18 feet high, is delicate carving, the doorway itself made of marble. The walls, 20 or 22 feet high, are covered in a reddish fabric. "Art conquers all" was my rough translation of an inscription over the door; and high along the top borders of the room other similar inscriptions in large letters on all three sides.

In the midst of this splendor—noncommercial splendor—in one of the most materialistic and money-mad cities in Europe sat the directors, about fourteen.

Directly across from me sat Spada. A huge man; enormous head, arms that press against the seams of his protesting coat. He hardly looked up the whole three hours, except now and then a fleeting glance of sardonic amusement at the volubility of some of his Board associates, chiefly the wordiest man, in *any* language, I think I have known: Baroncini of the great insurance firm of Assicurazioni Generali of Trieste.

I had to remind myself that Spada, this tough-looking man, was actually the representative of the vast financial resources of the Vatican, in this FIDIA ensemble.

To my left sat Jean Monnet, composed but intent, not missing a thing. Occasionally he would turn to me with a wink, when the talk got pretty excited, as Italian discussions not infrequently do without, as we say, "meaning a thing."

The discussions were chiefly in Italian, occasionally, where Monnet had raised a question, in French (he does not speak Italian, strangely enough). Then from time to time Cuccia would give me the gist in English, or would translate my comments.

Flying now over Greenland's icy mountains—and icy is not an understatement.

We had to stop in Iceland because of bad weather in New York. Head winds changed the course to the northern circle. So, in a haze of golden light we have been going over the heart of Greenland. My first sight of gigantic glaciers. How forbidding and yet how majestic and beautiful this land is. The chanteys of the New England whalemen about the no-good Greenland waters I can now understand.

NOVEMBER 11, 1961
PRINCETON

Yesterday, on an impulse, I went to the Institute for Advanced Study, across the common, to spend an hour with Robert Oppenheimer in his office.

What was behind the "impulse"? We live almost next door yet I have seen him very little since we moved to Princeton.

It had to do, I am sure, with what is going on these days in public emotions and official action about nuclear weapons. Particularly the hysteria (as I think it is) about bomb shelters (fanned into flame by public officials—the President, Governor Rockefeller, *et al*).

But why the impulse to sit down with Robert? Not because I thought he would have anything new or creative to offer about these troublesome things—his great creativity manifested itself sixteen years ago, when we first met as members of the State Department Board of Consultants, and nothing that has occurred since changes in any essential the analysis of the problem we then made, in our Report, largely through his imagination and understanding.

The sunlight poured on his head as he sat at the table in his office. What a different head than the one I found so striking and haunting when we first met, in a hotel room of the Wardman Park—or was it the Shoreham?—in Washington in early January, 1946. Then he was so thin and drawn, pacing back and forth, gaunt and haggard, smoking one cigarette after another. His wide-set eyes, so pale blue and prominent. Yesterday the gauntness was there no more; no pacing. The hacking cigarette cough still, though I noted that he is no longer a chain smoker.

The tension in him about the problems we were asked to face sixteen years ago is gone. It shows in his manner, in his face and voice. The reason: "There is nothing I can do about what is going on; I would be the worst person to speak out about them in any case."

I told him I felt "lonesome," watching the very things our Board of Consultants members had predicted sixteen years ago, the very things we had worried about and had tried to impress on the world's mind, now being discussed again as if they were *new*. "There is a repetitiveness about this whole thing that hurts, that almost sickens me," I said.

But two new factors have been added, both collateral to the main issue of what to do about nuclear warfare. These are the clamor about building bomb shelters and the issue about testing. Their importance, I thought, was that they might profoundly affect the emotional setting in which the main issues might be ultimately faced. And the emotional setting, the emotional ambiance of a people and a world is more important than the technical or specific facts or programs or proposals. Thinking *follows* emotion, in sequence, I thought, and emotions determine the prospects for something resembling rationality.

NOVEMBER 13, 1961
NEW YORK

Ebtehaj arrested and in jail! I can hardly believe the rather circumstantial story in the *Times* of yesterday. What does this mean? Questions, questions, questions.

NOVEMBER 16, 1961
NEW YORK

More has come in about the arrest of Ebtehaj. He was put in jail "like a common thief," as he said, and may still be there. He insists that the subject of the "investigation," the "crime" for which he is to be tried (if tried he is) is the legality of the arrangement with Lilienthal and Clapp for the development of the Khuzistan. This happens at the very time the Shah, the Prime Minister, and the rest are praising that venture so lavishly.

NOVEMBER 18, 1961
PRINCETON

Helen and I climbed the Nassau Tavern's two flights of stairs, shaking off the rain as we came. At the head of the narrow stairs was an old lady, sitting quite upright and composed, her eyes open but somehow looking not outward *at* things, but dissolved, eyeless. It was a second before I recognized F.D.R.'s great Secretary of Labor, Miss Frances Perkins. Was it because she wore a piece of veil over her hair, rather than the tri-cornered black hat she made famous as her trademark?

When I greeted her, she rose, somewhat bent but with that warmth of eyes and figure that have marked her, for the past thirty years, as one of the great public figures America has produced.

After extended negotiation I was there to meet with the senior seminar which she teaches at Princeton. She said "the boys" wanted to discuss TVA with me. Eight or nine young men. Only four or five said anything. Mostly the quizzing (more like amateur Congressional Committee questioning, this "discussion") came from three vocal ones. The others had little opportunity.

I came to the session full of the idea that the "young generation" would be represented by these Princeton seniors; that they would not be interested in reminiscence any more than I am, nor in old and now stale issues; that it would be what TVA meant for the *future* that would interest them. Once more I had built up a picture of what *I* *wanted* to be true. My opening comments were along that line.

What happened shook me. These three vocal young men argued with me. "Baited" would not be too strong a word.

And what did they argue about? The meaning of TVA for the future? The worldwide interest in it? Don't be silly. They regurgitated stale hackneyed arguments against the *theory* of TVA that were current in the twenties and early thirties. What had actually happened seemed to them irrelevant.

An example: One young man said that flood control and power could not be combined in a single structure; that is what A. E. Morgan believed. And after all he was a flood-control engineer.

I tried to keep from showing the full extent of my astonishment. I explained patiently I thought that whatever may have been the theory the *fact* was that for more than a generation now TVA dams had in fact been *operated* for *both* flood control and power. It had been *done*. This made no impression whatever; the young man went on to show that he had read somewhere that it couldn't be done logically; I don't know that he even heard what I said.

There were several students who tried to steer the discussion into less arid channels. But the three talkers took over, and Miss Perkins' efforts were unavailing.

I was disgusted. Helen was simply outraged! I made some satirical comments, apropos the abstractness of this discussion and its staleness. "Come on," I said, only half joking; "let's be young again; this kind of abstract, overlogical, high school debater's talk is old man's stuff. Where is this new generation I have heard tell about?"

It is good to be reminded of some facts. One is that because people are *young* does not mean they are youthful. Whatever the calendar says, I am more youthful in outlook and spirit than several of these men in their twenties.

Then, it reminds me that teaching college students is, by and large, carried on by men who have not been exposed to the kind of rigors and discipline—of facts and people—that has been the story of my life. This tends to make college teaching (except in science, perhaps) full of soft spots, where abstractions and argufying take the place of the bruising battle with real situations, the need to make decisions and be responsible for them, the imperative of making something happen, of getting things done.

This sounds like anti-intellectualism. Perhaps that is just what it is. But I prefer to think it is an effort to define intellectualism *to include action* or an understanding of the process of thought and emotion which induces action.

Pamela came home from her first class, when school opened, all agog. "When I gave the teacher my last name she asked me: 'Is your father the famous man?' I said no. 'Well, was it my grandfather?' I didn't know what to say." She asked her mother: "Mom, what did my grandfather ever *do* that he is supposed to be famous?"

NOVEMBER 19, 1961
PRINCETON

Cow manure on the peony hills, against next May. Bone meal (25 pounds of it!) and lime on the iris, including a new Temple Bell. Peat moss on the newly dug, widened herbaceous borders.

The more I read the portentous words of the "experts" the more I trust the deeply planted common sense of the race, of the human race, of the countless generations that have preceded this particular little flyspeck of time. Of course what is "eating" me is the rising tide of concern for a place to hide, preferably in a hole in the ground (called a "shelter"—what an ironic word *that* is) or escaping to the realms of outer space.

Should I publicly say my say on this? Would it do any good? Won't this shelter phobia recede like other fads; or is it a sign of a deep sickness?

NOVEMBER 21, 1961
NEW YORK

Board meeting of American Commercial Barge Lines Co. this morning. Once again I felt the fascination and the range of the "business life," the *activity* itself.

Those wordy people who have never actually managed anything but write books about how to be an "effective" manager make me slightly ill as I observe the skill and close thinking *about their particular* jobs these men of business display. A new man has taken over the Commercial Carriers division, concerned with moving automobiles chiefly by road trucks. A massive, powerful looking young man, quite bald, his head joining his shoulders with practically no neck in the back; wearing a ring the size of a paper matchbook, dark green with a huge diamond sticking out of it. *But* when he started to analyze the business in his charge, what he has done to cut costs, make people responsible for the right things, project into the future of this particular business, look realistically at the danger of competition from the rails, etc., here was a highly skilled workman.

The story in that outwardly prosaic business meeting ranged from huge wheat movements from the Dakotas to New Orleans; thence to the hungry of the world; chemical barges and the ups and downs of negotiating about them with the Du Ponts: a range of exciting subjects but carefully disguised with the matter-of-factness most men of business seem to *prefer* to clothe their daily work.

Whereas I seem to have preferred, through the years, to make my "work" seem anything but matter-of-fact. It may be the "ham" in me, or it could be imagination. Whatever it is, I persist in my conviction that there is excitement and drama in what I am doing, as a manager.

NOVEMBER 23, 1961
10 A.M.—THANKSGIVING DAY
ON THE "TRENTON LOCAL" HEADED FOR PRINCETON

I say that it is a wonderful world. High, or low, or even in between, in spirits or mood, I find the world a delight, a challenge every morning, a warming object to look back upon when night comes and another day is done.

I see so many dour, sour faces, so many shoulders slumped, hands that tell the same story. And this droopiness I see among the "success-ful," who at great cost of effort and strain and sometimes butchery of others, have got what they set out for, yet are embittered, or whiny, or lost; what they have struggled for turns out to mean nothing to them.

John Oliver got back from Iran Tuesday. Ebtehaj was still in jail at the time he left. The Government doesn't quite know what to do with him: they can't "spring" him and they can't keep him in jail. The "official" story from our Embassy is that the arrest was an "accident"— what this means, according to John, is that Ebtehaj was called in by official investigators of the Ministry of Justice, questioning him about engaging the "foreign experts Lilienthal and Clapp" and giving them such latitude. Ebtehaj exploded and stormed and denounced the inter-rogators. So they felt the only thing they could do was to put him in the jug, without any charges against him; what I suppose we could call a summary contempt of court judgment for misbehaving in the court-room.

NOVEMBER 24, 1961
PRINCETON

Stirred deeply by a longhand letter from Frances Perkins, written in her strong bold hand.

She sensed that the attitude of the "boys" at her seminar (i.e., the vocal ones) had stumped and baffled and rather distressed me, at least in the first hour or so. She wrote: "I think the boys (who have often substituted Economics for God in their thinking) finally got it." That is, what TVA was driving at. I'm not so sure. But it is nevertheless wonder-ful that her heart is so youthful—more so than some twenty-year-old ones. But part of this is their lack of experience of life—much of it is.

NOVEMBER 27, 1961
BOGOTÁ

Met at the airport by Enrique Penalosa. A remarkable young man. Has the shoulders, head, and neck of a fullback, the kind you give the ball to to drive for three yards through tackle, and know you can *count* on that. He has driven through tackle in his work too: a prodigious job of getting groups of young Colombian engineers to cull basic information about a new agriculture.

Now he needs help in knowing how to get the information put to use. He was very frank; none of this cagey business for him. "We urgently need you; not for surveys but to make this whole group of surveys we have made, on minerals, sanitation, economics, etc., into a working program."

Why is there such a man? What is it that moves men or, better still, what moves this man and that? This interests me deeply. Why should a man of thirty-five "love" what he is doing so ("love" is the word he used, and it is the best one there is)? Why does he work so patiently and wholeheartedly, when so many Latin-American young men are content with making money (and lots of money is to be made in so rapidly growing a country and region)? Well, I will know more about this before I leave, and it interests me almost as much—perhaps more—than the physical and technical and managerial questions they will throw at us, hour after hour, during my stay.

NOVEMBER 28, 1961
BOGOTÁ

With me just throwing off an intestinal bug, nevertheless a very full day, and an evening of conferences with all the "contractors" for the Corporación Regional† still ahead of us. I must be a healthy animal of almost unlimited reserves or it simply couldn't be done.

Met with President Lleras at 11:30, after I had spent more than two hours of meeting with the officers of the corporación. Then after luncheon spent from 1:30 until 6:30 on a trip into one of the primitive, unspoiled (physically) areas of this 9,000-foot plateau, the Subachoque Valley. Such beauty of mountains and clouds and sky and shadows and young faces topped off with a dying warm light on the mountains as the day crept softly into night. I shall see other valleys in my time, I have no doubt, few that give the illusion of having just been discovered,

† This was the Corporación Autonoma Regional de la Sabana de Bogotá y de los Valles de Ubate y Chiquinquira. Enrique Penalosa was Director Ejecutivo.

new and untouched. And the bouncing metropolis of Bogotá, busting its seams, only a few miles away.

I said "untouched." So now we may be helping our Colombian friends "touch" this valley with a dam. But that alone would leave a beautiful body of water hugged against the shoulder of the mountain. What is really hoped for is that some of the overcrowded industry of Bogotá will either move here or start up new plants.

NOVEMBER 29, 1961
7:30 A.M.
BOGOTÁ

The pattern of ideas in the head of this stalwart Penalosa and some of his friends of the corporación is becoming somewhat clearer to me.

What struck me most was how frustrated they are—and outspoken —about the *power for inertia* of the rich, the "six or eight men" who own most of the land of this savanna of Bogotá, and therefore own the banks, the newspapers, and run things.

These younger men are themselves sons of well-to-do families, have been trained in expensive universities, and have professions that earn them a far greater living than public service jobs or "contracts" can possibly do. Yet the desire to achieve something on this plateau is burning in them. And they have made great headway, in the preliminary stages. They have an understanding not shared by many of the foreign experts. They see that a study or a set of figures can mean very little; that these reports don't get things done but are only tools—and often unreliable ones—too often created for the satisfaction of these experts, to give them a basis for recommending *another* study.

12:30 P.M.

Just back from a flight over the sabana in a Piper Comanche—a single-motor plaything of a plane. What a rugged plateau, with ominous jagged elbows of unyielding rock jutting out suddenly from a gentle little valley *within a valley*. Our pilot was Gustavo Penalosa, younger brother of our host here.

This is heady stuff, this trip. For example, the Mayor of Bogotá, Jorge Gaiton Cortés, said to me at a big luncheon this noon: "Your book, *TVA: Democracy on the March*, and your fathering of Plan Lilienthal have had consequences I don't suppose you know. Now we are moving in Colombia toward autonomous corporations so that in a brief time the Ministries will be only political offices—the real work of the country will all be done by corporaciones like the CVC and the Corporación de Sabana."

This I doubt, though I don't say so. Still, such things are worth recording, because they do pierce my armor. For example: after the conference with the ten man Board of the corporación one member, head of the Industrial Finance Corporation, took me aside. A distinguished-looking man, gray hair brushed back smoothly from an aquiline intense face, a look of authority about him. "You can help us with our future, because you can say things to us with the authority of your experience and reputation that only an outsider can say; if one of us says the same thing it has no effect." I expressed surprise and said I thought it would be the other way around; that the kind of things (such as my urging increased local taxation to pay for this development) would be resented from a foreigner. He smiled quietly and said: "No. We know you in Colombia."

NOVEMBER 30, 1961
BOGOTÁ

A huge, oblong room, as big as a miniature golf course, 30 feet high, draped to the ceiling in the richest red velvety folds; in the center a beautifully set table for perhaps fifty people. This was the setting for yesterday's luncheon for me.

At my left was the youngish Mayor, Jorge Gaiton, a slender, rather short man, very serious expression behind his tortoise-shell glasses, a slow deliberate way of speaking. Graduate of the Yale School of Architecture, formerly dean of the Universidad de Los Andes.

The Mayor told me one fragment of what was an absorbing account of how a small group of young men (including Penalosa) had put some new ideas and vigor into the City Council.

I asked about national politics. He said that in Bogotá the Communists were extremely active. Were they homegrown or inspired from Cuba? They were Colombians, he answered, but received considerable support from Cuba, from Russia and China. All of this said in a matter-of-fact atypical way for a Latin, I thought. (In fact, the more I see of these men who have trained in the U.S. the harder it is to speak of a typically *Latin* reaction or outlook.)

"I can explain this best by showing you the daily report I receive from the police." With which he pulled out of his inside pocket a two-page carbon of a document, which he put before me to read, asking if my Spanish was good enough to get it—which it was except for the word for "disguised" (disfraz) which he translated "masquerading."

This was a detailed report of perhaps six meetings held last Monday of Communist-led groups, called such things as Committee for Support of the Cuban Revolution, or MLR. Names of speakers, numbers of people present, the sort of report that Agent 864 or Informant Y3 might make to J. Edgar Hoover.

But there was one that caught my fancy. It was reported that one of these groups was organizing a special Mass to be presided over by a priest. (The word "meeting" in Spanish is also "mass," I believe, but this was clearly the kind of service we in English would call a Catholic Mass.)

The police reported that other members of the church were prepared to prevent the Mass by force; therefore the police were going to have plenty of officers around in case of trouble.

This idea of a Catholic chuch being used to celebrate a Mass for the Cuban revolution which is so violently disposing of the Catholic clergy seemed to him as ironic as it did to me.

DECEMBER 1, 1961
BOGOTÁ

Last evening it was quite an experience to sit on the platform at a meeting of young men, perhaps one hundred of them, and hear an idea of mine that later became the CVC, the subject of exegesis, as if it were, say, the Bill of Rights or some pronouncement of principle by Bolívar. "Did Sr. Dr. Lilienthal mean this; or that?" Now everyone wants a regional authority; Senator Gomez last night said there were bills and proposals in for nine more! Absurd, but there is a feeling that here is some magic that will cure the near collapse of local or "state government."

DECEMBER 2, 1961
PEREIRA, COLOMBIA

After less than an hour flight from Bogotá we are in one of the richest farming areas of Colombia, and in a rather fine hotel. My window looks out to the dark-green hills. This kind of tropical landscape always seems to me somehow smug and self-satisfied. Nothing of the struggle inherent in seasons, for here it is one season virtually the year around.

Bernardo Garces met us; after a walk around the city we will drive to Cartago to "inaugurate" a transmission line. But this is no ordinary transmission line. It brings power northward from the Valle, the CVC, to Cartago, in a part of the Valle where there was opposition to CVC only two years ago. Manizales and other cities in the state of Caldas were to be part of a multistate region in my original plan; later they withdrew. Now they are headed back.

Just back from the "inauguration" in Cartago. Was the principal guest, and much to-do. The happy faces, the expressions of incredulity that things had actually happened they had dreamed of, the inevitable *eating together* without which it seems human discourse can't be successfully carried on, took me back to the great county-wide celebrations, sometimes lasting a full day, when TVA electricity came to some of the small towns and rural areas. A strange sense that I was reliving my life but in another language!

I pressed the red button that closed the switches and brought the power into the city. Flashlight pictures, governors, dignitaries, nervous electrical engineers, the same TVA story but in another setting.

Then I noticed something very exceptional and heart-warming.

A wire fence enclosed the switchyard where all this was going on. Through the squares of the fence, in the blinding lights, faces, scores of dark-eyed eager faces, mostly of children, rather small children, round-eyed and full of wonder at what was going on in their little street —if such a series of holes and ruts along their houses could be called a street.

I walked away from the crowd, crouched down and started to grin and talk to these kids. I wasn't conscious of what I was doing, what with the squealing delight of the kids in having this strange character walk over and squat down beside them. Then the flashlights popped behind me, the dignitaries moved over, and another crazy American was caught being himself. I hope it didn't embarrass my hosts, but for me it was easily *the* event of the inauguration.

DECEMBER 3, 1961
PEREIRA

It is Sunday morning. I *never* have heard such a clamor as the church bells utter here; they begin as bells, but go on to become a roaring, rumbling mess of decibels.

The Manizales' local paper was on the floor of my room when I got up, *La Patria.* A violent headline across the top—in the manner of Colombian newspapers even if a dog gets distemper. "Fidel Castro declares that he is and always has been a Communist."

Only a couple of years ago, when I was here last, would *anything* a

Caribbean political leader had to say be reported in Manizales—or Bogotá, for that matter, in a way that puts all the other news in the shade?

This Castro business is one of those "unforeseen consequences" that Planners with a capital P *can't* take into their reckoning, so that their attempts at precise Plans—to "quantify," as they say—become downright silly.

DECEMBER 4, 1961
CALI, COLOMBIA

Down the Valley all the way from Cartago to Cali yesterday, for an "inspection," a visit of love and remembrance.

The strongest reaction is an emotional one: that an idea born at a certain moment in this very room (410) of the Hotel Alferez Real not quite eight years ago is now a part of the life of many people, and of the body of the land that lies between the gentle shoulders that embrace the land and people of a *particular* valley, a *particular* spot on the earth. Not a general, abstract "plan" nor an expression of hope or a promise, but something that can be seen and felt and judged the way most men must judge and test the words and ideas of their fellows: with their eyes and their tactile senses.

But for such reflections it is pretty early in the day. Beginning of another day that will be full and busy and noisy, full of new faces, new hands to grasp and say "mucho gusto," as well as many now familiar faces. I am amazed the way I am again back in the habit formed, quite unconsciously, in the TVA, of remembering countless names, this time Colombian names.

Yesterday I began the day early, wandering about the streets of Pereira in the sweet sunshine and peace of a Sunday morning. People dressed in their best, streaming in from all points of the compass toward the huge and ungainly church, the women and young girls gracefully pulling their lace head-scarfs farther forward on their heads as they approached the church, the men throwing down their cigarettes at the entrance of the church and pulling off their wide straw hats.

We drove southward, between the hills. A mule-train station, the saddles and gear of the drivers hung on a line under the overhang of the veranda, the cowboys lolling, waiting for Monday and the next trip up the hills to bring down their trains of mules loaded with bags of coffee. Then for a couple hours Bernardo took us through an area he wants to provide with water for irrigation. Although this is still the rainy season (though the end of it) much of the corn looks bad; most of it will be a "failure crop."

DECEMBER 5, 1961
5:30 P.M.
BOGOTÁ

A call from the President's Secretary, "Habla espanol?" No. Then a perfect American voice: the President would be greatly pleased if you could have lunch alone with him tomorrow at one. There could hardly be a more important and interesting time to meet informally with Lleras Camargo: his Colombian Initiative proposal as a counter to Castro was voted on favorably yesterday by the Organization of American States.

Today Penalosa and I reached agreement on a basis for D&R serving the Corporación de la Sabana de Bogotá. D&R has a new client, and I have a new opportunity to be useful in this country I have come to love.

For certainly the idea of a public enterprise corporación has taken hold here. Indeed the trouble may be that it has taken hold too well, that it has encouraged the notion that to solve problems is just a matter of creating a corporación regional. Well, it takes a good deal more than that.

I was quite bushed when we arrived from Cali last night. The visit in Cali and the Valley itself was a whirlwind; then the plane was delayed a couple of hours; then the motors wouldn't start; then at a high altitude a baby became very ill, great rushing about by stewardesses, the father, weeping mother, carrying the child forward for oxygen into the pilot's cabin, a general air of tumult not particularly soothing to one and all over high mountains at 13,000 feet without pressurizing in an ancient DC-6.

DECEMBER 6, 1961
BOGOTÁ

I arrived at the Palace fifteen minutes before my luncheon engagement with the President. A band was playing. The Palace guard, dark-skinned, solemn boys were overshadowed by their Prussian-type helmets with the gold spikes, much too big for them. Was this platoon or two made up of helmets or boys—one couldn't be sure.

It was hardly five minutes until El Presidente de la Republica entered, alone, with that warm smile that lights up his whole presence, his eyes snappy, his manner easy.

He waved me to a sofa in the adjoining living room. A moment later Senora Lleras joined us. She recalled, in most correct English, "How beautiful a view was it from your apartment where we dined with you

in New York; do you still have it?" A few words about grandchildren—
they have eight.

The President began by asking: "How was your trip?" I told him
that we had seen the sabana from both the ground and the air; then
went on to talk a bit about the CVC and my visit to the Valle. What interested me most, I said, was the way in which the rather conservative
and intrenched people of Cali, Cartago, and so on, who had either
scoffed or fought the CVC, were now in the forefront as its friends
and "true believers." "This is the way it always is about new ideas;
until people can see some results, most of them are against change. If
they begin to see results, things that can actually be seen and therefore begin to be understood, they embrace the change. And then
these same opponents of change in turn are adamant against any
change in the change."

I was quite anxious to hear his views about what is here called
"the Colombian Initiative" within the Assembly of the Organization of
American States (OAS). For the resolution approved by the assembly
in Washington only a couple of days ago, and the strategy behind it,
was solely the creation of his mind. Indeed Lleras had not only had
the idea, and carried on much of the preconsultation; he had written
the text out on his own typewriter; shades of Woodrow Wilson.

So he began to talk about the "situation in Latin America." "It
is most unstable," he said, with a shadow dimming the light in his
eyes.

At this point he was called to the telephone, striding across the
room, looking at the floor soberly, as if this was a call of some urgency
which he had been expecting, and not happily.

I remarked to his wife that I was pleased to see how well the
President bore the great burdens of his office. She was definitely unhappy and worried. "Too great, too great," she said, shaking her head
slowly. "Colombia cannot be governed." A neat summary.

The President settled himself in the wing chair, sipped his drink,
and with apparent relish returned to the subject of the Colombian
Initiative, and its reception at the OAS meeting in Washington the
other day.

"I consulted with most of the larger Latin-American members,
months before the resolution was finally presented. This is important
to understand, this process of consulting and getting views. Some by
memorandum: Chile, for example. Some through our Foreign Ministers."

I got a strong impression that Lleras wasn't too happy with the
net result, even though to a newspaper reader it looked like a substantial
"victory" for his effort to clarify the issue. As I understand the issue it

was simply to decide within the OAS what criteria to apply to the member countries to determine whether they were truly members of the Western Hemisphere (or the OAS) or were actually controlled or dominated—as in Castro's Cuba—by forces outside the OAS and the Hemisphere, to wit, Russia or China.

Make the nations of the Western Hemisphere take a stand: are they *of* the Western Hemisphere or of Asia, that was the common sense of the resolution.

I commented to the President that I couldn't understand how it came about that Mexico voted *against* the resolution. "To understand Mexican political leadership, you must understand this: that every one of them are friendly to the U.S., every one in private, that is. But they all feel they must in public declaim against the United States; that this is a political necessity." Here he threw his right arm up and half-imitated a political harangue, an ironic twist on his countenance. "No, you're right, there is no issue of difference or tension between yourselves and Mexico, and hasn't been for years. The relations are friendly and understanding and I think will continue so. And they have nothing but a kind of contempt for Castro, the 'Caribbean.' Still, that is the way it is. I wasn't expecting anything else.

"Chile—that is another thing. Chile abstained from voting—in effect voted against the resolution—for reasons that they said were 'juridical.' Very complex set of reasons why this wasn't the way to go about the problem and so on and so forth. This was somewhat discouraging to me. I wrote the President of Chile months ago, a long letter.

"The President replied in a letter: As to paragraph one, I completely agree. I agree completely to your paragraph two. And so on, following every point of my letter. Yet Chile took this position the other day. The reason, the real reason, their Ambassador explained to me: an internal political coalition the President had formed with leftist groups, which might collapse if he took a stand.

"The story back of Brazil's position—well, Brazil is now in a strange situation, difficult to understand even by the Brazilians. Why the President resigned so suddenly, why the military refrained from taking over —the stories are conflicting and make little sense. Brazil is in a most difficult and shaky condition. So the new President apparently didn't want to take a stand on this or any other issue so long as he could avoid it."

I said that Argentina's lukewarm attitude was what might be expected, based upon my brief visit there about a year and a half ago, and the impression I got of Frondizi as a person, and the fear he had of stirring up either the Army or the unions.

"No, I don't agree that Frondizi's government is in danger of a coup. I think he is quite solid as those things go. For him at such a time as this to go off for a visit to *Japan* [he fairly snorted as he said "Japan," his eyes indignant], a month touring around away from his country at such a time!

"This story of Frondizi's conduct in this important matter is more a story of the character of the man, rather than of policy, I think.

"Argentina, it is true, feels that it is the only country to exert leadership in Latin America. Unless they propose a thing they rarely will join in with what some other Latin-American country does propose."

The President slowly and deliberately took a package of Parliaments from his side pocket, extracted his lighter, and was about to light up. A servant had opened the sliding doors to the adjoining huge dining room. Mrs. Lleras glanced at him; no word passed. Again with deliberation, the lighter was dropped back in his pocket, the cigarette replaced in the box of Parliaments, and we went out to lunch. I liked this so simple domestic touch.

"How goes it with the Corporación de Sabana?"

It was obvious, I said, that the conditions on the plateau and in the area of the CVC were completely different, though the device for furthering the development of each was essentially the same, that is, the autonomous corporation. One is a fertile valley with a thriving city— Cali—at its center; the other is a thriving and rapidly growing industrial city—Bogotá—with an undeveloped region, the sabana, that needs to be developed so it will fit into the conditions of the environs of an industrial city.

The sabana adjoining Bogotá provides the oportunity to achieve a well-balanced and not too crowded city, by dispersion of industry, careful attention to water (the chief limiting factor for Bogotá), and planned transportation. In fifteen years the whole plateau could be made into one of the best examples in the world of a great city of perhaps three million spread throughout its region in a way that would benefit both the city and its area.

The President was very happy about the forthcoming brief visit of President Kennedy to Colombia, on the 16th, next week. "And Haqueelean. She will be very popular here; Colombians like beautiful women."

Mrs. Lleras beamed. Also she looked a bit overwhelmed at the prospect of the social obligations of receiving Jacqueline and "the man who will accompany her" on her conquest of Colombia.

After lunch we returned to the living room, and talked another half hour. Then he walked me down the long corridor, lined with rather horrid paintings of former Presidents or leaders, and sent me off with that warm smile of his.

Outside the Palace I stopped to make the shorthand notes from which this long account has been written, long because I regard this man as one of the few men of the world who can genuinely be called "statesmen." I wondered, afterward, what a security officer might think of a man coming out of the heavily guarded Palace, pulling out a slim black book and writing away—especially if he could see, from overhead, that the writing was in squiggles that must be a spy's code language.

DECEMBER 7, 1961
8:30 A.M.
FLYING OVER SANTA MARTA, COLOMBIA
EN ROUTE TO ARUBA, N. W. I.

From the very waters of the sea the mountains rise, suddenly, fiercely. The tropical jungle below to our left; on the right so close that they seem to hem us in, the high Andes (the highest peak 18,500 feet!) snow and ice covered, with that majestic aloofness and monumental indifference, even snobbishness, that the highest mountains seem to have for the lesser creatures of plains and forests—and men.

DECEMBER 8, 1961
ARUBA

A fat envelope just received from John Oliver. The jailing of Ebtehaj is the theme of the documents and letters he sends.

Irony I have known, in almost all of its forms; not all *yet*. But this tale outdoes anything I know of, excepting only the most bitter and shameless irony of all, the questioning of the loyalty of the very man who had most to do in creating America's atomic weapon.

A long memo from Hanson dated November 29 tells of a press conference by Ebtehaj's counsel, when for the first time the charges against Ebtehaj were made known. The public prosecutor had refused to do so, so counsel did.

The "charges" for which Ebtehaj is under "detention" and a kind of trial are that he entered into the arrangement with "Lilienthal and Clapp" for the development of the Khuzistan; that this contract was illegal because it had not been approved by the Majlis, the High Council, and the Board of Control; that under the contract we had received excessive fees, squandered money, and anyway were incompetents and no damn good as managers.

These charges and Ebtehaj's arrest occurred almost exactly at the time the whole country was congratulating us and themselves over two major *results* of this arrangement. (1) The pouring of concrete at the Dez Dam, from which I returned four days before Ebtehaj's arrest, with the warm praise of the Shah, the Prime Minister, *et al.*

And (2) the completion and beginning of operation at Haft

Tapeh of the sugar cane plantation, mill and refinery D&R had responsibility for. Tomorrow the Shah and Prime Minister dedicate that result, with the man under arrest who took responsibility for starting D&R to get the job done. Even a postage stamp is to be issued commemorating the event: sugar cane restored as a major activity of Khuzistan for the first time since the Great Kings of many centuries ago.

Ebtehaj wrote me a letter dated December 2, just received, which adds to the unfairness dealt this remarkable and fiery man. The Bank of America canceled the line of credit they had extended his new Iranians' Bank, because of reports that "he was in trouble with the authorities." He asked: would I do what I could to get them to reverse their position, that is, the Bank of America's?

It is the contract with D&R that seems to be the sole basis of this charge. The charge that the contract wasn't formally approved, etc., is nonsense, as the written records showed, of course. But that isn't Ebtehaj's crime, of course. It is just that by shooting at us those Iranians whom he has so intemperately criticized think Ebtehaj can be winged.

Here at this resort hotel in Aruba I have been watching some oldsters (or senior citizens, if you insist) dancing the cha cha (or whatever) or glumly watching a spinning roulette wheel or brooding over a one-arm bandit. I think George Bernard Shaw's aphorism about youth should be revised to read:

Old age is so wonderful; it is a shame that it must be wasted on the old.

I grow curiouser and curiouser about what makes men do what it takes to make money, and the fascination there is in making it, or trying to, where there is no financial need whatever. I am no exception. For example, I went to some trouble this morning to get a copy of last Wednesday's *New York Times* and checked the stock prices, particularly of those stocks I have bought lately, on one kind of theory or advice or notion. Is it just the same kind of fun that the stony-faced, almost morose-looking people get at the tables in the Casino here, as they watch the roulette wheel spin or the cards come flying out of the hands of the operator of the black jack game?

DECEMBER 10, 1961
ARUBA

Long visit with John Burnett, a wide-ranging conversation. The unity or theme was: why the work D&R was invited to do, and has been doing, has meaning, and what that meaning consists of.

Burnett is a man of quite exceptional talents: that I knew. But this conversation, lasting from 7 until 10, gave me an increased respect for the depth of his understanding of what it takes to make a satisfactory lifework; moreover, he is articulate about what my role in the company's work needs to be to make the best use of my abilities and interests.

Burnett's chief point is that my unique contribution is *going to the scene*, being physically present at places where our kind of work needs to be done; that when I do this, the kind of people who are needed to get development work done gravitate to us. This proposition rests on the principle that the central issue and the very starting point of development is a man (or men) preferably youngish, *of the country concerned*, who knows the problems and senses the aspirations, knows the kind of methods that will work *in his country* better by far than any "missions" or study groups from American universities or the ICA or the World Bank. And it is the gravitation pull we have for such people, says Burnett, that requires that I show myself in the locale.

The Colombia trip was filled with episodes and anecdotes, some amusing in their way.

I was with the engineers for the construction contractors (Perini, an American-Italian firm) looking back toward the adit of the tunnel of the Calima dam. I was aghast (literally my knees shook a bit) to see two *women* visitors behind us in the tunnel. The wife and sister-in-law of Manuel Carvajal, I think, of the CVC Board. The engineer turned white, looked around to see how the crew of workers took it. When we got out he said he was as worried as I; once he had seen 400 workmen walk off a tunnel job because some newspaperwoman had entered the tunnel, thus violating one of the most solid, pure superstitions of this specialized trade of tunnel-making, namely, that it is asking for disaster for women to enter a tunnel. But here nothing happened; it may not be a Colombian "tradition."

With Bernardo Garces we rattled over a narrow iron bridge, across a little tributary of the Cauca. Such a clatter, as if the bridge were going to chatter itself to pieces any minute. "This bridge," said Bernardo, "was sold to the local authorities by an uncle of mine by marriage, long ago. He was a German, represented a German bridgemaking firm. After the parts had arrived from Germany and were installed, the bridge was opened to traffic. My uncle wrote the company in Germany that by some mistake more parts were sent than were ordered; they had quite a lot of material and pieces *left over*. It took quite a while for the letter to be received; then back came an urgent cable to my uncle: 'For God's sake stop anyone using the bridge; those were no spare parts or extras; those were parts of the bridge, we are sending a man to erect them; in the meantime stop everything.'" The bridge didn't fall down (though it sounds that way as you go over it) and the unused parts were put in when the "expert" arrived.

DECEMBER 12, 1961
ARUBA

Have been thinking lately somewhat more explicitly of a statement I should like to make to the people of the Tennessee Valley. The purpose: to "present a program for the future, more vigorous and less dependent upon past glories and past policies than what the present management now, and for some years past, has pursued."

The immediate occasion for this desire to say my say to the Valley is the stirring of citizen criticism in the Valley over current TVA policy about "tributary stream" development, and other causes of dissatisfaction. This Valley citizen initiative appeared at first to be regarded by the TVA staff with antagonism, even contempt, certainly disregard. This led to my speeches in middle Tennessee in the campaign in October, 1960. More recently the Pearce series of articles in the *Courier-Journal*, which aroused Gordon and the TVA people and wounded them.

The points I would make in such a declaration to the Valley are:

About the tributary dams: Those dams mean *water*; water could revive languishing areas of the Valley; they could put to use water resources for what in time may become their *primary* use, not power, but water supply. This looks forward to the time, not far off, when water in its 1933 connotation of water for "navigation, flood control, and power" gives way to the concept of the primary importance of supplies of pure unpolluted water for other purposes, such as municipal and industrial use and recreation sites.

Financing of future expansion of power generation I suggested years ago be by municipal bonds issued not by TVA, as now, but by the larger cities of the Valley, consumers of TVA power with TVA operating their municipal generating plants as part of the TVA system, under contract with those cities. The income of such state-agency bonds would be exempt from Federal income taxation, as are those of the Power Authority of New York State or the Nebraska Power Authority.

A part of the increased cost of TVA power in the future will be due to high interest costs on TVA borrowings.‡ But the interest costs on municipal or state bonds of Valley agencies would be very much lower.

‡ In 1970 TVA was required to pay in excess of 8 percent interest in order to market its power bonds. Municipality bond interest costs were very substantially less.

DECEMBER 13, 1961
AN HOUR OUT OF ARUBA, FLYING TO IDLEWILD

This voyage to Colombia has provided fuel for thinking specifically about the methods and "principles" of the World Bank in making loans to underdeveloped countries.

The basic shortcoming of the World Bank is that it is without criticism, effective criticism. Not "control" by the Banking and Currency Committee of the Senate, say, but it is just plain without criticism.

What made TVA strong and effective was not the praise of its friends but the attacks of its enemies. It was this that forced me to justify everything I did. Sometimes this did make me a bit sorry for myself: that so much energy and distress had to go into answering often foolish criticism and demand for justification. But criticism, whether in good faith or not, whether sensible or not, whether bitter and negative or not—it was this that kept the circulatory system of the TVA lively and even buoyant.

The World Bank suffers from lack of such constant public scrutiny and the gunfire of criticism. The Bank sells its bonds to private investors. Those bonds are salable—mostly in the U.S.—on favorable terms because of good management and an excellent earnings record and a huge surplus, but chiefly because of the U.S. Treasury's subscription to the Bank's capital, essentially the guarantee and backing of the U.S. taxpayer. Yet no committees of Congress call upon the Bank for a regular justification of its program. No U.S. budget officer probes into its affairs.

The Bank thinks of itself as a *private* bank. This is a fallacy of pervasive effect. For a private bank has depositors and stockholders who are relatively independent and able to ask questions, fearlessly, if not entirely intelligently. But look at the Bank. Its executive directors represent countries that, except for the U.S. and Britain, are chiefly applicants for loans *from the Bank* of which they are "directors." I daresay only rarely do they risk the displeasure of the Bank's management, and its insulated top staff, by being sharply critical, lest their own country's prospects for loans be jeopardized.

So much for general considerations. But one needs actual cases. The case of Colombia in its relations to the World Bank is illustrated by a defect in the Bank's operations.

The criticism one hears from the most responsible sources in Colombia is summed up this way: *too many Bank missions.*

A census of the "missions" from the Bank during recent years makes one ill. One after another they come trekking to Colombia. I wonder if *any* country has been so examined and measured and "missioned." The amount of time lost as a result of this succession of missions examining *pretty much the same thing again and again* is appalling. Say nothing more about cockiness and lack of humility in the earnest members of these missions—mostly West Europeans. And now two more missions. One, a "small one" in January. Another "general, country-wide mission" (so President Lleras told me, with the utmost sadness) set for later in the year.

The World Bank is insisting that the Planning Department of this Government have its "nationwide plan" ready, and expects to examine it and revise it. So sixty economists are working day and night on a document—it will not be much more than that. For what purpose: so they can say that there *is* a "country-wide plan," though any basis for confidence in the reality or practical usefulness of such a gawk into the mysteries of the future is negligible.

It is an exercise. But one presided over by the blind leading the blind. A gesture.

If these multiple missions had produced great results in Colombia in the past, had proved that outsiders—or Colombians—can foresee and weigh future events by the mystic processes of planners, then the case would take a closer examination. But look at some of the results.

The able Currie Mission, to pioneer in the important basic techniques of planning for an undeveloped country, recommended, *inter alia*, a railroad paralleling the lower reaches of the great Magdalena River. The Magdalena was already a most useful avenue of commerce into the back country, capable (with modern diesel tows) of carrying a great traffic. But the Mission recommended that a railroad was needed. Its purpose: to *colonize*, to provide a "place for the country people."

The railroad has been built and is in operation. Currie, who gave as a chief justification for the railroad a need to colonize peasants back in the hinterland, has just come forward with Operation Colombia, a strong case *against* colonizing, a vigorous, almost frantic plea that Colombia should, in every way, encourage the movement of the peasants from the hinterland into the cities!

The hemming and hawing about the "soundness" of Calima Dam (which we fervently urged years ago) delayed that project, with absolutely no compensation to Colombia for the false starts, the building at the Bank's insistence of small, high unit cost piddling little power plants at Yumbo, rather than going ahead strongly with that power resource in which western Colombia is so rich: the power of falling water.

The point in these comments is simple: missions of "experts" are far from infallible. Long-range "plans" drawn by such groups of "experts," often the ablest of men, but not infrequently, too, mediocrities who have escaped from the arena of competitive life or are from countries where opportunities to exercise this kind of heady raw power is limited—these missions and studies and surveys are often salutary, but they can become a vice, just as leaping ahead completely without facts or study can be a vice.

More than making a report is necessary. The strength of any plan or program is no greater than the men who are available *in that country* to take initiative, fight the battles, devise the policies that will fit that country or region at that time. Find the men. Look for the men. When they appear, encourage them: when they have zeal, enthusiasm, some skills, *develop those men.*

The heart of development is men, *the men of the country.* No plan or program on paper is any better than the quality of the men who will try to make a reality of those plans and programs.

DECEMBER 22, 1961
NEW YORK

We went to the Hamilton Fish Armstrongs' Christmas reception last night.

Santha Rama Rau, in a golden sari, very handsome indeed in a dark and flashing way. She has written a play, she said, based on Forster's *Passage to India.* "The only way to communicate with Forster —I wanted permission to use his great novel for this play—is to just go to his house in London and ring the doorbell. He refuses to have a telephone and his handwriting is absolutely illegible. No one can make out a thing. They sold the manuscript of the *Passage to India* some years ago: It was just a heap of scrawls, like the script of some kind of foreign language." Her buoyant husband comes from Oklahoma, Helen tells me, and, of all things, is a scholar in Japanese dancing.

John Oakes, recently made editor of the editorial page of the *New York Times,* handsome, a sturdy frame, topped with an iron-gray crew cut. Asked me whether I agreed with the *Times'* favorable position on the United States loan to Ghana for the Volta. Seemed a bit unsure, as if he had been criticized for it. Said "Jack" Fischer of *Harper's* thought we shouldn't give Nkrumah another nickel. I said I, too, had no longer confidence in Nkrumah nor any illusion that an aluminum plant in that country would benefit the villagers, and will not create a series of headaches, economic *and* political. But on the whole case I was clear—and said so—that things had gone too far for the U.S. now to withdraw its support of the Volta scheme. Could it be reshaped so that low-cost electricity came to the villages?

CHRISTMAS DAY, 1961
PRINCETON

The brassy sun seemed to be spinning along the horizon, not rising but rolling. The world had been reborn, begun anew: this was the effect of the off-white snow, the glint of low-lighting against the slender trees that thrust their way upward here and there on the stillness of the open common, yesterday a recognizable rectangle of green, this morning at dawn the paleness of a new start, a white-board from which the marks of a million years had been erased by some Celestial Eraser. The stillness could be heard. Fleeing from the cold of the winter is doubtless a wise thing for the old. But I would not have missed the feeling this winter's day gives one of being the only man alive, or being alone, present at the creation of a new world.

So much for a new beginning.

But this is the time of year when for more often than I can readily remember I look *back* on the "year": what was it like? what do I best remember on this day?

The year was a full one. Charged with emotional intensity: the emotions that come from new sights and new people, for there was a great deal of travel to far places. The emotions that are joy, and pain. The pain that seems so often to be the coin with which one pays for an overflowing sense of being alive, which *is* joy. But on balancing the accounts for this year at least there is a big fat *black* figure in favor of joy and satisfaction.

So very much has happened during a single year. Within and without. I ask myself: Put aside the series of events, what do you distill from this full and intense year? It is this: a conviction that somewhere within me is a possibility unrealized, a potential still not utilized, a labor for which my life and energies and experience fit me if I will but find what it is, and get about it.

What an egotistical thing to say! Not only because I am sixty-two and a half years old by the calendar, but because I have already had more than my share of things done, of not one career but several.

Cocky beyond endurance or not, I have this conviction that I am not at the end but a beginning of something new.

I recommitted myself to the basic objectives of Development and Resources. From an almost I-don't-much-care attitude early in the year I came to believe D&R is well worth a positive affirmation.

A second affirmation during this full-to-overflowing year: to continue to keep the journals, and to publish them.

It was a year in which some people—quite a few it seems—looked at me, the "controversial" ex-public servant, in a new way. *The New Yorker* Profile accounts for this quite obvious new light in which a good many people now see the passionate radical, a financially successful man of business. Has this "exposure" in a new role affected my own view of myself? I suppose so, perhaps in ways too subtle for me to recognize. Certainly having only minimal financial problems does something (just what I would not be able to define precisely) to almost anyone, so I am sure it has to me.

Physically it has been an exceptionally good year. I'm functioning, as an animal, with more vigor, less fatigue, less tension, and for the first time since I can remember, no illness for over a year. Strenuous exercise, so I *look* fit, and this affects my outlook.

The emotional ups and downs—especially the latter—I face up to quite well: frustrations, disappointments, causes for "sensitivity," fits of feeling alone—the assortment that a person of my temperament and way of living must expect. It isn't that I don't have these sensations, for I do, and now and then acutely. But I get through them better.

It *has* been a good year. But that isn't so important as this: at the end of a good year I'm looking forward eagerly, intensely, joyously to the next.

IV

1962

Fallout and bomb shelters—U.S. and Ghana—Education and World Affairs—Teodoro Moscoso—Fulbright on foreign policy—Dominican Republic after Trujillo—Before Senate Committee on Foreign Relations—Oppenheimer security case—Shah and Queen Farah in the U.S.— André Meyer—Drama of a business merger negotiation—President Houphouet-Boigny of Ivory Coast— D&R-Iran contract troubles resolved—World Bank and CVC—Roger Baldwin on the Africans—Trip to Iran: Vice-President Johnson in Iran; political situation—Trip to Mexico: peasant unrest

JANUARY 1, 1962
NEW YORK

Have just read the "booklet" the Department of Defense has issued to "instruct" people what to do in the event of an attack by nuclear bombs, how to obtain protection from fallout, etc.

What a picture!

But the pamphlet is better than I feared it would be, only in this: it does not follow the "line" that *Time* magazine and others were offering so recently: that 97 percent of our people could be saved by fallout shelters. The pamphlet is a somber, sober response to the need that some people probably feel that they must "do *something*." But I still am completely unpersuaded that the amount of energy and funds required to provide any significant measure of protection is justified, balanced against the diversion of energies and spread of fear and negativism such a program entails.

In spite of today's fanfare about shelters I doubt whether this will take hold, except among a very small proportion of the people. I still feel there will be no huge program; if I am right, this will be a triumph of common sense.

JANUARY 2, 1962
8:45 A.M.
NEW YORK

David and I spent almost two days drafting—and *redrafting*—a proposal—in the form of a letter—to Canfield of Harper's. The subject: my personal conviction about the publication of the *Journals* as a *continuous narrative*, as a "manuscript," as David put it. This concept differs from the concept of a "book," in which journal entries would be quite incidental.

William A. M. Burden, whose annual New Year's party is rather a legend, is a big bulky man of perhaps forty-five. He is chronically serious, even solemn—unless there is a side of him I haven't seen, which is entirely likely. He peers, rather than looks, through thick glasses; a great crag of a head. His wife is a friendly and handsome lady of about his age. She works at her job, at such an enormous gathering standing at the doorway to greet people, and never leaving her post to chatter with her particular friends, as most less experienced, or shall I say "pro," hostesses might, and do. Their apartment is also a kind of modern art gallery, in the best sense. Large, squarish rooms, on the walls of which are huge abstract paintings. (He is Chairman of the Museum of Modern Art.)

Burden was U.S. Ambassador to Belgium until Kennedy came in. So it was natural for me to recall to him that in 1959 and in early 1960 Baron Coppée had urged us to make up a multinational technical mission to the Congo, to be run by D&R; that in Coppée's house I had met some of the younger Belgians who were trying to make independence workable for the Congolese.

Burden bored through me with those intense and narrow-spaced eyes: "I don't agree," he said, "with U.S. policy in the Congo as it is now. It is the one place in the whole of Africa where something good could have been done; *that* chance we are throwing away and discrediting. Maybe you were lucky you didn't accept that invitation to go out there, the way things have turned out."

Many of the people at this huge affair were the very rich denizens, usually well along in years, of New York's Gold Coast. But there were many working people there too: Alfred Barr, Monroe Wheeler, and René d'Harnoncourt of the Modern Museum; Turner Catledge, who still has that extraordinary alertness of eye and visage that I like to think marks the country boy who has made good in the city; John Davenport of *Fortune*, who plays hockey still, a trim, handsome man, who says (with his wife's warm assent) that "I know nothing about making money, my business is to *write* about it! Now, Harry Luce has a great touch and flair as a journalist, but first of all he is a businessman."

Anyone who can find something affirmative and positive to say, with this gruesome nuclear threat hanging over us, should do so.

I feel that there *are* positive things that I can say: (1) to puncture the balloon of blind confidence in what the "experts" say—they have been wrong again and again, particularly about the atom; (2) to do what I can to prevent some people from hiding from the way the world is, either physically burrowing under the ground or, what is even worse, by hiding their souls behind shelters that do not exist, in a world that does exist. There *is* a world in which to live, if one will fight and take risks and seek experience, not run away from it; and (3) to propose *how* we should live, what we *can* do.

That is quite a program, but said with conviction it might share my perspective with some people who have not had my opportunity to gain one.§

JANUARY 3, 1962
NEW YORK

A medical checkup with Dr. Dana Atchley this morning, at Harkness. More a visit with a friend than a consultation with a physician.

The nonphysical side of my "condition" as his patient is something he always inquires into, since he is almost the "founder" of that body of medical knowledge that finds in the emotions the source—and the cure—for somatic or bodily conditions.

When you find a man who recognizes that taking risks is a part of an adventuresome life, a life that reaches out for what our David called "a total engagement with life," *there* is a wise and whole man. That is the kind of wisdom he has, that is the kind of physician this slight, intent man is.

Luncheon with X, a successful editor of a popular large-circulation, mass-media magazine, one he has brought to a level of serious purpose —which is quite an achievement.

§ In his Stafford Little Lectures at Princeton in February, 1963, Lilienthal set out his "positive" views. The Lectures were published by Princeton University Press in 1963 under the title *Change, Hope, and the Bomb.*—Ed.

He described the financial troubles that some of the long-established maganizes are having: *Life*, *Look*, even that Rock of Gibraltar, the *Saturday Evening Post*. The *Reader's Digest* has done very well; he ascribed this to the fact that the *Reader's Digest* is strong on "inspiration," and that it *looks* like a paperback book. But—measure of current American civilization though it may be—the two magazines that have "increased their advertising lineage" most in the past year were *TV Guide* and *Playboy*, Man's Boozum Companion.

There is a mystical streak in him that I can't fathom. For example, he said that when he had a weekend place in New England he discovered, by living with untutored men, what are the foundation blocks of men's lives: faith in God, use of the hands, working in the soil, etc. And yet he left his place in Maine and lives on Park Avenue. I fear the story illustrates an infirmity of those who are verbally fluent, a yen for sloganeering, that afflicts people in his business, which deals with words.

This editor is one of a special category that deserves study and analysis. They are not a part of the army of business that produces or distributes goods and services, which is after all the basic business of business. These mass-media men develop circulation (i.e., readership) in order that businessmen who *do* produce and distribute will buy space in which to sell their products or services. The *content* of their periodicals is secondary to its appeal to the potential customers of those businessmen who are producers and sellers.

A wonderful morning with Gordon. When we function together at our familiar and practiced best, I daresay there's never been a better team of quite different minds and temperaments. We went from one topic to another one quite unrelated with the kind of conversational grace that is rare in this world. The tendency he has, now and then, with some of our people, to indulge in a monologue or lecture, was completely absent, as was my own characteristic vagueness and diffusion. He has ideas and convictions, this man I've worked with so many years; and my occasional levity or irony he responds to with a twinkle that few people, I would guess, know he has.

Part of the responsiveness to my ideas I found so marked in him this week may well stem from me. He can sense that I have an increased sense of sureness: the boom in my voice, the quickness with which I sort out the things that are important enough to chew over and those that are not. The men of the staff feel free to walk in on me, a dozen times in a morning, to hand me something, to talk about something, to get a decision. That hasn't always been true, by any means, either here or in AEC or TVA.

JANUARY 5, 1962
PRINCETON

David and I were talking, rather solemnly and deliberately, about how best to go about *saying* what I felt I needed to say on current issues that stir me.

His conclusions: first, that writing a set article was difficult for me, that it took a great deal out of me. In contrast, the writing in my Journals he had found "free and loose," usually readable, often lively, and with a natural structure and sequence that carried one along in the reading. Part of this contrast between "set" writing and journal writing was that in the Journals I quite naturally *selected* those things about which I wanted to write, for the very good day-to-day reason that those particular subjects moved me at the time; the emotional impulse so essential to good natural writing was engendered by events that triggered me into expression in the Journal.

Though written in the most unlikely places (planes, trains, hotel rooms) and at odd hours and without painstaking revision after revision, writing in my journal has become such a habitual response to events that it has developed a style of its own, he said; and that style was superior to anything else I had written. So continue it. A highly personalized *form* of writing is what the Journals offered. Not a *literary* production, no conscious attempt at polished writing.

While we were about through kicking this around, a call from Cass Canfield. He was "very much interested" in publishing the Journals; could he send a young man of Harper's, named Jim Kraft, out to begin a reading of the Journals this coming Sunday?

So, after so many starts, some false and some not, we are about to get a publisher's judgment about this huge array of words—more than 1,500,000 of them, spilled out over many years.

One's life rises up out of these pages, pages I wrote, often a few moments after occurrences as the Japanese attack on Pearl Harbor, McKellar's latest ferocious assault on me, a long evening with Nehru, the state of mind in Washington before we got into World War II—and so on, a long string of the beads of my life. "Self-Portrait." But that isn't quite right. The Journals are that, but they are also a portrait of a time in the life of our country.

JANUARY 6, 1962
PRINCETON

The process of negotiation is at the heart of most administration. What hadn't occurred to me was that negotiating (using the term in the broad and multicolored feeling it has for me) is something that goes on within one's self. The evolution of a conviction, of a style of living, of the development of a set of measures, of values, these, too, are the product of advancing ideas, revising them, setting one set of one's own ideas up against another. This, in short, is also negotiating, negotiation within the house of judgment that is inside every man.

JANUARY 7, 1962
6 P.M.
PRINCETON

Kraft, of Harper's, arrived at 11:15; has been reading the Journals almost without a break since.

A fresh-faced, quite young man (about twenty-seven), slight and intense. When I learned from him that he had "majored" in English, here at Princeton, and had spent some graduate years on the Elizabethan-Jacobean *theatre,* I was nonplused. What would he bring to this record of events so far removed from all that area of literary scholarship?

On second thought I could see this as an advantage, for he could approach this MS without being—or thinking—that he was an expert in contemporary American history or a "New Deal specialist." He could look at the Journals as I now want them looked at: the record of an individual, a particular guy, his trials, tribulations, triumphs, mistakes, self-doubts, and all the rest, rather than a piece of "history." Most important of all, he looks at the world from the viewpoint of a new generation, of the young men and women. If this story excited him, it might have the same effect on other young people, and it is *they* I am most interested in; I think I could almost say it is *only* they I am interested in. If his reaction *as a young man* turns out to be that this is readable, understandable as a human document, and even perhaps inspiring in places, then that would settle the question: should we publish *now*?

JANUARY 8, 1962
NEW YORK

André was cordial in his greeting, but as the half hour wore on an underlying unhappiness in the man became more and more evident. So long as we talked about specific things there was that light in the back of his eyes that bespeaks an extraordinarily keen mind. But when I tried to lead him into what he thought of the "state of the world," such a pall of sadness I have rarely seen in anyone.

But, like many men of imagination and drive, the lights go out suddenly and come on again as suddenly, all ablaze.

In common with many others not nearly as well informed, he feels low indeed about the state of the world. "Kennedy is intelligent; very intelligent. He is popular in the country. But nothing happens. We are not making progress. In Europe he means nothing, nothing at all; he has no standing at all. This is not par-*ti*-zan, I hope. That is the way it is."

JANUARY 9, 1962
8:45 A.M.
NEW YORK

The early years of manhood are usually the years of greatest range of interest, the peak period of freshness, when the world stimulates even the moderately dull.

This is quite different than saying that a physicist, say, has his most *creative* period in his twenties. It seems to be true of scientists. But not of other creators. Some great painters maintained and indeed increased their creativity into their *old* age, and so with some writers (Goethe certainly).

But the pressure on the young these days to be like their elders, who are usually their bosses, is far too strong in the business and political world particularly to produce that swift-flowing curiosity and outlook that produce important ideas, that carry men through hard fights for those ideas. Here is a tragic loss. And ironically it is the very *elders* who complain that the young men of today are too preoccupied with "security" who themselves foster in the young this caution and middle-aged attitude about security; foster it by their own attitude toward life and change and risk and innovation, by their regarding people who do something out of the way (from the middle-aged viewpoint) as exotic or "beat" or radical.

Of course it must also be remembered that a good many of the very young are *born* middle-aged and cautious.

9:30 P.M.

In October, 1955, I spoke to an audience of big-shot Italian businessmen in Palermo, Sicily. Among the things I said apropos the "Problem of the South" (i.e., the South of Italy, of course) was: the solution of the poverty and underemployment in the South is *not* exporting people, the good solid South Italian workman. He is needed, not today, in the South but it will not be long before he is.

I learned years later that this became known as the "Lilienthal Doctrine." It was off the cuff, verbally, though actually born out of my experience in the Tennessee Valley where the same doctrine was being preached in 1933-1936.

In today's *Times* I find the following quite comforting support of this offhand hunch of 1955:

"Only a few years ago there were [in Italy] 2,000,000 or more unemployed out of a work force of fewer than 20,000,000. Unemployment was considered an incurable disease that the Italians had to live with. Now fewer than half a million are unemployed, mostly unskilled laborers."

Clearly labor shortage is what is now troubling Italy, not a surplus.

A long visit with Paul Manship, perhaps our greatest sculptor, a rotund Foxy Grandpa of a man. I told him with relish of Helen's and my pleasure in seeing his sculpture "as it should be seen, under the great live oak trees" at Brook Green near Georgetown, S.C. Like most older artists he was critical of the new artists "who don't have anything to say except an emotional itch in their guts. What I have always had was a *job* to do, some specific function—like a doorway to the Bronx Zoo, and so on. That was a thing that my sculpture had to perform, not just some vague desire for self-expression."

JANUARY 10, 1962
NEW YORK

In our work in D&R we produce ideas. These ideas, methods, techniques, are usually reduced to writing in some form; call them "reports."

I now find that our people are being asked for copies of these reports, the embodiment of ideas we have created, and those ideas or facts, produced with a good deal of effort by all of us, become available freely to our competitors, who get business in our field with the use of our ideas.

I consider this absurd process as one of the consequences of our noncommercial background. In private business an "industrial secret" is as much an asset or part of a company's property as its physical plant, not to be handed around free to competitors or anyone else.

For example, we have worked out some important advances in irrigation farming, and organization to that end, in Iran. These ideas and methods are set out in our quarterly and other reports to the Plan Organization, our employer. But why should other firms, now expanding into the agricultural field, come to our offices, as they do quite regularly, talk to our people as if they were coming to the Department of Agriculture, and walk away with ideas, some embodied in our reports, which they then sell to others for their own profit?

This is but one illustration, however, of the handicap of carrying over public service policies—and staff members—into a private competitive business venture. In public service the ideas of any kind developed by the use of public funds *belong* to everyone, and one spends a good deal of effort trying to make their availability known. But that isn't business.

Conference with Bill Voorduin, Gordon, and Adolph Meyer this morning. Meyer is that sturdiest of men, a German-Swiss (though long a resident of the U.S.); for years one of the chief dam design engineers at TVA, then in the CVC. With his cavernous eyes and oblong countenance and twinkling eyes and shambling gait, he is a kind of benign Boris Karloff—and one of the great artists of engineering in the whole world.

Subject: helping Bernardo Garces establish *his own* CVC engineering staff. This requires a decision by him that he get rid of an American firm. They don't believe, as we do, in using their engineers to train and season Colombians to be able to stand on their own; their advice always ends up the same way: CVC needs more and more of that American firm's engineers. This is not because they are the "bad guys" and we the good ones; any big engineering organization finds it necessary to keep its organization fully employed, sending out $35-a-day men on jobs that pay the firm $100. This is the way that kind of engineering business is run—and one of the best reasons I have for trying to keep our own organization from getting big, and therefore being forced to persuade foreign clients that they aren't "yet quite ready" to stand on their own with their own young men.

In D&R we *live* by our principle: "working ourselves out of a job" instead of making the job bigger for our own people. The transfer of management, step by step, to an Iranian organization is tangible proof not only of our motives but of our capacity to do an intrinsically difficult maneuver: substituting Iranians for our own people, while still keeping the job going full blast. It isn't fully accomplished, but it is going. And this will be a great story when it is a full reality.

JANUARY 12, 1962
PRINCETON

This week in New York one of extraordinary exertions. And much achieved. That warm, strong inner sense of fulfillment, of sparking ideas, of giving: giving others a new way of looking at things, of bringing out of them counterideas to my own. There is in this a kind of reassurance that makes all else, by way of accomplishment, pale into nothing.

When I got to Princeton last night I was tired. But it was such a healthy fatigue. A half hour's nap before dinner; an evening before an open fire; a walk, before turning in, under stars so bright in the cold northern air that they were in my very hands; listening to music; reading a bit, and then sleep.

That Nkrumah has gone off the deep end of worship of himself— the power disease was too much for him—and that he succumbed to adulation from the Soviet is part of the history of the past eighteen months or so. But I have just learned from a source with an intimate knowledge of Ghana what has been happening as a result of Soviet "assistance."

Here are some lines from this man's letter, actually part of his quarterly report from the Ivory Coast work on minerals.

"One of the surprises about Russian and other Eastern European technical assistance in Guinea and Ghana, is that it is, by Western standards, extremely expensive. The last British Director of Geological Survey in Ghana asked for fifty geologists for what was certainly a very complete and ambitious program. The Russians are bringing in a hundred and fifty for the same program. Many of the Russians are at a loss in these unfamiliar surroundings, and lean heavily on the few remaining Westerners in the Department. In addition Ghana has to keep the Russians as well as pay them: some of them are lodged in the best hotel, and monthly bills are about £200 per man, often inclusive of unreasonable quantities of gin.

"The Russians have not yet got the job of building the Bui Dam in Ghana (an auxiliary of the main Volta Dam), but they are dickering for it. As a first condition they require half a million pounds' worth of *air-conditioned housing.*

"The Ghanaians are looking askance at some of the industrial projects, inspired, built and financed by the Soviet. The work was often done in complete disregard of economic criteria, and some massive white elephants are the result—very expensive to maintain too. The legend of infallibility generated by the Sputniks may be wearing thin."

JANUARY 14, 1962
PRINCETON

Robert Goheen is compact, highly energized. He makes me recall the best of the smallish quarterbacks I have known. Seeing him across from me in the sitting room of the Jim Perkinses last evening and being asked to guess: what does that fellow do, the last guess I would have made would have been: he is President of Princeton University, and he is a classics scholar.

There were six of us at dinner, the Goheens, Helen and me and the Perkinses. After dinner Jim and Goheen asked me: would I become a board member of a new agency just formed by the large universities? Purpose of the organization, to give policy guidance for U.S. universities that are increasingly being called on to provide educational help to universities overseas in the less-developed countries. Name of the organization: Education in World Affairs, Inc. The university directors are the presidents of five universities: among them Princeton, Michigan State (John Hannah, my friend of years gone by, and one of the best anywhere), Franklin Murphy of the University of California at Los Angeles. I asked for a chance to think about it, to look at some documents.

At dinner "shelters" came up, as they do everywhere these days. Princeton's Trustees, Goheen said, had yesterday authorized converting the basements of existing buildings for fallout protection for 8,000 people, 4,000 of them students.

I took a very dim view of an extensive fallout shelter program. The point I made that seemed to shake them a bit was the effect of a real program on the inner strength and preoccupation of the country. Military preparations did not affect or involve the ordinary citizen, in his daily life; a shelter program of any magnitude would. Communities, schools, universities, churches, individual families, would be in the middle of this, with negative and frightening effects.

Moreover, the technology of war changes rapidly, as the enemy changes his metliols of attack and of *defense*. A substantial shelter program would be countered at once by weapons and strategy to eliminate or negate "defense by concealment," i.e., by putting a large part of the population underground. So the same circle we are in as to weapons of offense—the bigger or more lethal the other side's the bigger and more lethal ours must be, and so on—would be paralleled by the protective measures taken in a shelter program. The forced obsolescence of our weapons by new weapons of the enemy would be matched by obsolete shelter defense measures. But instead of only the military and scientific community being concerned about this kind of race, the *entire population* would be caught up in this maddening chase, never being secure, but always being obsessed with the problem.

JANUARY 18, 1962
WASHINGTON

George McGhee was a great contrast to Chester Bowles, as he greeted Gordon and me in the big office Bowles had occupied so recently. George is husky, has that unshakable, ruddy, casually dressed, well-padded earthiness that makes him look more like a top British labor leader, say, than any kind of intellectual among the more precious birds of this Administration.

Unshakable, unflap-able—but still his first comment was about "what a hell of a state the world is in." He is the central exchange—in telephone system terms—as the Under Secretary for Political Affairs, of all the upsets going on. Laos—"Well, we have some very difficult partners out there; and then the Dominican Republic, where all hell has been breaking out since the killing of Trujillo." The last report I read this morning was that a military group had seized power from the President and Council we were backing; the U.S. had issued a stern rebuke and prepared to stop payment on sugar. As we started talking he answered his phone, after which he said: "Well, there has been *another* coup in Dominica, and *our* people are back in there again."

An hour later, when we were conferring with Teodoro Moscoso, head of the Alliance for Progress, about the Dominican Republic, no one had yet told *him* that the tables had turned *again,* though he, Ted Moscoso, had just come back from a special mission to the Dominican Republic and had reported all was well.

Then Gordon spoke of D&R's report on the Peligre Dam in Haiti. That report on power in Port-au-Prince has been lying on the Inter-American Development Bank Executive Vice-President's desk for two months. None of them had the nerve to do anything about it, since our recommendation was that Haiti buy the American-owned power company, financing it by an Inter-American loan. McGhee said the President of Haiti was "pretty awful," not someone to be entrusted with anything; the question of supporting the program we recomended in our report would put more strength behind the Haitian President. The usual dilemma.

If they had electric power there was perhaps a chance for some industrial and tourist development. McGhee said it was conceivable that this might lead to a better government, though this was by no means sure. His skepticism is more than warranted.

JANUARY 19, 1962
WASHINGTON

Late yesterday Gordon and I met with Ted Moscoso, now head of the Latin-American economic aid program, and half a dozen of his aides.

Moscoso was the son of a drug supply merchant in Puerto Rico and was in that business when Rex Tugwell became governor. Tugwell's ability to see that this young man (as he was then) had what it takes may prove to be one of the most creative things that he did as governor. For Moscoso applied his impatience and drive and *insights* to the development of industry in Puerto Rico—the now famous Operation Bootstrap—with the greatest success.

Now he is a man in his middle forties, who even at the end of a *very* trying day (what with the Dominican crisis) has the hopefulness and sense of conviction that mark a real leader. (These cautious birds who take pains to hide their emotional commitment to what they are doing are not very interesting—nor effective, I think.)

A square, solid, outsized head, large luminous eyes that meet you eyes-on, brave shoulders that can carry a load, an impatient do-it-now kind of man, but without fidgets. He was appointed to head the Alliance program on the theory that a Spanish-speaking man from an island in the Caribbean would have an advantage. Gordon and I agree that this may in fact prove to be his most serious handicap. For to a good many of the Latin-American countries—particularly partly Europeanized ones such as Argentina and Brazil, or a sophisticated Spanish country like Colombia—Puerto Ricans, by and large, are *not* held in high esteem. Makes me think of the tough time American Negroes have in black West Africa.

Moscoso went to the Dominican Republic a couple of weeks ago; worked well with the National Council that replaced the shambles Trujillo left; dispatched an economic mission just the other day; reported enthusiastically to the President about converting the Dominican Republic into "something that would show that democracy works, right alongside that other place." (In the State Department I find there is a professional reluctance to mention Castro by name; curious psychological quirk, that.)

Then he had hardly got home until the roof fell in, a couple of days ago. A group of military officers seized control, put the Council in jail, took over. The State Department reacted immediately; recalled the economic mission, stopped payment on the sugar we agreed to buy from the new regime, expressed publicly great disappointment. In short, "intervened," though not with the Marines.

While the "good guys" he had dealt with were still in charge, during his visit to the Dominican Republic, a group of able, enthusiastic, middle-class younger men talked to him about a valley development. These Dominicans were steamed up about it. He ordered that as much information as possible be got together.

"Then I took the liberty," he said rather shyly, "of asking these local leaders, and the Council, what reaction they would have if I could get the TVA team [nodding to us] to take on the job of development with Alliance funds. Frankly, their reaction was most enthusiastic; they know all about you fellows. So that is why I asked you [looking at Gordon, whom he knows far better than he does me] to come down to talk about it, and that's why I have all these men here at this table.

"Then, yesterday, they threw out the Council. But I honestly believe that things will straighten themselves out. Let me tell you: the decent, intelligent, nonpolitical, middle-class people of that island have just had their fill of dictatorship, after twenty years or so of Trujillo. They won't go for another dictatorship, that's my belief.

"I saw a man who put the trigger to Trujillo, a quiet, decent man, a doctor who had spent his life saving lives, not killing people. He just said he would rather die than live longer under those thugs. And if any other dictator tried to take over, this doctor said 'he will go out like this' " —demonstrating with his hands, a pantomime for being carried out feet first.

Moscoso proposed that as soon as things quiet down a bit, but right soon he hoped, we do a "macrosurvey." "You mean 'take a quick look?' " Gordon asked. Yes, that's it.

We urged that the first visit, if it is made, not be "built up," lest expectations be aroused that a closer look might not support. Yes, he could see that; however, the men who are enthused about this valley will certainly not keep our presence a secret, by any means.

"Let me tell you how this idea of developing this Valley originated. Senator Bill Fulbright, Chairman of the Senate Foreign Relations Committee, was at the White House, with Under Secretary George Ball. Fulbright said what the Alliance needs is a 'mystique'; there should be a 'spectacular,' a 'valley development' that will demonstrate how well democracy can work in Latin America. Perhaps the best place for it would be in the Dominican Republic. And what about getting Lilienthal and Clapp to do it, with their experience and all the prestige and excitement the TVA has in Latin America.

"Now, I don't believe," said Moscoso, with a glint of humor in his eyes, "in discarding an idea because it comes from a legislator. But I thought it was a great idea. And so here we are."

For months some member of the Senate Committee on Foreign Relations has apparently been needling Fulbright to get a staff investigation under way about what D&R did with the $90 million of Iran's money we have disbursed for development of the Khuzistan.

All the material we have sent the Committee has not satisfied them, and the latest letter from Fulbright, received just before we left for Washington, was rather sharp. They want all sorts of figures of the kind characteristic of a Congressional fishing expedition.

This made Gordon quite mad; it was evident the Committee had singled out D&R for special "treatment" of all the American private companies abroad; even though *none* of the money is U.S. money, but Iran's. But it does you no good to get mad about how unfair legislative investigation is; you either have to fight it, which makes it appear that you have something to hide (which fortunately we don't), or comply and swallow the unfairness.

On the train down to Washington I broached a course to Gordon I thought might be more useful. We would provide the information about Iran's own money, if Iran had no objection (which they won't express even if they have). BUT we would like also to have the opportunity to appear before the Committee and tell of a distinguished American achievement in the rebuilding of the Khuzistan, now the pride of Iran, and a means of improving U.S.-Iranian relations even though no U.S. money is involved and even though we are a private, not a government, agency.

JANUARY 23, 1962
ON THE TRAIN TO NEW YORK

Notice that the *Wall Street Journal*'s leading article on the Common Market uses the word *"multinational."* So far as I know, my talk at Carnegie Tech in 1960, titled "The Multinational Corporation," was the first time the word had been used; I rather think I coined it, to mean that form of internationalization that is more than the conventional meaning of international. In any case, it is good to see that wholesome and meaningful term get into newspaper use.

In the same article Ray Vicker refers to an institution in being that Dave Schwartz and I projected, in that same "lecture," as something that would come: a multinational school to bring up the new race of multinational kids. I get a real satisfaction from seeing these cockeyed ideas, shot into the air of conjecture or prophecy, actually become realities.

JANUARY 24, 1962
NEW YORK

Fifteen minutes ago Shahmirzadi, working here with us from Iran, heard from the Iranian Embassy in Washington: General Bakhtiar, strong man of the Army security forces, had been arrested. "This," said Shahmirzadi, "is serious, much more serious than the student riots in Tehran, even than the closing of the bazaar, bad as these are."

So Iran will again be on the "critical list."

JANUARY 26, 1962
NEW YORK

Some people lose their verve and vigor with advancing years; *not* Eleanor Roosevelt. She greeted us at her new house on East 74th Street with warmth and composure; she presided over her table with dignity and a sparkle. I was seated at her right, an honor indeed from so great a lady.

We talked some about Persia. She had been distressed to find, on her visit to her daughter, Anna, in Shiraz, that people didn't have a sense of "community responsibility," of responsibility for others. Unless they developed this, the dams and roads and industry would do no good, she said. Of course she's right.

I said that the way we tried to meet this real problem was to try to make dams and irrigation provide *incentives* that would slowly create community and individual responsibility for others.

JANUARY 27, 1962
PRINCETON

Since early this morning have been listening to the chatter of the radio announcers as they try to hold America's attention until the big rocket goes up with a man aboard. A whole new vocabulary—blast off, burn off; all the words are of that colloquial kind that makes the American language so lively and the American personality so attractive. Like jeep, say. None of the Teutonic verbal heaviness of an earlier period of science.

My intellectual almost-disdain for shooting all this money and effort into imitation of the Russians has changed. Now the excitement of doing *anything* that has chance, risk, experiment, try-it-and-see has taken over; I am back in my best element: emotion.

I have a mental picture of Jim Webb this morning. As head of the space agency, this is a vital moment for him. Never a quiet man, he must have even deeper hollows than usual under his eyes; but his chin will be firm.

JANUARY 29, 1962
NEW YORK

Peals of thunder in Persia: "We must put an end to *foreign* consultants and luxurious and extravagant contracts." Gr-grr-grr. Even Asfia, but chiefly the Prime Minister. Bang, bang by the Minister of Justice: Ebtehaj stands accused of "crim-in-al acts" of permitting expenditures of this country's money by extravagant foreigners and for grandiose things like dams and irrigation.

And yet . . .

Leo Anderson, just in from Persia, reports: the Prime Minister heard that he, Anderson, was leaving his D&R post in Iran. Which he is, because his contract term is over and he and we want him available for other things. The Prime Minister sends for Leo; spends half an hour urging him *not* to leave; how will Iran get these things done that he does so well, etc.?

We didn't plan it that way at all. But Anderson's departure—which would have happened without regard to the fulminations and the Ebtehaj case—is a way of bringing home to them that, however much they growl for public consumption, actually they know we have done a good job and they need us. This is the kind of double-talk with which life is filled, and not only in Persia but in our own country as well. This is part of the business of placating—I guess that's the word—the nationalistic or local pride sentiments of a few, but often a very vocal few.

Accepted a formal invitation to become a trustee of Education in World Affairs, Inc. This will not be a "front" kind of obligation: the problem this new enterprise was organized to meet is far too serious— and fascinating—for that.

Today a long discussion with Gordon and Burnett at my initiative, on the question: Is it really feasible and workable to try to combine in one organization of the kind of people we are both the public service kind of thing we do and private ventures? This was my basic original idea of D&R back in 1955. But so far nothing—but nothing—of this private kind has actually developed that has amounted to anything at all.

The discussion was useful indeed.

Not because we came up with any pat solution. But it cleared the air.

Gordon, thinking out loud more or less, said that the price, in energy and preoccupation, of working hard at something that would or might make money out of business was more than he believed he was willing to pay, much as he would like to have money and much as he enjoyed spending it. John clarified his own position and that of others: we want a private profitable activity because we want to feel that D&R has an assured future, because this is the kind of work we love.

I have not given up the concept that consulting work and private entrepreneurial activities can be *combined* in D&R.

JANUARY 31, 1962
AT PENN STATION, NEW YORK, WAITING FOR
THE 9:30 A.M. TO WASHINGTON

A sensitive person who loves people just because they are people can make the whole world of the here and now clearer, sharper, give the most "commonplace" experience a tang and savor such as the cold clear air has on this very wintry morning. To look at people, in the street, scurrying to their work, not as a crowd or blur but as individuals, each different, each interesting, sometimes interesting because so dull, with a classic dullness.

Dr. Gremliza has been our visitor these past three weeks from the desolate wastes of Khuzistan. Like his "patients" and friends, the Persian Arabs, he folded his tent-office out on the desert below Dizful to come to New York. Purpose: to discuss with public health authorities here the concept and techniques he has developed after years of living with and working with some of these poor devils in the villages of the Gebli area, and before that in the harsh desolation of the region known as Susangard.

All of us have felt rather protective of him. Of course, we thought, he will feel lost, need guidance, a helping hand. For the first time in his life the visitor from Mesopotamia, seat of ancient Babylon's "wickedness," comes to the New Babylon.

Bug-eyed, Burnett told me a story of just how much Gremliza, the desert doctor, needed guidance in the big city. Gremliza came to a party at our house in Princeton last Sunday. On the way back, with Burnett, Gremliza said he enjoyed modern jazz. Suggested they go to a place where it was played. As they came into Nick's (don't know where this is) at about 11:30 P.M., the hat-check chick hailed him: "Hi, doc, glad to see you again," and gave him a big pat on the shoulder. As he and Burnett settled down in a seat, the trombonist sighted him, came over to sit next to him, complete with his trombone; old buddies.

FEBRUARY 1, 1962
PRINCETON

The distinguished Chairman of the Committee on Foreign Relations of the Senate of the United States was chewing off the corner of a sandwich, crouched over a knee-high table in the corner of his office in the Capitol. As we were swished in, Fulbright looked over the top of his glasses—as characteristic a gesture with him as shaking the remnants of his mane was for Tom Connally—and hailed me Arkansas fashion: "Hi, Dave. Just grabbing a bite [at which he gulped the last of the milk in the glass beside the crumbs of the sandwich]. Sorry about not being over there at my own office. The Senate is the most disorderly—no, that's not quite it—the most unpredictable place there is. We've just taken a vote on John McCone for head of CIA, confirmed 71 to 12. Even when you have an *agreement* to vote at a certain time you can't count on it;

some Senator gets up and starts off on something else. Anyway, glad to see you and Gordon.

"Well," the Senator went on, "I voted against McCone. Said neither I nor our Committee had been consulted about the appointment. Couldn't vote for him without knowing about his basic views on foreign policy. Made [Richard] Russell [Chairman of the Armed Services Committee] furious; said CIA didn't have anything to do with foreign policy. Just fact-gathering, that's all they do. Do you believe that, Dave?" This was not a question; just a comment. "I get the impression—the impression—that they're mighty *operational* in international affairs." And then that grin that is such a disarming and charming part of this remarkable and powerful man.

"But you came to see me about Iran." The usual questions: Will Prime Minister Amini be able to hold on? What about the Shah? "I think we give him too much military aid, but that's just my opinion."

Said the Senator: "All these detailed questions our Committee has been writing to you about how the money for your Iran project is spent, that all comes from Senator Hickenlooper. He has some reason, don't know just what, why he brings this up even though the money isn't from the U.S. Can it be said that *none* of the money for the project comes from the U.S., none of it?"

Gordon assured him this was true. I broke in to say that, though the funds were not American, *we* were, and the project had reflected credit on America because it had gone well. So we had asked for an opportunity to tell the Committee the story of the project, including of course all the detailed figures that any member wanted.

"Should it be an open or an executive hearing?" Bill asked. I said open, but fast.

"It will be a good thing to air these things, and maybe we can learn from your operation something that will be useful when the foreign aid hearings come along in April." So a tentative date was set for early March, by which time Fulbright will be back from a campaign trip. "Orville Faubus hasn't yet made up his mind whether he is going to run against me," Bill said, grinning like anything. "So until May 2, when he's got to make up his mind, I've got to be running like anything."

FEBRUARY 2, 1961
PRINCETON

The land was white, when I peered out through my curtains at 5 A.M., though it was still night; a gentle snow had transformed everything. At 6:30 I set out walking in the new world the snow had made, swinging my stick, absurdly happy for no particular reason. The kind of buck jump that Mac used to execute, me on his back, just because the air was a delight and he and I felt good. Down the middle of the street two little figures, one red parka-ed, one gray. The faces shining; shuffling the snow as we used to scuttle through leaves in the early fall, as kids. Great smiles, the wide, dark-eyed smile of Asian children's faces: the son and daughter of our neighbor, the young Chinese Nobel Laureate in physics. Children and fresh snow, those two go together. "Good morning," said the little girl, so formally. "Isn't the snow wonderful?" said I. "Yes," said the little beaming Chinese face, "we hope it will become much deep-er"—this said in careful, *spaced* tones.

FEBRUARY 6, 1961
NEW YORK

I was fifteen or sixteen years old when I began a "diary" in a slick-coated little school notebook. This has been going on ever since.

Today, at 11:00, in the austere offices of a most conservative publishing house—Harper & Brothers—the words "excitement" and "deeply implicit" (whatever that means) were applied to the more than a million and a half words written since 1915. In short, Cass Canfield, head of Harper & Brothers and D.E.L. have reached agreement on the publication of the *Journals*. The basis is publication essentially in their entirety. And this means five or more fat volumes.

I could not be more shaken with a sense of unreality. These acres of shorthand notes written late at night, on planes and in remote places. These years of trying to find some way of making these observations on life into something useful to others—all this has come to fruition: a decision to see them in print in my lifetime.

Of course, there is a great deal of work ahead. There are hundreds of questions of "good taste," there are hundreds of explanatory footnotes perhaps. But we are up the slope now; from here it is downhill.

One thing Canfield said that pleased me a great deal. As we were breaking up, he said: "You have a distinction that is true of very few authors that I know of. [It sounded strange to hear myself described as an author, even in a technical publishing sense as he used it, i.e., someone who has written a book.] All three of your books are still in print: I checked on this this morning. That shows the vitality of what you say."

Two energetic young Dominicans—Tomas Pastoriza and Louis Crouch—were in this morning. Their river and valley—Rio Yaque del Norte—is their great enthusiasm, their driving force. In a few days we shall see it, and perhaps help begin something that may prove significant for that troubled island.

The papers have been full of stories from India that the world was coming to an end: their horoscope—or whatever—said the stars and sun were lined up in just the right way to finish everything off quite neatly. The stores there were virtually closed (someone even had a "statistic" about how much "retail trade" had fallen off in anticipation of the event that would make buying things a futility). It didn't come off, this "end of the world."

I thought how disappointed many millions of Indians must have been. The kind of people who have it all figured out that on a certain day the world is coming to an end are people who *want* to have it over. Has anyone ever written a book gathering in one place all of the predictions of the end of the world? Not casual predictions, but serious, documented ones, where large numbers of people lay out their plans (or nonplans) very carefully because they *know* that it will soon be over for everyone. And how full of glee they will be that all the people they hate, including themselves, will be no more, and at an hour and day that they have predicted in the teeth of the unbelieving!

For many people every day of the year *their* world is done for. But that is not what "the world is coming to an end" means in these days of nuclear weapons.

FEBRUARY 7, 1962
NEW YORK

Gordon enjoys very complex crossword puzzles, and double-jointed supercrostics. He carries these with him on trips; flying across the forbidding mountains of Turkey, he is absorbed completely in working out these mental enigmas. Recently, so he told me, a distinguished engineering colleague, the fabulous Bill Voorduin, was sitting next to him in the plane; he was reading one of several books or pamphlets he subscribes to about how to make money in the stock market, about which Voorduin, I fear, knows less than nothing.

Bill looked at Gordon working on his crostics a time or two and said: "Why do you waste your time on *that*?" Gordon grinned, looked at the how-to-beat-the-stock-market stuff Bill was stewing over and said: "I like to waste my time *this* way; you have another way of wasting your time."

Everyone should waste time his own way.

FEBRUARY 8, 1962
FLYING TO SAN JUAN, PUERTO RICO

Thinking on this theme: The Faith of a *Humanist*.

The words or categories "liberal" and "conservative" have surely lost whatever clarity they may once have had. Then why not substitute *"humanist"*? The Faith that human beings come first; that they are the center of all. The test: what is the effect on human beings? A man is a man. That is the starting point. And the end.

Individualism has come to *mean* a form of *self*-centering, out of keeping with the nature of our *inter*dependent system. "Socialism" means that individualism is best served by concentrating on "society," which is putting the cart before the horse, I rather think.

Many of the things I believe—much of the "education of David Lilienthal"—can fit into this matrix or theme of humanism.*

FEBRUARY 9, 1961
ON A BENCH IN A LITTLE PLAZA, OLD SAN JUAN

Gordon and I spent perhaps an hour with Governor Luis Muñoz-Marín in his peaceful Spanish colonial office, looking out on the battlements of La Fortaleza and the bay.

He seemed almost a living definition of *power*. The compact figure, the great craglike head, set deep in the recess of heavy curved shoulders, like the head and shoulders of a proud bull. Quick in movement, youthful, springy with the stance of a boxer just as the referee starts the match. Actually he must be almost my age. A man of responsible power shows his self-assurance in different ways, of course. When he understates, when he can make ironic, gentle fun of himself and his position, when he can ask *you* what you think, make you feel he values your opinion, he increases that ambiance of sureness of himself that is the clearest evidence of strength.

I have used the word "power" in what I have written, sitting here in the now slanting sun, in this little plaza. But *strength* is the word, really. I admire and covet strength, inner strength as well as its outer manifestations. I'm not sure I admire power and doubt if I have ever coveted it. It exacts a high price, power, to any sensitive person. Strength can radiate strength; one man's inner strength can give strength to others by a process I recognize but don't understand.

There is no effective political opposition in Puerto Rico. "So I have to be my own opposition," he said, a rumble of a laugh shaking him. "In my message to the legislature I put in a paragraph of how I would attack my budget if I were the opposition: amounted to that," an illustration of the need for criticism even if you have to *invent it yourself*.

"I understand you are going to the Dominican Republic," he said.

* On this theme of humanism, Lilienthal delivered the Benjamin Fairless Lectures at Carnegie Institute of Technology in November of 1966. The Lectures were published by Columbia University Press in 1967 under the title *Management: A Humanist Art.*—Ed.

Gordon explained that our trip was "sponsored" by two private individuals, Dominican businessmen. The Governor said: "My advice to you would be *not* to talk about the important things that *private* enterprise can do for the Dominican Republic. We in Puerto Rico now know that is true, but we didn't at first, and we had to learn it in our own way. Well, let them find that out in *their* own way. Otherwise you will just give psychological ammunition to the Commies and extreme left. The Governor there now isn't leftish; moderate, somewhat conservative. The Fidelistas are looking for a chance to show that the men who are running the Dominican Government now are just arms of Yankee exploitation, and all that stuff."

I remarked that the land reform problem in the Yaque, and elsewhere, seemed to be easier than it might otherwise be, because, ironically, of the Trujillos. This was a subject I inquired into, in the first moments of our first visit with Crouch and Pastoriza in our offices. "How will the poor people who are squatting on the hillside get any benefit out of increased irrigation?" was about the way I put it to them. Their answer: Most of the best land the Trujillo crew had stolen and developed; the revolution returned that land to the country so it is owned by the country; what you would call public domain.

The Governor picked this up. With the irony he loves he said: "Trujillo is a demonstration of the principles of Marx! He stole everything, concentrated ownership in him, as Marx said the capitalists did, and then there it was, all nicely concentrated and developed when the proletariat arose and seized it."

"A Dominican Marx without the beard," I commented, and the big boom of a laugh shook the Governor. The item about the beard could have been developed further, since a beard—the trademark of Marx—is also the worldwide trademark of Fidel Castro.

Gordon said we would like to see him on one of his frequent trips to New York City, but realized how busy he must be when he is in that city where such a large part of his constituency lives. "Yes, Puerto Rico is one island in an archipelago of Manhattan, Long Island, and so on." Archipelago indeed.

FEBRUARY 12, 1962
9:15 A.M.
SANTO DOMINGO, DOMINICAN REPUBLIC

Such elegance! Not only this presidential suite of the late Generalissimo Trujillo, but *everything* since we landed a half hour ago. Six million dollar airport, a long parkway along the deep blue sea, the cluster of "modern" government buildings. And as we drove along the wharves the four masts of a magnificent schooner, the *Sea Cloud,* bought by Trujillo from Mrs. Joe Davies and *one* of the late "President's" several steam yachts.

I have never seen so many submachine guns, handled with aplomb, as in the President's "Palace," and particularly just outside the door of Dr. Bonnelly's rather spare office. Only a month ago, almost exactly, there was a coup that put the Cabinet in jail—we were in Washington at the time—and the next day *another* coup that put them back in authority. So no wonder about the machine guns.

President Bonnelly is a gentle, bland, graying man of about sixty, with a sweet smile and manner. Very cordial. Comes from Santiago, that is, he is a Cibao-an (as they call the region of the northwest, and the Rio Yaque). He spoke with enthusiasm about the future of that region; considers it, he said, as not just for the benefit of that region but as a place to begin building the country.

A talk with the young men who are part of the Water Resources Department; earnest, solemn; when we said good things about the maps and data they had about the Yaque River development, they smiled in the pleased way that you see on men who have been waiting a long time for their work to be recognized and attention paid to it.

But of course what strikes one hardest is to go through the main streets, and on the edges, and see the fresh marks of destruction and looting: almost every residence of the Trujillo tribe had been gutted, plenty thoroughly. In one beautiful house, a dozen families, squatters, had moved in, kids and all.

The very early colonial architecture is most appealing. Much of this is of the sixteenth century. And next to it a modern aluminum sheath building.

It's now 11:15 P.M. Have been going at it, hammer and tongs, since 5:30 this morning. Whew! And what an array of people, talents, viewpoints. What dramatic people are pointed out to us: "That man was hidden in a closet for seven weeks, after the assassination. That man is one of the men who defied the dictator, and hid, without food or water, for two days," etc.

Such excitement as there is all about us today.

FEBRUARY 14, 1962
SANTIAGO

This is a time when I get a bit weary of this 16-hour a day grind, washing my shirts, forever grinning at new people one meets—and wishing I'd stayed at home.

10:30 P.M.

Another very long day. Filled with the excitement of new faces, places, little dramas. In addition to everything else, this was "Helicopter Day."

Columbus was the first European to see this Yaque Valley. He and his crew set out, on foot, from his ship's mooring near here, to cross this island through the mountain passes. He was first. But he didn't do it by that strange bird known as the helicopter—and we did. Going up over the tops of the Cordillera between here and the blue of the ocean, a sea deep and mysterious and beckoning; skimming the trees on the very tips of the mountains' precipitous crests, all this proved to be one of the most dramatic explorations I have ever been part of. Our meeting last night with thirty eager young men, still dazed by the new freedom that has come to the island and to them, was equally dramatic and unexpected.

FEBRUARY 15, 1962
SANTO DOMINGO

A town meeting, almost in classic New England Anglo-Saxon style, in the Dominican Republic, only a month or so after the end of thirty-two years of a tyrannical, bloody dictatorship.

That sounds, as I write it, an absurdity or the product of a romantic imagination. But that is what I saw, and participated in as a guest, last night.

About thirty young Dominicans, who in their lifetime have never known anything *except* the iron and bloody and greedy hand of the Trujillos, so young were they. Presenting ideas, then listening to the ideas of others, discussing what was wrong with them, rejecting them.

At the outset, when a question was directed to me, we tried to answer it by putting another question to them. I said it would help us, as foreign guests, if these young men would tell us what was in their minds; what they were thinking now that their country is beginning a new course after a full generation of rule by a dictator.

One man said he thought there should be a coordinating junta for the nation (one even said for all the Americas!) which would *decide*, por ejemplo, whether pineapple should be raised, or tomatoes, anywhere in the country. With the greatest earnestness one extraordinarily handsome young man, perhaps twenty-six years old, when asked why anyone should stop a farmer raising tomatoes, replied: "There should be a study made first to see whether it would help or hurt the country if land were used for tomatoes or pineapples; there might be a better use of the land."

There was some fine rhetoric and verbal idealism. But what struck me was that almost every one among them joined, in an orderly way, in the discussion; that in the process of discussion the proponents of abstract ideas found they were answering their own arguments and freely changing positions.

Pastoriza, as moderator or chairman, took a vote. I found the picture of young Dominicans taking a *vote on ideas* an interesting one, with Trujillo hardly cold in his grave. They were unanimously for the creation of a TVA kind of regional authority for the Yaque Valley, with a national junta providing advisory services from the national viewpoint.

I have been brought up on the notion that if a generation lives under dictatorship, such as that in Russia, the brainwashing is complete; the generation that never knew anything else would be docile; completely gone would be the talents of independent thinking, open discussion, etc. This group certainly didn't support that proposition.

One should certainly not draw too broad conclusions from this experience. But the very fact of a Dominican town meeting in this provincial capital was heartening, just the same, and surprising.

Yesterday morning, early, we set off by car, heading northwesterly. When we got to the good-sized town of Valverde, we stopped suddenly to greet a stocky, very intelligent-looking young man, a Dr. Flores, a physician, the new Governor of the province, as impressive as he was black. He said to me in English: "We have had a rebirth. Now we in this town must accept our responsibilities. We must do things for ourselves. We know best what our problems are, what things can be done to make this a better town."

At a little village of Esperanza four helicopters were primed and waiting to take us down the Yaque Valley. The doors of the two-seater had been taken off. This put me out in the open air, literally (I put one foot on a stanchion outside the cockpit).

A spectacular flight up the Narrows and then, in late afternoon, across the high mountains. The sharpness of the ridges we skirted, the extraordinary effect of the white trunks of royal palms in the green and rugged setting, the sudden bursting over the last peak to be overwhelmed by the sight of the Atlantic Ocean filling the whole canvas, white breakers row on row, the very same blue body of water by which Columbus thought he had reached India.

Everywhere we sensed this: the atmosphere of a country emerging —or is it really emerging?—from one kind of dictatorship and frightened by the possibility of another, the uprising of the terrorists, the Castro-ites.

FEBRUARY 16, 1962
SANTIAGO

The boy was tall, almost my height; erect and slim; dusky shading of skin, a soft voice. Eager and alert. Seventeen years old, he said, president of the high school student body of 900. An eagerness to learn, great ambition. No self-consciousness in talking to the VIP, which he did at length, pouring out, in the English he had learned mostly "by myself," the interest he has in math-a-mat-ics and drawing. Critical of the school that required him to spend time on other useless things: "We had to learn 145 biographies and spend time on history and many other subjects; but what I want is mathematics. Culture I can learn sometime by myself. When I was fifteen I was arrested and put in jail for a long time. I read a speech of the Generalissimo to a meeting of students, about how good was life in our country. I made a laugh of it. What I saw in that jail was so terrible, the tortures, that I lose my mind, I become sick. After I was no longer in jail I had to take medicines for six months to get back my mind."

There drifted back across my mind, as I listened to this eager, ambitious boy, at a reception for us last night, the picture of another seventeen-year-old boy, in a small Indiana town many years ago. He was naturally shy; but when a "great man" came to the high school to lecture —the president of some school of education in Michigan, probably an obscure one—this shy boy went up on the platform and, waiting his turn, talked to this man about his own ambitions, asking his opinion, finding the lecturer so interested that he had him come to see him the next day at the hotel. Through this handsome young Dominican youth, a reunion between Lilienthal, age sixty-two, and David, age seventeen.

From the walls of the municipal Council chamber the faces of the nation's heroes stared at us, as we marched in last evening, the Council being in session in our honor. The portraits fascinated me: like the set and arranged expression of a not too expert product of the embalmer's art, complete with broad purple sashes across the chest, epaulets, mustachios, and the lusterless eye of a fish after the color of the deep has faded and it lies there on the deck looking up at you with disdain.

The Council members were lined up on each side of a long table, curious, friendly in a distant way—after all, these two characters are gringos. The questions were the usual ones: how much will the "proyecto" cost, how long will it take, what will it do for Santiago? I tried to explain that this was *their* project, not ours, but this did no good. We were the magicians, and that is that.

FEBRUARY 17, 1962
LEAVING PORT-AU-PRINCE, HAITI
FLYING TO MONTEGO BAY, JAMAICA

Yesterday afternoon in Santiago Gordon and I met with the Junta, the Citizens' Committee. I told them that our visit had amply *confirmed* in our minds their own convictions about the Cibao area and regional development of that area.

The bright-eyed high-pressure Tomas Pastoriza asked: "Will you help us; what kind of contract can we make with you?" I said, of course, we would help them, as individuals. But it would be "awkward" if discussions about a contract were held before the Committee had acquired some status. The status I suggested was that of a commission set up by decree of the Council of Ministers, the first function of which would be to prepare and recommend to the Council a charter for a permanent regional corporación or autoridad.

Yesterday they were drafting something along this line most of the afternoon, and far into the night. At 6:30 this morning Tomas and Alejandro Grullón, two members of the Committee, were to present these ideas to the President and prepare the way for the presentation to the Council. Pastoriza is confident to the point of cockiness that by the time Gordon and I have returned to New York the middle of next week we will have a cable that the first step has indeed been taken. I am far less confident as to how rapidly a dazed and burdened group of ministers will act, on what will be regarded—and rightly so—as a commitment to form an autonomous authority for that wonderful region.

A long, long cable from Oliver in Persia. Developments for the extension of our contract and the completion of the transfer of some functions to the Iranian regional agency moving along well. (Not a word about Ebtehaj.) Oliver urged Gordon to make a quick trip out to push things along, decide some things outstanding, etc. I commented that one argument *against* Gordon's going would be that if Oliver could handle this by himself it would do a good deal to strengthen his confidence.

Apparently Gordon didn't think much of this comment, for it is pretty clear that he will go. I can't be sure that this isn't essential. But the only way I know how to build up people is to toughen or test them with *sole* responsibility.

FEBRUARY 20, 1962
8 A.M.
MONTEGO BAY

We leave by BOAC at noon. The weather has been unbelievably good—cool at night, benignly warm during the day with a gentle breeze.

A full moon, silvering the water of the bay, making magic leprechaun shapes of the tropical vegetation. Flowers and birds at every turn.

APPROACHING NASSAU (BOAC 707) FROM JAMAICA
2:46 P.M.

Signia of the *new*, new world, reached us while we were over the very ocean that began a new era of the old world.

The captain of this huge airplane tells us, over the public-address system, that Colonel John Glenn has completed his third orbit of the earth and in a "few minutes" the "capsule" (meaning a courageous man) will drop into the Atlantic very near to our present position in this blue sea. (The young steward, way forward, has signaled with his hand —the fingers open and extended downward. I know this means that man has returned to earth, and a helicopter is now fishing him out.)

FEBRUARY 27, 1962
NEW YORK

Last night on Eric Sevareid's TV panel show, called *Challenges*. No one should miss the experience of being on at least one TV panel program; it's part of being in the mid-century. (One is enough.)

The backstage apparatus for a TV production has expanded until you think you are in a factory. The performance before a live audience, of which performance I was a cog, involved so much machinery and operatives that I could hardly believe it had anything to do with that little glass rectangle in people's living rooms.

I guess it went all right. Finally I felt I had to wade into a way-out character on the panel, Ayn Rand by name. I had never heard of her before the program went on. A terribly intense woman, a gifted writer and fuzzy thinker, she has founded a right-wing cult. A well-organized claque of young people scattered in strategic enclaves through the audience cheered her every word.

When I said that what she was saying was "nonsense" I found I had tangled with a high priestess, complete with her disciples and followers. That "nonsense" comment did it! My guess is she hates not only me— which she made clear—but life itself.

MARCH 2, 1962
PRINCETON

With the almost unreal closeness of a TV close-up the President's hair seems like a wig, so regular and heavy. A distraction I shouldn't have yielded to, considering that the discourse he held with me—and in

25 million other American living rooms—was why he was ordering the resumption of A-bomb tests.

His ordering the resumption of atomic tests was, of course, entirely to be expected. Much of the argument cited by Kennedy tonight was the jargon of the scientific weapons fraternity, the vested interests of the atomic labs. "Design," "efficiency," and a lot of parochial terminology directed to parochial technical concerns that do not go to the heart of the terrible issues.

If only we could come to grips with the real issues; I wonder if we might not be far along toward some kind of accommodation with the Soviets that would give a degree of confidence. But all these technical discussions so far are based on the *assumption* that these weapons, if improved, etc., *provide security*—for us, for the Soviets, for the world.

There is no evidence or reasoning to support this assumption any more.

MARCH 4, 1962
PRINCETON

The "life story of a business" continues to unroll. The degree of intellectual interest and emotional reaction I have in each succeeding chapter of Minerals & Chemicals-Philipp I find difficult for me to believe. For example, a Board meeting last week in the spanky new headquarters of the Philipp Division, in one of the new cathedrals of business along Park Avenue.

The high point was the decision to raise the dividend rate from 12½ cents a quarter to 15 cents. We spent a half hour exposing and examining the facts that argued for such action—or raised doubts about its wisdom. There was almost an absence of community "value" judgments, i.e., questions such as the effect of a dividend increase on the general welfare, on workers, on inflation.

A businessman has his troubles, God knows. But in comparison with the issues in Government they are relatively simple and not in the same order of magnitude of worrisomeness.

But what is interesting is that I, who for thirty years have been in the middle (and still am) of *public* issues, should find the *process* of reaching conclusions and agreement in business matters so intrinsically interesting, that is, interesting *as a process,* however unimportant, really, the particular decision is to all but a few.

MARCH 8, 1962
SITTING IN AN ANTIQUE PENN "LOCAL," PENN STATION

Great bold eight-column headline staring at me from the news-stands: "Anti-U.S. Riots in Domingo."

I heard the details of this from a news ticker Nate Greene read to Gordon and me an hour ago. Nate grinned in that boyish way—out of a face that, however worn, still has the flash of impishness in it; "You fellows don't seem to be afraid you'll get shot."

MARCH 13, 1962
NEW YORK

A letter from Pastoriza of the Valley of the Rio Yaque in the Dominican Republic. The Council of Ministers (pausing between street riots!) has indeed created a commission to create a regional authority for the Cibao; Pastoriza is going to visit and observe the CVC in Cali, and then up here late this month to work out the charter, and terms with us. So he says.

MARCH 19, 1962
PRINCETON

Uncovered the garden yesterday from its blanket of tawny salt hay. It is still cold, but the signs of green rebirth are *everywhere*. So it is with me: under an outer mask of wrinkles (every one of which I *earned* and cherish) the green shoots of life surprise me with their vigor, as undefeated by long living as the perennials are by the zero cold through the long winter.

MARCH 20, 1962
AT THE WASHINGTON AIRPORT, READY TO
TAKE OFF FOR NEW YORK

How many times in the past I have found myself in that lonely witness chair, facing the half circle of bored solemn faces up there on the raised platform, symbolizing political power—or the "Legislative Branch," or the Inquisitors, or however you want to put it. For years it was a large part of my life.

But this morning's testimony before the Senate Committee on Foreign Relations was different.

Why was this different? Because I was sitting in that seat of confrontation, answering Senators' questions *not* as a public servant but as a private citizen. But it all seemed familiar: the sly innuendo in the questions of Bourke Hickenlooper or Senator John Williams (of Delaware) or the comments of the porcine bloated Homer Capehart of Indiana, though this time I appeared as chairman of a private business corporation. "Private enterprise" is something they will never accept *me* as representing. There they are probably right at that.

The hearing was in the new chambers of the Senate Committee on Foreign Relations, my first appearance before *that* committee. Now and then a familiar and friendly face would pop up on the dais, give me a wave of the hand and a grin: John Sparkman, hair now gray but still with the red-cheeked face of a boy; Albert Gore, handsome, curly-headed. Senator Russell Long, bearing on his face the faintest suggestion of a likeness to Huey the Terrific, whom I shall never forget as I heard him, on the Senate floor, make a fiery, a withering attack on F.D.R. and Farley, at the very beginning of the New Deal.

The hearing was attended by quite a few newspapermen, but it was pretty tame for news. The only prospect of news was something Blair of the *New York Times* was there to get, if possible, i.e., Ebtehaj. Hick brought this in, of course: "There is a report that he is in jail because of his arrangements, these unusual arrangements with your company."

Bill Fulbright looked out from over his half-glasses, like an inquisitive benign bird. His humor is delicious: in the end he kidded me about acting "sensitive" that we were being critcized in Iran because we were Americans. Said Bill: "I get criticized all the time right here in my own state and I don't mind it. You fellows have been criticized here, too, so you ought to be used to it." Which we are.

I'm glad to say neither Gordon (who was good, clear, explicit) nor I was defensive or secretive or reluctant, even about our financial statement or our salaries. But it seemed strange just the same: from public servant back to *another kind* of public servant, it seemed; and this is not far from the case.

NEW YORK
6:30 P.M.

The complete story of the crucifixion of Robert Oppenheimer isn't in yet. Today Joe Volpe told me another episode, a sordid one.

When, in December, 1953, the AEC suspended Robert's clearance and prepared to "try" him as a risk to the national security, Robert went to see Joe Volpe, asking him to act as his attorney. Thus a lawyer-client relationship was created; the inviolability of this relationship of confidence has been a part of the common law and of common decency, too, for centuries.

Later Robert met in Joe's office with his other lawyers, Herbert Marks and Lloyd Garrison. They discussed the case, how to prepare to present Robert's defense—the usual things that a client and a lawyer confer about. Before the case came on for the "trial" before the now celebrated Gray Board, Volpe had withdrawn as one of Robert's counsel.

Just a week ago Joe learned this ugly fact: a verbatim transcript of a meeting in Joe's office, between Robert and his lawyers, was sent to the AEC, while the supposed "investigation" was in the hands of the Gray Board. The Acting General Counsel of the Commission, Harold Green, was astounded when this transcript came to him. There was only one way such a recorded transcript *could* be made, namely, by planting a microphone in the office of a lawyer representing a client in a proceeding involving his good name and his patriotism. Green was outraged. He left the AEC, though I'm not sure whether this was the only thing that led him to leave. Last week he told Joe this story, and Joe tells me both Green and one of his assistants at the time who saw the report have signed affidavits to this effect.

In addition to this planting of a microphone and thereby invading the lawyer-client confidential relation, Joe says the report shows that Joe's telephone was tapped. His conversations with me, in New York, and with others were included in this record.

Just how low can you get?

Joe's recital reminded me of the way I was treated before the Gray Board back in April of 1954, by those out to "get" Oppenheimer, not to investigate the so-called charges.

Knowing I was to testify before the Gray Board I asked the AEC General Manager, K. D. Nichols, for a chance to refresh my recollection by reading the file on the AEC's handling of Robert's clearance back in 1949, only a brief time after the AEC had assumed its duties. Nichols gave directions to the secretary, Roy B. Snapp, that this be done.

So a day or so before I was to testify I sat in an AEC office reading the file that was handed to me. I had requested, and was led to believe, that this was the *complete* file that we AEC Commissioners had before us when Robert's clearance had been confirmed by all the Commissioners, including Strauss, when I was the Chairman. This was in the fall of 1949, years before the Oppenheimer hearings.

Only later, on April 20, 1954, when I was before the Gray Board, being cross-examined by Roger Robb, counsel appointed by the Commission to "bring out the facts," it became evident that a number of records had been extracted from that file and were in Robb's hands before the "complete" file was turned over for me to "refresh my recollection."

So when Robb asked me certain questions about the Commission's action at the time we confirmed Oppenheimer—I testified I had no recollection of a number of episodes. The part of the early Commission files which could have caused me to recall those early episodes—one of thousands to remember—had been lifted from the file that, only a couple of days before I testified, had been represented to me as the *complete* file. Robb had these lifted portions before him in the Board hearing room, and he queried me about them.

Not remembering these episodes, or recalling them only vaguely before the Gray Board under Robb's crude police court kind of cross-examination, I was made to appear a liar or one with a very poor memory.† The legal term for misleading a witness in this way is "entrapment," and has been condemned by the courts since the early days of Anglo-Saxon justice. This kind of sharp practice, condoned by the AEC, transformed into a Star Chamber atrocity the fair administrative procedure we of the first Commission had set up for these security hearings.

"You aren't the kind who looks backward. If you spend your time reminiscing—about George Norris, or your *past* achievements in TVA—then you're through. You're not old enough for that. Those past experiences gave you the strength and toughness and understanding for what you have to do *today*, in the world as it is *today*.

"The past is important only because it tempered you, as a piece of steel is tempered by going through the heat of the furnace. That's why the past is important, and not as something to revel in or look back on." Thus Spake Beatrice.

Such thoughts as these were thrown at me too from quite another source and another experience. John Burnett reported that my "remarks" to the Conference on the Public Service at Princeton Friday night stimulated a good deal of the discussion of that sophisticated group of public managers and advisors on public management. These men, he said, expected me to be the elder statesman, recounting what "we" did about the public service years ago. It hit them that I said nothing about the past; instead I talked about new problems, the new condition of the country as I thought it would be in the seventies, as a way of telling them what these high-level administrators should be thinking about and working at now. John keeps pressing the idea that the reason I have something to say on the current scene is because I am still *working* in it.

Saw an exhibit of Willem de Kooning's paintings, and of Henry Moore's huge bronzes yesterday afternoon. The paintings I couldn't understand at all: the touch of realism is just enough to confuse me about the abstraction and the abstraction to obscure the objective touches. But the great silent shapes of the Moore bronzes almost stunned me with their power; like coming on an ancient Aztec or Mayan monumental figure in the jungle.

† Volume III of the *Journals* has an account of the hearing before the Gray Board, See Index: Oppenheimer case.

MARCH 22, 1962
4:30 A.M.
NEW YORK

Popped out of bed because a theme popped into my so-called mind, when I *thought* I was asleep.

The Heroic in American Life. The story of the achievements of America that are so magnificent and unique in human history that the word "heroic" seems appropriate. And this could provide the theme for a kind of "bragging" about where we have come, what we have done, that is paulbunyanish in more ways than physical—and particularly, where we are going or can go. An answer to the cynic and self-deprecator. And much of it drawn from what I know, what I have seen.

MARCH 27, 1962
NEW YORK

How exhilarating is a change so sudden and drastic as the Supreme Court decision of yesterday: that a citizen may sue in the Federal courts if he believes that the State laws do not give his vote equal weight with that of others in determining the make-up of the state legislature. With the careening, plunging course of the nation away from rural domination in economic affairs, this gives "urbanism" a decisive push forward in the political field as well.

A tingle of excitement to know that I am alive (and fully alive) at a time when such far-reaching changes are at their beginning. For that the Supreme Court decision will accelerate a change in the political character of the nation is perfectly clear.

APRIL 1, 1962
PRINCETON

The Shah and the Queen arrive on the 11th; Helen and I have been invited to the State Dinner at the White House for them. Tried my tail coat on this morning; first time I have had it off the hook for perhaps twelve years. The pants too big around the waist, to my surprise; the coat too tight across the shoulders, because in the past couple of years I have been exercising like mad. So I'll wear it, and try not to bust out across the back—or explode along the front either.

APRIL 8, 1962
AT THE WILLIAMSBURG INN
WILLIAMSBURG, VIRGINIA

"Tables forming a hollow square"—the symbol of a thoroughly established American institution: The Confer-ence.

This one‡ is about educational assistance abroad, but it could be on almost any similar subject, which attracts the people who think that when they have said that something *should* be they have said something. What should be and is desirable is a long way from doing something effective about it, but only a minority at such meetings—or anyplace else—seems to sense the difference.

A caricature from a lower echelon of the World Bank spoke up late in the afternoon; he described the "seven criteria" he laid down, at a big meeting at Santiago, Chile. These were to be the conditions which the Bank would insist upon in making educational loans. But it was obvious no country in the world could *possibly* qualify for a loan under these criteria. When he completed his list of "criteria" most everyone laughed, out loud.

I had about as much as I could take. I raised my hand, was recognized. "It is the part of prudence not to overcommit. Since we haven't done too good a job in capital formation and capital development abroad, nor in scientific assistance to underdeveloped countries, nor preinvestment, nor economic planning, wouldn't it be wise in this conference to ask some hard questions about whether we should add still one more item to an already full plate, the subject of educational assistance? Shouldn't we ask ourselves where in the world are the *people* qualified to provide educational guidance to underdeveloped countries? The ordinary man from Dubuque may say with Andy Jackson to his troops at the battle of New Orleans: 'Raise them sights a little lower, boys.' "

APRIL 10, 1962
WILLIAMSBURG

I contributed something to the meeting yesterday: I could tell this by the attention my words got from the "hollow square." The room had been ringing with one of these exhibitions of verbal acrobatics on the high trapeze, contributed by a rotund and unbelievably smooth-flowing and thoughtful professor from Dartmouth, Kalman Silver, and the articulate and witty Barbara Ward: all about very fundamental things, I'm sure. But to me it was *so remote* from reality or the action the world cries for.

I stood it as long as I could, seeing the gathering dismay on the faces of men like Frank M. Coffin (deputy director of AID). He had come here, from being a witness in the baiting ring of Congressional hearings "on foreign aid." Then he listens to this erudition about the meaning of meaning, the value of value, etc., etc. "Here in what I can

‡ This was a conference sponsored by Education and World Affairs, Inc.

only call the bosom of the Fluent Society," I began, "I would like to bring the subject back to one of the stated topics of this conference: the development of human resources; educational assistance overseas."

My "text" was a single sentence in the paper prepared by Professor Frederick H. Harbison, a forceful, experienced man; the neglected opportunities of employers in the underdeveloped countries to train men to be "*developers* of manpower."

I went back to the earliest TVA days in 1933, 1934. One of the chief reasons we decided to do our construction work by "force account" —by TVA employees—rather than by contract was that we conceived it to be part of our responsibility in developing natural resources also to develop human resources, about which so many words had been expended in this conference. Contractors did not care to accept that responsibility and had rarely qualified themselves to carry it out; said developing people was a nuisance, an added expense, a darn fool idea.

So TVA did the training.

But we find that foreign aid agencies and the international lending agencies, such as the World Bank, seem to have the same view as contractors about "developing" human resources. They select contractors because they are qualified *technically*, but ignore this strategic qualification: the experience and ability and willingness to develop, i.e., train, human resources of the nation *as* they build physical structures, dams, roads, bridges, etc., for these nations.

I said that private business of the better kind—such as Grace (represented here by an executive vice-president, Felix Larkin)—did train nationals in countries overseas because it was in their best interest as a company to do so. But I had not heard of ICA or the World Bank having effectively used this kind of *leverage* to further the development of human resources.

That phrase, "human resources," I said, in no time is going to "become just another of the fleeting slogans of the foreign aid succession of slogans, unless every bit of leverage is used, by *concrete action* to give content to the idea of development of people in process of developing their natural physical resources."

I concluded with a story about the hot line maintenance crews working on high-tension electric lines such as we have trained in Persia. These Iranians learned we were more than just out to repair a line when it was hot and dangerous, a tricky technical business. They learned, too, *how to work together as a crew.* For unless they did there would be a serious accident to a fellow member of the crew. Well, not serious; "fatal," I added.

This picture of the hot line maintenance crew appealed strongly. Partly because it was graphic, I think, after all the vagueness. Max Millikan of MIT, sitting next to me, told me in the evening session that in the afternoon the steering committee talked about the illustration as a theme; and Barbara Ward said later the "specialists" were at work turning the story into a formula to be called the HLML quotient, Hot Line Maintenance Lilienthal quotient.

APRIL 12, 1962
WASHINGTON

Thomas Jefferson and John Adams looked puzzled from their places on the wall of the East Room as Jerome Robbins' "kids" jerked through a series of jazzy ballets, if "ballet" is the word for young people in sweatshirts and black tights flinging their arms suddenly over their heads to music.

This was the Jacqueline touch, I gather; after Mamie, culture invades the White House.

The star of the evening was the President: looking bluff and commanding, and more self-possessed even than F.D.R.

The dinner was, of course, in the State Dining Room—a beautiful room, with Lincoln's musing countenance looking down on us. After it was over Kennedy rose at his place and made one of his miniature speeches, rather gems in their way. "The Shah of Persia and I have something in common. We both visited Paris with our wives recently, and *we* might just as well have stayed home."

Then some more about how the Persian people had survived all kinds of invaders: Romans, Mongols, friends from the South and enemies from the North. This showed how much vitality they had. The same kind of vitality and love of keeping their freedom that we have, except that—he paused—"we don't live as the Shah and his people have for twenty years in the belly of the bear."

For this masculine eye, however, the star was the Empress. A dress of gold, on a slender figure, eyes so beautiful they would dazzle any male at one hundred paces. She wore a crown; more than a tiara, with seven loops of jewels, huge diamonds, rubies, and emeralds.

I sat the very farthest south of the salt one can get; across from me was Jerome Robbins, the dancer and choreographer of the ballet presented as the entertainment for the evening. Slender diminutive man, with a quiet grin, no force. He began as a chemist, he said, and found that science is a creative thing; went from that to painting, then to dancing. I suppose this is all told in some biography, but it was new to me.

It was good to be greeted with friendliness and acclaim, of course; it was good to be in the middle of a formal State Dinner at the White House. But I must say New York seems to me so much more vital, alive, and modern than Washington. Washington is looking backward, for me. New York is part of that new man I have come to believe in.

A group of guests were gathered in the main foyer, just inside the big front portico, waiting until the Iranian party had departed in their cars. The President was chatting vigorously with some young and "high style"-looking people. Mrs. Kennedy came up, looking a bit lost, with that perpetual smile erased for a moment, and said to Helen and the woman who was with her, at my elbow: "Has anyone seen my husband? Where is Jack, do you know?" Where *is* Jack indeed?

APRIL 13, 1962
NEW YORK

When I am full of "ideas" and the tumult and desire to do something about them, sleep just isn't something I can manage. This isn't conventional insomnia, I guess, for when the itch subsides I can sleep like mad.

Well, way back in my mind the magnetic tapes of my brain or imagination are slithering around like the very dickens; it seems the sensible thing to turn on the light and try to order these thoughts, rather than just lie there looking out into the darkness of this by-now all too familiar hotel room.

The identifiable head of steam is centered on the immediate future of my Development and Resources child. I'm dissatisfied with the *tentative* outlook that has come to dominate our plans and structure. D&R is badly understaffed, with no "spare capacity." We should have capital resources adequate to "invest" in people, against the conviction that there will be important and compensatory things for them to do, compensatory in money and in satisfaction, even though we don't yet know just what work there is for them to do.

Here it is four o'clock in the morning. When I wonder how I can manage to continue the pace I'm setting I recall that this is about the way I have always functioned before at my best, with unbelievably little sleep and constant motion, mental and physical. Whether the years that have been added since some of those peaks of energy consumption in my public service years will make a decisive difference I can't be sure.

ON THE TRAIN TO PRINCETON

We were waiting at the south entrance to the White House, waiting for the absurdly huge Cadillac to take us to the Hay-Adams just across the street. (How silly can ceremony and appearances get? I ask you.) Standing with us was Secretary of Defense Robert McNamara. With his rimless glasses, extra-bright alert eyes, and perky brushed hair, he could have been a professor of economics—which I understand he once was. Could have been except for one thing: a line of firmness and strength around his chin and brow that marked him off from the ivory tower, or the ivory balloon that carries so many economists off on dream trips. I offered my hand, introduced myself. He recognized my name in the way a younger campaigner greets an older one. I expressed admiration for his willingness to tackle the job of really *running* the military establishment. He grinned rather soberly, thoughtfully. "Thank you very much; may be foolhardy, but that's what I'm going to do."

A real man, that one.

APRIL 14, 1962
PRINCETON

Apparently David has made a real breakthrough in his writing, bless his stubborn, talented heart. The *Cosmopolitan* story is to be followed by another. It has been a long hard winter of trial for him; this may indeed be his spring, too, as it has been mine, in quite other ways.

APRIL 15, 1962
PRINCETON

Rarely do I think about Money (with a capital M) these days. There was the period after I got out of AEC when I thought about it, because it had a kind of fascination for me. There was the stuff, all around, rolling in; without thinking about what it meant, it was a new experience, later it gave a certain sense of achievement (a temporary sensation, I must say).

Yesterday we signed our 1961 tax returns. I realized then that I had hardly given money a real thought since it was clear that I had all I would ever need.

I keep on pressing hard on ideas that might produce more money; but stirring up ideas is an old habit only remotely, if at all, related to making money. "Incentive," the driving force that the American business-man, and Khrushchev, and David Lilienthal all talk about: this is a complex idea, not a simple one, surely.

APRIL 16, 1962
NEW YORK

Queen Farah sat with her exquisite head tilted forward, like a blossom too heavy for its stem, all the while the Shah was making a touching personal preface to his "set" speech. I was on the dais just behind and to the right of her. (The "waxworks," as some rude poet called these dais arrays at the Waldorf public dinners.) As he talked softly to an utterly still audience in the Grand Ballroom, she took from the little finger of her right hand an enormous emerald and diamond ring; staring down at it, she turned that ring around and around. A strange little ceremony. He was talking about the very first days that he "ascended the Throne" when he was twenty-one, and the day afterward the armies of three nations occupied his country, the country from which his strong father had "departed"—by request, he did *not* add. At that time Farah, now twenty-three, was a child of perhaps three. Here she was: acclaimed as "The Empress."

I arrived at the hotel rather early, going to the room where the special reception guests are "kept" to meet the King and Queen. The backstage preparations for this endless procession of public dinners: how hard it must be to "impress" the Waldorf's red-coated waiters and the long-tailed supervisors by one more Head of State, one more testimonial dinner, one more round of speeches.

APRIL 19, 1962
NEW YORK

The Shah stood up before the most difficult of all audiences, the aristocrats of brains, the Council on Foreign Relations, and was an absolute knockout, a smash hit and no mistake. I have just this moment returned from the late-afternoon meeting and am still bubbling with the excitement and I confess, the pride that his performance gave me. He impressed that group as no Prime Minister or intellectual has in my experience.

Of course it added to the satisfaction this gave me that he spoke with warmth about the work that "Lilienthal and Clapp" are doing in "one of our provinces"; that when this is completely done in fifteen years or so "Mr. Lilienthal himself told me that it will be as grandiose and spectacular as your own TVA."

His answers to questions about the danger in which Iran stands, the amount of military equipment the Soviet has supplied to all those around Iran, the bitterness of his comments about "that man who heads Egypt," the ambiguity of the United States forming the Baghdad alliance and then withdrawing from it, the weakness of the literal terms of the bilateral defense pact between Iran and the United States—all these he handled in a clear, *forceful* way. If he had only thrown that official speech away that was handed him at the big meeting at the Waldorf, and talked this way, he would have wowed them as he did this sophisticated group.

As we were leaving Tom Dewey greeted me warmly and said, "Your friend certainly gave a great exhibition that he is a ruler as well as a king."

APRIL 21, 1962
PRINCETON

What do my fellow countrymen do for amusement these days?

This list is long, and much of it familiar. There is the number one indoor sport hallowed by ancient usage but still highly regarded—making love. More recent is TV watching. (The other day Pamela asked her grandmother: "What did people do before there was television?" She appeared astounded to learn that her parents did not have the blessings of TV when they were kids.)

But a new gambit. A cabbie gave me an insight into how the sport of *kings* is now for "the masses." I mean horse racing, of course. Rather, watching horses run. The cabbie said he went to the races "with the wife" at least two evenings a week, sometimes three. I don't suppose he ever actually touched a horse in his life, much less curried or cared for it, or rode it. Twenty thousand people do the same, he says, about every afternoon, 50,000 on the weekends. A group of women will put together a pool, $10 each. After they have paid for the expenses they bet the rest.

Somehow that picture of present-day America, in the big cities, sticks in my mind.

When I was a boy in Valpo, Deforest Muster's father trained trotters and pacers, kept some in his barn in our neighborhood. His dad used to seat me between his legs, so I was practically on the horse's tail, as he whisked us around the track at the Fair Grounds, in a frail little two-wheeler. But watching a trotting race was something that happened only during the County Fair season in the fall; everyone who sat in the grandstand and watched the races *knew* horses. It was part of the County Fair, and the Fair was for farm people, particularly the "retired" farmers who came to Valpo to live.

APRIL 22, 1962
5:45 A.M.
PRINCETON

The Lilienthal Journals in volume after volume seem now a thing certain. But how incomplete a "portrait of a man's emotional journey" this will in fact prove to be. Perhaps more complete—or so I hope—than that of any other public figure certainly of recent times, but nevertheless with gaps that leave unsaid those things without which this particular man at least is as incomplete as if the portrait omitted the head, or the eyes, say.

How would it be if—in imagination at least—I were to sit down some early morning, the sun barely up as it is this wondrous early spring day, and set down that part of the story of one man that has been so carefully elided or omitted—say it: suppressed.

And are those omitted or suppressed parts of importance only to the man himself? *Of course* not; the picture is distorted, just as the man was distorted when he pretended that he was made up only of the kind of emotions that are approved.

But no one tells it all. Who knows what kind of "private" emotional life the formidable, stern-faced, and proper Henry Stimson lived? I read what he says, I recognized the self-serving conventional sentiments of the "great man," but what about Henry Stimson? And Foster Dulles? And the man next door? Is it better that we carefully maintain the façade? Or are these repressions actually essential to health or are they part of the world's sickness?

I reached 44 Wall Street before nine, walking through the thinned onsurge of people with the new joy I get by being with city people and in the utter grandeur of those cliffs of lower Manhattan. Into the corridor of 44 walks André, his quite American casual-type hat jammed down on his head, relaxed and not looking at all like the international financial figure he is—or has become. He took my arm and put me in the elevator ahead of him—the French touch, I thought, but one that comports with his great instinct for the formalities of courtesy.

I talked to him about my ideas on coal, as a business opportunity. I had proposed the acquiring of a "position" in coal seven years before; but I had made the mistake of not carrying it directly to him, depending instead on a written memorandum which someone else in the organization apparently thought little of. Since that time Peabody and other coal companies have made great fortunes out of the basic idea.

But since that time, seven years ago, there have been further changes in the position of well-located coal, all favorable to its future: larger electric power stations at lower unit cost; technical improvements in transportation, e.g., pipeline for coal slurry, the prospect of much lower rail rates, the decrease in cost of power produced by coal to the point where the Ohio Valley now even had aluminum plants using coal, which meant power at perhaps 4 mills, a figure that many hydro stations would have difficulty meeting.

And so on.

I proposed that D&R had the facilities in such men as Kampmeier and Seymour to study the coal picture with precision, that Gordon and I could supply an over-all look that was special. That when we found something promising we could get the kind of men to go out and get options who were used to that specialization.

Object: to get options on land, and then to carry on explorations of the kind so familiar in oil wildcatting. A setup, financially like the oil lease apparatus: men with high tax brackets putting in the money, as a business expense; and if we found the kind of coal so located as to make commercial sense we could sell the rights or try to assemble a mining and transport enterprise based on the coal, and an electric grid to get the power to market.

My exposition went on for only fifteen minutes. Those glittering eyes behind the gold-rimmed glasses grew brighter, more concentrated. How glazed and wandering those same eyes can be when what you say doesn't appeal, somehow.

Result: "I'm all for it. I approve strongly. Now get going; don't lose any time."

There are many obstacles and uncertainties. But the start was good.

APRIL 23,1962
NEW YORK

Most of the day, today, with a group of professional educators of great repute, Franklin Murphy, head of UCLA; John Hannah, President of Michigan State, that wise educator-politico combination that the state universities demand; the keen sharp delightful Douglas Knight, head of Lawrence; the boyish, ever surprised-looking elder statesman of education, Herman Wells of Indiana University.

The occasion: the first meeting of the Trustees of a new enterprise known as Education and World Affairs, Inc. A big title, but no bigger than the need that brought this foundation-supported undertaking into being. The need: to try by discussion and thinking to bring some greater *sense of a goal* into the rapidly increasing amount of effort going into providing education and educators to underdeveloped countries.

What did I add to this meeting of distinguished and experienced educational administrators today, and foundation executives (Henry Heald of the Ford Foundation, John Gardner and James Perkins of Carnegie)? One "contribution," I think, was in questioning whether we yet know what the *objective* was of helping education abroad; is just any education a good thing, the more the better? I thought that was the assumption but that we had better test it, within this new organization, by hard critical discussion. The tendency has been for educators to concentrate on the administrative problems of their organizations (including money, retirement provisions for faculty, etc.), accepting the idea that the more faculty members seen abroad the better. But my experience cast a great deal of doubt on this.

These mildly iconoclastic things were received well—though with raised eyebrows—by most of the members.

APRIL 24, 1962
3:30 A.M.
NEW YORK

The very earliest glow of dawn gives the city a touch of innocence, of inanimate innocence. It seems never to have known hurry and the swirls of life that boiled around it twelve hours ago, for example. It is people who make a city, of course, not monumental buildings and great avenues.

My hotel room in the Gotham—a tiny one—looks to the north. In this half-light the gray steeple of the church at 55th and Fifth seems to have a presence of its own; is there really a church down there or is the steeple floating like the top of a gray iceberg? It is difficult to resist the temptation to see some symbolism in this eminence that rises between me and that part of Fifth Avenue which probably represents more elegance and ostentatious display than any other street in the world. A church in this setting is without the *roots* it had in another day and time.

Changes are so often best seen through the glass of men, of individuals.

I felt this strongly as I had a reunion with John Hannah yesterday, and thought what his adult and professional life stands for.

A poultry expert is the way he began, one of those men trained to know a great deal about something of immediate importance to the development of the Middle West. By extraordinary abilities in understanding human motivations, by the sense of wisdom this shaggy kind of man inspires, he became president of what was then still a "cow college," Michigan State. Today Hannah is looked upon by the legislature of that state as the man to turn to for such of its sticky political problems as reapportionment of representation, in a once agricultural state, one now dominated by the great industrial complex of Detroit. The basic job of the head of that once traditionally agricultural land-grant college is now to be the leader in a predominantly industrial state.

APRIL 25, 1962
NEW YORK

I have resigned from the Board of Trustees of Radcliffe. The ground: that there really isn't any *need* for a separate Board of Trustees for Radcliffe, now that it is fully "inside the Tiger" of Harvard—where it belongs.

"Polly"—so President Bunting signed herself—wrote me obviously not agreeing with my position that Trustees don't have a function (I said they had no *educational* function, and I'm right). But send along the resignation, she said, and closed with some kind words:

"I shall hope that whether or not you are on the Board you will continue to work closely with the Radcliffe Institute. . . . We are all greatly aware of our debt to you for your strong support of this venture when it was just a gleam in some of our eyes."

APRIL 26, 1962
ON THE 11:45 PENNSYLVANIA FOR PRINCETON

Of all the tests of human character and strength "facing up to reality" is probably the most exacting.

This demands an understanding of *what is reality*. In human affairs this is by no means a self-revealing fact, reality. What *is* reality in the subtle relations *between* individuals? They are the uniquely different and utterly "alone" and separate human vessels who carry the stuff of life. Individuals are each the *unit* by which I have come to measure almost everything, whether in the area of public affairs or "private" emotions.

APRIL 27, 1962
PRINCETON

Yesterday was a day of sadness for the whole world: America's new A-bomb tests began in the reaches of the Pacific near the place where fourteen years ago, from my desk in Washington, I had given the word that set off the Eniwetok atomic weapons tests! To most of the people of the earth it was no more sad a day than any other, to some perhaps happier, for only a few know what goes on or feel affected if they do know.

But for Robert Oppenheimer and for me it was unutterably sad. It happened that he and I were together—a rare occurrence—at his home, attending the annual meeting of the Twentieth Century Fund. He looked old, really old; those huge, expressive eyes were more melancholy than I have ever seen them.

We couldn't help reminding each other—more by manner than by words—how hard we had tried, in the winter of 1946, to find a way to stop "international rivalry" in the production of these weapons, weapons that came out of that strangely shaped head of his, and for the production of which for three years I was ultimately responsible.

The significance of the resumption of testing is that it is a declaration of diplomatic impotence, an impotence that is not made more bearable because it is the reckless intransigence of the Soviet that made it almost inevitable that the atomic arms race be continued and stepped up.

MAY 2, 1962
NEW YORK

On a drizzly foggy late afternoon yesterday, dropped into a movie. In the dismal darkened overheated foyer stood the most melancholy young person I have seen in a long time. A girl, an usher, perhaps twenty, dark circles under her huge eyes, her whole body drooped in almost the attitude of utter despair. A great deep sigh. "What's the matter?" I asked, sotto voce. "I am just tired of living. Terrible jobs I get. Nothing to live for." I was rather startled. Such a lonely, despairing voice.

After I had as much of the movie as I wanted—an hour perhaps—I went out for dinner. There she stood, slumped, a classic picture of ancient Mediterranean mourning. As I passed her I put my hand on her shoulder but said nothing. Stupid thing for me to do, but somehow she seemed part of a life I knew nothing of, being such a damned optimist and such a lucky guy; this was my way of saying "buck up," but, of course, it was meaningless to her.

A good reminder to me though. In this city of many faces, a kaleidoscope of faces moving, moving, moving, behind many of the carefully composed made-up grim faces there are people who don't see the magnificence of New York, this tower of light and life. They see none of this; they are looking inward.

MAY 7, 1962
SAN FRANCISCO, CALIFORNIA

Strode up Powell Street to the Hopkins Hotel, in the late afternoon sun and wind. As I reached the summit, two burly San Francisco motorcycle cops sirened their way into the Hopkins driveway, followed by a big car. Out of the car stepped a bedraggled-looking little man—diminutive and haggard. Two Russian guards on either side, big as Catherine the Great's studs. Gherman Titov, the Russian cosmonaut, no less, tottered toward me—I was in the way of the photographers coming out of the hotel. In his right hand he carried a bouquet of discouraged apricot-colored roses, their heads hanging as if they had been handled a bit too much.

So now I have practically rubbed shoulders with a man who has been out of this world. And I still say it is mostly a lot of expensive, distracting escapism—for both the Russians and ourselves.

MAY 9, 1962
SAN FRANCISCO

Negotiations *can* represent a high order of the art of living, something lived through with every sense awake. My long negotiations with Wendell Willkie,◖ for example, that determined whether TVA would die aborning or grow to maturity.

The years of trying to figure out Willkie (and vice versa!) were as great a seasoning in the art and bruising truth of living as almost anything I ever did, and this without regard to the specific public *issues* and the array of *facts* poured into us by our staffs.

Two men, facing each other in the amphitheatre, each intent upon prevailing, each sure that his passion to prevail was chiefly motivated by the desire to see that "right" prevailed, that fairness, etc., came out on top. But it was not by mere chance that two men strong enough and stubborn enough to be the antagonists stood toe to toe in such a combat for six long years; we were cut out to be strong protagonists by our very natures; we found ourselves in that arena because from the beginning of our careers our faces were turned toward just such a confrontation.

This was negotiation. But in quite a different sense than the one on which I spent twelve hours or more yesterday: exploring whether two major corporations could find a basis for a merger or a broad-scale joint venture: Utah Construction & Mining Co. and Philipp Brothers division of Minerals & Chemicals.

But even so—without the public issue Willkie and I were contending over, with antagonism plainly absent—it was negotiation in the sense that the play of individual personalities, backgrounds, and motivations were dominant in these business discussions yesterday. It was almost like the first draft of the script of a play.

Character A: Marriner Eccles. Actually and symbolically an amalgam of the pioneer West of his immediate forebears (who were prominent Mormons of Salt Lake) with the quick, sophisticated modern personality of a man of the world of business and government. Former

◖ Entries describing these lengthy negotiations between Lilienthal and Willkie are set out in Volume I of the *Journals.—Ed.*

head of the Federal Reserve, a rebel (a New Dealer among bankers!) and now quieting down, with years (seventy-one he said), the gentling of a remarkable wife, his deep gloom over how badly things have gone with the world—as he sees it—while his own personal and business fortunes have succeeded beyond imagining.

Character B: "Ed" Littlefield (the first-name basis comes very quickly out here in California). Gray curly hair. An exceptionally handsome, intelligent-looking man of forty-eight. Of a line of entrepreneurs, connected (perhaps by marriage) with the Wattis family who were among the rough-and-ready founders of Utah Construction. A "pro" among managers, coming up the financial side. So he is a cross between the professional but unmoneyed, self-made Charles Robinson, Character C (waiting in the wings), and Eccles, inheritor of an empire and also its builder.

Littlefield appealed to me at once. Warm, courteous, so modern that he made the voluble *reminiscing* Marriner seem of a different world. A shadow passed over Littlefield's expressive eyes when I said something that stimulated or puzzled him. A good listener, one who keeps his counsel, quite in contrast to the fiery and furiously *intense* Robinson, Ed has the assurance that goes with having won his way up in an organization dominated as is Utah by moneyed "families."

Character C: Charles ("Chuck") Robinson, president of Marcona, a big iron ore enterprise owned equally by Utah and Cypress Mines, and San Juan, a "Liberian" corporation owning a fleet of ore and oil carriers. This they call "The Marcona Complex." Both companies, and some other tax-saving affiliates (nonprofit service outfits, etc.) spring from the same resource: the iron ore mines in Peru.

Robinson looks young in a boyish way. Actually he is forty-two, slim, athletic, wavy hair, a driver but with an inner explosiveness.

All through lunch he just seemed an attractive and bright, but definitely *light*weight young executive. Was he *really* in charge of his huge iron ore operation?

All this changed as we sat in the Board room, and I veered to talk of ways in which Minerals & Chemicals-Philipp's Chilean and Marcona's Peruvian operations might get support from each other in some kind of intercompany arrangement, ranging from a conventional "merger" to some more specific partnership venture.

The smolder in the preternaturally bright hazel eyes began to burst in a controlled flame; the curly hair seemed to tighten on his head. He looked me full in the eyes across the table.

"I would like to comment about that. I know all about the Chilean operations you control. We looked them all over. I don't think they could do anything for us." A pause.

"I would be less than frank if I didn't say some things about how we [such *pride* in that "we"] do things in the Marcona complex differently than in Philipp.

"But I suppose I ought to say right off that I'm in a different position than you, and Ed, or Marriner, of course. I have no property interest and no financial stake in all this except what I earn. My job—and I suppose my bias—is to make my boss [looking at Eccles] worthy of being saved"—this with a grin. "So they'll keep on needing *me*. So the idea of turning that job over to someone else—well, I react against it."

But this is clearly the professional manager, who gets his incentive out of doing a good, hard job, and after he has built up something over eight years, he has no intention of losing it or having it messed up by someone who happens to own the stock. I have seen managerial pros in a hundred different circumstances; they all react pretty much the same.

I said I agreed they were good. After a long background with Utah, and the Utah experience to draw on, of course they were good, better than the shoestring entrepreneurs from whom M&C acquired the Santa Fe mines. But there were now new hands on the throttle. I had spent my life at management; I expected we would put in a kind of management that would be as good as there is. But it would take time and cost money. Perhaps we could work things out together to save that time and expense. And from there things got cordial and "constructive." That I think is where things will start off the next time we meet, if we or the officers of M&CP do.

The taxi driver who took me to the Eccleses wore his dirty-gray type hair *long;* but I mean *way long.* As we passed a rather morsel of a tall, long-legged girl, he asked my opinion of "*that.*" The hotel lobby was completely filled with PTA-ers, all badged and ribboned up, in for a convention, thousands, it seemed, and most of them weighing two hundred pounds on the hoof. "Won't have room for all of them; never can handle a convention here. What would you think if you found three of them in your bed when you get back tonight?" I told him I thought this unlikely, but definitely uninspiring, if that's what he meant. "Well, it would depend on how deesire-able they were, wouldn't it?" I lapsed back into silence. Then after long reflection he said: "I guess my libido is still active." I opined that it probably was.

Can you imagine a New York taxi driver talking about his libido? Maybe this San Francisco type is a poet in his spare time, or the other way around. After all this is the seedbed of the beatnik and the poet-reading coffeeshop.

MAY 12, 1962
EN ROUTE TO PRINCETON, FLYING OVER CHICAGO

I have had a good chance to think about the mission that brought me on this scoot across a continent that once was "vast."

Item: the puzzle of *why, why, why,* with enough money and more than enough to do, I reach out for business ideas such as those I presented to the Utah-Marcona people.

To say that it is a "compulsion" answers nothing. Why my compelling, zestful interest in a worldwide raw materials consortium or enterprise? *Why* the interest in trying to put together into a more effective functioning unit the special talents and capabilities of Utah, plus Marcona, *and* the talents and the functioning abilities of Philipp?

The answer, as of this day: that I have a strong instinct to make things work better, in a world where things that work are more rare than words and manifestoes.

To bring *together* parts of one's feeling about the world, whether in a painting or a poem or a novel, *or* in a program for an "underdeveloped country," or for a couple of industrial enterprises—among all these things there is a common bond. That bond is to make order, relationships, harmony, meaning closer to perfection, to that perfection which is unattainable but always an imperative of the creative person.

No wonder I find "business" so intensely interesting, emotionally absorbing.

But few people see this; they think "business" is dull but necessary. It is necessary but need not be dull. Only *people* are dull when their imagination is blunted.

MAY 15, 1962
NEW YORK

"I know about you and about TVA, so I know TVA isn't just dams."

So said the Minister of Finance of the Republic of the Ivory Coast, in a suite at the Waldorf this morning. Minister Saller is a square, rugged-looking man of about fifty, close-cropped hair, rimless glasses. The only Frenchman still in the new Government's Cabinet, I'm told. Born in Martinique. He runs half the Government. I was brought into his "presence" by the Ivorian Ambassador, a conspicuously short young man, Bedie by name, very jolly.

Saller said he had wanted to meet me for "fifteen years," not just because of TVA; "I wanted to know the man Lilienthal." He recalled sending two of his men to TVA in 1946 because "There was the center, the Mecca for planned development the world over." Of course, all this was good to hear.

Saller said the Republic wanted to know whether D&R would undertake a development program for the virtually uninhabited but potentially rich southwestern region of the Ivory Coast. "Yes," I said, "but on one condition. If it is financed by the American Government through AID we as a company would be responsible to and be directed by the Government of the Ivory Coast, not the United States Government. We do not want any question of divided responsibility."

He found this, as I expected, satisfactory. But it is an *important* point, not just some blarney.

MAY 16, 1962
NEW YORK

The President's Drawing Room at the Waldorf has seen many, many potentates, and I have seen a few of them in that room. Minister Saller, hard-bitten and orderly, met us at the hour we were to see President Félix Houphouet-Boigny; the President sent us regrets; he was tired and said he would "stay in bed" (actually, he did come in later).

We were given a big dose of personal kudos, fervent expressions of appreciation to me for "helping" the Ivory Coast, and a request that we extend the scope of our responsibility to include development of the southwest region, a subject brought up yesterday, but made explicit today.

The Waldorf was in the throes of a strike of service employees. No room service, no telephones, no elegance in the dining rooms, in fact no food. The handsome dark attendants of the President, and some of them probably assistant foreign ministers or something, were busily going out to the lunch counters on Lexington Avenue, coming up with paper cartons of coffee for the abandoned swells—and themselves.

The President of the Republic of the Ivory Coast is totally different from Nkrumah, in appearance and in the ambiance projected by his personality. Nkrumah rather struts; his eyes seem to protrude, he is constantly on the alert in the presence of such a stranger as myself. But Félix Houphouet-Boigny, also a short man, gives me the impression of some gentle creature of the forests. His eyes are quiet and turn up as he listens, say to Saller, as if he, the President, were just someone else in the room. But there is charm. When he talked directly to me, in French it is true, his intonations and the smile were warm. He expressed appreciation for my interest in his country in a low soft voice, the melodious voice of an African with the words of a cultivated Frenchman. "We want to develop our country; but when I see what you have done in America [here a pause for a fetching grin] I confess to envy."

I can't imagine Nkrumah talking this way, being this gracious. He is still the man who got where he is by revolution, and revolutionaries aren't likely to show a sense of appreciation to others. I wonder whether Nkrumah, however, doesn't perhaps talk the way Houphouet-Boigny does here when Nkrumah is feted *in Moscow*.

MAY 17, 1962
IN THE LEXINGTON AVENUE SUBWAY
NEW YORK

The journal of a man who works in the City of New York should be written on the subway, from time to time. As this note is being written. *Standing*, of course, back against a door, since I almost *never* get a seat, and if I do I give it to some hapless-looking female.

The faces—what a miracle of human mixture. At this hour there is room to breathe—not always the case. It is an exciting piece of modern life one sees and shares and senses and becomes a part of.

ON THE 4 P.M. PENNSYLVANIA TRAIN FOR PRINCETON

D&R is adding to our responsibilties rather markedly in recent weeks. This will mean increased work for me, until it could become a day-to-day preoccupation. Then what about the many other things I want to do? And without Gordon and me what would be left of D&R?

Is the solution to this dilemma to be thinking about merging the company with some long-standing firm, equipped with management and a backlog of work, a background of *related* experience? The objections to *any* merger or loss of complete independence—for that would surely be one of the results—are easy enough to formulate. But there is another side to the coin. Bill Voorduin doesn't have another big job in him, I fear, for the Dez took a lot out of that heroic man. Gordon is much younger (six years) than I, but his energies are not infinite, and I detect a strong and understandable tendency to watch his outgo of energy; this is reflected, I think, by a very conservative inclination about the expansionist tendencies of his associate, the writer of these notes. Which makes it relevant to recall what Dr. Kingsbury said about me this morning: that he could not remember a time during the past ten years he has known me when, physically ("neuromuscularly," he said—jargon) I was in as good condition. "Your muscle tone is firm and responsive; no matter how hard you appear to be working, your condition is extraordinary." He didn't add "for a man your age"!

I keep coming back to the idea that D&R needs a public relations firm, that I need a kind of institutional public relations advisor. I put this on the ground that we have no brochure about D&R activities, except a country boy mimeographed "thing" we have come to call "the non-brochure." No big splashy pictures, no shiny paper, just a bunch of rather heavy-footed words about what we do and whom we have to do it. And as for me, personally, I have many random invitations for speeches, appearances, articles, etc.; no one hired to stimulate the kind of invitations to write articles or make speeches that would be most useful.

This latter, of course, is what most companies and most "figures" have.

I got the hell beat out of me about this rankling notion—which I've rejected off and on for a couple of years—yesterday at lunch with Nate and John Burnett. Did they pound the dickens out of that idea! If we as a company or I as an individual had a "paid intermediary," that would be "the end of your now high standing with the press and magazines" was the substance of what they said.

Burnett was full of conviction on this subject. "How much would you have to pay a public relations man or firm to get Harrison Salisbury to make the kind of description of our Khuzistan work that he has made in his stories in the *Times*? *No* amount of money would do it; a professional intermediary would turn Salisbury against us."

This intense young man leaned over the table and gave me both barrels. How I enjoy having someone who is "working for" me show such spirit and vehemence with the "boss." It is almost worth taking a position I sense isn't quite tenable in order to see the fire rise in such a man.

MAY 22, 1962
WASHINGTON

The finest endorsement, and most highly prized, about the decision to publish the *Journals*, from a source I respect enormously, from Ed Murrow. We spent two and one-half hours at a leisurely lunch, talking about everything. Such unhurried, unbusiness visit is quite rare in this hectic city, or New York.

When I told Ed that the *Journals* were being prepared for publication he seemed so pleased; how reassuring this was. But apparently putting into print such personal and emotional reactions and reflections, while I am still alive, troubled *me* more than I realized. He said this about why I shouldn't wait for publication: "People in the Government and elsewhere, and particularly the younger people and those who are still getting over the McCarthy trauma need to hear how it was with you, as you experienced it at the time, and how you not only survived but emerged with honor and dignity, and gave the country a lesson in how a man with guts behaves."

12 MIDNIGHT

After the White House State Dinner (white tie and all) for the President of the Ivory Coast we, eighty people, sat down to watch the *Ballet of Billy the Kid.*

The three dance hall gals of the ribald West wore scarlet velvet down to the "vulnerable" parts, with a gold fringe dangling so you wouldn't miss the point; and the boots were red and high-laced. They postured, in accordance with the choreography of a Western dance hall, and it wasn't ambiguous, any more than it would have been at Minsky's. Right ahead of me was the dark silhouette of the back of the head (and quite a big head it is) of the man who as President holds all our destinies in that head. Lincoln, in that contemplative picture, was looking down, not too sure how he liked this in the White House, though he might well have thought it was a good thing out beyond the Illinois River.

We watched the President at close range as we were trying to get away, while he was still visiting with folks at the door; Helen remarked: "He doesn't act as if he had a thing on his mind, not a thing. He just seems to be enjoying himself."

In his remarks, after the dinner, proposing a toast to Houphouet-Boigny, this little man who commands all this attention, whose whole nation contains only about one third as many people as commute daily into New York City! Kennedy said: among the many accomplishments of our guest, one should be remembered. He won in a free election by the vote of 98 percent of the voters. "This is a somewhat wider margin than has recently been achieved in our own elections, and what is forecast for the future," which brought a spontaneous laugh, a witty sally of the kind he goes in for these days—kidding himself. A good sign indeed.

Most encouraging note: the President is more sure of himself. He is running strong.

FLYING TO NEW YORK

Across the aisle in this absolutely packed—jammed cattle car type airplane—is a dozing Allen Dulles. From what some of his now critics say about his handling of the U-2 spy plane and the Cuba Affair he has *been* dozing quite a while. Next to me is a haggard high-tension man I came to know first in my Public Service Commission days in Wisconsin: Arnold Zander. With his energy and dedication he has built the idea of a union of public service employees into a big union (over 200,000) affiliated with public employee unions in Britain and Germany, representatives in African and Latin-American countries.

MAY 24, 1962
NEW YORK

Two hours with Chuck Robinson of Marcona Mining this afternoon at my office. He embraces my global view (to use the Italian phrase) about the *necessary* future of raw material production and transportation, *but* he feels the Utah people are too defensive minded to accept it. The distinction between defensive minded and aggressive minded is a good one—a chasm, a cleavage between men in almost every walk of life.

MAY 25, 1962
ON THE PENNSY, TO PRINCETON

A session with André reporting and interpreting my meeting yesterday with Robinson.

Let's move ahead, he said, find out what Utah may have in mind, about a possible merger, as soon as possible. Marcona is negotiating for expansion in South Africa and in Japan. So my estimate of Marcona as someone to tie to, but soon, was borne out.

What has driven me ahead in this now not insubstantial beginning has been the fascination I have for my "dream" of a great world-wide raw materials company.

But as a valid *experience* of business, of trying to get a big idea into the realm of reality, of keeping green my skills of persuasion, I am sure it is well worth the effort, even if—as is likely—nothing comes of it in the end.

A telephone talk with Beatrice this morning that was memorable for one thing at least: Candor. On her part. And candor is a mild term. "I'm more realistic than you are; maybe this is because you have such an imagination, or because you have been so used to inventing things to believe in." I puzzled over what specific weakness or worse in me she was pointing out. On reflection, I guess there is something in what she says.

MAY 29, 1962
PRINCETON

Talked yesterday to Hank Dunne who handles my investment account at Lazard. "No," he said, "I still don't think there is any reason to sell; as I said last week, what is happening is emotional and psychological."

"What you mean is we are having a panic," sez I. This was the first time I have even heard that good old-fashioned word for a long time. It is always "recession" or "technical readjustment" or some fancy term. But it used to be called panic.

As it turned out—though I didn't know it at the time I spoke to Hank—the stock market, after several weeks of decline busted loose with a big bang yesterday: 11 million shares, paper "losses" of $29 *billion.*

There are so many small stockholders today, and so many ordinary guys have been playing the market for a kick, as they would bet on a horse, that a cave-in of the stock market affects the outlook of people generally. That the drop in stock prices has as slender an immediate cause as did the tremendous rise of the past three years hasn't much to do with it. These things are in people's minds and emotions, and fears and hopes, more than in some stodgy "research department" report.

In a suite in the Waldorf Saturday Minister Saller, looking the worse for wear, as I did too, we both signed the extension and enlargement of our Ivory Coast minerals program agreement, and then read through and he approved the program for the development of the southwest. This latter a great and unique venture that will be years in the making.

I warned him that this latter task was at this stage more an *exploration* than a job of normal "studies." For we are going into unknown and virtually uninhabited country. He agreed. We would have to have a fleet of helicopters, tents, the equipment of an explorer's expedition.

MAY 31, 1962
NEW YORK

Achievement is a process of one little step at a time. For an inherently impatient man, this is a lesson not easily accepted. It is as true of business as of public affairs.

All of this apropos of an hour this morning with Ullmann and Jesselson of Philipp. The centuries of shrewdness and toughness in the eyes of these so utterly different men of business!

Yes, they said, my discussions with Robinson of Marcona looked promising enough to continue. A big concession, I thought, rather half-bitterly; but this cautious attitude is the way of the trader. The next step: a meeting between Robinson and the Philipp people. I have my fingers crossed about anything coming of such a meeting. For more utterly and dramatically different types of businessmen than these it would be hard to imagine. And yet as business becomes more and more international it will be the capacity to make such utterly different backgrounds work together that will fashion the structure of the great international enterprises I envision in the raw material field. So this is a challenge I find myself accepting, after a period of half-sulking.

The rhapsodies about New York are endless. Yet it is given to me—a big city "hater"—to see with the eyes of a country boy what to blasé city-bred people is commonplace.

Item: from the window of my taxi this morning, I saw a big truck, marked: "Mrs. Herbst's Strudels." How my mother would have chuckled: a whole truckful of those wispy delicacies she produced on the kitchen table, with the preoccupation of the artist—and with the artist's need for an audience! A *truck* for strudel!

Another truck (one *sits* in a taxi more than one moves, in New York): legs, naked female legs horizontal, sticking out of the half-open doors of a small truck. *What* is this? And on the outside of the truck: "Manny's Mannikins."

JUNE 1, 1962
NEW YORK

The Persian Tale continues to provide dramatic, even hammy episodes. But they are not of the Arabian Nights variety: they concern matters of the most deadly seriousness.

Item: A cable the other day about the redoubtable little scrapper, Asfia, to whom we have all become devoted for his guts and integrity. The public prosecutor came into his office to demand that Plan Organization activities be "held up" until he, the prosecutor, could "investigate" this or that. This gent is the "wise guy" the Shah referred to in his speech here a month ago, as being the moving force behind the jugging of Ebtehaj—another piece of Oriental drama. Asfia, so our word has it, rose quietly from the chair behind his desk as head of Plan Organization, made a little gesture, and said: "Here, you take this place," and walked out of the building and out of his job. He was followed, according to newspaper accounts, by most of the other Plan executives, the men who want the job to succeed.

He didn't resign: he did what seems to be an accepted form of resistance, just "went home" and didn't come back. He was later prevailed upon to come back, and is again on the job.

All of this theatrics has behind it some serious issues in Persia, about the steady erosion of development funds to make up the operating deficit, particularly in the Army.

It is in the midst of this that we are discussing an extension of our contract out there, which expires in September.

JUNE 3, 1962
PRINCETON

This was to be a two-day shutdown: no work, no stimulation, mental, emotional, physical.

Yesterday I carried out this negative program to a T. Lolling, reading trifling mysteries, even dozing in a hammock. No one can be restless in a hammock, can he?

But this morning a basic idea about the deeper meaning of the Atom has been crawling up and down my spine. I tried the usual antidote to shut off the idea machine: physical labor, i.e., digging hard in the garden. No go. Perhaps trying to state the essence of the idea will quiet the damned stallion.

Here's a try: The Atom has forced us, as individuals and as peoples, to look into our hearts and souls, to inquire into what life means, in that solitude given us only by vast and unmistakable *change*, change in the foundations of our beliefs and in the structure of our world. So the Atom is a test, a challenge to our beliefs, a shaking of assumptions, premises, long held.

It should in this philosophic respect be compared to other events in history that have caused man to look anew at himself, alone and unprotected.

JUNE 5, 1962
NEW YORK

"Last Thursday I was sitting next to Khrushchev at a Benny Goodman jazz concert; now that couldn't have happened three years ago, that the head of the Soviet Union would possibly listen to American jazz." This was the rather mousy U.S. Ambassador to the Soviet, Llewellyn Thompson, speaking at a dinner meeting tonight. And now, he says, you see Russian girls wearing pony tails and the latest Western bouffant hairdo. What such things have to do with our foreign policy was only made vaguely clear. But it was pleasant, albeit wishful, listening: things *are* changing in the U.S.S.R. and in the right direction.

He expressed great surprise—with Jack McCloy nodding agreement in the background at the head table—that the Russians seemed to show no interest whatever in any proposals we are making for cutting back on arms, though they terribly need the resources going into arms for increasing farm production. What we heard was a very charming optimistic picture of evolution, of great failures in the Soviet system (except in industry) all going our way. Somehow it wasn't convincing, to me.

Sat next to Keith Glennan, who had been the first head of the Space Agency. When the Ambassador predicted that the Soviet would cut back on their space program, leaving us "holding the bag," Keith whispered to me: "That is what I predicted a couple of years ago. I am not in sympathy with the present space program."

Neither am I. Why we plunge headlong into such a hunk of meaningless flypaper I can't figure, unless it's Lyndon Johnson and his passion for building things in the Southwest.

I had a beer with Dick Hottelet of CBS. He and I agree about the unwisdom of this "compulsive talking that is called negotiating." Talking about disarmament now seems to me risky and unwise.

JUNE 6, 1962
NEW YORK

Tante Marie* died in the very early morning yesterday. The death of a unique personality, as she certainly was, forces an emotional summing up.

I remember Tante. I remember a charming, warm, gay, laughing, songful, bouncy, wide-eyed gal. My mind tells me her death, ending a long illness, is a blessing. But as Beatrice said yesterday: "Yes; but the heart hurts."

David's first book of fiction has been accepted for publication, by Random House. It is as impossible and yet stirring a story as any he will write, this victory, against odds, this beginning of a solid writing career. I am astounded by the endurance he has shown. Months and months, all alone, writing, writing, writing. Nothing but rejection letters, nothing but that little room and that staring typewriter—and his self-confidence that he would indeed become a writer. That Helen and my son should have proved himself *to himself* is the greatest joy of all. Other sons of "successful" fathers could quite naturally and readily go into their fathers' businesses. But this huge, very special, tense, and driven young man simply had to make his own niche. And he has. He told us yesterday late afternoon that yesterday he had finished the draft of a second novel, quite different from the first.

And again: I remember. I remember a roly-poly baby, round-faced; a long-legged lad; a charming young man. And now the beginning of a writing career, the kind of achievement he most wants.†

* Marie Szanton was the sister of Lilienthal's father, and the mother of Beatrice Tobey.—Ed.

† Under the pen name of David Ely, as of 1970 David has published four novels and a collection of his short stories.

JUNE 12, 1962
NEW YORK

The "business life" has added a new episode. Read the other day in the *Times* that Commercial Carriers had been indicted for violation of the Taft-Hartley Act, with Jimmy Hoffa as codefendant. What this actually meant was that Commercial Carriers, a truck subsidiary of American Commercial Barge Lines, had been accused of bribing Hoffa to lay off a strike, or something of that kind, through the device of a trucking company Hoffa's family would own.

This mess is made all the harder to take, for me as a director of American Commercial Barge Lines, because no report that I can recall was ever made to the directors about this transaction, nor in our recent Board meeting was there any reference to the pendency of a grand jury investigation which must have been going on at about the time of the meeting.

The trucking business has been notoriously crude, partly because of the character of the labor leaders, partly because of the nature of the business, I guess. But it doesn't sit well with me when I hear people in business say that "you have to be realistic and live with bribery and go along with it." But that a good deal of paying off goes on in American business I suppose one must recognize as a fact, a miserable one.

JUNE 13, 1962
NEW YORK

When the little man was in repose, his fat hands across his comfortable paunch, his head and torso and legs formed a series of globes one atop the other, like a certain kind of toy I've seen. But when Pierre Weill, French lawyer extraordinary spoke all you saw were those twinkling, knowing eyes behind the heavy glasses. There was something Chinese about the tilt of the eyes, the acceptance of the world's foibles, as if he had witnessed these himself through hundreds of generations, like a Chinese Wandering Jew.

He was in my office because the King of Morocco had asked him to see me in New York. This is the new Sultan, Hassan, son of the late King whose friend and lawyer and protector this mild French lawyer Weill was for many years.

It was Weill who fought the French when the French Governor of Morocco picked up the former Sultan and packed him off, with only a dozen wives or so, to Madagascar. It was Weill who helped get him back his throne, and it was he who arranged the visit to the Valley of the Sous by Voorduin, Helen, and me, and Jean Guyot of Lazard Paris and his two keen young men. How long ago was that? Three years I guess‡

The new King, Weill said, telephoned his office in Paris: Get Lilienthal and the others to come back to Morocco. "But," said Weill, "nothing was done about their report and recommendation." Oh, that was the fault of the Minister of Finance at that time, who "hated" the royalty and was a leftist. Now things are different, "although the new King doesn't think too much of me; when he was Crown Prince I stopped him from doing a number of foolish things."

He talked on, in the most entertaining way. "I told André Meyer: You do business with a Negro President of the Ivory Coast who has been in office only five months. Why, the Kingdom of Morocco is so ancient that when they speak of the 'two wars' they mean the war with Charlemagne and at Poitiers."

I left it this way: If the King wants us back, he should be explicit about it; they should give assurances that this time something will be done about our recommendations; we should not be confined to the pathetically underresourced Valley of the Sous, but something more extensive than that, affecting a larger and more likely aspect of the country.

We shall see. Anyway, it was a delightful hour. The man may look as if he might be, say, a Chinese sage, but his humor, of which he has an abundance, was definitely French, with the grace and style of French humor or irony or amusement with the absurd ways of the world.

A visit or consultation with Dr. Atchley this morning. As before, he didn't "examine" me, except orally.

I said: "Here I am, in another month reaching my sixty-third birthday, and I sometimes act, and feel, as if I were a damned eighteen-year-old."

The spark in his eye: "And so you *are*: at the *same time* eighteen and sixty-three."

JUNE 14, 1962
6:30 A.M.
PENN STATION
NEW YORK

Remarkable that this train, which has just come out from under the river should at this ungodly early hour already be filled with people, people whose lives I know nothing about. The world is made up of concentric circles of people, lives in each circle hardly touching those

‡ The account of this trip is set forth in Volume IV of the *Lilienthal Journals*.

of people in the next circle; indeed those of us in one circle not even realizing the existence of the people in the next ring.

Talked to David yesterday by phone. He was working on the *Journals*. "I am at about June 1941," he said, with that wry, delightful lilt in his voice. "Things look bad. Looks like there's going to be a war." I chuckled and said: "Hm. Tell me how it comes out."

JUNE 15, 1962
PRINCETON

Ebtehaj released from jail after six months, on his pledge not to leave the country, supported by a "bail" (this is the *Times* report) of $140 million. That story gets to be more of a whopper all the time.

Gordon and John are seeing him tomorrow, in the Tehran jail, so on their return we will have a blow-by-blow account.

JUNE 16, 1962
PRINCETON

A man, and his son and namesake; a man and his almost-seven-year-old grandson and namesake.

What stirrings deep within a man this tall sober man, my son, evokes, full of the sense of accomplishment and the light in the eye that comes from a taste of glory.

And that slim, beautiful, blond grandson. An extraordinary-looking lad, a head taller than other kids his age, lithe and graceful as a young gazelle. He spent the afternoon with me here, and I am full of him.

The joy one feels on a magic June day. The shadows this early morning; the sun so warm and generative. Hard, rough work in the garden, turning under borders, breaking up the clods of earth with my hands. With Helen solemnly planning future plantings. And feeling around me invisible as the air yet every bit as real and essential to life, the ambiance of love.

JUNE 19, 1962
NEW YORK

Chawmping your breakfast perched on a stool, waitresses fluttering back and forth behind the counter, an air of let's-get-it-over-with throughout the coffeeshop. Down here in the "financial" district that is the way thousands of people begin their day, as I did mine.

What is the effect of this gulping way of beginning the day on people accustomed to the leisurely breakfast of the British upper class, or the home-type breakfast which I was brought up on?

Nate just phoned: Celia died at midnight last night. The cancer that has been pursuing her for seven years, sometimes with severity, other times apparently under control, finally wasted her away. Sad. Nate is as close and dear a friend as I have, or have ever had.

"The house fell in" is something that happens to everyone who engages in risky (i.e., challenging) ventures, either of the mind, or public affairs, or business.

How well I remember the gloom that settled over the five AEC Commissioners at Bohemian Grove in the fall of 1946. Carroll Wilson said: "Just had word that there has been a strike in the Congo uranium mines. The mines are flooding. It will take months and months to get them pumped out and operating again. We are out of business." Wham. Actually we hardly lost any momentum.

The house that fell in on me this morning, however, was another crisis in Iran. Our contract expires in late September. Gordon and John went out, reasonably confident as we all were that there was agreement on all essential points of an extension agreement. This morning a cable from Gordon: "I am coming home right away. Asfia and Ansari are 'incredibly optimistic' that a form and kind of contract they want—and we don't because it regurgitates some issues long since 'settled'—can be worked out before the expiration date." Evidently Gordon is very low in his mind about the outcome.

Here is where Burnett is such a source of strength. He understands that it is only when we take a close look at the terms that might be acceptable to them, and that we could swallow, that we know where we stand; that abstract principles and rigidity can only be dealt with by specifics; that the sooner we get down to those specifics and away from general propositions (however strongly held) the sooner we make that tortured, often tedious progress toward success.

But what about the 110 D&R Americans now out there? Can we honorably let them *assume* that they will be employed after September 22, when we know now how narrow a squeak it will be?

9 P.M.

Called Nate at 6; said I wanted to come out to see him, and would he have dinner with me? The picture of his sitting there in that oh-so-empty apartment where he and Celia had lived so long—and happily—overcame my reluctance to appear to imply that he needed my "support."

He seemed deeply pleased, and we had a talkative couple of hours. Once in a while a great shadowing would settle over his face, poor man. "Thirty-three years; we were together almost twenty-four hours a day. That's almost ten ordinary marriages."

JUNE 21, 1962
BEEKMAN TOWER HOTEL
NEW YORK

A rousing good session with André this morning, about another of my preoccupations: COAL.

I have given up the idea of arranging the optioning of coal in the Mississippi Valley area and have turned to the Rocky Mountain area. The crux is: Can we establish a judgment that the great needs of the Pacific Coast for electricity in the coming decade can be met in competition with oil?

I asked Burnett to go with me to 44 Wall Street for my coal talk with André. I asked John to make part of the presentation. He came through brilliantly on all counts. André's eyes gleamed with appreciation; he gave Burnett his full attention, and gave him an accolade when we left.

From this tower on the East River at 49th Street I see such grandeur as even the imagination of poets of another age could not have fashioned. None of the great builders of marks of royal splendor—the builders of the Pyramids, Persepolis, Angkor Wat—ever attempted such a mortal defiance of the heavens, such a fierce sign that man could outlast, outdo, outpower the gods of time and death and decay and weakness and mortality. The massive bulk of Manhattan 1962 seen at this blue-gray hour at this height is man's most outrageous nose-thumbing of mortality.

These feelings come from a pretty tired guy. It has been a hard, intense two weeks; this afternoon Gordon is due to return from his trip to Iran, in what I fear will be a pretty discouraged frame of mind. So I must pull on my reserves of strength and guts, to see if there isn't something that can be done to get the Persian venture rolling again. And if that proves beyond me, to see to it that we go out on a note that will be neither bitter nor pettifogging. "Finish with style."

The stock market fell apart again today, I see by the headlines. Apparently very badly—I haven't bothered to read the gory details.

This is a good time for perspective. One thing is sure; if we are indeed in a Kennedy Depression (as the term is beginning to be used!)

I will never be as poor as I once was, because there is nothing lower than nothing.

The big rich fellows—like André, say—will look on this as breathing out, after a strong inhalation, knowing that in time "things" will correct themselves.

But it does illustrate a thesis I have long spoken of to my friends among the economists who regard inflation in itself—per se—as a form of original sin. You simply *can't* maintain things at a *level keel* in a free economy, or in a free human society, for that matter. Therefore, things are either going up or down. Inflation—going up—is stimulating and within limits can be controlled. But if that control is in the hands of those who fear inflation unreasonably, almost hysterically, then you will have deflation. And deflation is almost impossible to control, because its major components are the minds and emotions of millions and millions of people. We have nothing to fear but fear itself said some phrasemaker—probably Ray Moley. But that fear is plenty, for it spreads, one fear engendering others.

But *this* deflation won't get out of hand for any period of time. Kennedy is no Hoover, the U.S.A. 1962 isn't 1929. But it may get tough, tough indeed, for many people.

JUNE 22, 1962
ON THE PENN TRAIN

Gordon back, looking none the worse for a long (16,000 miles) and frustrating trip to Iran and back.

He gave me and John Burnett a careful story on what happened—and didn't.

Net fact: Three months before our contract with Iran expires we still have no agreement on an extension. Somehow I am confident that if we are not too inflexible we will still be in Iran after September 22.

Asfia (head of Plan Organization) suffered a severe slipped disc, so he was in pain and flat on his back while Gordon was there. Not only did his disc slip, but his judgment suffered an injury. He should know us well enough to know that we will indeed leave Iran rather than go on in a state of utter uncertainty from day to day.

The facts are simple enough: They want to write a contract that will exclude those provisions that Ebtehaj has been criticized and jailed for: D&R disbursing funds, making contracts without prior Plan Organization approval, able to declare accounts settled unless specific objection is made within sixty days, etc.

What we want is a simple time extension.

But such a simple extension, if signed by Asfia and Ansari, would open them to the same criticism leveled at Ebtehaj.

Gordon talked to Walsh, Economic Counselor at the U.S. Embassy, and the Prime Minister. From these talks he deduces that the U.S. Government is getting fed up with Prime Minister Amini, that Amini is discontented with the extent of U.S. aid on their general budget—a perennial feeling for all Iranian Prime Ministers and the Shah of course; that if the United States gets more unhappy about Amini, a new Cabinet will come in; that the Shah is vacationing on the Caspian and letting Amini go down if he can't manage to pull out of his mounting troubles.

And that both the Persians and the U.S. expect to use *us* as a card in the poker game between them. Amini wants us to plead Iran's case to the U.S. Government (which we most certainly won't) because, as he says, if more U.S. funds aren't provided, we, i.e., D&R, an American institution, will suffer; the United States wants us to yield about the kind of contract we insist on so Iran won't have us as a card in Iran's hand.

Wow, what a spot to be in—and how I love it!

JUNE 24, 1962
PRINCETON

It simply isn't like me to sit on my hands—and my dignity and personal pride—while we wait for something to turn up to solve the ugly impasse about Persia. I'm just not built that way, haven't lived that way. Our completing the Khuzistan program, or letting it die by default, is an important and even fateful issue.

During the afternoon Nate talked to me at length, by phone. I phoned New York for strength and reassurance. It was clear: I must take over from Gordon responsibility, active responsibility, for reaching a workable agreement. That this means that I, a pretty tired man, must persuade a beloved colleague that I should step in, and that I should then be ready to go to Persia myself and there settle the contract dispute, doesn't seem to faze me—though Friday when I got home I was bushed, and no wonder.

It is in the inner recesses of men's character that decisions are made—not by staff papers or pure logic. "What manner of man is this?"—that is the question when the chips are down. So I look upon this as another voyage of discovery: how much strength, patience, humility, and devotion to an idea can I show, here in my sixties—as much as I did in my forties?

JUNE 27, 1962
NEW YORK

I have my troubles tonight. Gordon and I don't see alike on what to do to end the uncertainty about an extension of our arrangement with the Iranians, on which the future of our company rests—and we just about to move into new plush quarters. These differences are something of a strain between two different temperaments, and a cause of distress to me; for I know how much depends on our not letting the work in Iran end in chaos.

My "problem" so often turns out to be conquering myself: fighting off the impulse to sulk, to be envious of others, to use a verbal whip on others because *I* am in some way being frustrated, not by them but by circumstances.

I think I have pretty well succeeded in winning this battle *with me* over the way the Iran "negotiations" were handled by Gordon—if one can call his delivering a virtual ultimatum "negotiation."

So much of public affairs and private business is determined by these internal inside-human-hearts considerations: pride, greed, vanity, and all the rest. The philosophers are right, and the economists are usually just carpenters, assemblers of figures *after* the fact.

JUNE 28, 1962
IDLEWILD AIRPORT

A painful two hours this morning with Gordon, John Oliver, and John Burnett. Subject: review of the terms of an extension of the Iran contract.

An impasse, a tough deadlock; this is where things stand only three months before the contract expires. The usually, quietly optimistic Asfia says they must rewrite the existing contract rather than merely extend its terms. Gordon was equally and grimly adamant that it is "futile" to consider rewriting the present contract because there won't be time to complete such a renegotiation.

My conclusion is that we should go along with Asfia, submit to them a rewritten contract, i.e., one incorporating the provisions of the earlier contracts, rather than a mere extension of time. Gordon believes deeply that this would be construed as a sign that we were prepared to "break." "My experience," he said, "is that the party that tried to bring the other to the bargaining table shows by that initiative that he expects to *give* the most." This theme of depending on what he called "showdown" runs through his philosophy, depending on *their necessities* to force an acceptance of our simple extension. I have a quite different view: that we should go out there and negotiate; in my experience as a negotiator I have often without hesitation "taken the initiative to bring the other party to the bargaining table."

JULY 2, 1962
MARTHA'S VINEYARD, MASSACHUSETTS

"The man has *everything*." This is what people said about my class-mate, even as a college student. "He knows where he is going and has the drive and personality to get there." This they also said. And they were—well, as it turns out—only partly right.

He spied me, sitting on a bench in the Idlewild Airport, waiting for the plane to the Vineyard.

The greetings over—God, how long has it been since we saw each other, etc.—he pushed his crushed, worn-in-looking hat on the back of his head, slumped into the seat, gave his face a dry-wash, a kind of hard, thorough rubbing of his eyes and brow. He had something very much on his mind. So I stopped the "have you heard from so and so" of our class and listened.

All he said was: "I thought when I got to be our age the life inside of a guy would be simple. No problems, no conflicts, inside, any more. It's just the reverse. The things I have I don't particularly care for any more, or take for granted. The woman I want most of all I can't have. No; I guess what I mean is I'm not willing to pay the price, in hurting people, in remorse, in what my kids and grandchildren and my law partners will think. Who would ever think this could happen to me? Why, Dave, I've been an adult for over forty years."

I made no comment. What *can* you say, even to a friend; especially to a friend, over sixty, reputed to be wise, experienced, successful per-sonally and in his work, in vigorous health. So it's not simple.

FOURTH OF JULY, 1962
MARTHA'S VINEYARD

Last night I slept beneath stacks of blankets. Yet this morning, at 5:30 (a morning of such beauty as to make the heart leap), temperature 52°, I put on bathing trunks, put down the top of the car, and went down to Miss Emma's beach for a swim. Exhilarating it was too, and so too the walk across the dark-green moor, twinkling with grass flowers, with the soft sea spreading out from the tawny crescent of sand. Made me tremble happily with the beauty and the glory of the enveloping earth and sky and sea.

JULY 9, 1962
MONDAY, 4:30 P.M.
NEW YORK

Spent much of this day in a land new to me, the private kingdoms of the World of the Foundations.

The occasion: a meeting of a kind of ad hoc Executive Committee of the about-to-be-born "Education and World Affairs, Inc." consisting of Franklin Murphy, Chancellor of the University of California at Los Angeles (UCLA), Robert Goheen, President of Princeton, and myself. Result: secured the consent of Herman Wells, the great man of Indiana education, to serve as Chairman and Executive Officer, part time, and William Marvel as President of the fledging organization.

This result we submitted to and received the approval of John Gardner, head of the Carnegie Corporation, and Henry Heald, President of the Ford Foundation, these two being the source of funds and the origin of the idea that this organization is needed to bring some order into the overseas education picture, rapidly growing more and more chaotic.

Philanthropy (now so highly organized, as in these two great foundations) has many of the same problems that are so common in government and in business. Human sensibilities—pride, ambition, resentment, and all the rest—are at the core of one's dealings with the *people* in the Foundations; and of course it is the people, the wondrous variety of people, that make any institution, whether its purpose is profit, giving away money, governing, or education.

These three men—Heald, Goheen, and Murphy—I found almost impressive and extraordinarily interesting, "special" men.

Heald listened to us with hooded eyes, jaws down on his chin, the finger tips of his hands joined before his face, not a single expression for a long time. It is revealing that the only decoration on his wall is a drawing of Abraham Lincoln, whom he strongly resembles, with his great height, his shambling gait, the deep hollowed eyes, the sudden lighting of his face—and his Illinois background.

Goheen has a twinkle in his eyes that lights up his whole face. When he concentrates (as he did when the outcome with Heald was in question) there is a deep frown and great power in that face. He takes the built-in inertia, the "vested interest" problem of his faculty (*any* faculty) with a grin but doesn't believe there is any quick or simple solution to this faculty stuffiness, such as creating, as an antidote, the "centers" or "institutes" that are springing up all over the place, including Princeton. A sturdy and very likable man.

JULY 10, 1962
NEW YORK

Today private business all day long, from 9 until just a few minutes ago, when I left Chuck Robinson of Marcona Mining Company after a dinner meeting alone.

My hunch was advanced today, namely, that M&C-Philipp and the Utah-Marcona complex could find ways whereby, working together, they could make two and two equal five and somehow divide the added plus.

Whether agreement on a joint venture will ever be reached between such utterly different men—Robinson and Jesselson—is still much in doubt. But I found it personally a good satisfying exercise. Testing one's wits, bringing people together to see if they do not have common ground, and then trying—as I did rather patiently—to lift their sights beyond the nuts and bolts of the pragmatic things business must deal with, and grace the discussions with a broad concept. The "concept," of course, is my conviction, expressed earlier in these notes, of the internationalization of raw materials.

JULY 11, 1962
NEW YORK

Just outside my hotel window the men in hard hats (and are they *all* man) who are building the colossal Pan Am Building have been at work now for a half hour. One man, stooped over, walked a steel I beam, his feet on the lower flange of the beam, his hands used like the hands of a monkey on "all fours." He's scrambled way up on the roof of Grand Central now; now he's out on the fancy wreaths (in concrete or stone) that some architect once thought were pretty. (The new Pan Am is smack dab against the Terminal.) Now I can hear the riveting.

Below that crawling man was the crisscross of steel beams, in the spectacular light of early morning—and no place to stop en route if he fell. No huge circus crowd to ooh and ah, no net as most acrobats have. This is the *day's work* for these guys. Critics may well think that the cubes of buildings that are going up in every direction in midtown Manhattan are ugly, or uninspired. But they are built by men, tough guys like that figure out there who crawled hand and foot so he could begin his day's work.

JULY 12, 1962
PRINCETON

It was *coal* for several hours in my office this morning. A report from our new hopeful, John Allen, just back from two weeks of exploration for coal in the Rocky Mountain area. Then the kind of clearheaded analysis, discussion, differences and their resolution, narrowing of issues —restating of objectives—the give-and-take of ideas in a specific matrix I so enjoy. We came out with a decision, a step ahead, by 1:30.

Gordon was at the very top of his form, and that is very good indeed. Narrowing things down, bringing things to a focus. When he does this there is no one better. The clarification of what we should *do* next was due largely to his concise questioning and wearing the issue down to a fine, precise cutting edge.

I am so relieved tonight that I am completely over the disaffection that I found myself entertaining for the rather arbitrary and roughshod way he viewed the Iran contract extension. He has mellowed since the first discussion of this issue and so have I, so we are each able to think more clearly, ready to reassess the cliff-hanging tableau we find ourselves in about the September 22 contract expiration date.

These personal relations are at the very root of administration. This is just another of a long line of illustrations of a truth that many managers don't yet see.

JULY 17, 1962
NEW YORK

I have just come in from a long dinner-visit with Nate Greene. He warned me of the danger of adopting the values (by imitation or osmosis) of the financial community in which I was to work and thereby lose my own. More specifically, he insisted that I ask myself how much it really *means* to me to spend days and days on a possible merger of Utah Construction and Minerals & Chemicals, or even on coal. That these ideas I have generated should excite me, that my sense of workmanship should lead me to want to make these ideas *result* in something—this is understandable. But that I should commit myself to objectives that are not part and parcel of my past disturbed him. I listened to his eloquent though simple words almost with awe, so honest and forthright is this remarkable guy.

"Their standards—these bankers and industry men—aren't yours. You have created a unique record of things that you stand for in people's minds. Don't squander your good health or your time without being sure that what you are doing—such as this merger business—fits into the scheme of your life, of what you most want out of life."

JULY 18, 1962
ON THE PENNSYLVANIA HEADING FOR PRINCETON

The Cabinet of Iran's Prime Minister, Amini, resigned last night.

Why the sense of relief and satisfaction I feel that a Cabinet crisis has hit Persia just two months before our contract expires? Because *perhaps* this will precipitate the issues of the Third Plan, the budget, the relations to the United States (a central issue indeed), an issue that will be solved, if it is, by U.S. dollars, rather than in basic ideologic differences.

"Incredible Iran" enters a new chapter—unless this is one of those "one-day" resignations.

JULY 20, 1962
IDLEWILD AIRPORT
ON THE WAY TO THE VINEYARD

A visit from Bernardo Garces, that redoubtable, composed, and whimsical genius of the Cauca Valley (CVC). With him José Otoya, handsome engineer and CVC Board member, and Caldes, a CVC engineer. After an hour we seem to have agreed to take on certain responsibility to guide and approve the safety of design of Timba, the next dam in their series. We would replace a tough U.S. "commercial" engineering firm, to use Bernardo's words, TAMS.§ TAMS has not worked out, Garces said, chiefly because they simply will not try to train Colombian engineers nor carry through on the proposition we feel so strongly about, which is that CVC has reached the place where it should have its *own* design engineering organization, as it has now its own administrative and other staff, a course we helped to initiate years ago. So there is a principle at stake.

JULY 22, 1962
MARTHA'S VINEYARD

In the mail awaiting me a letter from Fred (Newton) Arvin, enclosing a chapter from an autobiographical book in which he describes the Valparaiso [Indiana] of his (and my) early boyhood. (Our family left Valparaiso when I was about eleven.)

His statement of facts (churches, stores, etc.) and names of people of those now faraway days (1905-1912) conformed to my recollection. But as I read this smooth-flowing account I saw that the Valpo of my boyhood and of Fred's were two utterly different places, peopled by different human beings, so differently did he and I look out on the world. We did live in the same town, knew the very same people and places, and were friends. But the story I would write of the Valpo of our boyhood would be a wholly different one.

In this chapter about Valparaiso and northwestern Indiana, he makes a good deal of the many lakes that surround Valpo, and the part they played in the life of the children of that time. One of these lakes, he said, was Sager's Lake, on the edge of the town. But Sager's Lake

§ Tippetts, Abbett, McCarthy, and Stratton.

was not a lake but the pond back of a small dam. I recall so well the mill below the earthen dam, the water flowing in a flume through the mill to grind Sager's wheat into flour, the dustiness inside the mill (a flour mill like hundreds, I suppose, throughout Indiana of that time). In short, Sager's Lake was my first exposure to "water power."

Here in my "isolation ward" to which I have retreated, I have, incongruously, been thinking about wealthy men.

I have known many men of great wealth, particularly since I have been in private life. Can I say of any one of them that his wealth has made him happy, given him more than a momentary satisfaction, or perspective on life, or joy?

Go down the list, one by one. Are they fearful, uneasy, jealous of the kudos that comes to *others*, dissatisfied with the kudos *they* receive, with all their expensive and elaborate public relations devices? The satisfactions they have do not derive from wealth.

On the other hand, Owen Young, who died just the other day, maintained a balance and serenity by living simply and by forgetting his money.

Plenty of poor men are unhappy. Of course. But no one ever claimed that being poor in itself is a source of deep satisfaction, except the kind of poverty we associate with the ascetic or saint. Just being poor is sordid, often; but no great transformation is expected in the spiritual life of a man solely because he is poor. Wealth does not have that power to transform either; on the contrary.

JULY 23, 1962
MARTHA'S VINEYARD

Doers and sayers: this division of men continues to explain much, and to fascinate me. This morning, reading *Pilgrim's Progress* again for the first time in many years, I find Faith says to Talk: ". . . Indeed *to know* is a thing that pleaseth talkers and boasters; but *to do* is that which pleaseth God." The italics are Bunyan's.

JULY 29, 1962
MARTHA'S VINEYARD

A prayer from the heart of a man of experience as he casts an eye backward:

Oh, Lord, may Thy servant remember that there is no one more tiresome or untrue or transparent than the man who was always right, his critics and opponents always wrong.

AUGUST I, 1962
MARTHA'S VINEYARD

The path of the innovator is not an easy one: I learned and re-learned this "the hard way" as they say, over a span of many years.

The World Bank's upper staff has just provided another example of the roadblocks that are put in the way of anyone honestly trying to do things differently. Yesterday I learned that Bernardo Garces of CVC had a World Bank money-pistol put to his head, forcing him to give up his plan—and ours—for establishing a Colombian staff of design engineers in place of a foreign U.S. firm.

The Bank people, led by a department head, said that thay were "for" the training of Colombian engineers; in fact, they were about to suggest it themselves! Then he takes a position that effectively prevents this happening. The day when Colombian engineers would be "experienced" enough would, of course, *never* come, if the holders of the moneybags, the Bank, never lets them get that experience.

The stuffy hypocrisy of those who oppose innovation is what makes me boil—and I have been boiling these past days. Their tactics are never to oppose change in what they *say*. They are always for change; it just is never the right time or the method is wrong. The World Bank is just one more instance of an institution *created* to bring about change (International Bank for *Reconstruction* and *Development*) but which in a few years became as conventional and cautious as the most nervous or timid or unadventuresome Victorian who ever preached the doctrine of the white man's burden.

I have thought for several days about what I could *do* to help CVC actually start on this road of their own engineering organization, something they have been working toward for years. We thought we had done something when we agreed to recruit foreign engineers to be part of *their* staff. We found six good men and engaged them on behalf of CVC. Then the Bank vetoed this; said there must be a foreign engineering *firm* responsible. So Bernardo asked if we would take responsibility that the CVC staff's design work was well done. The Bank vetoed that a day or so ago: the foreign engineering firm must have full responsibility. In other words, the idea of a CVC engineering staff was thrown out of the window. It is a foreign *firm* or no money.

What help can older people be to the young? I think of this a good deal, off and on. Of one thing I am sure: to be helpful they must have preserved, within them, the youthful way of looking at the world that *they themselves had* when they were young.

Nancy Tobey had her eighteenth birthday a couple of months ago. A remarkable, talented, eager young one, versatile to a degree and "temperamental" in the best, as well as the more difficult, sense.

I thought of Nan by reason of reading a bitter letter from Dylan Thomas' widow to her eighteen-year-old daughter: it appeared in *Harper's* this month. So I sat down the other night and wrote Nan a letter, some of which I want to insert here as a reflection of how I see this important relation between the oldsters and the youngsters:

"David and I were tossing a football back and forth, in our front 'yard' at Norris [Tenn.]; this was years ago, when he was fourteen or perhaps fifteen. Tossing a football so it will spiral *just so* takes concentration, so it is a silent kind of conversation, which is the best kind, if you're lucky enough to find someone or some way to communicate without words that way. . . . He tucked the ball under his arm, walked up to me almost belligerently and said: 'Dad, I bet you don't know how you felt when *you* were fourteen. You don't, do you?' It seemed an important question to him, and I took it that way.

"Older people, if they are going to be any good whatever to young people (a debatable proposition, I grant), must try to keep green within them NOT how they at sixty-three or fifty-three or forty-three see the world of the eighteen-year-older, but how *they*, the oldsters, felt when they were eighteen."

AUGUST 4, 1962
MARTHA'S VINEYARD

"The World of the Decision Maker"—the subject continues to fascinate me. The weighing and balancing of facts, the tossing and turning of emotions, motives, fears, hopes, all these make the *process* of deciding almost the peak of human activity, that is to say, of living.

This seems to me clear even if the "decision" is on what would seem to be wholly an objective issue: Should the United States resume atom testing? Should taxes be cut? Should Isabella put her prestige and money into this fellow Columbus' idea of a voyage to the Indies? And the process is even more fascinating and interesting, because closer to the springs of human behavior, when the issue is a personal decision, a decision an individual makes that changes the whole course of his life.

I saw an almost classic case of this kind last evening here in our "seasonal house" (as the insurance company describes our cottage).

We had Nat Elias and his wife, New York Health Commissioner Leona Baumgartner, to dinner; no other guests.

I knew she had been considered for an important role in the AID (foreign aid) program. I think she has already made up her mind that she will accept the new AID chief, Fowler Hamilton's, proposal that she become an important program deputy. Otherwise I might not have so unequivocally urged her to take the job on when she asked me what I thought. It would be a great break for the AID program, now still staggering under the almost impossible load.

She is a person who is candid not only with others but with herself. This is a special and rare quality; I fear I have little of it in my system, preferring to see myself as I *want* to be rather than as I am.

Almost as if she were soliloquizing, she recited the reasons or pressures for, and some against, making a firm decision in favor of taking the job on.

Her fears: that the job is literally impossible; that morale at AID is desperately low, that she doesn't want to stay more than a year, and that this would militate against her ability to recruit top people; that it would mean she would be away from home and Nat.

On the pro side: "I feel uncomfortable that so important a thing is going on, that I'm asked to be part of it; just how can I say no, just because I probably will get my throat slit?

"I have been Commissioner of Health of New York City longer than any other person in the history of the city; a lot of good things are going on, dandy things, but perhaps it's time to move into something else. I'm going to be sixty soon, and I want to make the best use of what I have learned for the years of active work I have left.

"I am expendable; if I get fired, it won't hurt my reputation, which has been made, for good or otherwise, and I don't need to worry about how to earn a living.

"Things aren't very good in AID; if I can keep them from being worse, maybe that would be enough justification for trying." No euphoriate she.

Then she said, about the job I'm pretty sure she has agreed, with herself, to take: "Well, I guess I'm getting ready to trade one set of frustrations [meaning in the New York City Government] for another [in Washington]." A good, healthy-minded woman.

The Aphorisms of Atchley: Phoned him the other day at Harkness Pavilion; a "switch" (as they say) since *he* is a patient there, after surgery. Asked me how I am; said O.K. "Not yet unraveled," said I. "Well, you don't want to get *completely* unraveled." And then: "I find that the way to be less tense about one thing is to get tense about something entirely different. That's why sailing [I had said I had done quite a bit of spirited sailing] is so good for you. Makes you tense about something else than the usual, and there is the air and water and sun."

AUGUST 6, 1962
MARTHA'S VINEYARD

The Persian sword of uncertainty (or certainty of a debacle, perhaps I should say) no longer hangs over my head. Burnett has just phoned: Ansari has transmitted a contract providing for D&R's continued work in Khuzistan for another two years. In substance and in form it is so nearly what we wanted that what remains to discuss isn't of consequence. The great big question mark in my future is virtually removed; all that is left, ironically, is to *do the job,* a difficult, tough one. But *that* I shall enjoy, for it is what I wanted most to do and had begun to think might end in an unthinkable breakdown before the finish line of nearly seven years of hard and, on the whole, effective effort.

"I told you so's" are an indulgence I rarely permit myself (I hope). This will be one of those rare occasions. The Iranians' insistence on a long-form or consolidated contract was *not*—as my partner had insisted —simply a subtle way of renegotiating the basics of our contractual relationship. The contract they have sent to us, received today, makes that plain. My hunch has been justified by the event.

But there is more to this than a petty "I told you so." There is a basic proposition of human relations involved, and of negotiating technique. We offended our Iranian friends by an arbitrary attitude. Let's get going, and stop this self-righteousness.

AUGUST 8, 1962
MARTHA'S VINEYARD

In a report from Blumberg in Tehran the following about "planning" in Iran. These, as Blumberg reported them, are comments of Dr. Thomas McLeod, head of the Harvard Advisory Group for Plan Organization, made as he is departing from Iran:

1. Iran is not looking for solutions to its problems (principally budgetary in this context) but rather for a "big pill" that would cure everything easily and at once.
2. Sending Iranians abroad for training, except in specific areas like technical engineering, etc., results in very little. Most of the returnees spend all their time figuring ways to return to the U.S.
3. The major flaw in the Third Plan drafting is not the plan itself, but the fact that nothing was learned by the Iranians themselves and this did not prepare them for future planning efforts.
4. The country does not have the necessary administrative skills or machinery to carry out a national scheme like the Third Plan. It is too much for them.

5. The Third Plan is something alien; prepared by foreigners, for foreigners, and in the interests of foreigners.

D&R's experience leads us to a quite different view. I believe time will prove that we are more nearly right about Iran's future than is indicated in the above disillusioned comments.

AUGUST 9, 1962
MARTHA'S VINEYARD

It is not my inner purpose on this holiday, evidently, to cut myself off from the life that sustains my spirit. When I first came, in July, I vowed I'd not talk to the office. But I don't remember any other summer when I have been on the phone to New York so often and at such length. But these days I am exhilarated and full of the joy of my "work"; for me excitement masks fatigue.

So I have been "unraveling"; this is an unpleasant process for one so ill equipped to be passive; or, to put it another way, one who is almost obsessively active, and, moreover, likes activity for its own sake: cutting down trees on the obviously flimsy excuse that we need firewood, or opening the Wilderness Trail (as Pammy and I called it last summer) through the dense brush beyond the rock wall, or even less useful busynesses.

5 P.M.

Just back from the woods: split the trunk of a tree I felled last summer, using a ten-pound sledge and two steel wedges.

What *sensual* pleasure I get out of swinging that sledge over my head, bringing it down with a clang on the face of the wedge. (Would a psychologist make something unflattering of this?) Then actually to *hear* the log protesting as it splits, separating slowly, fiber by tough fiber. The low petulant voice of the wood, as I stand over the rending log, just waiting, has a quality I can't describe.

I'm fascinated by *natural* sounds, anyway. Sounds of the machines of man often annoy or distract me. I think of the machines, not the sounds alone. But natural sounds, of the woods and shore, have a personality of their own.

A high wind (35 knots) out of the northeast today. The treetops swish and roar in such a wind. The sounds the waves make as I walk the beach are part of the air and the sky. Such sounds were here before there were men to hear them: that thought sticks in my imagination. An island of sounds, a world of sounds with a life of their own.

I continue to swim at Miss Emma's deserted west beach, usually before breakfast. The sun is low, and when, as now, the wind is easterly, the cove is in the lee, and the water so utterly clear. Or is it water? Or air? Or something that is neither?

Most of my swimming is what is called "under" water. *Within* water would be a better word. The difference between the words "under" and "within" are more than verbal.

After I dive I see my hands ahead of me—are those mine?—my arms stretching forward, preparing to sweep back to propel me through that special strange transparency. I live in an ambiance that is neither air nor land nor sea. I, a land animal (or *is* man a land animal?). I am living within that strange substance which partakes of all three, sea and land and air. A net of golden cords, undulating, spreads over my arms and legs as I move within the water. My *mind* tells me the cause of this beauty is the optical effect of the low-lying rays of the very early morning sun that designs this abstract pattern of a net of gold. But does my mind really know? That part of me that is pagan is sure that the gods fashioned this net in which my legs and arms are caught, for my delight.

Isn't this net, far from being explainable as an optical effect, part of the mystery of the substance in which I move, defying matter-of-fact explanation?

Carl Sandburg would scorn what I have just scribbled, in my shorthand, as "fine" writing; and when I see it transcribed I'll probably feel the same. But isn't a man entitled now and then to *feel* as well as to reason, to be effusive (if that is the verdict) as well as sensible?

AUGUST 10, 1962
MARTHA'S VINEYARD

On the phone steadily for three hours today. Our new contract draft, to submit to Iran, contained provisions that troubled me a great deal. I agreed with the objective. So it is ironic that I should find that the *way* that objective was to be put before the Iranians should raise such deep doubts in me.

But *how* a thing is done, I have long since learned, becomes important in determining whether it is, indeed, the thing to do. But these long talks about *how* will, I think, clarify our own minds. Do we truly *want* to relinquish the functions we have been carrying of *managing* (that is, accepting full responsibility for results)? If we are halfhearted about this relinquishment, of course the provisions will seem as odd to the Iranians when they see them as they were to me.

I believe we should *push* the job onto the Iranians even if it isn't going to be as well done as we think—and know—we can do it. And then stand by to help—but help, advise, etc., *only*.

AUGUST 15, 1962
NEW YORK

Monday morning, with me navigating on that steady, even keel that this skipper does not always manage, we reached decisions and positions about the proposed contractual renewal with Iran, the contract that is basic to our company. The gist is a simple one: the process of transferring functions *from us to the Iranian KWPA* must be speeded up.

We discussed "what is there in our draft that is negotiable?" *This* is the way to prepare for such discussions, instead of laying down an ultimatum. We decided that to settle the matter one way or another we shall have to go to Iran.

Just before we were shuffling around toward getting lunch I suddenly decided to drop an explosive. What would be the over-all financial consequences if we decided to convert ourselves into a non-profit corporation? In view of the big tax bite we would save (52 per-cent), I suggested that the results might not be much different than what we now have, i.e., the officers and staff would receive their salaries and a substantial retirement equity. Gordon and I, as 20 percent owners each, would be adversely affected; but would we or would we not *as a company* be in a better position to acquire the kind of work into which we could put our hearts and minds if it was known that we were non-profit?

To my surprise, the group took it quite seriously. The idea will be studied, and produce ideas sparking off perhaps in *other* directions; this was my essential purpose in raising the isuue.

Today we decided to engage the Research Foundation of the Colorado School of Mines to prepare a study of likely areas for filing claims to coal reserves. What seemed to appeal to Gordon (whose interest in "business" is tepid, to say the least) was that we here would be entering a field with a strong public interest and natural resources basis: the minerals of the West, and the rapidly growing need for energy supply in the underdeveloped empire which is the American West.

AUGUST 19, 1962
MARTHA'S VINEYARD

The Friday *New York Times* had a front-page story: Dr. Baumgart-ner to be made deputy in the foreign aid program, etc., and continued: "She will have her sixtieth birthday on Saturday." As Katharine Cornell came in to Leona's party, bringing *her* birthday gift, those eyebrows of hers so world famous lifted particularly high, she said: "Well, I never heard of anyone announcing their birthday on the radio every hour on the hour for a whole day so *everyone* would be compelled to bring presents. Leona, really!"

AUGUST 22, 1962
MARTHA'S VINEYARD

A press report from Iran: a high authority in the Iran Government stated that the contract with D&R would *not* be renewed. The reason assigned: that the U.S. Government had not provided the necessary amount of funds in the aid program.

Vice-President Johnson will appear in Tehran very shortly. The Washington report is that he is going out to tell the Shah that our military aid to Iran will not be increased, may be decreased.

The redraft of an Iran contract with D&R we sent a week or so ago has been received and is being reviewed.

As I write I don't know how the plot will unfold, in the fourth act. The story of crises resolved at the very last moment has become sufficiently familiar in my life, and in the Persian picture, that I feel rather foolish to say that I don't know how the story "comes out."

6 P.M.

How does one behave at one's time of "triumph"? A cable just in from Ansari that our draft of contract is acceptable to him, and to the Shah. Our Iran problem now is not whether we are going to continue to be there but whether we can *deliver*, positively and strongly, on the commitment we have made—to the Persians and *to ourselves*. I am so sick and tired of this fussing and negative pecking and pettifogging over "terms" that it will be a great relief to be *doing* things that look to the future.

Spent two hours with Leona Baumgartner this afternoon, discussing some of the things on which she wants guidance about her new AID post. Leona is over the euphoric stage of a new appointment, with everyone crowding around congratulating her, the papers calling, etc., and is beginning to see what she has got into. Her instinct is that of the experienced and natural *doer*: not just what is wrong, ineffective, etc. But where do we start, where are the places where something can be done, first?

She is a first-rate public servant, which means she is a first-rate human being.

I made gentle fun of the latest fad of calling *everything* "the development of oooman resources." I urged her to make people be *specific* about what that meant to them. Such a bunch of fluent word tossers are attracted to that phrase. And the role of the American universities, and of "education"—that too needs defining in concrete terms.

I used the Ivory Coast assignment of D&R as an illustration of how a *limited*, defined, and doable task could produce good "human resources" results, broader than the particular physical undertaking. But a big amorphous nationwide "movement," vague and beyond doing, could do nothing but raise and dash expectations. This is an important part of my basic philosophy of how to go about the overseas aid program, but it will be some time before *necessity* compels its adoption.

AUGUST 24, 1962
MARTHA'S VINEYARD

The waves bore down on my little boat from all sides, licking their white crested chops, hissing as they rolled under me and on. A strong tide was running to the east (the Nun #20 off the Falmouth shore way over on her side) and a spirited wind from the east. From the time I left the lighthouses on the Chops behind and was in the Sound, the swells were stronger than anything I had ever experienced.

Once I got out into this turbulence I couldn't come about to return, without broaching and being swamped. Anyway, a perverse devil had got into me: that mainland shore became something I just *had* to make, crazy or not. Mediocre sailor that I am, and singlehand, I did make it, and then set out to return.

Taking risks is something I do all the time, and relish. But actual physical danger is something else again. The "risk" is often an intellectual thing, something in the mind; the consequences of having risked unwisely are usually slow in becoming apparent. But danger such as this, with little *Lili-put* careening wildly, just barely getting over the crests, water coming over by the bucketful—and no chance of doing anything but seeing it through—that kind of danger is immediate and elemental. And so was the period of fear, for I was afraid more than once during the worst part of the crossing, and the beat on return.

Since I made it, it was a wonderful experience. There is something cleansing about fear, about that kind of danger. Living the kind of life I do—and most people like me do—we can only *read* about danger, which is too remote from my own innards to suit me.

Still it would be just as well if I didn't make a fetish of this sort of thing. Then it becomes "showing off" [What are you trying to prove?] and just plain insanity.

But I wouldn't have missed it. Three hours on the water to be in a battle with the water, the wind—and myself!

Rita Benton stirred the pasta in the bubbling boiling water, dipped a ladle now and then into the pan with the sauce. One of Rita's famous Italian meals was approaching the on-the-table stage last evening.

This unself-conscious woman, with the bright and undismayed eyes, is fun to be around at any time or place; but in her kitchen, performing the rites she knows so well, and with the perfumes of delicious food cooking, the vapors of her particular kind of Delphic oracle, there was something evocative of the best of the Italians, and also the best of the Middle West pioneer women in her stance, her words, her warm acceptance of the life she has lived, with Tom Benton, great painter of the American Western scene.

There is still about Tom, at seventy-three, some remnant of the peppery gamecock, the belligerent banty rooster. The strain of the whole tribe of Missouri Bentons is strong within him.

What an extraordinary pair, these two. A visit with them on their hilltop overlooking Menemsha Pond is always a treat, and always a paradox. Tom, the mercurial, the temperamental. Yet he it is who has the qualities of the rough, tough, profane American pioneers; and yet the sensitive artist recording the earthy side of American history: the great Indiana University murals; the Independence, Missouri, murals for that other cocky Missouri giant, Harry Truman; the Niagara Frontier murals; the murals of a ripsnorting vital America in the New School in New York.

Rita, born in Milan, in this country only since she was twelve, very Italian. Yet she, "the Latin," is the solid, stable, enduring one of the two, almost a picture of Mother Earth, with her magnificent girth (of which she is rather proud), the way she seems to be planted, rooted like a great oak to stand against the gales of Tom's tempers and moods. Without Rita's strength would we ever have had the treasures Tom has created?

I tried, at the table, to get Tom to talk about the future of his work. "No more contracts for me." This refers to such big mural jobs as the Truman Library one.

"But I'll keep busy. Reading. I want to know the philosophy of the American Catholic."

I agreed this was probably interesting, but what about work in his field of painting? "Oh, that too. Lots of problems I want to work out, never had the time. Formal problems."

I tried to get him to say what he meant by "formal." He went into a kind of lecture tone that pretty well lost me: everything for the artist must be brought into a unity, etc., things I could have read in books about "art appreciation," and indeed have. But I hoped he would give it a special Benton flavor; no luck.

When Tom and Roger Baldwin are in the same room, the decibel count is high. Roger emits a boom, or blast, when he talks. Such rigor, such a man! He must be close to eighty, if I recall correctly, but an auctioneer of thirty would do well to match that volume. A refreshing mark of the intense love of life there is in this man.

And then, over brandy, his face somehow shrank, the eyes seemed to be closer together in his face, a sadness and confusion that I have never seen before in this very sure positive hot-blast gent.

"Dave, I have spent my life learning about democracy, standing up for what I believed it was. And now, do you know, I am not at all sure I know what democracy means. Do you?" The question was rhetorical, I thought, so I waited, after this remarkable admission of humility in a great man who has no cause to be humble.

"My African friends from the new states—and I have many of them and I think they trust me—my African friends say to me: 'Yes, we believe in democracy all right. But for our new countries it won't work at all. We have to work out a national purpose that we still haven't had time to develop. We have to do so many things, and don't yet know how. So we can't possibly have an opposition party. It would destroy us. Everything must be worked out within one party; it is hard enough to have one party; if democracy means more than one party, and elections and rowing that goes with it—well, democracy isn't suited to us.'

"Now, Dave, what do I say to my African friends?"

He looked so sad. A lifetime of championing civil rights, and here he sees these black men, who have "thrown off the shackles" of white colonialism, putting critics of their own color and citizenship in jail for daring to exert the basic civil right of democracy—to criticize.

Has there ever been a deeper, more biting irony than this picture? Of all Americans, in Baldwin we have the flesh and symbol of "human rights," for fifty years. And yet, being told these things, he confesses he has no answer that is persuasive to his black "liberated" friends.

We talked about the transformation of Nkrumah, the hopeful signs in Nigeria. But he kept coming back to the picture of critics not being tolerated, being put in jail. As we were leaving, he took my arm (he had been brooding, so uncommon for such a sure, confident man) and said: "All my life I have thought that everything is relative; that there are no absolutes. But I think I agree with you: the right to criticize, the duty to allow and even encourage criticism—that *is* an absolute. Perhaps you are right, Dave, that nationwide elections are not, at this stage, a necessity of democracy. But the right to criticize and question is." He shook his head with a thoughtful sadness quite moving.

AUGUST 28, 1962
NEW YORK

Back to reality, the roaring passionate city, from the serene change-lessness of the routine of the Island. Or is *that* reality and this great city something made up, invented in men's minds? It is hard to be sure. But my *work* is real and there is here a fire that is very real; no pale easy serenity about that.

The Persian story goes on apace, since my return just yesterday. A morning of talk, with Gordon and John Oliver, about how we "dispose" of our forces: who should go to Iran for the contract discussion, who stay and "keep the store."

How often it happens that, after thoughtful discussion a conclusion is reached—and then a fact quite out of context, not known to us, changes all the pieces on the chessboard. We decided that the first group should be Gordon (rather at my insistence, for he has had this on his soul now for months), John Oliver and Nate Greene. I called Nate at Rockport to tell him. In the saddest tone (and in his voice he can summon a kind of Old Testament Hebraic sadness at times), he said: "I had expected to go, but I can't. André says he must have me 'by him' while a securities episode—a potential scandal—which the SEC is investigating is pending. I can't say No to him on what may be the most serious trouble he has ever been in, affecting his pride and worrying him sick."

The "strong man" reaching out for the hand of Nate because now he needs a man who unlike most advisors of the rich will not just say Yes but give it to him straight.

So when I told Gordon we gathered again. "Let's all three go." And it was decided. Gordon, John, and I leave Thursday of this coming week.

A delicious bit of modern informality in an Oriental regal setting in one of Blumberg's recent letters from Tehran: "It seems that one evening at a private party, Mr. Ansari and his wife were on the dance floor. Suddenly he noticed that His Imperial Majesty the Shah and Queen Farah were dancing at elbow range. H.I.M. the Shah leaned toward Mr. Ansari and asked: 'How is the sugar cane?' Mr. Ansari replied that it was fine. 'I hear you have had some difficulties, some disappointments in the result,' continued H.I.M.

"Mr. Ansari replied that this was true, but there were very good reasons for this. 'Such as what?' asked H.I.M. By this time Mr. Ansari was about to give up his dance and asked H.I.M. the Shah's permission to submit a written report on the matter. H.I.M. agreed."

SEPTEMBER 3, 1962
LABOR DAY
PRINCETON

Horrible news from western Iran: a great earthquake centering near Hamadan and Kazvin, to the north of "our" area. Villages leveled, men, women, and children buried under their mud-brick dwellings.

Such news anywhere would be sad in the extreme. But when I hear the figures of so many villages, so many dead, etc., in this case I can see and feel: dark-eyed little people wandering, bewildered. Among the bullet-shaped heads of the men, the women with their dragging chadors, clutching the crying children, misery ten times compounded. What mankind must "take" at times from the hands of a beneficent Nature.

Two other dams—the Karaj and Sefid Rud—are not far from the area that felt the quake, though not at its epicenter. One responsible for the safety of great dams, as I have been for years, cannot help having it pass through his mind: is that double-arch thin dam, set in the vast canyon of the Dez River, engineered to take such shudders. such throes of the earth as this convulsion?

SEPTEMBER 6, 1962
ABOARD PAN AM EN ROUTE TO LONDON

This morning a cable from Williams, D&R's project manager on the Dez. A tremor was detected at the time of the great earthquake. A fissure of "micron" size discovered in one of the tunnels; it is being dug out and grouted. A tunnel is the weakest part of the canyon, of course. But that this quake was strong enough to leave *any* kind of mark in a thin arch dam is, well, somewhat disturbing. Until the dam is topped out, the whole weight bearing down against the arches that drive the double eggshell of the arch into the sides of the canyon, the dam is not at its greatest point of stability and strength. After that (say, December 1) the dam is as strong as the canyon itself—it could hardly be stronger, I suppose.

A fissure even if invisible to the eye (as a micron crack would be) is something that engineering can undoubtedly do something about, objective and direct and measurable.

But a fissure of character, even micron in depth—that is another matter. And it is human character cracks in myself and others that have made up most of my career.

SEPTEMBER 7, 1962
ZURICH, SWITZERLAND

There is something disembodied, in time, space, and ideas, about this kind of air trip. This may account for my latest gambit about saying my say about the atom, in the Princeton lectures over which I am laboring.

Satire is what the atom and the atom-ers need more than that solemn "new approach" the need for which I'm writing about. But not the fierce satire of a Swift but the bumbling belly-laugh kind of a Bob Benchley, or even Ring Lardner at his best.

When solemn scientists keep saying the same damn thing about the atom year after year, that is occasion for planting in their path a banana peel of ridicule; that calls for a real burlesque pratfall. Perhaps I ought to begin my stuffy appeal for a "new approach" to atomic dangers by saying this calls for a farce; but that would seem in bad taste from me. But where *is* the ridicule-maker who could bring this all back to the *human* comedy? And it is *this* we must remember; that neither the atom nor any other "outside impersonal force" can change things—only human beings can do that, juicy, warm, humor-loving, ironic human beings. Where are they?

SEPTEMBER 10, 1962
TEHRAN, IRAN

I slept very poorly last night worrying that we were bearing down too hard on Ansari.

There is a time in the course of negotiation toward agreement when one can be *too successful* in pushing one's views through to acquiescence or acceptance. This I think is where we stand this morning.

Yesterday and the day before, in our sessions across the table from Ansari and his staff of perhaps eight Iranians, we insisted on changes, and after much seemingly excited Farsi confabs, in the end Ansari did say: "We accept your language."

We have, I suppose, the power to exact almost any terms as things now stand. This is the very time, I think, when one must be moderate, yield on every point that seems important to them. After all, we are not "negotiating" with a foe but with a partner with whom we shall be continuing to work, a partner new to the role of responsibility of a huge enterprise which we have built. "Easy does it."

But the short-perspective mind, harassed by day-to-day annoyances, always wants everything set out in a contract that will eliminate those annoyances by giving him *his way*, always.

The specific emotional issue I see raised by a provision our people want: if funds are not advanced on time, we give notice that we terminate the function we have assumed responsibility for. I don't like this sort of rubbing their nose in this.

After a long talk with Gordon we agreed that we shouldn't insist on this if our Iranian friends had as much trouble with it as I believe they have.

A call from Oliver confirms this: they were affronted by it. So the provision that kept me awake much of the night is out, and we are almost out of the woods.

Ambassador Holmes looked more like a general in mufti than ever: "The earthquake: I've been running a command post here since last Monday a week, ordering blankets, bringing in a hospital unit and so on." This man is an operator and is happiest when he is operating, that's clear.

How often irrelevant details hit my eye in the midst of portentous events. The hole in the Ambassador's socks, for example. He was sitting there, his legs crossed, and staring up at me was a hole in the *front* of one sock. (Later, when he asked us to a small dinner, he explained that his wife was in Europe with their daughter, and my mind returned to the hole in that sock.)

It's not only the earthquake that has kept him busy, he said: "We had Lyndon Johnson here and that took a lot of doing, organizing that."

Then he went into a description of the way Johnson's warmth and outgoing manner took the place, wading into the crowds, talking to peasants in a village near Varamin so they "communicated" without an interpreter, etc.

"It isn't only the man's warm manner, but he really wants poor people to have a better time of it; he's come from poor people himself. He *believes* in these things, and people sensed this without words. When he talked to the Shah about the importance of planning, he spoke of his home town of 700 in Texas. 'We built us a steam plant and it was too small and we had to build it over and it cost more that way; wouldn't have happened if we had planned ahead a bit.' "

You could sense his career Foreign Service officer's appreciation of the qualities of a skilled politician who cares about people. I thought to myself that if more professional people in the Government could understand the special functions of a politician who can "get to" people, the pros would be happier and less frustrated with Congressional "interference." For a man with a way with people has something to contribute without which the pro and the technician couldn't operate under a democracy at all.

"Lyndon said some very complimentary things about Lilienthal and Clapp in his talk with the Shah while he was here, " Holmes said. It is evident that we are beginning to be an asset—that is, our work is —on both the Iranian and U.S. sides.

The Third Plan has been approved, Holmes confirmed, but they don't have enough projects ready to go—costs, economics, basic facts— a problem in finding such. So he would guess that the Khuzistan program will be able to get more money for immediate expansion because it is good and because it is *ready*. Here is stellar proof of the virtues of planning ahead in a country that is often pretty weak on getting ready, except verbally, to do anything.

SEPTEMBER 11, 1962
2:51 P.M.
TEHRAN

A tremor, a definite but gentle one, just massaged our living room, while Gordon, John, and I were having a drink.

If there weren't the great earthquake disaster in the Kazerun area we would hardly have noticed this. Now we can think: Well, there may be another big one somewhere.

At 10:15 this morning we sat along the table in the KWPA conference room, opposite the seven or eight Iranians. At 10:45 a contract had been agreed upon. So the vigil is over. Only the *work* remains! And it will be tough work. But when Gordon said this morning that it is nothing less than a "miracle," that despite the wave upon wave of difficulties the program is now reality, he was "saying true."

11:15 P.M.

Last evening Ambassador Holmes had shown Gordon and me about the spanking new Residence with pride; it is a beautiful modern design with a Persian flavor, a fit place for the representative of the President of the United States. He had settled us on a little roof "porch," with an almost full moon through the dark bulk of the great Tehran pines. A red fez appeared through the door, slipped among the chairs silently (like a character in a Durrell novel) and handed the Ambassador a message, whispering in French. (The servant in the fez is a carry-over from the Ambassador's days in the Foreign Service in North Africa.) The Ambassador put on his pince-nez. "You will have to excuse me; it appears that this is a message I must attend to at once."

The lights were turned on; he read the paper, then grinned. "Let me read you this urgent cable—from Rome. 'Send urgently my two blue chiffon dresses put them on board plane tonight. Love,' signed by my wife." Being an orderly and obedient soldier, after we had our chuckle, he sent for his wife's French maid, gave her explicit directions ("Yes, monsieur, I know what dresses she means"), and then we resumed our discussions of the state of affairs in Iran.

There are a number of things the Ambassador said that he identified pointedly as "in the family," and these I omit from this entry: the security preparations for Johnson's visit to the bazaar here; the methods the Ambassador employs to learn what goes on among the peasants and their relations to their landlords, etc. Mostly, however, he spoke with the utmost candor, brisk, colorful; a man who felt rather lonely and got as much benefit out of trying out on us his ideas about Iran and its leaders as we could benefit from such opinions: for most of what he said was opinion, but the opinion of a pro.

His disappointment about the departure of Prime Minister Amini was profound. "He was finished as much by just plain physical exhaustion as anything else. By the time he resigned he was an empty wineskin."

But what ended the hopeful regime of Amini ("He was a real Persian, for all his Western manner and education") was "the merciless pressure of the Persian tradition that anyone who had a grievance or petition had a traditional right to present it to the head of the Government."

I could testify to this, for I recalled the early-morning appointment I had with Amini when I was here last November. His outer and inner office lined with merchants, landlords, peasants, traders, etc., who had been waiting there since 5 A.M., all of whom he saw, and would see all day long, on any and all subjects.

The Shah knows—or senses—that the days of the landlords' power is over its peak, that "Minister of Agriculture Arsanjani and his land reform program" is going to be the strongest tide in Iranian affairs; and "the Shah is apparently getting ready to align himself fully with the forces that have brought about the decline of landlord political power."

How much more interesting and useful such a dinner for three, with no formality, no servants about (some of whom I always assume are part of the Soviet apparatus in a place like this) than a big party, where one just chatters.

Two hours with Leo Anderson this afternoon, hearing the latest report on the "pilot irrigation project." This man is full of savvy, and knowledge, and the ability of a teacher who cares a hell of a lot about his subject. When a hard-bitten farmer out of a Scandinavian North

Dakota background uses the word "exciting" about the use of berseem clover on these ancient lands—how it provides feed for the peasant's own sheep and cattle and donkeys, so the landlord can't take a hunk of what the peasant raises—well, then you are in the presence of the kind of human being that makes the world move along.

SEPTEMBER 12, 1962
TEHRAN

Oh, land of the exotic Orient! Oh, loaf of bread and Omar's houri beneath the bough. I have just come back to my elegant hotel room from a feast of cheeseburger, at a Hot Shoppe (operated by great huge Persians in dinner jackets, at high noon), followed by a shopping trip to an American-style supermarket, complete with the little wire wagons and packaged meat—even hamburgers ready to fry, in cellophane bags. All around are the older style markets, with the meat, fly covered, hanging from hooks; the little men carrying a handful of limes, hawking them outside the swank women's clothing stores, and all the rest.

The change to Western-style living—and the Western-style housewife—comes exceedingly fast in these parts.

SEPTEMBER 13, 1962
(OR SHAHRIVAR 22, 1341)
TEHRAN

Perspective. An even keel. Working with day-to-day realities and still seeing to the far horizon. All such copybook words are important to keep repeating to myself, and to my associates who must face and overcome the frustrations and emotional wear and tear that always comes when (1) one can't always have one's own way—which is mostly —and (2) when things don't work out as one has planned or hoped. And this is mostly too.

These homily-like thoughts are prompted by the efforts I have been making the past two days to accommodate myself and my friends to the subtle and the wearing difficulties of getting things done here in Persia.

Difficult enough at best. More than ever difficult now, in these latter days, when the "foreign consultant"—often with great reason—has become such a popular target. Add, too, the transition we are in the process of making—at our insistence—of turning over to Iranians the task of doing what we believe needs to be done, with ourselves only what are called "advisors." (What a euphemism, that term "advisors.")

It is hell on wheels and no mistake. Last night I slept badly because I had one of those low dips in which I wondered whether it was something that could be done at all, except at a cost of wearing ourselves out completely with frustrations, and of course gettting blamed for everything that didn't work out according to the most rosy expectations, now that it is under *their* direction.

But confronted for the past hour with the specific causes for my associates' anguish I did what I so often do: I became the calmest man in the place, tried to spread the spirit of adjustment. Gordon, too, was terrific: his ability to analyze, find the crucial point is phenomenal. I think we were of real help to John Oliver, who as D&R executive vice-president bears the full brunt of the frustrations and confusion inherent in this anomalous *new structure of relationships* we are now in process of working out with the Iranians.

In the strong light of specific troubles, the D&R rhetoric fades; the fine words about wanting to "work ourselves out of a job"; the importance of having Iranians run the Khuzistan program (the biggest thing going in this country, incidentally).

The cane sugar project at Haft Tapeh illustrates the crunch we are in. The *first* season's harvest, last winter, was far from meeting the predictions and expectations we had for it. Not by half.*

The American sugar company we hired to do the job, under our supervision, is probably the best available, the Brewer people of Hawaii. They were harassed with interruptions in the Iranian flow of funds, and other circumstances, some but not all of them attributable to their own managerial limitations. But most of the difficulties were inherent in the first growing of sugar cane in *many centuries* on that plain. Their contract expires October 31, just as the new harvest, the second, is due to begin. For weeks we have been trying to get approval of KWPA, the Iranian agency, to the terms of a new contract we think is the best we can get, and protect the interests of Iran. The Iranians (speaking through Ansari) want Brewer to agree that if the production doesn't come up to a certain level they, Brewer, will be liable for damages in a major amount. Of course Brewer won't agree to that. There isn't much profit or prestige in the operation for them at best. So nothing happens, and the calendar moves on inexorably, the day of the ripened sugar cane isn't far off. If Brewer withdrew, there would be a real mess: an unharvested cane plantation and an idle mill and sugar refinery.

For such a debacle we would bear the "responsibility," so our contract reads; yet it is Iran's KWPA, our principal, that seeks to impose conditions we don't think can or should be exacted of Brewer. Confusion and stalemate.

No wonder John Oliver is indignant; no wonder last night I thought

* In subsequent seasons cane production at Haft Tapeh rose dramatically; the 1969-70 harvest produced 120.4 tons per hectare, among the very highest in the world.

of telling Ansari we had changed our minds and wouldn't sign the new contract after all!

But if we stand by our guns this particular crisis will pass. We'll go on to the dozen others, almost equally troublesome. Troublesome because of this imposition of responsibility on us yet without authority to deal with the situation as we think best.

I can see the Iranian position too. It is their money; it is their sugar; the first results weren't up to what they should have been; they will be blamed (indeed, the Old Shah would probably have had Ansari shot) if Brewer—our choice—doesn't come through on the second harvest. So they feel, too, that they should have a voice in the new contract terms, even though D&R has the "responsibility."

For such a specific managerial impasse the glib writers of books on "the executive" are totally ignorant; the fact is there are no neat "solutions."

I bore something of the same kind of duality in the AEC. The General Electric Co., for example, was under contract with us to run the atomic plant at Hanford. Their way of handling labor relations (the Boulware style) wasn't my way; their cost controls were creaky; their discrimination against Negroes made me furious. And for the bad results I, as AEC Chairman, was held "responsible" by Congress. But having given G.E. the job of running that place, I could hardly change their way of doing things and still hold them accountable. Not a satisfactory solution, but better than having two hands on the same tiller.

A big party for us tonight, at the home of an Iranian family, with important roots in the Khuzistan. A lovely garden, within the walls of the traditional compound, the center a rectangle of water in the Persian manner, roses, extraordinarily beautiful dark-eyed Persian women, mostly young married gals, and the colorful food—the best in the world—the Persians prepare so well, set out on a heavily laden table. As we were piling our plates (and some of us thinking of the poor devils in the earthquake area), the electricity went off—not a rare event in Tehran.

But then the *full* moon in the glowing desert air lighted the garden like a million stars. The host was embarrassed about the electricity failure; but we rejoiced to see a Persian garden by dazzling moonlight. All we lacked was a nightingale.

SEPTEMBER 14, 1962
TEHRAN

Eng. Asfia, now head of the Plan Organization, has just announced the details of the new Five-Year Plan, the Third Plan, which had been formally approved a day or so before by the Council of Ministers, and was therefore "law."

This was an official government action. It was also, as we saw with unbelievable poignancy yesterday late afternoon, a personal drama, tragic and very Eastern in its intensity of expression.

Ever since young Khodadad Farmanfarmaian was summoned back from the U.S. perhaps five years ago, at the call of Ebtehaj, he has been the intellectual and emotional leader of a coterie of young patriots, the "intellectuals." He used that word himself, as meaning men who are not only trained and exceptionally able but capable of looking at the affairs of their country *apart* from its effect on their own personal fortunes. A definition of "intellectual" that would bear imitating in our country.

When Ebtehaj was dismissed as head of Plan Organization, Khodadad stayed on with Asfia. Passionately loyal to Ebtehaj, they were determined to carry out the "only thing that is important in this country, its economic development." Khodadad made the fashioning of the Third Plan the focus and center of the human flame that he is. For a year his flashing dark eyes, the outpouring of eloquent words—and hands—the thrust of his noble head—everything in his whole being he engaged in this task of the Third Plan, and its consequences. His ideas were accepted; he was sent by the Prime Minister as his personal representative to explain the Plan to President Kennedy and Prime Minister Macmillan, etc.

Then last May suddenly he resigned. Why, we never knew until today.

For the months since he resigned he has paced the rooms of his home on the edge of the mountain, where he lives with his American wife, brooding, sulking, in pain from his ulcers and humiliation, overwhelmed with fear for his country, trying to nurse the wounds of his great disappointment, or what he, in his resonant voice, called his "betrayal."

Just as Gordon and I were about to leave, after a social call on him in the twilight, he in slacks and jersey, the smolder in his eyes burst into flame, and he told us the story of the "betrayal."

I can't remember any "performance" more moving. The differences he had with those from whom he parted may or may not be as deeply vital as he believes. But the depth of the tragic feeling he displayed with such *power* made this an unforgettable episode. Perhaps it throws a good deal of light, too, on the most important factor in the "economic development" of this country, that is, the emotional dimensions of the Persian.

"I built up Asfia; when my first cousin, Amini, became Prime Minister he had never heard of Asfia. I believed in him. Asfia agreed with my ideas and those of my men about the basic proposition of comprehensive national planning and a budget that would put teeth in that plan. He agreed in the basic idea of Ebtehaj that to leave the commitments on the national revenues to a single Minister of Finance would mean that all the Ministers would jockey for position and again we would face disaster, each starting projects of their own on their own, and all the rest.

"Then suddenly Asfia called me in and said: 'I can't go along; it is too much for me to stand out against the enemies of comprehensive planning.' What a betrayal! I resigned. The men around me, the only completely competent group in the country, came up here and said: 'We will resign with you.' I would not permit it. I looked at these men, looked into their faces. [Here he named them; the only one I recognized was "Cy" Samii.] For over a year I had poured into them the two qualities this tragic country needs most: hope and dynamism. I stormed, I cursed, I praised—for a year I played on the great qualities of these men until we had an esprit such as had not existed since the early days of Ebtehaj. All gone, all disappointed. I would not let them resign; they have families. But one by one they have departed. Samii has accepted the post of economic advisor to Syria, the others have gone to the States. Gone. Disappointed."

In a dead silence I asked Farmanfarmaian: "What were the forces that made it insupportable for Asfia to stand by the concept of the Plan?" "One man only: the Prime Minister. I said to Asfia: 'If you had only been willing to fight, for a day or a week, even if you knew you couldn't win. But to give up something you believe in without any fight at all—that is unforgivable.'"

No, he said, when Gordon and I tried to give him some consolation and perspective, no, he won't leave the country as the others have done, though several foreign governments have offered him jobs, and Princeton wants him back. "I will stay here in my country and fight this out. If only Ebtehaj would take the lead, but he won't. He says: 'They know my address if they want me; they know my terms.'"

So, sadly, we left this patriot, confident that he and his convictions would prevail.❰

SEPTEMBER 17, 1962
AHWAZ, IRAN

About to leave for the Dez canyon, to see what a year has done to that narrow chasm where a year ago—with much Oriental cum modern splendor the Shah "poured" the first concrete.

❰ In 1963 Khodadad Farmanfarmaian became Deputy Governor of Iran's Central Bank (Bank Markazi Iran) and Governor in late 1968. In June of 1970 he was appointed Managing Director of Plan Organization. The young men he referred to also later returned to posts of great public responsibility.

Gordon has been such a good companion on this trip: good-humored, interested in talking to people, full of laughs. And *what* a mind!

11 P.M.

"What hath *Man* wrought?" This variant on Samuel Morse's first message by the now almost obsolete miracle of telegraphy is what went through my mind and my insides when I first looked down on Dez Dam. A towering evidence of man's temerity, creating a mountain and jamming that mountain into the somber scarred cleft of the Dez canyon.

The swelling curve of the upstream face of the dam moves the heart. It has the beauty and the symmetry of the curving edge of the surf as it curls and breaks, propelled by the far-off turbulence of a storm at sea. It was hard to pay much attention (though I should have, I suppose) to the complaints of the Impregilo representatives, the contractors, about our rejections of their claims for added compensation because of this and that. Somehow that seemed so irrelevant today, as this great structure (on which the Italians have done such a prodigious job) nears its completion.

For years I have worn a "hard hat" on a construction site reluctantly, considering it mostly "show." Today I learned what a good idea it really is.

Walking in a tunnel, wriggling past a huge truck holding a concrete mixer, I felt something hitting my hard hat, my shoulder and back. Some of the concrete poured out of the mixer when we were being carelessly piloted past the truck to one of the openings in the tunnel. I was well clobbered, but of course not hurt. I might have a different story to tell if that much concrete had hit me on an unprotected head.

SEPTEMBER 18, 1962
AHWAZ

After an early coffee, my head still throbbing with that sight of the dam yesterday. The irresistible impulse to put what I saw and felt down on paper, in the long, long habit of journal writing.

People, not the Gargantuan engineering feat, become the keynote in one's thoughts.

We visited the Dez at noon, when some of the Iranian workmen were taking time off for a bite to eat. Down from the flying carpet of a shaky platform suspended by a cable that brought me across the canyon on the cableway, a thousand feet or more above the bed of the stream, delivered me to the mouth of two huge man-made caves in the face of the canyon wall: the flood spillways. Numinous, awesome as the interior of a cathedral, chewed right out of the ancient rock. In these "caves" Persian workmen—Bakhtiari, I was told—had built little fires on which their tea was heating. Black-smoked kettles lined up on the fire. The men themselves on their heels, in the manner of all mountain people, I guess, for this strange, and for me strained position, sitting on one's heels I recall from the hills of eastern Tennessee. Chewing and tearing hunks out of the flat pebble bread, that in the darkness looked more like a coarse cloth than the traditional food of these hard-working men. One older man was cutting a melon into pieces for the little circle squatted around him; the aroma of the fresh-cut melon incongruous amid all the compressed-air hoses and machinery. As if we had surprised a long-hidden band of prehistoric men.

Other kinds of men too.

The light in the eyes of the "educated" Iranians, the new way of carrying themselves. Monshizadeh, for example. Now the Iranian Comptroller of KWPA, with self-assurance, conversational ease, that special glint and pitch required for kidding, for humor. When he first came to "KDS" (which then simply meant a company of "expatriates" as Shahmirzadi calls our people) as one of our first Iranian employees he was as shy as an antelope colt, eyes always cast down when you talked to him, head slightly bowed in the courteous manner of Iranians. Though in their *hearts* they have as little sense of inferiority or servility as any people I know; but they have a tradition of good manners that to an ignorant outsider may give the appearance of submission.

All that is changed now in this bespectacled, very bright-eyed youngish man. I asked him question after question about accountancy, how his profession is progressing in Iran. His responses were given looking me right in the eye, delivered with strength and confidence.

In an hour we see the bouncy unpredictable strange figure of Mahdavi, the Governor General. This very short square little chunk of a man has caused the Khuzistan program as much trouble as a battalion of enraged landowning sheiks. He came to the Khuzistan on the special train, on Gordon's and my very first trip. His pet project, as head of an Irrigation Bongah, was an absurd little dam on the lower Karkheh River, to the west of here. Billed as a model, approved by a team of above-the-battle FAO "experts," it was to provide irrigation for 70,000 hectares. It was a terrible flop, managing to bring water to barely 5,000 hectares, the dam's abutments washing out more than once (once while we were here). Ebtehaj asked us to take a look at the project, see what we could do to salvage it. Reluctantly we did; concluded that it should be cut down to 500 hectares. There simply wasn't enough water in the Karkheh to sustain more than that.

Mahdavi never forgave us, nor gave up the idea that the whole

Khuzistan program should have been the Karkheh baby of his. Now that he is Khuzistan's Governor General he organizes landowners (who had previously agreed to the pilot irrigation program's conditions) to renege, writes to the Prime Minister that the whole scheme is no good, and generally makes Ansari's life a torment of distraction from his substantive jobs.

The merits of Mahdavi's ideas are not really the issue. How, for example, can anyone not a schoolboy justify encouraging government agencies in this provincial capital from neglecting to pay their power bills, and thereby bringing KWPA into financial disrepute? Yet this he does.

No, Mahdavi is but one more illustration that the public affairs of this world, in Persia, or in Valparaiso, Indiana, or around the conference table at Geneva, are dominated by human emotions and men's individual molds of personality and character.

But to return to the Dez Dam.

The Italians'—the famed firm of Impregilo—ideas of safety and construction housekeeping are shocking to those of us brought up differently, in TVA. George Jessup, builder of TVA's Kentucky Dam, for example, would have exploded if he had seen the debris, the shaky planks in the cable car that took me across the canyon, the lack of protective guardrails on the edge of a 1,000-foot drop; the scaffolding out in the middle of the air.

So do some of the Italians' own skilled workmen, apparently, not find the firm's construction sloppiness quite to their liking. John Blumberg tells a story of an Italian skilled carpenter. He was working way below, not far above the river bed. A hundred and fifty meters above an Iranian workman felt the call of Nature, as they say; impromptu-like "he dropped his pants and took care of his needs. The Italian below was hit full square, not only on his hard hat but all over him, with the impact of 150 meters of drop. He took off his hat and clothes, walked to the office, turned in his badge and started back for Italy."

SEPTEMBER 19, 1962
TEHRAN

Rosebushes set in the greenest of grass (not beds, like mine) rimming irregular emeralds of water pools, level after level of them in the brilliant crisp sunlight of a Persian mountain morning: these were still in my mind as we were bowed into the Shah's office in the Summer Palace this morning. And as the warm greetings were exchanged, the big grins, the opening questions, I was more conscious of the sounds of a gardener's pruning shears, clip, clip, clip through the open windows than of the soft rather gentle voice of the gray-haired ruler of this country.

The King began the talk by asking me how I found the work progressing. I said it was on schedule, that we were within a few weeks of the first harvest of the Dez River, electricity and water for irrigation of the Pilot Irrigation area. I reminded His Majesty of the dream we had described to him six and a half years ago. A redeveloped Khuzistan, of 2.5 million acres of very productive land with water enough to supply that land, 6 million kw of hydro power (at this the King broke in: "You first said 4 million and that is what I told Khrushchev; later you changed it to 7 million"—I think his recollection is right about the 4 million) and a considerable industrial complex at the Persian Gulf, access to the seas east and west. Nothing had happened, in the intervening years, to weaken our conviction that these things were within reach, not all of them within my time but certainly within his as a much younger man. "The first fruits are in our hands," he commented, in that soft almost inflectionless voice, and some other comment about how fortunate "my country" was in securing my services and energies and those of Mr. Clapp and our organization.

I said: "The fact that the plan has proceeded to the first stage of actual reality is due chiefly to the fact that you, as the sovereign of this country, have made it your baby, and have seen it through many difficulties. You have been a good boss; a good boss wants his workers to tell him the problems and obstacles, as well as the favorable things, and with your permission that is what I would like to do. The difficulties are not in the nature of things; they can be cured."

Behind his dark glasses he showed amusement at this way of putting things, fidgeted a bit as if to brace himself for one more set of complaints and grievances (of which he hears a lot), and asked me to go into them; also to tell of the part the Khuzistan development would be able to play in the Third Plan.

"For this land program to work we must start with a limited area for intensive irrigation, just as an industrial concern with a new process will build a small plant to find out the best way of operating a big full-size one. That is why we call the first stage of irrigation the pilot project. It is not so small; 58 villages and 50,000 acres, but small in comparison to what the Dez water can later serve.

"To make this work required the agreement of landowners to make certain improvements and to pay the water charges. Those agreements were made with most of the owners, and it was on this representation that the World Bank made the Dez and irrigation loan.

"But within the past year the Governor General of the province, Mr. Mahdavi, has taken a position that the whole scheme is wrong, a

waste, and this has encouraged a large number of landowners to withdraw their approval.

"So this is the obstacle: Unless all branches of Your Majesty's
Government cooperate, the first step, the pilot operation, can't succeed,
and if that fails there may not be a second step. We have talked to the
Governor as recently as yesterday; he does not believe in the course
the Government has taken, and says so in ways that greatly increase the
chance that Ansari will not only be distracted from his tasks but the
whole enterprise will fail. I haven't minced words, though I am talking
about one of your appointees, not for personal reasons but because this
goes to the heart of the future of the Khuzistan."

He took this as if he had heard before that Mahdavi was a nuisance.
Under a new law just enacted the Provincial Governors will have greater
functions; this will require a different kind of governor general than in
the past. "This will be taken care of." I got the impression it had already
been decided.

Gordon described how well equipped the Ansari organization of
Iranians (with our "help") were *now* to carry out projects or extend
existing ones, such as irrigation, under the Third Plan to the tune of
$140 million in the five years ahead. It was an excellent summary, and
held the King's interest, particularly our investigation of the next dam.
He was obviously disappointed that the full capacity of Dez probably
wouldn't be used up until 1967 or perhaps 1970; he is impatient in the
right way.

Most of the rest of the hour was taken up with a quite different kind
of subject, though a related one: How can Iran get an increased share
of the new and added markets for oil?

The Shah was emphatic: "Kuwait with only 200,000 people is able
to sell, chiefly to British concerns, $400 million of oil. They don't know
what to do with the money, so they buy up real estate in Switzerland
or keep it in Swiss banks. Here is Iran, so important to the interests of
the West, not a neutral but an active ally; why should not Iran get the
principal share of the added market year by year and thereby save the
necessity of outside loans to keep developing our country."

It is evident he thinks that I, and "other outstanding Americans"
should start a "public campaign" to this end. I agree it doesn't make
sense, the present situation about Kuwait vis-à-vis Iran. But I did remind
him of the great power the international oil companies have acquired
through the years within the foreign services of governments of Western
countries having a stake in Persian Gulf oil. "Yes, of course; but where
would they be if Iran fell and the Persian Gulf became a Red lake; how
would they get their oil out, I ask you," he said with real pain.

During the latter part of the talk I again became conscious of gardening sounds outside, and the color through the windows, matched by the splendid colors of the huge rug in his heavy office, heavy with the kind of mediocre European paintings I gather his father found to his liking, his stern father who built the great Palace, perhaps the last palace of its kind to be built by an Asian monarch.

10 P.M.

Was told today that a dozen foreign construction or engineering contractors, some of whom have been doing work here for a generation (Kamsax, the Danish port builders, for example), had heard of the cancellation of their contracts without notice. ("Get rid of the foreigners" is a popular slogan hereabouts.) While we were received in state at the Palace, and our contract extended. So we still stand well and aren't treated as just another "contractor." The fact is we really aren't. For one thing, we don't try to make a fortune out of this country. More than that, it is recognized by the Persians that we are delivering the goods on schedule, within the cost estimates, and with idealism and practicality.

SEPTEMBER 20, 1962
PARK HOTEL
TEHRAN

The Shah (I have been ruminating on our meeting with him yesterday) has a mannerism while he is speaking of a half-sigh, an indrawing of breath. When I do this "sighing" I have been told that this may be a sign of fatigue or stress, reaching for more oxygen than ordinary breathing provides.

Why lovers sigh—as they always do in novels—or why Congressional witnesses do—or this one did, anyway—well, there are different reasons. Boredom, in the case of the latter, I would say. The sighing of lovers, that is more complicated. But when a monarch half-sighs—what does that mean? My own guess is that here is a very disciplined man, a man who has himself under a tight rein of self-control; that he is using up a great deal more in worry and concern than a man with normal responsibilities.

Well, such speculations are the kind of detail that run through one's mind after closely observing a man who holds the destiny of 20 million people in his hands and whose country may hold the destiny, in our time, of the whole Middle East, perhaps of Africa, too, if the Middle East is the military road to Africa as the Shah keeps insisting.

This morning I was pounding away at a typewriter in our office on Avenue Pasteur. A background of noises in the spacious courtyard. Went to the window. Almost the entire courtyard was dark with the sleek heads of young Iranians, in clusters of three or four, waving papers, talking together most earnestly.

The explanation: a couple of days ago we advertised that we had need for *four* trainees, to become operators at the Dez Dam; we got *four hundred* applications and most of the applicants were there this morning, filling out their papers.

It is quite a story, actually. For those four Iranian high school graduates (later there will be more) will be working in the powerhouse or the control room, under the tutelage of a group of *Canadians*. These are the seven or eight elite of the Ontario Hydro Commission's crew we contracted to train Iranian successors.

I get great satisfaction out of such a sight of young men, not a few the sons or grandsons of peasants or small teahouse operators, eager to move into the modern world of technical objects, and particularly so wonderful a symbol of change as is the great Dez Dem.

Difficult, indeed quite impossible to keep out of my mind the agonies of the people whose homes and lives were struck down in a few seconds by that terrible earthquake. The pictures appearing in the many Persian magazines are beyond imagination. Tortured faces of grief and shock. Men hauling their crushed young children out from under their collapsed homes, their faces so torn as hardly to be faces at all. The mothers are the saddest. "What has happened?" The ultimate in despair and confusion of spirit.

SEPTEMBER 21, 1962
TEHRAN

Today "Sunday or no" we go into the nuts and bolts of a budget for the ensuing period of "our" (i.e., D&R *and* the Iranian KWPA) year. The mundane affairs of supporting services, costs, the why and wherefores of pedestrian things are what are required to bring about these dramatic and sometimes flamboyant results about which I write what I fear are at times purple passages.

No limit to these old issues, familiar to me as a manager, but here in entirely new dress, so strange in attire that for a moment one doesn't recognize them as old friends—or old antagonists.

For example: I asked the Australian, Kerr, who is supervising the cane sugar growing in the second season: how much hand labor will there be in this season's cutting? Kerr is a bouncy, breezy man. He bounced: "All of it." Gordon and I did a "double take," asking Kerr for more details. He assured me that my concern about adequate supply of labor was nothing to worry about. But, I protested, it was lack of experienced labor for cane cutting that Brewer (the Hawaiian sugar company we engaged to run the plantation) blamed for much of the disappointing results of the first harvest a year ago. Why, we asked, do you think you can get skilled labor for all the cutting when last season you did so badly on only part?

Kerr gave us a sly grin. "We have contracted with the sheiks. They will guarantee to deliver us the labor."

My blood pressure dropped. Do these people know what they are doing? If we transfer our responsibilities to such men as the feudal sheiks, how can we then hold them responsible for results?

I was shocked. If our contractor paid the sheiks, who kept the money, this would be simply serf labor, to which they have been accustomed in times past in the Khuzistan. If, however, the sheik paid the once-serfs, but not enough, the men might just not show up; we'd get no cane cut or the sheik would have the gendarmerie called out to force the men to work.

We talked to Ansari about it. If the labor contracts were exclusively with the sheiks, this wouldn't work out. Our contractor should pay the men directly, and pay the sheik for his service in recruiting the men, if necessary. But the sugar operators must also offer to make direct contracts with cane cutters, so if the sheiks tried what might be called a "sheik-down" the sugar operation would not be entirely dependent upon the sheiks for labor supply.

This is one kind of worrisome and tiresome problem, far from a philosophical one, that one confronts all the time. The great big vague generalizations one reads in smart-aleck books about management overcome mighty few such day-to-day obstacles to results.

SEPTEMBER 22, 1962
TEHRAN

Is it possible for such a person as I am to fix a "program budget" *for myself* such as we devise for the orderly priorities and choices in such an undertaking as the Khuzistan development or as we used to, with such care, in the TVA? Since there isn't and can't be enough time and energy to do *all* the things I want to do and consider important in my life, how do I choose? That is essentially the budget process applied to a restless man.

The selectivity I insist upon as an administrator I seem to brush aside in making up my own budget of energy. I do far more than good sense will approve. Yet my strongest impulse is not to "budget" but to add new fresh experiences, particularly if this includes coming to know more people.

SEPTEMBER 23, 1962
CROSSING TURKEY BY PAN AM

An incandescent glow touches the folds of these mountains, so forbidding and gray in the full light of the sun. The shadows deep blue, the cliffs and peaks half gold, half rose.

Friday night an interesting party for us at the home of Soltani's parents. He is a former deputy in the Majlis from Bebehan, in the southernmost Khuzistan; now one of Ansari's deputy administrators. A square-built man of about thirty-five, big head on massive erect shoulders, a tough, straightforward, blunt manner, quite un-Persian.

During the evening he pointed a short index finger at me and said: "When I was in the Majlis I spoke for two days attacking *you*." He went on to explain, with no soft-soap or indirection, that our insisting on buying the fine land of Sheik Kalaff of Hosseinabad to raise sugar cane, when there was all that unoccupied "public domain," outraged him. Then he added: "I learned the facts, that you couldn't raise sugar cane on any except a particular kind of land. Now, as you know, I'm one of the whole program's strongest believers."

As we had stood and stood and stood for two hours, and I began to wonder whether we would *ever* get fed, the explanation for the long preliminaries appeared in the person of a smiling young man whom I recognized at once, even in the dim light of the garden, as the new Prime Minister, Amir Alam. Some four years ago we had a long luncheon at his home. A friend of the Shah's, he was then full of a project to organize an opposition party, a loyal opposition, to be sure, a party that would seek the suffrage for women and other reforms.

He was just back from a week's tour of Azerbaijan Province. The absurd centrifugal force drives *everything* into the Prime Minister's lap, under the Iranian system. Yet there was nothing in the face or demeanor of this lithe, laughing young man (perhaps forty-two) that would indicate that he wasn't getting ready to go on one of his many hunting trips. He has the words of the reformer, the rich man (a great landowner) who has picked up the emotions and slogans of help to the oppressed, feels quite virtuous about his genuine magnanimity but has still only a limited understanding of the agonies the slogans exact of a public official or political leader when they are translated into something real in people's lives.

10 P.M.
HOTEL PONT ROYAL
PARIS

Three hours of happy immersion in French middle-class (there is no more "middle" they say) late-summer holidaying in the parks of Paris. Babies (usually having their own way, in the best tradition of European parents, I have discovered), "characters," particularly wispy old ladies as grim as fallout, with hats that surely are out of a film; students (for I wove my way through the Left Bank college area); lovers nuzzling each other in a tender self-centered way, but hardly passionate, more awkward than passionate; intense men playing a kind of bowling game with steel balls that they hurled and twirled with utter concentration, and most colorful of all, a great circular pond (near the Tuileries) filled with tiny sailboats, the perimeter alive with young boys watching their bateaux go from side to side.

I could write a love letter tonight, a love letter to life, to the utter joy in seeing people, so many diverse people utterly absorbed in the enjoyment of a pleasant Sunday afternoon among their own kind. Once more I was awed by the windows of Notre Dame in the afternoon sunlight; once again I was enchanted by the elegance and grace of Paris. But it is the people, the unrolling processional of faces, everyone unique and different from every other, outside and in; it is this that renews my love affair with just being alive.

I was aware of a great satisfaction in not having a single soul to talk to, not a single face I knew or who knew me. It was glorious to be alone and yet in the very midst of bubbling life. I didn't see how I could ever be really lonely with so much to see. Perhaps I'd get over this, with a vengeance; but it wasn't so on this glorious day in Paris.

SEPTEMBER 24, 1962
HOTEL PONT ROYAL
PARIS

The reason I like this hotel—far from elegant itself, with no Swiss pros in long-tailed coats, their blood as chilly as their native Alps—is that it is in an area swarming with young people. College age. After sundown, and I suppose long after this old geezer has turned in, they sit around the tables of the sidewalk cafés gabbling like mad. A few girls, too, but mostly young men. An occasional couple, transfixed by the Parisian convention that they must walk with their arms about each other, he occasionally giving her a solid whack on the rump, she looking into his eyes as if he weren't buck-toothed, usually wearing glasses, hair in the present mode way down over his eyes like a Kerry blue dog.

Beards among young men have quite taken over, and those with heavy fierce ones sit rather apart, glaring like a young Confederate major or precocious brigadier of the Civil War. A delightful mixture, too, with a good many black young men spouting French, of course, and occasionally sitting off in a corner stroking the hand of a white French girl; this particular mixture is and for a long time has been the thing in Paris. But this area, because of the colleges, is full of tiny, delicate little people from what was once Indochina, ,and right attractive they are.

SEPTEMBER 25, 1962
PARIS

At the concierge's desk, as I was getting ready to leave, I saw the *back* of a man I recognized as Roy Wilkins, National Secretary of the NAACP, in Europe on his vacation. In ten minutes of relaxed talk the thing that impressed me most was his comment that the struggle of the Negro in America is only part of the worldwide, universal "resistance to change." The *foreign* aid program, Kennedy is finding out, is resisted "by the same people within America who keep on opposing TVA, after more than a quarter century of outstanding success."

SEPTEMBER 29, 1962
PRINCETON

The papers have been full, in the past month or two, with events in the "South"—the Italian Mezzogiorno—that are good to read. They seem also to demonstrate that the recommendations and impressions Gordon and I put together back in 1956-57 about that underdeveloped European region were not far from the mark, despite the cold reception they got at the time from Italian officialdom.* Perhaps that cool reception was the best sign that we had hit the nail on the head.

For example: the importance we placed on electric energy upon the future of the South. The other day the electric utilities of Italy were nationalized. This wasn't, I believe, wholly a *political* decision; or, rather, if the private utilities had been doing their job of keeping up with the great need for additional electric energy there wouldn't have been such fertile soil for the political issue.

Another example: Clapp's and my recommendation that heavy industry in the South was the only way to begin to come out of the sloth and stagnation of that region. This has now been confirmed—the big iron and steel works at or near Taranto is the latest example—that what we were saying wasn't nonsense, though unpalatable to the Ministers responsible for the country at the time of our expedition.

* The details of this work for the Cassa per il Mezzogiorno are set out in Volume IV of the *Lilienthal Journals*.

The same for the region known as Apulia. After our firsthand person-to-person inquiry we concluded that just doing more of the same, i.e., the processing of more and more wine and olive oil, would never revive that area. The recent stories from that region indicate that the industrial route is the one now being taken as a high priority.

Another instance is the concept I developed while we were advisors to Italy that restoration of southern Italy should rest in part on its historic position on the ocean routes east and west. This is beginning to take hold too.

There is some satisfaction in now and then being somewhat ahead of people's thinking.

OCTOBER 8, 1962
NEW YORK

A talk today with Jim Conant. Had I read Lewis Strauss' book? No, not yet. "Well," said Conant, "*his* recollection and mine are quite different. But he claims credit for having suggested that the AEC institute a system of detection of atomic explosions. Actually that was my proposal, made first in a meeting of the General Advisory Committee. But then I suppose there is no particular point in going back over things of that kind." I warmly agreed to that.

Said Conant: "In all that controversy about the H-bomb back in late 1949 and early '50, I don't remember any serious weight given to *delivering* the things. That's where the Russians were smarter than we were; with all our hullabaloo about a crash program to produce the H-bomb, the Russians saw that such a bomb without an intercontinental missile to deliver it was a lot of nonsense, and that's where they got their start on rockets. Do you remember anything being said about rockets to deliver the H-bomb if we were able to make one, which at the time seemed doubtful anyway?"

"No," I said, "I didn't, certainly not in that precise form. The nearest thing was Sumner Pike's opposition to the H-bomb until he had an answer to his question: what do the military say is the strictly military value of such a hypothetical bomb? He never got a clear answer. Also, he insisted we should be told whether we had planes or could make them that would carry such a weapon."

OCTOBER 10, 1962
NEW YORK

The possibility of a merger between Utah Construction and M&C-P perked up today. This is the off-again on-again way of so many business transactions of such a complex character, complex for one reason, among others, that the people who own each of the two enterprises are complex. Both want a marriage, for very good reasons of their own, i.e., that they would be better off together than as separate concerns. But each is full of fight talk that they don't want to surrender their respective right to boss the show to anyone else. If there is enough natural, i.e., economic, affinity between them, such very human objections can be worked out, I believe (though I am still a neophyte at mergers), by what I can only call corporate and financial carpentry. But if there is no basic reason for their being together, and it is only a financial maneuver, then it shouldn't be attempted.

OCTOBER 16, 1962
NEW YORK

Richard Heffner, since I first knew him six or seven years ago, has become a solid fullback-appearing man, with the marks on his face that show that he has been living through the fires that life lights and with which it also can burn her restless and imaginative and stubbornly dedicated children.

He is the general manager of New York's first "educational" TV station, WNDT-TV, now in its early days. We were lunching together, talking rather casually about the hourlong "interview" with me that is going on live the night after tomorrow. He told me a story about Ed Murrow, a man we both rather idolize, in our different ways, since Heffner is a TV "professional" and a young man, and I know Ed chiefly as a "reporter" and a friend.

"We had labor trouble—a strike—when we were finally to open our TV station in September. Strike by the union I am a member of; Ed too. Ed had promised he would open the station and preside over the first program—two and a half hours long. Then I heard that he was reported ill; I thought to myself: He doesn't want to cross the picket line, and I can't say I blame him. No; it was a very painful bursitis—is there any pain that is worse?—in his left hip, and he was bedridden and pretty miserable. But, sure enough, came the time for the program he didn't cross the picket line; he *dragged* himself across. He had two big codeine tablets with him, but he wouldn't take them because he was afraid it would make him drowsy. He had to sit, couldn't move, but he went through the two and a half hours. *Then* he took the codeine and dragged himself home. What a man."

OCTOBER 18, 1962
NEW YORK

One of the most excruciating experiences in my "life as a witness" came to my mind this morning, as I read that President Kennedy had signed legislation "repealing the requirement that college students who applied for loans under the National Defense Education Act sign an affidavit prying into their political beliefs and opinions. The bill also applies to graduate fellowships of the National Science Foundation."

My stand against inquiring into the political beliefs of the students having fellowships from the AEC in nonsecret atomic work, or even medical research, raised such a storm of criticism against me that even such friends as Brien McMahon and, God forgive, Lowell Mellett, called me aside in the big Senate hearing room to say this: "Dave, you are your own worst enemy. I don't see how you will ever get confirmation taking that kind of a position. You have to be practical about these things." And Lowell said I should testify the next day about how "rough" I had been on Communists in labor unions doing atomic energy work, as debasing a proposal as I can remember and yet coming from one of the purest-hearted liberals in the world. But that is now all water over the dam, rather dirty water over a leaking dam.†

I may be hopelessly naïve for this world. But if a position is wrong in principle, and you know it is wrong, what considerations of expediency can possibly justify approving it?

OCTOBER 23, 1962
NEW YORK

If the air is heavy with the smell of war it isn't discernible to me. This burnished and shining city, sharp and luminous in the brilliant light of the first almost-winter day, seems too sumptuous, the women too handsome, the men too elegant or preoccupied with "deals"—or women —to show outward signs of fear. I suppose Paris was not unlike this on the eve of other wars, and so was the little village of Norris on the Sunday that the amazing word interrupted the Philharmonic concert on the radio: the Japanese are attacking Pearl Harbor.

The President's order: stop Russian ships on the high seas bound for Cuba, twenty-four hours ago, Helen and I heard here together looking out over this glowing city. It was a strong, forceful statement, with no embellishment of anger or braggadocio.

In my NANA piece in the *New York Times* on July 8, 1960, and one on May 15 (at about the time of the U-2 episode) I called for an end to the wishful thinking then rampant that tensions should be and could be relieved by generalities, that "peaceful coexistence" was something worth taking seriously on the part of the Russians. I predicted a series

† See Volume II, pg. 528 et seq., for entries on the attack on Lilienthal for the AEC opposition to FBI investigations and loyalty oaths of recipients of AEC non-secret scientific fellowships.—Ed.

of incidents of which the turning of Cuba into a military base of the Soviets was one.‡

I don't foresee more "war" than we have been having for some time. But certainly a series of showdowns are bound to follow on the President's order to stop Russian ships on the high seas.

In our new D&R offices at One Whitehall Street for the first time. A dazzling view: the East River wharves, the tugs busy with their white trailers of foam; the Statue of Liberty almost in my office, she is so close, the harbor and Battery Park: a breathtaking office it is.

OCTOBER 24, 1962
NEW YORK

I have just come from a long evening at André's home at the Carlyle, talking merger with Littlefield of Utah and the Philipp people.

"Merger among the Masterpieces" should be the subtitle of this chapter of the Life Story of a Business—*if* the "dream" I laid before André Meyer last spring really moved as far along tonight as I sensed it *may* have. For the discussions of a merger between Utah Construction and M&C-P were conducted tonight with a Gauguin, a Cézanne, a Picasso, even a Rembrandt looking down at our grubby efforts at creativity. Grubby they are compared with those dreamers with brushes in their hands.

I keep saying "dream" because at dinner André, Ullmann, and Jesselson made so much of my "imaginative creativeness" in the original concept out of which these discussions of merger grew. I found to my modified delight that the original conception, and the reasons I thought these two companies could join with benefit to both, held up through all the mauling they have had. "Modified" delight because I am not really as interested in the *result*, pleasant as it would be to see increased value of my stock, as delighted with the fact that I can now and then come up with ideas of very broad scope that have a practical impact and have some appeal to men of affairs.

Ed Littlefield was clear, candid, handsome in a manly way, which helps; it is evident that the seeds I planted in San Francisco back in May in his mind and Marriner's have been sprouting. It is just plain *fun* to see this process, whether anything comes of this in an actual merger or not, and of course the odds are against it. And a tougher job of bringing two different kinds of people together I have never tackled.

‡ The article included the following statement: ". . . our minds should be prepared . . . for such possibilities or probabilities as the following, among others: the leasing by Cuba to the Soviet Union of air bases and missile launching sites . . ."

OCTOBER 26, 1962
PRINCETON

A footnote to my entry late Wednesday night after the merger discussion at André's home. The two groups of men represent a picture of American business that is waning, and someday (within a generation, I should guess) will be as rare as the bison, or the whooping crane.

Take Utah Construction first. Owned by two family tribes, not utterly dissimilar to the family tribal owners of a cluster of villages in Persia. The founders of Utah sixty-odd years ago were sons of pioneers to Utah. They made their great stake in construction, in a developing country, finally stepped out, with five other Western families of much the same kind, and got the government contract to build Boulder Dam, a highly creditable and very profitable job it was. There are now two distinct family groups, the Eccles, represented by that strong and powerful personality, Marriner, and his younger brother, George. They own about 15 percent of Utah. Most of the balance is owned by another "tribal" group, the Wattis family. Litttlefield, president, is a grandson of one of the original Wattis family. Though his group have the largest ownership, and therefore "power" to control, the real power is in the strong hands of Marriner.

Is this an anomaly of power? No, because, as Littlefield found it necessary to explain the other night, it was Marriner who had the ability and force and drive that brought Utah out of an internal row some years ago; it is his word that governs now, though he and Littlefield always consult, and Littlefield carries the actual operating responsibility.

So even in a closely held, old-fashioned kind of business institution, power isn't synonymous with ownership. But this setup is a far cry from Alcoa or Union Carbide, say, where the managers have very little of the ownership, the ownership of shares is so widely scattered among many shareholders that no one person or institution has power to control, or anything approaching that. This is the familiar picture that A. A. Berle drew as to Big companies, a generation ago: ownership of property and control separated. But here we have it in a company where ownership is *not* diffused, where it can be established that the Wattis group's stockholdings mean they *could* exercise power; but they don't. Eccles controls, i.e., has the power, because he knows how to run things or get men who can.

On the other hand, the Philipp Brothers group is about as different from Utah as can be imagined. Yet it, too, reveals the anatomy of power. Ullmann *owns* 16 percent of the M&C-P company, since the merger; Jesselson less, but still a large part. The Philipp group together, taken as a kind of tribe, and they are certainly a tribe, though not quite a family, certainly have the power.

Eccles says: "I don't want to merge Utah, where we know each other and can make decisions, with a group who could outvote us, precipitate a proxy fight, or serve as a rallying center for an opposition to us." He obviously would like the advantages of a merger with a "public" company, with Philipp's worldwide listening posts and trading capacities; but he wants assurance about the exercise of the power of large stock-ownership in the hands of this other tribal group.

Ullmann said with great emphasis and sincerity: "Power lies with those who can manage well. I would be prepared to work out some method that would remove power from my hands, because I know that I would not use my shares against a management that shows it knows what it is doing, as Utah does." The proposition about "power" is, Ullmann said, an academic kind of issue.

André was displeased that anyone, Eccles or anyone else, should expect that men like Ullmann and Jesselson, who had many millions in a company they had spent their lives building, should not be given proper consideration, in order to achieve a merger, however otherwise desirable. He made such an issue of it I thought things might break up without trying to see if these two views couldn't be reconciled. Perhaps they can't. But it is worth trying.

These variants of power in business terms, in human terms actually, are no longer real issues in the very big publicly held corporations, like General Electric, etc. The issue of power between these groups wouldn't continue to be an issue very long, should this merger produce a new small-giant, for the shares would be bought on the market until the proportion held by any one person would be greatly reduced, and after a few selective funerals the whole issue would disappear.

Whether agreement is possible—still highly dubious—to me this is a fascinating business drama to see at first hand and not in a book: the actual human actors before one's eyes.

OCTOBER 31, 1962
NEW YORK

Dictating three mornings in a row on the nuclear weapons "lecture." Hard work; even to dare to question "disarmament" (as I am doing) is like being against Home and Mother.

A talk with Lester Markel of the Sunday *New York Times Magazine*. Proposed that he consider an article about the Khuzistan as a *case*, a hard, discrete example of what goes on in the world, as a balance to the general, polemical, and philosophical articles about economic development by other professional writers.

Many people who submit articles to him say they find Markel a very difficult, even a mean man; but I get along well with him, partly because I never press: either he wants what I write, or suggest, or he doesn't. He has been on that job forty years, and in that time has pretty well stuck to the same line for his *Magazine*; it certainly has flourished, so the style and standards he has set must have merit.

NOVEMBER 6, 1962
NEW YORK

Scribbled off a note to André the other day, as a footnote to the evening's discussion of merger, to create a big international mining and trading company. The essence: international, yes; but the theme of such a natural resources company should be that the greatest underdeveloped country is the United States of America. To my surprise back came a note from him: I just want to say that I agree with your approach, and always have.

If there is excitement about today's elections I haven't detected it around here, sans the gubernatorial contest in California between the plodding but solid Pat Brown and that puzzling perennial in American political life, Richard Nixon, who was defeated.

The alarm about the confrontation between Russia and this country over the Cuban missiles has rather drained the country of its excess emotional energy; perhaps that is why the apathy about the elections.

NOVEMBER 7, 1962
NEW YORK

A cable from Iran: "River closure satisfactorily effected three a.m. Wednesday November seventh Williams."

God, what a relief.

NOVEMBER 8, 1962
NEW YORK

Deep asleep last night when the phone rang insistently. "Do you have any comment on Mrs. Roosevelt's death?" This brought me out of my dopiness right away, for of course I hadn't heard this news.

After prodding me with the usual questions the reporter then said: "We have been taking down what you have said on a tape recorder attached to the phone. Do you have any objection to our using parts of it on ABC radio?" What a thing: putting a recording device on your phone without telling you in advance that this is what you are doing. Good manners and electronic news-gathering need not be so inconsistent as all that.

Decisive times for our proposed expedition in the southwestern no man's land of the Ivory Coast. We should know by the end of the week whether it is possible to conclude arrangements with the U.S. AID organization in time to begin this winter. The rigmarole AID requires is so complicated and detailed that just doing the "processing" of papers, personnel, clearances, etc., will take darn near as much effort—if we do it their way—as carrying on the actual investigations.

This again emphasizes Gordon's question: Should D&R do *any* work that is paid for directly by U.S. money? A fine state of affairs. Most of these regulations, designed to satisfy critical Congressmen and the General Accounting Office, are so onerous and time consuming that they probably cause much of the inadequacy of the programs the critics complain of.

NOVEMBER 15, 1962
NEW YORK

Exciting talk this noon with Gordon about another possible avenue for our interests and talents: acting as management advisors to American universities. This came to him out of a talk with Raymond Kettler, financial Vice-President of the University of California, just back from Iran, where he acted as our consultant to KWPA.

Kettler sees that American universities are more and more the prisoners (my interpretation) of their huge research contracts with the U.S. Government, on the one hand, and legislative control, on the other. They need help to protect the basic purpose of the universities as Gordon and I see it, i.e., the students.

NOVEMBER 16, 1962
PRINCETON

Half alive.

The way so many people live. Just half alive. Drifting, like sleepwalkers. One day follows another, then a year is gone, then a lifetime.

Tonight, lying full length before an applewood fire, it hit me that I, too, am fully alive only part of the time. Am I, too, the prisoner of acquiescence, dragged down into the murkiness of that demi-life by those who don't have the spark of joy of life? Yes, the truth is I am, and without the wit or guts—or toughness on others—that it would take to stop this tragic waste.

"Spendthrift trust." That phrase, concept, from the law of trusts comes to mind. Alas, there is no spendthrift trust yet devised that can prevent a sixty-three-year-old inheritor of a finite number of days of full life from being a spendthrift of that legacy.

The Utah-Minerals & Chemicals merger idea has hit a rather unexpected kind of snag. I expected resistance from the Utah owners to any detailed and serious discussions. On the contrary, Littlefield reported on his return from Peru that they were prepared to favor the idea and go on to the next step. Jesselson was quite enthusiastic; Ullmann, anxious to retire, was still favorable. Then they talked to some of the lesser men in the Philipp organization. No enthusiasm at all. Could not see the "business reason" for such an alliance. The reason is a very human one, I think. With a Utah merger these men would not know anything about an important segment of the business, the business that Utah does. Trading in minerals is their life, these men; they know almost nothing else. They would feel unsure and less important in an organization that presented a new set of circumstances and challenges. At least this is the reason I ascribe for their feeling.

So these months of trying to make this work may have been spent to no concrete result. I wouldn't say to "no purpose," for the *experience* of trying to understand the men and the institutions involved was "worth" a lot to me.

NOVEMBER 20, 1962
NEW YORK

Luncheon at Sweets—grilled bay scallops, ever so sweet. Then wandered along South Street, imagining the days when the bowsprits of square-riggers jutted out into that famous street. Having just reread *Two Years Before the Mast* and part of *Moby Dick* I'm full of visions of the great clouds of sail that once must have stopped men's hearts with joy. And broke their spirit and body with hard labor.

Restless, after this and that, and lonesome, went tonight to Stravinsky's *Rake's Progress* at the beautiful Carnegie Hall. Place was jammed with opera fanciers or men dragged there by ennui or restlessness or their wives. I'm not an opera buff. Though the music was spirited and good, the posturing of the singers bored me stiff, so I left at the intermission with half my $9 ticket unused. That is just not my style, either the fancy-fancy audience or the artificial flavor of that kind of operetta. Waxworks, they seemed to me.

5:35 A.M. (IT IS NOW THE 21ST)

Being unable to sleep—quite wide awake in fact—have been reading those delightful scraps of a very young French country-bred girl's emotions: Colette's *In My Mother's House.* How I wish I could even now and then have the art that finds just the right word forever to snare and fix the moods that Colette so deftly and poignantly sets before a restless "elderly" gent, in a hotel room in the great city, so far, far removed in time and place from the sprouting young soul she writes about.

NOVEMBER 27, 1962
5 P.M.
NEW YORK

A rip-roaring sunset across the waters of the harbor, with the Lady of the Lamp peering out over the dark waters: a dramatic view it is.

Arthur V. Davis died the other day, at ninety-five. Made me recall the long sessions I had with him and his people of Alcoa, just before the war, working out the intricate transaction under which I was able to get the Fontana damsite owned by Alcoa made part of the "unified" Tennessee River. I shall never forget his eyes, which *never* batted, and his pudgy, short legs that just barely touched the floor in our rather crude offices in the Woodward Building in Washington, where these complex (and successful) negotiations were concluded.

DECEMBER 3, 1962
PRINCETON

Just back from a walk across the Common, to top off a day of intense mental activity. The world in its beauty overwhelms me completely. That moment of magic between the day and the night: the embers of the last rays of the reflected sun in the whole western sky and the evening star already having taken over the sky. The night belongs to the hard masculine light of the stars, not the soft feminine glow of the setting sun.

What made it all almost beyond bearing was the haze, a haze so smoke-blue and gentle that made things so familiar to me seem utterly new—the silhouette of the now leafless trees, the glow of the Institute alight with genius and electric lights. How positive and sharp the outlines, the patterns of those trees (I really think trees are more moving to the heart without their leaves) and yet the haze-light softened them without blurring. How happy such things can make a man.

Two Board of Directors' meetings last Thursday and Friday, the 29th and 30th, of such contrasts as to be hardly believable.

Thursday, from 8:45 a.m. until after 2, a rather stormy, wearing meeting of the full Board of Minerals & Chemicals-Philipp. On Friday, from 9:30 on until 3:00, the Trustees of Education and World Affairs.

In the corporation meeting hardheaded, intelligent, quick-witted, and transaction-tested men. By that strange latter term I mean men who live their lives in particular transactions—of buying and selling, of bidding on sales, of the terms of leases and exchange rates the world over, of a multitude of *particular* issues. Each one of these requires a kind of pragmatic concentration, a quality of judgment about particulars, only occasionally about a general proposition. Yet general principles can't be kept out of any activity, even though the participants may not fully recognize that what they are reaching for is some principle. Usually in business this is called not principle but "policy."

For example: Should the company buy its own stock? This comes up as a question of *at what price* does it make corporate sense to do this, in other words, can the company's money be better, i.e., more profitably, employed in buying its own stock at the current levels than in some other kind of investment, an apparently pedestrian and matter-of-fact issue. Yet this involves questions of principle too: "What will the stockholders think?" and from this one is first to consider what are the merits of an objection they might raise, or question they might ask, which must be answered on a platform of principle.

Or, again (and this discussion went on interminably), should the company stop its practice of declaring annual stock dividends as well as a cash quarterly dividend? Several of us thought it was "unfair" to stop the stock dividend policy abruptly without notifying stockholders of such a change, so they could sell out their holdings if they didn't like that. Others thought that since stock dividends make no sense, i.e., simply a further division of the equity into more pieces of paper, the practice should be stopped as not sound and an increase made in the cash dividend. Here again a specific transaction decision turned into a discussion—whether they knew it or not—of *principle*, i.e., fairness.

The Education and World Affairs meeting was of a startlingly different character. I thought the Princeton University President—Bob Goheen—most impressive. Then, too, John Hannah of Michigan State, big, gray, easy, but with strong conviction and experience showing in those remarkable eyes, pale blue, his whimsical half-smile; young Doug Knight, newly elected President of Duke, across the way, jolly and poetic but still sure of himself; Herman Wells, our Chairman, an almost round man physically but with the light in his eyes of a boy, so eager and happy, and with such savvy.

Ellsworth Bunker, austere and quiet, not popping off, as I fear I did, until he knew just what he thought. A businessman, Ray Eppert, with a single theme of "trade *and* aid" which he kept repeating as a kind of speech he had once made that he thought was good—and it was good.

I found it comforting that I felt at home in both of these quite different groups. But the big difference is this: the stakes and issues in the M&C meeting aren't really important, not really. In the other they darn well are.

A call from David. Another long stride ahead for our writer son. Bennett Cerf of Random had asked to see David. Cerf, David said in his restrained way, was very cordial. Said he found the story idea in David's second novel, *Seconds,* very interesting; that he hoped this was the beginning of a long association with Random House; asked how he was coming with his third novel; said he was exploring with motion-picture people the possibility of sale of the story as a movie, prior even to its publication, which occasionally happens, but not often.

DECEMBER 20, 1962
HOTEL MONTEJO
MEXICO CITY

Mexico City as we have seen and sensed it these past couple of days is so utterly different from the Mexico City we visited seventeen years ago as to be almost beyond either recognition or believing. The sickly-gray churches ("shrines") and the Cathedral are familiar, and so is the handsome stately Palace, the first structure of the conquering Spanish. But almost everything else, especially the faces, quite changed.

Helen and I walked in the park along the Paseo de la Reforma. Alive and gay and happy with Christmas: huge elaborate exuberant balloons and an incongruous figure among the camel, elephant, and three king figures: Santa Claus.

I bounced along in the swarm, and over my shoulder said to Helen: "Isn't this wonderful? I'm having a glorious time." She said: "You always feel wonderful when you are with the great unwashed." Said with some irony, but it's true in a strange way. I sometimes think my chief drive is to see that people have "a higher standard of living," as we used to say, and then after they get it, lose interest in them because then they get stuffy.

When I want to get some idea about a place I head for the markets, so this morning that is what we did; we went to the biggest one, Mercado de Merced I think is the name.

Four squat Indian women, in shawls, etc., discussing a purchase with a woman in the stall, all looking very earnest. The article under discussion was a brassiere; the saleswoman was pulling it way out to show how it stretched, I guess, while the Indians watched, with the most serious look.

The oldest customer for a brassiere was gray-haired, with the worn-out look of women who must work so very hard; the ages then ran down to a quite young girl. This thing about a bra you could tell was a mighty serious business.

I was amused; but actually it has a serious side. These women—and millions of others—are now able to do things that increase their self-esteem, and strapping themselves up so they look or think they look like the gals in the magazines, is one way of increasing their self-esteem. I remember seeing something like this in an open market in Nigeria, except there the big fat black woman was trying the thing on, also very earnestly, right in the middle of the stream of traffic.

Late today visited for an hour with a remarkable Mexican, an engineer, Adolfo Orive Alba.

Seventeen years ago he had taken us through the country to see some of the feeble beginnings of a water conservation and irrigation program. We had found him a warm and passionate man about the needs of poorer people. He had read about TVA, particularly my book, and was greatly stimulated about what "integral" development (the word the Latins use for what we call *unified*) could do for Mexico. A few months later Miguel Alemán was elected President, and appointed Orive Alba his Secretary of Hydraulic Resources, as the post later became. Hardly had Alemán been inaugurated when he made a trip to TVA with Orive Alba, who gave me, today, more detail about the result of that trip.

"Mr. Alemán," he said, pointing to his picture on the wall, "became very excited. On his return he said we should pick two regions in Mexico that needed help badly and develop them like TVA. So he established Comisiones—our word for Authority—in the basin of the Papaloapan, in the tropics, on the east, and another in the Tepalcatepec basin in the west. He gave us the money and told us to go ahead: dams, irrigation, health, schools, roads, everything *put together,* integral. That was the essence of TVA to us. He put the former President Lázaro Cárdenas in charge of the western TVA and he wrought a miracle. Where before people were sick of malaria and exhausted from the heat, and starving to death, now they export melons, fruit—the place is a kind of paradise. All of this," he said with Latin gusto and exaggeration, "came from your book and your work, Mr. Lilienthal."

Orive Alba is by descent a Basque. Tall, lean, stooped, saturnine, with the profile of a very earnest hawk; the most brilliant of eyes, eyes that burn when he talks about the tough time people have in his country, how the rich and the landowners are *again* dominating the country.

I had remarked on what great progress Mexico had made; half the food of the country comes from land irrigated since he became Secretary of Hydraulic Resources. Things look different in the city, and I assume all through the country.

"Yes, but don't be misled. There is great discontent. Many people can hardly live; peasants revolt and are shot down, but you don't read about this in the papers; you only read in the papers what the Government wants printed."

He was obviously a disturbed man. He thinks Mexico is better in this disparity between the rich and the poor than any other Latin-American country, but it is far from safe from revolt. "When people get hungry they say they are Communists. They don't know what Communism is, these poor people; they just want to eat."

Quite bitter and upset and so intense he fairly made the room— his dark-paneled office—burn with his passion.

DECEMBER 22, 1962
SATURDAY
MEXICO CITY

Saw my first *New York Times* in two weeks here in Mexico City: it contained a story about Mexico that tended to confirm the basic facts that accounted for Orive Alba's cry of outrage the other day.

The story simply said that a peasant-labor group was organizing to speed up the lagging land reform in this country and to protest to the Government about the treatment of peasants in some of the country areas by the police and military, going on to say that there was distress in these areas "and even some hunger."

This dissipates the feeling I had that Orive Alba was overstating and overdramatizing when last Thursday he described the dark clouds of revolt he feared might descend over his country. Of all Latin America I thought Mexico had moved further toward social reform than any other.

Indeed, this has been a country built upon a social revolution. I had in mind not only the political independence bought with the blood of martyrs against outside foreign oppression, or the expropriation of the Rockefellers' and other oil barons' holdings that shocked so many people in the U.S., or even liquidation of the Church's temporal power. I knew that the peasants had been given land, and the workers' modern social benefits and the right to organize; in both of these areas my impression wasn't wrong, but as to rural areas apparently the reforms were not effective; more promises than fulfillment.

Orive Alba spoke almost in anguish about how badly the U.S. Alianza para el Progreso had fallen from its original purposes. The blame for this he put squarely on "the men in your Government two or three, how shall I say it? layers? down from the top. President Kennedy— what he said the other day—if you wrote it down on a piece of paper [and Orive Alba went through the motions of writing on an imaginary piece of paper] I would sign it, word for word, just as he said it. And with such sincerity and feeling.

"No, between what he wants for Latin America and what is happening—it is very sad.

"I was in Santiago, in the Dominican Republic, last winter; arrived just a day after you had left. The Inter-American Bank asked our firm for our opinion about a thermal electric plant at Santiago.

"What did I see? Trujillo gone, dead, killed. But the rich families that were part of Trujillo's system, the people he had made rich and powerful—*they* were the ones your ambassador and your foreign aid people were working with hand and glove, like this [demonstrating with those intense flickering long fingers, as he fairly crouched to emphasize his feeling].

"So, that is the way all through Latin America. Your President is for just the right things, that these very, very poor people get a chance. And your State Department people are doing just the opposite.

"A man of your stature—you should go and tell President Kennedy what is happening."

On our walk back to the hotel tonight, a bus stopped in the middle of the block, and a happy bouncy Mexican family, papa, mama and two small children jumped off, ran and skipped back of the bus to dart across the street. A flash of a car, a terrible sound, and the whole family was stretched out in the street. Only one of the little ones seemed hurt badly, it seemed.

When I had absorbed this and got to the hotel, the clerk handed me a cable. Both Helen and I drew a sharp intake: *now* what.

"What," however, wasn't something bad; on the contrary. A cable from Gordon that after two nonstop days of negotiation the new project in southwest Ivory Coast had been worked out and finally approved; so "now we can start the work. Merry Christmas." I must take back what I have said that nothing but paper work came out of any kind of dealings with the AID organization.

DECEMBER 23, 1962
ISLAND OF COZUMEL, MEXICO, OFF THE YUCATÁN PENINSULA

This noon we flew into this *once* isolated spot, an island about the size of the blessed Vineyard, perhaps fifteen miles from the mainland.

What impresses me most, I think, in coming to this place so far from home is that it is filled with middle-class income Americans, coming distances that would have been considered out of the question not so long ago. Two of the people on the tiny handkerchief of a beach identified themselves to each other as elementary schoolteachers. My heart doesn't bleed quite so much at the low salary of our teachers if they can afford a trip of this length for a ten-day vacation.

DECEMBER 24, 1962
5:15 P.M.
COZUMEL

Sundown: Christmas Eve, 1962. An orange sky, with the edge, the last edge of sun at this very moment slipping into the Golfo de Mejico. The mountains of billowed clouds are still pink, but soon it will be colorless and the early twilight will be followed by the early night of the Caribbean.

Sitting out here on the sand, only the gurgle and splash of this tideless calm sea as it strikes the coral, that is all, all but the blue-gray of the sea. But not all: I can hear the deep half-roar of tractors up the beach, preparing the way to turn this "remote" island into another busy vacation playground. "Affluence" thrusts its frenetic diversion-loving finger farther and farther into the remote parts of the world.

DECEMBER 25, 1962
COZUMEL

I was sitting crosslegged on the coiled anchor rope in the very bow when a flash of steel blue arched right under the bow; El Capitán—at the tiller—yelled "Porpos." A pair of huge porpoises then began a game with our boat, swimming under the bow where I could almost reach over and touch them, then arching out of the indigo water and back again. A perfect ending—for we were chugging back in the 40-foot local motor-sailor—after a day I enjoyed, actively and wholeheartedly, as much as any expedition on water and beach that I can remember.

I am still rather bewitched by the experience of living, for a half hour or so, in another world, and yet a world that lies no farther away than the difference between the surface of the water and the underside of that surface. In my snorkel I saw such a sight of caverns, absurdly garish fish and schools that were pale green, delicate as the first touch of green on the willows in early spring, a sluggish huge grouper along the bottom, 30 feet below—a galaxy of gliding beautiful motion amid the coral and fans of a tropical underseascape.

The men and young boys who were with us on the schooner were delightful companions. We had a great time toasting Feliz Navidad to each other, in beer and Bacardi rum, of which later I had more than "necessary" in my enthusiasm for celebrating Christmas in a pair of minimum trunks; the animal joy of being on the water along a jungle coast.

The isolation I was so disappointed *not* to find the first day here I found to the *n*th power today.

These Mexicans we find extremely attractive, charming people. Their dignity is impressive and pleasing. On the boat the diver, a sturdy handsome young man, the engineer and the captain, all members of the same family, invariably addressed each other in this way: "Señor."

DECEMBER 26, 1962
COZUMEL

Do I have enough courage or insight to set out in the journals how I feel about the life *within*: those fragile but powerful and real— terribly real—emotions that are apart from the things one does?

Thus far in the long history of these journals there have been mighty few such entries.

I have not spared myself in being candid and even overcritical about my work, my relations with the people I worked with and for or against, and so on. I didn't "edit" at the time to make me "look good," or conventional, or respectable.

But that part of a man's life—the outward one—is only a part. And as time goes on and I gain what I believe is a truer sense of what is most important I realize how little did I face up to my emotional storms and deficits; how impossible it was for me to write down some of the efforts I made to break out of spiritual ennui or frustration.

Fictional writing, great and mediocre, for centuries has recorded agonies that go on inside a man that have nothing—or little—to do with his work, his responsibility, his movement through his days.

One might point to Pepys and Boswell to the contrary. They did write it *all*, so it is said. But their journals aren't on the precise point I have in mind. What makes their self-revelation most distinctive is that they wrote of what they *did*, not the least what they did as male animals, with extraordinary candor and explicitness. It is not the absence in my own journals of this kind of recording of sexual adventuring that is a challenge to me. After all, sexual explicitness, often deliberately written to excite, this one can read about in scores of novels or dull how-to-do-it manuals. But what about a man's feelings (or a woman's) when he pits his basic urges, whether "good" or "evil," against the expectations and restraints and *institutions* that have been built up to keep those basic urges within what society considers permissible limits?

The constant drive of ambition, or vanity, or waves of self-pity about things that have nothing whatever to do with one's love life (or lack of it!) are things I have difficulty in writing with utter frankness. This kind of reflection has led me to speculate on whether I could, now, write an emotional memoir, either contemporary or retrospective. The kind that I would have to put away in a safe for fifty years.

More than once in the past twenty years I have been attracted to the idea of writing fiction, a novel. Now and then I recall putting down fragments of a plot or theme, or situation, or even a splinter of a scene. The impulse to do this occurs more and more often recently; part of the reason is that I feel I have more to say than a factual or first-person record would enable me to say.

The role of fiction as a *release* I can now see more clearly. But the people I would "invent," the situations I would roll out would be more a way of saying the otherwise unsayable than the more customary way of the fictionist, who after all can never completely exclude from his fiction his own story.

But a writer of fiction is first and foremost a storyteller. What fiction I might write—an unlikely possibility—would be not so much invention or storytelling for its own sake (which is what fiction should be) but an effort to overcome the inhibition I have to tell my own story and tell it *completely*.

Relationships become institutionalized—that is what happens. What an individual once *felt* becomes congealed, caught in the grip of an institution, a *formal expectation*.

An example: near us, on this little island, is one of the runaways from the rigors of an institutionalized life: an American of about forty (he has the corroded look and shamble of a much older man). He has but little money; he lives here the life of freedom he wanted, in revolt against something back home. For some time he has been sleeping with a tall, exotic-looking Mexican girl. We saw them having drinks in the dining room the other night. But it is evident—or was to me—that this apparently casual and *free* kind of emotional relationship has also become institutionalized. She isn't his wife; he isn't her husband. But the expectations and conventions of *the* kind of freedom they have take on a shape that can only be described as conventional. It was written on his face so plainly.

There is no escape, perhaps, from living by the world's expectations, or your own; the notion of an existence that is wholly one's own is probably a myth.

DECEMBER 27, 1962
COZUMEL

Returning from our expedition along the coast of this island day before yesterday we saw, in the harbor of San Miguel (the only town on this island) a ship so huge that it could only be a cruise passenger ship—until we got closer. It was a private yacht, at least 200 feet long, flying the flag of Liberia. On her upper deck were *two* power launches, each not less than 30 feet. The yacht is owned by the multi-millionaire David Ludwig, the same ship we had seen in Manila Harbor three years ago.

This morning we drove into San Miguel. Our driver, whom everyone calls Oscar, looked out at the white cloud of the huge Ludwig yacht with a wry grin on his face. "This morning the man who owns that ship came to my boss; he said to my boss: 'I need a boat. Can you get me a boat?' " Said Oscar with a belly laugh: "*He* needs a boat."

The year 1962 is fading. These are the days of the year when for so many years I have almost invariably *looked back,* to review and cast a judgment, add the accounts, for the year that is dying.

But this time I'll leave the year-end look-back for some later day.

Why this sense of impending vigor and excitement in the twelve months *ahead*?

The heart of the reason is that I have great expectations of challenge, risk, danger, controversy, uncertainty, the driving of personal, deeply felt guidelines of a new road for the "new man" who has been coming alive, emerging, since the hibernation period that followed my leaving public life thirteen years ago.

I find I have an eagerness *about the future* that makes my past "achievement" marks along the road, warmly satisfying as they are, less on my mind at "appraisal time" than the prospect of things ahead.

Some of these unpredictable events ahead will likely taste once more of the smoke and tension of battle. For example, my re-entry into the atom controversy, and particularly the challenge I lay down to the phony of the "peaceful atom," or disarmament. When these Stafford Little Lectures appear in book form later in the year I will probably find myself attacked for the first time in years, or criticized, forced to defend and support my views.

When the first two volumes of the *Journals* appear in February, 1964, they may bring down on my head a swarm of buzzing hornets, sticking out their stingers for reasons varying from the "good taste" of publishing these intimate records while I am still alive to attacks on the veracity or fairness of what I wrote so long ago and am now publishing.

But perhaps more than these reasons lead my mind and imagination and sense of anticipation to the future.

I am convinced that I am better prepared at this moment to run *to* life, rather than running away from it, than ever before since I can remember. I feel I have been through a period of refreshment that makes me able to fulfill the life force within me, not halfheartedly but wholly.

No more for me, I hope and believe, the caginess, the caution, the holding back, the fears, the shutting out of those vistas of life that would not further what I used to call "my work," as if living *fully* was not my primary "work."

In short, I have been through a several-year course of re-education in living itself. To that kind of fuller way of living I look forward with an ardor and an eagerness that even the somnolence of this tropical island and the setting, designed for that strange phenomenon "planned rest," cannot wholly dampen.

DECEMBER 29, 1962
COZUMEL

I came up the sharply rising beach where my two Mexican non-descript, beat-up "crew" had anchored an equally beat sloop we had sailed from San Miguel yesterday morning. Under the palmetto thatch, seated at a kind of picnic table, was a very tall lumbering fellow, per-haps ten years younger than I. He called to me, in the irrepressible friendliness of the American away from home: "Speek Eenglis?" This tickled me. I said I did, a little, and laughed. In the American routine he spoke his name, introduced his wife and a younger American with them, and then waited for me to say "I'm So-and-so" and shake hands —which I did, of course.

Was I the Lilienthal who had been in the Federal Government?

Which then started him off, leaning forward, and quite intense; about how I had contributed so much to my country and to others. He had been brought up on a farm in Kentucky, and later in Missouri. His speech showed it, pleasantly, in the drawl that has fooled so many people into thinking that slow speech means a slow wit. Hog-killing when the frost comes. Tough going in the depression years. The hollows under his eyes were deep as he recalled all this, hardly paying me any mind. "Then because I was overweight I got to go to college as a foot-ball player [a wry countryman's reference to his really magnificent giant's frame—what an end he probably was] and went on to California, where we live now."

"Everything that has happened to me since has been something *coming to me*. Citrus raising. Buying real estate and developing shopping centers. My country has done so much for me and I haven't done any-thing back. I think of a man like you, who has done so much to build up this country, and getting abused and criticized for it too, and I just feel there ought to be some way that men like me can give three months or six months a year 'without compensation.' " (He underlined this more than once, this theme of a penitence you drop through a slot in the box at church.) "A young lawyer that works for us came to me the other day, said he was going to join the Peace Corps, wanted to do something useful that practicing law wouldn't give him. I think our young people are wonderful, wanting to go out into other young countries and help. There's a lot more of this feeling among us *older* men than you might think."

He still can't completely believe it: that the lanky farm boy who saw his parents struggle through the dark years of the thirties now can make a trip to a kind of South Sea paradise right in the middle of the winter. All coming one way, he says, never paying it back.

How much of this is relieving a mild sense of "guilt"—that was the word he used—and how much is just making conversation to a man he unexpectedly comes on, stepping out of a native sailing boat on that beach I can't say. Just the same, even to have such feelings is a good thing.

A very full year indeed it has been. As I walked the shore this morning these things about 1962 ran through my mind:

That in this year there has been no decline of zest nor of joy and excitement nor of looking ahead; that curve continues to point upward; not living immersed in "blandness" nor the beginning of mental retirement: quite the contrary. When I was told—with conviction: "You can do anything you *want* to do" or "You haven't yet used to the full your potential" I found myself believing this and acting accordingly.

This is an emotional more than an intellectual attitude. The *events* of the year confirm this feeling of a beginning rather than the orderly retreat of an "elderly man," a retreat known as "preparing oneself" for "retirement."

Of more *specific* things these stand out, almost in this order:

The recognition that came to David as a writer—two novels accepted, several stories. The decision of Canfield that Harper publish the *Journals,* in six or seven volumes. The achievement of our first goal in the huge Persian job, with the dream of seven years ago now an unfolding, visible reality after incredible difficulties. The greater self-confidence, born of a deep feeling of being needed, of being always in the presence of profound warmth. The decline of interest in being a private businessman in the conventional Minerals & Chemicals sense and an increasing interest in the special kind of private-public business that is D&R; an increased appreciation of the qualities that Gordon Clapp and John Burnett possess to a degree, qualities that, too, must be called a kind of genius, a genius for public service.

I have added to the number of distinctive people I know, always one of my measures for any period, whether a year or a decade. But it has not been new people so much as the discovery of *new dimensions* in people I already know well, qualities of depth and beauty and strength. Most of all Beatrice, whose facets of wisdom and understanding seem infinite. She, during the year, has opened my eyes to the vividness of the world of things and of people which she herself sees and lives, the world of the artist, not only in paints but in living. Gordon is another example: A new warmth of personality, almost as if I had found a new friend instead of rediscovering an old and tried one.

DECEMBER 31, 1962
MÉRIDA, YUCATÁN

A memorable year, one that grew out of earlier years, earlier lessons in living, earlier skills, earlier trials and harassments and joys.

Did the year *resolve* anything at all for me, as an individual? No. The most important questions remain unresolved.

Such an assessment could have been written at the beginning and the close of *every* year I have lived. When I breathe my last will I even then have come closer to a resolution than when I was a boy of seventeen, writing the first florid sentences in that old leather-bound account book back in May of 1917?

I am one who wants everything; whose life has been a full one, restless and seeking. Such a person can never find answers. Only new questions.

V

1963

~⟨0⟩~

JANUARY 2, 1963
FLYING TO MEXICO CITY FROM MÉRIDA

A gentle-mannered soft-voiced man raised his hand in the salute
that among Americans means "Hi"; I did the same. Somehow it didn't
seem at all remarkable that this was Roger Blough, president of U.S.
Steel, sitting at a table with other Americans by the pool of the Hotel
Pan Americana in Mérida. Blough rose, met Helen, and invited us to
meet his friends. One a gray-haired man with the darting fierce eyes
of an eagle, James Black, chairman of Pacific Gas and Electric, utility
boss of California for many years, with his wife, a lively and attractive
woman. While we were in that crummy hotel at Cozumel they had been
on Ludwig's huge yacht.

Yesterday was a big day, for I had set my heart on having Helen see *some* ruins, so dear to her heart. After false starts—at Oaxaca there was no room at the inn—we saw the remarkable remnants of the Mayans at Chichén Itzá and the day before at Uxmal.

The young Mexican father across the aisle has just performed the classic and explosive rite of making things *exactly* equal between the shrieking demands of siblings, his two kids. Two nursing bottles of milk, opened, judicially part of one poured into the other, demonstrating that the amounts in each were equal, while the dark-eyed kids followed the ceremony intently, solemnly.

I said to Black: "I saw your announcement that PG&E is to build a large atomic power plant." "Yes," he said, "we already have a small one operating; the next one will be 350,000 kw. Congressman Holifield of the Congressional Joint Committee wants us to accept a subsidy—$10 million, whatever you want, he said to me. They want to get their political hands into it. I said 'nothing doing.' "

JANUARY 4, 1963
FLYING TO NEW YORK FROM MEXICO CITY

If you are eager to get back to your work, they say, then your vacation has been a success and you are "rested."

In a couple of hours more we set down at Idlewild, and the pressures of an active, responsible, exciting life begin again. I cut our stay short a day so I could have "contact" just that much sooner.

Mexico I left with a good optimistic feeling: friendly, handsome people; a country that is changing itself, yet with an undertone of uneasiness—and I hope of a kind of guilt—about the way in which the poor devils, particularly in the rural areas, are struggling with the kinds of problems of bare subsistence that brought on a series of revolutions in an earlier period.

Somewhere during the recent I don't quite know how many weeks, my old feeling of the iconoclast, the man who speaks up for the underdog, has returned full force. I never have lost it entirely, of course; but I must be honest with myself: it did diminish. The Tennessee Valley had become a success before I left; the AEC was off in a humanless kind of world of the unseen and the overintellectualized. The business experience with Lazard and with Minerals & Chemicals, etc., stirred me up to the excitement and intellectual and money rewards of business life. I honored businessmen more because it seemed to me—perhaps mistakenly—that they, rather than the present-day labor leaders or big farmers, had become certainly not "underdogs" but the misappreciated men, the undervalued *function* in society, in social reform even.

Now I feel myself sensing afresh the meaning of what drives me in the D&R enterprise, and should drive me in the years to come *within* my own country: the fate of the people who have a hard time of it.

The impersonal song of the economist—GNP, figures of production, etc.—is an alluring one. It disguises by its facelessness the human condition of *individuals*. And it is to individual human beings that one's commitment should be, first, last, and always.

JANUARY 5, 1963
PRINCETON

Early this morning Nate Greene phoned. He had read and reread the manuscript of the Little Lectures; was in strong disagreement, strongly expressed. My attack on disarmament is of course what upset him, as it did David and Joe Volpe when they first knew of the position I was considering taking. David and I analyzed this opposition again today; he has no doubt about it, after two weeks of letting it cool, nor have I. But I can see that it will cause considerable pain among my friends, and those who believe that the *first* thing in this world is to "contain" the nuclear arms competition, to use Nate's word, and who will consider my position as putting me in bad company.

I anticipated Nate's reaction; but I didn't believe he would feel so strongly about it, for he customarily takes a professional advisor's position of not becoming emotionally committed: giving his opinion and letting it go at that.

So I find myself faced with the temptation to soften the impact of the position to avoid stirring up a hornet's nest. I must be sure I say what I mean reasonably clearly and that I believe what I say; then take the consequences.

JANUARY 14, 1963
PRINCETON

For three consecutive days Helen and I have been going through a husband-wife routine begun nearly forty years ago: whipping out the final versions of a piece of thinking and writing. As always, her steadiness and patience have helped enormously, together with a willingness to do whatever needs to be done, such as typing and retyping and retyping an endless series of changes. This rewriting reflects my determination to make the Little Lectures (for that is what it is all about) as nearly clear and difficult to distort by critics as possible.

Finding one's way through the maze of ideas, counterideas, the difficulty of expressing an idea without understanding it—the whole can of worms involved in a serious discussion of a most serious problem—have made this one of the toughest thinking and writing assignments of my career.

Read David's first book, *Trot,* yesterday. I was completely gripped by the story, a true "novel of suspense." But what most impressed me was the insight into all facets of life that shone throughout the telling of a fast-moving narrative, an adventure. His *understanding,* his sense of compassion, his recognition of the evil there is in the good people and the good in the evil goes far beyond my comprehension of life at that—or my present—age. He is way, way ahead of me at his age, in understanding of what the world is all about, both more realistic and more imaginative.

As Peggy says, he is extraordinary because he combines a sense of fantasy and imagination with an almost fanatical sense of "deadline," to use her expression. When he takes on an assignment it is done, you can count on that, on time, or else; and everyone else around him must adjust to his sense of precision. And yet he can write an almost surrealist story like *Seconds,* his second novel.

JANUARY 19, 1963
PRINCETON

Dinner last evening, Helen and I, with Leona Baumgartner and Nat at their apartment in Washington Mews. She has had a more than usually frustrating beginning of her career as deputy director of AID. No luck at all in recruiting people—this is the tough part for a good administrator who left a well-operating organization, as she did, to take over an ailing one.

Leona doesn't let things get her down very often, even momentarily. But this truly distinguished person told us that she was so discouraged by this impossibility of getting a good staff, and the attitude of the other government agencies toward AID, that as she left for Washington from the Mews a couple of weeks ago she cried, a bit. "Something I haven't done since I don't know when," she said with that captivating grin of hers. But she will lick this problem too.

Leona told a wonderful and revealing story about President Truman. "I was at a White House function of some kind—a small group— and the President was brought into the room, and I was presented as 'a gal from Lawrence'—which out there in Missouri means the University of Kansas at Lawrence.

"The President's face lighted up. 'Did you go to the basketball games?' Oh, sure, of course I did, all of them. I knew Fogg [or was it Goff?] the coach. 'You knew Fogg! Say, I never missed a game that I could help—Independence is just across the state line.'

"Whereupon we got talking about this game and that, the crowds; he even reminded me of how hard it was *to park*. There we were, the President and I, going to it about basketball in Kansas when an aide came along and said, 'Mr. President, I wonder if you shouldn't step over and greet,' well, someone, an ambassador maybe. Truman's face fell; he was having such a good time reliving the days when a big basketball game was the center of his attention. I thought it was a wonderful kind of light on that remarkable and unassuming man."

JANUARY 21, 1963
WASHINGTON

(Written while sitting with the Trustees—mostly university presidents—of Education and World Affairs, Hay-Adams Hotel.)

If this discussion we are hearing at times seems pretty pedestrian and aimless, remember that the same thing goes on in meetings of Boards of Directors of *businessmen*—such as the most recent one of M&C-P I attended.

I am here today in a world of "educators"—a world as new and strange to me as nuclear physics was on that fateful Saturday afternoon in Norris back in 1946 when I faced the fact that in a few days I would be asked to take over atomic energy.

The big event today: a couple of hours watching a really first-class public servant as he met with the EWA Trustees, and responded to questions about the AID program.

David Bell, when he came into our EWA conference room at the Hay-Adams, preceded by Leona Baumgartner, gave the same physical impression that our son David does: of a pleasant crane, leaning forward a bit to compensate for being so much taller than most people.

The thing that most struck me, as he talked and listened, was his serenity. Here was a man who, as director, had just prepared the largest budget in the history of the country, and had then been shanghaied to take on a discredited and unhappy huge program, foreign aid. His demeanor showed that he was serene inside. This will stand him in good stead, even if it is only the *appearance* of sureness: I recall that after weeks of watching me as a witness, the magazines almost always referred to me as the "soft-voiced unruffled Lilienthal." I was in fact *plenty* ruffled; but it is important to keep that under control.

In the morning session I kept reminding my university fellow Trustees that an administrator has to begin with the problems that face him urgently; that he will want to know: What can I, as the man in charge, *do* about this or that problem? What can you fellows do about them?

JANUARY 26, 1963
PRINCETON

"The public dinner at the Waldorf" is as much a part of New York as the chronic traffic constipation. But the public shindig I attended last Wednesday night, as one of the wax works on the dais, was a very special and memorable one.

For the "honored guest," as all the introducers say, was that mighty little personification of anonymity, Jean Monnet. The occasion: the Annual Award of Freedom House, an award I received in 1949.

Last Monday I thought to myself: He won't be there; it will have to be awarded in absentia. De Gaulle, fresh from his triumph at the polls and hard-nose at Washington and London, had thrown his biggest roadblock to date into Monnet's years of work in developing European unity. In 1950 the British told the French that they, the British, were really not of Europe, but of their world empire, the Commonwealth. So they weren't interested in joining the Schuman Plan. Last Monday De Gaulle turned the tables: the U.K. couldn't be admitted.

And *at such a time* here was Monnet coming to America to receive an award for his work in unifying Europe.

He not only did not renege; he stood up (all 5 feet 3 of him) before that big audience and said: Britain must of necessity be a part of the Common Market, the same thing he said in 1950 when we were his guests in his country house near Paris. The French Ambassador, sitting next to him, didn't move a muscle of his face, fearing the fiery blast from those huge De Gaulle nostrils, no doubt. The Ambassadors of the other countries did not join in the applause. But Monnet knows more about the tidal currents of history than any other man I have ever known, not excluding F.D.R. He knows that, whatever setbacks there may be this week or month or year, the tide is running, and in time the British despite De Gaulle and other setbacks *will* become part of one of the greatest unions in history.

Personal recollections are stirred by all this. For example, Helen reminded me that in June, 1950, I was asked to consider becoming the "emperor" of the Coal and Steel Community; this morning I found a story in the London *Mail* to that effect.

I was seated on the dais at what would be left end if this had been a football lineup. Next to me Paul Hoffman, then Harry Gideonse, then Walter Lippmann, one of the speakers. The presiding chairman was Roscoe Drummond, who is a bright, delightful little cricket of a man, hardly 5 feet, I'd say. The lectern before him was massive; the long necks of the dozen microphones sticking out at him were like the hissing of geese. When he stood up to open things it was apparent from where I sat looking down the line that out in front in the audience no one could see him. So a box of some kind was provided hastily and he stood on this. Monnet too is short, and what people in the audience could see was apparently a disembodied red-cheeked, imperturbable face; no body back of it. That indomitable Christian Herter, poor fellow, now terribly crippled from arthritis, was brought a stool on which he *sat* while he made his remarks.

The sight of all these mechanics from the sidelines was a diversion, but not so much that I wasn't greatly moved by the occasion. For Monnet has a quality not too often honored and recognized: he has *always* been content to get the job done and let others have the kudos. Which is perhaps one reason why he has got so much done.

I was particularly struck with what George Ball said. His was not the kind of speech someone else writes, I thought; it had a ring that seemed to come from the innards of a man I didn't know could show so much power and conviction.

A brief talk with General Lucius Clay about the foreign aid program: he has been named chairman of an advisory group of pretty tough characters, such as Robert Anderson, etc. Yes, he agrees, he has a good impression of David Bell. "But I think the foreign aid program right now is a salvage operation." I think I know what he means and, unhappily, agree. I remember I predicted in what deep trouble it was getting three years ago, in the TV program I did for Ed Murrow in Tehran.

A call from André, would we come over and see him? Gordon and I and Nate met him Wednesday morning. André relaxed, exuding the charm that is something he has lots of when he is out to "charm."

"What would you think of a possible merger of D&R with Utah Construction & Mining Co.? David brought this important idea forward as a possibility between Minerals and Utah. At the time I thought it might become a constructive thing for a three-way merger. You have things that would strengthen Utah and they could make you more secure, broaden the things you would like to do, improve the financial picture for you by trading your shares for theirs. But the Philipp people thought the idea, as to Utah, wasn't good, after considering it very carefully, partly because it would mean too much of the income of the two companies would come from South American iron ore, Chile and Peru.

"So now I wonder if you feel like considering such a merger, leaving out the Minerals side of it? I think it has great possibilities for you; it would not mean much one way or the other to Lazard.

"The first thing is whether you two men want to do it."

To my surprise Gordon did not immediately shy away from the possibility, as he did when I first vaguely suggested it last summer. The financial advantages may seem more clear to him now, though I doubt if that will ever loom very large to him—or to me either, I guess, since we don't need money. If either Gordon or I should die, our widows will not get much out of the not inconsiderable surplus we have managed to accumulate on D&R's books, because the shares have a restricted market, can only be sold to other stockholders, which would mean Lazard or the survivor as between us.

A similar situation occurs in almost every closely held or family-owned enterprise. Indeed a good many mergers these days are made because the shares of a family business must be sold under a kind of duress on the death of important holders, whereas if the business can become part of a bigger undertaking, with shares that have a market, this problem is not present.

I have come to know André's methods well enough to know he will do what he says he will do, i.e., approach Utah and try to make this work out, giving of that terrific strength and ingenuity that he has.

"Deterrent."

How this term has been used as if it were a form of arms control, a step toward disarmament and peace. As I follow the nuances of the cult that is erected on man's anxiety for peace I sense that all of this preaching of the doctrine of deterrence by large stores of arms is just a variant of an old-fashioned doctrine of an earlier world: Balance of power.

That mankind's noble desires should find themselves back on the old cynical discredited circle of "balance of power."

"Balance of power" is what such high-minded men as Lippmann and George Kennan preach, but it was also the stock in trade of the most cynical crowd of people who ever ruled the world, in the late nineteenth and the early twentieth century. Wars, wars, wars—they are the spawn of balance of military power.

JANUARY 29, 1963
NEW YORK

How refreshed and renewed I feel when the fresh air of the Tennessee Valley blows over me!

This morning I called Barrett Shelton, partner in many a joint venture in the TVA. Said that May 18 was the 30th anniversary of TVA; that Helen and I were planning a visit to the Valley at that time; that I had some things about the *future* I wanted to get off my chest. What were his ideas about the place and time to say them, directed to the Valley and to the country?

"Of course it should be Decatur, young fellow," he said. We had one of our robust give-and-takes. How it stirs me to feel that I am still in the hearts of some people down there, so far away from the great harbor I look out upon here from my office, that there are in the Valley people who still trust me and remember me. So to Decatur we shall go, in May.

FEBRUARY 2, 1963
PRINCETON

My mind keeps coming back to a circle of faces I met with yesterday, the career men known here as "Princeton Fellows in Public Affairs."

They are quite unusual men to find at a university. All are in important "middle management" jobs in different agencies of the Federal Government, from the naval station at Hawaii to the Science Research Division of the Pentagon.

They had been selected—or nominated—by their agencies, to accept a kind of study sabbatical here in the Woodrow Wilson School, and then return to government service.

As I visited with them they wanted so hard to have other people understand why government service can be so rewarding because of the satisfactions it gave them in doing something that was important, exciting, full of responsibility. "The wives?" said a graying slight man, Wilbur Bolton; "Why, my wife, I don't know what she would do if I told her one night I was going to GE or some other company, leaving my work in the Government. She gets enormous vicarious satisfaction out of what I am doing. Always has."

A flashback, as they say in the movie scripts, came back to me. Almost exactly forty-two years ago Phil La Follette had asked me to come to Madison to see him; he had just been installed as governor, at about thirty-one years of age. Would I quit my law practice in Chicago and go on his Railroad Commission, reorganize it, bring public utility regulation up to date, "take on Sam Insull"?

I left the Governor's Residence about eleven; the train back to Chicago and back to Helen didn't leave until 4 A.M. I walked all that time, in the frosty Madison night, around and around the Capitol square. What to do? What would Helen think of leaving our newly rented house in Wilmette, and our growing income, pull up stakes at my new law office, to go off on a binge like that, at $5,000 a year; moving the children out of school—and so on.

How simply Helen met all these "complications," when at last I got back to Chicago and home. "If that is what you want to do, and believe in it, then the rest doesn't matter; I can manage on the money and we can adjust quickly to the other changes." How right Bolton was: the wives, this work we do is *their* way vicariously of getting the kind of satisfactions that public service holds.

The long preparation of the Stafford Little Lectures on the atom is over at last, the culmination of ten years of trying to understand how I feel about nuclear weapons and atomic energy. A week from next Monday night, at eight, I will walk onto the platform here at 10 McCosh and put my name right on the line on the most difficult problem any of us have ever confronted; try to point the way, the way that is dangerous, the way that holds hope.

FEBRUARY 5, 1963
NEW YORK

Word just in that the dam on the Dez is to be named after the Shah. The most explicit kind of endorsement of the seven years we have put in—a biblical seven years. Wasn't that the length of time one of my "ancestors," Jacob, worked for Rachel only to get Leah? While my Bible memory isn't so good, the recollection of all the ups and downs of the last seven years is fresh and clear.

FEBRUARY 11, 1963
PRINCETON

To hold an "audience" so that at times "they" seem quite unable to move until you choose to release them; to weld 500 who before you began to talk to them were 500 individuals, into *one* individual—I wonder if there is anything in the gamut of man's satisfactions that compares with this kind of experience.

This is the experience I had tonight, in the first of the Stafford Little Lectures.

I am moved by a good audience, and this was a good one. The place was filled almost to the last seat, the gallery included. And such attention. This stimulates any speaker, this close, almost breathless attention, so you are tempted to hold the pauses long, driving your points home by the silence itself. All these months and months of wrestling with what my convictions are about "the atom" seem repaid tonight.

It was wonderful to see David out there, his long Lincoln legs filling the aisle, looking surprised when he saw that I had cut something that we had worked on so long, or catching some phrase of *his* that I would direct right at him. It was good, too, to see others out there who have borne with me during these months as I have tried out ideas on them: Beatrice, with her great faith in me, looking anxious at first, quite pleased as things went on; Helen, who has borne with me in the years and months of sweating out these ideas, through the endless revisions, the endless tossing about of one new draft after another.

It takes a lot of people to make one man, and one man's work.

FEBRUARY 15, 1963
PRINCETON

Dr. Atchley phoned me yesterday morning, from his room at Harkness where he is convalescing from some "plumbing" problem.

He had just read the first two Lectures. Such a hearty agreement with the outlook, the theme. "This is true leadership," he said. "Spiritual cognizance." Well, what he said made me feel almost as if the months of digging this out of my guts had been worth it for that telephone call alone. Then he said something that moved me: "Will you send copies to my three sons?"

When a man thinks first: I want my *son* to be exposed to an idea—or a person—I have learned that this is the test of his own commitment to it.

Dr. Atchley, able to judge me objectively as a scientist-physician, knows more of my emotional geography than any other person; it was evident that he thinks that I am alive and functioning; that the pulls and strain of my work have not constricted my capacity to do the things I was put into the world to do.

FEBRUARY 17, 1963
PRINCETON

Feeling terribly let down these past several days. For distraction, went yesterday to see the Harvard fencing team in a match with Princeton at Dillon Gym. I had never seen intercollegiate fencing before. When they attached a long electric cable to the backside of each of the fencers —literally to his tail—I thought I had gone out of my mind: *electronics* taking over this ancient and ceremonial sport. When a fencer touches his opponent in one of these lightning-like exchanges, a bulb lights on a desk. But what a travesty—these graceful young men each dragging something that looks for all the world like an ambulatory enema hose out of his rear end as he lunges and parries. What won't the technicians take over next. (Half the time during one match was taken up with testing and fixing the electrical system, which apparently wasn't working too well, which with electronic gear anywhere—computers included—is par for the course.)

6 P.M.

A wave of ennui, almost of despair swept over me; I threw the book I was reading at the wall. (Orwell's *1984*, as it happened—and this dismal picture seemed to be Pollyanna-ish compared to the ugly blackness and emptiness I felt so acutely.) Then a self-administered spiritual shot in the arm, a "sei ein Mensch"—be a man—fight talk, a round of pounding the squash ball around in our basement court, shouting out the numbers of continuous bounds off the wall (I reached ninety) and now I think I am "in charge" again.

A serene life apparently isn't the thing I crave. I live on enthusiasm, zest; and when I don't feel it, the bottom sags below sea level, and it is agony, no less.

Talked to Fred [Newton] Arvin by phone this noon from his hospital room where he is dying. Apparently he doesn't know that he isn't going to get well; he speaks of other books than his Longfellow, just out, that he hopes to write. Or perhaps he is saving me by talking this way.

Wrote him another letter today; perhaps it will be the last in a long line, going back fifty years and more, to our early boyhood.

A brisk walk today, to the Institute grounds. As I got to the corner of Battle, the familiar shabby Cadillac convertible came up the hill; inside I could barely see the outline of that flat porkpie hat that *is* Robert Oppenheimer. I raised my walking stick in salute; the car stopped a few yards beyond me, and I went back. The door opened: Kitty, her eyes larger than ever, against the ravages that time and trouble, poor dear, have committed against her.

Robert, leaning earnestly over the wheel, said: "How are the Lectures going? I get something of the spirit of them from the titles [he grinned] and from what people who have heard you say."

Kitty: "Good to know you are on our side." A really Kitty comment, out of her fiercely pro-Robert feeling, against any who raise even an eyebrow against him.

"Well," I said, a little taken aback by this impression of representing a position, "while I was working them out I didn't come in to talk to you about them, so I wouldn't find myself using your ideas rather than my own. When they are over I'd like to come in and talk about them."

A tragic pair. The trail from Los Alamos, and Alamogordo is a long and terrible one, a Golgotha indeed.

Suppose, I thought as I continued my striding into the sparkle of the winter air, suppose he had *failed* at Los Alamos; suppose some of his calculations had been wrong. Suppose the Alamogordo test had then been a dud. The world would be a different one today; far different. There would be nightmares, but not nuclear ones.

FEBRUARY 18, 1963
PRINCETON

"David, this is Baruch calling from Kingstree [South Carolina]. I have read your thing on disarmament, the first one, and I wanted you to know—tried to reach you yesterday—that I agree with you completely. Nonsense to think you can settle these questions until we are a more civilized world. Just a lot of propaganda, that's all."

And so on.

His voice continues to be strong and firm—he is "going on" ninety-three.

He spent some time saying that the "plan" we proposed long ago was a sound idea. I said the principle wasn't dead, but it would be a long time until that could be recognized.

"And how is your son?" He never forgets to ask about him, recalling the time that David, lean and rumpled, spent the night with a young companion of his, at Baruch's swank, butler-filled apartment, years ago.

"Do you see Oppenheimer? I had a wire from him the other day that he wanted to see me. I had offered to be a witness for him. Always had a high regard for him. Do you ever see him?" I said he was my next-door neighbor, but I see him very little these days.

FEBRUARY 22, 1963
10 A.M.
IDLEWILD

So I am going to Persia for the "dedication" after all, it would seem.

A cable yesterday that Ansari thought our absence would be "subject to misinterpretation."

What he should have said is that it would be subject to the correct interpretation, namely, that we were not happy with the way their payments have been delinquent, their rowing with Oliver about our overheads, and some "pique" (Gordon's word for his own state of mind) that D&R would barely be mentioned in the ceremonies.

BRADLEY FIELD, NEAR HARTFORD
6 P.M.

Fred, in his room in the Northampton hospital, seemed more composed and serene than I can remember. I had prepared myself to see him wasted and apprehensive, since "normally" angst has been his state, for so many years. Outwardly not at all. Now and then, as we would walk the groves of boyhood recollections—strangely enough, as he dies his youth is very much in the front of his mind—his eyes would mist up; I could see the cloud of realization come over him: "I am near the end" it almost said. But this was only now and then.

FEBRUARY 23, 1963
PRINCETON

Dr. Eugene Rabinowitch, founder and editor of the *Bulletin of the Atomic Scientists*, asked to see me; he has just left.

Very short, stocky, portly man, with the brightest, most alert eyes; perhaps fifty. Born in a Russian village, he said.

Agrees with my Little Lecture that the scientists are "barking up the wrong tree" with their emphasis on disarmament. "But neither at Pugwash [the international conference he originated] nor in the pages of the *Bulletin* can I get other scientists to agree *in public.*"

When I pressed him on this he said: "But I can't say those things. Everybody all over the world—Nehru, all the rest—everybody, all the governments, believe that disarmament comes first. The Russians believe this; they say, the Russian scientists, 'but first we must disarm.' Then the other things, the other kinds of cooperation. So how can I say anything to the contrary?"

Well, I thought this was just plain shocking. But all I said was: "What good does it do to be a private citizen as you are and not be able to say what you believe?"

No, your position in the Little Lectures is just not "politically possible," he kept saying.

More than once the things he said confirmed the cutting edge of my thesis: that you can't carry on both disarmament discussions and also move in the other nonweapon areas that are the only ones that will count; the first makes men lose their interest in the second, because it is less dramatic, less of the limelight falls on scientists who talk about health or food, say, as an instrument for relieving international tension, than the silly "black box" dogma—a technical gimmick for detecting atomic tests—now at the center of the stage. Temporarily, I'm sure, as with all such technical bright ideas.

"*Why* should scientists, of all people, be so swayed by the appeal of disarmament; surely they are too intelligent to believe that this is the *one way* to get the world moving in the right direction?" I asked.

"Well," he said, somewhat taken aback by the vigor with which I went after the scientist-god, "the scientists and the scientific revolution have produced these weapons; governments have relied upon them, and governments now expect them to solve the problem."

"But solve it through getting rid of the weapons—is that the way?"

"No, I agree it isn't. The syllogism is false: wars are fought with weapons; therefore get rid of the weapons and you get rid of war. But scientists are asked to help on disarmament, so that is what they do."

I felt rather physically ill, after this.

Rabinowitch himself is a very likable brownie of a man. He sees things more clearly than the *Bulletin* would indicate. "We scared everybody about these weapons; the *Bulletin* helped to do just that. Now we believe our own story and don't seem to be able to talk sense— nothing but disarmament, that is all the scientific community seems to want to talk and think about."

"And what is your political program?" This from Rabinowitch.

It must be a political *program*. Damn. The illusion of European reformers: a neat and complete program. Marx, darn your whiskers, but you *have* left a trail.

The idea of a diverse, multiple, untidy way of getting along toward a goal somehow doesn't seem worth considering to this warmhearted intellectual. It must be a *program*. Is it not arrogant for people to think that human beings can look ahead so clearly, when all of human development—so it seems to me—cries out that man's progress comes along on a completely different, random road?

MARCH 1, 1963
PRINCETON

I don't know when I have so utterly revised a chapter of my own life long, long after the living of it, been so overwhelmed with how much more drama there is in real life than in anything seen upon a stage.

This emerges from a reading—far into the night last evening—of the typescript of Fred Arvin's autobiography he sent me as a parting gift. It was only the first five chapters, but almost certainly all he will be able to write, since his death is imminent.

The story as he has written it goes only until the time when our family moved away from Valparaiso (Indiana) about 1913. "Dave" is woven through all of it. The manuscript draws a picture of this brilliant literary man, as a boy, that was utterly new to me, one that I didn't recognize, at that faraway time, nor since. I clearly remembered him as a very bright boy; he had read everything; had an enormous vocabulary; knew the great names and places and battles and kings, all the things I, in my slower plodding way, didn't know, but thirsted to know. The other boys of the neighborhood—and I—thought of him as a "sissy"; he wasn't good at baseball, didn't go in for our perpetual roughhouse. We didn't take this very seriously; that was just Fred. But that he was "different" in the sense of being some way inferior never crossed my mind; certainly I never thought of him as having what today we would call worries or problems.

Now, as a distinguished critic, in his sixties, he describes himself, as a boy of seven and nine and twelve years of age, as "misbegotten" because of differences that to me at that time were simply marks of his inability to excel in rough games, which was more than balanced, to me, by his extraordinary mind, from whom I could and did learn so much about literature, words, history, etc.

I was amazed that, in writing of this long-ago time, he recalled the protection that a tough hulk of a boy, I, gave him from the normal bullying of other boys. I took that role for granted; the sort of thing I did for *any* boy who was being put upon—I being quite able to take care of them if it was a fight they wanted. To Fred I played a kind of "elder brother" role—indeed he used that term in these memoirs. He was explicit in saying that the friendly feelings we bore each other were completely without what he in his sophisticated Freudian older age called "homoerotic" feelings, in contrast to the beginnings he had of a different kind of emotional stirring he felt—or thinks now in retrospect he felt (which may be two quite different things)—for another little boy in our neighborhood.

I have a feeling that in these few hours of reading his extraordinary memoir I have traveled back to another world, an aspect of boyhood I didn't recognize when first I passed that way.

The reactions to my skepticism about the priority to the disarmament part of the Lectures continue to come in. A letter from E. B. White, of the *New Yorker Magazine,* one of my heroes. I include the letter here in this journal, for it is a kind of payment for the risks that no one would be listening, and that I would be chided by everyone I respected. There will be plenty of brickbats, but if Dana Atchley, Gordon Clapp, Dr. Bob Loeb, and E. B. White are for me, it will take a lot of cussing out to bother me much.

"Thanks for sending me the copies of your Stafford Little Lectures. I am reading them with a good deal of interest and agreement.

"To be against disarmament, these days, is like being in favor of influenza—people don't seem to grasp what you're talking about. I think the popular acceptance of weapons control, or weapons reduction, as the road to peace is easily as alarming as the power of the accumulated weapons themselves. You've done a great service in your attempt to dispel these fantasies of life."

MARCH 3, 1963
PRINCETON

A golden afternoon living again in that gay, heady time of boyhood. David III and I, alone, strutting along the roadways, each carrying a walking stick with which to punch the snow, jab at attacking Indians, twirl at the head of the band we were leading, building *two* dams (not one) along the gutter where the melting snow was rushing downhill, playing darts and ping-pong in the basement, drawing.

David is not only an extraordinary-looking boy—at seven and a half he now reaches my shoulder (he will be a giant!) but he has a range of interests that overwhelms me. One of these continues to be the Stone Age, and the creatures thereof. This noon on our first walk he rattled off the names not only of dinosaur (the only one I know) but a whole roster of these multisyllabic creatures. And he wants to know *how* things work, *how*, just how. How does the baby inside mommy get her food; how does that wire on the pole bring electricity to run the refrigerator, how does a jet plane "eject" a pilot in midflight?

He never condescends to me, when we are without other adults, so that for an hour at a time I am lost, with him, in that world within a world where little boys live.

So the afternoon was a joy. Such a joy that when David left I fell into a deep dreamless sleep for two hours.

MARCH 5, 1963
NEW YORK

We are having our first experience with the U.S. AID organization, which finances our Ivory Coast work; previously this had been a rather tiresome paper-pushing one. So that a paragraph or two in a memorandum from Tom Mead, heading our work in the Ivory Coast, of a meeting in Abidjan with the U.S. Ambassador warms my heart:

"The Ambassador went on to say, with some jocularity, that when Mead had told him earlier that D&R would get to work in January he found this difficult to believe. However, it had happened. He was surprised and he was delighted by the speed and efficiency of our operation; that it was completely unprecedented for a company to launch an undertaking of this sort within three weeks of contract signature.

"The Ambassador said it had come to his notice that this had already made a considerable impression on the Ivory Coast. Our readiness to act had been of very great help to the Embassy in helping it over a very awkward period in its relations with the Ivory Coast Government. . . ."

MARCH 6, 1963
8:20 A.M.
IDLEWILD AIRPORT

How is it to live in the U.S. of A. in 1963?

I continue to marvel—or shudder at what this means, in a very specific way.

Par example: taxiing out to the airport this morning, at an early hour (7 A.M.) the roadway leading to the city, at that hour, was filled with cars, their lights on (it is a rainy, foggy morning). Where have they come from? Long Island, says the driver. Hundreds, thousands of cars pouring into the city, each with one person to a car, headed for a day of work in the city. Their wives must have to be up at five or so, preparing breakfast, getting them off. And then at night they repeat this long drive, again bumper-almost-to-bumper, an hour and a half each way probably. This goes on all over the country.

Item: a waiter in a "chain" coffee shop, telling another waiter of the cussing out a "spotter" for the shop had given him for sitting down during business hours; his reply: "But when no one is here, yes. But when I see someone, a customer, I run to take care." The eye of the Lord is everywhere, only it isn't the Lord, it's the "spotter," a man you never see, like God, but he may be watching you *right this minute*.

MARCH 8, 1963
PARIS

It is a downright *pleasure* to watch the French eat.

It's not only the sociability; the food is a matter for earnest attention, inspection, conversation, and of course gusto in the eating. The waiters share in this excitement.

I stopped for a late luncheon at a small restaurant—Café Bosc— going there for no particular reason. A single room, narrow, the walls lined with eaters. Without French I had to do some improvising about my order, but I got fed. I couldn't help contrasting this with the *fierce* way we lunch in New York, where the food is the least important thing.

The Plaza Athénée is a rather elegant place compared to the Hotel Pont Royal where I usually stop, on the Left Bank. Elegant or not, the automatic elevator doesn't work, so I climb the broad, marble staircase quite happily. Somehow getting into a strange empty box of an elevator and poking a button for your floor is a substitution of machine for man that is singularly cold-blooded, one that doesn't breed too much confidence in me.

Our offices at 50 Broadway were not as handsome or convenient as those at One Whitehall. But at 50 we had a red-beaked jolly elevator man who never failed to have a wisecrack to trade with us. Riding the elevator was actually fun. A month after we had moved, a half dozen of us, on our way back from lunch, saw our elevator man on the street. We clustered around him the way the Princetonians do when they find a classmate at reunion time. He looked quite different, with a gay pea-green little cloth hat, but the jokes and grins kept coming. All of us came back to work happier. Score at least one for man versus "the machine."

MARCH 9, 1963
BEYOND ANKARA, TURKEY

The mountains of Persia are white and serene, under a full moon; the lights of the city spread out like no magic carpet Omar ever dreamed of.

And here we are—landing this minute—seven years after we had first arrived, to leave an imprint on this ancient country that will last a long, long time.

MARCH 11, 1963
ROYAL HILTON HOTEL
TEHRAN, IRAN

An inspiring session this noon with Reza Ansari.

I asked him to give his assessment of the effect of the "land reform" objectives on the Dez irrigation pilot operation which I regard as perhaps the most important single thing we have undertaken. This morning the flaming and erratic spearhead of land reform, Hassan Arsanjani, resigned from the Ministry of Agriculture, so the topic was particularly timely. I made the point that water for the land would be available this summer, in quantities, from the Dez Dam. If there continued to be uncertainty as there still is about who was to get the water, what the charges would be, about who owned particular tracts of land, etc., a great opportunity would be lost to make the new water serve the goals of land reform for the peasants.

The confidence and clarity with which Ansari handled this issue and responded to it showed how much he and his associates have grown in these past two years. He said he agreed that land reform must not be merely a political slogan as it was with Arsanjani; it will be made a reality by the creation of democratic organizations of peasants, under the KWPA, to provide a means for distribution of water and better use of the land. Greene said afterward: "The student was speaking to his teacher with great respect but with a sense of having learned much from his teacher." I couldn't be more pleased; I felt something of the satisfaction that *my* teacher, dear Dr. H. A. Morgan, must have had when he heard *me*—half his age, and quite ignorant—take his teachings and expound them to the Valley in a way that he himself was not articulate enough to do; what pride there is in having an apt pupil.

MARCH 12, 1963
7:15 A.M.
AT "GHOLESTAN," NEAR AHWAZ

On the plane to Abadan I read the printed booklet issued to commemorate the "dedication" of the Dez Dam on Thursday. It tells a story of beginnings and has pages of statistics about how many cusecs of water it will release, etc. What struck me, hard, was that this recitation of things now *in being* had little to do with the reality; and I asked myself: What has this got to do with *you*? Nothing.

Not that my name and Gordon's aren't scattered all through the booklet, as well as the name of Development and Resources. It's just that somehow a *finished product*, like a dam in a canyon or a sugar plantation, does not convey the idea of the dynamics, the ebb and flow of discrete problems, crises, debates, disparate *decisions* that brought it into being. That texture of decision-making, little and big, by many people over a period of time is somehow obscured by the smoothly finished result toward which all of these separate acts—and teeth grinding—were heading.

This morning Gordon, Nate, John Blumberg and I set out for the Dez (now the Pahlavi).

6 P.M.

Back from a great experience: "our" dam now controls the Dez River.

When I *first* saw that great canyon from the plateau looking down one-fourth of a mile below, the ribbon of water came from the plains and plunged into the gorge, almost disappearing. Today a great lake spreads back between the battlements, towers that reach toward the sky like a Gothic cathedral; way below the graceful curve of the dam.

MARCH 13, 1963
7:45 A.M.
AHWAZ

We are quartered in a house on the banks of the serene Karun River with the poetic, lilting name of "R-5."

A report last night that the Queen had a daughter yesterday. If she had "decided" to delay this event until late tonight all the diplomats, VIPs, ex-TVAers and the lot of us would have had to dedicate the dam without the King—or have it delayed.

A wonderful Gremliza story: He had been hammering away at the people in a woebegone village about refuse (or its equivalent) without much luck. Just throw it into the stagnant water that seems to mark so many of the Arab-Iranian villages. A man came to the "Doctor" and said: "Tell us where should we throw our refuse."

Such a question in itself, so Shahmirzadi asserted, represents a new outlook on the part of the villagers. This is the "sense of responsibility" that Mrs. Roosevelt used to preach as an essential of progress; what perhaps she didn't see, when she spoke despairingly of its fatal *absence* in the parts of Iran she saw, was *how* that "sense of responsibility" develops. Gremliza's activities as a doctor living with the people these years is one answer; in specific ways he has been able to make plain that there is a *relation* between throwing refuse around anywhere and your baby's illness—or health.

Shahmirzadi, the Deputy Managing Director, is an earnest, sensitive young man. He told me how greatly life and outlook had changed in the dusty provincial city of Ahwaz. "Why, a *flower* shop has just been opened. Now some people might not think that is important—and economically it isn't. But what a change in the way people think that that stands for. These are—what do you call them—the intangibles?—that are so important and that don't show up in figures."

How right he is.

5 P.M.

On the plateau: in the house of one of the Italian construction staff.

The place up here is positively jumping; soldiers against the skyline, squads of Iranians in civilian dress at the engineering center, putting on aluminum hard hats while they grin like kids at each other, off to wander around—and off to clutter up—the dam construction area down below. Poor Williams, our Chief Engineer on the job, looking sadder by the minute as he, once lord of the manor, sees himself even this early engulfed with strangers whose only interest is to look, not to work, and who wouldn't obey his instructions even if they understood them.

MARCH 15, 1963
GHOLESTAN, AHWAZ

When we had our visit with Ansari the day after our arrival in Tehran he was glowing with pride about the forthcoming dedication, the official stamp of "royal" approval of the Khuzistan program. "Next to the Shah himself you are the most important person at the ceremonies. The father of all of this; if it had not been for your idea and force, there would be no dam and no Khuzistan program and therefore no dedication." Of course, he meant Gordon as well.

This is taking too serious a view. I was reminded of this by a rueful comment of a man (Charles Williams) from the American Embassy AID staff, with whom we had dinner last night, here. Said he: "I couldn't help noticing that the dedication platform was filled with Iranian officials, some of whom had never been here or had anything to do with this program. The men who conceived the idea and did the work were way back in a remote corner, and probably no one saw them. I mean you men. Rather ironic, I thought." Not really; being out of sight at a ceremony is a symbol of the way we want to behave, in important matters as well, in a country not our own.

This is the Persians' country; it is their morale that needs boosting, *their* confidence I believe should be built up. Besides, there is credit enough for everyone, even those Iranians who bitterly fought the whole program, some of whom were right at the Shah's heels all day yesterday.

The absence everyone must have noticed—certainly Gordon and I did—was Ebtehaj. He was the man who really made it possible to get the job far enough along so it was hard for its enemies to stop it.

But it is a good sign that he is coming to Khuzistan the end of this week, for a three-day visit, when he will be given every honor.

MARCH 16, 1963
TEHRAN

The Elburz mountains, white and black it seems, look serenely and a bit contemptuously into my room. How abruptly they rise from the scattering of elegant new homes at their base.

MARCH 17, 1963
HOTEL PLAZA ATHÉNÉE
PARIS

Me phoning down to the concierge. "Would you please send me a copy of this morning's *New York Times*?" "Yes, m'sieu."

This is not a request I could make *in New York* this morning, ex-except "for laughs." To have to go Paris to see your own newspaper. That newspaper strike goes on and on.

MARCH 20, 1963
AT WATERLOO STATION, LONDON

Left Nate at the hotel, feeling closer to him than at any time since we became friends more than ten years ago. A very companionable man, honest and thoughtful, but fun too. He believes in me, in what I stand for, which I now see accounts for his almost big-brother concern that I think carefully, prayerfully, before writing or doing things that will trouble and confuse those people he insists look to me. There are others who share this concern—Helen, first of all—but from so sophisticated a man from another world I find this difficult to resist. Though I must add that I do resist, as when I rejected his deep disagreement with the thesis of my disarmament lectures.

MARCH 21, 1963
LONDON

Yesterday I suggested to Nate that we visit the Queen's Bench, more particularly the trial of a libel action, since libel is one of the areas of the law that professionally he knows so much about. So we went to a trial reported in the *Times* as having just begun. It would have been an exciting thing—the panoply of a trial in England is in itself an invitation to one's imagination—but the judge was an unbelievable be-wigged old aunty. He wrote continuously, as the witnesses testified, so in the end a witness was not so much testifying as *dictating* slowly (for the judge wrote a labored longhand). Stupid. The jurymen resented this waste of their time as much as we did. And the court stenographer, who could write as fast as the witness could talk, sat there and re-peatedly opened her wide mouth in yawns.

MARCH 22, 1963
AT SEA, 24 HOURS OUT OF CHERBOURG, ABOARD
RMS QUEEN ELIZABETH

I think perhaps I have slept myself out now. A good passage thus far; even some sun and warmer weather this morning. I fully intended to be bored as apparently the only alternative, the way I am constituted, to being stimulated. But there was a period this morning when I thought: God, how can I put up with four more days of this *nothingness*?

It has been less than a week since I left Persia; a week since the "big day" of the dedication of the Dam.

What made the most powerful impression on me during this seventh anniversary visit?

Not the giant bridle we had put on the river, the lake reaching its fingers out into the hills; not the ceremonial of the slight-built, soft-spoken Shah and his Court peering at this reality most of them never thought could be.

No, it was the evidence that this time the people are wakening to their strength. The people in the village of Kutyan, in the "pilot area" are the same people Helen and I saw two or three years ago. But there is a difference which I either imagine or correctly sense. All these young fellows of ours, with their talk of fertilizers, of summer water, of medical help, of a big something that will collect water and big ditches to bring it to them—these things are no longer just talk. The people themselves are as dirty and bedraggled as ever; the way they live in this village hasn't changed markedly. But the burros were bringing in load after load of the greenest, most abundant forage you ever saw; the animals look different. A trial farm is under way nearby. The word that the landlords are no longer supreme and that their headmen are never to be questioned is no longer to be taken wholly for granted, like the pains and weakness that they (and most of their ancestors) have always had to bear.

Bob Harkens, one of our agricultural men, is a curly-headed, wide-awake product of a California agricultural college; in Khuzistan about a couple of years. I asked him to take us into some of the villages I remembered from an earlier trip, when we were here with that delightful Iranian Vakilzadeh. Harkens, full of enthusiasm because of the increased yields, the beginning of better cattle, etc., seemed completely at home with the headman, the "owners' man," and the villagers. But with no condescension on *either* side.

One story Harkens told brought into focus the sense I get that a new independence, a new vitality may be surging in this country. I had asked about any change in the relations between the peasants and the landowners. This will be crucial to getting increased productivity, when before long the water of the controlled Dez comes into the pilot area.

"Well, ever since the referendum campaign, when the Shah's land reform program was discussed and voted on, there certainly has been a change. Yesterday in one of the villages in the pilot area the peasants just threw the landlord out."

"Threw him out? What do you mean?"

"They did just that. They grabbed hold of him and his khadokah—

his village manager—and carried him out of his own village and threatened to kill him if he came back.

"But that is the rare violent case. A good many of the landlords are leaving before they get thrown out, just leaving.

"This means that there is no one left in such villages to do what the landlord and his people have done, the managing of things. Then the villagers come to us and ask us for help, about planting, harvesting, getting things to market, arranging about water. There's a vacuum developing and we are asked to fill it—we of D&R, we Americans. We don't see any other way out but to help the peasants, for the time being, until there are Iranians, *now* being trained, to do the helping."

These grass roots happenings are the key to the role the KWPA can perform to make land reform work in this one area anyway.

"Land reform" has begun to produce social fluidity in a country that has had precious little of it. And it is when the winds of change are blowing that I am happiest and most effective.

It is just possible—it is indeed likely—that what I was witnessing in Persia is one of those rare things: a deliberate conscious social revolution *set off at the top*. The American Revolution was begun at the top, but that was not a social revolution; it was a separatist revolt.

But whether it is a genuine revolution or an attempt by the Shah and his political associates to lead a parade that could not be stopped, the picture is that of a Peasant King, a King heading a peasant and workers' party. The man who detonated the feeling beneath all this was Minister of Agriculture Arsanjani, a Populist type. Irony in the fact that the day we arrived Arsanjani's resignation was accepted—which probably means it was called for—and he left for Europe.

Ebtehaj, whom we saw on that same day, scoffed at Arsanjani's concept of land reform as simply breaking up large landholdings. This, he said, did not increase productivity. He is right if this is all that is done.

Ebtehaj, brave leader for a new Persia, is right about "efficiency" and "productivity" à la the West. But I hope he does not miss the essence of the best in modern Western civilization—as so many Americans do. That is an understanding that the road to the economist's "productivity" must—by my lights—be by bringing out the latent vitality and spirit of people.

At the end of our visit, in our two-and-a-half-hour session with Ansari, Gordon and John were disappointed that Ansari insisted on terminating the contract with the Brewer people of Hawaii for supervision of the sugar cane plantation. Ansari cited his reasons again. He wants no part of them. Insisted he wants D&R to take responsibility the

Brewer people have had. "No, thank you," said Gordon. "You'll have to find some other solution." We went round and round on this, I holding my tongue. Getting people from the sugar industry who will consider the social consequences of such an undertaking, be concerned with more than getting the cane cut, "irregardless," is very difficult. We don't know where we would find such people if Brewer is not continued.

Ansari was very unhappy about this; asked if we would think about it further. Gordon, quite redfaced with understandable annoyance about the unfairness to Brewer, said Yes we would think about it, but not to be too optimistic.

I had said to Gordon I thought the land reform atmosphere gave us an opportunity to do a challenging job with that sugar plantation, an opportunity that didn't exist before, when the sole issue was thought to be getting out the cane at the lowest possible cost and in the best physical condition for the mill.

This harvest will be a quite good one, greatly improved over last year, the first, which was not a good performance. We can then begin pointing to a new or *added set of goals*: making the plantation serve as a major demonstration of how to transform a kind of corporation farm into an enterprise that will give the workers some stake in their work.

The plantation at Haft Tapeh is already an operating unit, with the necessary *common* mechanical units, common housing, common technical services. In short, it is about where some of the land reform activities now being gestated will be after a generation of what I hope will be something quite new, i.e., peasant farm corporations.

MARCH 23, 1963
QUEEN ELIZABETH

As I reflect on a great change in a historical Asian land I hear my shipmates talking and visiting. They are part of a big "cruise" (*Mauretania, Caronia*) to dozens of countries. They think, darling old dears, that they have actually seen all those countries in which they were put ashore for a day or two or three. Do they know more about them than if they had stayed at home, for unless you are in the middle of a country's problems, do you really have a chance to learn more than the inadequacies of tourist accommodations, the prices in the shops? Moreover, don't you acquire that deceptive smattering (called "impressions") that makes you think you know, when you can't possibly?

A half-gale today, from the southwest, which I like, for it turns this floating hotel into something like a genuine boat tussling with the sea.

Through the portholes the white horses plunge, as this huge ship pushes through the water, horses that throw their manes high and dive and rise again. Inside emotions plunge and fight the conflicts, the yearnings, the desires of a man who thought thirty years ago—or less—that now all would be serene; in the broadest sense: "all passion spent."

MARCH 24, 1963
QUEEN ELIZABETH

Sons and fathers.

Nearly everything, in fiction and in reminiscence, has been written on this theme. Osbert Sitwell used his old man's crotchets to do a five-foot shelf; I note that Evelyn Waugh is letting his father "have it" in the current *Atlantic*. Story after story.

Has what has happened between my greatly talented son and his father ever been the basis of a piece of fiction? Our story, David's and mine, has two sides. I can only surely know the father's side, and only surmise his.

What has happened on my side, to my great joy, is that I have found a friend, a wise and knowing man, a separate individual with insights and talents and characteristics entirely fresh and original in my experience with people, and I have actually known a good many talented, interesting people. But this talented man is different, full of interest to me because at almost every turn in our *work* together I find something in him I hadn't seen before.

"Work" is the key word. I have discovered this person, this distinctive individual, because we have worked together now for a year and a half. The relationship of a friend dominates the relationship, almost superseding that of father and son.

Not entirely, of course. A little thing. Now and then I reach out in a parental role, to set his collar straight, say, or am tempted to invite a confidence about how things go with him. These are things one would do with a friend not one's son—Nate, let's say—but not in the half-proprietary way that dominates the relations of a father and a son in his youth.

But, on my side, I find the exchange of a son for a friend, an interesting, talented, intense human being, a good bargain.

I have oversimplified, but this is the essence of it. The pride and joy I get out of seeing him succeed in writing, and in getting it accepted as good writing, well worth publishing, is a resounding joy; but I sense that it is more the joy and pride of having your judgment about your friend ratified by others than the sense of proprietorship that is, I fear, the basis of so much parental pride.

"He did it; he made the team; he won the prize, etc., so *I*, his father, glory in *my* achievement." This is an overdrawn picture of the element of parental pride, but there is a great deal of truth in it just the same. Parental pride (or humiliation and frustration) is almost wholly *vicarious*. What it means *to the child* is secondary and in many cases forgotten. From this flow many of the ills in the parent-child relationship, when the child is grown but the parent hangs on, or tries to, because in that child the parent lives.

I might find it something of a shocker if David's reaction to this (to me) transformed relationship turned out to be entirely different. One of these days I may find myself the thinly disguised subject of a novel or play by this man and learn that he sees me as the parent who seeks to dominate his son, in the conventional pattern. But as I look back on the evolution of the ideas in the book on the atom we are now preparing I think that if there was any "domination" of ideas by either of us it was the weight of David's ideas that prevailed, through their sheer soundness.

What has been running through my mind suggests a theatrical or fictional device! Act I is through the eyes of the father. Act II is the very same set of circumstances as Act I, but through the eyes of the grown son. Why does a scene from Miller's *Death of a Salesman* cross my mind at this point?

MARCH 25, 1963
AT SEA, 36 HOURS OUT OF NEW YORK HARBOR

A long and satisfying visit on shipboard with Fowler Hamilton, recently deposed as head of AID, and his radiant, intelligent wife, Kitty, at their invitation.

Hamilton is very much the lawyer, with an ability to marshal facts and the lawyer's inclination to make the facts prove some point or other. A forceful man who has intense convictions about foreign aid. I wonder if he wasn't rather casually dealt with by Kennedy, or perhaps his positiveness didn't set well. Or it simply may mean that since foreign aid wasn't well received on the Hill and in the country, Hamilton had to take the presidential disfavor.

He didn't mince words about General Clay's Presidential Committee which has just served up a report that drives one more nail in the foreign aid coffin. I said that when you pick a jury made up as that committee was you shouldn't be surprised about the verdict. Hamilton confirmed that the Clay Committee had the answers before they looked into the question of foreign aid. As Clay said to me in January: "This is a salvage operation."

What the President thought he was doing in naming that kind of committee Hamilton didn't say, though his face indicated he didn't think much of the reasons. If Kennedy thought he could negotiate with the enemies of AID by such a maneuver he isn't the experienced politician I think he is. Having had a quart of blood, they will now want the whole bloody carcass.

Hamilton is a fairly common phenomenon: a small-town boy (western Missouri), then Kansas City, who came to New York and blasted a big place for himself as a lawyer, by the force of an excellent, logical, well-ordered mental apparatus. His wife appealed to me very much; so proud of him, trying to keep out of her manner her resentment that he was given short shrift, delighted with their experience among the big shots. Washington life quite evidently got into their blood. It *is* heady stuff, public service at that level, with eighty countries to affect and billions of dollars to control.

The essence of the Clay Committee report is to call overseas economic development a failure, to be liquidated. Well, in the short term— say, for this Congress or two years hence—this may represent the governing mood.

But this view of foreign aid runs into a stubborn block. For the issue isn't just a matter of money, or "dollar drain," or whether "aid" should go to those who are or we want to be our "friends." No, it's not that easy. It would be a good deal to expect a brilliant, logical, essentially military administrator like Clay or a banker-type like Robert Anderson to see this.

Our foreign aid policy springs from an ethical need and responds to an ethical impulse. As such it goes deep into the fiber of American life, reaches back far into American tradition. We are not just a nation of soldiers or traders, at our best.

So the aid issue won't down. As long ago as the Murrow TV program on Iran (more than two years ago, wasn't it?) I said foreign aid was in bad trouble. But the issue will remain. The unexpected success of the Peace Corps testifies to that: there is a latent impulse, a strong American instinct at work.

After all these years of having the experience, it still shakes me a bit to wake up during the night or even in the midst of a heavy nap with some new idea, which I scramble to jot on paper. The mind is a mysterious presence. One is unconscious; then suddenly a compelling idea breaks through, wakens one, there it is. Does anyone understand how this can be? I find it inexplicable, *even* though more often than not the ideas really aren't remarkable. Somehow, though, they show marks of analysis, show evidence that in the midst of sleep the mind has been weighing, putting things together, resetting them.

7:20 P.M.

Have just taken a quick turn along the boat deck. We are headed full tilt into the setting sun. There is a pride about this great ship as she pants and thrums her way into the final lap of the crossing, the sea now almost calm, the glorious, glistening wake stretching out astern almost as far as one can see, in the twilight.

I've been thinking how jolly (that being a good British word for a vague feeling of half amusement, half mischief) it is to be a "controversial figure" (the usual term applied to me these many years) *after* I have managed to achieve enough things so I need have no defensiveness about being "controversial." But there was a time when it was different. All through my early years with the TVA—even *after* Willkie decamped leaving me on the field—I was, inside of me, quite defensive. A sensitive chip on my shoulder because I was said to be "controversial." This usually meant, in the lexicon of my enemies or critics, "socialistic" or "radical" or something of the sort. This effort to make me feel that I was a wild man didn't soften me up on the public issues I was responsible for. But inside me it took a toll of making me overly sensitive, belligerent to cover up that sensitivity, and often half-withdrawn.

A funny instance of how such a reputation can reach into far places was retold to me by that master of the anecdote, my Oklahoma colleague, John Oliver. It seems that Shahmirzadi, Ansari's deputy in the Khuzistan, gave a luncheon the day after the Dez Dam dedication, at Ahwaz. One of the guests was a former Cabinet minister. After lunch he noticed a copy of my *This I Do Believe* on Shahmirzadi's table. The former Minister, at home in English, turned to Oliver and said: "The book is about Communistic ideas, isn't it?" Oliver said: "Well, no; it is about democratic principles." "Well, isn't that about the same thing?" Oliver said he didn't think so. "And how did the trial come out?" asked the former Minister. "The trial?" asked John. "What trial?" "Well, Lilienthal's trial for writing the book."

Why did you write these millions of words, in your journals, through the years? The reasons vary, of course, from period to period, from year to year, from mood to mood. But when I note the instinct to reach for this shorthand book and to pour out these vagrant, random thoughts, after all these years, I can see that part of the answer at least is: I wrote these journals because the experiences through which I have gone *would not be complete* until I have somehow recorded my feeling about those experiences in this way.

For a "lit'ry" person—which I certainly am not—this is not an unusual response. To a writer it is the expression in words that is the heart of the experience itself. But for a man who has lived by action as I have this is not so readily explained.

What shall I say to the people of the Valley on May 17, at Decatur? Thinking of the Valley, and the way I have spent much of my life, I was greatly moved this morning to come on this sentence from William James:

"The great use of a life is to spend it for something that outlasts it."

MARCH 27, 1963
9 A.M.
ON THE PENNSYLVANIA

Reached Princeton by 10:30 yesterday. Helen looking fine; serene and still relishing the visit with Nancy and her boys.

Fred died last Thursday, so Helen told me. Dead but not gone. For he left a name and a place in American literature. Edmund Wilson's appraisal of him in a current *New Yorker Magazine* apropos of Fred's just-published *Longfellow* book places him with Van Wyck Brooks, among the immortals of American criticism and writing.

My boyhood friend suffered through most of his life; but he did something great with his talents, something that will outlive him.

Part of a letter of this date from Khodadad Farmanfarmaian to Gordon and to me:

"I had earlier expressed my most earnest desire to see you both, primarily to show my gratitude as a citizen of this country, for your long, tedious, and I hesitate to say thankless, efforts to bring to reality a vision which only a few years ago was considered impossible, even by people like myself. I am sure the job has not been thankless, and you have been rewarded amply by the process of transforming a dream into reality. There stands a monument, which represents yours and Ebtehaj's faith, courage and ability. God bless you for what you have done for this country. I am sure, in a few years' time, the Iranians and, in particular, those of them who inhabit Khuzistan will, in chorus, voice their gratitude to two Americans who made a very important contribution to their happiness, and to a Persian who never gave up."

MARCH 30, 1963
PRINCETON

When André Meyer is at his best ("best" by my lights, of course) there is hardly anyone any better: imaginative, relaxed, concentrating on the important; gracious and at times full of a kind of wit that is carried off with style. Last night he was at his best.

The occasion: a dinner meeting at his apartment in the Carlyle. The guest who occasioned the meeting was Yves Boël of Brussels, grandson of the founder of Solvay, who has succeeded to the leadership (Administrateur-Délégué) of the great international firm known by its initials as SOFINA. In his early forties, tall, handsome in a kind of British way, with the manner of a European but the way of thinking of an American—quite a cosmopolitan figure. SOFINA (of which André for many years has been a director) needs new avenues of activity: driven out of Barcelona, Argentina, etc., where their electric properties—pioneers in their time—have been virtually confiscated and their engineering work curtailed, they have a good name—and a great deal of cash needing utilization.

Said André: "Water—pure water—is a commodity absolutely essential to life, to industry, to communities. It is becoming scarce, and in many places polluted. Surely here is a field that calls for the kind of talents of David and Gordon. Development and Resources could do for water what they hope and plan to do for coal and have done in the Tennessee Valley. What ideas do you have?"

Gordon thought he meant irrigation, but after it became clear he was thinking in broader terms—water in densely populated areas, not for growing of crops—the possibility stirred recollections in me of ideas I tried to express to the American Mining Congress in Chicago years ago.

So, over a delightful meal, and with André's great paintings looking down on us, we had a stimulating and perhaps a fruitful beginning of a new set of ideas to which to try to apply our skills and imagination. Successful or not, it is the stimulus of such ideas that keeps me going.

MARCH 31, 1963
PRINCETON

A beautiful warm spring day. Spring! God, how good it is to have my hands in the warming earth again, to exult in the improved feel and texture of the soil my efforts have "improved," to see the long-sleeping perennials come green from the dark earth in the greatest miracle of this whole miraculous world—spring after winter.

Overrationalization.
The ills that flow from this so-human failing. Is it a modern notion that because reason is a good thing all things can be explained and analyzed and affected by reason, by rationality?

Is overrationalizing an aberration that grows out of modern intellectuals' loss of immersion in the way things *actually happen*, his alienation from earthy reality? Is this overrationalization the cause of my distrust of theoretical economists of a certain kind, and their formulae, of scientists when they apply their abstract intellects to such issues as human behavior or military strategy and disarmament?

APRIL 1, 1963
NEW YORK

Lunched with Boël, more than ever impressive and likable. We got right down to cases with him—and soon agreed on the terms of a joint venture: what we, i.e., D&R would do, who would supply the money, how we would divide the profits if any, or if and when. A new venture for D&R, in a field about which we know next to nothing, actually, i.e., the *upgrading* of water, the phrase I used. But if we apply ourselves to it we will come up with something, perhaps something important, dealing with an intensely *timely* need.

APRIL 2, 1963
NEW YORK

The *Times* again! The strike over. Yesterday morning, when I got the first issue after months of goneness, it really came over me what it meant to be without a morning *Times*. Absurd, in a way; in another, a great tribute to what Arthur Sulzberger has accomplished in building a paper that is far more than a paper: a repository of serious people's trust, a spring from which they draw the daily sense of renewal that "information in depth" provides.

What astounds me still, however, is that when night descended on *one* paper in one city, as it did during this long shutdown (however great that city), it was as if the *nation's* entire source of information had been obliterated. The *whole* country. That is ridiculous, yet this was the effect on me and I doubt not on many, many other people.

APRIL 3, 1963
NEW YORK

I get quite a chuckle out of the circumstances of my first appearance before the Joint Committee on Atomic Energy since I left the chairmanship: "voluntary involuntary appearance" describes it. Chairman John Pastore phoned last week. He was hot under the collar. "Why are you being so difficult about our invitation that you appear before our committee; your lecture on the atom at Princeton has caused us here no end of trouble; the things you said are being quoted at us.

We insist that you come down to answer some questions; maybe we will take you apart but you don't mind that." I told the Senator I would look at my schedule; later told the secretary of the staff that I would come next week, not this. The Committee had what John Conway, the secretary, described as a "hot session" Friday afternoon; an urgent call from him. "The Committee has authorized a subpoena for your appearance and the Chairman has signed it, and directed that a Federal marshal serve it on you. But if you will come without that service, I don't think he will insist on having the marshal serve you with the subpoena."

Well, of course I said: "I'll be there if I must." It ought to be interesting!

APRIL 4, 1963
WASHINGTON

A crowded standing-room hearing room; a belligerent scowling Committee, a paraphernalia of cameras, the stenotypist looking frozen, the press, lobbyists, angry AEC Commissioners: this was the setting all morning when Chairman Pastore called me from the back of the room to take the witness chair.§

It was a rowdier session even than I had anticipated. The Joint Committee and the AEC were obviously expecting to give me a going-over. As happens with an antagonistic committee I had little chance to testify in a coherent pattern on my Princeton Lecture views on the peaceful atom. This peppering was a mistake on their part, for they pushed me into an extemporaneous emphasis on atomic power plant dangers I had not planned◖ and this had them worried. And they didn't at all like it when I said the Government should stop prodding and dominating the atomic industry; let the private companies who expect to make money out of these plants put up their own development money. Well, this brought down defensive speeches from the Committee, the familiar kind: "No one believes more strongly in the American free enterprise system than I, but . . ."

The concluding note came from a new member, a young Congressman, John Anderson, who said he thought I had performed a public service in raising these questions. Chet Holifield was so mad he even imputed that I had some kind of personal financial interest in expressing

§ The text of Lilienthal's testimony and the questioning by members of the Joint Committee are set out in Hearings Before the Joint Committee on Atomic Energy, 88th Congress, 1st Session, on Development, Growth, and State of the Atomic Energy Industry, 1963, Part 2, pp. 704 *et seq.*—Ed.

◖ The questions and answers concerning the dangers of atomic power plants are at pp. 717 *et seq.*—Ed.

my reservations about atomic energy plants. As he left the hearing room he said to me in a tone of one betrayed: "You have hurt the program, hurt it badly." But from the bench he was, as usual, gracious and friendly.

But what seems important is that there be public discussion of whether the "program" is right to move ahead at such a headlong pace with a new technology.

The whole point of being a knowledgeable *private* citizen is that you should be prepared to say what you think and then be willing to absorb this kind of going-over; many men are not equipped by experience or temperament to take it. Joe Volpe said I "fielded" the questions well—and I think on the whole I did—and I certainly avoided yielding to the temptation of showing outrage or being cute or brittle.

APRIL 5, 1963
ON THE CONGRESSIONAL

I reached for the lunch check at the Carleton; Ted Sorensen, the reserved, scholarly, almost solemn-looking counsel to the President, gave me a look which I interpreted as meaning that he wished to pay for his own lunch. So I asked him if he preferred that: an old TVA leaning-over-backward attitude about never having anyone else pay even for a lunch. "No," he grinned, "but I ought to be paying for the lunch; I have been 'lobbying' you, rather than the other way around."

We had such a good, simpatico time together. "You say that your experience in public service is the thing you are most proud of and from which you get the most satisfaction—and I can readily see why because you did a more *lasting* and controversial thing than anyone has done or is doing, high or low. Well, since you feel that way about it, would you consider coming back into the Government? This isn't an offer but is a direct question."

I hesitated, lest what I would say—and I knew what I would say— might seem too offhandish. "I think what I am doing now is a form of public service in private life and that there is a time in one's life for both forms of public service."

Then with this rather stuffy response I referred to my appearance before the Joint Committee about the atom: he was aware of this and wanted to know more about my views, went on to tell me about the White House's troubles with pressure from the Joint Committee.

"What I said about hazards, and going on and on with programs that should not be continuing to expand—well, it made the Joint Committee mad at me, and the AEC too."

Sorensen warmed up. "Making them mad may be real public

service; maybe they needed that prod. Frankly, we at the White House think they did."

I went on to say that I thought the AEC hadn't told the President fully what it would mean to the safety of the American people to have the country dotted with huge atomic plants *until* and unless they had more adequately faced up to and solved the radiation waste problem.

APRIL 7, 1963
PRINCETON

Spent most of a sunny afternoon yesterday with David III. Long legs, a mat of yellow hair down in his eyes. We set off on an expedition to see the horses in the Oppenheimers' field next door, and what else we could turn up. Said he, looking solemn: "Grandfather, what interests you best?" Well, that caught me off balance, so I improvised about the *many* things that "interest me best" but which the most I couldn't quite say: books, people, etc. "No, but what interests you *best?*" he insisted. So I asked him what was *his* answer, because I finally realized that all this was an introduction to something he had in *his* mind. "Space." "But," I said, "David, only a couple of weeks ago you said it was dinosaurs that interested you most." "Yes, but now it's space."

Just back from Morven, the Governor's Mansion.

As I pulled my car in, there were several young men and boys "shooting baskets." Out came a strongly built, curly-headed, youngish man who introduced himself as "Dick Hughes." The Governor apologized for interrupting my Sunday afternoon, and we went into the Mansion. A more informal scene in official residential circles I've never seen. Children of all ages and sizes dripping all over the place (Helen says they have twelve children). A smiling dark-haired woman in a red housecoat and slippers was introduced by her first name: the Governor's wife. Arranging a big dinner for her college class and patting the children on the head as they zoomed by.

The Governor said he wanted me to be a member of a committee he had promised, in his campaign, to set up to report on the future of the system of higher education in the state. We talked a bit about the place of higher education in furthering the economic development of a state—the Wisconsin idea, I called it, though that idea has been inert I fear for a good many years now—and something about the other people on the Commission. I said I feared I had "too much on my plate already"; he said he realized that but would I talk to the chairman of the group before deciding.

As informal and unstuffy a man as I have seen in a governor's chair since I can remember.

As he walked me to my car he looked into a service yard back of the Mansion; a bright and laughing baby was jouncing madly up and down in one of those springy chairs, up and down with squeals of delight. The Governor stepped in, leaned over the baby, then rejoined me. "That's the blind one," he said in a matter-of-fact way; "but he's getting better, I think. The other day I thought he reached for my wristwatch [at this point he fingered the gold watch on his wrist] as if he could see it. I think he's getting better."

I could have wept.

APRIL 13, 1963
PRINCETON

I have just read some clippings of the AP account of my appearance before the Joint Committee. "Flayed . . . twitted . . . accused of loose talk," etc. People say to me in terms of respect: "Of course it never bothers you any more, being criticized or jumped on, you are an old hand at this"—Volpe's expression of the other day. But, Volpe went on to say, think of the ordinary private citizen who isn't toughened, doesn't know what it means to be hopped on by a Congressional Committee, with no chance for decent treatment and rejoinder—think how reluctant such supposedly independent citizens are to state their views.

Well—whisper it not in Gath—I *never* will get over a kind of resentment, and a dialogue within myself (an imaginary he-said and I-said with Congressional baiters). After reading these clippings today, more than a week after the hearing, I had to tell myself to control my indignation. I resolved long ago how I would conduct myself during and after such one-sided assaults one must endure in Congressional hearings, and I will continue to keep my outward composure. But the tenderness is still there; might as well face it.

All the more reason not to shirk the obligation to face such committees if I must, and stand up to them.

APRIL 19, 1963
PRINCETON

Day before yesterday spent a couple of hours with Dr. Atchley: a half hour about my health (he just asks questions: no stethoscope, etc.) and the rest of the time, including lunch, talking about my Little Lectures and particularly my appearance before the Joint Committee on Atomic Energy. The president of Babcock & Wilcox, manufacturers of nuclear and other electric generating equipment, had sent Dana pages from a recent issue of *Nucleonics*, exposing what a dope I proved to be before the Committee. The job *Nucleonics* did on me, printing only part of my answers, etc., got Dana mad. "The issue of the dangers of radiation, and how relatively little is really known about it," he said, "is an important one. I have thirteen grandchildren and three sons; this is important for them. You can't just let this rest with your appearance down there and your statement of the issue. *Professional skepticism* is scientifically right, it is right in medicine and in any of the scientific disciplines," etc., etc.

This *is* an important issue, and I shouldn't run away from it.

APRIL 20, 1963
PRINCETON

A walk, early, the sun slanting low, making almost black shadows on the almost synthetically green of the grass. The leaves of the elms are tightly closed, like the fingers of a tiny baby, clutching tightly. Pale and almost gray they are; those leaves that are not yet leaves will unloose their hold in a day or two of this warmth, festooning the long "dead" trees. As I walked past the Oppenheimers' (Olden Manor it is called) I saw a crab tree with scarlet fiery-red tiny globes all over. In a few days those globes will slowly part and be blossoms. As I look out my bedroom window I see the graceful fronds that are in fact the still-inert branches of the ancient apple tree; in my room I seem to live in its top branches.

APRIL 21, 1963
PRINCETON

Out for a walk in the Institute woods, bright with early spring wild-flowers, with "Eddie" Greenbaum and Harold Hochschild's old dog Rex.

Yesterday's paper reported that a certain Mrs. Murphy, wife of a Rockefeller Institute doctor, had been granted a divorce, and that her lawyer was "Edward S. Greenbaum." Also, Governor Rockefeller was interviewed: Was he going to marry Mrs. Murphy, etc.? All of this has been widely gossiped about.

And all the time not a *single word* on this subject from General Greenbaum, whom I see a good deal of here. "Even my office associates didn't know about my connection with this matter during these past two years," he said. A man of a vanishing tribe among lawyers: the family solicitor of great wisdom and dignity.

APRIL 22, 1963
NEW YORK

Listening to a TV program (Augie Heckscher's) on Thoreau. Only once, Thoreau said, had he felt lonely. But Thoreau's aloneness and capacity for solitude was in the midst of Nature, of "living in the woods." This evening I have been living in solitude in the midst of a great, crowded city. *That* is a different kind of solitude. It is interesting to contrast the aloneness of a man in the woods and on the Avenue of the Americas in New York.

APRIL 26, 1963
PRINCETON

Yesterday afternoon David asked to come over "for a talk." He and his mother and I sat out in the sunshine while he told us that he had decided "to move the family back to the Vineyard." The personal reasons seemed to him "compelling." He was composed and strong, but it is evident that he has been going through dark deep waters of anxiety, the troubles that do pursue even so gifted a man; perhaps it is because he is so gifted that this is so.

So draws to an end another chapter, for me, one that held great stimulation and satisfaction; for working with this remarkable man (forget the "son" bit) has been one of the great experiences of my life.

Dinner at the Robert Oppenheimers' last night, with the Trustees of the Twentieth Century Fund and their wives. A very happy gathering of very worthwhile people.

An interesting passage of arms—a bit too vigorous for my taste for after-dinner conversation—on the subject of Emmet Hughes's piece of journalism called *The Ordeal of Power*. The question: Is it proper for Hughes, a confidant of a President (Eisenhower) to write about his observations so close upon the event, observations that deflated Ike and some of his Cabinet?

Arthur Schlesinger asserted strongly that such a book should be written while the principals are alive to deny the truth or accuracy of what was written. Arthur's view is the "bias" of the historian, I suppose, but affected no doubt by the fact that he is himself now in the White House making notes like mad for a book. Arthur Burns, having been Ike's economic advisor, quite understandably took a different view. Adolf Berle sensibly, I thought, said that if writing about confidences as an adviser to the President made the *process* of asking and receiving advice from a brains trust unworkable, then such a book should not be written, or not written so close to the event. Jim Rowe, once an assistant to F.D.R. dismissed the whole idea of such writing, on the ground that "no one in the future will ever trust Hughes again; he is through, ruined."

The bearing—though not direct or parallel—on the publication of my *Journals* was not lost on me!

Time magazine this week has a one-page story on TVA's thirtieth birthday, a very favorable, friendly one. A week or so ago I had a visit from a *Time* researcher, a Mrs. Dorothea Bourne. She made much of the question: Is the *original spirit* still there? I said I thought it was and added that many people *today* took for granted the results of TVA without knowing what TVA had faced in the beginning. I told Helen's story about the lady visiting TVA from Louisiana; she flew over some badly eroded country en route to the Valley. "How lucky you were," she said, "that you put TVA in such a pleasant green valley." This anecdote became the closing line of the *Time* piece, and the title.

APRIL 28, 1963
PRINCETON

Less than an hour ago a phone call from John Oliver: Gordon is dead.

No way of saying how numb I am; it doesn't seem real. So close, so intimate a friend, so much a part of me, suddenly gone: I simply can't take it in. A man who was so much a part of my life and thinking will not be there tomorrow morning when I go to the office.

Years ago Gordon and I were at a meeting with the World Bank, in Washington. A frantic phone call: my mother was dying in Daytona Beach. I started at once for the airport. Gordon, outwardly always so impersonal, with such compassion, said to me as I left: "Into the everlasting arms. Remember that, Dave."

MAY 1, 1963
PRINCETON

My first day of being fully in charge at D&R. Gordon cremated only yesterday. But with man's work there can be no hiatus—not with my temperament anyway. The people in the organization must *know* that the sailing order is full steam ahead. So this morning and early afternoon I talked to all the seniors, in my office, with a freedom and vigor I wouldn't have thought seemly with Gordon in charge. A new dimension to the company is what I want, less emphasis on work overseas, more on our own "underdeveloped country."

I have enough money and enough other interests so that I could say: Oh, to hell with going ahead with a hard worrying task of strengthening this company without Gordon's strong right arm, now that the Persian job is so well begun. But where would I get more satisfaction?

MAY 5, 1963
PRINCETON

When men give up a fragment of freedom of mind and independence of thought it rarely happens because they are on some kind of police rack; it is just that in their innocence they put their arms around this loss of freedom as if it were a benefice.

I am stirred by a cold sense of the ominous about how it is that men lose their freedom. In a new chapter in my forthcoming book, *Change, Hope, and the Bomb,** I expressed strong misgivings about the nonprofit corporations and institutes organized to provide the Government with the wisdom of scholars, particularly on "strategic policies" of war. I singled out the sacrosanct Rand Corporation and Dr. Herman Kahn, the high priest of such organizations.

My point is that without perhaps being fully aware of it many of the scholars and technicians who work for Rand (and similar organizations) lose their independence because for most of them their sole client is usually the Defense Department; the Federal Government. Therefore they are impelled to follow the Government's current policy—or dogma —on whatever subject they are studying and writing about. This doesn't happen to particularly strong and independent men, such as Bernard Brodie, a well-known strategy expert.

Can't help feeling that Rand and such corporations as are created by the Defense Department are just respectable fronts for the Government, since the Government hires them, directs them, pays their bills and fees, and gives them latitude to use the profits they accumulate (they pay no Federal income taxes) for such research ventures as they choose to go into.

MAY 7, 1963
NEW YORK

We have just come from a VIP-type voyeur party to end all celebrity-gawks-at-celebrity gatherings. Harry Luce's celebration of the 40th anniversary of *Time*. Such a conglomerate: from Rex Harrison to Justice James Byrnes and everything in between. A couple hundred of the people who have been on the cover of *Time*, including yours truly.

* Published in 1963 by Princeton University Press.

A session in the late afternoon with a tired André Meyer, shepherded by that wonderfully balanced and wise friend, Nate Greene. I said I was willing—indeed, wanted—to take on the Presidency of D&R and to direct it into a somewhat different path than the past, including the idea of a merger with a larger company, etc.

Since I have only had a week to get oriented, after the blow of Gordon's death, I thought my description of the program I envisaged for the company was clear and hopeful; whether it will work I said I didn't know; if it doesn't we will recognize that and fold it up. But I have no intention of having it fold.

No one—except perhaps Nate and Helen—know how much energy I used up not in running D&R, but in *not running* it, in making sure that Gordon as president had a free hand, letting him do and not do things in a way that I wouldn't have done them.

MAY 8, 1963
NEW YORK

My "coal idea" is developing in the pattern of other ideas I have had, that begin I don't know from where and then move I don't know exactly how, into something tangible, something you can get your intellectual teeth into, either to make it into something visible, like the Dez Dam, or into that collection of discarded and undoable things that lie like whitened bones across the track of my working life these many years.

At this moment the coal idea does look like one of those that just might amount to something. This afternoon our pioneer John Allen returned from the trek on which we sent him through the badlands that form the southwestern part of Utah. He told a remarkable story of *finding* billions of tons of coal—great seams near the surface—coal that the Geological Survey and even the Colorado School of Mines people had not correctly calculated.

MAY 12, 1963
PRINCETON

Two weeks ago at just this hour Helen handed me the telephone and with horror in her voice said: "It's John Oliver. It's Gordon."

What a different way of living and thinking that message introduced. Now I am in the middle of daily decisions of my work that for long Gordon handled. The full effect, however, has been in the vigor I have brought to plans for the future of the company. Whether I can maintain this and bring it to fruition is another matter. But having this sole responsibility now has somehow released a tide of energy I hardly knew I had.

MAY 16, 1963
NEW YORK

What a strange and delightfully unpredictable spinning thing is the wheel called Fortune. I have read something like that—usually in less gummy words—in books. But in real life, my own real life certainly, even what appears in books of high imagination seems prosaic.

Here I am. "Established"; a reputation, blah blah blah, a fortune, a wide range of interests and of friends, and enemies too. And what am I doing? For two weeks spending every waking hour, virtually (and many of the "waking hours" are in the early morning when they should be sleeping hours), trying to put new life into a little private company when I could so readily walk off, without a scratch, and go my way. But D&R's future is the kind of puzzle that sasses me to my face: Can you lick this one? And I dig in, feel the compulsion of pride, and say: Get in there and pitch, you old bastard. No sense to it on the surface. You have enough income from investments to live as you now live. But the inner springs of a man aren't that simple, by far.

Now, with John Oliver so thoroughly agreeing with me, a new chapter of D&R can open. It may be a short and final chapter if we can't make it go, but the prospect of a radical change in outlook does excite me.

MAY 16, 1963
QUALITY COURTS MOTEL
DECATUR, ALABAMA

So we drives up to this here now big splendiferous motel, and there it was, in great big two-foot letters:

WELCOME
MR. AND MRS.
DAVID LILIENTHAL

Barrett Shelton and Maynard Layman met our plane at Huntsville; since that time Helen and I have been exclaiming, audibly and to ourselves: *Can* these be the same places we knew even five or six years ago? The Arsenal (as they still call the Space outfit at Huntsville) and all the industrial development and shopping centers as big as a stadium, all over the place.

MAY 17, 1963
DECATUR

Just back from a look at a microcosm of this transformed northern Alabama county, that TVA and Barrett's leadership transformed. Maynard Layman as our mentor.

As we drove along the back roads I knew and loved so well, years and years ago, I would ask Maynard who now lived in this new (or old) house, refurbished, or shack at times; with his countryman's gift of expression he would give us a thumbnail sketch of each individual and his history. In this person-by-person story of what development has done to *individual*s I can see, and understand, better than in any other way what is meant by change.

MAY 18, 1963
7:30 A.M.
DECATUR

My speech at the high school auditorium last night celebrated TVA's thirtieth anniversary. I had titled the talk "Look Homeward, America"; that title summarizes what I called for: the rebuilding, the strengthening of *our own country*, in every way, in the spirit in which this Valley has been rebuilt and strengthened. An "isolationist" speech? I thought not, but others might see it that way.

After the big doings at the high school auditorium, the Sheltons, Layman, and a couple of others went to the home of Johnny Caddell, once attorney for the Power Board here and one of the most intelligent and kindly men I have ever known. He is now a trustee of the University of Alabama at Tuscaloosa, and on the Executive Committee of Trustees.

The conversation, inevitably, was about "race." It was quiet, not bombastic, earnest. But out of it I got one strong impression: *even* the moderates among Alabamians (and they may or may not be in the majority), agree with Caddell's solemn conclusion: Integration won't work and experience will show that it won't work. Even the Negroes don't want it.

If this decent fellow Caddell represents—as I surmise—a moderate "let's work it out" sector of opinion, then I fear the South is in for some disappointments and surprises and frustrations of a major kind. They will try to get a constitutional amendment passed permitting the states to establish the principle of "separate but equal treatment" and go back to a distinction that I don't believe in, that wouldn't work, and that the Negroes won't accept.

Caddell looks on terrorism and the works of the Ku Klux with disgust; "these Ku Kluxers around Tuscaloosa" are the ones who may make the resistance to the admission of Negroes to the University dangerous; it will be much more bloody even than in Mississippi for that reason. As a university trustee, appointed by a firebrand governor, George Wallace, Caddell would be glad if Negroes were admitted to the University at Tuscaloosa. But in the back of his mind is a conviction that we *must* go back to the separate but equal treatment—with emphasis on separate inevitably—and that just won't happen.

The upper strata in the South I have just visited have long wanted to think that the Negroes really love them, really prefer to be "taken care of" by white folks who are kind and generous, in the way of an indulgent parent.

But I note they are beginning to doubt this. One rather chatterbox kind of Southern woman I recall, in the past few days, remarking that Mattie, who had been their help for years, etc., *really* sympathizes with the Negroes in Birmingham who are showing how much they hate the whites and resent the way they have been and are being treated. "I declare, I think Mattie hates us as much as they do!"

What a long-suffering people they are, our Negro brothers.

5 P.M.

Sitting on the platform a few feet back of *this* President as he made a speech at Muscle Shoals today to a great crowd was in such contrast to times when I was on the "platform" behind F.D.R., his pants' legs looking as dead as the legs within them, his great hands gripping the podium. For Kennedy has the figure of a man about to jump from a springboard. I was fascinated—as a longtime speaker—to notice that he kept his heels severely together and never moved his feet as he turned from one side of the audience to another, as a speaker normally does.

It was a very strong speech of praise for TVA and exulting in its success. Delivered with great force, too, I thought.

One rather sad note for me.

On the platform in the front row were three men—now Senators— who had been the young fighters for TVA causes. Estes Kefauver, looking pudgy, soft, the fire completely gone, the face of a man who was so tired he wasn't quite there. Lister Hill, gray and slowed down, but with that familiar sparkle in his eyes. John Sparkman, still apple-cheeked, but without the boyish eagerness of years ago. And Albert Gore—where was Gore? I never heard. Apparently he wasn't at the President's speech at Nashville yesterday either. There is probably quite a story back of this; for Gore is so much for Gore (and he comes up for re-election this fall, I believe) that he wouldn't want to be a second player to his rival, Tennessee's Governor Frank Clement, or be in the Kennedy parade if he thought being so might affect his chances to be re-elected.

Politics brings out the best in men of great character, such as George Norris. It brings out the soggy spots in lesser men.

The President's appearance at Muscle Shoals in George Wallace's Alabama, which in a memo to Ted Sorensen I had strongly recommended, turned out to be a success, despite the foul racial conflict in Birmingham—which erupted after I made that recommendation.

The President's appearance was scheduled by the press to be a dramatic "confrontation" of the violently anti-integrationist Governor Wallace and the young President on the other side of that issue. Actually, the President strode up the steps to the platform with TVA's Chairman, Aubrey ("Red") Wagner, having been greeted by the Governor, in a dignified way, in the chemical plant lobby below—the whole thing quite undramatic. And *then* after his speech the President took off into the crowd—in which there were many black people—shaking hands right and left, people jamming in around him like mad, a friendly and carnival-like crowd. If there was antagonism to the President, this crowd certainly didn't show it. When the Secret Service finally got him out of the crowds and behind the iron fence that leads to the nitrate, etc., plants, Kennedy went along from iron bar to bar sticking his hand through and shaking hands the whole length of the fence.

A week after he had ordered Federal troops into Alabama, and with violence and ugliness all about, the President of the U.S. strides into one excited, jammed mob of Southerners after another, grinning, shaking hands, utterly fearless and relaxed.

That was quite a picture. If one hundred years years ago, in South Carolina, Lincoln had been capable of so natural and gay a gesture as Kennedy's today it just might have made things different on the brink of war between brothers.

The public address system was so lousy that the press section couldn't even hear well enough to know whether he was following his text—and were they *mad*. I could hear, back of him on the platform. But Helen, down in front, and Maynard said they had heard hardly a word. Why is it that people who conquer really difficult technical problems of dam building or chemical engineering can foul up simple ones like making a microphone work?

MAY 19, 1963
AT THE KNOXVILLE AIRPORT, TAKING OFF FOR NEWARK

"Don't hang on to anything after you have done your job, done as much as there is for you to do."

The above is me talking (silently) to myself this morning, as I think back on the excitement and the warmth of my homecoming to the Valley and the joy of hearing a young President of the U.S. (he was seventeen when I began my TVA work) extol TVA as a great established achievement known the world over, etc.

I laid down the foundation stones of TVA, drew a rough pattern, fought a good fight, left the enterprise healthy and with a sense of direction. That is enough, more than enough, for any man. Now I must put out of my mind the things I would like to see done by TVA that haven't been done, the feeling that these TVA men don't seem to have fire in their bellies. Wagner *knows* a great deal; he may prove to be an innovator and driver.

But in my time I did my part, did everything I could do, and on the whole it was well done and much of it will live. Now *let go*, not only actually but in outlook.

Now back to the challenges that *are* mine, that are looking forward not backward. All are bound up with emotion: whether fighting hard to return D&R to the pattern that I fear was lost along the way since I dreamed of it first eight years ago.

Down below is the lake back of Douglas Dam. A lot of my "blood" in that water. That *was* a bloody fight with Senator Kenneth McKellar about that dam.

MAY 21, 1963
NEW YORK

Last Saturday night we had drinks and dinner with Johnny Caddell in Decatur. A worried, distressed man. The next morning he was to leave for a meeting of the Board of Trustees of Alabama University of which he is chairman of the Executive Committee. He had explained to me *why* he was worried. He was making up his mind under the pressure from Governor Wallace whether he should vote to bar Negroes from the University of Alabama. "For a long time," he told me, "we were able to *avoid* the issue because none of the Negro applicants were qualified. But now there are two or more who are definitely qualified. Can we defy a court order for their admission? I am sure we can't."

Now here, back in New York, a few minutes ago, on TV in the Huntley-Brinkley Report was Johnny, reading the statement of the Trustees, directing the admission of two Negroes, followed by Wallace saying that he was head of the state and he would prevent any Negro going to a state college no matter what a court or the Trustees said.

MAY 22, 1963
NEW YORK

Walter Lippmann's face glows with the kind of incandescence that marks a good man. And such a youthful face—not serene as might become a sage but radiant with the pleasure of living.

This ebullience of mine, at midnight is the aftermath of a delightful party at the John Gunthers'. I distinguished myself by being the only man who didn't wear a dinner jacket (for which I was mistakenly given credit for being a strong individual). Lew Douglas was so warm and friendly. We reminisced about our first meeting—it was nearly thirty years ago! The issue between us then was whether TVA should use the usual copper—which of course as an Arizona man he favored—in TVA's very first transmission line, between Cove Creek and Muscle Shoals, or experiment with an aluminum conductor. (At some risk I opted for aluminum.)

Adlai Stevenson seems more composed, relaxed, and healthier than I have seen him since I can remember.

Of course the acute race troubles in the South were the center of most discussion, even when we were at table. My having just come from darkest Alabama made my comments seem a bit closer to reality than most. Adlai said the Alabama issue was the subject of a long Cabinet meeting today. His description of the ideas put forward sounded more like politicians trying to put out this week's fire than any thought, in depth, of where all this is headed and what basic new ideas can be advanced to prevent a serious crisis.

One young woman (perhaps thirty-five), whose name I didn't get, was full of fire about how ruinous it had been for Africa to throw out the hated colonialists in so precipitous and hateful a way. A lawyer by profession, apparently she has lived and traveled through much of Africa for years. Except for Houphouet-Boigny in the Ivory Coast, she was filled with apprehension, horror, and a passionate rage at what she had "seen" (she said) of the brutality *and* the left-wing extremism of much of Africa under the enlightened policy of "freedom." We hit it off very well together on one point, at least: that U.S. support of Nkrumah was a ghastly travesty. Nkrumah being rewarded by the U.S. with all that private capital and the support of the World Bank (the Volta River project) because of the itch for profits of the Kaiser industrial empire's private interests, and then Nkrumah turns around and becomes what I called a Typhoid Mary of Communism and tribal brutality throughout West Africa.

MAY 23, 1963
NEW YORK

A sleepy over-age seagull sitting on the shore trying hard to keep awake after a too-large meal, propping his eyes open, and looking about him sternly: this was my impression of Norman Thomas, after a big dinner. But what a warm, fully alive old boy he is.

The dinner (from which I have just come) was given to a small group by the African-American Institute, for Kenneth Kaunda, the to-be Prime Minister of North Rhodesia.

I always enjoy Norman Thomas, as who doesn't. He will never forget me because of a remark I made to him at the *Time* dinner a couple of weeks ago. The comment was that I was so proud to meet him again because he was the *father* of Evan Thomas (of Harper's). This is not the usual salutation, indeed in exact reverse. But being myself a man who someday expects to glow with pride at being introduced as the father of the noted author and playwright David Ely, the flavor of my crack seems on the understandable side.

Kaunda is a startling-looking man: a great cliff, a shining crag of forehead topped by a crop of bristling hair; eyes that smolder. Too good a man to last long in the new African setting, I fear.

I overreacted about Ghana to one of the guests. The occasion: his effort to rationalize our support of Nkrumah on the ground that we had made a mistake in not supporting the Aswan Dam, so when the Volta came along our State Department, represented by Inland Steel's Clarence Randall *et al.*, felt we *had* to go along. I thought this was a poor effort to disguise the reality: that it was Kaiser's private interest in the Volta and the aluminum that will come out of it that was the real push, not the political reasons ascribed to our support of Nkrumah, a man who one day, we shall learn to our sorrow, is a really evil man.

MAY 28, 1963
NEW YORK

Lunch in a tiny dining room at Rockefeller Center this noon, with John D. Rockefeller III as host; at his right, and next to me, the Indian Minister for Defense and Economic Coordination (whatever that means). John, in his considerate, gentle way, asked the Minister and the two Indians with him whether they would have vegetables only, or meat, aware of the diverse Indian religious prejudices about food. The Minister got vegetables, and how amused I was when I looked down at what was served *me* (without consultation about *my* food prejudices). What I saw was a poached egg looking up at me, a rather discouraged-looking one, perched atop HASH. Which reminded me of luncheons at President

Roosevelt's desk, years ago. Almost invariably it was HASH. But the Roosevelts were completely oblivious to food; it was just something on a plate to accompany talk.

The Minister, T. T. Krishnamachari, rambled on about everything: the state of Nehru's health (not so good, but he still works until 1 A.M., "gets tired," said the Minister, as if this is a remarkable thing for a man of seventy-two); who his successor would be; how Nehru would not consider the idea of a successor and cut down everyone suggested as a possibility; how the Indians *didn't want* to receive sufficient arms from the West as would cause the Chinese to be afraid of them and so drive the Chinese Reds back once more into the arms of the Soviet (this was too subtle an Indian bit of reasoning for me!). Hardly a dynamic man and not one who would arouse American public opinion, but he saw everyone—President Kennedy, Senators, etc.

I referred to the fact that the Indians had utterly miscalculated the Chinese, so perhaps their judgment about other Asian matters might be subject to some qualification too. Yes, he said, a bit peeved. Nehru feels this deeply; it is a psychological wound, what the Chinese in attacking India have done to disprove Nehru's oft-repeated estimates of the historic brotherhood between the Chinese and Indians. What a way of being dismayed by a major international crisis: that it was a *personal* disappointment to Nehru.

Ansari and I had good talk today. He has more savvy about how to present a budget to his government people than we have shown; I made myself a bit obnoxious to our people in criticizing the *way* we put our figures together. The figures themselves are probably sound; but the method of presentation doesn't take into account the problem of defending them, a problem I lived with in my government service. We have not been operating a tight ship, and I made that plain this morning, in discussing the way the D&R engineers are building up an organization to mother-hen the construction equipment left over at Dez, and thereby keep men on the payroll who are no longer essential to the job at hand. One must be ruthless about this sort of thing. If you want to do an effective, efficient job with other people's money, you can't form attachments for individuals. There is a lot of pruning to do and I am very much in the mood to do it fast.

MAY 29, 1963
NEW YORK

A visit with John Rockefeller early this morning, in his little office at Rockefeller Plaza. John said he thought our Indian visitor yesterday was rather a disappointment.

I agreed; said it is not just that Indian leaders are getting older. They are simply overwhelmed as they begin to realize, vaguely, the magnitude of their miscalculation of what kind of world they—and we —are living in; that Nehru's misleadership, though growing out of humane compassion and the purest of motivations, has put half a billion people in jeopardy; that this is dawning on him and his "revolutionary" colleagues and that they can just not bear to face it, and therefore escape it in intellectualism and hairsplitting rationalizations.

In the midst of a historic crisis out-dated Indian intellectuals are unwilling to face up to the world and prefer to come whining to Washington to ask for ammunition, for small arms and machine guns, as if this had much to do with the crisis of confidence which their superintellectualization and abstraction has produced.

Nehru can blame some of his country's present troubles on the worship that some Americans (and some British) intellectuals have lavished on him. He has been an admirable, a great man in many, many ways. But American India-idolaters who play up to his softness, his vagueness, his cosmic view when confronted with specific problems, his dreamy rhetoric, his politician's resort to the mystique of that sophisticated British barrister—the great Gandhi and his spinning wheel—all this reaching back *into the past,* is something that a young and vigorous country should never have admired and encouraged, nor should we.

Ansari and I picked up a taxicab after leaving the Olivers' attractive new home in Brooklyn Heights last night, and I was dropped at my hotel, Ansari going on to his. This morning Ansari, who has a bit of hero worship in him for me, I gather, told me he had said to the young taxi driver as I left: "Do you know who that man is?" Of course, the taxi driver did not know and Ansari continued, according to his story: "That is Mr. Lilienthal, you know—the TVA." The taxi driver said: "Oh, that's the guy that everybody used to be against." Perfect identification.

JUNE 1, 1963
PRINCETON

This must be something like the way a woman feels *just before* she has a baby. She has carried it so long that it is hard to imagine everyday life without that bulge amidship; yet what a relief that it will soon be over, this mixed with a strong curiosity and anticipation: what will people think of the product once born?

This apropos of the last days of writing the atom book, begun more than the statutory nine months ago—and now in the last stages of completion. Now in the finishing stages of a new chapter (new, that is, from the Little Lectures) about the AEC and the Joint Committee: twin anachronisms. It will not win many friends in those quarters, God knows, but it may stir up the kind of no-holds-barred discussion I believe is needed.

Long, long ago, when I was AEC Chairman, I warned, in an article in *Collier's* against a fate for the great Atom Adventure: that it become "a nesting place for industrious mediocrities." One of the reasons it is becoming just that is the cozy footsie relationship that has grown up between the Congressional Joint Committee and the AEC. It began with Gordon Dean, McMahon's partner, who when he became Chairman decided that there was no reason why the Joint Committee and the AEC shouldn't get along beautifully—no disputes. Well, they got along so well that the lady was soon inside the tiger—Joint Committee—and the mediocrity began.

Big headline: "Riots in Tehran." But the reasons were "honorable" to the Shah and my own convictions: protests by religious leaders against land reform, women's rights, etc. Blumberg cables the fighting is right around our offices, which are a block or so from the Palace.

JUNE 9, 1963
PRINCETON

Tomorrow afternoon I see Herbert Bailey of Princeton Press, with a complete text of *Change, Hope, and the Bomb* in his hands this weekend.

What tears at me, as the last mile opens before me, is a *pull and haul* on my innards, a strain quite familiar in my public career days.

Pull: To speak moderately, be a "statesman," understate your point, thus not alienating those who might be made to agree or build a picture of you as a reckless guy.

Haul: Be yourself, state your convictions so full of fire and bounce and vividness of phrase that people will listen, and argue and fight, and therefore think.

Is there really a middle road between these two impulses?

JUNE 18, 1963
NEW YORK

A call from Lester Markel of the *New York Times Magazine* early this morning: he had read the chapter of the new book on Science and Scientists; "It's an important article, a very important one, and I agree with it thoroughly. We want it; we'll try to carve out 3,500 words for an article."

Very reassuring, that message. For Markel is a tough editor, very hard to please—which means he is a good editor.

Beatrice's huge abstract painting for my office greeted me this morning when I arrived; she and Barney and a professional "hangman" put it up Sunday. Stunning: great color effects. How it lights up the room.

JUNE 19, 1963
NEW YORK

Quite tired by noon. So, I called Beatrice: how about playing hooky for the afternoon. She was fed up with a morning of hard painting, so we did. An ocean voyage to Staten Island, total round-trip cost, four nickels! To see the towers of Manhattan rise through the Japanesy mist on a summer afternoon is a sight indeed; how do you suppose some visitor from Burma or Albania must think seeing that for the very first time?!

JUNE 20, 1963
HAY-ADAMS HOTEL
WASHINGTON

"I never saw a more rigid institution—it is an institution, not a bank, why they call it a bank I don't know." This was George Woods, Black's successor as head of the World Bank, sitting back in his most relaxed manner in the huge Mussolini-sized President's room in the new addition to the Bank building.

I now see why George Woods phoned asking me to come in to see him: I had written a note that I only wanted to stop by to "pay my respects." He is thinking his way through his new job, and wanted someone to "swap ideas" with—which is a super-VIP's way of saying he wanted someone to *listen* to him. Which I did, with fascination and admiration.

"These people around here have become hipped on industry—guess that's because they really think they are a bank. And they set down amortization rules and that is that, no budging. Well, they have built up a surplus—they call it a reserve but it's a surplus that in a year or so will be a pretty dramatic figure of a billion dollars. Can't we relax and do some things with that surplus that are part of *development*? That's in the Bank's title, you know.

"Well, on this agricultural thing, I don't know much, out of my personal experience. What I know is that in the U.S. it has become a good business. What you in D&R have been doing I guess is down that line."

George's critical attitude about the workings of the Bank will be healthy, I'm confident, but how it will be effective against the imprisoning power of an entrenched staff I don't know; he is very close to the retirement age, makes sounds of fatigue. But to have someone who will ask questions and not bow the head to what some in the Bank's staff insist is "sound banking"—that will be something to watch.

"Credit-worthy," said George scornfully; "that's the word they use. That means saying *No*. That's the way the insurance company officers are around New York. All they want, those insurance fellows, is to hold their jobs and never make a mistake; so they always say No. That's the way it is too often around here." Here he looks out on the Potomac and smiles.

I made some reference to the Kariba Dam in Rhodesia as an example of how the Bank's rigid rules sometimes make little sense. As a result of a fifteen-year amortization rule on a hundred-year dam, the power rates are so high only one third of the power is salable. He looked troubled as hell, murmured something about "political troubles between the Rhodesias so the load didn't develop as forecast." The fact as I get it from an American firm that is an industrial user of power is that the Kariba is limping badly.

Jerry Wiesner makes me think of one of the ancient heads, sculpted, one sees in Bari or some other Apulia museum, heads carved by the Greeks and left in Italy when that part of Italy was a tributary of Greece. Very bright, darting eyes, wavy, tousled hair; the rocky lines of a face that two summers ago, when I sat with him through an evening at Leona Baumgartner's on the Vineyard, seemed satisfied, almost complacent, over-relaxed, the pipe going constantly, the reserved MIT professor. But not today. As science advisor to the President there are too many desperate *decisions* the man must participate in to permit that kind of composure—or abstraction.

It seemed strange to have my once young and obscure law clerk, Joe Swidler, and later the often "difficult" TVA counsel, sitting in the seat of the Chairman of the Federal Power Commission, with an influence over energy in this country that is enormous.

But Joe hasn't changed much. He worries about things that involve people—apparently he is having some kind of "trouble" with one member of his commission and this upsets him.

He was apologetic about the headline in the *New York Times* last Sunday in which it appeared that he thought a big atomic power plant in New York was "safe"; he says he won't be led into that kind of loose statement again. And he took very much to heart my warning that the issue of safety of these reactors is a dire one, a responsibility the FPC should not accept by saying that the AEC "presumably" knew whether they were safe or not. "Your name is too precious to you to permit you to stamp something as safe because someone else says it is so; you have to face this issue in your forthcoming national power survey this winter."

He was so impressed and troubled that he called in the other members of the Commission and we had a round of discussion about it. I hope the warning I gave and the similar one to Wiesner (though I think Wiesner is pretty aware of this anyway) will do some good on an issue that is bound to be a serious one for years to come.

JUNE 21, 1963
HAY-ADAMS HOTEL
WASHINGTON

When magnolias last in the doorway bloomed . . . in Washington, that once sleepy Southern town. Just outside this familiar room in the Hay-Adams, I look into the top of a blossoming magnolia, in the midst of a transformed Washington, building like mad, tearing down, traffic jams that at times seem incredible in what in my recent memory was a place "where you can get to your office in ten minutes from your home," etc.

Magnolias may be blooming here "last" in a way more significant than the physical transformation of this Southern city. The curtain is about to go down on the South of magnolias and mammies. These brave black people, who almost throw themselves against the tanks as Hungarian patriots did, are going to bring legislation—but more than legislation—they are about to break the spell of the South that Negroes *love* to be deferential to "our white folks."

AT UNION STATION
3:30 P.M.

David Bell, head of AID, is right in the middle of the toughest, roughest of fights with an antagonistic Congress. As I sat there in his big office this afternoon he seemed a different kind of public servant than I can remember: a fleeting grin, an unassuming manner, not a bit of the rhetoric or "manner" or rumble that almost everyone in so high a government post has; such *simplicity* of manner.

Nothing casual about him, just to put in the time because he had a "distinguished" visitor; every question he put, every point of mine that he followed with a sharp eye bore directly on one question: *how* can what you do provide lessons for us in this organization? He kept pursuing this; I made up my mind to concentrate on one set of facts:

our D&R way of doing things in a single set of circumstances; decided it should be Colombia. With the news just in that we are "back" in Colombia in a big way (*three* contracts, instead of virtually none of a couple of weeks ago), I had something fresh and stimulating to say, I thought; in any case both he and Frank Coffin, his square-built, intense deputy, showed every sign of thinking so, took notes.

Coffin asked: "Can you provide everything Penalosa, head of the land reform agency INCORA, needs in the way of technical assistance in Colombia or is there something AID in Colombia can provide?" His question led Bell to say that he liked the idea of having *one* group of advisors or managers working directly with the country's own staff, instead of a number. This is the way through the Khuzistan Development Service we had made headway in Iran, he thought; and probably would in Colombia. But we both wanted time to think over the idea of D&R essentially providing the range of technical assistance in Colombia AID normally would.

In the morning for an hour and a half with Felipe Herrera, the dapper, bright-eyed little head of the Inter-American Development Bank. He has been thinking about opportunities for multinational development projects in Latin America, where economic coordination might lead to political integration. The one he wanted us to consider was a joint undertaking between Colombia and Venezuela, at the point where they are contiguous, i.e., the western border of Venezuela. The next step would be to ask us to represent the Inter-American Bank in a look at the opportunities for a joint undertaking. I said that if this meant conferences between the central planning bodies of the two countries I would have my doubts. What usually happens is that planning is thought to be the *end result;* nothing gets done. As an alternative I proposed that one man from each of the two countries meet together with us and explore what there is that could be *done,* where it could begin; and then if it could not be avoided, get into this sterile round of singsongs with formal planning bodies.

ON THE TRAIN TO PHILADELPHIA

Footnote on the Age of the Tax Deductible:

A card on my table at the Hay-Adams where I had lunch alone. In big letters the card says: "It's still Deductible." Inside a brief treatise on how you can "entertain" people and let the Government pay most of the bill, complete with citations, this sentence being typical:

"A nightclub will probably be treated differently than a typical restaurant and generally would not be considered a suitable environment for business discussion." And concludes: "But a record should be made of business discussions necessary to justify other types of good will entertaining."

I hope fifty years hence history will not record this *solemn* preoccupation with what is tax deductible as a fair sample of our current state of civilization.

JUNE 26, 1963
NEW YORK

George Roberts, sitting next to me at the long table at the Century tonight:

"Dave, I have a strong impression about you. I have the impression that you are a happy man. Am I right about that?"

"It may sound old-fashioned and smug to say so, George, but I am a happy man; you are right."

This *was* a strange bit of conversation. I met George for the first time when he was one of the country's leading lawyers for the utilities— member of the Winthrop, Stimson firm—and I was a young, brash new member of the Wisconsin Commission, the center of a good deal of curiosity among utility lawyers at the American Bar Association meeting at Atlantic City in 1932. I made a speech critical of utility holding companies; shocked the pants off the assembled lawyers, not the least shocked of whom was George Roberts.

JUNE 27, 1963
NEW YORK

Dexter Keezer, across from me at the long table last night, watching me answer questions about Persia—and asking them too—said: "Dave, on a graph of satisfactions in your life, would you say that TVA was the highest point? I suppose so." Since life *today* means so much to me, I said something like this: "The first, the formative years of TVA, say the first five, were very high on such a graph of satisfactions. But I really believe that my most recent five years, up to right now, would be the most satisfying of my entire life."

Of course I was questioned about this—it was all in the mood of relaxed postprandial conversation—and the things I had in mind were several, some personal, but personal, inner things are just as much a part of the process of deriving satisfaction from work as the work itself; indeed, they are interacting. Working in other people's countries I found added a measure of satisfaction that measured high, perhaps higher than anything I had ever done, since in both Colombia and Persia initial resistance to new ideas from foreigners had changed to acceptance, and more than acceptance.

A chart of a man's life, divided into youth, middle and old age, with the line on the chart rising and slipping depending on "satisfaction" is an interesting idea. My journals will give a more accurate picture of this, for me, than anything I think today, for we *remake* our recollections as we go along: that is the reason memoirs are suspect, to me, compared to a faithfully kept journal.

JUNE 28, 1963
NEW YORK

To *resist* disagreeing "across the board"—or exploding with indignation—with anyone who has opposed you is a talent of living I have in recent years consciously tried to cultivate. This is in contrast to earlier days of my public service when in my mind there were only good guys and bad guys. So it is with some satisfaction that I note I can now read Arthur Krock and not dismiss *everything* he says because for so many years he was and still is so opposed to me, the things I tried to do, and such a supporter of my enemies.

Which is a reaction to his column in this morning's *Times* taking Kennedy to task for his lashing out at De Gaulle and France, during his current trip abroad. In the longer view it is to French initiative that we must look for European unity.

ON THE FERRY AT WOODS HOLE,
WAITING TO PUSH OFF FOR THE VINEYARD
11 P.M.

I'm "let down" already, way down, and more than ready to fold for a while. These past six months have had packed into them a great deal of living—and I have enjoyed almost every minute of it, including the rough spots. The *habit* of enjoying has taken me a long time to develop. True, occasionally I backslide. But how good it is, that "habit."

The waters of the Sound again!

JULY 4, 1963
MARTHA'S VINEYARD

I don't see how I could live without my work. Stay alive, yes, I suppose so. But live? I think not.

Why I should have such a thought, recurrently, today puzzles me. For it is a day of days up here on our hill; a cool, brilliant day of magnificent distances, the Atlantic almost in my lap as I look to the south, toward Portugal. And to the west the Sound, the cliffs of the Elizabeth

Islands standing high, carved and three-dimensional, the blue of the water touched by sails scudding along in a 25-knot breeze.

Then why today, of all times, this recurrent theme about not being able to live without the prospect of work? Back of this strangely timed notion is a lifetime of self-consciously taking time off for "re-creating," playing, etc., with the sole purpose of thereby being better able to *work*. Absurdly enough, to me relaxation is not an end in itself.

JULY 14, 1963
MARTHA'S VINEYARD

What makes a companionable person? Well, one thing certainly: a wide range of interests combined with a zest and enthusiasm for what he sees and thinks and hears. That is Ged Bentley† to a T; so his several days' visit with us here was a pleasant one for both of us. Two or three sails, one a very spirited one, much good conversation.

During the week I plugged away at a review of the journals covering 1941 and part of 1942.

At first I felt that the length and detail of the entries about aluminum would be tiresome to others. These entries relate my agonies and maneuvers to get the confused and often timid "defense" authorities in Washington to *move* on what it would take to get the aluminum needed for the wartime aircraft program. Then, as I thought about it further, it was clear that to portray every facet of *one case* (such as aluminum) was the best way to describe the American state of mind and heart and resolve (and *irresolve*!) of that critical time for our country's survival; and incidentally it also gave a picture of the inside of me. So I didn't cut out the aluminum entries.

To portray the inside of any one person in the midst of issues— of preparedness for war, of public affairs, of love, whatever—fully and honestly is what a journal should be. A memoir or autobiography is likely to be a picture of what *in later years* the writer would like other people to believe he was like; an honest journal is an unretouched record, as of the time things or emotions took place.

I must recognize that to include entries that record the effusions, the self-praise, the angers, the harsh comments on contemporaries, the predictions that didn't come off, will doubtless make me often look foolish or vain or intemperate or just a bum prophet. The author of a "memoir" can and usually does avoid this.

† Gerald E. Bentley is Murray Professor of English at Princeton University, and a celebrated scholar.

JULY 15, 1963
MARTHA'S VINEYARD

A letter from Bill Fulbright in response to one I wrote about the Rand Corporation and its project for the Air Force "to develop techniques which will deal with expert intuition in an organized manner . . ." Bill comments: "If something like this were undertaken by any other department, I am sure it would be the subject of considerable interest in the Congress and the press." And in a longhand postscript he says: "There is little wonder that they need more that [*sic*] $50 billion."

Bill senses that such a nonsensical way of spending public money is a way for him to prod the Defense Department, just as I hoped he would; if such a piece of tripe is part of their program over there, perhaps there are other programs, too, that need to be justified on a sensible basis.

JULY 16, 1963
MARTHA'S VINEYARD

Professor Sidney Hook has a lengthy and careful essay in the *Times* book section about Walter Lippmann's ideas as set out in a new book of Walter's writings: *The Essential Lippmann.*

Lippmann's criticisms of democracy, writes Hook, "go to the quick of the entire conception of the role of popular rule in the *democratic or parliamentary process* itself."

I underline these words because it is evident that Hook and, presumably, Lippmann think that the democratic process and the parliamentary process are synonymous, that the terms are interchangeable.

It is blindness to equate the parliamentary legislative process with the whole sweep of the people's way of expressing their will and carrying out their will. It is an error, I think, to have one's eyes only on the kind of "governing" that is expressed in laws and their execution, or treaties between governments. What they miss is the day-to-day operation of our society *outside* the relatively narrow (though often crucial) area of the legislative ("parliamentary"). And it is these thousands upon thousands of decisions in "the private sector" that also constitute "governing," the process by which the public aligns itself with ideas, people, leaders. My journals are full of such instances.

No, I think in this instance both the political analyst and the philosopher miss a good deal by the necessarily abstract and high-level air they breathe.

JULY 18, 1963
MARTHA'S VINEYARD

For several days my mind has been troubled. A sense of being cut off from the flow of emotional vitality that sustains me. So sleep goes badly, and even the delights of a rousing sail out into the Sound in a sturdy westerly is not "singlehanded" (as one says in the sailing jargon) for that haunting unease rides along with me.

And then as if by magic reassurance flows through me, the unease is gone; I "let go" and even slept, hard, for an hour this afternoon, feel pleasantly drowsy and ready to take on whatever lies ahead.

How strange is the complex known as a human being. And when I was twenty I thought this was the sort of thing that only happened to the young and "unproven," part of the life of a youth who had not yet been engaged on the field of combat.

JULY 21, 1963
5 A.M.
MARTHA'S VINEYARD

The earliest hint of the dawn. Pale blue and mauve of sky and dark of woods; so quiet, so serene as not to be real. The birds are just beginning a tuning up that is not song but more an earth sound. Not a leaf stirs, so that one can't be sure that wind—the moving that is invisible—has yet been invented by God. So vague the sky with its paleness and immobility of form and faintness of no-color that it is a fair question whether color, too, has yet to be invented, as if God were making up His mind: should the sky then be gold and reds and orange? Or just be a shell, a backdrop of pale, serene blue—is this kind of silent blue a color at all? An hour will change all this, I happen to *know;* but can I be sure?

The predawn is an unreal world. So uninhabited a world. I see not one single sign that man, during the night, didn't decide just to decamp; to leave the whole damn world to me. Gone to the moon perhaps, without leaving a note on the pillow: "Have given the world up as a bad job; it is all yours, my boy. The blue-gray of the Sound is all yours; the forest too. We have taken the wind, and the color of the sun, and the sounds and the ambitions and rewards—it's all yours; we've *had* it!"

But in an hour all will be stirring again; there will be birds scratching for breakfast and men scratching like mad for what they think *they* want. And people who want a piece of you, and you of them, it will be back in an hour or so.

I *think* it will.

JULY 25, 1963
NEW YORK

Made a decision yesterday in the life story of Development and Resources, one that could change the course of this "idea-child." After a year or more of thinking about it and two hours of discussion with Jack Franklin of Lazard, Nate and John Oliver, I authorized Jack to begin a definite exploration with Utah Construction & Mining people of their acquisition of D&R: merger is the term ordinarily used, but acquisition is a more forthright term.

Utah may not find the idea interesting at all, in which case that will be that. But if they do we will be launched upon discussions that will probe the potentials of this "unique" enterprise, D&R, and its prospects for continuing beyond the time when I will be around.

My critical remarks before the Joint Committee about the safety aspects of a Consolidated Edison nuclear power plant in New York City have certainly had repercussions far beyond anything I remotely conceived, particularly after the Joint Committee gave me such a "scolding" for saying such naughty things.

The public relations corps of Con Edison has been hard at work— you can tell this because the same story appears, at the same time, in *Time*, the *New York Times*, etc. The facts that come out strengthen the doubts I expressed of a nuclear power plant in Queens, a densely populated borough of New York City.

A few days subsequent to my appearance before the Joint Committee there was testimony about safety by members of the AEC expert staff that obviously shook the Committee badly, so much so that one member of the Committee, Representative Jack Westland, remarked on the record: "I think Lilienthal was right, then."

The issue before the Committee was an item of $19 million for a "standard pressure shell that you see all over the country." In this shell it is proposed to duplicate "the maximum credible [nuclear] accident and find what the causes are."

The colloquy between the AEC experts and the Committee members confirmed my hunch, that these experts and Con Ed's people have not told the public, or the Joint Committee, the whole story about the safety of such a plant in the heart of the city because they *just plain don't yet know* the causes that might produce a nuclear accident, nor just what damage such a "credible" accident would entail.

Here is one excerpt from the testimony that runs several pages:

REPRESENTATIVE WESTLAND: How have you got your siting criteria now? We had Consolidated Edison appear before us the other day and they indicated that the containment building that they were proposing, which is to be located in a very highly populated place, was going to be adequate.

Now you come in and say you are going to blow up some of these things in order to provide information or criteria.

The two do not seem consistent to me.

DR. WILSON: Do you not think we ought to know something about things like that?

REPRESENTATIVE WESTLAND: Sure I do. But I would assume you would know something about it now, or you would not be telling Consolidated Edison—you have not actually told them, but you have indicated you have told them—that it was going to be all right.

DR. WILSON: No, we did not indicate anything of the kind.

REPRESENTATIVE WESTLAND: I think Lilienthal was right, then.*

The whole testimony is chilling; it confirmed what I said in my own testimony about why we laymen should remain skeptical of technical experts—and of Members of Congress who are too impressed with them.

I had testified only a couple of days before this astounding confession by the AEC that it didn't yet really know about the effect in a populated area of a "maximum *credible* accident." I expressed then the basis for my doubts; my comments to one member of the Committee as expressed in the following testimony puts it about the way I see it today.

REPRESENTATIVE HOSMER: Let me ask you specifically with respect to the Con Edison plant that you used as an example: Are you fully familiar with the proposals respecting engineered safeguards against radiation and reactor hazards which have been proposed with respect to this particular plant at its particular location?

MR. LILIENTHAL: No, I am not.

REPRESENTATIVE HOSMER: You charged, however, that you would not dream of living in Queens if that plant existed there.

MR. LILIENTHAL: Yes. I will give you my reason. It is not on the basis of what the engineers have to say. It is on the basis of thirty years of experience with engineers and with scientists whose prescience and knowledge upon subjects frequently turn out to be less than their own estimates of their prescience or their own view of what they say they know.

REPRESENTATIVE HOSMER: You are speaking from your general low estimate of the engineering profession rather than the specific knowledge of details with respect to this plant.

* Hearings before the Subcommittee on Legislation of the Joint Committee on Atomic Energy on AEC Authorizing Legislation Fiscal Year 1964, 88th Congress, First Session, April 9, 1963, p. 91.

MR. LILIENTHAL: No, I am speaking from a long conviction and experience with technical people that they are human beings. Sometimes I doubted this, but they are human beings who are fallible. When it comes to safety, I take these predictions with a grain of salt.

There was a [nuclear] runaway at ARCO [a materials testing facility in Idaho]. This was exactly contrary to what we [of the AEC] had been told would be possible. In other words, engineers are fallible human beings. I myself would not want to live around one of these plants.†

JULY 26, 1963
11:30 A.M.
ON NORTHEAST PLANE

The news this morning: a "treaty" by the U.S., U.K., and U.S.S.R. agreeing not to test atomic weapons on the earth's surface.

The "treaty" turns out, on reading the text, to be a moratorium such as the one Ike had in effect, or Kennedy has put into effect recently, each party saying it will abstain from tests as long as it believes it is to its interest to do so.

How much it will amount to as an indication of a desire to "reduce tensions" raises a large degree of skepticism in me. If this agreement not to test above ground is taken to mean too much, and reinstates the relaxation, "the spirit of Geneva," which will be taken advantage of by the Soviets, they can make fools of us again.

JULY 29, 1963
MARTHA'S VINEYARD

A deeply moving experience walking the moors this morning about dawn, through a very heavy Vineyard fog. Perhaps fog is what it was. But to me it was something *more real:* a walk through a dream. As I climbed the hill, following the undulating path to the highest point of this so familiar moor along the shore, there was nothing I had ever seen before, nothing I would ever see again, nothing familiar, all with the strangeness that is the heart of a dream. And yet I have walked that path, I have stood on that hill, I have seen those boulders strewn along the shore time and time again. That is the fact, that is what my mind should have told me. But, as in a dream, it isn't the mind, it is something *beyond mind* that functions. And it is this dream quality that moved me to sense the unreality of reality, the double, the multiple

† Hearings before the Joint Committee on Atomic Energy on Development, Growth, and State of the Atomic Energy Industry, 88th Congress, First Session, April 4, 1963, Part 2, p. 734.

way of my life; my "real" life at 88 Battle Road, Princeton, or One Whitehall or here on Topside, just a role, the reading of a script prepared by others, while the unreal, the life of the imagination and the spirit, is the flesh-and-blood life.

Last week in New York I saw Federico Fellini's new film 8½. A disordered moving in and out of people, places; not a sequential march of events as in a story that has a structure and a chronology, but the way the imagination, the inside of a man functions, the random movement from one thing to another. The dream quality of that film (autobiographical of the director, I assume) and this morning's walk through the fog on the moor seemed to fit together.

AUGUST 1, 1963
MARTHA'S VINEYARD

Jack Franklin in San Francisco is seeing Littlefield of Utah Construction today about a possible merger with D&R.

Mergers or joinings together, in business, have some of the same pitfalls and anomalies of other mergers or joint undertakings, those called marriage or close friendship. The most unlikely alliances sometimes come off, and grow, or survive; some of the logical ones run into trouble.

The mergers I have had a part in bringing about, beginning with the desiccated Minerals Separation North American Corporation, way back in 1953 and the immediately subsequent years, these were sensible, improved the strength of both parties, supplied management and technical talent the "mergees" needed, and have since proved financially quite successful.

Actually the M&C side of M&C-Phillip is the best part of the business today. The merger—or absorption—of M&C by the ore-trading group known as Philipp Brothers has not yet worked well. The earnings of the combined companies continue to increase, but from an artistic craftsman viewpoint it was more a financial maneuver for the Philipp owners than a substantial improvement in a management sense. The reason: neither of the two merging groups knew or understood the habits of mind and background of experience of the other. The trading mentality is a thing apart, as I have come to see; the industrial management and research mentality is something else entirely. On paper and in theory the merger made very good sense; in practice there are still two companies, not one. This doesn't mean at all that it will always be so.

It is with this background of fruitful and logical mergers, and also one that has yet to prove itself, that I think about the possibility of a joining with Utah—or, if that doesn't appear feasible, some other group. For to give some long-term stability to this unique D&R enterprise, that grew out of my head, is worth a lot of thought and experimenting. I'm not naïve enough to believe, however, that *any* merger is better than going it alone for D&R. Definitely not true. It would solve some of our present problems—providing a marketable security or cash for Gordon's widow's D&R shares, and rather promptly, but that obligation could be taken care of in other ways.

What a merger would do to my freedom of action and my fun in the work is the decisive factor. If it doesn't maintain my motivation and happily even increase it, then it would be a mistake for me and for Utah, for they wouldn't be getting what they would be paying for, which is the prime energy and drive I could—and have—brought to the work.

AUGUST 2, 1963
MARTHA'S VINEYARD

My reflections—about self, about "the world as it wags"—these reactions, broodings (not formal enough to be called by the old-fashioned word "meditations"), most all of these seem to be sparked by *events* in which I have or have had some part as an actor, a participant. In short, my thoughts about self mostly spring from *outside* myself. But this is not the classic pattern of reflections, is it?

Have just been reading from Bernard Berenson's diaries, notebooks, etc. The excerpts seem so exotic to me because so many of them spring from *within* the man of reflection, an inner man without much of an outer man to go on. Aesthetics was the driving interest of his life. But the contrast with the things I had to write in my journals over the years is a startling one. Because the examination of self to be found in those pages of shorthand, and now of typescript, are reflections that *grow out* of what I do, trying to get others to do, or was having done to me.

Today Rusk *et al.* leave for Moscow to sign the treaty agreeing to end nuclear explosions on the earth's surface. Surely it should be ratified by the Senate, and probably will be overwhelmingly, if for no other reason (and it is a good one) than to turn it down would be a repudiation of the President at a bad time. On its merits the agreement is a good one.

But I have had some second thoughts up here on this serene hilltop about what this negotiation teaches, what kind of precedent it may set for further discussions on many other topics that I hope will continue with the Russians.

There is a sour note here that I can't disguise from myself. The formula for agreement with the Russians, so this negotiation says, is *easy*: just accept what they offer. For years this test ban business has been going along its dismal way, every proposal we make being stalled or denounced or rejected. Then suddenly they accept a treaty that meets *their* views, long sustained and repeated: that there should be *no* international or UN participation, but instead a direct deal between the U.S. and its junior partner, the U.K.; not a foot to be put on Russian soil in the administration of the treaty; no agreement to suspend their nuclear weapons research and testing (and ours) if underground; and freedom for the Soviets to terminate the treaty and resume testing in the air, and lay the blame on some act or other of ours.

That the timing of agreement by the Soviets should so often be when it suits their needs and when we are in trouble in making an agreement our European allies will find troublesome and worrisome: this is the old story of Russian skill in keeping the initiative. France is further from us, as a direct result of this treaty, at a time when a repair of damage to our French relations might have been in sight; West Germany is going to exact a price that may disturb other relationships in Europe. The Soviet will be acclaimed, as they were in the Cuba missile confrontation, as the initiators of this move to cease polluting the atmosphere.

Well, these are the things that make one less than happy, even though on the whole case there is much to gain in the achievement of a treaty.

AUGUST 3, 1963
MARTHA'S VINEYARD

Shocked and disturbed by a page-one story in today's *Times:* Jim Landis pleads guilty to failure to file an income tax return for five consecutive years.

Of all the intense, brilliant, ambitious young men who made up my contingent at the Harvard Law School in the twenties, the fierce, hawk-like Landis was easily at the top. President of the *Law Review,* a legend while still a student because of his swiftness of mind and his fabulous marks: to the School's Faculty and students marks were the *sole* measure of a student, an unfailing yardstick of his worth and his future. (My own marks, except in my third year, were merely mediocre.)

He was a man of ardor and impetuousness. The driving force within him made his path as a person and as dean of a conservative faculty anything but smooth. That is understandable. But just blandly neglecting to report his income tax for five years: how in the hell can you explain that in a first-rate *lawyer?*

Reminds me of the strange career of another Harvard Law star: Edward ("Prich") Prichard. Another of Felix Frankfurter's favorites, close to Fred Vinson before and after he became Chief Justice. A huge, genial man, superbright, definitely headed for the top in the law and politics. Then how explain his getting involved in a cheap ballot-box stuffing charge, in his home state of Kentucky; going to jail?

Another shock and another mystery. Phil Graham, also a star in the Harvard Law constellation, a close friend of Nate's, and head of the Washington *Post* and *Newsweek* killed himself this morning. Oh, ye successful men, what goes on behind that curtain of self?

At the Eliases' for a fish chowder dinner: among the guests Jerome Wiesner, Kennedy's science advisor, and John Oakes, of the *New York Times*.

Wiesner was not reluctant to volunteer things about the test ban treaty. Defending the ninety-day termination of treaty clause, he said this was *our* idea, not the Russians', intended to draw some of the fire out of the American die hards against any cessation of big bomb testing. That *we* were the ones who wanted a quick out—and therefore a much milder treaty—surprised me. Perhaps it should not have, considering that apparently the whole Administration was surprised out of its boots that the Russians were ready to agree to anything about testing.

He moved to a place on the sofa next to me and talking tête-à-tête said he noticed I had not made a statement favoring the treaty's ratification; that they all hoped I would as they will need everything that can be done to get a strong vote in the Senate: "a defeat would be as serious as the reservations clause in the League of Nations fight in the Senate in Wilson's time."

I said of course I believed the treaty should be ratified, but that I would delay saying anything until what I thought was the right time, which isn't now.

He spoke in the familiar terms: a first step. I agreed, of course, but found myself, to my surprise, talking like an elder statesman to the President's science advisor that the second and other steps should *not* be in the area of weapons; trade with Russia would be a much wiser direction. "The greatest Congressional lobby this country has ever known, the combination of the defense industry with the military, the greatest vested interests of all time, are involved in disarmament; for that *political* reason if for no other—and I think there are other reasons equally strong—let's try the next steps along *economic* lines."

I said I thought we should not rejoice over the signs of a split between Russia and China and give the appearance and reality of trying to isolate China for a temporary advantage to us; we did this to the Soviets after the revolution in 1918 and have been paying severely for it, in hatred and other ways, ever since. And after World War II we literally *forced* the Russians to become self-sufficient industrially, with our embargo on strategic material; look what that got us. Let's not let the Chinese, with their harsh statements and intransigence, taunt us into "punishing" them, for this is a long, long road, and twenty years from now we will pay heavily for such shortsightedness.

Oakes found this viewpoint puzzling; he said the *Times* believed in recognition of China, but they have been so impossible to get along with, how can we make any decent headway with them?

So I said: Begin with little things. There have been only half a dozen Americans inside Red China in the past decade or so. Half-joking, I said: "How about TVA Lilienthal going to China to report to them on the development of power from their rivers, as we provided engineers to Soviet Russia in the days of her early struggles?" More Americans traveling in China would be a healthy beginning.

Wiesner said: "Have you suggested that to the State Department in this Administration?" No, I hadn't; didn't think there would be any chance. "I suggest you write Secretary Rusk and suggest it; you might be surprised at the response you would get."

I think he meant this seriously. Might be worth trying. I thought that the important thing was to find a way to get the Chinese to agree first, and then go to the State Department. I remember how George Marshall as Secretary turned down the idea of my making such a trip years ago when Harry Luce proposed it. But perhaps our State Department is the place to begin.‡

Oakes wanted very much to find out what had led me to "take out" on the proposed Con Ed nuclear plant in Queens, in mid-New York. He certainly starts with the usual assumption: that it *must* be safe or the experts would have warned against it ("you are the only expert who has even mentioned the danger, so far at least"). Moreover, he said, "we at the *Times* hate to be 'against progress,' like the people who were against the railroad because it was dangerous, and so forth."

I assured him I thought the damage, if anything substantial went contrary to the experts' expectations, would be very serious and that therefore there was a great risk; what was there to justify that risk? There are other ways of producing electricity without taking that risk right in the *heart* of the city.

‡ But Lilienthal never did make such a proposal to State.—Ed.

The problem of getting rid of the atomic wastes apparently he had hardly heard of. "I thought they would just take them out to sea and dump them." I must assume that Con Ed is pushing this idea: but whether the wastes are transported through the streets on their way to the reprocessing site or to ships and then to sea, the danger of an accident is there. Think of New York Harbor or the Narrows with such a cargo going through, to say nothing of the risks of putting these containers in the sea where sooner or later they will corrode.

I thought the Con Ed nuclear power plant worth speaking out about because it clearly brings out the central issue, one of *timing:* Has it yet been established by experience that it is sensible to depend upon atomic energy as the major source of added energy for the country, as the AEC is projecting, in, say, a couple of decades? Not on the basis of demonstrated safety so far, I thought. And it is not solely a question of plant safety but also of how *dependable* are these large plants as part of a network, at this early stage. I mean dependable in an operating sense. Therefore the whole future of electricity in America one or two decades hence is at stake.

Atomic energy as *the* major source of energy means we must think not simply about the suitability or economics of a plant, at a specified site. We must think about a great proliferation of these plants all over the country. The pressure of engineering convenience and costs will bring these plants more and more into densely populated areas. To start down that road without first completely licking the problem of risks, or *dependability in a regionwide system,* is a foolhardy course.

AUGUST 4, 1963
MARTHA'S VINEYARD

I am oozing just plain sweat from every pore. Cause: a couple of hours cutting away viburnum and sumac growth along our east stone wall, to expose its sturdy color and design.

Whether I do this because I am a ham and like to show myself that I am tough enough for such work on a muggy summer afternoon or to get rid—or transfer—my hostilities or frustrations—to use the modern idiom, I don't know. But I like it.

I'm not the only one who likes this strange form of fun. I remember going out to Dean Acheson's place in the country one Sunday afternoon to see him on some urgent matter about the atom control business. That usually very elegantly dressed and groomed gent I found up in a tree, wielding big pruning shears, even as I did today, sweat running down his face and wilting that really quite becoming mustache. He had a light of real pleasure in his eyes; he was having fun, and damn little of it he was getting in those trying days of his secretaryship. He hailed me, with that half-laugh so characteristic of him in social exchange, said he wanted to finish that particular spot and would be down in a minute. We had already finished our business when here came another visitor, Walton Butterworth, fresh from the agonies of the Marshall Mission to China.

AUGUST 6, 1963
NEW YORK

As I boarded the plane on the Vineyard I was hailed by a diminutive lady in a rather elaborate hat with veil (elaborate for the Vineyard, I suppose I mean, where even wearing *shoes* is being elegant). Lillian Hellman on her way to New York for a few days. Visited with her as we waited for luggage at Idlewild. When I remarked that she continued to be productive (I had a vague recollection that a play of hers had done quite well last season), her eyes looked so sad and troubled. "Oh, I haven't written a line for six months. In my work that is forever."

AUGUST 11, 1963
MARTHA'S VINEYARD

A stately Jaguar sedan came rolling up our hill. A soft-spoken lady got out: is this the Riggses'? No; I gave her directions. The man behind the wheel, swarthy, a light in his eye, looked me over. "From the photographs I would guess you are David Lilienthal; is that right? Well [shaking hands through the window], I'm Jed Harris."

As a pushover for sentimental theatre, I could hardly have been more impressed: the producer of some of my corny favorites: *The Front Page, Our Town, The Royal Family,* etc.

"It's your son I read in the *Gazette;* is he going to settle down here?" "Yes," I said, "and one day you will produce one of his plays, though now what he is writing is novels, under the name of David Ely."

"He's not writing under his own name; that's old-fashioned, doing that. That's not done any more. Well, tell him for me to stay away from writers; this island is *full* of them. Talk to the garage man or anyone but not to other writers. He's how old? Thirty-five almost. He's old enough to have something to say. But he'll get nothing from other writers." And abruptly down the hill they went.

Seeing Harris up here reminded me of Nate's story about Harris. It seems he was having a business conference with a noted lawyer, Mr. X, at X's elaborate country home. X, the story goes, is a devout nudist, goes around his home without a stitch. Harris, known to go in for nudism himself, made no comment about X's attire or utter lack of it. As he was leaving he turned to X and said: "Oh, by the way, Joe, your fly is open."

AUGUST 13, 1963
MARTHA'S VINEYARD

A great storm!

For hours now this big open unfinished living room has been rattling and shuddering; even the floor has been visibly trembling as a particularly determined gust roars into the open garage beneath our feet. How many young farm boys from this island and across the Sound, near New Bedford, sailed out "for to catch a whale." Their vessel lashed and plunged through the awful Pacific seas in a gale like this!

Took Helen in for a festive sort of lunch in Edgartown. Edgartown was fun. We slurped cherrystone clams in the fish market with a long, lanky, middle-aged gent in shorts and a sailing sou'wester, probably chairman of a big bank or something. On a foggy day with a storm in the offing, the harbor is full of towering yachts—some of the greatest pleasure ships in the country, I suppose—and the streets are filled with their owners and their guests, their faces very top-drawer and rich, their clothes scandalously ragged. Reminded us of the time we were at Pawleys Island, in South Carolina; some of the crummiest dressed young people, the girls barefooted, the boys too, dancing the Big Apple. Our hostess explained that we were seeing "some of the bluest blood of the South." The bluest—sometimes the thinnest—of the North here, in the streets of Edgartown in the sailing summertime.

AUGUST 14, 1963
6:30 a.m.
MARTHA'S VINEYARD

A roaring night it was outside. The roof of our house—being without ceilings beneath, or "finishing," acts like the head of a tight drum, so that a sudden burst of rain that in an ordinary house one would hardly hear is like the roll of Dave Brubeck's drummer, getting off the kind of solo that "sends" the young people.

Why do people do what they do? Why do *I*? The items on the agenda for that question could be very long.

Example: Why do I take such satisfaction in being able to chin myself, pulling my now 190 pounds off the floor by grasping the top

of the door of my bedroom and heisting. What use have I for muscles?
I *feel* better when I use my muscles, that's true. But a brisk walk
would do that. No, this is a kind of personal vanity of an immature
kind. This is but one puny example of the gyrations people go through
that can't be explained by reason, logic, a set of rules, formulae.

The human being, even at his best, is a strange duck, but a wonderful one, because he *isn't* logical and always sensible and "objective."
To see this in oneself is important because then one is less likely to
commit the sin that was so omnipresent as I was younger: judging
others. Judge not. Judge not because that makes you less understanding
of others; the biblical reason: "lest ye be judged" (it *is* biblical, isn't
it?) misses the point, a kind of "deal."

9 P.M.

Tony Young is eight, and David III's constant companion. Looks
for all the word like the bumptious little character in the old *Our
Gang* movie scenes, enormous freckles on his nose, a permanent mischief tilt to him. Last week I took him and David to the town wharf;
they began to be obstreperous, kid-style, so much so that the frail old
docktender asked me: "Are them yours?" And when I said they were
(they tearing up the dock steps, yelling like drunken sailors on leave),
the old boy said: "Git them out o' here."

So I grabbed David by the hand and Tony, resisting, I threw my
arm around his middle and carried him along, he kicking and furious.
When I put him down—out of the dock jurisdiction—he glared at me
through his freckles and looking me right in the eye said: "I hate *you*."

Which no doubt he did.

Today we were at Topside. They scrambled up Signal Rock, the
great boulder, like monkeys. They talked me into climbing up too; I
dug my toes and fingers in, and with shouts of encouragement from
my young friends above, heaved myself up with an arm push and was
on top. Tony yelled: "We *made* him do it." Then we all stood up on top
and crowed like young or old roosters, Indian-yelled to Helen across the
valley, and told tall tales.

AUGUST 16, 1963
MARTHA'S VINEYARD

The annual Fair is going full tilt at North Tisbury nearby, with
a tightrope walker act no doubt. But there is no more regular tightrope
act (no nets!) than the Persian financial crisis we teeter across three
or four times a year. The most recent one was over, or eased, almost

as soon as we had sent a cable saying we would give notice of termination to our people out there if we didn't have money in our bank in New York by August 20. Well, a quarter million came through, and the balance (a large figure) seems very likely. One of these days we may slip on that tight wire, but so far no casualties worse than an occasional set of slightly frayed nerves as the deadline we set approaches.

Another chapter in D&R's life story appears definitely happening. Franklin, talking to Littlefield and Eccles of Utah Construction & Mining, found that they are serious about acquiring an interest in D&R and working together with us. The basis for a price of the shares was agreed to; they don't want 100 percent or even 51 percent, i.e., control; instead, they want the greatest possible incentive to remain for me and the others who make this little company interesting to them, and similarly want Lazard to continue to have an ownership position to increase their interest and incentive.

AUGUST 17, 1963
MARTHA'S VINEYARD

As she greeted me, late this afternoon, at her new home on the harbor, Lillian Hellman seemed like a pair of eyes without a body, a pair of the most knowing, wise, hard, and deeply sad eyes, eyes that are without "sentimentality" and without illusions. That this look should be attached to candy-stripe pants and blouse made it all the more impressive.

With some encouragment from me she spoke about the "bad shape" of the present theatre, and getting worse. The trouble? Simple. It doesn't require a big Twentieth Century Fund "study" (which we Trustees have just authorized§) to find out what is the matter: the theatre has lost its audience. In its place are middle-aged expense account and theatre party groups. Young people don't go to the theatre, because it is so bad, and the less the young go to it the worse it gets.

AUGUST 25, 1963
MARTHA'S VINEYARD

Last evening we had as a dinner guest Dr. Jerry Wiesner, just back from Washington and the Senate hearings on the nuclear test ban treaty.

§ This study was published in 1966 under the title *Performing Arts—The Economic Dilemma.*

He looked very sad; as he said: "The hearings are stirring up more ill will and more fear than I would have believed possible, and that about a *minimal* measure of disarmament; if this tiny step can cause so much warlike talk and exhortation to 'keep ahead' of the Russians, then how can anyone hope that something significant would have a chance?"

It was this kind of stirring of the competitive race and of charges of bad faith that I had in mind when I took a dim view of negotiating for disarmament now, the kind of thing that has already happened in these hearings, the kind we shall unhappily hear more of soon.

Yes, he had just read the galleys of my new book; knew what I had said. "But we have to start sometime, and someplace, and the test ban seemed the best chance for that start."

As a measure to protect the health of the human population, yes; but putting it forward as a way to slow up the arms race or as a form of disarmament—that is what I thought was a mistake. I'm for the treaty, strongly now, but I can't help reflecting on how quickly the note of hope for the future that the President expressed has not only evaporated but been replaced by an ugly note, in the hearings.

SEPTEMBER 2, 1963
PRINCETON

Thursday night last, August 29, dinner with Dana Atchley. It was memorable, one of the happy joinings in a sense of common understanding and purpose that happens so rarely and is long remembered.

He said that my course has always been one of challenging "what you thought was in error, or wrong, or didn't fit." A recent example: a nuclear power plant in New York. But my whole adult life has been founded on that premise: challenge it, re-examine, reassume, re-examine.

"Well, our two lives have followed very different paths, but they haven't been divergent. Years ago I fought against the medical idea and precept that the practice of the healing art consisted of gathering *facts*, what I called *secondary facts*: ulcer? blood pressure? and so on. I insisted that those were really secondary; the primary thing is the patient's *personality*, that is the decisive thing. I was attacked as you have been in your own fields. Now this is being more and more accepted. But I feel that you and I have come together in our basic outlook of never accepting as beyond re-examination anything however many 'important' people believe it."

I suppose this thesis about the primacy of the individual personality is why he is considered the founder, or one of the founders, of

psychosomatic medicine. And it is why, because he has come to understand my "personality" even better than I do myself, he has been able
to help me so much. People are aghast when I say that only once a year,
actually, does he take my blood pressure, etc.; the rest of the visits he
just asks a few questions about "secondary" facts, if any; the rest of
the time he is observing as a sagacious, compassionate friend might,
the vital matter that collecting physical facts does not disclose.

"Conserve your energy"—he looked away almost with disgust.
"Conserve it for what? For your business? For God's sake! Conserve
it so you can write your memoirs? If you do that your memoirs wouldn't
be worth writing—or reading."

SEPTEMBER 3, 1963
NEW YORK

A day of balancing the pluses and minuses, the advantages and
disadvantages of taking Utah in as a stockholder of D&R. Hard work,
and trying.

What is involved is more than an "investment" (as it is largely for
Lazard and Utah). With me it is how I spend much of the rest of my
active days. But the trial of making a new set of facts work, of confront-
ing new faces and problems, is always tempting to me.

SEPTEMBER 4, 1963
NEW YORK

A "peasant and workers' revolution," headed by the King, is under
way in Persia, what His Majesty calls a "White Revolution."

There was ample basis for believing it is genuine in how both
peasants and workmen in the city of Tehran behave, as contrasted
with, say, five years ago.

But *political* democracy? Well, hardly; not yet. But that will come.

Just read one of Blumberg's staff reports from Iran (dated August
29), one paragraph of which is on "Elections," for the Majlis (now a
nonexistent body).

"The Tehran press is full of reports of election meetings of women,
tribespeople, leading citizens, etc. But the readers are bored to tears
with the whole thing.

"The prospective candidates do not yet know whether they will
be permitted to be candidates. As you may know, there is approval required by certain offices: Governor General, Security, Gendarmes and
Justice. The list for each area, with approved names, is forwarded to
Tehran for study."

SEPTEMBER 11, 1963
NEW YORK

How the King of Afghanistan appears to his subjects in his royal robes I don't know; most impressive and kingly, no doubt. But two seats removed from me at the head of the table at the Council on Foreign Relations dinner tonight, his glistening, highly-polished bald head looked like a *melon*, a had-been-burnished melon. Long ceremonial slashes in his thin and delicate face; a distinctly Semite profile. As for his "answers" to questions put to him by what is called a "distinguished audience of representative citizens," if anyone got any information it was unwitting on his part. He spoke in Farsi (Persian), then the handsome UN Ambassador of Afghanistan rendered it in English; the same with questions. The question: How does he feel about the danger of Chinese invasion of his country, or of the row between Russia and China? Perched where they are on the map, how could he be expected to answer such questions, even if he had some foggy idea about what the answers were. Which he didn't.

Left the Vineyard for the last time this season on a day of splendor. The *light*—my God, how alive the light is on such a day, with a northerly breeze, the cliffs of the Elizabeths so you could reach out and touch them, each oak leaf a bit of polished bronze throwing out a flash of gold.

SEPTEMBER 18, 1963
NEW YORK

The youthful President of Princeton University came into the private dining room at the Princeton Club, grinning like a boy, opened his briefcase and said: "I hand you the first copy of your new book, *Change, Hope, and the Bomb:* I am the Princeton Press special messenger service."

SEPTEMBER 21, 1963
PRINCETON

A day of heavy gardening. Digging the earth still gives me a sensual delight; wheelbarrowing loads of mellowness from the ripening compost heap, dropping it into the newly upturned border, next spring to be bursting with life and color; and best of all, redesigning, trying to picture what clump over here I should dig up in the moist heavy fallish earth and put over *there*. This is such fun that I came into the house gurgling with it all, Helen wondering if I had left my senses. Which I had, I suppose; my workaday senses, but not the best ones.

I have just read a short story by Louis Auchincloss called *The Single Reader*. It is the story—ironic and well done—of a man who needed someone with whom to "communicate," his wife having left him years before and he never taking human relations seriously since. So he began a journal or diary; and the diary became a substitute for intimate relations with others, until it ate him up—and drove off a woman who might have loved him but was terrified that she would simply be a *subject* of a journal, which would always be the most intimate communicant he could have. So she rushed off, and he went to the Century Club, secure and *content*.

The story does have a twist for me; but my story doesn't end the way Auchincloss' did.

One does not feel or think imaginatively until one finds a way of *transmitting* feelings and the fruits of one's imagination. The pages of this notebook on which I am now writing these shorthand outlines, and the literally millions of those outlines that preceded this, these *words* are one way of transmitting feelings and ideas as the words set out in his journal were for the character in Auchincloss' tale.

But there are other ways than by words to express feelings to those you love and who love you. Without *that* emotions become just words, not poetry, the imagination more intellect than creativeness. Just "communicating" facts and ideas and reasons isn't enough. I confess that for a long time I thought it was.

SEPTEMBER 23, 1963
6:30 A.M.
NEW YORK

How a modern Marco Polo might exclaim over Manhattan as I saw it this morning, just as the sky in the east began to glow as if a great celestial forest fire was burnishing the shell of blue, the dark blue of just before the dawn on a first day of northerly autumn.

This is what I imagine Marco might have said on such a morning as this:

"I, Marco Polo, tell thee, Venetian unbelievers in miracles, what these eyes have seen of the wonders of the golden city of Cathay, a city of towers rising to the sky all in gold, each pinnacle bathed in gold; gold and the purple that is royal is that city of wonders caught between two broad ribbons of water, blue on the west and blue on the east. But I tell you, my fellow Venetians, this great city of might and splendor is too much for the heart to bear in this morning silence, empty of any living thing."

What I myself saw from this hotel aerie yesterday early afternoon was almost equally unbelievable: the sun made white the great buildings that border the green of what I can believe is Sherwood Forest; the white irregular pile is an Italian hill town in the valley of the Po. And then lights came on, and it is *another* city entirely.

SEPTEMBER 26, 1963
IN PENN STATION, WAITING FOR THE 5:30 P.M. TO PULL OUT

Bushed. A week that would bush almost anyone. Worst part, made me prickly. "Complaining," to Nate, that Lazard participated in organizing a development bank in Iran, with no credit nor benefit to D&R for our "opening the door" by our work there. Nate bristled, told me off for being a "resentment collector," said my "assumptions" of fact were wrong. He got up in a considerable huff and left. I felt badly that I should lose my temper with someone I like as well as Nate. Sign of fatigue, I think. So I decided to call it a week (and what a week).

Asked Beatrice to take me to an exhibit at the Whitney Museum: "60 Years of American Art," partly because I wanted to see it with so knowledgeable an artist, partly because I had had more than enough of D&R *et al.* for the week. She suggested I drop by first to see some of the paintings she has been doing lately. It was the first time I had seen her recent work (she and Barney have a "thing" of not allowing anyone to see paintings in the process or unhung—say it is not "professional"). I thought her ironic touch in some of her paintings (society women gabbling or female singers in velvet) was damned good, and to my lay eyes better than many of the paintings that we then scurried down to the Whitney Museum to see.

Eruption in the Dominican Republic, with the military "taking over" for the group that didn't win the election when Bosch was made President. I suspect that some of the relatively conservative and prosperous young men who got Gordon and me to visit the Yaque del Norte, if they didn't have some hand in this certainly would find it more to their liking than the Bosch regime. The strange workings of events which I somehow get to see at first hand.

This morning's paper had a picture of two "generals" of the junta that has just taken over. Both in civilian dress. I recognized one of them as the sensitive, tense young doctor we met in the office of the Provisional President in February, '62. He was described as one of the men who, taking their lives in their hands, had shot Trujillo dead when he was on his way to visit one of his many mistresses. This earnest young man now shows up to oust another ruler.

OCTOBER 1, 1963
WASHINGTON

Hutchinson, "in charge of Africa and Europe" (wow!) in the AID, is a neat, slender, rather short man, reputed to be icy. But I found him warm and, more than that, receptive and a "quick listener" to my idea. The "idea": making the Niger River a symbol of the coming (or hoped-for) unity of the West African "nations" formerly part of French West Africa.

I brought him up sharp by saying: But this idea isn't worth much unless there is some *place to start*. Where should that be? I said I would spell out why a charter between the countries might be the place, if the charter had something like teeth in it, that is, could be made to produce something, with a Planning Agency for all the nations in the group as the possible beginning. He agreed that unless the French could take the initiative in this it wouldn't go.

Pageantry we Americans may not have, but what I have just seen, standing on the curb across from the White House, is a pretty good facsimile. The Emperor of Ethiopia was the occasion (each week there is a visit by a different king or emperor or "president" of some tiny new country). A gay sight. Certainly motorcycle cops with pennants on their cycles *aren't* like the magnificent white horses of the King of Morocco's honor guard we saw in Rabat. True the shako on the leader of the Marine Band did look a bit strange; the little fellow in the Air Force bagpipe ceremonial band *did* have a cap twice his size, as he tootled on a little horn. And the crowds along the Avenue were file clerks from St. Petersburg or Fredericksburg out for the sun, rather than worshipers of the Lion of Judah (a dried prune, in his red cap).

But it *was* a good show. There are so many of these potentates and "heads of state" these days that I don't see how the President gets anything else done (God knows he *does*). But the load of visitors is so large it requires that a part of the armed forces be organized as greeters (with their bayonet-tipped rifles, and the very careful inclusion of the right proportion of Negro faces in the ranks).

OCTOBER 2, 1963
ON AMERICAN FLIGHT TO NEW YORK FROM WASHINGTON

The World Series opening game was going on while I was scheduled to talk about my new book to a Contemporary Affairs-Princeton Press luncheon. So I was surprised that so many of the "media" were on hand to hear what *Change, Hope, and the Bomb* is about, and to put questions to me.

Among the guests: David Brinkley of the famous Huntley-Brinkley Electronic Twins. To my surprise he is a *tall* man, with a very boyish look and grin: I wasn't prepared for how he actually looks by having seen him scores of times on our living room TV screen. And despite that one-sided pleasantly sardonic look he was certainly warm and friendly.

And Art Buchwald was *exactly* as I had pictured him, in appearance: roly-poly, a Brooklyn-type Will Rogers with huge glasses and a delightful laugh. But so *serious* when he was serious. A look of pain came over his face when he asked me such a question as: But isn't there *anything* good about the peaceful uses of the atom?

A number of these men had followed me in my work and had attended my press conferences for a long, long time as a public servant: Mark Childs, looking terribly worn, I thought, and as despairing of Congress as ever, but charming with that explosive bark of a laugh. A great soul, Mark, torn by what he wants the world of public affairs to be but with so few things in recent years to hearten him. Ernest Lindley, now special assistant to Rusk, slender and more handsome than ever, with his mound of iron-gray hair. He was unhappy with my comments about the unrealism of the Administration and the Joint Committee's handling of the French request for information and help on their atomic energy program. I had made it strong; that France was perfectly capable of an atomic program and for us to try to delay or hamper it when so much was at stake with France in *other* directions I thought was absurd and risky to the alliance.

At breakfast this morning Walt Seymour and Tom Mead reported on their dinner with Diawara of the Ivory Coast: The Government (which is the President and Minister Saller) is publicly and firmly committed to the southwest development program we have recommended. But the AID people haven't yet made up their minds. This is causing pain.

Day before yesterday President Houphouet-Boigny made a speech saying the southwest program was going to go ahead and that the Ivory Coast had selected the "firm of Lilienthal of world renown." We may get this thing off the ground at last.

This overseas work takes patience, and more patience.

OCTOBER 4, 1963
8:30 A.M.
NEW YORK

To go to bed after an exhausting kind of day without fear; to awake with the love of life strong in you: this is what has happened to me, so I must conclude that it happens to many people, despite the evidence to the contrary of these long, unhappy inward-looking faces I see so much on the streets of New York.

OCTOBER 8, 1963
PRINCETON

David has been here for the past several days, working away at the *Journals*. Last evening he said he would like to see some of the old family movies. And so we brought them out and watched for two hours: David, a chubby boy of four in Knoxville and Norris; running a motorboat on Wilson Lake as we saw the foundation for Wheeler Dam being dug; Penny, our cocker, frisking, and Dinah, that cat of the long, long ago, rolling about asking that her tummy be scratched—and so on.

NEW YORK

Bernardo Garces of CVC just back from a two-month holiday with his whole family in Europe. "Tell me," said I to this eternally smiling, sophisticated man of what he himself calls "the ruling class" of Colombia, "tell me what the devil is going to happen in Latin America; it looks pretty grim to me."

"Latin America; well, that is not anything one can say much about. Too big, too different one part from the other.

"Colombia: well, in Colombia even the strongest man, say, Lleras Camargo, is too reluctant to use force; afraid, timid about taking hold of trouble. Now our present President, Valencia, is an elemental man; no particular background, no understanding of history, and so on. But for the first time the Government is shooting at the bandits instead of the other way around. So we may get some order, and with order much can be done."

Bernardo confirmed the worst stories I have heard about how the "ruling class" behaves—but always in some *other* country than Colombia! When they go to their estates, in Chile, say, they go with a complete cavalcade as a grandee of the Middle Ages might. Spend six months in Europe each year. Men who work in the sugar cane fields getting one-third the wages they get in Colombia, where the fields are operated the year around, whereas elsewhere it may be two months and then there is nothing for the poor devils to do. Couldn't be worse.

"Look at me. I own only sixty acres of sugar cane, just sixty acres. Some of these people in Chile or Brazil own thousands of hectares. We pay far more to the workers than they do. Yet on sixty acres we do quite well. But the income of some of these big landlords in Latin America is enormous."

"What will happen?" I asked.

He puffed at the long cigar, looked bemused but not sad, and said nothing for a long time. Then, "It is a terrible mess."

Which for Bernardo is a very strong, unequivocal statement.

What happens, he says, is that in so many of these countries— Cuba under Batista, for example—the police get 250 pesos a month ($25). Who wants to be a policeman? So the police come from the dregs, sooner or later, and then they take over.

When I think of the high hopes for social reform so eloquently expressed in the Punta del Este Declaration of August, 1961,◖ and the *Harper's* article of Peter Drucker about the new young men who are going to bring about the Kennedy Revolution in Latin America, and my own euphoric article for *Harper's* (which, *happily*, was not accepted), I am amazed at how those bright hopes have so completely collapsed.

OCTOBER 9, 1963
NEW YORK

A phone call from Ed Littlefield: The Utah merger transaction is approved by their Executive Committee, he said; they want to call a special Board meeting to ratify it. But clearly it is settled.*

A fiery, dramatic Oriental gal, Madame Nhu, has set New York by the ears. Pouring her scorn on the U.S., whom she blames for the assassination of President Diem of Vietnam; her husband killed at the same time. The crowd at the Overseas Press Club to hear her was so great they had to move the luncheon to the Waldorf. How the State Department must be fuming, which is one of the reasons, I fear, why the Dragon Lady is such an attraction to the press, which would like nothing better than to embarrass the Kennedy Administration.

I was much touched by a comment of a Mrs. Jane Cutaia, science

---

◖ At the Punta del Este Conference the U.S. agreed to provide $20 billion over a decade for economic development in Latin America; nineteen Latin nations pledged to increase their contributions to economic and social development, and to make far-reaching social reforms.

* The transaction was ratified and the shares transferred in December, 1963. D&R reacquired the Utah shares in June of 1966.

editor of *Business Week*. She had left my book about the atom out where her seventeen-year-old son Stephen saw it; he sat up through the night and read it through; found it very encouraging and hopeful. This impressed Mrs. Cutaia—and me. She said: "I think you will find that in a year it will be that generation that will be reading your book and following you on this issue."

OCTOBER 10, 1963
NEW YORK

The Century dinner for new members was a relaxing, happy kind of gathering. It is an extraordinary club. Where else one could meet such a *diversity* of excellence I don't know: painters, writers, doctors, musicians, and of course, lawyers. Whitney Seymour, presiding, quoted Clarence Day's definition of the Century Association: "The ragtag-and-bobtail of the best in the country," which has the element of kidding in which the more or less "arrived" can indulge.

OCTOBER 11, 1963
IN PENN STATION WAITING FOR THE 11:45 A.M. TO LEAVE FOR PRINCETON

Word just in that a great thin arch dam on the Piave River in the Italian Alps overtopped: a great tragedy. (The first word was that it had *failed*.) Designed, probably, by the same great Italian design engineer (at Bergamo) who was the genius behind the basic design of the Dez Dam. Built by an Italian construction firm, no doubt, and it was such a group we selected to build Dez.

I didn't question Bill Voorduin about this yesterday; thought he would be too upset right now.

But I am responsible "period." If there had been a failure of any of the twenty-odd dams of the TVA, the responsibility would be on me. Not because I was the engineer; but final responsibility is the lot of a man in charge. And so with the dam on the Dez.

On the Piave apparently an earthquake caused a landslide and a sudden rise of water at the dam. We tested the Dez design for earthquake forces several times greater than ever experienced. But if for any reason that dam should be overtopped by such a slide, or fail for any reason, the blood would not be on the designer, nor our eminent consulting panel, nor Bill Voorduin, but on *me*.

Which sounds as if (1) I thought this likely, which I definitely don't, or (2) that I am brooding about it, also not true. But such thoughts do move into your consciousness whenever you take great responsibility.

Those of Con Ed or the AEC or the Joint Committee on Atomic Energy who give us to understand that a nuclear plant is "absolutely safe" located in the heart of New York City should ponder what would happen if some unforeseeable human or physical failure occurred, in a hotbed of radiation!

OCTOBER 13, 1963
6 A.M.
PRINCETON

Up at five; the stars as big as loving eyes. It is mid-October, and in my calendar the beginning of a new year and therefore the end of the one just past.

It was a very full and happy year, happy because the willingness, yes, eagerness to "take on" all comers was so strong in me, the juices of the forward look running strong.

The new book—the Atom Revisited it might have have been titled—is evidence, to me at least, that the sense of drive and desire for excellence is still greater in me than the desire to let things drift—in the intellectual area at least. The importance of the book to me is that I was willing to say my say knowing full well that it would produce controversy among powerful and often mean forces, that it would shock and disappoint people who thought they had me classified as one thing or another: proscientist, prodisarmament, pro-"peaceful atom."

Deliberately and fully aware of the consequences to take on a whole area of controversy, standing up to the disapprobation of friends and former associates, and the renewed enmity of old enemies who thought I was completely out of their hair, marks the year as one in which the moral stamina I once had has reasserted itself. As to public issues this is true. But on my course and choices in my private life I am anything but brave, or candid with myself.

One spring I cleared the debris from the old spring on our place in Redding Ridge, scratching out the accumulation with my hands. Through my digging fingers the spring came bubbling up once more, cold and strong as it had decades before when the spring had been well tended. Since Gordon's sudden death in April I have found that I am ready to start all over again with the company about which I had begun to have a sense of half-feeling. Like our Redding Ridge spring, my own springs of vitality and chance-taking had become clogged, not dried up at all.

OCTOBER 16, 1963
NEW YORK

A bellowing, grating voice on the phone today, out of the past: Colston Leigh, the man who arranged a series of lectures all over the country for me thirteen years ago. "What about commiting yourself to two or three months of lectures in the next season . . ." This in that terrifically forceful manner of his. Before he got through talking to me I agreed not to say No right off (which is rather silly considering how much I have to do with my company) but to talk to him about it next week. The argument that caught me was that if I felt I had something to say—and my book and articles showed I did—a lecture trip would get me once more before college audiences, which I found was a wonderful way to get a feel of the younger generation, the new younger generation. I would have supposed that hootenanny, a pop music jamboree, would be more to their taste than a lecture (as it is mine, for that matter) but perhaps I'm wrong.

I get letters and invitations to speak from all sides these days. I am back in circulation again, or about to be. An interesting letter from Clare Boothe Luce, very approving; a snappy and very Trumanish one from "Harry"; a pleasant one from the President; a most reassuring letter from Jim Conant. I seem to have hit the issue of a crisis of confidence in the scientist and science right on the head so far as timing is concerned. Almost uncanny considering that we wrote that chapter months and months ago.

OCTOBER 23, 1963
NEW YORK

Luncheon with Marriner Eccles. Lean, spare, eyes that bore right through you. He does look a bit weather-beaten, but when he told me of the many things in business and pro bono he is doing, and doing well, and then said: "You know, I'm the same age as Eisenhower: seventy-three," I thought to myself: I only hope I can be doing as many things with as little thought of "retiring" ten years from now as this guy.

Charles Collingwood talked to me while I was waiting for Eccles, about Ed Murrow. The words of praise he used were so full of feeling, but the thing he said I liked the most was: "Ed was *never* afraid of anyone in CBS. He wasn't always right—though most of the time he was—but he was never afraid. And his leadership in USIA and in CBS came from a quality he has of giving a *moral* fervor to what he is doing"—and by that he meant moral in its true and broader sense. Ed is in real trouble, physically; having a very rough time of it. To be held back by his body's infirmities is what Ed would be able to tolerate least.

When Collingwood first saw me he hailed me: "Still controversial. Still fighting." The picture of me as a "controversial" person has always been hard for me to recognize, and I said so to him, who has, professionally, seen me through so many free-swinging public fights. I certainly am back in that squared circle and can stay there (on my back occasionally perhaps) for quite a while if I persist in the issues my book on the atom has raised, issues that according to a *Business Week* two-page review, have "jolted" people. Conant says I should now start a "crusade," but somehow that doesn't fit either.

OCTOBER 24, 1963
NEW YORK

Had a lengthy session with the SOFINA men, and our staff, plus the fabulous Abel Wolman of Johns Hopkins, as our consultant, on water improvement as a field of consulting service. Western Europe, Wolman says, "is just about at the end of its rope" so far as water for industry and even public use is concerned.

OCTOBER 28, 1963
PRINCETON

Governor Robert Meyner has been an almost next-door neighbor of ours ever since he left the governorship, a couple of years ago. But last evening, at a cocktail party at the Greenbaums', was the first time I have talked with him. A ruddy, hearty, full-throated, handsome man he is, and utterly relaxed. We had a good time talking furiously about the rehabilitation of the Jersey Meadows. If any one person could work out an agreement between the many municipalities of the Meadows, all of which claim rights to these swamplands, he is the man.

OCTOBER 29, 1963
NEW YORK

Those few men who, as the saying has it, "rise to the very top" in any sector of a society are in their own persons perhaps the best reflection of the particular time in which they live.

If this be true, then I have seen much of the essence of our society and standards, for I have seen so many of these "at the top" characters. Today noon was an example. The occasion: lunch in the dining room of the Empire Trust Co., as the guest of Dean Mathey, a Princeton friend and charter Trustee of Princeton, chairman of Empire's Finance Committee. The guests—about ten—a varied lot. Jack McCloy, of all the perennials the hardiest, compact, handsome, outwardly self-assured, widely experienced; Lew Douglas, also of the Establishment, with the gentlest manner of any man I know who has been through the competitive mill, in Government and in business as he has, so warm and friendly and moderate always. John Cahill, grown so heavy since he stopped smoking that I actually didn't recognize him at first; a layer-on of soft words, never unaware for a minute of his role as a great legal "business-getter." John Fennebresque, a tense man, recently made head of the Chemical Division of Socony Mobil, a very sure, aggressive, alert man, who found his own smaller company sold out from under him and bounced into a far "bigger" job, full of ideas about the defects of oil companies which operate under the Standard Oil system of committees. Mathey, now half-retired, shrewd and genial, with the sharpness in his face that told of years of intense competitive life. An interesting group it was, in the Stock Exchange Building.

This time I didn't ask myself: "And what are *you* doing here?" But I might have, for much of the talk was gossip about Goldwater versus Nixon, in other words, "Who can we get to beat Kennedy?" The Republicans disagreeing among themselves on every name. Amused to find Empire's president, Henry Brunie popping up with Tom Dewey, but I suppose *everywhere* those who don't want Goldwater, and those who do but don't think he can make it, are looking for someone. This has long been a great American political pastime.

The case of the secretary of the Senate Majority, Robert ("Bobby") Baker, is very much in the press at the moment, complete with rumors of orgies à la the British current scandal of Profumo-Keeler. Baker is charged with finagling his way into a personal fortune by appearing to dispense influence, etc. This is, of course, a kind of stock figure in American politics, Administration after Administration. I was nevertheless somewhat dismayed that the much-honored Jack McCloy, a genuine authority on public service, distasteful as the episode is to him, seemed so resigned, giving the impression that of course this sort of thing happens. Bothers me to see the knowing look on the faces of some of those businessmen of the first water that *of course* this is the way it goes.

McCloy was indignant, in his quiet way, that the savings bank executives of New York had engaged the great liner *Rotterdam* to entertain a group of State Senators while legislation affecting the banks is pending before the New York legislature. He had met with a half dozen of the leading savings bank executives recently, and they were mad as hell at the *Times* for printing the story that told of this shindig; called the *Times* all kinds of names. Not ashamed of themselves for what they did but furious that the *Times* reported it. In that passionless lawyer's way he has, on the surface, this kind of ethics disturbed Jack: "This expense account business is bad, thoroughly bad. Wish we could do away with it *entirely*."

Amen.

OCTOBER 30, 1963
NEW YORK

Mr. Morris Solowich of Brooklyn and I had a discourse about our respective philosophies of life this morning; he told me with a pride and detail most moving about his son Paul, fifteen, winner of every kind of intellectual honor in his high school. "But his mother died six weeks ago, and he needs her."

A taxi driver, of course; how otherwise would I get to hear the sounds of a man's heart who lives so far out of my own little orbit? Much fun is made of Gallup polls based on the loquacious New York taxi driver; but they are every bit as much a part of living and working in this unbelievable city as the cubes of aluminum and glass that are transforming the city these days.

NOVEMBER 1, 1970
NEW YORK

One characteristic of this particular time in which I am living—and so fully!—is this: People's shadows on a TV screen become more real, more the substance of them, than the real person. Item: Larry Spivak, inventor of the *Meet the Press* program, who had me to lunch in the celebrity-heavy atmosphere of "21" yesterday noon.

In point of fact Spivak is almost diminutive in height. See him in a close-up filling the whole TV screen on a Sunday night (and now in "living color") and he looks enormous.

He spoke in great agreement about the first chapter of my atom book. The point that particularly appealed is the total theme of the book: the Grand Solution fallacy, and those who, thinking they are actually "scientific," further that idea. People are too various for that, and within each person there are so many, many different forces from day to day—he restated this point, in a very impressive way, as growing out of his own experience.

Mostly we enjoyed talking about what has become one of my favorite topics: the independent man. On this theme he was clear and quite personal. For as a pioneer among the new-style electronic newsmen and before that as editor of the *American Mercury* (following the fabled Henry Mencken) he knows at first hand about the pressures. He summed up his own philosophy: Never hold any job, get any "position" in life which you are not ready and willing and able to quit rather than give up your right to say and do what you believe to be the right thing. It is a counsel I myself believe in. But in Government, where you have others to consider (your President, your associates on a commission, etc.) it may not always be workable.

NOVEMBER 7, 1963
NEW YORK

The transformation of a scientist, full of the purity of genuine humility, into a know-it-all: this is the picture Joe Volpe brought to me today. The scientist: that lovable man I dragged away from his lab and almost literally shanghaied into becoming a member of the first AEC, Bob Bacher. He phoned Joe: "What the hell is eating Dave? Hear he wants to junk the atom, just when we are beginning to make some real headway. What's wrong with him?" Joe asked: "Have you *read his* book; have you read what it is he is saying?" "No, I haven't; but that's what people say."

Not a very "scientific" reaction, I thought. I wondered whether he is no longer able to maintain that calm, dispassionate, almost child-like open-mindedness that made him such a delight and such a good commissioner too.

Joe says he is disturbed by the number of my friends who are either puzzled or hateful about what they *think* is what I want done about the peaceful atom. Jim Ramey, now an AEC commissioner, John Finney of the *Times,* a friend of Ramey's who was his pipeline into the Joint Committee, even Al Friendly. I'm not inclined to take all this as tragically as does Joe, nor do I want to become defensive about it. What I said is what I believe, and by that I stand.

I would like to take the initiative, the offensive, rather than just "explain" my views in a defensive way. I'm inclined to say that science and technology are in for a bad time; it is the job of the scientists to persuade the public that they know what they are about, in the public sphere.

In the Sunday *New York Times* review of *Change* by Adolf Berle, he states my "philosophy" as being the important thing in the book— as indeed I think it is—and praises and endorses it. A most favorable review by a very experienced man.

NOVEMBER 11, 1963
PRINCETON

Spent an hour Friday morning with the executive head of the famous art dealers, M. Knoedler on 57th Street, a Mr. William Davidson. He called in the head of the house, Mr. Roland Balay, just in from Paris.

We talked about the "Szanton paintings"—a group of five or six of Beatrice' recent work which I had arranged for them to look at perhaps a month ago. They asked to have them for a somewhat longer time. Now and then such dealers try to "discover" artists who are relatively unknown.

As these two men talked to me—and I to them—I felt I was peeking into a world of its own—the world of "collectors" of paintings. They apparently had a similar feeling or said as much: that my kind of *lay* thoughts about art had what they called a "breadth" they didn't have, being so close to the business side and the art critic side of art as they are. So it was a refreshing episode.

These distinguished dealers in art are first of all businessmen; that's clear from their appearance and the necessities of their work. But businessmen with a special slant on the world: a love of the things they have in their gallery or in their office; a feeling that the world of art is broadening out rapidly, the zest of occasionally finding some contemporary new painter.

I am a two-headed curiosity to them, which accounts in part for the exuberance and hospitality they showed; they are a new breed for me. Getting out of the groove of one's life, however interesting that groove, is one of the best ways to enjoy life more fully, I find.

A cardinal in our Franklin tree. As it turns, in swift little movements, the low-angle light of the waning sun seems to set the whole tree, now bare of leaves, into a beam of flame. So long as you can enjoy life through the warmth of a cardinal's color on a November afternoon you are still alive.

The seventy or so men I spoke to tonight at the Princeton "Y" are about as varied a cross section as I have ever known, and in this respect characteristic of Princeton itself. The owner of a restaurant, the headmaster of a fashionable prep school (Hun), the president of one of the country's biggest corporations (RCA), Dr. Elmer Engstrom; a former U.S. senator, Alexander Smith; a real estate lawyer; a handsome young Negro, president of the High School Student Council.

Two men I found extraordinarily interesting, in different ways.

John O'Hara in a blue sports jacket, eyes close together, long, almost distorted face, sad, sad looking, and very shy. He had warned the chairman, Dean Mathey, he wasn't to be "recognized," and dashed out as soon as the meeting was over. I thought it strange to find him taking an evening off to attend a meeting sponsored by the "Y"; he should have stayed to read some of the juicier sexy passages from one of his books to the kiddies.

A huge mountain of a man, looking like the university wrestling coach, and with the affable manner of a Texan running for the city council, came crashing through the entrance, shaking hands right and left. Fairly young, perhaps thirty-five. Who should he turn out to be but Dr. James McCord, the President of the Princeton *Theological* Seminary!

NOVEMBER 14, 1963
NEW YORK

I have just come from an hour or so with Bernard Baruch, age ninety-four (or is it ninety-three? no matter). All in all a wonderful man, such warmth and alertness, so alive and quick and wise with the wisdom of both long experience and a mind that sorts out the important and the unimportant.

As I prepared to leave he looked at me in the quizzical, worldly-wise way he has and asked: "Did you have something particularly on your mind?" No, I said, I just hadn't seen you for a long time, knew you would be off to Carolina soon, and just wanted to see you. *But,* I added, as is always the case when I see you, "I may not have anything on my mind when I come here, but I always have by the time I leave."

In this case what I "got" from the old boy was some advice about my papers. He has just decided to give his own extraordinary papers to Princeton to become part of a Center for Studies in Twentieth-Century American Statecraft and Public Policy.

The Library of Congress, he said, "wanted me to give them my papers. But I didn't want them to be put in a mausoleum and that's what the Library of Congress is. I want the papers to be somewhere where they will be used by students so we put all that into the contract with Princeton." He advised me to do the same when I give my papers to Princeton.

He reminisced hardly at all. He has lost a good deal of weight, which gives him a less powerful look than fifteen years ago. His mane of white hair looks as if he had just been tossing around in a blanket.

My book he has read and agrees with completely, he said. "Clare called me about that book; I guess you know she thinks it is quite a book." Clare? said I. Oh, Mrs. Luce.

"Our wheat, our stocks of food—there is a lever that, like that fellow, who was it—Archimedes—there is a lever that could move the world. Better than gold. We could use the threat of selling that wheat below world prices to puncture Argentina for the way they are treating us on those oil contracts; we put a lot of money in and make something into a good business, and then they come along and take it away. Well, let's use our wheat to show them that they can't push us around."

Baruch is so full of energy and plans it is hard to think of him as being of any particular age; this is a long way from the brash kind of judgment of him as a hopelessly vain and antiquated dodo I made years ago when the Acheson-Lilienthal Board was at work, and he entered the picture as the American representative before the UN on atomic disarmament.

A long session about D&R's future now that Utah is about to "join" us, with Jack Franklin, Nate Greene, and John Oliver. Jack is one of the best things that has ever happened to this company. As a director he gives us time—and close attention to detail, has a sound idea of management, and stirs me up so I put out ideas: about coal, about Italy, about how to make use of our engineers' skills, etc.

NOVEMBER 17, 1963
PRINCETON

A big football game between traditional "rivals" on a brilliant autumn day is a zestful experience even if the game itself may not be good football. Yesterday's game between Princeton and Yale was both pageant *and* exciting football. Princeton won 27-7 but there never was a time when Yale could be "trusted" not to break out with a long pass or a march down the field. As his guest, sat with Frank Glick, an all-time Princeton football hero and all-American. We sat among his 1916 classmates. They are a species all their own: the look of youth comes through the wrinkles, the paunches disappear, the light comes back in their eyes, they are once more back on that field.

NOVEMBER 18, 1963
2 P.M.
PRINCETON

"A man who is trained in the law is not surprised to find—is quite prepared to find—that public affairs, public questions, are not tidy. But the problems of Nature, the problems that a scientist studies, while the subject is not tidy, the way of studying it is. And this misleads scientists when they apply themselves to a question of public policy."

This is Robert Oppenheimer, puffing away at his pipe, looking much, much better physically than I have seen him in a long time. ("It's because Kitty is feeling so much better," he explained.)

I phoned his office this morning asking to see him because, though we are almost next-door neighbors, we rarely see each other. So I took the initiative; the hour with him (I have just this minute returned) was not only pleasant but relaxed. I can see that the awe of him I once felt, that made relations with him those of a high school sophomore talking with a college professor, no longer prevents me from being natural, or being able to differ, or offer a variant viewpoint.

He still thought what we had done years ago (the Acheson-Lilienthal report) was right; we got into a broader issue or issues (and even machinery of how to bring things about) than we of the Board of Consultants ourselves wanted to get into. Still, he said, it had been a good thing for our Board to get people thinking about how to bring the world toward peace. Where he doesn't agree with my new book, *Atom Revisited*, is that he thinks only good can come from thinking and talking about disarmament, even though we know that nothing much can come of it.

"Where I do agree with you thoroughly are the pretensions [here, at this word, a particularly vigorous puff of the pipe, a particularly blue flash of those remarkable eyes], the pretensions of the *social* scientists, as if it is not people we physical scientists are also concerned about."

NOVEMBER 19, 1963
4 P.M.
NEW YORK

Just back from making a speech to the American Nuclear Society in which I seriously questioned whether there was enough known about the hazards to the public of atomic power plants in congested areas.

The antagonism so obvious in that crowded hall was understandable and anticipated. I was about to express to the men whose careers and livelihood are wrapped up so wholeheartedly in atomic power some most unpleasant opinions and raise unorthodox questions about their life's work.

I knew how they would resent this—some of them friends and former coworkers. But I stepped into the pitcher's box and threw as hard and straight as I felt, which is plenty. Some of them were just plain mad. It was strong medicine to expect them to take without some reaction; in fact it is my purpose to make them think hard, whether they like it or not.

I was literally booed by a few in this predominantly scientist audience—the first such in a long time.

A typical hurt comment from a wonderful man who commands my respect and that of most scientists: Manson Benedict of MIT, now head of the AEC Advisory Committee. He thought I had not been "fair" to Chairman Glenn Seaborg to say, as I did in my speech, that Glenn had "prejudged" the New York atomic reactor case simply because he said *he* would feel safe living next to a reactor: that is "just his *personal* view, how he feels about it personally." I said that a man who sits in judgment in an important government post cannot express a purely personal view on an issue that is before him for his decision. If Chief Justice Warren is sitting on a case, and off the bench expresses a "personal" opinion about the case, he becomes disqualified to sit; so it is, I said, with Glenn and his personal opinion on the question of an AEC permit to build and operate a nuclear reactor in New York City. Manson looked as puzzled by my comment as I would be if he rattled off something esoteric in his field of science.

Well, after this rowdy session, no "honorary degrees" or kind words for me from here on. That's clear. It's also clear I intend to keep on saying my say, because I believe it.

After the speaking was over, there were angry "questions." A cluster (including the AEC "truth squad," as they called themselves, and a group from Consolidated Edison) plus one strange Socialist hung on to me and I had to break away or I would be there yet answering mostly angry or injured questions.

The hectoring from Commissioner Jim Ramey's "truth squad" of AEC employees seemed a stupid, reckless stunt. I can imagine the uproar if as TVA Chairman I had set government employees on the trail of a private citizen making critical speeches about TVA! But the AEC will hear more and more of this issue of protecting the public and the environment from the hazards of atomic power plants; just booing me, or having Senators bark at me won't make the very real issue go away.

NOVEMBER 22, 1963
9:30 A.M.
PRINCETON

Wednesday morning's papers—the *Times, Tribune,* and *Wall Street Journal*—carried accounts of the essence of what I said Tuesday to the American Nuclear Society and people from the industrial manufacturers' side: "the Atomic Industrial Forum." The *Times* and *Journal* reported about as much of an "angry" outburst ("angry" is the reporter's term) by Jim Ramey, now an AEC Commissioner, holding an "informal press conference" in the foyer after my speech. It was angry and a personal attack on me and my motives.

The atomic equipment industry was urged yesterday, by Westinghouse, to launch a "national campaign" to "rebut" me and educate the public. But even that will probably be a bunch of ads; it takes quite a lot to sustain a rebuttal about safety, for the more you talk about it the more people are troubled that something is wrong: which in this case there is. If my advice were requested I would say that they'd be better off *to do more effective work in the laboratories,* take this issue more seriously as a *technical* problem to be overcome, and talk less, *negatively,* against my position.

2:45 P.M.

How utterly horrible, how evil.
President Kennedy dead, murdered.

The TV voice is still booming away. But why listen to anything more. Irrevocable. God forgive the hatred in men's hearts that produces such cowardly barbarism.

About fifteen minutes ago Dr. Lively phoned. "Have you heard the news bulletin?" he asked. No; what is it? "President Kennedy has been shot, is in a critical condition." I turned on my little radio, shouted to Helen, she turned on the NBC-TV, and we listened, she with her hands over her face, I lying face downward on the living-room sofa, paralyzed as the statement was read from the White House: The President had died at two o'clock—Texas time.

What a grievous blow to us all.

7 P.M.

So shaken not only by the shocking lightning that has struck our President but by the ominous sickness of hatred that brought on this horrible deed, with the seeming inevitability of Greek tragedy. I set out, with my heavy stick, to walk off some of my grief and anger. On the roadway, toward the Institute, a car sitting by the roadside. A square-built man, a workman with heavily muscled arms and bulky shoulders, was rubbing down his car, out in the middle of the Common. A dirty athletic shirt with the number 2 still visible on the back and, strangely, a beret on his head. Wild-eyed, he was. "Can't hardly believe it, can't believe it," he said, as his auto radio blabbed on about the event, unheeded. "This ain't going to be the end of it. Did you know that them Negroes in Trenton, Black Muslims they call them, walked along next to a white kid leaving school, just a kid, say, fourteen, and beat the living shit out of that poor kid. There's going to be trouble in Trenton and don't you forget it. Real trouble. We won't take that lying down."

When hatred starts on its terrible journey no man can predict where it will end. God help us all.

Just sent a message to President Johnson: "Because I have seen at first hand those qualities of strength of spirit and skills of government you possess I know all of us can count upon you in the trials ahead."

The television pictures that are coming through: the casket being lowered from the plane, the new President leaving by helicopter for the White House; how different from the sad hours when F.D.R. came home. How I still remember that cortege through the streets of Washington, the services I attended in the East Room.

But F.D.R. was old and exhausted in the service; this President was *young*, full of vitality and eagerness and joy; shot down without mercy for him and his family, or for his country.

This day ends in anguish.

NOVEMBER 23, 1963
PRINCETON

Began the morning as I usually do, a bit groggy; through my bed-room exercises: push-ups, etc. In my pajamas to the kitchen, putting on the water and measuring out the coffee into the percolator. Suddenly I found myself leaning against the cupboard, my arm across my face, sobbing like a child. It had come up from my subconscious: the President has been killed in the midst of the exuberance of his manhood; how utterly meaningless.

I write this because there must be millions upon millions of people beginning this day with much the same pain and sense of incredulity. It is not just another man who has lost his life; a great symbol of vigor and the fullness of life has been cut down. And through it all runs my deepest conviction of faith. For this tragedy is a blazing instance of my conviction that we live in a world in which nothing can be precisely foreseen, and therefore we cannot make rigid plans and schemes; "chance" and "change" rule us. And how much better this is, I try to persuade myself, than that we be ruled by omniscient men, or even by an omniscient Power who will look out for us, when to be really men we must be *strong enough* in our faith to stand on our own, as individuals, yes, but more especially as a people, as mankind.

Yesterday afternoon I talked to Dr. Lively about the program for making a gift tó Princeton of my papers. He has ideas about how the papers can be used for academic and scholarly and teaching purposes. This is what I most want: that somehow a generation of young people will find these papers, among others, as a source of understanding of how it is in this world, in statecraft, yes, but even more so in the emotions that pulse through the inner man confronted with the kind of trials and issues that faced me.

So that decision is made, and soon the documents will be drawn, and "The Lilienthal Papers" (as Lively refers to them quite imper-sonally) will be the object of a two-year job of classifying, filing, etc., ready to be opened to scholars. And by January 15 the MS of the first two volumes of *Journals* will be in the hands of Harper.

NOVEMBER 24, 1963
5 P.M.
PRINCETON

Just back from a luncheon given for us by former Governor and Mrs. Meyner at their gay and tasteful house just around the corner. They moved into that little house, in the best of democratic traditions, directly from the huge, sprawling Governor's Mansion, "Morven," when his eight years as governor were over in 1961.

The other guests were the delicate and sensitive-faced Chief Justice of New Jersey, Joseph Weintraub, and his wife, and the Attorney General, Arthur Sills, a sober-looking man, and his dark, intense wife.

Bob Meyner deplores many of the same things I do—the draining out of the smaller communities of the best young brains, either into the huge Washington bureaucracy or into the large law offices or business centers of New York; a regard for public service and particularly for the kind of service that requires a man to submit himself to the approval of his fellow citizens, i.e., elective office. This is something I have never done or attempted, of course, but I know something of the measure this can be of a man's inner capacities.

The Meyners apparently still feel the sting of the way the Kennedy machine rode roughshod over the other candidates—especially Johnson and Humphrey—at the Los Angeles Democratic Convention. Probably President Johnson hasn't forgotten that either, particularly the "ruthlessness" of Bobby Kennedy.

Helen and I went to the University Chapel this morning; I felt the need to be in a place of worship, after the horrible things that have happened to our country and our people since Friday at two o'clock or so. The quiet beauty of the chapel, the organ music, the faces of the young students of the choir, as they walked past us, gave me comfort and restored some balance.

Then I came home, about 12:15, and turned on the TV for the first time since about this hour yesterday—when I had had about all of that I could take. A crowd of frantic newspapermen hammer questions at a mixed-up Dallas policeman, wildly milling about. Just a few minutes before the man suspected of shooting the President, Oswald, had been shot at point-blank range in the basement of the police station itself, while flanked by Dallas police taking him from the station to the county jail. Later a film of *that* shooting was shown—in slow motion!

At lunchtime at the Meyners' the Chief Justice was much disturbed by the "pretrial by TV"; the police chief commented in a way that was, of course, prejudicial and which no prospective juror could ever forget; the pictures of "the gun," etc. Of course, all of this makes a lawyer who believes in certain procedures cringe. And then the "suspect" shot while in the police station by the keeper of a night club called Strip Tease. What a picture for the world!

NOVEMBER 25, 1963
NOON
NEW YORK

Before me is a spectacle by electronics such as has been seen by no man before: a Requiem Mass for a slain President. A whole people in mourning.

Went directly to the office, looked out upon the glory of the view of the harbor on this crisp, sunny prewinter morning; then concluded I couldn't really work, feeling as I do, and set out for the hotel and a TV set.

Phoned Helen a few minutes ago, to tell her that we were together, looking at this sad and yet proud national event. Yes, she was watching it too, said: "I sit here weeping."

Mrs. Kennedy, erect and unflinching, began the march behind the riderless horse, walking behind the casket on the caissons. The gay laughing society girl with the finishing school voice and manner was gone; there walked all women upright in their strength in the face of sorrow. When she reached the Cathedral, she left the group and moved toward the two little children: what a touching thing to see, the little boy only knowing that there was much to look at, and then taking his mother's hand, walked up the steps of the Cathedral.

3:20 P.M.

And now the Captains and the Kings depart; the flag folded ceremonially from the casket resting over the open grave, Mrs. Kennedy has lighted a flame, the mourners from all over the world are getting into their cars.

What a sad thing indeed for a man so full of the juices of life to go when his job was only begun. May he be in peace, And may his *country* be in peace.

NOVEMBER 27, 1963
NEW YORK

Scotty Reston's column this morning begins a tattoo of frank comments about the new President, predicting that he will *not* like the column, as he is thin-skinned about criticism, according to Scotty; he has, so Reston says, "tended to regard dissent as perversity, and to fret and worry about it, as if criticism was not a duty in a free society, but a crime."

This reminded me of the outbursts now going on against me, personally, because I dare to deal critically with the atomic power program. I have just seen the *Christian Science Monitor* issue of November 21; the four-column headline reads:

A-Experts Launch Attack on Lilienthal

The story reports the meeting of the Nuclear Society, and the big manufacturers of nuclear power equipment, saying that it was decided it was no use trying to wait until I had "talked myself out," as the story puts it; that "the experts would have liked to have the atomic energy issue worked out in private." No doubt.

ON THE BROADWAY LIMITED, EN ROUTE TO CHICAGO
9 P.M.

In the womb of a roomette (what a name for a train compartment!) set to read and doze off; Helen across the aisle in *her* little cubicle. All very aseptically cozy.

This must be Harrisburg. I hope I'll wake as we go around the Horseshoe Bend near Altoona—what a firm impression on my memory of youth that made.

NOVEMBER 30, 1963
CHICAGO

Three thousand teen-age high school youngsters have turned a middle-aged hotel for middle-aged harried businessmen and their hair-shellacked female counterparts (for such is the type that usually inhabits this convention-style hotel, here and anywhere) into a giggling, pimply-faced, twittering, wriggling mess of kids. A national convention ("Conference" is the word they use) of the high school newspapers and "annuals"; predominantly from small towns, I would say. Boys and girls together, racing like a herd of heifers and immature bull calves through the corridors, day and night. Another evidence that the America of my own youth is in some respects as far away from the present as if I had been brought up in the Administration of William Henry Harrison.

Helen and I went to the University of Chicago's Oriental Institute Museum, toward noon. In a dark mission oak, heavy leather chair kind of office, visited with the new Director, Dr. Robert Adams. A couple of years ago we had breakfast with him at the Gholestan "Club house" near Ahwaz, while he was prospecting in nearby archaeologically fascinating areas, physically and intellectually: trying to find prehistory villages based on the earliest kind of organized agriculture.

Adams is very tall, dark-haired, piercing, knowing eyes, eyes that smolder when you show a strong interest in what he is doing; this latter isn't difficult, since both Helen and I find his kind of passion one we respect enormously and indeed Helen shares it, so strong has her interest in archaeology become.

Helen referred to our visit to the Euphrates reed villages, not omitting, naturally, my unplanned and hilarious dunking in the waters of the marshes: "David among the bulrushes."

"I envy you having visited the reed villages in that area, in the marshes; do you suppose we could possibly arrange to have motion pictures taken of the manner of life in those villages?" I assured him this could be done. His purpose? The Educational Services, Inc., are now trying to develop an elementary school curriculum in the social sciences that will be as much a departure from the conventional pattern as the new math and the new science (physics, for example) developed by Killian and others. To show motion pictures of *contemporary* primitive organization such as those villages would fit into the theory of this new way of teaching about social organization to young kids.

The Curator, Dr. Delougaz, showed us through his treasures, as well as the "study exhibits." A very short, square man, whose eyes behind his glasses would brighten and glow whenever we showed special appreciation of something or other—and this happened often.

At the end of a long hall, against the end wall, is a huge Assyrian deep bas-relief of a bull (with five legs, I noticed) with the head of a king or general. Perhaps 15 or 18 feet high, about the same in length. The Curator, beaming up at this creature, told us a story about it. A long time ago he was in Mesopotamia (Iraq it is now) as a young assistant to the immortal James Breasted, who was anxious that the party come up with a big find to stimulate the flow of funds for the Oriental Institute. "Only this far [motioning about two feet with his hands] away from where the French had been digging for a long time we found this mammoth figure. We dug it out. Then I was left with the job of transporting it. We got hold of a truck, somehow, built a big wooden platform on it. It took us a month to get that thing loaded and transported to a place where we could get it on a boat." Pride and the memory of a big challenge of his youth made this scholarly, absorbed, diminutive man seem ten feet tall, as he told this story.

DECEMBER 1, 1963
11 A.M.
CHICAGO

Late this afternoon I fly to Washington, and tomorrow late afternoon to the White House to witness the new President pouring the sacramental water of absolution on Oppie, in the form of the Enrico Fermi Award.

Now Helen and I, at my suggestion, are going to spend an hour at the Art Institute, where so many years ago we used to go to admire the Innes landscapes (now probably in a warehouse somewhere, the fad for that kind of naturalism having passed, I suppose), the Lorado Taft sculpture and so on. Then another purely sentimental journey to 67th Street, just east of Stony Island, where we began our life together more than forty years ago. This is not the kind of backward looking one should indulge in often, but once in forty years does not seem excessive!

DECEMBER 2, 1963
8 P.M.
WASHINGTON, ABOARD AN EASTERN "SHUTTLE" FOR NEW YORK

Robert Oppenheimer was a figure of stone, gray, rigid, almost lifeless, tragic in his intensity. We were in the Cabinet Room, the tall rangy, relaxed President was reading the citation and speaking about the great contribution of this man who seemed, beside the huge figure of the President and the altitude of Seaborg, almost diminutive.

It all seemed to me a ceremony of expiation for the sins of hatred and ugliness visited upon Oppenheimer, now, belatedly, being given a gold medal, a plaque, and a check for $50,000 from the Government of the U.S.

My own little "moral crisis" I came through well, indeed with a mark of A. I confess cringing a bit at the prospect of shaking hands with (or being openly "cut" by) these men I had been creating such a "fuss" about (to use the expression John Palfrey, now a commissioner, used in describing my recent activities). There were more people I had publicly criticized—and with extraordinary coverage—than are ever gathered in one room—and later at the Academy of Sciences at a reception even more: pouting Chet Holifield, urbane Leland Haworth, Jim Ramey, now controlling his angry explosions of two weeks ago, Frederick Seitz of the Academy of Sciences, Edward Teller, who shook my hand as if it were a poisonous reptile, Teller with his strange, overcast, passionate face, he who had refused on a TV program to say that Robert was *not* a security risk and who was extremely sensitive to my ironic description of his atomic shelter ideas; Jim Webb, whose space program I had criticized—a whole range of people with whom I have recently tangled—all there. And I went out of my way not to duck seeing them on their own territory.

Kitty Oppenheimer was a study in joy, in exultation almost. She hugged me just before the ceremony at the White House and then as I passed down in line at the National Academy of Sciences, Robert having gripped my hand in both of his bony hands, a grip so frantic it frightened me, she next to him said: "Another buss, dear Dave," and gave me a smack.

The two Oppenheimer children were so embarrassed, particularly Peter, a shy and tender-looking teen-ager. I think it was more painful than happy for them.

My hero of the whole Oppenheimer story was Harry Smyth. I only wish there had been some reference to him; perhaps later there will be. What steel it took in him to stand up in that Commission and dissent. Lewis Strauss wasn't present at the ceremonies.

Only one member of the Joint Committee, on the Senate side, was represented: Clint Anderson. Pastore absent, perhaps for no particular reason. Hickenlooper made a big thing of refusing to come, and objecting to the award.

The way the photographers have multiplied! It was almost impossible to get into the Cabinet Room from the White House lobby, so dense was the jungle of newsreel, TV, still photographers, etc. There were more men of this calling in the Cabinet Room than guests.

President Johnson looked extremely fit; when Robert made his "response" the President's face was in repose, and this showed the dark clouds under his eyes. But he looked every inch a President, I thought— assurance and a sense of power in his manner, even when he quipped about the fact that Robert had taken the medal and plaque but he noticed that the "wife" was holding the check.

One of the delightful dividends of making this trip was the visit with Sumner Pike. He has not lost his genius for telling a tale. Now a member of the state legislature of Maine, he still lives in his huge house in Lubec. What a rare bird he is, robust, colorful, eloquent, romantic and sentimental under that down-East exterior. We relived some of the past. With the same gusto that made him such a warm companion in the "old days" he told of his experiences in Persia when he was a young stalwart with White & Case, acquiring oil concessions, and wheeling and dealing through that country.

I was lined up along one wall of the Cabinet Room, getting as far out of the range of the multicamera horde as I could; next to me, standing on the lower rung of a ladder used by some of the photo fraternity, was a beaming Eugene Wigner, the big rosette of the Nobel Prize he had just won gleaming in his buttonhole. All of a sudden Wigner's eyes opened wide; he was looking at the books President Kennedy had lined that wall with: history, biography, etc., but one title stirred him and he read it under his breath: *"Elements of Physics*. In the President's office!"

He reached on tiptoe and brought down the volume. Sure enough, a *beginner's* text in physics. Wigner leafed through this book, turning his back to the crowd, to the ganglia of electric cords, to the aggressive TV cameras. Completely absorbed in his "find."

DECEMBER 4, 1963
NEW YORK

Last night reading Bernard Berenson's Diaries, *Sunset and Twilight*, the "terminal" ones, as the doctors' antiseptic phrase has it for an illness that will finish you.

The zest and vitality of the man is contagious despite the sense of doom that crops up so often, and the preoccupation with his aches and pains and fatigue, etc.

That I should find in the highly personal reflections of a professional art critic so much that is relevant to me, a man so much younger and still full of the juices of physical vigor which Berenson did not have (at any age) is somehow baffling. He keeps saying that *writing* about what he thinks and feels is essential because it is the *functioning in the outer world* without which he feels lost. I find it difficult to believe that writing is functioning *in the outer world*. Am I missing the main point about the artist, whether he be writer, painter, or musician? For to me functioning is action and seeing the results of action is the breath of life for me; the writing in this journal about that action and my feelings about it simply *completes the action*.

DECEMBER 5, 1963
NEW YORK

All morning at a regular Board meeting of Minerals & Chemicals-Philipp.

These directors and officers are all exceptionally quick-witted men; some of them have established by their works that they have a great sharpness and a form of mental acuteness or cunning about buying and selling. Yet set this group to discussing a question involving management and, so it seems to me, some of them show a naïveté and even a kind of obtuseness that after a couple of hours I find very tiresome. I had somehow thought that a group of men of great and proven talents in competitive business could move a discussion along with a sense of proportion, getting to the *issue* quickly, keeping the discussion on the vital points. God, how disenchanted I have become about that illusion; there seems to be no essential difference on this particular score than the discussion in, say, a neighborhood PTA meeting.

DECEMBER 12, 1963
NEW YORK

Lively session in my office this morning, discussing a letter from SOFINA, proposing that we immediately form an international company to promote the water improvement idea. The proposal puts the ball in our court; I didn't think our boys showed as much drive as Mechelynck of SOFINA, and said so; a good thing to have outside forces at work on an organization, pressing, stimulating, making it possible for the man responsible (which happens to be me in this case) to make comparisons of how his people are functioning when put alongside others.

An organization can quickly develop the staleness of inbreeding; the same people talk to each other, go to lunch with each other, watch out not to step on each other's toes. I have seen this happen even in TVA. It develops a kind of parochialism that isn't healthy. One way to prevent it is by having new groups to work with. This is one of the reasons I welcome the SOFINA initiative; one of the reasons I look with considerable hopefulness to the new partner, Utah's entry on the scene. All of us will have an outside basis of comparison, a source of criticism, of ideas, of challenge. All to the good, for everyone.

DECEMBER 13, 1963
4 P.M.
ON THE TRAIN FOR PRINCETON

At the Twentieth Century Fund Trustees' lunch this noon Mrs. Berle descended upon me with an excited look in her eye and began telling me she thought my new book was very good, has been making it "required reading" for . . . and here she told me firmly of the people into whose hands she had put the book and said: This you must read. Of course I was *that* pleased. With Jim Rowe and Ben Cohen she went on to cite an example from the medical world (she is a practicing physician) to support my thesis that it is the human being we are concerned with. A woman patient in a hospital; the resident looks at her chart and the lab tests. The woman says: "I'm so unhappy, desperate. My daughter is pregnant but not married—a blight on us all. [She described this with gestures, quite an actress, I thought, for I could *see* the bedside scene.] You must do something for me, doctor. I can't bear it." The resident looks up from the chart and says: "Madam, you have nothing to worry about; your cholesterol level is absolutely normal."

A newish member of the Fund, Georges Henri Martin, editor of the *Tribune de Genève*, spoke to us with such quiet eloquence about the "sorrow" in Europe over the death of our President. Never had been a time when the French Government had sent a representative to any ceremonial: coronations, state funerals, etc. But the feeling about President Kennedy was so strong, *from the people*, that after searching frantically all of Saturday after the killing for a precedent, and not finding one, it was decided that France would indeed be represented—and De Gaulle himself found it necessary to come, and join that disorganized-looking little group that followed the strong, erect Mrs. Kennedy on the walk behind the casket from the White House to the Cathedral. Amble it was, rather than a march, despite the fact that it included the desiccated, bemedaled Lion of Judah, the towering, gloomy gus that is De Gaulle, and the rest of the "heads of state."

Martin is a squarely, solidly built man, as befits a Swiss, but with an intensity and sense of irony unlike any of the Swiss I happen to have known. He talked to me about Romania (where he visited this summer). What he wanted so much to have me understand was that Romania was tasting the beginnings of an industrial development that was more important to them—and should be to us—than the fact that for the present there was only limited freedom of action. "About Communism as an ideology they couldn't care less," he said, with a gleam in his eye. What really interests them: (a) becoming "autonomous" vis-à-vis the Russians, (b) and becoming industrialized. To them industrial expansion is the road to lessened control by the Russians.

Jim Rowe talked to me about President Johnson. (I remembered, of course, that he was one of the F.D.R. alumni who had worked hardest to get Johnson the nomination in 1960.)

Agreeing with my comment that Johnson was one of the very earliest of the original New Deal young men, he said: "Johnson is going back over his past. For example, the other night he heard that Aubrey Williams was in town; the President went right over to Aubrey's house to see him." Aubrey was a highly controversial and utterly dedicated man, in the literal sense of that overworked term, in the crusading New Deal days (days that lasted only a short time, actually). "You'll remember that Lyndon's first public work was as head of the Texas NYA—the National Youth Administration—way out on the very edge of the forest, of the F.D.R. New Frontier of 1934 when Aubrey was the national NYA head."

In the dusk of a winterish landscape, the "interior" of a commuter train swishing people home is as typical a reflection of U.S.A. 1960's as a teahouse is along an old caravan route in Iran or the circle of light and talk about the stove in the general store would be in my Middle West boyhood.

The last place I would have expected to hear a discussion about betting on horse races would be in the chaste, gleaming white Board room of the Twentieth Century Fund, in our splendid quarters on East 70th Street, a remade, elegant home of some very rich man of the early part of the century. But so it was yesterday forenoon.

Berle, presiding, asked our new member of the Board, Lawrence Miller, to say what was most on his mind. Miller is a very tall, lean man in his early forties, I would say, a crew cut sprinkled with some gray, eyes somber behind his glasses. He runs (perhaps owns) one of the best of the smaller dailies of the East, the *Mercury-Eagle* of Pittsfield, Massachusetts, in Berkshire County, near the New Hampshire line.

"What's most on my mind in Pittsfield—it's almost traumatic on my paper—is the effect of big-scale gambling now authorized by a new law in New Hampshire right next door. Horse racing, it's called. But it's really an animated roulette wheel. Like a sweepstake, so if you hit the right horse the amounts you could win are enormous. What this will do in taking money out of our community and putting it in the hands of these gambling syndicates worries us. A great deal it worries us. New Hampshire expects to get a large part of its tax support from this track, so it is very appealing to them. The corruption that always goes in the wake of these things—well, it is something new in our part of New England."

A good deal was said around that beautiful round table about the economic and fiscal consequences of this spreading custom. With a New Hampshire lottery—which is what it is—going, other states would have a hard time resisting; in fact, New York State is very likely to go for what is technically called "off-track betting." " But don't think." I said, "of this only in terms of the economics and the political consequences; people want to go to these races; it's the answer to a great many, many people of what to do with themselves, with the new leisure and added income they now have. Are we going to provide some other and perhaps better ways of spending leisure than getting into a taxi and going out to Aqueduct to gamble on the horses and share the centuries-old excitement of the sport of kings, brought down to the level of the ordinary guy?"

DECEMBER 14, 1963
PRINCETON

Governor Bob Meyner, looking like a pro fullback with charm, arrived as "scheduled"; we had a splendid lunch, prepared and served by Helen, who left us pretty much to ourselves.

He spoke feelingly of the lure of political life, the excitement of attending six or eight meetings in a single evening, of *putting out* to audiences in the glow that they sense in having the Governor as their guest and speaker, and, more important, having them return what you give with the electricity an audience can send through a man: these things he still looks forward to, I'd guess.

He commented about how little of this Jack Kennedy had felt. "I went with him throughout the State when he was campaigning. When he'd finished talking he would mutter under his breath that *that* was over; or when people would swarm up to shake hands he didn't enjoy it a bit. Why then did he fight so hard for elective office, going through all those campaigns in Massachusetts and two primary campaigns before he was elected? [It was a question I had put.] Well, I think it was the old man, Joe. Jack Kennedy was like the kid that just *had* to bring home an A or the old man would raise hell. His father was a very competitive man, but very, and it was Joe that set the pace for the whole family of the boys."

That Kennedy didn't seem to lap it up, with audiences and hand-shaking, as Phil LaFollette did when I remember him campaigning, I can believe. That he didn't get the energizing effect of crowds that F.D.R. so obviously did, giving him a radiance and a freshness instead of wear-ing him down—that too I can believe. But it seemed to me that as the months went on Kennedy began to enjoy crowds and people. That scene after his speech at Muscle Shoals last May will always be fresh in my mind: his going out into that big crowd, shaking hands and grinning and joking; I never saw a man so obviously having himself a happy time.

So I take Meyner's interesting appraisal with that reservation.

How do men become great men? he asked. What is this "verdict of history" about public men; where does it come from? Comes from historians, who create that verdict pretty much, don't they? He wasn't being argumentative, just puzzling about the sudden "canonizing" of Kennedy that he feels is going on now.

"Take Woodrow Wilson, for example, one of my predecessors. Here in Princeton you can't say a critical word about Wilson these days. Well, what about the record? He always was just about played out in one job at the time he went on to the next. They were about ready to fire him as President of Princeton when he ran for governor; he was about washed up as a governor when he ran for the Presidency. But do you hear any of that in the adulation, this professional historians' 'verdict'?"

The "business" I wanted to talk to Meyner about concerned land development in the Meadows, the tidal marshes that lie vacant and sorrowing along the Hackensack and Passaic Rivers. A dramatic thing it seemed to me that there should be 25,000 acres, more or less, within a few minutes of Manhattan's density, unused. Such development as has occurred has been largely bit by bit, covering some of it with garbage fill. An important business opportunity that could be done constructively if well done.

The fire in our upstairs living room hissing and sputtering and singing; the wind of a cold winter's night moaning and breathing in the chimney. Outside the outline of the garden sweet and protected under its coverlet of snow. The first of the year. My roses all tucked in, compost piled about their feet, salt hay wrapped and stuffed about the now wilted leaves of the canes where only a very short time ago—two weeks about—Sutter's Gold and Queen Elizabeth were still spunkily putting forth their glories, telling the calendar that it was spring, not autumn.

I say the same these days: autumn indeed! And conceding as one must that the arithmetic of the years says unmistakably that for me it is indeed autumn, it is the time of life when the joys that one was too shallow to savor in one's spring, too full of oneself to taste fully in the summer of life, can in the autumn be of the best flavor of all.

DECEMBER 15, 1963
PRINCETON

In the *Times* today an article by Elia Kazan. His father—why had he left Turkey? The old man, Kazan wrote, had almost forgotten. Did he want to make a visit back to the old country with his famous son, Elia? "No; what's wrong with New Rochelle?" As I read this, in the secure and timeless atmosphere of our living room, deep, nostalgic currents about my own father swept over me.

My father *never* forgot for one moment why as a very young man *he* had left Austria; his passionate disdain for the "old country" was expressed all the more forcefully because throughout my memory of him he was so blunt and unself-consciously pro-American ("100 percent American," as we now say). He, too, refused my suggestion of a visit to the old country as a present. "Never want to see it again."

How people yearn to come to America. Kazan speaks of it in his article; I have observed it in my travels the world over. This yearning, I assume, will be the theme of the World Premiere tonight of his new biographical film called *America, America*.

I was reading aloud scraps of this beautiful essay to Helen—while she was reading something else, a trick a long marriage can teach you

—when she riffled the *Times* and said: "Had you read that Molly Kazan died Friday night?" I was stunned. How I remember that happy evening at our apartment in New York when Elia and Molly Kazan dined with me (Helen was away) and with what respect as well as gentle affection they held each other. I sent Elia—one of my heroes in the world of theatre—a wire and wrote him a note. Sad, this, on the very eve of a professional triumph.

DECEMBER 17, 1963
NEW YORK

There is a good deal to be said for the joys of being alone. "Loneliness" is not a synonym, an interchangeable term, for "being alone."

Which comments arise from my having my lamb chop dinner in the men's bar at the Biltmore. I was alone but far from lonely. For on either side of me talk going full blast out of worlds not mine. Being by myself, no one I *had* to talk with or "entertain"; I could eavesdrop to my heart's content, drinking in the flavor of what goes on with people I would not ordinarily run into in a lifetime.

The young men on my right, for example, engaged in the business side of technical books: the lure of the chase after authors, the hot breath of competitors (the names of McGraw-Hill, Allen, etc., bandied about as a chemical salesman would toss off Allied Chemical, etc.). What zest these fellows got out of what in my ignorance I would have thought would be just a notably uninspiring aspect of the commercial, competitive struggle.

An hour in the Biltmore Turkish baths. The middle-aged giant with the sun-reddened face wound a small towel around his *forehead,* making him look like an oversize Navajo extra in a Cecil B. De Mille movie. Except that below the turban were glasses, and in his hands the stock-market page of the paper. The huge guy was Gene Tunney, not so long ago the greatest boxer in the world, a modern gladiator who continues a rigorous regime of exercise. Despite which—I was stupidly reassured to note—middle age and a sedentary life have awarded him with a midriff even thicker than my own.

DECEMBER 18, 1963
11:30 P.M.
NEW YORK

Not to have seen midtown New York at Christmastime, as a slowly paced snowfall mingles with gay lights and the bright-faced crowds (intent on entering every brilliant store and spending every last cent), is not to have seen a great city at its most colorful.

Tried to phone Dr. Atchley to let him know how struck I was by an article of his, *The Evolving Art of Medicine*. Once his "answering service" answered; then a long pause. I decided that now even an answering service (abomination) itself has an answering service—the height of automation or impersonality, a prediction of things to come à la Huxley or Orwell.

DECEMBER 19, 1963
NEW YORK

George Woods, beginning as a bond salesman, become a fabulously successful and trusted New York banker (but still with the eyes of a mischievous boy), now head of the World Bank, sat in the tiny foyer of the D&R office, arriving alone, with no entourage, hatless. Certainly not a trace of the Wall Street stuffed-shirt "personage." George grows out of a genuine American Midwest soil, like Willkie.

It was agriculture he wanted to talk about to me. Why had he decided to press on this? Practical reasons: the World Bank was vulnerable to what had once been the "mutterings" of the new nations, who now (in theory only) control the Board of Governors, and could do what they wanted if they decided the Bank wasn't doing enough for the new and nonindustrial countries. He knows what others have chosen to ignore—so he said—that the World Bank isn't as independent as they preferred to think. And "a very high official of the U.S. Government" (probably, I guessed, the Secretary of State or Treasury) had phoned him that an eruption was in the making. Anyway, agricultural projects were now to be given a high priority, at last.

I said we knew how to get agricultural results and had done so. Iran was the proof and his organization knew it. You couldn't get results except by a comprehensive kind of project—piddling around with a little loan for a storage silo here or a little agricultural credit facility there would get exactly nowhere.

"You have not told me anything that I haven't learned from others" —which encouraged me. "And everyone around the Bank says in agriculture your firm is good; perhaps one of the best in the world. The British ex-colonial people are as good, probably, but you are the best in this country. But if you want to get new business—and you say you aren't coy about saying that is what you want—you will have to persuade my top staff."

About "that thing you started, David, in the Indus Valley. Have just come back from three weeks in Pakistan. It is quite a story. I told President Ayub it was like a big wedding, that treaty about the dividing of the waters of the Indus. Everybody gets high, has a wonderful emotional spree, and then when it's over the parents had to stop and see how much the party cost and how to divide the expense."

Sir Alexander Gibb, the English engineering firm, gave the Bank a figure of $850 million as the cost of the idea of physically giving three tributaries to India, three to Pakistan. The figure today is more like $2 billion. (I'll bet it will turn out to be more.) The amount pledged by the various nations of the West is not even enough to develop the Jhelum, much less the Indus itself. Woods seemed undisturbed. "If we had had a better estimate to begin with the whole thing might never have gotten off the ground."

So bad an estimate of cost with so much at stake—a potential scandal—would keep some men awake nights. One day the record will come out and some reputations may suffer. I doubt it though: The Alexander Gibb firm has such a cozy standing with certain members of the staff of the World Bank this will be forgotten. As has happened more than once with bum estimates of cost by our own Army Corps of Engineers or Bureau of Reclamation, the crushing steam-roller momentum of a big bureaucracy can roll over almost anything, even overrun a bad estimate of this colossal magnitude.

Lunch with André and Jack Franklin mostly about the Jersey Meadows. André began by saying that "You and Clapp were the only ones I saw who had a good word for Kennedy. You told me he was very good, long before the Convention, and I said you were completely wrong. Do you remember? Well," André continued, "I was 1000 percent wrong. Such intelligence, such sensitivity, such understanding of the world!" I was reassured.

All of us are wrong at times, but very few of us ever admit it.

DECEMBER 20, 1963
10:15 A.M.
ABOARD PAN AM, AT IDLEWILD

Yesterday afternoon a phone call from Helen. She said, in a muted, puzzled voice: "Well, I have just had a call from our travel agent. He said Katharine Cornell was to have been on that same flight we are taking to Jamaica; would we be willing to take a big Christmas package with us for Noel Coward, whose house guest she was to be? She can't go, because of illness."

Helen had said that we would. At the gates, an hour or so ago, sure enough there was Nancy Hamilton (Kit Cornell's staunch friend) looking for us.

"We're so pleased, " she said, "you are willing to take that carton of Christmas presents to Noel. You will be met at Montego by two of Noel's men. The carton is marked—I hope you won't mind—it's marked: 'Noel Coward care of David Lilienthal.' " We all agreed that this was funny.

DECEMBER 21, 1963
OCHO RIOS, JAMAICA, SHAW BEACH "CLUB"

Sleep, deep wholehearted sleep, and sleepiness in between sleeps. In a heavy rain, by sundown, we reached this South Sea paradise— paradise, physically, for those who *have*—and a nagging unrest for the black people of Jamaica, most of whom have *not*. Even the water of the Caribbean breaks on the sand shore with a hushed, discreet shush, not the vigorous, "to hell with you Jack" commanding roar of the South Beach on the Vineyard.

Now to do *nothing* is not a natural thing with me, with my need for *doing* things, for an exciting, demanding kind of atmosphere. Looking out over the water Helen speculated: "Now I can do nothing quite happily. I'm quite good at doing nothing. It takes talent of a sort and I have it."

It *is* a talent of a sort. And it is not, as Helen, with a deliberate touch of irony, pictured it, as wholly a negative thing, a vacuum. How different we are, the two of us; mostly in temperament.

DECEMBER 23, 1963
JAMAICA

A sentence in Evelyn Waugh's precious and dated *Brideshead Revisited*: "I could tell him [his cousin Jasper, who had remonstrated with his behavior at Oxford] that to know and love one other human being is the root of all wisdom."

The key is "to know"—really to know. To truly know another human being is the road to knowing oneself, and to know oneself is the root of wisdom. The root of wisdom but not happiness. That is another matter entirely. Truly to *know*, so that the stones in the wall between one human being and another come down, a stone at a time—this is something rare and wondrous—and when stones *do* come down there is a special kind of wisdom; but when that happens and there is also love, then something so uncommon has happened that it can only be called a miracle.

DECEMBER 24, 1963
JAMAICA

Helen and I reading, under the shade of a coconut tree on the beach in front of our two rooms. High noon. A man approaches me:

"You are David Lilienthal; I'm Louis Nizer." A friendly and distinctive face, curly hair, eyes that take in everything, a small, slender man in red-checked swimming trunks, by all odds the most illustrious trial lawyer of the day.

He took us over to the Spences, whose house guest he is. A delightful couple. Mrs. Spence has fair hair and—well, fair presence. Derek, her husband, very English, an exceptionally handsome, middle-aged man, full head of silver hair, a discreet full mustache; robust fellow.

CHRISTMAS DAY, 1963
IN THE EVENING
JAMAICA

It is quite impossible to get a full picture of what it is like in the mid-sixties by going to the winter "resorts," such as the north shore of this island has become in the past ten or fifteen years.

Poverty, strain, tension, ugly slums—these you won't find at a winter resort, but they exist aplenty.

But the "resorts"—summer and winter—the cruises, the tours, the theatre parties to New York from Des Moines and Logansport, filling buses and trains—these have become so common and characteristic of the times that without grasping their meaning and observing this side of American life one simply gets no whole picture of what goes on in our country these days.

Not so very long ago it was little wooden Chick Sales, called "tourist cabins" that lined the roads; the rental at first $1 per person per night; then later "motels." Now the elegance of these "accommodations" throughout the country, and especially, of course, in Florida. An astounding change. More impressive is the drive to go farther and farther south, to the warmer places, during the winter. Florida still is full to bursting, but now the Caribbean islands are becoming as built up—for use only a few weeks or months a year—as Florida became thirty years ago.

Reading Francis Parkman's *The Oregon Trail*, the story of a "privileged" young Bostonian among the rough characters that crossed the prairies and mountains of the West. The American movement is still west, but what difference. Nancy and Sylvain's story of the thousands of camping sites along the way as they motored to the Coast, fully equipped, most of them, with running water, toilet facilities, etc.

But now the push is not only west, as for a century or more, but south, and south not for adventure or curiosity, or to find a piece of land to settle on, but south to swim in the warm water, escape the cold for a time, get a suntan, snooze and loaf—as I am doing.

What a restless creature is man.

DECEMBER 26, 1963
JAMAICA

Up a winding mountain road in a driving, blinding rain, to the Derek Spences for dinner. The great house, with its deep, broad balustrade, was like the stage set of a melodrama. That it wasn't real was confirmed by the "guardians of the portal," six huge, lugubrious great Danes. Each was in an open wooden box. There they stayed during our approach, baying in a basso profundo but not moving out of these ominous boxes. Our driver, a Jamaican, paid no heed to the servant who assured him in dialect that they are not going to bite; he simply wouldn't get out to open the taxi door for us. Once inside, a magnificent room, nearly 50 feet square; lovely Japanese or Chinese screens on the walls, Chinese carved cabinets, a huge deep-blue curved sofa, a fire crackling.

We were welcomed by the Louis Nizers, our hosts being delayed by the downpour. They soon arrived, in identical garb: tomato-red toreador pants and blue shirt, barefoot. And barefoot they remained throughout the formal dinner.

I had a sprightly talk with Kitty, as she insists she must be called. She has convictions, is lively and witty. I can't say so much for my social graces, in support of which judgment I submit the following:

D.E.L.: "I was so glad to have the chance, thanks to you, to meet Louis Nizer. The only other great trial lawyer I ever knew was when I was a very young lawyer, when I was a very junior associate of Clarence Darrow."

Kitty Spence: "Oh, yes, Clarence Darrow. Yes, he and my grandfather were opposed to each other in a trial once."

D.E.L., suddenly waking up to what he knew, from Leona Baumgartner, but had forgotten: this fair lady with the pony tail, elegant English husband, and "seat" in Jamaica, is the granddaughter of William Jennings Bryan, the "Great Commoner."

D.E.L. (coloring at his gaffe): "Uh-huh. The Scopes trial."

DECEMBER 27, 1963
JAMAICA

Just a few moments ago I read the final paragraph of Elia Kazan's book: *America, America*. Suddenly was convulsed in sobs. The hard lump in my chest is still there. "You have a new chance here," Stavros had written to his family in Anatolia, "so get ready. You're all coming." Which evoked the picture of my seventeen-year-old mother, holding the hand of her eleven-year-old brother Sam, clutching the package of food from home, as this young girl, barely five feet tall, left her home village for America, knowing she would never see her beloved mother again. And, too, a picture of my father, rebelliously shedding himself of the brutality of the Austrian army and of the heavy labor he was put to even as an eleven-year-old, in Vienna, off to America. Such pictures swept over me and replaced those of the boy of Kazan's story, the Greek boy who had to fight his way to America against the same cruelty and heartlessness and ignorance that stood in the way of a whole stream of young people, their hopes kept alive by the song "America, America."

Kazan's story for me was a renewal of understanding of what America has meant, continues to mean, not only to me but to people wherever in the world I have gone.

DECEMBER 31, 1963
JAMAICA

These journals began long, long ago as a more or less annual ritual: a self-audit by a very young man at year's end, a quite self-conscious summing up of the year.

The "very young man" is no longer young; in six months he will reach the age that is identified with "retirement," sixty-five.

I find it difficult to think about what *happened* during the year as a measure of the quality of the year. Actually a good deal did happen: Gordon's sudden death, the sorrow that brought, the need to consider anew what to do with myself: go ahead with D&R with a slant more nearly my own or call it a day. The Stafford Little Lectures were delivered, they were transformed into a book, the book produced articles and controversy and approval, in short, I emerged again as a voice to be heard, in my old role (always so surprising to me) of a "controversial figure."

But the question I keep asking myself (and my answer is certainly not "objective"—how can it be about one's self): not what did you *do* during the year but did you develop, did you grow, did you look ahead, did you take risks, or "settle" for what you have accomplished, "settle" for less than you desperately want?

How does one "measure" whether a man is still growing or his growth has stopped? To do this objectively is for others. But I can say how I *feel* about it. I feel that in the past year I have grown, grown stronger; better able to take blows, crises, even gross causes for irritation and anger; more decisive, less given to "look up" to people because they are rich, or glib, or have status of one kind or another, a bit more able to *be my own man*.

The worst thing about a holiday taken to "rest and recharge" oneself is that it encourages a tendency even normally too strong: to be chiefly concerned about me. The best thing about the life I lead when I am at work is that it quite naturally encourages a tendency to be more concerned with what is outside of me, with challenges, issues, tasks, troubles—and best of all, people other than myself.

Perhaps that is as good a resolve for the New Year as I can make: so to live, a day at a time, so that the balance of concern should always be outside me. And by so doing to find myself.

INDEX

[545]